Bureaucracy and the State in Early China

Ancient Chinese society developed a sophisticated and complex bureaucracy which is still in operation today and which had its pristine form in the government of the Western Zhou from 1045 to 771 BC, ranking among the oldest administrations in the world. Li Feng, one of the leading scholars of the period, explores and interprets the origins and operational characteristics of that bureaucracy on the basis of the contemporaneous inscriptions of royal edicts cast onto bronze vessels, many of which have been discovered quite recently in archeological explorations. The inscriptions clarify the political and social construction of the Western Zhou and the ways in which it exercised its authority. The discussion is accompanied by illustrations of the bronze vessels and their inscriptions, together with full references to their discovery and current ownership. The book also discusses the theory of bureaucracy and criticizes the various models of early-archaic states on the basis of close reading of the inscriptions. It redefines the Western Zhou as a kin-ordered and settlement-based state.

LI FENG is Associate Professor of Early Chinese Cultural History in the Department of East Asian Languages and Cultures at Columbia University. He has undertaken extensive fieldwork on Bronze-Age sites in China and is the author of *Landscape and Power in Early China: The Crisis and Fall of the Western Zhou 1045–771 BC* (Cambridge, 2006).

Bureaucracy and the State in Early China

Governing the Western Zhou

Columbia University

CAMBRIDGE
UNIVERSITY PRESS

CAMBRIDGE UNIVERSITY PRESS
Cambridge, New York, Melbourne, Madrid, Cape Town, Singapore, São Paulo, Delhi

Cambridge University Press
The Edinburgh Building, Cambridge CB2 8RU, UK

Published in the United States of America by Cambridge University Press, New York

www.cambridge.org
Information on this title: www.cambridge.org/9780521884471

First published 2008

Printed in the United Kingdom at the University Press, Cambridge

A catalogue record for this publication is available from the British Library

Library of Congress Cataloging-in-Publication data

Li, Feng, 1962–
  Bureaucracy and the state in early China : governing the western
Zhou/Li Feng.
      p.   cm.
  Includes bibliographical references and index.
  ISBN 978-0-521-88447-1 (hardback)
    1. Bureaucracy – China – History – To 1500.   2. China – Politics and
government – To 221 B.C.   I. Title.

  JQ1510.L47484 2008
  931'.03 – dc22

                                                    2008025653

ISBN 978-0-521-88447-1 hardback

Contents

List of figures   [vi]
List of maps   [viii]
List of tables   [ix]
Acknowledgments   [x]
Scholarly conventions   [xiii]
Chronology of the Western Zhou kings   [xv]

Introduction   [1]

1   The historical context   [24]

2   Structural development of the Zhou central government   [42]

3   The administrative process of the Zhou central government   [96]

4   Managing the core: local society and local administration
in the royal domain   [149]

5   Official service and career development during the Western Zhou   [190]

6   The regional states and their governments   [235]

7   Reconceptualizing the Western Zhou state: reflections on previous
theories and models   [271]

Conclusion   [300]

*Appendix I: A list of official titles in Western Zhou bronze
inscriptions*   [305]
*Appendix II: A bibliographical list and index of inscribed bronzes cited
in the book*   [315]
Bibliography   [354]
General index   [374]

Figures

1 The Ling *fangyi* in the Freer Gallery of Art   [46]
2 Inscription of the Ling *fangyi*   [47]
3 Organizational map of the Western Zhou government (royal domain: early Western Zhou)   [50]
4 Cover of the Fansheng *gui* in the Nelson-Atkins Museum of Art   [64]
5 Inscription of the Fansheng *gui*   [65]
6 Organizational map of the Western Zhou government (royal domain: mid-Western Zhou)   [68]
7 The Li *fangzun* and its inscription   [80]
8 The Maogong *ding* in the Palace Museum, Taipei   [86]
9 Inscription of the Maogong *ding*   [87]
10 Organizational map of the Western Zhou government (royal domain: late Western Zhou)   [89]
11 Inscription of the Shi Song *gui*   [100]
12 The Song *ding* and its inscription   [106]
13 Illustration of the appointment ritual with respect to the Yuntang temple-structure   [108]
14 Military personnel surrounding Hu (Shi Hu)   [134]
15 The hierarchy of authority in the Zhou government during the mid-Western Zhou   [138]
16 Condition of properties of the aristocratic lineages   [156]
17 Itō's demonstration of land transaction recorded in the Fifth Year Qiu Wei *ding*   [157]
18 Idealized compositional model of the city of Zhou   [165]
19 The administrative structure of the "Five Cities"   [170]
20 The Guo Cong *xu*   [175]
21 Inscription of the Guo Cong *xu*   [175]
22 The composition of *Yi* and transaction of land   [177]
23 The Sanshi *pan* in the Palace Museum, Taipei   [184]
24 Inscription of the Sanshi *pan*   [185]
25 Social structure of the Royal Domain   [188]
26 The Shi Hu *gui* and its inscription   [193]
27 The Yihou Ze *gui*   [239]

28 Inscription of the Yihou Ze *gui*   [240]
29 The Ke *lei* and its inscription recording the establishment of
      Yan   [242]
30 Model of the regional states   [244]
31 The recently excavated Shu Ze *fangding* and its inscription   [258]
32 The Mai *fangzun* and its inscription   [261]
33 Inscription of the Shi Yuan *gui*   [267]
34 Pattern of settlement organization of the regional states   [289]
35 Conceptual map of the Western Zhou state   [298]

Maps

1 Prominent regional states of the Western Zhou [32]
2 The Zhou royal domain and its adjacent areas [102]
3 Zhouyuan, the settlement of Qi [161]

Tables

1 Relations between the *youzhe* and appointees/awardees [124]
2 Regularity of the Zhou king's visits to building compounds under official authority [146]
3 Officials with responsibilities for the Five Cities [167]
4 Official appointments in Western Zhou bronze inscriptions [202]
5 Percentage of official appointments [213]
6 Career development of seven Western Zhou officials [222]

Acknowledgments

If the study of history is anything, it is a system of interpretation of the relationships between events that happened in the past and of the reasons why they were related in such ways. The present book interprets the political institutions of the Western Zhou state (1045–771 BC), which made a fundamental mark on East Asian civilization and was one of the earliest documented attempts to construct a government and manage the affairs of a state. For such a work to emerge, the field of research has to have gained a firm base of sources and has to have been honored already by a long series of pioneering works that have established the basic facts of the period and clarified its overall historical development. Therefore, although intended as an interpretative analysis, the present book is constructed on the collective merit of numerous previous evidential pieces of research in paleography, history, and archeology of the Western Zhou period, and it does only what they can support.

My own interest in the sociopolitical institutions of the Western Zhou state has grown in parallel, and indeed cognate, with my interest in its political geography. In fact, even before *Landscape and Power in Early China* was planned, and continuing through the intervals in my work on that book over many years, I have devoted most of my time available for research to reviewing inscriptions and contemplating their implications for the Western Zhou government. It was natural that the study of geography based on current archeology would clarify the spatial dimension as well as divisions of the Western Zhou state as a political organization, and a thorough understanding of the various complex political and socioeconomic relations based particularly on the administrative inscriptions could lead to promising opportunities to explain how the space or spaces conceived as the Western Zhou state were managed through a coherent political system. Emerging from these interlocking processes of research were a number of articles that gradually appeared in journals from 2001, and the negation of the doctrine of "Western Zhou feudalism" has provided me with a new ground to rethink the nature of the Western Zhou state and to reinterpret its political system along a new line of theory. The present book incorporates the contents of some of these articles, but it attempts a more comprehensive analysis of the governmental practice and political system of the Western Zhou state based on information in the currently available bronze inscriptions.

A number of scholars have generously helped this interpretation to develop before reaching its present form. But I owe my utmost debt of gratitude to two scholars who served as the first readers of the still rough first draft of the manuscript of this book in spring 2005: Professor Edward L. Shaughnessy of the University of Chicago has for a long time served as the first reader not only for the present book but for many of my previous works that provided the foundation for the present one; Professor Barry B. Blakeley of Seton Hall University sacrificed many beautiful, sunny California days of his retirement to toil over pages full of difficult ancient inscriptions. I thank them for their very constructive comments as well as the criticisms that challenged me on a number of critical issues concerning the book. At Columbia University, I am particularly grateful to Professor Madeleine Zelin, who has taken a large amount of time from her pioneering research into the socioeconomic history of later imperial China to read most of the chapters of this book and provide constructive comments. Professor Emeritus Cho-yun Hsu of the University of Pittsburgh, respected Academician of the Academia Sinica, generously offered his comments when parts of the book were presented in conferences we both attended; but I thank him even more for his advice and support for my work and research over the years. I am indebted also to Professor Ken-ichi Takashima of the University of British Columbia for his professional linguist's advice on the English translation of a number of key terms in the inscriptions. I have benefited from my continuous conversation with Professor Hirase Takao of the University of Tokyo, who has provided timely updates on recent Japanese scholarship on the early Chinese states. I am also grateful to Professor Quentin Skinner of the University of Cambridge for the opportunity to consult him about a number of key political terms used in the book such as "state" and "sovereignty." Finally, I thank the graduate students of Columbia University who attended my seminar on Western Zhou history in fall 2006, where a number of chapters from the manuscript were circulated for discussion in the class. One student, Nicholas Vogt, went on to compose the bibliographical list of inscriptions (Appendix II) for this book, and I thank him for his hard work.

My thanks for institutional support must go first to the Chiang Ching-Kuo Foundation for International Scholarly Exchange for its generous granting of a Junior Scholar's Grant in 2004, which enabled me to extend my sabbatical leave to one year, during which the first manuscript of this book was completed. I thank the Department of East Asian Languages and Cultures of Columbia University and its chair, Professor Robert Hymes, for the continuous and strong support to me and this book.

Finally, I would like to express my gratitude to Marigold Acland, Senior Commissioning Editor at Cambridge University Press, for her professional charisma and personal kindness, which have encouraged me to continue to work with Cambridge on the publication of this book. My thanks go further to the following scholars and colleagues who have helped me to obtain photographs for the illustrations used in the book: Xiaoneng Yang of the Nelson-Atkins Museum of Art, Cao Wei of Shaanxi Provincial Institute of Archaeology, and Chen Chao-jung and Hwang Ming-chorng of the Academia Sinica. I have made every effort to contact copyright holders for permission to reproduce previously published images and would like to thank the following publishers for their generous permissions: The Freer Gallery of Art, Smithsonian Institution (fig. 1); Zhonghua Books Co. (Beijing) (figs. 2, 5, 9, 11, 21, 24, 28); The Nelson-Atkins Museum of Art (fig. 4 and jacket); Shanghai Chinese Classics Publishing House (figs. 12, 26, 33); Institute of Archaeology, Chinese Academy of Social Sciences (fig. 29); The National Palace Museum, Taipei (figs. 8, 23). The author and publisher apologize for any errors or omissions and would welcome these being brought to their attention.

Li Feng
Columbia University
August 30, 2007

Scholarly conventions

1. For bronze inscriptions cited in the book, references are unitarily made to the *Yin Zhou jinwen jicheng* 殷周金文集成, 18 vols. (Beijing: Zhonghua, 1984–94) (hereafter, JC) and *Jinchu Yin Zhou jinwen jilu* 近出殷周金文集錄, 4 vols. (Beijing: Zhonghua, 2002) (hereafter, JL). Those that are not included in these two works, usually these very recently discovered ones, are separately noted.
2. References to bronzes reported in the monthly or bimonthly Chinese archeological journals are given only by the name of the journal followed by the year and issue number, and by page numbers (e.g. *Wenwu* 1996.9, 20–35). Archeological reports, monographs, and catalogues of bronzes are listed by their titles alone; their institutional authorial names are given only in the bibliography.
3. References to the Classical texts such as the *Shangshu* 尚書, *Shijing* 詩經, and *Liji* 禮記 are commonly made to the *Shisanjing zhushu* 十三經註疏, 2 vols. (Beijing: Zhonghua, 1979). For the Chinese texts cited for which English translations are available, page numbers in both the Chinese texts and their English translations are provided. For the widely read Chinese texts such as the *Analects* and *Mencius*, their English translations alone are referred to.
4. For smooth reading, the Chinese text is not provided for the bronze inscriptions translated in this book. But Chinese characters are provided for critical or difficult terms as well as personal and place names rendered in Romanization.
5. Official titles are directly given in English with parenthetical notes provided at first occurrence introducing their original inscriptional forms in Chinese, such as "Supervisor of Land" (*situ* 嗣土), "Superintendent" (*zai* 宰).
6. Inscriptional names such as Jinhou 晉侯 (Ruler of Jin), Jingbo 井伯 (Elder of Jing), Rongji 榮季, as well as lineage designations such as Sanshi 散氏 and personal designations such as Sufu 俗父 will be treated as one term. Thus, I will render a full personal designation as, for instance, Guoji Zibai 虢季子白 or Sanbo Chefu 散伯車父.
7. Translations of aristocratic titles such as *hou* 侯, *bo* 伯, *zi* 子, and *nan* 男 with medieval European titles are avoided, but the well-established

translation of *gong* 公 as "Duke" is maintained, along with "King" for *wang* 王. In addition, I also adopt the translation of *hou* as "Ruler" and *bo* as "Elder," both with initial capitals.

8. In general, the conventional rules for *Pinyin* Romanization are observed. Alterations are made only to differentiate some frequent homophones, such as Han 漢 and Hann 韓, Wei 魏 and Wey 衛, King Yi 夷王and King Yih 懿王, Shanxi 山西 and Shaanxi 陝西.

Chronology of the Western Zhou kings

Kings	Dates	Periodization
King Wen	1099/56–1050 BC*	PRE-CONQUEST
King Wu	1049/45–1043	
Duke of Zhou	1042–1036	EARLY
King Cheng	1042/35–1006	WESTERN
King Kang	1005/3–978	ZHOU**
King Zhao	977/75–957	
King Mu	956–918	
King Gong	917/15–900	MIDDLE
King Yih	899/97–873	WESTERN
King Xiao	872?–866	ZHOU
King Yi	865–858	
King Li	857/53–842/28	LATE
Gong He	841–828	WESTERN
King Xuan	827/25–782	ZHOU
King You	781–771 BC	

* Absolute dates for Western Zhou kings proposed by Edward L. Shaughnessy; see Shaughnessy, *Sources of Western Zhou History* (Berkeley: University of California Press, 1991), p. xix. Shaughnessy's system of dating accepts the theory advanced by Nivison that each king had two "First Years," that in which he started his new reign and that which came after the completion of the mourning period for his father. Therefore, two first years are provided here for the majority of the kings. See also David Nivison, "The Dates of Western Chou," *Harvard Journal of Asiatic Studies* 43 (1983), 481–580.

** Periodization follows the widely accepted system proposed by Chen Mengjia. See Chen, *Xi Zhou niandai kao* (Shanghai: Shangwu, 1945), p. 55; "Xi Zhou tongqi duandai I," *Kaogu xuebao* 9 (1955), 138–39.

Introduction

China was a bureaucratic empire for a long time in the past, and it still has one of the most complicated bureaucratic systems in the world in the present. In the Former Han dynasty (206 BC – 9 AD), the total number of officials in the service of the empire reached 130,285 (exclusive of military officials) in the year of 5 BC, as recorded in the *History of the Former Han Dynasty*.[1] It was remarked by historians of the Classical West that the Chinese Han Empire employed roughly twenty times as many officials as did the Roman Empire of the same time.[2] This figure, though it looks purely mathematical, suggests in its own historical context the fact that the Chinese in such an early stage of history had developed a culture that was deeply committed to ruling through constructing an elaborate bureaucratic machine. Needless to say, this profound reverence for bureaucratic order is still an essential part of contemporary Chinese culture. Because of its immense size and extremely long duration, the imperial Chinese bureaucracy has always been cited by social scientists as an example of the most thoroughly developed of ancient bureaucracies.[3] How did bureaucracy originate in China? A number of recent studies

[1] For the total number of Han officials, see *Hanshu*, 19a, p. 743; see also Hans Bielenstein, *The Bureaucracy of Han Times* (New York: Cambridge University Press, 1980), pp. 156, 205–6. This figure is strongly supported by a recent calculation conducted by Michael Loewe based on records on the bamboo strips from Yinwan, Jiangsu, that resulted in the account of a total of 99,214 officials at provincial level alone in 15–10 BC. See Michael Loewe, "The Administrative Documents from Yinwan: A Summary of Certain Issues Raised," 4 (posted at the website of the Society for the Study of Early China [http://www.lib.uchicago.edu/earlychina/res]; visited on February 15, 2005). On the magnitude of the Han government, see most recently, Michael Loewe, *The Government of the Qin and Han Empires, 221 BCE – 220 CE* (Indianapolis: Hackett Publishing Co., 2006), pp. 71–85.

[2] See Peter Garnsey and Richard Saller, *The Roman Empire: Economy, Society, and Culture* (Berkeley: University of California Press, 1987), p. 20. Even a comparison of the above figure with the thoroughly bureaucratized later Roman Empire of the fourth and fifth centuries AD would yield four times more officials in the Han Empire than in the Roman Empire. See S. E. Finer, *The History of Government from the Earliest Times*, vol. 1: *Ancient Monarchies and Empires* (Oxford: Oxford University Press, 1997), pp. 65, 479. See also A. H. M. Jones, *The Later Roman Empire 284–602*, 2 vols. (Oxford: Basil Blackwell, 1964; repr., Baltimore: Johns Hopkins University Press, 1992), p. 1057.

[3] See, for instance, Eugene Kamenka, *Bureaucracy* (Oxford: Basil Blackwell, 1989), p. 22. Indeed, China has been recently again credited as the inventor of "modern-style bureaucracy," while Europe is its re-inventor. See Finer, *The History of Government*, pp. 87–90. For such a view, see also earlier, Herrlee Creel, "The Beginning of Bureaucracy in China: The Origins of the *Hsien*," *Journal of Asian Studies* 22 (1964), 162–63.

have indicated that the origin of the Chinese bureaucracy is to be found in the governmental practice of the Western Zhou state (1045–771 BC), one of the early dynastic royal states in Bronze-Age China before empire and the acknowledged fountainhead of the ancient Chinese political tradition.[4] The period is rich in literary evidence, in particular the numerous contemporaneous inscriptional texts cast on bronze vessels, many of which have been brought to light by archeology in the past two decades. Archeology has also revealed the cultural and geographical perimeters of the Western Zhou state, centering on an increasingly clear political structure. Thus, the Western Zhou provides us with a critical time context in which we can investigate the conditions for the rise and early development of bureaucracy in China. It certainly also provides one of the well-documented contexts in which we can explore the concept of the state and the role of its government in the ancient world.

THE PURPOSE OF THIS BOOK

The purpose of this book is to discover the structural as well as operational characteristics of the Western Zhou government on the basis of the contemporaneous bronze inscriptions. These inscriptions cast on bronze vessels, large numbers of which have now been accumulated (13,371 in total by 2002 for all periods from Shang to Han, but the majority are from the Western Zhou) as the result of ongoing archeological excavations,[5] contain authentic records of the Zhou government. In fact, many inscriptions preserve portions derived originally from the royal edicts issued during the court ceremony of appointment that were transferred onto the bronzes. Thus, the condition of sources of the Western Zhou period is quite similar to that of early Mesopotamia, where information on the archaic state and administration can be learned from the contemporaneous cuneiform texts. By examining these archaic records with conceptual tools developed by modern political scientists, I hope to achieve a systematical understanding as well as an analytical presentation of the fundamental characteristics of the Western Zhou government as the first bureaucracy in China, and one of the oldest bureaucracies in the ancient world. Through the study of the Western Zhou government, I hope also to clarify the nature of the Western Zhou state and the unique ways in which it achieved political authority

---

[4] See Cho-yun Hsu and Katheryn M. Linduff, *Western Chou Civilization* (New Haven: Yale University Press, 1988), pp. 245–49, 54–56; Edward L. Shaughnessy, "Western Zhou History," in *The Cambridge History of Ancient China: From the Origins of Civilization to 221 BC*, ed. Michael Loewe and Edward L. Shaughnessy (Cambridge: Cambridge University Press, 1999), pp. 323–26; Li Feng, "'Offices' in Bronze Inscriptions and Western Zhou Government Administration," *Early China* 26–27 (2001–2002), 51–54.

[5] A total of 12,113 inscribed bronzes are included in the *Yin Zhou jinwen jicheng*, 18 vols. (Beijing: Zhonghua, 1984–94), of which roughly 350 are long inscriptions with more than fifty characters. Another 1258 recently discovered inscriptions are collected in the *Jinchu Yin Zhou jinwen jilu*, ed. Liu Yu and Lu Yan (Beijing: Zhonghua, 2002).

and exercised administrative control, exemplifying the early royal states in China before the rise of empire.

All studies begin with a set of questions. The questions that have much motivated the present study and that will be subsequently discussed in this book include the following: What was the social and political reality in the Western Zhou that had conditioned the rise of the bureaucratic way of government? Was it a strategy adopted by the Zhou state to cope with outside stress caused by either the need for expansion or the loss of territory through the effective internal refinement of administration, or was it a process driven by internal new forces emerging from structural changes in Zhou society? What was the rationale behind the organization of the Western Zhou government, and in what way and to what extent had the functions of offices become specialized and their operation regularized? How was the relationship between the Zhou king as the ordering authority and the bureaucratic body of the Zhou government constructed and modified over time? Were there discernible official hierarchies in the Zhou government providing the principle by which administrative authority was also stratified? What was the nature of government service during the Western Zhou, or what was the social background of the Zhou officials selected for such service? What was the relationship between the central court in the Zhou capital and the numerous regional governments? What role did the regional states play in the overall political operation of the Western Zhou state at large? How did the Western Zhou bureaucracy transform or evolve into imperial bureaucracy, or was there such a process of linear transformation and evolution at all? Ultimately, was there awareness among the Western Zhou officials of the institution of the "Zhou state" rather than the royal house? What was the nature of the "Western Zhou state"?

Not all of these questions that one can legitimately ask about the Western Zhou can be satisfactorily answered on the basis of our present evidence. However, I believe that the current condition of our sources does allow us to answer many of these questions in such a way as to acquire a general understanding of the ways in which political authority was achieved through systematized administration. In this regard, the present study will be one that lays out clearly what we know and what we do not about the many interrelated aspects of the Western Zhou political system. As such, it certainly presents the first book-long analysis of the Western Zhou government based on the contemporaneous inscriptional evidence.

BUREAUCRACY, WEBER, AND CHINA

What is bureaucracy? Can the concept of "bureaucracy" be applied to an early state in China such as the Western Zhou? The discussion among the political scientists of the concept of bureaucracy and its applications in the twentieth century has not moved too much beyond the conceptual net cast by Max Weber (1864–1920) at the turn of the century. However, Weber, the father figure of "bureaucracy," never produced a statement that could be considered a definition of it, but has characterized in a number of places in his writing how "bureaucracy" should ideally work.[6] These character- istics have been summarized by Martin Albrow in his most systematical modern exposition of Weber's theory of bureaucracy and its influence on social sciences, including:[7]

1. The staff members are personally free, observing only the impersonal duties of their offices.
2. There is a clear hierarchy of offices.
3. The functions of the offices are clearly specified.
4. Officials are appointed on the basis of a contract.
5. They are selected on the basis of a professional qualification, ideally substantiated by a diploma gained through examination.
6. They have a money salary, and usually pension rights. The sal- ary is graded according to position in the hierarchy. The official can always leave the post, and under certain circumstances it may also be terminated.
7. The official's post is his sole or major occupation.
8. There is a career structure, and promotion is possible either by senior- ity or merit, and according to the judgment of superiors.
9. The official may appropriate neither the post nor the resources which go with it.
10. He is subject to a unified control and disciplinary system.

However, these characters make only a paradigm[8] – the *ideal or pure type* of "rational bureaucracy" – that, according to Weber himself, was only closely approximated by the modern governments and only in the most advanced capitalist societies.[9] It is clear that Weber's description of the *pure type* of bureaucracy was based on modern Western governments and, as pointed out by David Beetham, reflects the perspectives of the liberal and non-bureaucratic European elites in the special intellectual context of the nineteenth century.[10] Weber, in that regard, clearly saw the "rational-legal" authority of the modern state that promotes impersonal rules as the foundation of modern bureaucracy, and even considered the process of bureaucratization as having paralleled the progress of modern

---

[6] For Weber's theory of bureaucracy, see most importantly, Max Weber, "Bureaucracy," in *From Max Weber: Essays in Sociology*, trans. and ed. H. H. Gerth and C. Wright Mills (New York: Oxford University Press, 1946), pp. 196–244.

[7] See Martin Albrow, *Bureaucracy* (New York: Praeger Publishers, 1970), pp. 44–45. In a more sim- plistic way, other scholars such as Richard Hall summarized six points of Weber's characterization of bureaucracy, including division of labor, hierarchy of authority, system of rules, system of pro- cedure, impersonal relation, and promotion on condition of competence. See Richard H. Hall, "The Concept of Bureaucracy: An Empirical Assessment," *The American Journal of Sociology* 69.1 (1963), 32–40.

[8] See Kamenka, *Bureaucracy*, p. 2.   [9] See Weber, "*Bureaucracy*," p. 196.

[10] David Beetham, *Bureaucracy*, 2nd edn (Minneapolis: University of Minnesota, 1996), p. 6.

democracy.[11] On the other hand, scholars have also identified a Marxist influence on Weber, very clearly in his characterization of bureaucracy as an institution that separates officials from the means of administration, closely paralleling Marx's notion of separation of workers from the means of production.[12]

While characterizing the *ideal* bureaucracy in the modern context, if not as a part of modernity, Weber clearly took also a historical-sociological approach, identifying a number of pre-modern bureaucracies: (a) Egypt during the New Empire; (b) the later Roman Principate; (c) the Roman Catholic Church; (d) China since the Qin unification.[13] Weber called them "patrimonial bureaucracies," especially in the case of China, in contrast to the *pure* form of bureaucracy, because they employed "unfree" officials and were based on "traditional authority" but not the modern "rational-legal authority"; in the Chinese case, although officials were selected for qualification through written examination, they were qualified for humanistic learning and not the technical proficiency needed for administrative work.[14] Despite these differences, Weber still regarded them as "distinctly developed and quantitatively large bureaucracies." In other words, even for Weber, bureaucracies do not have to be *ideal* or *pure* to be called such, and China had developed bureaucracies. Therefore, the issue is: How bureaucratic does a "bureaucracy" have to be? This aspect of Weber's theory certainly left ways open for further research.

The study of bureaucracy after Weber has taken many new directions, but has evolved in two main ways. The first took the form of debate against Weber, questioning on a number of key issues the validity of his characterizations as criteria even for bureaucracies in the modern European states.[15] The severest case has been brought against Weber with regard to the total lack of concern with bureaucratic inefficiency: there have been a number of studies that show why and how the "superior bureaucratic machine" as described by Weber can instead result in actual administrative ineffectiveness and even failure.[16] Through such debate, scholars have significantly modified Weber's original descriptions and have produced new definitions of bureaucracy, such as:

"Bureaucracy" means a centrally directed, systematically organized and hierarchically structured staff devoted to the regular, routine and efficient

---

[11] See Weber, "*Bureaucracy*," pp. 225–26.

[12] See *ibid.*, p. 197. See also Albrow, *Bureaucracy*, p. 41.

[13] See Weber, "Bureaucracy," p. 204.

[14] On this distinction, see Max Weber, *The Theory of Social and Economic Organizations*, trans. and ed. A. M. Henderson and Talcott Parsons (Glencoe: Free Press, 1947), pp. 62–63, 331–35, 351; see also Richard Bendix, "Bureaucracy," in *International Encyclopedia of the Social Sciences*, ed. David Sills (New York: Crowell and Macmillan, 1968), pp. 206–7.

[15] For a synthesis of these debates, see Albrow, *Bureaucracy*, pp. 50–61.

[16] See David Nickinovich, "Bureaucracy," in *Encyclopedia of Sociology*, ed. Edgar F. Borgatta (New York: Macmillan Reference USA, 2000), pp. 233–34; Albrow, *Bureaucracy*, pp. 89–91.

carrying out of large-scale administrative tasks according to policies dictated by rulers or directors standing outside and above the bureaucracy. Such a staff, as Weber rightly saw, tends to become rule-bound, functionally specialized, elevating impersonality and esprit de corps.[17]

This definition suggested by Eugene Kamenka (1928–95) considers most of the widely accepted modern meanings of bureaucracy and emphasizes the core structural and operational characteristics of the bureaucratic government. It is adopted here as the working definition of bureaucracy in the present study.

The second way in which the post-Weberian study of bureaucracy has evolved is directed at examining the internal properties of the bureaucratic organization. Since no actual bureaucracies had ever matched exactly the Weberian *ideal* or *pure* type,[18] there is certainly the issue of *degree* to which they approximated it. In a number of studies called "empirical assessments," Weber's characterization was recast as a number of variables including, most importantly, division of labor, hierarchy of authority, system of rules, system of procedure, impersonality, and competence, and bureaucracy is thus viewed as having existed in degrees along these variables (or dimensions).[19] So, the degree of bureaucratization can be actually calculated quantitatively, as exemplified by the Aston University project.[20] It should be noted that all of these studies were based on modern governmental and industrial organizations, but their implication surely goes beyond the confines of the modern period. Not only should all ancient bureaucracies be studied in the same way, but all the variables of bureaucracy should and can also be studied historically to show how they appeared and grew in degree.

Putting China in this context (not that China has been left out of the modern discussion of bureaucracy), in fact, the Australian political scientist Eugene Kamenka has written a long treatment of the development of bureaucratic elements in China, drawing mainly on the works of Etienne Balazs and Hans Bielenstein on the imperial Chinese bureaucracy and Herrlee Creel's study of the pre-imperial Chinese bureaucracy.[21] Creel is widely acknowledged for his study of the origin of the territorial administrative unit *xian* (county) in the sixth century BC, which he considered as the beginning of bureaucratic administration in China prior

---

[17] See Kamenka, *Bureaucracy*, p. 157.

[18] See Stanley Udy, "'Bureaucracy' and 'Rationality' in Weber's Organization Theory: An Empirical Study," *American Sociological Review* 24.6 (1959), 792.

[19] For a comparison of different variables given by different scholars, see Hall, "The Concept of Bureaucracy: An Empirical Assessment," 34.

[20] See D. S. Pugh *et al.*, "Dimensions of Organization Structure," *Administrative Science Quarterly* 13.1 (1968), 65–105. See also, Nickinovich, "Bureaucracy," p. 232.

[21] See Kamenka, *Bureaucracy*, pp. 22–39. See also Etienne Balazs, *Chinese Civilization and Bureaucracy: Variations on a Theme* (New Haven: Yale University Press, 1964); Herrlee Creel, "The Beginning of Bureaucracy in China."

to the unification by Qin in 221 BC, the time that Weber regarded as the beginning of the Chinese "patrimonial bureaucracy." Kamenka further traced the origin of bureaucratic officials to as early as the Shang dynasty (*c.* 1500–1046 BC). Unfortunately, his treatment of Western Zhou officials as "feudal administrators" was completely misguided by Creel's conception of the Western Zhou government as "feudalism,"[22] and his presentation of the Shang and Western Zhou states was very often inaccurate.

A generally better-informed presentation of the Chinese form of bureaucracy was written recently by the later British political scientist S. E. Finer in his masterful and highly praised comparative study of "all" governments.[23] While granting the Chinese bureaucracy of Han times a prominent position as the earliest "modern-style bureaucracy" in world history that was rationally organized, trained, and paid, which he recounted in detail with regard to both its central apparatus and local administrative framework, Finer was apparently unable to demonstrate its historical development in the pre-Qin periods. Simply, such scholarship was not available to him. Like Eugene Kamenka, Finer's treatment of the Western Zhou state shows the strong influence of Creel's "feudal" interpretation, which I have recently examined in detail and have shown to be an inadequate characterization of Western Zhou China.[24] Working on the "feudal" premise, and indeed unlike Kamenka, Finer shows little interest in considering the significance of the Western Zhou government.[25] However, as new archeological discoveries in the last thirty years have outdated many of Creel's theses on the Western Zhou, it is important and indeed inevitable that any study of the origin of bureaucracy in China must take serious consideration of the governmental practice of the Western Zhou. The historical position of this crucial period in the development of bureaucracy and bureaucratic government in China can now be reasserted on the basis of new evidence.

[22] Creel clearly saw "bureaucracy" and "feudalism" as two opposing institutions and contrasted them in the following words: "'Feudalism' is a system of government in which a ruler personally delegates limited sovereignty over portions of his domain to vassals. 'Bureaucracy' is a system of administration by means of professional functionaries, whose functions are more or less definitely prescribed. The distinction depends chiefly upon the locus of initiative and decision. A feudal vassal, in governing his domain, may do anything that he is not expressly forbidden to do. A bureaucratic official may not properly do anything that is not part of his prescribed function." See *ibid.*, 163–64.

[23] See Finer, *The History of Government*, pp. 473–527. For two reviews of Finer's book, see G. E. Aylmer, "Review: *The History of Government from the Earliest Times. Vol. I: Ancient Monarchies and Empires. Vol. II: The Intermediate Ages. Vol. III: Empires, Monarchies and the Modern State* (by S. E. Finer)," *The English Historical Review* 113.453 (1998), 953–55; Donald A. Bailey, "Review: *The History of Government from the Earliest Times* (by S. E. Finer)," *Sixteenth Century Journal* 30.2 (1999), 601–3.

[24] See Li Feng, "'Feudalism' and Western Zhou China: A Criticism," *Harvard Journal of Asiatic Studies* 63.1 (2003), pp. 115–44.

[25] See Finer, *The History of Government*, pp. 488–50.

THE STUDY OF THE WESTERN ZHOU GOVERNMENT

Compared to other aspects of the Western Zhou, the Zhou government has received relatively more attention in previous scholarship, especially in China and Japan. However, the contribution of this scholarship has been limited by a number of key factors. The first negating factor is the reliance on some later ritual texts such as the *Zhouli* 周禮 "Zhou Rites," known also as *Zhouguan* 周官 "Zhou Offices." The text registers a total of 379 officials with their duty specifications divided into sections, each bearing the name of a season or of Heaven and Earth.[26] The text purports to describe in detail the royal government institution of the Western Zhou time, but it is nothing but a Utopian construction by political philosophers of the Confucian School in the late Warring States period.[27] Since the publication of Guo Moruo's insightful study of the text in 1932,[28] certainly most scholars who use the *Zhouli* to study the Western Zhou government are aware of the pseudo-historiographical nature of the text, but it has been quite normal for scholars to use it as a manual to interpret the functions of the Western Zhou offices. To some degree, such references can even be justified because the text does describe many offices that we find in the Western Zhou bronze inscriptions, and it has also been suggested that even some archaic terminology as well as graphs are preserved in the text.[29] However, given the highly ritualistic nature of the text, and given the fact the named offices are constructed within a projected system that could be very different from that of the Western Zhou, such references could sometimes be very misleading, especially when evidence in the bronze inscriptions has not been fully analyzed; very unfortunately, this seems to have often been the case.

Secondly, there seems to have been a significant lack of conceptual tools in previous studies of the Western Zhou government, particularly in Chinese and Japanese scholarship. No study there has been conducted in the light of contemporary discussions of bureaucratic government, and no scholar has bothered to even bring Weber into the context. For this reason, most of the studies, as exemplified by Zhang Yachu and Liu Yu's 1986 book,[30] have proceeded in a way the main purpose of which was to determine the specific functions associated with each official title that appears in Western Zhou sources. Such studies fall largely in the category

[26] The original entries in the "Winter Offices" section had long been lost and were substituted with thirty-one officials in charge of craftsmanship. See *Zhouli* 39, pp. 905–42.

[27] In Western history, one may think of the *Notitia Dignitatum*, which describes the offices of the Eastern and Western Roman Empires after the reform of Diocletian, but the *Zhouli* is bound to be more illusive and ritualistically constructed. On the date and textual history of the *Zhouli*, see Michael Loewe (ed.), *Early Chinese Texts: A Bibliographical Guide* (Berkeley: Institute of East Asian Studies, University of California, 1993), pp. 24–32.

[28] See Guo Moruo, "Zhouguan zhiyi," in *Jinwen congkao* (Tokyo: Bunkyūdō, 1932), pp. 80–87.

[29] On this point, see Chen Hanping, *Xi Zhou ceming zhidu yanjiu* (Beijing: Xuelin, 1986), pp. 208–19.

[30] See Zhang Yachu and Liu Yu, *Xi Zhou jinwen guanzhi yanjiu* (Beijing: Zhonghua, 1986).

of traditional encyclopedic study of the "system of offices" (*guanzhi* 官制) that goes back to at least some medieval works.[31] Efforts have been made to recover the overall structure of the Western Zhou government, such as in the works by Yang Kuan and Kimura, who have brought to light some important organizational features of the Western Zhou government.[32] However, while such studies contributed some important insight on the structural characteristics of the Western Zhou government, they also left out other aspects of the Western Zhou government, especially its operational characteristics. Certainly, the study of the Western Zhou government is much more than just the recovery of the system of offices, and only a fully fledged study addressing the various interrelated aspects can succeed in capturing its nature.

Thirdly, very often, the Western Zhou government was studied in isolation from the broad context of Western Zhou society, with little attention paid to the way in which the government was embedded in the overall political system of the Zhou state and the way in which the administrative structure was related to the distribution of power. Many of the studies were conducted within the Marxist framework in which the Western Zhou was conceived as either a slave or a feudal society. However, Marxist theory provides little if anything about the internal organizational and operational principles of government as part of the "superstructure" in a class-divided society. This lack of a theoretical foundation has led to a major break in Marxist interpretation between the construction of the Western Zhou government and the general configuration of the Western Zhou state. Certainly, the Marxist interpretation of the Western Zhou either as a slave-owning society or a feudal society has serious problems in itself that cannot be solved without reexamining the intellectual basis of these theoretical models.[33]

Western study of the Western Zhou government has taken a much broader, and at the same time over-ambitious, approach as so manifestly shown in the work of Herrlee Creel. In his renowned book, Creel wrote three chapters dealing with three important aspects of the Western Zhou government: organization, finance, and justice.[34] At the same time, he wrote a long chapter on the so-called "Western Zhou feudalism,"

---

[31] Such study has been an integral part of the versatile learning in medieval China; for instance, both the *Tongdian* 通典 and the *Taiping yulan* 太平禦覽 offer a section on the organization of offices. See *Tongdian*, 5 vols. (Beijing: Zhonghua, 1988), pp. 462–1119; *Taiping yulan*, 4 vols. (Beijing: Zhonghua, 1960), 4, pp. 981–1260. Studies by the Qing scholars of such official titles are best found in Huang Benji, *Lidai zhiguan biao* (Shanghai: Zhonghua, 1965). For a modern study of historical official titles, see Deng Delong, *Zhongguo lidai guanzhi* (Wuhan: Wuhan daxue, 1990).

[32] See Yang Kuan, "Xi Zhou zhongyang zhengquan jigou poxi," *Lishi yanjiu* 1984.1, 78–91; adopted in Yang Kuan, *Xi Zhou shi* (Shanghai: Shanghai renmin, 1999), pp. 315–35. See also Kimura Hideumi, "Sei Shū kansei no kihon kōzō," *Shigaku zasshi* 94.1 (1985), 38–66.

[33] On this point, see recently, Li Feng, "Ouzhou Feudalism de fansi jiqi dui Zhongguo lishi fenqi de yiyi," *Zhongguo xueshu* 24 (2005), 8–29.

[34] See Herrlee Creel, *The Origins of Statecraft in China*, vol. 1: *The Western Chou Empire* (Chicago: University of Chicago Press, 1970), pp. 101–93.

providing a general theoretical framework for the whole book.[35] While seeing the Western Zhou government as structurally confused and operationally chaotic, Creel had the clear idea that the centralized administrative control was set up through, for instance, the implementation of a unified taxation system.[36] While the first view was necessitated by his "feudalism" premise, under which the Western Zhou government had to be judged non-bureaucratic or at best a "proto-bureaucracy" as in any "feudal" state, the second point actually created a contradiction with it and led to his suggestion of a "dilemma," which he attributed to the Zhou state. Creel indeed had a hard time reconciling the two poles by making Zhou feudalism more "limited" and at the same time the Zhou centralized royal control more "elusive."[37] Creel raised many meaningful questions regarding the Western Zhou state and its government that are still inspiring today, but in answering those questions, based indeed on very little evidence he also created a massive contradiction, owing much to his misconceived theoretical framework, "feudalism."

Earlier, Cho-yun Hsu paid special attention to the actual workings of the Zhou administration. In an English article published in Taiwan in 1966, Hsu made a number of insightful observations such as the existence of jurisdictions attached to established offices, the succession of assistants to senior officials, and a possible separation of the royal household from the government.[38] Although at the time when these good points were made, and in the three decades that followed, the support of more inscriptional evidence was needed, such as that which the present study provides, it must be recognized that Hsu's inquiry suggested a new dimension in the study of the Western Zhou government. Then, in his 1986 book co-authored with Katheryn Linduff, while accepting Creel's position on "feudalism," the two authors clearly thought that the Western Zhou government was a bureaucracy and spoke of a process of "bureaucratization" from the mid-Western Zhou, taking place first in the specialization of the official roles associated with the Secretariat.[39]

Most recently, Edward Shaughnessy has also spoken about the process of bureaucratization of the Western Zhou government, which he thought had started first in the expansion of military offices as a part of the so-called "Middle Western Zhou Reforms."[40] My own work was previously focused on recovering the operational characteristics of the Western Zhou government. Quite contrary to Creel's view on Western Zhou government, I have found that there were certainly bureaucratic rules that had developed in

---

[35] See *ibid.*, pp. 317–87.   [36] See *ibid.*, pp. 114–21, 134, 152–53.

[37] For such discussion, see *ibid.*, pp. 423–24.

[38] See Cho-yun Hsu, "Some Working Notes on the Western Chou Government," *Zhongyang yanjiuyuan lishi yuyan yanjiusuo jikan* 36 (1966), 513–24.

[39] See Hsu and Linduff, *Western Chou Civilization*, pp. 245–49, 54–56.

[40] See Shaughnessy, "Western Zhou History," pp. 323–26.

the Western Zhou government, both in the administrative process and in the way in which Western Zhou officials were selected and promoted.[41] However, in order to understand the process of bureaucratization, we need to make a systematic effort to recover the many interrelated aspects of the Western Zhou government on the basis of a general understanding of the political tradition and power dynamics of the Western Zhou state, which is the assignment of the present book.

THE BRONZE INSCRIPTIONS: THEIR CREATION AND THEIR SOCIAL CONTEXTS

The bronze inscriptions constitute the base for the present study of the Western Zhou government. The contemporaneous and nearly contemporaneous received textual sources, though valuable in that they offer the historical outline of the period, are generally uninformative on the Zhou government. Why were the numerous bronzes cast and inscribed, and what is the purpose of the texts they carry? To what extent are the bronze inscriptions valid historical sources? These questions must be addressed before we can use them as sources for the study of the Western Zhou government, but the clarification of the questions will need a long discussion.

About twenty-five years ago, in a very insightful study to reveal the background of the creation of the Western Zhou bronzes, Matsumaru Michio proposed a theory that departed quite radically from the traditionally held views on the nature and function of the inscribed Western Zhou bronzes.[42] Matrumaru's theory was quite historical in the way that he tried to construct a large social-political framework in which the production as well as ownership of the inscribed bronzes could be interpreted. Contrary to the conventional view that the inscribed bronzes were cast by their named owners to commemorate the favors they received from the Zhou king, Matsumaru argued that most long inscriptions that mention the Zhou royal personnel were composed instead by the royal scribes and cast, though possibly at their owners' cost, in the royal foundry. Therefore, the named owners of the bronzes were more precisely the *subscribers* of the bronzes but not the *composers* of their inscriptions, who were normally the royal scribes and hence speaking from the standpoint of the Zhou king. As such, the inscriptions actually reflect the royal view on the events they record, but not that of their owners. On the other hand, there is a small group of inscribed bronzes that were cast by the owners themselves and therefore reflect the owners' point of view, but these inscriptions, as

---

[41] See Li Feng, "'Offices' in Bronze Inscriptions," 1–72; Li Feng, "Succession and Promotion: Elite Mobility during the Western Zhou," *Monuments Serica* 52 (2004), 1–35.

[42] See Matsumaru Michio, "Sei Shū seidōki seisaku no haikei: Shū kinbun kenkyū, joshō," *Tōyō bunka kenkyūjo kiyō* 72 (1977), 1–128; reprint in Matsumaru Michio (ed.), *Sei Shū seidōki to sono kokka* (Tokyo: Tōkyōdaigaku, 1980), pp. 11–136.

manifest in the case of the Zuoce Huan *zun* 作冊睘尊 (JC: 5989), which was produced by attenuating the inscription of the Zuoce Huan *you* 作冊睘卣 (JC: 5407), cast in the royal foundry, were calligraphically less well formulated and technically inferior.[43] Thus, the casting and distribution of inscribed bronzes actually constituted a political system of royal control over the various local lords who received the bronzes, and a relation between the Zhou king and his subjects reemphasized through the production of bronzes.[44] Furthermore, Matsumaru suggested that such political relation constructed through the production of inscribed bronzes also existed in the regional states, where the regional rulers cast bronzes to assert their political superiority over their local subordinates.[45]

Ten years later, Itō Michiharu wrote a lengthy introductory chapter to his book that constituted a systematic reply to Matsumaru's theory.[46] In an apparently empirical way through the examination of a number of key terms, Itō reasserted the traditional view among the scholars of Western Zhou bronze inscriptions. In conclusion, Itō argued: The Western Zhou bronze inscriptions are essentially documents in which the Zhou nobles who have received royal favors or official appointments swear their loyalty to the Zhou king through the recording by themselves of such historical facts. As such, the inscriptions reconstituted a political relation that was forged through, and facilitated by, the offering of favor by the ruler to the ruled and the repaying in response of loyalty by the ruled to the ruler. Thus, importantly, the inscriptions speak from the standpoint of their named owners.[47] As for the difference between the Huan *zun* and the Huan *you*, Itō suggested that, while the former was cast under the casual circumstance of a military campaign, the latter was cast in a more formal way when Huan returned to his own base.[48] However, while considering the inscriptions as "manifestos" of loyalty composed by scribes commissioned by their owners, Itō also admits that in cases such as the He *zun* 冏尊 (JC: 6014), in which the Zhou king delivers a long speech addressed to He, a large part of the inscription was copied from a document initially composed by the royal scribe.[49]

This debate, though it has raised little concern in the West, has deepened our understanding of the possible social roles the inscribed bronzes played as well as of their political agenda. Today, in reviewing this debate, it is quite clear that inscribed bronzes were cast in areas beyond the Zhou royal domain and even in some non-Zhou cultural contexts,[50] but it is still

---

[43] See *ibid.*, in *Sei Shū seidōki to sono kokka*, pp. 48–51.   [44] See *ibid.*, pp. 122–29.
[45] See *ibid.*, pp. 137–84.
[46] See Itō Michiharu, *Chūgoku kodai kokka no shihai kōzō* (Tokyo: Chūō kōronsha, 1987), pp. 13–76.
[47] See *ibid.*, p. 71.   [48] See *ibid.*, pp. 40–41.   [49] See *ibid.*, p. 61.
[50] On this point, see examples recently discussed in Li Feng, "Literacy Crossing Cultural Borders: Evidence from the Bronze Inscriptions of the Western Zhou Period (1045–771 BC)," *Bulletin of the Museum of Far Eastern Antiquity* 74 (2002), 210–421.

unclear, within the royal domain, whether the inscribed bronzes were all products of the royal foundry or whether some of them might have been cast in family workshops. It should be noted that what the debate concerned most was a type of inscription recording communications between the Zhou aristocrats and the Zhou king; nearly 100 such inscriptions fall in the category of the so-called "appointment inscriptions" – records of the court ceremony of appointment (*ceming* 冊命) in which the Zhou king personally appointed officials to various government offices.[51] Since the core statement of such inscriptions likely reproduces the royal edicts used in the ceremony, they are important testimony on the Western Zhou government. However, as will soon be clarified below, the bronze inscriptions were composed and cast for a variety of reasons relevant to the life of the Western Zhou elites and are primary evidence for almost every aspect of Western Zhou society.

In the West, the recognition of the bronze inscriptions as historical documents of the Western Zhou period goes back to an article written by Herrlee Creel in 1936,[52] and this position was reconfirmed by Edward Shaughnessy.[53] However, this basic point has been questioned by Lothar von Falkenhausen in a long review article that was published in 1993.[54] Since the debate closely relates to the social role of the inscribed bronzes and the circumstances surrounding the creation of their inscriptions, and since it is relevant to the basis of the present study, which intends to use these inscriptions as primary sources for the Western Zhou government, the issue has to be discussed in some detail here. It is my hope that this discussion, intended here as a healthy scholarly discourse, will deepen our understanding of the complex social contexts in which the inscribed bronzes were cast and put to use. It has been suggested by Falkenhausen:

The bronze inscriptions are not accurate historical records, or are only incidentally so: they must be understood primarily as relics of ritual activity. It is because the ancestors were deemed literate – approachable through a literary medium that had quite possibly been initially devised with the specific intent to address them – that events and circumstances of significance were committed to writing. The "meaning" of the inscription

---

[51] Typically, an appointment inscription is introduced by phrases that describe the time, place, and the relevant etiquette of the ceremony. The core statement is the royal command, which is followed by a list of gifts or accoutrements. Finally, there are phrases specifying to whom the bronze was dedicated. According to a multi-faceted survey conducted by Musha Akira, ninety-one appointment inscriptions were known by the end of the 1970s; see Musha, "Sei Shū satsumei kinbun bunrui no kokoromi," in *Sei Shū seidōki to sono kokka*, pp. 49–132.

[52] See Herrlee G. Creel, "Bronze Inscriptions of the Western Chou Dynasty as Historical Documents," *Journal of the American Oriental Society* (1936), 335–49.

[53] See Shaughnessy, *Sources of Western Zhou History*, pp. 175–82.

[54] See Lothar von Falkenhausen, "Issues in Western Zhou Studies: A Review Article," *Early China* 18 (1993), 139–226.

emanates from the function of the inscribed object in ancestral sacrifice; what mattered was not that messages were inscribed, but that the rituals of communication were performed according to rules.[55]

Thus, the Western Zhou elites are described as having cast hundreds of inscriptions on the bronzes primarily for the supernatural beings to read in the imagination of their casters, in religious services dedicated to the ancestors. In other words, the bronze inscriptions as such, as Falkenhausen explicated, must be understood "as essentially religious documents" with the ancestral spirits in Heaven as their intended recipients, instead of as archival ones aiming at delivering information to later descendants.[56] The reasoning behind this is as follows: (1) the inscriptions were placed on the "ritual vessels, implements, and toned bells" to be used in ancestral sacrifice; (2) such ancestral ritual is described in the poem "Chuci" 楚茨 (Mao no. 209) in the *Book of Poetry*, which actually mentions that the ancestral spirits were entertained with food offerings and music performance, and ritual prayers were pronounced by the official invocators; 3) incidentally, on bronze bells such as the Jingshu *zhong* 井叔鐘, we do actually find such a prayer to the ancestors to grant good fortune to their pious descendants, seemingly suggesting that the inscription was cast for a religious purpose.[57]

Falkenhausen raised important questions with his admirable and sharp thoughts regarding the social role of the inscribed bronzes and what their inscriptions were intended to do, and for whom they would do it.[58] Indeed, he has highlighted one important social context – the "religious-ritual" session of ancestral worship – as the cause for which the inscribed bronzes were cast and the environment in which they were used.[59] My own view on this issue has been stated briefly in a previous study – that the bronze inscriptions were cast for an indefinite set of purposes such as the commemoration of administrative and military merits, the facilitation of marriage relationships, religious prayer to ancestral spirits, the recording

---

[55] See *ibid.*, 167.   [56] See *ibid.*, 146–47.

[57] The inscription of the Jingshu *zhong* was published in *Kaogu* 1986.1, 25–26.

[58] All of the above points have been reiterated more forcibly by Falkenhausen in a recent article in Chinese. See Luo Tai (Lothar von Falkenhausen), "Xi Zhou tongqi mingwen de xingzhi," in *Kaogu xue yanjiu* 6 (Festschrift for Professor Gao Ming) (Beijing: Kexue, 2006), pp. 343–74. The English version of the article, titled "The Nature of Western Zhou Bronze Inscriptions," was presented at the Columbia University Early China Seminar on February 24, 2007, on invitation by the author.

[59] Most scholars draw little or no distinction between the concept of "religion" and that of "ritual," which is rarely defined when used; this has contributed to many misconceptions in the field. To me, "ritual" is a set of acts performed not for their utilitarian value but for their symbolic meaning in a common proceeding prescribed by a religion or by the tradition of a community. Ritual does not have to be religious – religion normally has an underlying belief system involving supernatural beings. There are various forms of social ritual, from the "investiture ritual" performed for the presidents of American research universities to most weddings in contemporary China (without going to the church or the ancestral temple), that do not normally involve supernatural beings. Therefore, I adopt the term "religious-ritual" for those religion-based ritual performances such as the ancestral sacrifice.

of family history, the preservation of important treaties or deals of territorial or material exchange, marking their owning families or origins of
manufacture (as often on weapons and tools), and so on. As such, no single theory can and should explain the creation of all inscribed bronzes.[60]
In general, I see a much larger social context, or more precisely multiple
social contexts, pertaining to the creation of the inscribed bronzes. In what
follows, I will present social contexts different from the religious-ritual
sacrifice to the ancestors in which the inscribed bronzes were used and will
explore reasons other than communication with the ancestral spirits that
might have conditioned the casting of the bronzes and given meaning to
their inscriptions. I will do this by reading the contents of the inscriptions,
which fortunately do sometimes say things for themselves.

For instance, the Mai *fangding* 麥方鼎 (JC: 2706), a bronze cast by
an official in the state of Xing 邢 during the early Western Zhou, says
that Mai would use the bronze to follow the ruler of Xing in (military)
campaign affairs and to entertain his many friends. In another case, the
recently published Shoushu Huanfu *xu* 獸叔奐父盨 says explicitly that
the bronze was used to serve four different types of grain to the honorable guests (*jiabin* 嘉賓) and that, with food in abundance, its owner
can enjoy long life of ten thousand years without limit.[61] Another very
illuminating case is the Wu *gui* 戲簋 (JC: 3827), the inscription of which
says that the bronze was to be used to serve grains to the owner's own
grandsons and sons (*Wu zuo baogui yong fen jue sunzi* 戲作寶簋用𤔲厥
孫子). This is a clear case of a bronze intended to be used to serve food
to the offspring of an elite family, but not for use in ancestral worship, or
at least not explicitly so. Sometimes, we find that the Zhou king was the
intended recipient of such service, described by the line "With which to
feast the king and to welcome the receipt of award (or command)" (*Yong
xiangwang nishou* 用饗王逆逳 [受]), seen for instance in the inscriptions
of the Zhong Cheng *gui* 仲爯簋 (JC: 3747) and Bo Zhefu *gui* 伯者父簋
(JC: 3748). In addition to all these cases, it has been convincingly demonstrated that a group of bronzes with inscriptions in our current corpus
of inscribed bronzes was cast actually as toys for the amusement of the
Zhou elites.[62] Such bronzes, even those with the inscriptions cited above,
certainly could not have been always locked away in the lineage temple,
but must have been always present in the domestic space of those who
commissioned their casting, and hence owned them after their manufacture, for their material as well as cultural functions.

---

[60] See Li Feng, *Landscape and Power in Early China: The Crisis and Fall of the Western Zhou, 1045–771
BC* (Cambridge: Cambridge University Press, 2006), pp. 9–10.

[61] See *Wenwu* 2004.4, 90.

[62] See Huang Mingchong, "Yindai yu Dongzhou zhi nongqi jiqi yiyi," *Gujin lunheng* 6 (2001), 67–88.
Putting this matter in a larger context, there are more than 1500 inscriptions placed on bronze
weapons that were used in warfare or on bronze tools and chariot parts.

These examples suggest that the employment of inscribed bronzes by the Western Zhou elites was by no means restricted to religious-ritual offerings in their ancestral temples, but might also have occurred in other social contexts such as domestic feasting, solicitation of friends and colleagues (whether private or public), outdoor travel, warfare, and even leisure time amusement. Therefore, it is dangerous to determine the collective "nature" of all inscriptions by any single context some of them might have served. If anything like the *nature* of bronze inscriptions does exist, it must be remarkably diverse, or perhaps is the combination of many different *natures*. In all likelihood, the home space of the Zhou elites constituted a prominent social context in which the bronzes were used together with lacquer and perhaps also ceramic containers (particularly glazed ones imported from the south) in food-offering and drinking, as the archeology tells us,[63] paralleling their uses in the religious-ritual sessions that took place in the ancestral temples. Itō Michiharu has further suggested that even bronzes self-identified as "sacrificial vessels" (*zunyi* 尊彝) could reasonably be used in other social contexts. For instance, the Ling *gui* 令簋 (JC: 4300) bears a line of dedication to Ling's father, but the inscription explicates three ways in which the vessel was intended for use: "In ritual offerings in the august temple, in feasting the Zhou king and welcoming his awards, and in entertaining the subordinate officials of the Ministry" (用尊事于皇宗用饗王逆受用鄦寮人).[64] Particularly, the occurrence of the word *yong* 用 three times in the inscription clearly defines the three social spheres – "religious," "domestic," and perhaps "public"– in which the bronze was used. This is certainly also true for other bronzes such as the Duoyou *ding* 多友鼎 (JC: 2835), a sacrificial *ding* cast for its marked purpose to "entertain the friends and colleagues."[65] These cases indicate that the social context of the inscribed bronzes was not only diverse, but could indeed be very fluid, and an inscribed bronze could be freely transferred between different contexts, hence obtaining multiple social meanings. Understanding this complex situation, we would not expect that all inscriptions be cast for communication with the ancestors in the strictly religious-ritual sessions dedicated to them.

[63] It is not rare that the *Book of Poetry* mentions such scenes of family banquet or entertainment for guests and friends; see for instance, the poems "Luming" 鹿鳴, "Famu" 伐木, and "Liuyue" 六月. The first two were probably songs sung at such occasions; particularly the "Famu" mentions that eight *gui*-vessels were deployed to serve food to the family relatives, in addition to the offering of alcohol, doubtless served in wine-vessels. See *Shijing*, 9.2, pp. 405–6; 9.3, pp. 410–12; 10.2, pp. 424–25 (Arthur Waley (trans.), *The Book of Songs: The Ancient Chinese Classics of Poetry*, ed. Joseph R. Allen [New York: Grove Press, 1996], pp. 133, 137–38, 150–51).

[64] See Itō Michiharu, *Chūgoku kodai kokka*, p. 59. See also Ma Chengyuan, *Shang Zhou qingtongqi mingwen xuan*, 4 vols. (Beijing: Wenwu, 1986–90), 3, pp. 66–67.

[65] Certainly such domestic feasting or entertainment could sometimes be "ritualized." But they do not have to be "religious," and there are good grounds for thinking that such domestic events were differentiated both by their physical location and their social meaning from the "religious-ritual" sessions taking place in the ancestral temple.

Therefore, it is my conviction that in order to understand the *natures* (or more precisely functions) of the bronze inscriptions, which cannot and should not be assumed from any single context they served, we must investigate the specific motivation behind each particular case of casting. Again, reading the inscriptions will provide the key to this question. Let us first look at the inscription of the Pengsheng *gui* 倗生簋 (JC: 4262):[66]

唯正月初吉癸子，王在成周。格伯取良馬乘于倗生，厥貯卅田，則析。格伯邊。殹妊彶托厥從格伯叐（安）彶田：殹谷杜木，遷谷旅桑，涉東門。厥書史敄 武立區（甶）成壄（壘），鑄保（寶）簋，用典格伯田。

It was the first month, first auspiciousness [of the moon], *guisi* day (no. 30), the king was in Chengzhou. Gebo took four fine horses from Pengsheng, and he compensated [him] with thirty fields; hence [he] split the [contract in halves]. Gebo regretted. Yiren and Tuo followed Gebo to settle [the borders of] the land: from the birch-pear trees in the Yin stream to the mulberry trees in the Yu stream, crossing the eastern gate. His (Pengsheng) Book Scribes Shi and Wu shoveled earth to build up a mound, and cast the treasured vessel, in order to document the transfer of fields from Gebo.

As in a number of other inscriptions that document such land transactions, the thirty fields were carefully inspected by Gebo himself and two officials, probably from Pengsheng's side. When the borders were determined, Pengsheng's secretarial officials themselves labored to erect an earth mound as a landmark and subsequently cast the bronze to *dian* 典 (to document) the fields that were transferred from Gebo. This is such a good example of an inscription that unambiguously describes the circumstances under which the bronze was cast and for which it was inscribed. In this case, the word *dian* points directly to the archival purpose of the inscription-that is, it was cast to preserve information about a significant deal, whether for the owner himself to reflect upon or for his later generation to observe. One should also note that the composer of the inscription did not use the term "sacrificial vessel," but instead he used "treasured vessel," suggesting that, though the vessel could still be used in a religious context at some point of its lifetime if its owner wanted to, it was not, perhaps, primarily intended as such.

The referential function that we see in the inscription of the Pengsheng *gui* can also be found in some other inscriptions. For instance, the Shi Tian *gui* 史䛇簋 (JC: 4031) records the receipt of cowries by Scribe Tian from the Zhou king; thereupon, Scribe Tian cast the bronze to "fix (the memorable event) onto the vessel, so that he can observe it every morning and evening" (古[固]于彝其于之朝夕監). The term *dian* (to document) expressing the purpose of inscriptions also appears in the Rong *gui* 榮簋

---

[66] For the inscription, see also Ma Chengyuan, *Shang Zhou qingtongqi mingwen xuan*, 3, pp. 143–44.

(JC: 4241), which records Rong's mission to deliver the royal award of a group of slaves from the Zhou capital to the ruler of Xing in present-day Hebei. In the inscription, Rong asserts that "I am the servant of the Son of Heaven, and in order to document the royal command, I cast this vessel for the Duke of Zhou" (朕臣天子用典王命作周公彝). In this case, although a sacrificial vessel was cast, it was cast for the particular purpose of documenting the royal command. In more cases, although the term *dian* is not used, the inscriptions were also clearly cast for the purpose of commemorating significant historical moments in their casters' lives. For instance, the Taibao *gui* 太保簋 (JC: 4140) records the Grand Protector's campaign in the east, for which he was awarded the land of Yu by the king. Thus, the Grand Protector "used this vessel to respond to the royal command" (*Yong ziyi duiling* 用茲彝對令). The Chen Jian *gui* 臣諫簋 (JC: 4237) describes Chen Jian's battle under the command of the ruler of Xing against the Rong people, during which his son was probably killed and his nephew was called in to serve the Xing ruler. To commemorate this event, Chen Jian thus cast a bronze dedicated to his father and "uses it to [?] the peaceful command in (with respect to) my august monarchic ruler" (*Yong X kangling yu huangpi hou* 用□康令于皇辟侯).[67]

Certainly, the need for ancestral sacrifice did not motivate the casting of these inscriptions; instead, they emerged from the desire of their owners to commemorate important historical events. Particularly the first three inscriptions suggest that it was the historical events themselves, regarded by the owners of the bronzes as significant and critical enough to warrant the energy and economic resources to record, that they were committed to writing and cast on the bronzes that carry them. Had the above events not taken place, clearly the inscribed bronzes that document them would not have been manufactured.[68] The archival function of these inscriptions is beyond question, and this point is even more obvious in long inscriptions that were cast either as a record of treaty or legal cases such as the Sanshi *pan* 散氏盤 (JC: 10176) and Hu *ding* 曶鼎 (JC: 2838), or as testimony to commodity sales of high economic value such as the Ninth Year Qiu Wei *ding* 九年裘衛鼎 (JC: 2831); indeed, I have found that many of the extra-long inscriptions were cast without an ancestral dedication.[69] Although I do not think that this can and should explain the creation of all inscriptions, as they could have been cast for various reasons in various social contexts, hence their social role could change depending on the

---

[67] For the inscription, see also Li Xueqin, *Xinchu qingtongqi yanjiu* (Beijing: Wenwu, 1990), pp. 60–62.

[68] Falkenhausen agrees that it was the appointments or the rewards granted by the Zhou king that usually occasioned the manufacture of the bronzes and the casting of their inscriptions. See Luo Tai, "Xi Zhou tongqi mingwen de xingzhi," 362.

[69] This is the case with the Maogong *ding* 毛公鼎 (JC: 2841), Duoyou *ding* 多友鼎 (JC: 2835), Yu *ding* 禹鼎 (JC: 2833), and Sanshi *pan* 散氏盤 (JC: 10176); for instance, the first three rank as the first-, sixth-, and seventh-longest Western Zhou inscriptions on *ding* vessels, while the Sanshi *pan* is the longest among all *pan* inscriptions.

particular context they served, I do think that this explains the motivation behind the casting of most long inscriptions of commemorative contents in what Falkenhausen calls the "documentary mode." Certainly, there are inscriptions that were cast primarily for religious purposes, as there existed hundreds of short inscriptions composed merely of an ancestral dedication or of a simple statement that a sacrificial vessel was made, not to mention the many long religious prayers constantly found on bronze bells that can be best considered "religious documents."[70] But religion is not the only social context in which the inscribed bronzes were cast and were subsequently put in use during the Western Zhou, much less the only way they need to be understood in the present.

Why were the commemorative inscriptions cast on the bronzes, whether or not intended for use in the religious context? I think the answer could be both simple and more complex. The simple answer is that it was the most durable way to preserve the historical memory that the Zhou elites considered worth recording-the bronzes were intended to be used by subsequent generations (子子孫孫永寶用). Although the bronzes eventually vanished at certain points of time and in any case no later than the fall of the Western Zhou in 771 BC, this is specifically the reason we still have these commemorative texts today. The more complex answer, however, is that, particularly because of the multiplicity of social contexts that the bronzes were to serve, by transferring onto them the texts written on perishable materials originating either from the royal court or preserved in the family archive, these texts could be circulated to a larger elite audience and contribute to the social standing of those who owned them. When they were presented in lineage temples on designated religious occasions, the messages they carried would be witnessed and adopted by the lineage community including the imagined, but sometimes most important, participants in such religious sessions, the ancestral spirits (even though the messages might not be particularly addressed to them), and thus sink deeply into the mental memory of its members, as the inscribed texts would certainly be carried down to the later generations as a part of the lineage's literary possession.[71] When the bronzes were displayed at luxurious

---

[70] I have noticed that most inscriptions that Falkenhausen cited in his 1993 article as examples of "religious documents" are those on the bronze bells; bells account for only about 3 percent of all inscribed bronzes. In fact, such long religious prayers, seen for instance on the Jingshu *zhong*, rarely appear on the food and wine vessels. Therefore, we must be aware of the special cultural role the bells played as musical instruments in the life of the Zhou elites, hence the unique *nature* of the bell inscriptions. See Falkenhausen, "Issues in Western Zhou Studies," 150–67.

[71] In the second part of his recent article, Falkenhausen actually comes quite close to the position expressed here. Arguing that all constituent parts of a documentary inscription were derived from oral presentations taking place either in the royal court or in the lineage context, he suggested that, by putting the edited texts onto the bronze, public privileges could be transferred into lineage contexts, thus serving as long-lasting material manifestations of these privileges. But in his theory, the privileges had to be validated by the ancestral spirits first. See Luo Tai, "Xi Zhou tongqi mingwen de xingzhi," 369–70.

banquets attended by colleagues of the owner and friends of the family, the bronzes were themselves the showcase of the family's wealth and power. The texts therein inscribed in beautiful calligraphy, which doubtless had a display function, could be viewed and appreciated,[72] whether before or after the consumption of the food or alcohol they contained, by the Zhou elites in the owner's social circle, hence contributing significantly to the social prestige of his family. When the Zhou king happened to be among the guests, as a number of inscriptions would suggest, the inscribed texts, which normally included a line extolling the Son of Heaven's beneficence in the events of previous royal appointments or rewards, could indeed be very pleasing to the king. Viewed from this broad perspective, the appearance of such commemorative inscriptions in the religious-ritual context would seem quite incidental, because there were also other social contexts in which they appeared. It is inevitable that the bronze inscriptions were means of communication, but they must have communicated to the living at a much larger social scale and on a more regular daily basis than they did to the dead.

Although the purpose of these commemorative inscriptions was to record and communicate historical events that their owners considered important, they might not always record history as it was. Instead, they only record what their composers think the history is or should be and how they want it to be remembered, as is true of all kind of historical documents that came into being as the work of human brain. There are certainly prejudice and subjectivity in the recording of the bronze inscriptions, as I have recently discussed fully in another place.[73] While the reader is encouraged to read the relevant discussion there, it should just be noted that, with full awareness of their subjectivity and of the complex social contexts in which they were produced and employed, we can use the bronze inscriptions, especially those that were products of political relations, as valuable primary sources for the study of the Western Zhou government. The present study will fully explore their meaning in such context.

ORGANIZATION OF THE BOOK

The book is composed of seven chapters. Except for Chapter 1, each addresses a special aspect of the Zhou government based on the bronze inscriptions.

Chapter 1 is written particularly for readers who have no grounding in the study of Chinese history, or are not familiar with the time context of the Western Zhou. The chapter provides a short introduction to the Shang

---

[72] On the issue of calligraphy and its relevance to the creation of Western Zhou bronze inscriptions, see Li Feng, "Ancient Reproductions and Calligraphic Variations: Studies of Western Zhou Bronzes with Identical Inscriptions," *Early China* 22 (1997), 1–41.

[73] See Li Feng, *Landscape and Power in Early China*, pp. 9–10. For an earlier discussion on this point, see Shaughnessy, *Sources of Western Zhou History*, pp. 176–77.

government and Shang state that preceded the Western Zhou. Then it discusses the circumstances of the Zhou conquest of Shang and the process through which the political Zhou state was constructed in the geographical space. The rest of the chapter is devoted to a review of the main historical developments during the Western Zhou period, highlighting a number of important political as well as cultural changes. More importantly, it discusses the whole range of changes that occurred concurrently during the mid-Western Zhou, of which the "bureaucratization" of the Zhou government was an integral part. The chapter offers the readers a necessary basis for understanding the subsequent chapters.

Chapter 2 addresses the organizational characteristics of the Western Zhou government through examining the development of its official roles. Unlike previous studies of the Western Zhou government, the chapter situates the Western Zhou government in a chronological framework divided into three periods. It shows that the Western Zhou government was a continuously changing institution with official roles gradually added to the existing structure. The chapter also shows that the early Western Zhou government might have marked a significant departure from the religion-focused Shang model of government; this is most evident in the establishment of some collective government bureaus bearing a generic name such as the "Ministry." Thus, the "Three Supervisors" as the primary functionaries of the "Ministry," together with the numerous secretarial officials, the "Scribes," formed the main body of the Zhou government. It also demonstrates that during the mid-Western Zhou, the organization of the Zhou government was rapidly compartmentalized and the hierarchy of authority was largely developed. The result of this change was a government that shows the clear organizational features of a bureaucracy. The clarification of the structural characteristics here lays a foundation for discussing other aspects of the Western Zhou government.

Chapter 3 studies the administrative process of the Zhou government, aiming at recovering its operational regularities. The chapter begins by defining some general characteristics of the workings of the Zhou government such as the spatial dimensions of Zhou administration, the appointment ceremony, the use of writing records, and the location of government offices. It suggests that official appointment to the Western Zhou government was a very routine and bureaucratic procedure. It also shows that writing was used extensively for administrative purposes both in the central court and beyond in the local areas. The chapter further demonstrates that some administrative divisions had been developed in the handling of affairs, corresponding roughly to its structural separation between the Royal Household, civil administration, and the military. It clarifies also that there was a defined hierarchy of order in the actual execution of tasks with respect to both civil and military matters. The last part of the chapter studies the administrative role of the Zhou king, suggesting that not only did his visits to the various building compounds seem to display a seasonal pattern, but his visits to particular "offices" seem also to have followed a certain routine. In sum, the chapter shows that evidently some basic rules and regulations had been developed in the administrative process of the Western Zhou government.

Chapter 4 deals with the social and political structure of the Zhou royal domain and the corresponding local administrative system. It clarifies that there were different ways in which the landed properties in the Wei River valley were held, representing three largely different systems of management. While the royal properties were managed separately by the household officials of the king, the local administration of the government was most developed at the major city level. On one hand, officials with collective responsibilities were appointed for all five major cities and formed a special stratum, and on the other, there was an administrative body existing in each of the major cities. In the rural area, the *yi* settlements constituted the basic social units of Zhou society. The inscriptions suggest that by the late Western Zhou the roles of the Three Supervisors had been established in the management of the *yi* communities. In the state-managed areas, the *yi* settlements were organized into a higher structure: the *li*-district. On the aristocratic properties, the *yi* settlements were managed through the lineage structure called *bang*.

Chapter 5 examines the nature of government service during the Western Zhou. With detailed analysis of the bronze inscriptions on a statistical basis, the chapter suggests that at least from the mid-Western Zhou on the Zhou government recruited officials from both hereditary sources and non-hereditary sources. In fact, the bronze inscriptions show that a minority of officials (37 percent) had entered government service with an acknowledged family history of service, and even for officials who had come along this line, there was no guarantee that he must serve in his father's office. The bronze inscriptions suggest that not only was promotion of officials regularly practiced, but there seems to have also been a career structure: it was quite common for a young official to start his service as assistant to a senior official and then, after some years, to be promoted to an office of full capacity. The study strongly suggests that the Zhou government was a relatively open system that allowed promotion of, and competition among, the social elites.

Chapter 6 moves beyond the royal domain, exploring the nature of the regional states and their governments. It clarifies that the regional states were political organizations comparable to the Zhou state at large and the regional rulers had the full rights of a ruler in their own territories. A regional state was formed physically by a cluster of *yi* settlements scattered around a central site that was the residence of the ruler and the location of his ancestral temple. The population within a regional state was necessarily stratified based on ethnic distinctions. However, the regional states were not independent "kingdoms"; instead, they were active participants in the large Zhou state. At the fundamental level, the regional states held their territories and defended the Zhou state against foreign enemies. The regional governments, on the other hand, replicated the roles of, and performed the same tasks charged by, the central government. But the regional governments do not seem to have undergone the process of bureaucratization; therefore, they remained largely personal and non-bureaucratic.

Chapter 7, based on the new ground acquired in the above six chapters, reviews a number of social-political and anthropological models hitherto applied to the Western Zhou state: "city state," "territorial state," "feudal state," "segmentary state," and "settlement state." The chapter clarifies that none of these models can be directly applied to the Western Zhou; on the contrary, some of them are hindered by theoretical problems in themselves. Rather than forcing an existing model on the Western Zhou state, I suggest that we characterize it on the basis of its own inscriptional and material evidence. In my view, the Western Zhou state comes close to what we may call a "delegatory kin-ordered settlement state." This implies that there was a set of depository rules that determined the position of the Zhou king and the many regional rulers. While the Zhou king delegated his power to the regional rulers, the regional rulers served as the king's agents. This also implies that the nature of state control was essentially the control of the *yi* settlements, which were organized along a kinship structure with its center located in the Zhou capital.

Two appendices are provided at the end of the book: Appendix I lists all official titles seen in the Western Zhou bronze inscriptions and the bronzes on which they appear; Appendix II presents bibliographical information for all inscriptions discussed in the book.

The historical context

The chronological framework of the period – the tripartite division of the Western Zhou into early, middle, and late, proposed by Chen Mengjia in 1945 – has been commonly accepted by scholars across disciplines.[1] The archeological discoveries in the past fifty years have indeed put us in a position where we should no longer view the Western Zhou period as a whole, but should study it in a more sequential way by first breaking it down into sections. The transition between the three sub-periods is fully demonstrable with respect to both the material culture of the period and the political history of the Western Zhou state. It is demonstrable also, I believe, in terms of institutional history, as the present study of the Zhou government will fully explore. In order to enable such a study, we must first clarify the historical context in which the Zhou government was founded, bureaucratized, and eventually diminished. For this purpose, I will first discuss the overall historical development in China before the end of the Western Zhou with a focus on political and institutional history. The chapter is written to clarify and in a number of places to reconstitute the historical contexts of Shang and Western Zhou China in which the development of bureaucracy and bureaucratic government took place, and is mainly for non-specialists of the Western Zhou period. Scholars who are well equipped with knowledge of the Western Zhou period can choose to go directly to Chapter 2.

THE SHANG PRECEDENCE

In order to understand the rise of Zhou to the main stage of Chinese history and its possible historical inheritance, we must first understand the

---

[1] Put this in the royal timeline, the early Western Zhou covers the reigns of Kings Wu, Cheng, Kang, Zhao; the middle Western Zhou covers Kings Mu, Gong, Yih, Xiao, Yi; and the late Western Zhou includes King Li, the Gonghe Interregnum, and Kings Xuan and You. See Chen Mengjia, *Xi Zhou niandai kao*, p. 55; "Xi Zhou tongqi duandai 1–6," *Kaogu xuebao* 9–10 (1955), 1956.1–4, 1.138–39. While this timeline is commonly observed by scholars, to my knowledge, only some art historians differ from it in the arrangement of royal reigns. For instance, based on a threefold stylistic division of the bronze art, Jessica Rawson pinpoints the beginning of the late Western Zhou to the accession of King Yi, but not King Li. See Jessica Rawson, *Western Zhou Ritual Bronzes from the Arthur M. Sackler Collections* (Washington, DC: Arthur M. Sackler Foundation, 1990), pp. 1.20–21.

Shang state, which dominated the political life on the northern China plains for centuries prior to the Zhou takeover. Despite the recent attempt among some scholars to downplay the political power of the Shang state,[2] the archeological reality remains compelling: the Shang capital in Anyang 安陽 had an area of 2400 hectares (24 square kilometers), called on the oracle bones as the "Great Settlement" (*dayi* 大邑), was at least forty-five times bigger than any second-level settlements and perhaps 200 times bigger than the small village sites that existed at that time on the northern China plains.[3] Such a huge settlement could not have existed without an elaborately constructed network of political-economical support and hence control, and certainly the Shang had power and influence beyond Anyang. If the later Shang state was nothing but one among the many communities on the northern China plains, it must have been the most eminent and far exceeded others in both power and influence. The oracle bone inscriptions suggest that the network of the late Shang state probably reached regions as far as the Fen River valley and possibly even the Wei River valley in the west and the western periphery of Shandong in the east, as communities probably located in these regions were periodically called on by the Shang kings for coordinated military operations.[4] The Shang state was also able to conduct military campaigns against the so-called *Fang* 方 enemies located even farther in Western Shaanxi, northern Shanxi, northern Hebei, and Western Shandong.[5] Some of these *Fang* entities might have from time to time allied themselves with

---

[2] See Robert Bagley, "Shang Archaeology," in *The Cambridge History of Ancient China: From the Origins of Civilization to 221 B.C.*, ed. Michael Loewe and Edward L. Shaughnessy (Cambridge: Cambridge University Press, 1999), pp. 124–25.

[3] See *Yinxu de faxian yu yanjiu* (Beijing: Kexue, 1994), p. 40. Second-level settlements, for instance, the Taixi 臺西 site in Hebei that overlaps the early phase of Anyang, yields a total area of roughly 30 hectares; the Caoyanzhuang 曹演莊 site near Xingtai has an area of 50 hectares. See *Gaocheng Taixi Shang dai yizhi* (Beijing: Wenwu, 1985), p. 4; Li Liu and Xingcan Chen, *State Formation in Early China* (London: Duckworth, 2003), p. 110. The Laoniupo 老牛坡 site in Shaanxi has a total area of 50 hectares. See *Laoniupo* (Xi'an: Shaanxi renmin, 2002), p. 5. Another major site is Daxinzhuang 大辛莊, located in northwestern Shandong and excavated recently, which has an area of 30 hectares. See *Kaogu* 2003.6, 3; *Chinese Archaeology* (Beijing) 4 (2004), 29. Beyond the plains and valleys of North China that might have been accessible to the Shang, in South China, for instance, there are also relatively larger sites such as Sanxingdui 三星堆 (about 400 hectares) on the Chengdu plain in Sichuan. However, Sanxingdui belongs to a totally different cultural tradition and is geographically segregated from the north; hence it was not a part of the settlement system and political network of North China. On the Sanxingdui site, see Robert Bagley (ed.), *Ancient Sichuan: Treasures from a Lost Civilization* (Princeton: Princeton University Press, 2001), p. 26.

[4] See David Keightley, "The Late Shang State: When, Where, and What?" in *The Origins of Chinese Civilization* (Berkeley: University of California Press, 1983), pp. 540–43.

[5] See David Keightley, *The Ancestral Landscape: Time, Space, and Community in Late Shang China (ca. 1200–1045 B.C.)* (Berkeley: Institute of East Asian Studies, 2000), pp. 66–67. For a recent analysis of the geographical locations of the various *Fang* polities, see Zheng Jiexiang, *Shang dai dili gailun* (Zhengzhou: Zhongzhou guji, 1994), pp. 283–335. It must be noted that Zheng's geopolitical reconfiguration of the pro-Shang communities and *Fang* polities to the west of the Shang center, following scholars in the past, overwhelmingly favors the Fen River valley in Shanxi. It is quite possible that some of these communities and polities might have indeed been located in Shaanxi further west, but this issue should be discussed in another place.

the Shang, and their leaders hence held the title "Elder of the *Fang*" (*Fangbo* 方伯), granted or recognized by the Shang king.[6] However, it is largely agreed that the area of the Shang kings' personal activities, based on the locations of their hunting trips, seems to have been essentially confined to the narrow belt between the Taihang Mountains and the ancient Yellow River, the core of the late Shang state.[7] This seems to contrast sharply with the Western Zhou situation, where the bronze inscriptions document the Zhou king's personal presence far away from the Zhen center in the Wei River valley even at a time when Zhou royal power was virtually waning.

Thus, the real question concerning the Shang state is not so much about its geographical "sphere" over which the Shang king exercised political control, but about the way in which political relations were constructed to support such control. In other words, we must first ask about what the structure was before we can ask and answer questions about the "sphere" such structure could and should have supported. However, we must admit that we do not know the political system of the Shang state well, as we do that of the Western Zhou. Nevertheless, based on previous studies by paleographers, historians, and archeologists, we can perhaps offer the following sketch of the Shang state and the way in which it operated, as a precedent to the Western Zhou state. The political relationship within the Shang state between the royal lineage in Anyang and the various local groups that recognized the supremacy of the Shang king was one of negotiation and power-balancing that demanded the Shang king's continuous display of power through royal hunting and military campaigning. In the view of David Keightley, these various local groups of the Shang state basically governed themselves, and as a result the Shang state was an aggregation of self-governing communities.[8] If this is true, the power that the Shang king possessed can be better characterized as "hegemonic" than "legitimate," and there was no other source of power to support the Shang king's authority than that embodied in Shang military might. According to an earlier analysis conducted by Matsumaru, the Shang state was also constructed along religious lines in that the originally independent local groups worshipped the Shang ancestors as their own ancestors, and local leaders were fictionally accepted as sons of the Shang kings and were called "son" or "prince" (zi 子) in the royal divination records from Anyang.[9] However, other scholars think that zi communities were

---

[6] The pre-dynastic Zhou 周 was apparently one of these *Fang* polities. The term "Elder of the *Fang* of Zhou" (Zhou Fangbo 周方伯) appears on the oracle bones from Zhouyuan 周原; see Edward L. Shaughnessy, "Extra-Lineage Cult in the Shang Dynasty," *Early China* 11–12 (1985–87), 186. The Fang of Gong, after a long period of war with the Shang, also came to assist the Shang. See Zheng Jiexiang, *Shang dai dili*, pp. 284–85.

[7] See David Keightley, "The Shang: China's First Historical Dynasty," in *The Cambridge History of Ancient China*, p. 275. See also, Zheng Jiexiang, *Shang dai dili*, pp. 155–56.

[8] See Keightley, *The Ancestral Landscape*, pp. 56–57.

[9] See Matsumaru Michio, "In Shū kokka no kōzō," in *Iwanami kōza: Sekai rekishi* (Tokyo: Iwanami shoten, 1970), pp. 72–79.

members of the Shang royal lineage,[10] while the "Archer-lords" (*hou* 侯) were the leaders of the various distant local groups, the constituents of the Shang state.[11] Whether the *zi* communities were originally descendants of the Shang royal lineage, or merely fictionally so, it seems true that the Shang state at large was composed of such initially independent communities brought together into a loose federation by the hegemonic power of the Shang king. No political relationship higher (or more permanent) than this level can be confirmed with the current sources, and consequently beyond the royal center there was no government that was either originated from or integrated with the Shang royal government.[12] The geopolitical perimeter of the Shang state, if there was one, can indeed be very elusive, extending very far, as mentioned above, when a Shang king's power was prevailing, but more limited when a king's power diminished. These pro-Shang communities might have shared a common cultural background, manifest in the archeological entity usually called "Shang culture," although communities that shared the "Shang culture" may not necessarily all have been parts of the Shang state. The political geography of the Shang state could change from time to time, depending on the actual power of the king and on the responses of the various local leaders to that power. There was no permanent membership in the Shang state as there was no permanent enemy of it.

As far as the Shang royal government is concerned, Keightley used to think that it depended completely on the personal rule of the Shang king, who was assisted by a large group of diviners who were little more than his

[10] See, for instance, Shirakawa Shizuka, "In no ōzoku to seiji no keitai," *Kodaigaku* 3.1 (1954), 19–44; Shima Kunio, *Inkyo bokuji kenkyū* (Hirosaki: Hirosaki daigaku Chūgokugaku kenkyūkai, 1958), pp. 442–51.

[11] The translation of *hou* as "Archer-lord" here follows Shaughnessy, and this translation is used only in the Shang political context. See Shaughnessy, "Extra-Lineage Cult in the Shang Dynasty," 184–87. Although the same word *hou* was inherited by the Zhou, it designated a role that was significantly different from the "Archer-lord" of Shang particularly in its relation to the Western Zhou state. Therefore, in Western Zhou political context, *hou* is rendered as "regional ruler." See Chapter 6, pp. 256–64 for discussion of the political role of the "regional ruler."

[12] Starting with Hu Houxuan's renowned 1944 article, there has been a long effort among some scholars to argue that the Shang might have "enfeoffed" the *fu* 婦 ladies and *zi* 子 princes with tracts of territory beyond the Shang capital, a system that resembles closely the "Fengjian" 封建 institution practiced by the Zhou. Without going into detail here on this argument, which is based mostly on very circumstantial evidence, it will suffice to note that, given the high uncertainty of Shang political geography and the difficulty in locating particular place-names, there seems little ground for such a claim. Although it is possible that some of the *zi* princes might have held land as did the nobles in the Zhou royal domain, there is no evidence that they ever functioned as the regional rulers of Zhou. On this issue, I believe Creel's objection still stands firm, although his effort to make the Zhou "Fengjian" system something like medieval European "feudalism" had resulted in confusion. See Hu Houxuan, "Yindai Fengjian zhidu kao," in *Jiagu xue Shang shi luncong* I (Chengdu: Qi Lu daxue guoxue yanjiusuo, 1944), pp. 31–111; Si Weizhi, "Fengjian kaoyuan," in *Xian Qin shi lunwen ji* (Xi'an: Renwen zazhi, 1982), pp. 33–42. For a most recent attempt to make the case of Shang "Fengjian" system, see Li Xueshan, *Shang dai fenfeng zhidu yanjiu* (Beijing: Shehui kexue, 2004), pp. 22–122. See also Creel, *The Origins of Statecraft in China*, pp. 32–34. On the issue of Zhou "Fengjian" system, see discussion below, pp. 277–78, 288–90.

personal attendants.[13] On the other hand, the later Professor K.C. Chang described the Shang government as a gathering of roles filled by Shamanistic officers in service of the king who was himself the "head shaman."[14] While differing on the issue of "Shamanism,"[15] the two authorities on Shang seemed to consent on the point that religious officials played a very central role and formed the main body of the Shang government. At the same time, Keightley also thought that, though not in the actual practice of government, a "bureaucratic logic" can be detected in Shang theology, as we see that deceased Shang ancestors were organized into a huge hierarchy and promoted in their ranks according to certain procedures.[16] In recent years, Keightley has begun to bring the same approach from the realm of divinity into the realm of actual government, suggesting that even the divinatory process of the Shang government itself reveals the existence of bureaucratic routines. Therefore, Keightley thought that, despite the fact that the Shang government was still centered on religious roles, the actual conduct of these religious offices exhibited what can be called an "incipient bureaucracy."[17]

We must, however, at the same time be alert to the possible bias of our sources, since what we know about the Shang government is overwhelmingly from the oracle-bone inscriptions, which are themselves records of religious conduct. If we rely solely on such sources, then the divinatory process would seem to have been the only way in which the Shang king entered into contact with his officials, but this is probably not true. In fact, the late Shang bronze inscriptions record secretarial officials such as "Document Maker" (*zuoce* 作冊) and functionaries such as "Superintendent" (*zai* 宰) who were in service to the Shang king.[18] The two offices continued to exist during the Western Zhou and had no known connections to royal divination. On the other hand, the oracle bones may still constitute some kind of "reality" of the Shang government, for although the bones themselves are not testimony to the "action" of administrative officials, the records they carry are not limited to religious affairs, but could be about anything meaningful to the Shang king and Shang state, hence offering good opportunities for

13 See Keightley, "The Late Shang State," pp. 548–58.

14 See Kwang-Chih Chang, *Shang Civilization* (New Haven: Yale University Press, 1980), pp. 192–94; *Art, Myth, and Ritual: The Path to Political Authority in Ancient China* (Boston: Harvard University Press, 1983), pp. 44–55.

15 See Keightley, "The Shang," p. 262.

16 See David Keightley, "The Religious Commitment: Shang Theology and the Genesis of Chinese Political Culture," *History of Religions* 17.3–4 (1978), 214–20.

17 See Keightley, "The Shang," pp. 286–88.

18 *Zuoce* is mentioned in the Sixth Year Yiqi *you* 六年切其卣 (JC: 5414) and *zai* in the Zai Hao *jiao* 宰椃角 (JC: 9105). Another example is the recently reported Zuoce Ban turtle 作冊般黿. The inscription of the bronze turtle is very interesting, recording that the Shang king shot four arrows to kill a turtle on the Huan River that flows along the north and east of the royal place. Zuoce Ban was rewarded by the king and hence cast the turtle with exactly four arrows attached to its back. See Zhu Fenghan, "Zuoce Ban yuan tanxi," *Zhongguo lishi wenwu* 2005.1, 6–10, pl. 1.

the administrative offices to have a fair share in the divinatory records. Indeed, the Shang king divined about a very wide range of topics that concerned him, and yet he seems to have paid very little attention to the establishment of administrative offices. True, the oracle bones do offer such terms as, most importantly, *duoyin* 多尹, *duoma* 多馬, *duoya* 多亞, *yushi* 御事, and *xiaochen* 小臣, and an early analysis by Chen Mengjia claims to have identified twenty-four such "official titles" in Shang oracle-bone inscriptions; the number was expanded to sixty-five by others.[19] However, most of these terms such as those given above are clearly names of certain categories of people or designations of status, but not specific official titles that should be associated with specifically demarcated administrative jurisdictions.[20] A more cautious analysis was conducted by Wang Guimin, but Wang could not move much beyond identifying only some broad functional groups.[21]

This situation certainly cannot be explained only by the bias of sources, but most likely reflects the rudimentary level of organizational development of the Shang government. In all likelihood, except for the secretarial role of the "Document Maker," which appeared towards the end of the dynasty, specific administrative offices had not been differentiated in the Shang government or separated from the religious roles of the royal diviners who staffed the royal court and transmitted royal commands to the targeted groups of officials. It is possible that these diviners occasionally also handled administrative matters that were brought to the royal court and helped the Shang king make decisions about them, whether through personal consultation or the divinatory process. The royal court that represented the body of the Shang central government, or at least of a part of it, might have been frequently away from the Shang capital

[19] See Chen Mengjia, *Yinxu buci zongshu* (Beijing: Kexue Press, 1956), pp. 503–22; Zhang Yachu, "Shangdai zhiguan yanjiu," *Guwenzi yanjiu* 13 (1986), pp. 82–114.

[20] For instance, "Many Horses" (*duoma*) were probably officers that controlled horses; "Many *Ya*" (*duoya*) were military officers, more or less like captains of certain units in the Shang army. The term *ya* 亞 (as *zouya* 走亞) is found also on a mid-Western Zhou inscription, the Xun *gui* 詢簋 (JC: 4321), where by context it refers to captains of certain military units stationed in Luoyang area during the Western Zhou; the term *ya* had a clear Shang origin. While the term "Overseer of Affairs" (*yushi*) could refer to anyone with some administrative responsibilities, the term "Many Chiefs" (*duoyin*) has been interpreted as secretarial officials, based on reading the same term in Western Zhou inscriptions. This is problematic because, despite the continuing use of the term *yin* 尹 from Shang to the Western Zhou, in the Zhou case the term is usually modified by other words designating specific offices (see Chapter 2), hence different from the Shang case where *yin*, used in a plural sense more often than not, could refer to the "head" of any group of officials. The title "Little Servant" (*xiaochen*) appears on numerous early Western Zhou bronzes, apparently inherited from Shang, but even in the Western Zhou context, the term seems to have designated the domestic servants of the king or of the regional rulers, but not a specific government office. On the interpretation of *yin*, see Chen Mengjia, *Yinxu buci zongshu*, pp. 517–18.

[21] According to Wang, such groups included administrative officials, religious and cultural officials, agricultural or crafts-production officials, and military officials. Wang presents a mixture of oracle-bone terms with "Shang" offices mentioned in post-Western Zhou texts, and the analysis is generally problematic. See Wang Guimin, "Shangchao guanzhi jiqi lishi tedian," *Lishi yanjiu* 1986.4, 107–19.

on the king's hunting trips.[22] This, one may speculate, and the fact that political and administrative decisions needed only to be pronounced, if not actually made, in a secret manner through/by royal divination, might have been meaningful factors that restricted the development of bureaucratic administration in Shang. The Shang state, on the other hand, was not managed through a network of administration directed by the central government that was itself obscure in structure and limited perhaps also in size, but was loosely bound together by the hegemonic power of the Shang king.

THE FOUNDING OF THE WESTERN ZHOU STATE

The oracle-bone inscriptions from the pre-dynastic Zhou capital in present-day Zhouyuan, Shaanxi, show that the Zhou people were doubtless one of the local groups that performed sacrifices to the Shang ancestral kings and might have also at some point of time participated in the loose federation of the Shang state.[23] Among these inscriptions there are also records that the leader of the Zhou people was called *Fangbo*, "Elder of the *Fang*," in reference to the overall political system of the Shang state.[24] However, in the twelfth century BC, Zhou was but a small community among many others on the western edge of the Shang state, which had its immense capital located in Anyang in northern Henan. However, the Zhou, from their center in western Shaanxi, secretly expanded their influence over communities in the adjacent areas and undermined Shang authority in the west until they probably attracted Shang attention, as the textual sources suggest that the leader of Zhou, Ji Li 季歷, died in the hands of a Shang king. The official founding of the Zhou state was credited to his father, the Grand King (or Danfu 亶父), who is said to have set up the Zhou government and the Zhou capital upon the historical move to Qiyi 岐邑 (present-day Zhouyuan).[25] However, the tradition credits Ji Li's son, King Wen, with initiating kingship and for having achieved the regional hegemony of the Zhou state.[26] It so happened that in late May of 1059 BC, when the five major planets of the solar system gathered in a narrow strip in the northern sky visible from the Zhou homeland, a rare astronomical phenomenon that was taken as an auspicious sign

---

[22] This aspect has recently been stressed by Mark Lewis commenting on Shang administration; see Mark Lewis, *The Construction of Space in Early China* (Albany: State University of New York Press, 2006), p. 137.

[23] See Cao Wei, *Zhouyuan jiaguwen* (Beijing: Shijie tushu, 2002), pp. 1, 78.

[24] See *ibid.*, pp. 62, 64. On the oracle bones from Zhouyuan, see also Edward L. Shaughnessy, "Zhouyuan Oracle-Bone Inscriptions: Entering the Research Stage?" *Early China* 11–12 (1985–87), 156–63. On pre-dynastic Zhou relation to the Shang state, see Hsu and Linduff, *Western Chou Civilization*, pp. 44–49.

[25] See *Shijing*, SZ, 16.2, pp. 509–12 (Waley, *The Book of Songs*, pp. 232–33).

[26] See *Shiji*, 4, pp. 115–19 (William H. Nienhauser ed., *The Grand Scribe's Records*, vol. 1: *The Basic Annals of Pre-Han China* [Bloomington: Indiana University Press, 1994], pp. 57–59).

of Heaven's Mandate to Zhou, Wen declared himself "King," officially breaking away from Shang.[27]

The conqueror was King Wu, the Martial King, who elevated the Zhou state from a regional power to universal rule in North China. The time came in the eleventh month of 1046 BC, according to the post-conquest calendar of Zhou, when the Zhou troops left their base in the Wei River valley in Shaanxi and embarked on a long march that was to take them across the Yellow River to the north of present-day Luoyang, striking into the heart of the Shang state. The last Shang king had massed a large army to meet the Zhou invaders but was defeated in a place called Muye 牧野 on the *jiazi* day of the first month of 1045 BC;[28] subsequently he committed suicide and the Shang capital fell instantly into Zhou hands. The conquest had come probably as suddenly for the Zhou as for the Shang, because the Zhou leadership apparently did not have a plan for the post-conquest era but had to adopt a temporary occupational policy, leaving two royal brothers stationed near the former Shang capital when the main body of the Zhou army returned west with King Wu. The conquered Shang subjects, on the other hand, were left to be ruled by Wugeng 武庚, a son of the last Shang king.

However, when King Wu died two years after conquest and power passed to his younger brother, the Duke of Zhou, the two older royal brothers stationed near the former Shang capital responded with rebellion, together with the subjugated Shang population. For a time, the Zhou regime seemed to be crumbling, and its survival depended entirely on the determination and capacity of the leadership. The bronze inscriptions suggest that with the active and collaborative roles of the Duke of Zhou and the Duke of Shao, the Zhou state was able to crush the rebels and to restore Zhou authority in the east. Within three years, the Zhou not only recaptured the former Shang capital, but had conquered the entire eastern plain and its peripheral areas.

The importance of the above historical development can be seen in a series of institutional inventions that came as the result of the Zhou's successful suppression of the rebellion. In fact, it was the second conquest that actually gave the royal Zhou state a new shape and a political

---

[27] The conjunction of the five planets gave legitimacy to King Wen's role; more importantly, it gave the Zhou people a theory of their state (see discussion in Chapter 7). On the event of 1059 BC and its relationship to the founding of the Zhou state, see David W. Pankenier, "Astronomical Dates in Shang and Western Zhou," *Early China* 7 (1981–82), 4–5; Shaughnessy, *Sources of Western Zhou History*, 221–25.

[28] On the dates of the conquest trip, see Edward L. Shaughnessy, "'New' Evidence on the Zhou Conquest," *Early China* 6 (1981–82), 66–69. The very day *jiazi* (# 1) is confirmed by the inscription of the Li *gui* 利簋 (JC: 4131), discovered in 1976, as the date of final combat between the Shang and Zhou troops, although other scholars think that the it took place in 1046 BC instead of 1045. On 1046 BC as the date of Zhou conquest of Shang, see Pankenier, "Astronomical Dates in Shang and Western Zhou," 14–15; *Xia Shang Zhou duandai gongcheng 1996–2000 nian jieduan chengguo baogao* (Beijing: Shijie tushu, 2000), pp. 48–49.

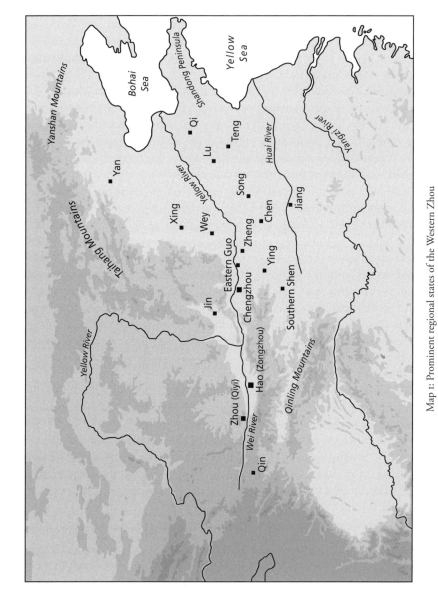

Map 1: Prominent regional states of the Western Zhou

system that was unknown to the Shang. First, an eastern capital was constructed in present-day Luoyang, called "Accomplishing Zhou" (Chengzhou 成周, also known as Luoyi 洛邑, "Settlement of Luo"), where a government branch was set up. Thus, the political reality of the post-conquest era gave rise to a "multi-center" structure, in contrast to the late Shang state, where all political authority was derived from Anyang. Second, the Zhou created what then came to be referred to by the Warring States historians as the "Fengjian" 封建 system,[29] by sending royal kinsmen and relatives to the most strategic locations in and around the eastern plain to form regional Zhou states. Some of these states were located far beyond the eastern plain, such as Yan 燕 near present-day Beijing, and Qi 齊, Lu 魯, and Teng 滕 in western Shandong, for which we have clear archeological evidence (see map 1).[30] The founding of the regional states marked a fundamental departure from the hegemonic religion-focused Shang state, which pursued political supremacy without changing the structure of the local societies. In contrast, the Western Zhou state installed Zhou elements in every corner of the conquered world as part of a unified program of governance; in turn, each regional polity by its very existence marked the presence of the Western Zhou state and provided a new structure in which the local society was reorganized. Third, the Zhou military was divided into two halves, with the Eight Armies located in Chengzhou in the east, and the Six Armies of the West located on the Wei River plain, although the latter armies could also be sent to the east for joint military operations with the former, as is fully evident in the bronze inscriptions. The above changes established the Western Zhou state on a totally different basis from Shang, and determined the fundamental political structure of the northern China plains for the next several centuries. And this new basis was the Heaven's Mandate – it was not merely that the Zhou were hegemonically strong enough to rule, but rather that they possessed the legitimacy to shape a new world and to create a new people.[31]

The first century after the conquest was a period of rapid expansion when the Western Zhou state continued to pursue military goals in all directions. The bronze inscriptions report major military campaigns launched into the lower Ordos region in the north, where the Zhou troops captured a huge number of prisoners along with domesticated animals. In the east, the focus of expansion was placed on the Shandong peninsula, as

---

[29] For a long time, the term "Fengjian" has been translated by the European term "feudalism," which suggests an unjustified comparison of Western Zhou to medieval Europe. In a recent study, I have systematically discussed problems with this translation and the misplaced comparison. See Li Feng, "'Feudalism' and Western Zhou China." See also discussion in Chapter 7, pp. 288–90.

[30] For a systematic analysis of the political geography of the Zhou regional states based on archeological evidence, see Li Feng, *Landscape and Power in Early China*, pp. 66–76, 82–88, 300–342.

[31] This concept of a new world and a new people was manifestly expressed in the "Kanggao" chapter of the *Shangshu*; see *Shangshu*, 14, p. 203 (James Legge, *The Chinese Classics*, Vol. 3: *The Shoo King, or Book of Historical Documents* [Hong Kong: University of Hong Kong Press, 1960; reprint of London: Henry Frowde, 1865], p. 388).

the inscriptions report a series of military operations directed at subjugating the indigenous communities in the region, called Dongyi 東夷 "Eastern Barbarian" by the Zhou in their inscriptions, and by the closing of the early Western Zhou, the Zhou had evidently established their stronghold in the eastern part of the peninsula. It seems that many if not all military operations were conducted through the collaboration between the royal forces and the various combatant units supplied by the regional states, a very interesting pattern of warfare that we see in the bronze inscriptions throughout the Western Zhou dynasty. The gain from such expansion must have been enormous, as slaves and goods continued to flow into the royal domain in Shaanxi and new land continued to be conquered and transferred into regional states. However, when the Zhou moved on to the south during the reign of King Zhao, the last of the early Western Zhou kings, they met formidable challenges in the middle Yangzi region. While the archeological evidence confirms Zhou expansion into this region, the textual records suggest that the Zhou suffered a major military defeat in the nineteenth year of King Zhao that not only ended the life of the king, but put a stop to the long period of great early Western Zhou expansion.[32]

THE MID-WESTERN ZHOU TRANSITION

The mid-Western Zhou had five kings who together ruled for a time that was shorter than three generations of an aristocratic family.[33] In fact, one of the kings, Xiao, was probably the founder of a minor branch of the royal house, being a brother of King Gong and uncle of King Yih, whom he had strangely succeeded. Due to the lack of information, the background of this very peculiar succession is unknown, and in general the received texts have very little to say about the political history of the mid-Western Zhou period except for King Mu, who is reported to have pursued luxury and pleasure rather than safeguarding the long-term interests of the Western Zhou state. Nevertheless, the short reigns themselves may be good indications of political instability, possibly caused by King Xiao's accession to royal power. Another king, Yi, who came to power after the abnormal rule of King Xiao, was reported to have been physically ill and possibly ruled for only seven years.[34] The bronze inscriptions, when compared to the early period, tell us a great deal more about the political institutions and social conditions of the mid-Western Zhou, but add little detail to the bold outline of political history of the Zhou state.

---

[32] For a discussion of King Zhao's southern campaigns and relevant inscriptional evidence, see Lu Liancheng, "An di yu Zhao Wang shijiu nian nanzheng," *Kaogu yu wenwu* 1984.6, 75–79. See also Li Feng, *Landscape and Power in Early China*, pp. 93–95.

[33] According to the chronology recorded in the newly discovered Lai *pan* 逨盤, the three generations of Lai's family had served six Zhou kings from King Zhao to King Yi; see Wenwu 2003.6, 26.

[34] The sources for this tradition are the *Bamboo Annals* and *Zuozhuan*. See *Zhushu jinian*, 2, p. 12 (James Legge, *The Shoo King*, Prolegomena, p. 153); *Zuozhuan*, 52, p. 2114.

However, the available sources offer us an informed view of the transition in the political power and institutions in the Western Zhou state as well as in its relations with the external world, a transition that is marked by a number of signs of weakness and disorder. The bronze inscriptions offer us some evidence of the bureaucratic abuses that might have occurred in the Zhou central government.[35] They also suggest that the Zhou court was no longer able to keep its allies on the borders and even some of the regional states in line by exercising political authority alone, but had to subjugate them to the royal will by military means. A typical case was a dispute between the Zhou court and one of the most prestigious regional states – Qi, located in Shandong, the self-appointed ruler of which, Duke Xian, not only was able to survive a possible royal military attack directed against him, but had ruled many years against the Zhou royal will.[36] Certainly Qi was not the only state that had problems with the central court during the mid-Western Zhou; the inscriptions and texts suggest that even some polities located probably in the upper Jing River valley near the royal domain might not have been obedient and were attacked by the Zhou royal forces.[37] These incidents evidently suggest the loss of control by the royal court over regional elements in a political relationship predetermined by the key institutions set up in the early decades of the Western Zhou dynasty.

War with foreign communities or polities continued to be reported in mid-Western Zhou inscriptions, but we find the Zhou court was no longer in a position to organize full-scale attacks in multiple directions; instead, the Zhou armies often had to fight defensive wars launched by foreign enemies. By far the largest group of military inscriptions from the period was cast in the reign of King Mu in relation to a war that was not a part of Zhou's effort to expand, but a defense of the Zhou state from the invasion by the Huaiyi 淮夷, an indigenous people in the lower Huai River region of the southeast. The inscriptions show that for once the Huaiyi were able to break the frontline of Zhou in the middle reaches of the Huai River and march very close to the Zhou eastern capital, Chengzhou, on the Luo River plain.[38] This was the first major foreign invasion in the century after

---

[35] The evidence for this comes from the inscription of the Mu *gui* 牧簋 (JC: 4343), which records a speech made by a mid-Western Zhou king, possibly King Xiao, in which the king accuses those officials in the central government for betraying the teachings of the Zhou founders and condemns them for abusing the common people in legal matters. For more details, see Li Feng, "Textual Criticism and Western Zhou Bronze Inscriptions: The Example of the Mu Gui," in *Essays in Honour of An Zhimin*, ed. Tang Chung and Chen Xingcan (Hong Kong: Chinese University of Hong Kong, 2004), pp. 280–97.

[36] The campaign against the state of Qi is recorded in the inscription of the Fifth Year Shi Shi *gui* 五年師事簋 (JC: 4216). The inscription and its relation to the turmoil in the state of Qi have been discussed by Shaughnessy in *Sources of Western Zhou History*, pp. 267–78.

[37] See Li Feng, *Landscape and Power in Early China*, pp. 97–98.

[38] For a detailed analysis of these inscriptions, see Xia Hanyi, *Wengu zhixin lu: Shang Zhou wenhua shi guanjian* (Taibei: Daohuo, 1997), pp. 152–55, 158–61. See also Qiu Xiqui, *Gu wenzi lunji*, pp. 386–92.

the Zhou conquest, and it marked a major watershed in Zhou's military history. It is possible to see the declining political control in the Western Zhou state and the loss of advantage on its borders as interrelated aspects of a weakening political-military giant.

The mid-Western Zhou was also a critical period of political-institutional and social changes in the Western Zhou. The mid-Western Zhou saw the rise and popularity of one special type of bronze inscriptions – the appointment inscriptions.[39] From the time of King Mu on, the Western Zhou elites took great interest in casting inscriptions that tirelessly recount the ritual sessions taking place in the Zhou central court, in which the Zhou king personally granted them appointments of service in various government offices. The appointment inscriptions are themselves good indications of major changes in the political culture of the Zhou state: government service had become regulated and there had developed a standard way to document and appreciate it. In general, the majority of the early Western Zhou inscriptions are concerned with military matters, but a much larger number of inscribed bronzes, particularly those with long inscriptions, were cast during the mid-Western Zhou to commemorate merits in civil administration (including official appointments). This strongly implies a shift of concern of the Zhou government, which, as will be examined fully in the following chapters, underwent a process of expansion and reorganization, and as a result, became fully bureaucratized during the mid-Western Zhou.

The political changes highlighted above took place in a society that was itself undergoing profound socioeconomic changes during the mid-Western Zhou, particularly in the Zhou royal domain in Shaanxi, which offers us the most evidence. It is likely that the favorable conditions brought by the political-military success of the state power during the early Western Zhou gradually gave way to a new epoch that was marked by intensified competition, conflict, and struggle among the Zhou aristocratic lineages. The loss of capacity to acquire new lands in eastern China would have meant the loss of opportunities to transfer the Zhou nobles out of the Wei River valley as a way to accommodate the growth of lineages in the Zhou homeland. The Zhou court, having probably already exhausted marginal and virgin lands in the Wei River valley to cope with population pressure, was no longer able to grant the lineages large areas of land as it had done in the early period, but had to hand out lands in a piecemeal fashion often located some distance from each other, as the inscriptions tell us.[40] The lineages,

---

[39] An early example of such inscriptions is the identical text on the Li *fangzun* 盠方尊 (JC: 6013) (figure 7) and Li *fangyi* 盠方彝 (JC: 9900), cast possibly during the early years of King Mu. For the implication of this inscription for the mid-Western Zhou transition, see Shaughnessy, "Western Zhou History," pp. 325–28.

[40] The inscriptions show that during the early Western Zhou, the Zhou king often granted an entire unit of land bearing a single place-name that was expressed as "land" (*tu* 土), such as grants of land recorded in the Qian *you* 趞卣 (JC: 5402) and the Shao *huanqi* 畐圜器 (JC: 10360). In contrast,

while growing ever stronger in power, also developed in a way that would allow the management of land in small parcels by branches or sub-lineages that would in turn develop into new lineages. This development, which was itself the result of land competition, created both new opportunities for social conflicts and new administrative demands. A number of inscriptions document sales of such small pieces of land between different lineages, monitored by officials sent from the central government, while many others record law suits brought to the royal court by nobles whose fields had been invaded by farmers of the neighboring lineages or by low-ranking officials against their superiors.[41] The inscriptions suggest that during the mid-Western Zhou competition over economic resources in the royal domain reached an unprecedented level and probably provided the cause of intensified social conflict and unrest.

In addition, the bronzes themselves, as the media through which we know the social and political history of the Western Zhou, underwent significant changes marked not only by the rise of appointment inscriptions, but also more ostensibly by their design and ornament. When entering the reign of King Mu, the Zhou elites seemed to have become overwhelmingly interested in one subject, the bird, and reproduced it in various forms that fitted the often streamlined body of the vessels. On the other hand, the various types of animal masks that had their origins in Shang and dominated bronze decorative art during the early Western Zhou were gradually abandoned. However, after King Mu's reign the interest in birds also seemed to have diminished quickly, giving way to simplistic and bold-lined geometric designs developed either from the birds or the masks, and this change set the standard for the next 200 years.[42] However, the changes were not merely decorative, but more fundamentally involved the

---

the mid-Western Zhou inscriptions often record lands in the form of "field" (*tian* 田), undoubtedly a much smaller unit, granted in multiple numbers by the Zhou king to his officials. The extreme case is the Da Ke *ding* 大克鼎 (JC: 2836), which records the king giving seven "fields" to Ke, each located in a separate location marked by a single place-name. The latter pattern of land-granting was carried into the late Western Zhou period, as indicated by the recently discovered Forty-second Year Lai *ding* 四十二年逨鼎 (*Wenwu* 2003.6, 14–15), which records Lai receiving a total of fifty "fields" divided between two different locations. For details of this transition in the patterns of land-granting by the Zhou king, see Li Feng, *Landscape and Power in Early China*, pp. 123–25.

[41] For instance, the Hu *ding* 曶鼎 (JC: 2838) records a law suit filed by Hu to the crown prince against Kuang Ji 匡季, who was accused of allowing a group of his farmers and domestic servants to steal crops from Hu's field. Hence Hu demanded satisfaction from Kuang Ji to the sum of five "fields" together with one farmer and three servants. The Zhen *yi* 朕匜 (JC: 10285. 1–2) records a law suit brought to the court by Muniu 牧牛 against his own superior, but Muniu lost the case and was himself punished. For discussions of these cases, see Laura Skosey, "The Legal System and Legal Tradition of the Western Zhou, CA. 1045–771 B.C.E.," unpublished PhD thesis, University of Chicago (1996), pp. 96–99; Matsumaru Michio, "Sei Shū kōki shakai ni mieru henkaku no hōga: Ko tei mei kaishaku mondai no shohoteki kaiketsu," in *Nishijima Sadao hakase kanreki kinen: Higashi Ajia shi ni okeru kokka to nōmin* (Tokyo: Yamakawa, 1984), pp. 49–64; "Sei Shū kinbun chū no hōsei shiryō," in *Chūgoku hōsei shi: Kihon shiryō no kenkyū*, ed. Shiga Shūzō (Tokyo: Tokyo daigaku, 1993), pp. 21–29.

[42] For this important change in bronze art, see Rawson, *Western Zhou Ritual Bronzes from the Arthur M. Sackler Collections*, pp. 75–83; Lothar von Falkenhausen, "Late Western Zhou taste," *Études chinoises* 18 (1999), 155–74.

way bronzes were used in ritual or ceremonial contexts: through the mid-Western Zhou, the traditional set of burial bronzes that included multiple wine vessels gradually gave way to a new set that was essentially devoid of such types. Thus, by the late part of the mid-Western Zhou, Zhou bronze culture had been completely transformed from its origins in the Shang tradition.[43]

In sum, the current evidence gives us the strong impression that the mid-Western Zhou was an important period of reorientation of socioeconomic and cultural trends, reordering of political relations in the Zhou state and beyond, and reorganization of the Zhou government and the other political institutions that came after the end of the great early Western Zhou expansion. It was also a period in which the seeds of the dynastic decline evident in the late Western Zhou, were first sown.

THE LATE WESTERN ZHOU STATE

We are better informed about the political history of the late Western Zhou period. The period began with the accession of King Li, who presided over a period of deep crisis in Zhou history. In foreign relations, the Zhou position had apparently shifted from that of invaders to that of defenders, as the Western Zhou state was meeting serious challenges on two fronts. In the south, the Huaiyi had never ceased to be a major threat to Zhou security since their war with the Zhou in the time of King Mu; but it was the rebellion of the ruler of E 鄂, a former Zhou ally who held the title "Border Protector" (*yufang* 馭方) in the Nanyang basin, that incited extensive attacks by the Huaiyi together with the Dongyi on Zhou's inner states, pushing the Zhou state almost to the edge of collapse. In the northwest, the Xianyun 玁狁, a society that inhabited the highlands of Gansu and Ningxia, launched repeated attacks on the Zhou royal domain in Shaanxi, directly threatening the Zhou capitals. Internally, the king had serious troubles with the Zhou elites and was reported to have adopted harsh measures against those who dared to disagree with him. Under such pressure, King Li's government collapsed and the king

---

[43] The change in bronze art has been taken by some art historians as an indication of some kind of "ritual reform" or "ritual revolution." While this is certainly not impossible, we have no written evidence that such a "reform" took place as a social program planned and implemented by an agent or agents; if it did take place, it must have been a small part of the much wider sociopolitical transformation that is analyzed above. As for the date of this "reform," Rawson pinpoints this change in the reigns of Kings Yih, Xiao, and Yi, from 899/97 to 858 BC, largely within the confines of the mid-Western Zhou; see Jessica Rawson, "Statesmen or Barbarians? The Western Zhou as Seen through their Bronzes," *Proceedings of the British Academy* 75 (1989), 89–93; "Western Zhou Archaeology," in *The Cambridge History of Ancient China*, pp. 433–40. Lothar von Falkenhausen, on the other hand, insists on calling it the "late Western Zhou ritual reform," a transformation that he thinks occurred around 850 BC, during the reign of King Li. See Falkenhausen, "Late Western Zhou Taste," 155–64; *Chinese Society in the Age of Confucius (1000–250 BC): The Archeological Evidence* (Los Angeles: Cotsen Institute of Archaeology, UCLA, 2006), pp. 56–64.

himself was driven out of the capital in 842 BC. In the next fourteen years before he died, it was a minister named Hefu 龢父 in the bronze inscriptions who was in charge of the Zhou court. Traditional historians have apportioned a great deal of blame to King Li for the failure of his government, but I have recently suggested that it was rather the policies, especially the granting of landed properties to the aristocratic lineages pursued by all previous kings, that had long since undermined the power of the royal house. It is possible, and indeed probable, that the incident of 842 BC resulted from a failed attempt by King Li to restore power to the royal house.[44]

This very unusual political incident gave rise to the young King Xuan, who was able to rule for forty-six years, the longest reign of the Western Zhou. Our inscriptional and textual records suggest that King Xuan was quite successful in the first half of his reign. The royal armies were again active on the borders, taking offensive against enemies particularly in the northwestern highlands and in the Huai River region in the south. It is also likely that the central court made systematic efforts to reorganize the Western Zhou state. This includes, first of all, the reconnection with some regional states in the distant east and north that had hitherto been alienated by the passage of time or even by their political quarrels with the Zhou court; some of these states, such as Qi and Ji, were again found in the inscriptions fighting alongside the royal army against their common enemies in the Huai River region. Further steps were taken by the Zhou court to transfer states from place to place to meet the needs of territorial security; this included most importantly the movement of the states of Shen 申 and probably also Lü 呂 from the upper Jing River valley to the Nanyang basin in the hope of filling the power vacuum left possibly by the rebellion of the ruler of E. It is also likely that, in this process of state reorganization, King Xuan might have even revived the early Western Zhou practice of the "Fengjian" institution by sending recent royal descendants to form new regional states, such as the establishment of the state of Yang in the Fen River valley, recorded in the newly discovered Forty-third Year Lai *ding* 四十三年逨鼎.[45] These strategies seem to have provided stability to the Western Zhou state. However, in the later part of King Xuan's reign, the received texts record, the Zhou royal forces suffered another series of major defeats, and the bronze inscriptions make clear that the Xianyun were again on the offensive against the Zhou royal domain.

The late Western Zhou bronze inscriptions continue to record official appointments granted by the Zhou king, suggesting continuity in the practice of government and administrative control. However, there seems

---

[44] For this historical development, see Li Feng, *Landscape and Power in Early China*, pp. 102–7, 131–34.
[45] See *Wenwu* 2003.6, 6–15.

to have been a subtle but significant change in the power structure of the Zhou royal court as we see again a few eminent officials exercising overwhelmingly strong control over court politics, as the Dukes of Zhou and Shao probably did during the early Western Zhou, but a phenomenon that was not evident during much of the mid-Western Zhou. For instance, Duke Wu was probably in such a position in the time of King Li, and so probably was the Duke of Mao, to whom King Xuan entrusted the supervision of the entire Zhou government.[46] Certainly, we also know the case of Hefu, who actually occupied the role of the king and was responsible for one of the only two non-royal appointments recorded in the inscriptions.[47] On the other hand, we find that the Zhou king more often tended to send his domestic officials of relatively lower status such as the Provisioner or Scribe on important business trips beyond the royal capital as perhaps a method to counterbalance the influence of the powerful ministers.[48] At the societal level, social conflict continued to be the topic of records in the inscriptions, as is most typical in the case of the Sanshi *pan* 散氏盤 (JC: 10176).[49] Overall, the late Western Zhou appeared to have been again a time of very frequent wars that the Zhou fought to defend their own territory against invading enemies, or that were instigated by the Zhou court in an attempt to regain control of the previous geographical perimeter.

The problem that eventually brought the Western Zhou dynasty to an end had its deep roots in a generational change in the Zhou government. The transition to new government after the death of King Xuan did not go smoothly but resulted in struggles between the last king, You, and his supporters, and a group of senior officials led by the "August Father" (Huangfu 皇父), who had served a long career under King Xuan, and in all likelihood this partisan struggle in the Zhou court seems to have been accompanied by a series of catastrophes that ravaged the Zhou royal

---

[46] In the long inscription of the Maogong *ding* 毛公鼎 (JC: 2841.1–2), the Duke of Mao was given authority over both the Ministry and the Secretariat, the two main branches of the Zhou central government, and the royal kinsmen, the marshals, the praetorian guarding units, and even the king's own domestic officials. See more discussion of the inscription in Chapter 2, pp. 86–90.

[47] This is the Shi Hui *gui* 師毁簋 (JC: 4311), which records Bo Hefu's 伯和父 speech commanding Shi Hui to serve his family. Hefu is also mentioned in the First Year Shi Dui *gui* 元年師兌簋 (JC: 4274), Third Year Shi Dui *gui* 三年師兌簋, and the Shi Li *gui* 師𩰲簋 (JC: 4324.2). On the identity and Hefu and his regency, see Guo Moruo, *Liang Zhou jinwen ci daxi tulu kaoshi*, 8 vols. (Beijing: Kexue, 1958), p. 114; Shaughnessy, *Sources of Western Zhou History*, pp. 272–73.

[48] For instance, we find in the Shi Song *gui* 史頌簋 (JC: 4232) that Scribe Song was sent to inspect an area called Su 蘇 to the north of Luoyang in the east. We also find in the newly discovered Wu Hu *ding* 吳虎鼎 (JL: 364) that Provisioner Fengsheng 豐生, along with a Supervisor of Construction from the court, was responsible for a land transfer ordered by the king. See *Kaogu yu wenwu*, 1998.3, 69–71.

[49] The Sanshi *pan* records the process of a land demarcation as the result of a raid carried out by the polity of Ze 夨 on the settlements belonging to the lineage of San 散, both located in the Baoji area at the western end of the middle Wei River valley in Shaanxi. For the implications of the inscription for Zhou local administration, see Chapter 4, pp. 183–87.

domain in Shaanxi.[50] In fact, the "August Father" can be identified with a group of important inscribed bronzes that was discovered in Zhouyuan in 1933.[51] This struggle eventually led to an open split between King You and the senior official, who left the capital with his supporters in 777 BC to reside in the east. The problem led to further political conflict between the Zhou court and some local polities including Western Shen 西申 and Zeng 鄫, located in key positions on the northwestern border that offered protection to the exiled crown prince, probably supported by the senior officials. With his control over the Zhou court fully consolidated through the installation of new officials, King You decided to take a further step to eliminate the crown prince and to secure the future succession of his younger son to the throne. However, when he sent the royal army to attack Western Shen and demanded the prince, the Zhou army was defeated by the joint forces of Western Shen and Zeng, assisted by Zhou's longtime enemy, the Xianyun. The allied forces subsequently marched on the Zhou capital, capturing it and killing King You in 771 BC.

When the prince was installed as King Ping after the war that destroyed the Zhou capital, he decided to reestablish the Zhou court in Luoyi in the east, hence beginning the Eastern Zhou period (770–256 BC) of Chinese history.

[50] On the historical circumstances surrounding the fall of the Western Zhou dynasty, see also Hsu and Linduff, *Western Chou Civilization*, pp. 279–84.

[51] These are the Han Huangfu 函皇父 bronzes, including two Han Huangfu *ding* 函皇父鼎 (JC: 2548, 2745), four Han Huangfu *gui* 函皇父簋 (JC: 4141), and Han Huangfu *pan* 函皇父盤 (JC: 10164). For the discovery of these bronzes, see *Qingtongqi tushi* (Beijing: Wenwu, 1960), pp. 20–21.

CHAPTER 2

Structural development of the Zhou central government

Regarding the government institution of the Western Zhou, a systematic analysis on the basis of the contemporaneous bronze inscriptions was conducted by Zhang Yachu and Liu Yu in 1986. From their extensive survey, the two authors reconstructed the Western Zhou government in each of the three sub-periods.[1] While we must deeply appreciate the efforts of the two authors in producing the most up-to-date account of inscriptional evidence at that time in the hope of rationalizing the structural changes of the Western Zhou government, the fruit gained from the study was very limited. In general, I think we know much less about the organization of the Zhou government, even with the help of the new inscriptions discovered in the last twenty years, than Zhang and Liu thought we did. Much of the problem in their study derives from a methodological deficiency – they drew little distinction between a person's official title and his official duty. To some extent, the language of the bronze inscriptions allows such ambiguity, as the term *si* 嗣 "to be in charge" is used in both ways. As the result of a large number of terms describing official responsibilities being treated as official titles,[2] the bureaucracy reconstructed by Zhang and Liu is indeed very greatly inflated.

In order to clarify the structural characteristics of the Zhou government, objective criteria must be first developed. In the present study, the following three points are closely observed: (1) when a person is appointed to *zuo* 作 "to be" something, the term that follows *zuo* is accepted as an official title; (2) when a personal name or designation is prefixed by a title that clearly describes a governmental function, as in the case of *Sima Jingbo* 嗣馬井伯, the term is regarded as an official title; and (3) when such titles appear independently representing an individual whose name is not given

---

[1] See Zhang Yachu and Liu Yu, *Xi Zhou jinwen guanzhi yanjiu*, pp. 105–10. Zhang and Liu were members of the research team in the Institute of Archaeology, CASS, responsible for the compilation of the monumental corpus of bronze inscriptions, *Yin Zhou jinwen jicheng* (Beijing: Zhonghua, 1984–94), which gave them full access to inscriptions down to the early 1980s as basis for their study.

[2] Just to give an example to show the nature of the problem: the inscription of the Mian *fu* 免簠 (JC: 4626) says that Mian was appointed *situ* 嗣土 "Supervisor of Land" with the responsibilities of 嗣鄭還林眾吳眾牧 (in charge of the forest, marshes, and hunting ground in the vicinity of Zheng); here, all of these terms – *lin*, *wu*, *mu* – are treated by Zhang and Liu as official titles, logically conflicting with his explicitly named official title *situ*. See Zhang Yachu and Liu Yu, *Xi Zhou jinwen guanzhi yanjiu*, pp. 68–69.

in the inscription, whether as the subject or object of an action, the title is accepted as an official title. An official title is understood as the name of a government role that is embodied in a particular office, whether physical or virtual, and is customized with a certain jurisdiction determined by the way in which responsibilities of the government are divided and integrated into a structural whole. Besides clarifying the official titles and their associated responsibilities, it is more important to consider the rationales behind the arrangement of government roles. Therefore, the study presented below is concerned not only with the general organization of the Western Zhou government, but also with the way in which such organization was conditioned by the political and social circumstances of the Western Zhou state. It will not take the path of traditional studies of *guanzhi* 官制 "system of offices," which focus on determining the responsibilities of individual offices, but will proceed in a way that aims to reveal the structural configuration of the Western Zhou government as an organized body through which political authority was expressed and achieved over time. For a fuller analysis of the range of responsibilities associated with each office based on a survey of the inscriptions that mention it, the reader should consult Appendix I: "A list of official titles in Western Zhou bronze inscriptions."

THE BIFURCATION OF THE WESTERN ZHOU STATE

In order to understand the organizational characteristics of the Western Zhou government, we must first understand the overall political structure of the Western Zhou state for the management of which the government was set up. As has been briefly discussed in Chapter 1, the Western Zhou state was the product of two conquests: the first took place under King Wu and the second was achieved under the regency of the Duke of Zhou. A number of early Western Zhou inscriptions testify to the "colonization" process by which the Zhou royal kinsmen and relatives were established as rulers of the regional states, often accompanied by Zhou or allied migrants to the new states, to control the vast, newly conquered territory in the east.[3] While leaving discussions on the nature of the Zhou regional

---

[3] At least four inscriptions that we know of were cast on occasions when a regional ruler was established on order of the Zhou king: (1) the most typical case is the Ke *lei* 克罍 (JL: 987), commemorating that Ke 克, a son of the Duke of Shao, was established ruler of the state of Yan 匽 (燕) in Liulihe 琉璃河 near Beijing where the bronze was found; (2) the Ta Situ *gui* 大嗣土簋 (JC: 4059) mentions that the Zhou king, upon attacking the Shang capital, commanded Kanghou, a brother of his, to be the ruler of Wey 衛 near the Shang capital Anyang; (3) the Mai *fangzun* 麥方尊 (JC: 6015) records a series of events beginning with the Zhou king's sending out of the ruler of Xing 邢 to his own state in Xingtai, Hebei province; (4), the Yihou Ze *gui* 宜侯夨簋 (JC: 4320) carries a detailed account of the Zhou king's command to Ze 夨 to be the ruler of Yi 宜, although the location of the named state is still debated. There are also incidences of the establishment of the regional states by the Zhou court recorded in the received texts; see the systematic analysis by Itō Michiharu, *Chūgoku kodai kokka*, pp. 78–83, 98–105. The inscriptional term for establishing regional rulers is *hou* 侯, used in its verbal sense. I borrowed the term "colonization" from Shaughnessy; see Shaughnessy, "Western Zhou History," p. 311.

states to Chapter 6, it should be noted here that rising from this process was a bifurcated structure of the Western Zhou state. It was mainly a division between the conquered east, placed under the authority of the many regional rulers, and the west, mainly the Wei River valley in central Shaanxi and the small area surrounding Luoyang, over which the Zhou royal court exercised direct administrative control. This division represented two separate areas of administration that remained fundamental to the Western Zhou state throughout much of the dynasty.

In the past twenty years, more than a half dozen regional states have been investigated by archeologists, and the inscriptions on the bronzes from the tombs in their respective cemeteries customarily refer to the regional rulers as *hou*, such as Yanhou 燕侯, Jinhou 晉侯, Yinghou 應侯, Xinghou 邢侯, Luhou 魯侯, and Tenghou 滕侯, etc. These inscriptions leave us in no doubt that the rulers of the regional states in the east were conventionally referred to as *hou* (hereafter translated as "Ruler", with a capital).[4] We also have inscriptional evidence that some of the eastern rulers might have been referred to as *nan* 男, such as Xunan 許男, the ruler of the state of Xu, located in southern Henan. With only two exceptions, which can be explained by special circumstances surrounding their provenance,[5] we can almost say that the title *hou* never appeared on bronzes discovered in the Wei River valley in Shaanxi. Instead, the heads of the local aristocratic lineages in the Wei River valley are refered to more often as *bo* 伯 (hereafter translated as "Eldest"), and sometimes as *zhong* 仲, *shu* 叔, and *ji* 季, all terms designating their seniority. The reason that we have many more *bo*, such as Jingbo 井伯, Rongbo 榮伯, Dingbo 定伯, and Shanbo 單伯, is because of the practice of primogeniture under which the first-born sons had a better chance to succeed their fathers as the heads of the families and to enter government service, and therefore they cast many more bronzes.[6] It is certainly possible that the ruling elites

---

[4] The etymology of the word *hou* 医 (Yanhou *gui* 燕侯簋; JC: 3614) provides us with a basis for understanding the function and status of *hou* in the general political structure of the Western Zhou state. Most scholars consider that, as suggested by the *Shuowen jiezi*, the character *hou* originally depicted the target used in archery rituals with an arrow hitting it; it was extended to mean people who were skilled in martial arts. This meaning well reflects the military role of the regional rulers as primarily the defenders of the Western Zhou state. See Zhou Fagao, *Jinwen gulin* (Hong Kong: Chinese University of Hong Kong Press, 1975), pp. 3464–65; see also Liu Yu, "Xi Zhou jinwen zhong de sheli," *Kaogu* 12(1986), 117–20. The term also appears in the Shang oracle-bone inscriptions and has been translated as "Archer-Lord" in the Shang context. See Li Xiaoding, *Jiagu wenzi jishi* (Taipei: Academia Sinica, 1965), pp. 5.1810–11; Shaughnessy, "Extra-Lineage Cult in the Shang Dynasty," 186.

[5] In both cases, it is certain that the bronze was not cast locally but was transported to the royal domain from the east. The first is the Xunhou *pan* 荀侯盤 (JC: 10096), discovered in Zhangjiapo, cast by the Ruler of Xun, whose state was located in the lower Fen River valley of Shanxi. The second is the Chenhou *gui* 陳侯簋 (JC: 3815), discovered together with the famous Li *gui* 利簋 (JC: 4131) in Lintong, Shaanxi, but cast by the Ruler of Chen in southern Henan for his daughter, who married the Zhou king.

[6] Zhang Yachu gives: 5.8: 2.5: 2.8: 1. Zhang's figures may not be accurate because they include bronzes cast by/for women whose names sometimes contain such words referring to their husbands' birth order, but I trust that the rate offered by Zhang reflects the actual balance of people who referred

in a regional state in the east could use such seniority titles to differentiate their siblings, but it is quite conventional for a regional ruler to use the official political title *hou*. So far none of the lineage heads who had their bases in the Wei River valley is known to have used the title "Ruler" on his bronzes.[7]

This distinction between *hou* and *bo* in the language of the bronze inscriptions with respect to the geographic regions in which they were used suggests a conceptual differentiation in Zhou political thought between the eastern states and the polities in the west. This distinction is well reflected in some inscriptions that describe the general organization of the Western Zhou government. An interesting case is the inscription of the Ling *fangyi* 令方彝 (JC: 9901; translation below, p. 51) in which *hou* and *nan* appear together in the context of "*zhuhou* 諸侯: *hou* 侯, *dian* 甸, *nan* 男," suggesting that they all belonged to the group of dignitaries generally called *zhuhou*, the "Many Rulers," although the three might well have been of reduced rank or significance in the Zhou political system of regional states. Juxtaposed with this group were other groups of dignitaries, such as *zhuyin* 諸尹 "Many Ministers," *lijun* 里君 "District Administrators," and *baigong* 百工 "Hundred Officials," all officials in the royally directly administered zone including whose who served at the Zhou royal court (figures 1–2). Furthermore, this binary arrangement is paralleled by another list of dignitaries who attended an important meeting in Chengzhou in which the Duke of Zhou announced the founding of the state of Wey 衛 near the former Shang capital Anyang, recorded in "Kanggao" 康誥, one of the genuine Western Zhou chapters of the *Shangshu*: "*hou* 侯, *dian* 甸, *nan* 男, *bang* 邦, *cai* 采, and *wei* 衛"; all of these titles represented people who had authority over certain areas of land.[8] Further comparison of this list with another slightly different list found in the "Jiugao" 酒誥 chapter of the *Shangshu* suggests that *bang* 邦 here actually stands for *bangbo* 邦伯, the head of the local polity called *bang*.[9] Correlating these

---

7 to themselves by such seniority terms. See Zhang Yachu, *Yin Zhou jinwen jicheng yinde* (Beijing: Zhonghua, 2001), pp. 1511–12.

7 For a more systematic study of the various aristocratic titles, see Li Feng, "Transmitting Antiquity: The Origin and Paradigmization of the 'Five Ranks'," in *Perceptions of Antiquity in Chinese Civilization* (Würzburger Sinologische Schriften), ed. Dieter Kohn and Helga Stahl (Heidelberg: Edition Forum, 2008), pp. 103–34.

8 Although the last three terms, *bang*, *cai*, and *wei*, literally designate certain territories or lands, in this context they refer to authorities over such territories. See *Shangshu*, 14, p. 202 (Legge, *The Shoo King*, pp. 381–98).

9 In the "Jiugao," the terms appear in the order: *hou* 侯, *dian* 甸, *nan* 男, *wei* 衛, *bangbo* 邦伯. See *Shangshu*, 14, p. 207 (Legge, *The Shoo King*, pp. 399–412). However, there is a historiographical problem in this source because the line in question appears in the middle of the "king's" speech that praises the officials of Shang for their virtue and diligence, in contrast to those who lived under the last Shang king. This would appear to some scholars as if it is suggesting that the Shang had practiced something like the "Fengjian" system of Zhou. See Xu Zhongshu and Tang Jiahong, "Lun Yin Zhou de waifu," in *Xian Qin shi lunji* (Xian: Renwen zazhi, 1982), pp. 53–54; Wang Guimin, *Shang Zhou zhidu kaoxin* (Taipei: Minwen, 1989), pp. 132–36. However, given the chapter's close relationship to the "Kanggao," it is quite possible that the speaker is trying to interpret the Shang situation

Figure 1. The Ling *fangyi* in the Freer Gallery of Art (Freer Gallery of Art, Smithsonian
Institution, Washington, DC: Purchase, F1930.54; reproduced with permission)

sources, but following more importantly the geographical distribution of
hou as revealed by current archeology, we have every reason to believe that
in the political thought of the Zhou elites this was a conventional way
to configure the Western Zhou state, which was composed of two zones:
(1) *hou, dian, nan,* all regional rulers located in the east and in control
of numerous regional states; (2) *bang, cai, wei,* all polities located in the
west, mainly the Wei River valley of central Shaanxi, over which the Zhou

according to the Zhou system, or in Zhou terminology. This possibility has also been pointed out
in Zhu Fenghan, *Shang Zhou jiazu xingtai yanjiu* (Tianjin: Tianjin guji, 2004), p. 289. In general, as
noted earlier, the idea of a Shang "Fengjian" system is very doubtful.

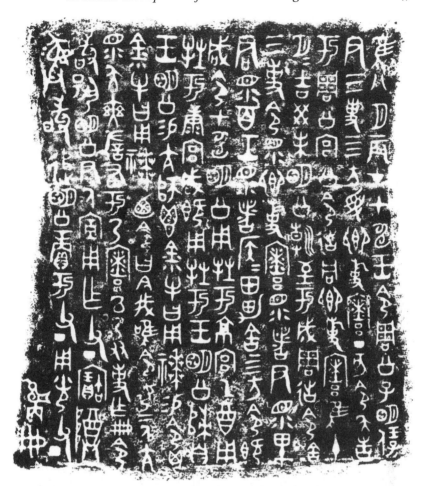

Figure 2. Inscription of the Ling *fangyi* (from *Yin Zhou jinwen jicheng* [Beijing: Zhonghua, 1984–94], no. 9901.1)

royal court exercised direct administrative control. By the same token, the government apparatus of the Western Zhou state was also conceptually divided into two parts, founded on very different principles and manifest in the inscription of the Ling *fangyi*.

Furthermore, two institutional differentiations might have also originated from the same binary conceptualization of the Western Zhou state. The first is a distinction between the terms *guo* 國 and *bang* 邦. In this regard, it is safe to say that, although *bang* was sometimes used in a more general sense, such as in the term *zhoubang* 周邦, referring to the Zhou state, and at such level it cannot always be differentiated from *guo*, in its narrow sense it was primarily used to designate the polities located in the Wei River valley, such as Jingbang 井邦 in the inscription of the Yu *ding*

禹鼎 (JC: 2833), but it was never used for particular regional states in the Western Zhou context. On the contrary, *guo* was used frequently in such terms as *dongguo* 東國, *neiguo* 內國, referring to the regional Zhou states, but it was never used for the polities located in Shaanxi. This suggests that *guo* and *bang* were probably different geographical units as well as different levels of administrative construction. Although a *bang* also had a defined area, and in middle to late Western Zhou times more precisely it referred to a cluster of areas with settlements under the political control of a lineage (see Chapter 4), it did not constitute that kind of jurisdiction and political power associated with the geopolitical entities that were called *guo*. Furthermore, the action of establishing an aristocratic polity such as *bang* in the Wei River valley is described with the term *feng* 封, meaning planting trees to demarcate borders, as frequently seen in inscriptions from Shaanxi. In fact, the characters *feng* and *bang* are semantically closely related.[10] On the other hand, the action of establishing a regional ruler is often described in the inscriptions with the character *hou* 侯 in its verbal sense "to become ruler." Professor Qiu Xigui's convincing analysis of the character 🀥 as *jian* 建 "to establish" in the inscription of the Xiaochen X *ding* 小臣𦉢鼎 (JC: 2556) has left us little doubt that the action of establishing a regional state is called *jian*.[11] This usage became even clearer with the recent discovery of the Forty-second Year Lai *ding*, where the Zhou king is quoted as literally saying: "I initially established Changfu as ruler at Yang" (余肇建長父侯于楊).[12]

    The above analysis indicates that the regional states located in the east constituted an entirely different order from that which was formed by the aristocratic polities scattered in the Wei River valley in central Shaanxi that, together with the small area surrounding the eastern capital Chengzhou, also under direct royal control, can be properly called the "royal

---

[10] Creel has correctly interpreted *feng* as one or two hands holding a plant, meaning "to plant it," but took it as an indication of "fiefs" in European sense. See Creel, *The Origins of Statecraft*, p. 322. The character *feng* appears on the bronzes as 🀙 (Sixth Year Zhousheng *gui* 六年琱生簋; JC: 4293) and 🀚 (Sanshi *pan* 散氏盤; JC: 10176), and is graphically related to *bang* 🀛 (Yu *ding* 禹鼎; JC: 2833) and 🀜 (Maogong *ding* 毛公鼎; JC: 2841). While *feng* signifies the action of "planting" trees to define borders, the component *yi* 邑 (settlement) in *bang* suggests that it refers to the area of residence defined by such trees, resulting from the action of *feng*. For discussions on the etymology of the two words and their graphical relationship, see Zhou Fagao, *Jinwen gulin*, pp. 4099–4100, 7450–52.

[11] The inscription of the Xiaochen X *ding* (JC: 2556) says: "The Duke of Shao established the state of Yan" (召公🀝 匽). The bronze must have been cast very close in time to the Ke *lei* 克罍 (JL: 987) mentioned above, which records the granting of the state of Yan by the Zhou king, most likely King Cheng, to a son of the Duke of Shao. See Qiu Xigui, *Gu wenzi lunji*, pp. 353–56. For the Xiaochen X *ding*, see also Chen Mengjia, "Xi Zhou tongqi duandai," 2.94–95.

[12] The character *jian* appears as 🀞 on the Forty-second Year Lai *ding*, cast late in the forty-second year of King Xuan (786 BC); see *Wenwu* 2003.6, 6, 17. However, it should be noted that the meaning of *jian* was expanded later and was used also in relation to *bang* in a more general sense, such as in the phrase "*jian wo bang guo*" 建我邦國 on the Caihou *zhong* 蔡侯鐘 (JC: 210) cast in the late Spring and Autumn period where *jian* is written 🀟.

domain."[13] The former was a political order that was conceived and was only meaningful with the Western Zhou state as its system of reference, while the later was a social order that was based on the ethic value of the Zhou people and that regulated the relations within the lineages. These two orders had very different political and social roles in the Western Zhou state.[14] In other words, the two zones of the Western Zhou state were founded on different principles and were organized and governed in different ways, associated with which there was a whole range of institutional differentiations. Although the actual boundaries of the royal domain cannot be determined with accuracy on the basis of the information we have,[15] discovering this fundamental division in the political structure of the Western Zhou state can provide us with an important new basis for studying the Western Zhou government. While the governments of the regional states in the east will be discussed in Chapter 6, the following analysis will focus mainly on the Zhou central government that operated in the royal domain in the west.

THE EARLY WESTERN ZHOU GOVERNMENT

Even though the bronze inscriptions constitute the primary sources for our analysis of the Western Zhou government, they are not balanced for every period. In fact, it is not until the mid-Western Zhou period that we

---

[13] Previous scholars have already noted the existence of a "royal domain" (*wangji* 王畿) based on descriptions in later texts such as the *Zhouli* 周禮 and *Liji* 禮記. However, few have considered the institutional differences between it and areas controlled by the regional rulers on the basis of archeological evidence. On the contrary, it has been commonly held that the lineage heads in the royal domain were also *zhuhou* 諸侯, hence not different from the regional rulers in the east. See Lü Wenyu, "Zhou dai wangji kaoshu," *Renwen zazhi* 1992.2, 92–101; Wang Jian, *Xi Zhou zhengzhi dili jiegou yanjiu* (Zhengzhou: Zhongzhou guji, 2004), pp. 52–53, 82–103. Alternatively the lineage heads were called "Inner Rulers" (*nei zhuhou* 内諸侯) or "Rulers in the Royal Domain" (*jinei zhuhou* 畿内諸侯), but this is completely to misunderstand the Western Zhou state and to misinterpret the nature of the regional entities. See Yoshimoto Michimasa, "Kokusei shi," in *In Shū Shin Kan jidaishi no kihon mondai*, ed. Matsumaru Michio *et al.* (Tokyo: Kyūko shoin 2001), pp. 63–88; Matsui Yoshinori, "Shū no kokusei: Hōkensei to kansei o chūshin toshite," in *In Shū Shin Kan jidaishi no kihon mondai*, pp. 89–112.

[14] David Sena, agreeing with the fundamental distinction analyzed here, has recently noted an interesting point regarding the transition from lineage to statehood. He suggested, though not very explicitly, when the heads of the Guo lineage were referred to as Guo Xuangong 虢宣公 and Guo Wengong 虢文公 (rarely used in the inscriptions for the lineage heads in the west), particularly with the latter's receipt of royal mandate in the fifteenth year of King Xuan, this indicates Guo's acquisition of regional rulership, corresponding to Guo's migration to the east, hence the founding of the regional state Guo in Sanmenxia, Henan. See David M. Sena, "Reproducing Society: Lineage and Kinship in Western Zhou China," unpublished PhD thesis, University of Chicago (2005), pp. 169–74.

[15] It should be noted that later Confucian texts actually describe the Zhou royal domain as having a square area of 1000 *li* on each side, located at the center of the idealized royal state. See *Zhouli*, 33, p. 863; *Liji*, 11, p. 1322; *Mencius*, trans David Hinton (Washington, DC: Counterpoint, 1998), pp. 181–82. There has even been a recent attempt to use this figure, when converted to modern units, to demarcate the Zhou royal domain in actual geography. See Lü Wenyu, *Zhou dai caiyi zhidu yanjiu* (Taipei: Wenjin, 1992), pp. 13–19. However, there seems little basis for such a study.

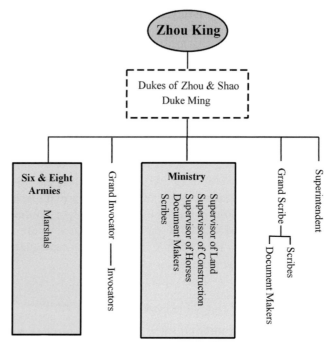

Figure 3. Organizational map of the Western Zhou government (royal domain: early Western Zhou)

have enough information to suggest a reliable reconstruction of the organization of the Zhou central government. In contrast to the mid-Western Zhou inscriptions, which offer such an excellent continuum of information about official appointments, the early Western Zhou inscriptions are much more diversified in content, and the largest group of commemorative records are concerned mostly with warfare. This certainly suggests the militant character of the early Western Zhou government in an age of great territorial expansion that provided reasons for the young and senior elites to cast inscriptions to celebrate their military contributions to the Zhou state. Although the available inscriptions do not allow us the freedom of a full structural analysis, we can perhaps recover some fundamental characteristics of the early Western Zhou government in its historical context (see figure 3).

General structural divisions

The key to understanding the organization of the early Western Zhou government lies in the long inscription cast identically on the Ling *fangyi* 令方彝 (JC: 9901) and Ling *fangzun* 令方尊 (JC: 6016) that records in detail the mission of Duke Ming, son of the Duke of Zhou, to the eastern

Zhou capital Chengzhou (present-day Luoyang) to inspect the Zhou officials as well as regional rulers present there. In fact, the bronzes were found
in a group from a small village located about some 5 km to the north of
Luoyang.[16] The inscription has already been mentioned above, but a fuller
translation of it is warranted here (see figure 2):

It was the eighth month, and the time was the *jiashen* day (no. 21). The
king commanded Ming Bao 明保, a son of the Duke of Zhou (Zhougong
周公), to take charge of the Three Affairs in the four directions, receiving
the Ministry (*qingshiliao* 卿事寮).

On the *dinghai* day (no. 24), [Ming Bao] commanded Ze 夨 to report
to the palace of the Duke of Zhou; the duke ordered [him] to go out
and join [the officials of] the Ministry. It was the tenth month, on the
month's auspicious day *guiwei* (no. 20), Duke Ming (=Ming Bao) arrived in Chengzhou in the morning. [He] sent out commands. [He] gave
orders regarding the Three Affairs, and the Ministry, and the Many Officials (*zhuyin* 諸尹), and District Administrators (*lijun* 里君), and Hundred Craftsmen (*baigong* 百工), and the Many Rulers (*zhuhou* 諸侯):
hou 侯, *dian* 甸, *nan* 男. [He] gave orders regarding the Four Directions.
After sending all the orders, on *jiashen* day (no. 21), Duke Ming offered
sacrifice to the Jing Temple. On *yiyou* day (no. 22), [he] offered sacrifice to the Kang Temple. When all done, [he] offered sacrifice in Wang
(Royal City).

When Duke Ming returned from Wang, Duke Ming awarded Kang Shi
black fragrant wine, metal, and a small cow, saying: "Use them in entreatment!" [He] awarded Ling black fragrant wine, metal, and a small cow,
saying: "Use them in entreatment!" [He] thus commanded: "Now, I am to
command you two people, Kang and Ze, to assist each other in the affairs
of your Ministry and of your colleagues."

Document Maker Ling dares to exalt Duke Ming the Chief for his beneficence; herewith [he] makes for [his] deceased father Ding [this] treasured
sacrificial vessel. [Ling] dares to forward the award of Duke Ming onto
father Ding, and to glorify father Ding. Emblem.

---

[16] On the provenance of the Ling *fangyi* and Ling *fangzun*, see *Zhensong tang jigu yiwen* (1931),
pp. 4.49–51. The Ling *fangyi* is currently stored in the Freer Museum, Washington DC, and the
Ling *fangzun* in the Palace Museum, Taipei; see *The Freer Chinese Bronzes*, 2 vols. (Washington DC:
Smithsonian Institution, 1967), pp. 212–21; *Gugong tongqi tulu*, 2 vols. (Taipei: Palace Museum,
1958), pp. 2.209–10. The date of the Ling bronzes involves a major debate in the study of Western
Zhou bronzes. Guo Moruo and Chen Mengjia date the bronzes to the reign of King Cheng, while
Tang Lan, on the basis of the appearance of the term Kang Gong, which he thinks was the temple
for the deceased King Kang, dates the bronzes to the reign of King Zhao. See Guo Moruo, *Liang
Zhou jinwen ci daxi tulu kaoshi*, pp. 6–10; Chen Mengjia, "Xi Zhou tongqi duandai," 2.86–91; Tang
Lan, "Xi Zhou jinwen duandai zhong de Kang Gong wenti," *Kaogu xuebao* 1962.1, 15–48. For a dis-
cussion of the Kang Gong debate and the related dating of the Ling bronzes, see also, Shaughnessy,
Sources of Western Zhou History, pp. 193–216.

Despite the grammatical ambiguity in its middle portion,[17] the inscription in a quite explicit way provides us with a description of the administrative structure of the early Western Zhou government. This hierarchy is topped by a body of officials associated with the Ministry (*qingshiliao* 卿事寮), which is apparently the most important segment of the Zhou government. Below it are the Many Officials (*zhuyin*) whose status the inscription does not explicate but who were obviously officials of the central government, more important than the District Administrators (*lijun*) who come after them; as will be shown later, the *lijun* were local civil officials in charge of delimited areas controlled directly by the Zhou central court. At the bottom of the hierarchy were the Hundred Craftsmen, perhaps those who had worked in the government-operated workshops located in the eastern capital. Following these officials who belonged to the central administration, the inscription then lists the many regional rulers of the various statuses such as *hou*, *dian*, and *nan*, whose own states were located on the vast eastern plain, beyond the administrative control of the central court. Since these are all officials present at Chengzhou upon Duke Ming's arrival from the Zhou capital Hao 鎬 (or Zongzhou 宗周) in the Wei River valley, there is a question about whether the inscription can be taken as a description of the general structure of the Zhou government. However, since Chengzhou was the main administrative and military base of Zhou in the east, it is quite possible that an administrative structure similar to that of the capital was developed.[18] In any event, the importance of the Ling *fangyi* inscription is that it reflects a general conceptualization of the administrative body of the Zhou state and a basic classification of its functional roles in an overall structure through which the Zhou state was governed.

Certainly, this structure will become more evident in the analysis of the various official roles below. But it is above all significant that the Ministry with its particular name *qingshiliao* 卿事寮 had apparently become an established institution during the early Western Zhou and is mentioned in the inscription of the Ling *fangyi* three times. Since we know that the Ministry continued to exist through the entire Western Zhou period, appearing again in one mid-Western Zhou and another

---

[17] Although the order for the Four Directions was almost certainly given to the many regional rulers including *hou*, *dian*, and *nan*, it is not at all clear to whom the order regarding Three Affairs was given. Previously, some scholars listed *zhuhou* among those who received the command of Three Affairs, while others treated all people from *zhuyin* to *zhuhou* as receivers of the command for Four Directions. See Chen Mengjia, "Xi Zhou tongqi duandai," 2.89; Ma Chengyuan, *Shang Zhou qingtongqi mingwen xuan*, 3, p. 68; Shirakawa Shizuka, "Kinbun tsūshaku," *Hakutsuru bijutsukanshi*, 56 vols. (Kobe, 1966–83), 6.25:305. It should be correct that the order of Three Affairs was a domestic policy addressed to all listed officials, including those in the Ministry, the Many Officials, the District Administrators, and the Hundred Craftsmen.

[18] Yang Kuan suggests that the *qingshiliao* existed in both Chengzhou in the east and the Zhou capital in the west. See Yang Kuan, *Xi Zhou shi*, pp. 327–28.

late Western Zhou inscription along with the Grand Secretariat (*taishi-liao* 太史寮),[19] it was evidently one of the most enduring institutions of the Western Zhou government. The emergence of the Ministry as a routinely maintained "bureau" that was not a particular office, but was a congregation of multiple offices conceived relevant to each other and needing a collective management by/through an institutionalized structure in a particular location, the "Bureau" (*lao* 寮), was a very important step in the development of the Zhou government, or government institutions in general.[20] It was probably one of the most important institutional inventions of the Western Zhou state and placed its government far beyond the rudimentary level of development of the Shang government. It suggests first, and at least, that certain definitions of roles as well as "standard administrative procedure," to borrow the Weberian term, no matter how basic, had already been developed in the Western Zhou government. It was only through a recognition of the distinctions between, as well as the compatibility of, such roles that they could be grouped into a particular "Bureau" bearing a general name that suggests its function. Second, such a standing structure occupying a specific space could not have existed in a government that handled affairs only on temporary basis, but must have been the product of a government that was intended to manage its affairs on a day-to-day basis with a permanent body of administrative officials. Furthermore, the establishment of such a standing structure also implies the existence of a body of clerical officials that was needed for its routine maintenance, referred to in the inscription of the Zuoce Ling *gui* 作冊令簋 (JC: 4301) as "Staff of the Bureau" (*liaoren* 寮人), cast in the same period as the Ling *fangyi*. Indeed, a mid-Western Zhou inscription, the Pu *yu* 㴰盂 (JC: 10321), suggests that there were even female and male servants (*liaonü liaoxi* 寮女寮奚)

---

[19] These are the Fansheng *gui* 番生簋 (JC: 4326) and Maogong *ding* 毛公鼎 (JC: 2841), respectively; see below for more discussion. Some scholars have advocated the existence of the Grand Secretariat during the early Western Zhou, thus making the Zhou government a binary structure from the beginning of the dynasty. See Yang Kuan, "Xi Zhou zhongyang zhengquan," 88–89; *Xi Zhou shi*, pp. 331–32; Kimura, "Sei Shū kansei," 59–60; Zhang Yachu and Liu Yu, *Xi Zhou jinwen guanzhi yanjiu*, pp. 104–5. Despite the mention of "Grand Secretary" (*taishi* 太史) in a number of inscriptions (see below), there is no solid evidence for the existence of the Grand Secretariat as a government division during the early Western Zhou.

[20] We can simply exclude the possibility that *liao* 寮 refers merely to a collective body of officials (if the graph stands for *liao* 僚 as some would wish), and not to a physical space such as a "bureau" where they conducted their work. Although terms such as *nailiao* 乃寮 (Ling *fangyi* 令方彝; JC: 9901) and *bailiao* 百寮 (Mu *gui* 牧簋; JC: 4343) raise ambiguity as to whether *liao* means "officials" or "bureau," it clearly means "bureau" in such contexts as *liaoren* 寮人 (staff of the bureau; Ling *gui* 令簋 [JC: 4300]), *liaonü* 寮女 and *liaoxi* 寮奚 (female and male servants attached to the bureau;

Pu *yu* 㴰盂 [JC: 10321], see more below). Consistent with this usage, the graph *liao* ▌ (Ling *fangyi*), which combines the graphs *gong* 宮 and *liao* 燎 (the palace where fire is kept), clearly represents the "place" where officials worked, probably with fire kept overnight, commanding a strong sense of continuity and routine. On the etymology of *liao*, see Zhou Fagao, *Jinwen gulin*, pp. 4813–14. For reading *liao* 寮 as *liao* 僚, see Ma Chengyuan, *Shang Zhou qingtongqi mingwen xuan*, 3, p. 68.

recruited for work in the Ministry.[21] More meaningfully, it indicates a possible separation of the public lives of at least some officials who performed their duties in the Ministry from their private dwelling quarters, for the simple reason that, whereas some could make them their personal property, others certainly could not. In short, the existence of such a routine administrative structure is a very important feature of the Western Zhou government.

The development of official roles

It is generally agreed among scholars that the most important offices in the bureau of Ministry were the three supervisors: Supervisor of Land (*situ* 嗣土), Supervisor of Construction (*sigong* 嗣工), and Supervisor of Horses (*sima* 嗣馬).[22] As the name suggests, the Supervisor of Land managed affairs related to the land in the royal domain that provided the main revenue for the Zhou court; he was also probably in charge of the populations attached to the lands under his management. The office of Supervisor of Construction managed public works carried out by the Zhou court, while the Supervisor of Horses was responsible for military affairs and local security. However, none of these functions can be confirmed by the current early Western Zhou inscriptions as having been parts of the Ministry until we arrive at the mid-Western Zhou. Nevertheless, the inscriptions suggest that these offices certainly did exist during the early Western Zhou, and the definitions suggested by their names largely meet their roles documented by the inscriptions, although a certain degree of overlap can be found between the jobs of the Supervisor of Land and that of the Supervisor of Construction (see Appendix I). As far as the early Western Zhou is concerned, the office of Supervisor of Land is mentioned in the Situ Si *gui* 嗣土嗣簋 (JC: 3696), and the office of Supervisor of Construction is mentioned in the Sigong Ding *jue* 嗣工丁爵 (JC: 8792), both being early Western Zhou inscriptions.[23] The role of Supervisor of Horses does not appear in early Western Zhou inscriptions discovered to date. Two

---

[21] For an interpretation of the Pu *yu*, see Shirakawa Shizuka, "Kinbun tsūshaku," 49.*ho*3:311–20; Huang Shengzhang, "Pu yu xinkao," *Renwen zazhi* 1982.5, 98–102. In an early study, Cho-yun Hsu noted the possible existence of some kind of staff for each of the many offices in the Western Zhou government based on a mid-Western Zhou inscription, the Shi Kuifu *ding* 師奎父鼎 (JC: 2813), which records that Shi Kuifu was commanded to supervise the "former colleagues of his father," very likely staff that once assisted his father. See Cho-yun Hsu, "Some Working Notes on the Western Chou Government," 520.

[22] See Itō Michiharu, *Chūgoku kodai kokka*, pp. 241–43; Kimura, "Sei Shū kansei," 44–45; Zhang Yachu and Liu Yu, *Xi Zhou jinwen guanzhi yanjiu*, pp. 102–5.

[23] In addition, two other early Western Zhou inscriptions, the Ta Situ *gui* 渣嗣土簋 (JC: 4059) and Zhou Situ *zun* 螯司土尊 (JC: 5917), mention the office of Supervisor of Land. But the former was clearly an official of the regional state Wey 衛 located on the eastern plain, and the latter was a local official in a place called Zhou 螯, probably located in the Wei River valley. For the location of Zhou 螯, see Wang Hui, "Zhou jinei diming xiaoji," *Kaogu yu wenwu* 1985.3, 26–31.

chapters of the *Shangshu* mention the office of Supervisor of Horses along with the Supervisor of Land and the Supervisor of Construction, but it is difficult to judge the date of the office on the basis of these records; we may have to await future discoveries of inscribed bronzes for confirmation.[24]

Outside the Ministry, a well-developed government function centered on the role of Scribes (*shi* 史), or perhaps Secretaries. In general, it is evident in numerous inscriptions that Scribes performed clerical roles in the Zhou government, including producing and keeping written records.[25] The early Western Zhou bronze inscriptions mention a fairly large number of individuals with the title *shi*, such as Shi Lai 史逨, Shi Yin 史寅, Shi Tian 史臨, etc., far exceeding other official titles of the time.[26] This phenomenon seems to suggest that even in the early days, when military expansion was the central concern of the Zhou court, the Zhou government had already acquired a strong civil character, with a large number of officials performing clerical functions at various posts. Furthermore, there seem to have been even more delicate differentiations among such clerical roles. For instance, in addition to the ordinary office Scribe (*shi*), the inscriptions of the Taishi You *yan* 太史友甗 (JC: 915) and Zhong *fangding* 中方鼎 (JC: 2785) mention the office of Grand Scribe (*taishi* 太史). The term *tai* prefixing Scribe certainly suggests a higher, more prestigious position

---

[24] The "Mushi" 牧誓 chapter mentions a group of officials who took part in the conquest campaign including "*bang zhongjun* 邦冢君, *yushi* 御事, *situ* 司徒 (=*situ* 司土), *sima* 司馬, *sikong* 司空 (=*sigong* 司工), *yalü* 亞旅, *shishi* 師氏, *qianfu zhang* 千夫長, *baifu zhang* 百夫長." The "Zicai" 梓材 chapter mentions "*shishi* 師氏, *situ* 司徒 (=*situ* 司土), *sima* 司馬, *sikong* 司空 (=*sigong* 司工), *yinlü* 尹旅." Both lists combine military and civil offices of which Supervisor of Land, Supervisor of Construction, and Supervisor of Horses are the main roles. In the first lists, the heads of the aristocratic lineages, *bang zhongjun* (similar to the expressions of *bangjun* 邦君 or *bangbo* 邦伯) were also included in the conquest troops. See *Shangshu*, 11, p. 183; 14, p. 208 (Legge, *The Shoo King*, pp. 300–305, 413–19).

[25] Some scholars have made efforts to trace the semantic origin of the "Scribe" (*shi* 史) in the military, archery, or religious context of the Shang dynasty. See Wang Guowei, "Shi shi," in *Guantang jilin*, 2 vols. (Shijiazhuang: Hebei Jiaoyu, 2001), pp. 159–66; Shirakawa Shizuka, "Shaku shi," in *Kōkotsu kimbungaku ronsū* (Kyoto: Hōyū shoten, 1974), pp. 1–68. However, the semantic origin of a graph in Shang does not necessarily explain its role in the Zhou system. In fact, on Shang oracle bones, *shi* 史 stands almost always for *shi* 事 or *shi* 使, and never appears in a context where it prefixes a personal name (except in causative relations where it is used as a verb, *shi* 使); hence it may not designate an official title. In other words, the meaning of *shi* 史 in Shang was quite different from that which we should translate as "Scribe" in the Western Zhou context. For the role of *shi* in the Western Zhou government, it is important to look at what they actually do in the inscriptions (Appendix I). We find no convincing example that *shi* was a religious office; instead, clear cases suggest that the Scribes were actually handling administrative documents. The essential role of the Scribe was secretarial and clerical, although such a role could take place in different social contexts. For *shi* 史 on the Shang oracle bones, see examples gathered in Matsumaru Michio and Ken-ichi Takashima, *Kōkotsu moji jishaku sōran* (Tokyo: Tokyo daigaku, 1993), pp. 4–5. For the causative use of *shi* 史 as *shi* 使, see recently, Ken-ichi Takashima, "The Causative Construction with *shi* in Shang Chinese," paper presented at the Sixteenth Annual International Conference on Chinese Paleography (Guangzhou, November 2006), pp. 1–20.

[26] The *shi* appears also in the Shi Lai *jiao* 史逨角 (JC: 9063), Chen Chen *he* 臣辰盉 (JC: 9454), and Shi Tian *gui* 史臨簋 (JC: 4030), all cast during the early Western Zhou, and most likely in the Cheng-Kang period. See also Zhang Yachu and Liu Yu, *Xi Zhou jinwen guanzhi yanjiu*, pp. 76–77.

than in other cases where the term is not used. And this is entirely true with regard to early Western Zhou inscriptions that sometimes the office of Grand Scribe was held by people with very high status such as *gong* 公. For instance, the inscription of the Zuoce Hu *you* 作冊魖卣 (JC: 5432) mentions the Duke Grand Scribe (*gong taishi* 公太史) as a very prominent official who received orders directly from the Zhou king and inspected the many officials in the Zhou capital. In fact, many scholars believe that the Duke Grand Scribe mentioned in the Zuoce Hu *you* was none other than King Wu's brother, the Duke of Bi (Bigong 畢公).[27] Moreover, as opposed to the frequent mention of Scribe followed by a personal name, there are inscriptions that mention Scribes modified by a prefix, such as *Qianshi* 瞉史, *Yangshi* 羕史, *Shengshi* 省史, and *Yushi* 御史.[28] Some of the terms may identify the superior official under whom the particular scribe served, or the administrative "unit" to which he belonged, as in the mid-Western Zhou case "Scribe of Qi" (*Qi shi* 齊史).[29] But, based on the usage of the relevant terms in other contexts, it is very likely that *shengshi* "Inspecting Scribe" referred to scribes on a royal mission of inspection to the local areas, and *yushi* "Attendant Scribe" were probably scribes who attended the Zhou king on important occasions.[30] This suggests that the function of the Scribes might have become somehow even more specialized during the early Western Zhou.

Despite the numerous occurrences of the Scribes in the early Western Zhou inscriptions, it is quite difficult to assess the extent to which the organization of these clerical officers had developed. It is not even clear whether or not the numerous scribes appearing in the early Western Zhou bronze inscriptions were all officials of the central court; probably not. However, given their association in the inscriptions with other known officials of the central court, many of them must have staffed the offices in the central government. For instance, in the Zhong *yan* 中甗 (JC: 0949), Scribe Er 史兒 served as a messenger of the Zhou king; in the Shi Shou

---

[27] On the identification of Gong Taishi 公太史 with the Duke of Bi, see Chen Mengjia, "Xi Zhou tongqi duandai," 2.112; Zhang Yachu, "Lun Lutaishan Xi Zhou mu de niandai he zushu," *Jianghan kaogu* 1984.2, 24–25. The Duke of Bi is actually mentioned in the Shi Tian *gui* 史唘簋 (JC: 4030), where Scribe Tian received awards of cowries from him. According to traditional records, the Duke of Bi was a half brother of King Wu; see Hayashi Taisuke, *Shōkō to sono jidai* (Tokyo: Ōkura shoten, 1916), pp. 15–16; Chen Pan, *Chunqiu dashi biao lieguo juexing ji cunmie biao zhuanyi* (Taipei: Academia Sinica, 1969), pp. 328–30.

[28] These terms are seen on the Qianshi *ding* 瞉史鼎 (JC: 2166), Yangshi *zun* 羕史尊 (JC: 5811), Shengshi *zun* 省史尊 (JC: 5951), and Yushi Jing *gui* 御史競簋 (JC: 4134), respectively. The Qianshi *ding* was excavated in Liulihe, Beijing, and the caster must have been an official of the state of Yan; see *Liulihe Xi Zhou yan guo mudi* (Beijing: Wenwu Press, 1995), p. 120.

[29] See Qishi Huan *gui* 齊史逗簋 (JC: 3740).

[30] The reading of *sheng* as "inspecting" is generally agreed among the scholars. See Zhou Fagao, *Jinwen gulin*, pp. 2209–24; *Yu* 街 (馭) literally means "chariot-driving" in the inscriptions, but sometimes also, by extension, means "attending" the king (Yu *gui* 逗簋; JC: 4207) or a group of guests at a banquet (Shen *ding* 申鼎; JC: 2732). See Guo Moruo, *Liang Zhou jinwen ci daxi tulu kaoshi*, p. 55.

ding 史獸鼎 (JC: 2778), Scribe Shou 史獸 was also on a mission from the central court to the eastern capital Chengzhou, sent by a chief official. Furthermore, even if many scribes recorded in the inscriptions had actually worked in the central government, it is still not clear whether they formed an independent "bureau" or any kind of "bureaucratic" arrangement with the Grand Scribe as their head, or served as clerical staff in the various government branches, including the Ministry, or even in the military sector. The existence of such a prestigious title as "Grand Scribe" may suggest the growth of clerical roles into an independent government organ, but it is also possible that such a title was granted because whoever held it had served the Zhou king directly. In other words, it might have been a mark of prestige but not an actual institution.

Moreover, the clerical function of the Zhou government was also performed by another well-known office – the Document Maker (*zuoce* 作冊). Since the job of the Document Maker was closely related to that of the Scribe, there has been a debate regarding whether the two government roles can actually be differentiated.[31] However, since both Scribe and Document Maker are regular offices, I believe that they certainly would have been differentiated during the early Western Zhou; in fact, the distinction between them may well reflect the level of specialization of the Zhou government. The difference is probably that, while the Scribes were generally responsible for producing and keeping records in the various branches of the government, the Document Makers were probably the ones who had particular responsibility for composing and writing official documents such as royal decrees and other letters that emanated from the central government. Such written exchanges, called *ce* 冊 or *shu* 書 in the inscriptions, were used frequently in the official ceremony of appointment and carried with them administrative authority. If this is true, the Document Makers, due to their direct control of the channel of written communication between the superiors and their subordinates, might have been in a more prestigious position than the Scribes. While this latter point has to remain hypothetical at present, there are signs that this may be true with respect to a number of Document Makers known to us.[32] In two cases, the Zuoce Zhe *zun* 作冊折尊 (JC: 6002) and Zuoce Huan *you* 作冊睘卣 (JC: 5407), the Document Maker was apparently sent on a diplomatic mission by either the Zhou king or the Zhou queen. It has been noted previously

---

[31] On this issue, see Zhang Yachu and Liu Yu, *Xi Zhou jinwen guanzhi yanjiu*, pp. 34–35.

[32] This can be seen in the fact that three Document Makers known from the early Western Zhou were associated with eminent figures at the court: in the Zuoce Zi *you* 作冊𩼧卣 (JC: 5400), Document Maker Zi receives fragrant wine and cowries from Duke Ming during the duke's office in Chengzhou; in the Zuoce Hu *you* 作冊魑卣 (JC: 5432), Hu receives the gift of a horse from the Duke Grand Scribe; in the Zuoce Da *fangding* 作冊大方鼎 (JC: 2760), Document Maker Da receives the award of a white horse directly from the Duke of Shao (Shaogong 召公). It is very likely that they were the Document Makers who worked directly under the prominent dukes whose commands they would transmit and send out in writing.

that there might have been multiple individuals serving concurrently as Document Makers in a given time, for instance, during the reign of King Zhao;[33] this would seem natural if we consider that the Document Makers might have worked in different branches of the Zhou central government. While some Document Makers apparently were in the immediate service of the king, we have good evidence that others were probably working in the Ministry.[34] But the differentiation of their role from that of the Scribes is above all significant in the development of functional roles in the Western Zhou government.

As is true for all early governments in history, the Western Zhou government was also charged with an important religious function. This religious function of the Western Zhou government was centered on the role of Invocator (*zhu* 祝), and was probably also carried out by others we do not know from the inscriptions.[35] The Grand Invocator was responsible for the various state rituals and sacrifices to the Zhou ancestors. While the office of Invocator certainly had a long duration, as we know of some individuals who held the position in a later context, our evidence for the early Western Zhou is from only two inscriptions. The first is the Dazhu Qin *ding* 大祝禽鼎 (JC: 1937), a bronze cast by Qin 禽 who used the title "Grand Invocator." The identification of this Qin as the oldest son of the Duke of Zhou and subsequently the founder of the state of Lu 魯 is well supported by the fact that he appears also as Invocator in the inscription of the Qin *gui* 禽簋 (JC: 4041) that was apparently cast on the eve of the conquest of Gai 蓋, known in the texts as Yan 奄, which then became the base of the regional state Lu.[36] Later texts also attribute the office of Grand Diviner (*taibu* 太卜) and other divinatory officers to the Western Zhou government, and in fact, Zhang and Liu offer a position for the Grand Diviner in their reconstruction of the early Western Zhou government. However, as far as the inscriptions go, there is no firm evidence that the diviners ever held a regular office.[37]

---

[33] See Zhang Yachu and Liu Yu, *Xi Zhou jinwen guanzhi yanjiu*, p. 35.

[34] This is shown by the inscription of the Ling *fangyi* translated above. Ling, who refers to himself as Document Maker and actually had the character *ce* 冊 as part of his family emblem, was ordered by the Duke of Zhou to work in the Ministry, following Duke Ming to the eastern capital. Later in the inscription, Duke Ming commands Ling, together with Kang, to assist in the affair of the "bureau" (*liao* 寮), undoubtedly the Ministry, mentioned earlier in the inscription.

[35] For the religious role of Invocator in the ancient historical tradition, see Lothar von Falkenhausen, "Reflections on the Political Roles of Spirit Medium in Early China: The *Wu* officials in the Zhou Li," *Early China* 20 (1995), 288–94.

[36] The inscription records King Cheng's attack on the ruler of Gai 蓋 (Yan 奄), a former ally of Shang in Shandong. On this occasion, the Duke of Zhou served as the king's advisor, and Qin, his son, served as Invocator. Qin conducted a session of *chen*-invocation, and was awarded a hundred *lue* of metal and hence cast the bronze to commemorate the award. For this identification, see Chen Mengjia, "Xi Zhou tongqi duandai," 2.75. On the Qin *gui* and its relation to the founding of Lu, see also Edward L. Shaughnessy, "The Duke of Zhou's Retirement in the East and the Beginnings of the Minister–Monarch Debate in Chinese Political Philosophy," *Early China* 18 (1993), 48–50.

[37] See *Zhouli*, 24, pp. 802–5. See also Zhang Yachu and Liu Yu, *Xi Zhou jinwen guanzhi yanjiu*, p. 105.

The title "Superintendent" (*zai* 宰) appears in the inscription of the Zai Chen *ding* 宰䍐鼎 (JC: 2010), which according to its calligraphy should be an early Western Zhou bronze but which provides little historical context. Since dating by calligraphy is risky, our evidence for the office is indeed very weak. However, since the office of "Superintendent" evidently existed during the Shang Dynasty,[38] and since our evidence from the mid-Western Zhou period suggests that the Superintendent played a prominent role as the head of Royal Household administration, it is reasonable to expect that it also existed during the early Western Zhou as part of the Shang influence. Furthermore, the Shang sources do not actually explain the responsibilities of *zai* 宰, so the translation of it as "Superintendent" in the early Western Zhou context can also be very tentative. In any event, the Superintendent does not seem to have played any significant role during the early Western Zhou, and we are not even sure if the Superintendent was in indirect service to the Zhou king as were officials bearing the same title during the mid-Western Zhou.

In contrast, a more prominent role that characterized the early Western Zhou government was the Protector (*bao* 保). We know two individuals who had held the title "Protector": the Duke of Shao, who is referred to variously as the "Grand Protector" (*taibao* 太保), "August Heavenly Chief Grand Protector" (*huangtian yin taibao* 皇天尹太保), and "Protector Ming" (*mingbao* 明保), or Duke Ming, who appears in the Ling *fangyi*. After the retirement of the Duke of Zhou, the Duke of Shao played a dominant and long-lasting role in the Zhou court through much of the reign of King Cheng and King Kang.[39] But because of the extremely important role played by the Duke of Shao, one would suspect that *bao* was probably an honorable title confined to a very limited number of eminent officials, but, perhaps, not a regular administrative office; it may not be even wrong to say that the role of *bao* might have come very close to something like "regent," superimposed on the entire government.[40] As this is

[38] See, for instance, the Zai Hao *jiao* 宰梄角 (JC: 9105), which was cast in the twenty-fifth year of the last Shang king.

[39] For the important role of the Duke of Shao in early Western Zhou court, see Edward L. Shaughnessy, "The Role of Grand Protector Shi in the Consolidation of the Zhou Conquest," *Ars Orientalis* 19 (1989), 51–77. On the retirement of the Duke of Zhou and the rise of the Duke of Shao to prominence, see Edward L. Shaughnessy, "The Duke of Zhou's Retirement," 51–64. For bronze inscriptions related to the Duke of Shao, see Yin Weizhang and Cao Shuqin, "Zhou chu Taibao qi zonghe yanjiu," *Kaogu xuebao* 1991.1, 1–21.

[40] However, Yang Kuan viewed the titles of "Grand Protector" (*taibao* 太保) held by the Duke of Shao and "Grand Marshal" (*taishi* 太師) held by the Duke of Zhou as representing two paramount offices in the Zhou government. The Duke of Zhou was responsible for the Zhou government centering on the eastern capital Chengzhou, while the Duke of Shao was supervising the Zhou government in the capital Hao in the west. In Zhang and Liu's reconstruction of the early Western Zhou government, the Duke of Zhou supervised the Ministry, while the Duke of Shao supervised the Grand Secretariat. However, these reconstructions are based on fragments in later historical texts that reflect on the political roles of two figures, and there is no proof for it in the contemporaneous inscriptions. After all, as mentioned above, there is no inscriptional evidence for the existence of the Grand Secretariat as a government bureau during the early Western Zhou.

probably the case, Protector Ming's role in the Ling *fangyi* was clearly to supervise the entire government with authority over both internal policies described as Three Affairs and the regional states beyond the royal domain described as Four Directions. Certainly, not every title was an official title. In the case of *bao*, or at least the "Grand Protector," my judgment is that it was a prestigious title designating certain high status, but not a regular administrative official title.

Organizational characteristics: a historical perspective

If, as discussed in Chapter 1, the Shang government was indeed an incipient (or religious) bureaucracy as suggested by Keightley, or a Shamanistic theocracy as suggested by K.C. Chang, we must recognize that the early Western Zhou government may represent a significant departure from these models. Although the contrast may be adjusted with respect to the possible limitation of the Shang oracle-bone inscriptions as primary sources for the Shang government, it nevertheless holds true that the Shang king had very little involvement in the establishment and operation of the Shang administrative offices, and this actually fits well with the hegemonic nature of the Shang state as well as with the peripatetic nature of the Shang royal court; the early Western Zhou government, on the other hand, exhibits some important changes from Shang. This does not mean that religion was not important in the Zhou government – it certainly was important, as the Zhou state was founded on the theory of the Mandate of Heaven, and we can imagine that a large number of diviners might have served in the Zhou government, as we know for sure the Zhou also practiced oracle-bone divination in their pre-conquest time.[41] However, the fact is that our current evidence, both from the Zhou bronze inscriptions and Zhou oracle-bone inscriptions, does not show that religious offices such as the Invocators played a preeminent role, overshadowing other executive offices, as in the Shang case. The early Western Zhou government was centered on the executive roles of the Three Supervisors as members of the Ministry, both their offices and the administrative structure in which they served being evidently Zhou inventions.[42] This tripartite formation of the

See Yang Kuan, *Xi Zhou shi*, pp. 315–21; Zhang Yachu and Liu Yu, *Xi Zhou jinwen guanzhi yanjiu*, p. 105.

[41] In fact, we do know an official from the mid-Western Zhou period by the name Hu 曶 who was commanded by the king to take charge of affairs of divination in the Royal Household (Hu *ding* 曶鼎; JC: 2838); however, in this case the term *si bu shi* 嗣卜事 cannot be regarded as a regular official title. The same Hu later might have gone on to serve as the Superintendent of the Royal Household. For the career of Hu, see discussions in Chapter 5, pp. 222–23.

[42] There is no evidence for the Three Supervisors in the Shang inscriptions. The received Zhou tradition, for instance, the poem "Mian" 綿, attributes the creation of the offices of Supervisor of Construction and Supervisor of Land, or in general, the beginning of the Zhou state, to the Ancient Duke, Danfu 亶父, grandfather of King Wen. See *Shijing*, 16.2, p. 501 (Waley, *The Book of Songs*, pp. 232–33).

administrative roles is found thereafter in the middle and late Western Zhou period at every level of Zhou administration. What is more important is the founding of the Ministry, which stabilized the roles of the Three Supervisors by organizing them into an institutional structure. The Ministry itself was an important development because it defined the role of the government and classified its functions according to actual administrative purposes, and because it was a routine government bureau that was intended to manage affairs on a continuing and uninterrupted basis. Certainly, it was an important step towards the development of the impersonal role in the Zhou government that is characteristic of all bureaucratic institutions.

The salience of secretarial offices is another major feature of the early Western Zhou government. Although the title "Document Maker" (*zuoce* 作冊) might have had a Shang origin, it is unlikely that it was an office very popular during Shang.[43] In the early Western Zhou, "Scribe" and "Document Maker" were clearly regular and very active government roles. Although it is possible that some Scribes might be involved in religious procedures, particularly those that were carried out in/by the royal court, whether in the context of reverence to Heaven or worship of ancestors,[44] the inscriptions show that they were essentially administrative assistants and performed clerical duties under varied circumstances in a civil administrative setting, but not, at least not primarily, religious offices. In Shang, to a large extent the clerical roles might have been played by the royal diviners. The high frequency of appearance of officials with the titles of "Document Maker" or "Scribe" in the Western Zhou bronze inscriptions suggests an indisputable Zhou emphasis on the administrative roles of the secretarial officials in the government. The middle and late Western Zhou inscriptions show quite clearly what kind of documents they handled. In fact, some of these documents were handed by them as administrative commands to the recipients of offices and were then copied onto the bronzes by the officials who received them; it is entirely possible that they were produced by them (particularly the Document Maker) in the first place. The important role of the Scribes and Document Makers together with the prominent role of the Three Supervisors suggests that the Zhou might have had a very different approach to government, an ostensible commitment to civil administration – although the political Western Zhou state was fundamentally destined to fulfill the will of Heaven, the Zhou had instituted a government

---

[43] *Zuoce* 作冊 appears in the inscription of the Sixth Year Yiqi *you* 六年𠃐其卣 (JC: 5414), cast in the last reign of Shang.

[44] In fact, Western Zhou texts do offer a few examples of secretarial offices being involved in ceremonial contexts. For instance, in the "Luogao" 洛誥 chapter of the *Shangshu*, Document Maker Yi 逸 conducted the invocation with a written document in a religious-ritual session held upon King Cheng's arrival in Chengzhou, in which cattle were offered to King Wen and King Wu. See *Shangshu*, 15, p. 217 (Legge, *The Shoo King*, p. 451).

that was mainly a practical, civil administrative machine to fulfill actual goals, rather than primarily a religious institution that handled their relations with the divinity and only in passing performed civil duties, as some have suggested for Shang. If we think that this was the government that achieved the great early Western Zhou expansion, we must admit that the commitment to civil administration might have provided Zhou with great practical strength to overcome their enemies. This was an important starting point and provided the initial condition for the development of bureaucracy and bureaucratic government. In this regard, the early Western Zhou government may represent an important turning point in the political culture of ancient China.

On the other hand, the real power to command the government lay in the hands of the royal princes with the honorable title *gong* 公, whose authority was derived from their genealogical positions in the Zhou royal lineage. In the first century after the conquest, the Zhou continued to benefit from the leadership not so much of the king, but of strong-willed ministers such as the Duke of Zhou, the Duke of Shao, Duke Ming, and probably also the Duke of Bi. This created a privileged stratum of political magnates superimposed on the entire government. In some way, this structure of authority came very close to the early Manchu state of the seventeenth century, where the royal princes were put in charge of each of the six bureaucratic departments and were members of the State Council hosted by the emperor where policies were decided. It was a bureaucratic structure that was supervised through a family structure.[45] In the Zhou case, the way in which power was structured at the Zhou court had most to do with, and was also subject to, the principle of lineage segmentation. As mentioned in Chapter 1, many of the regional rulers were either the Zhou royal princes or sons of the royal princes who had formed their own lineages such as that of the Duke of Zhou and Duke of Shao. In the latter case, as the inscriptions show very clearly, when their sons were established as regional rulers their lineages were split into two parts: one was located in the east and the other remained in the capital. Since the honorable title *gong* was passed down the line in the capital after the death of the lineage founders, this provided a basis for the lineages to continue their dominance over the early Western Zhou court. This transaction of political power can be fully seen in the case of Duke Ming, who supervised the Zhou government after his father, the Duke of Zhou. The other duke, Shao, himself lived well into the third royal reign of the Western Zhou. Therefore, during most of the early Western Zhou, the lineages of the Dukes of Zhou and Shao were the most dominant powers in the Zhou court.[46] However, as time went

---

[45] See Xiao Yishan, *Qing dai tongshi*, 5 vols. (Beijing: Zhonghua, 1986), pp. 224–25; Zheng Tianting, *Qing shi*, vol. 1 (Hong Kong: China Books, 1994), pp. 144–48, 204–7.

[46] For the political dominance of the Duke of Zhou and Duke of Shao, see Edward L. Shaughnessy, "The Duke of Zhou's Retirement," 41–72; "The Role of Grand Protector Shi," 51–77.

on and more and more recent royal princes joined the rank of *gong*, the dominance of the Zhou and Shao lineages was naturally broken down, hence giving rise to a government that allowed competition for political power among the numerous lineages, as was probably the situation during the mid-Western Zhou. This also created a hotbed for the development of bureaucratic rules in the operation of the Zhou government as well as in the selection of officials.

THE MID-WESTERN ZHOU GOVERNMENT

As discussed in Chapter 1, the mid-Western Zhou was an important period of transition in terms of both Zhou's political power and the sociopolitical condition of the Western Zhou state. Changes in the Zhou government are an important aspect of this wide-ranging transition if not the leading force behind it. In this regard, a number of previous studies have identified the mid-Western Zhou as a period during which the Zhou government was significantly bureaucratized.[47] However, bureaucratization is a very complex process that comprises multiple dimensions, and it was achieved through both the structural sophistication of a government and its operational specialization and standardization. While the following chapters will gradually clarify these dimensions, the present chapter concentrates on the organizational development of the Western Zhou government.

General organizational expansion

For the mid-Western Zhou government, a general organizational statement is found in the inscription on the lid of the Fansheng *gui* 番生簋 (JC: 4326), currently housed in the Nelson-Atkins Museum of Art in Kansas City, Missouri (see figures 4 and 5). The bronze does not itself have a year number or identifiable clues connecting it to a specific royal reign, but since Guo Moruo constructed the first chronology of the Western Zhou bronze inscriptions, the Fansheng *gui* has been placed in the late Western Zhou period, particularly in the reign of King Li.[48] This

---

[47] See Hsu and Linduff, *Western Chou Civilization*, p. 227; Shaughnessy, "Western Zhou History," p. 326; Li Feng, "'Offices' in Bronze Inscriptions," 51–54.

[48] This is based on the unsafe connection with the historical figure Fan 番 mentioned in the poem "Shiyue zhi jiao" 十月之交 (Mao no. 193) in the *Book of Poetry*, which is dated by Zheng Xuan's commentary to King Li; see Guo Moruo, *Liang Zhou jinwen ci daxi tulu kaoshi*, pp. 131, 133–34. Other scholars date it to the time of King Xuan, based solely on the similarities between its inscription and that of the Maogong *ding*; see for instance, Rong Geng, *Shang Zhou yiqi tongkao*, 2 vols. (Beiping: Harvard-Yenching Institute, 1941), p. 57. It is now clear that the poem speaks about the politics of the reign of King You, but this provides no ground for dating the bronze. See Li Feng, *Landscape and Power in Early China*, pp. 205–9; *Shijing*, 12.2, p. 445 (Waley, *The Book of Songs*, pp. 170–72).

Figure 4. Cover of the Fansheng *gui* in the Nelson-Atkins Museum of Art (Courtesy of the Nelson-Atkins Museum of Art, Kansas City, Missouri; photograph by Jamison Miller, March 2007)

late Western Zhou date was revised by Ma Chengyuan, who moved the lid to the mid-Western Zhou period, particularly to the reign of King Xiao.[49] The color photo now available to us courtesy of the Nelson-Atkins Museum shows clearly that the lid carried decorative patterns very similar to those on other mid-Western Zhou bronzes.[50] Although a specific dating of the bronze to a royal reign cannot be established based on internal evidence from the inscription, the bronze must have been cast during the mid-Western Zhou period and probably some time after

[49] Ma identified Fansheng with the caster of the Fan Jusheng *hu* 番匊生壺 (JC: 9705); the latter bronze shows clear mid-Western Zhou features, coming very close to, though perhaps slightly later than, the Third Year Xing *hu* 十三年瘨壺 (JC: 9726). See Ma Chengyuan, *Shang Zhou qingtongqi mingwen xuan*, 3, pp. 224–26. See also Shirakawa Shizuka, "Kinbun tsūshaku," 27.159:417–27. 160:432.

[50] For instance, this is closely matched by that on two *hu*-vessels discovered at Zhangjiapo in 1964. See *Kaogu* 1965.9, 447, pl. 2; see also, Chen Gongrou and Zhang Changshou, "Yin Zhou qingtong rongqi shang niaowen de duandai yanjiu," *Kaogu xuebao* 1984.3, 268–69.

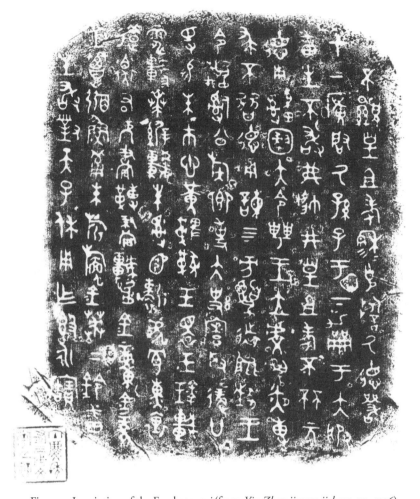

Figure 5. Inscription of the Fansheng *gui* (from *Yin Zhou jinwen jicheng*, no. 4326)

King Mu. Thus, we are fortunate to have a clear statement of the general structural divisions of the Zhou central government as of the second part of the mid-Western Zhou period:

Greatly illustrious are my august grandfather and father! Solemnly and solemnly [they] were able to make their virtue wise. [Their] sternness is above, [that] broadly opened up [ways for] their grandsons and sons below, [and that] harmonized the great service. Fansheng 番生 dares not to not-follow and take [as his] model the greatly felicitous prime virtue of [his] august grandfather and father, with which to extend and promote the Great Mandate, supporting the position of the king. [He is] respectful morning and night, extensively seeking for the great upright virtue, with which to persuade (*jian* 諫) the four quarters, softening those that are far and bringing to court those that are near. The king commanded [Fansheng] diligently to take charge of the Royal Kinsmen (*gongzu* 公族), the Ministry (*qingshi* 卿事), and the Grand Secretariat (*taishi liao*太史寮). [Fansheng] extricates twenty *lue* of *zhuan*-metal ingots. Award [him] scarlet knee pads, a green demi-circlet, a sheath of knife, a jade-circlet and a jade *hu*-tablet, a chariot with wooden baseboards under the riding-box, decorated and woven side-rails, chest-trappings and a front-rail of scarlet leather, a tiger-skin canopy with a reddish brown lining, a yoke with inlaid bronze fittings, and right yoke-saddles, painted leather yoke-bar bindings and patterned axel-coverings, a bronze heel of the draught-pole, a box-bottom bronze part, a box-pad with gilding,[51] a fish-skin quiver, and a scarlet banner on a bronze-fitted pole with two bells. Fansheng dares to extol the benefice of the Son of Heaven, with which [he] makes [this] *gui*-vessel. [May he] eternally treasure it!

Apparently, then, Fansheng was not assigned a specific administrative duty, but was entrusted with authority over the entire Zhou government. The inscription states that the king commanded Fansheng to supervise the Royal Kinsmen (*gongzu* 公族), Ministry (*qingshi* 卿事), and Grand Secretariat (*taishi liao*太史寮). Only the Duke of Zhou's son Mingbao 明保, or Duke Ming, is known from the early Western Zhou inscriptions such as the Ling *fangyi* to have held such an overall responsibility for the Zhou government. The argument has been about the number of bureaus (*liao* 寮) mentioned in this inscription. While some scholars think that *gongzu*, *qingshi*, and *taishi* were three independent segments of the Zhou central government, others accept only two: the Ministry (*qingshi liao*) and Grand Secretariat (*taishi liao*).[52] Although grammatically the Fansheng *gui* strongly suggests three segments of the Zhou central government, this cannot be certain because in the Maogong *ding* 毛公鼎 (JC: 2841), which will be discussed for the late Western Zhou, there is an equally high clarity that the royal kinsmen are mentioned separately from the Ministry and the Grand Secretariat; they are a gathering of

---

[51] For the terminology of chariots and their bronze fittings, see Lu Liancheng, "Chariot and Horse Burials in Ancient China," *Antiquity* 67 (1993), 824–38; Anthony J. Barbieri-Low, *Wheeled Vehicles in the Chinese Bronze-Age (c. 2000–741 B.C.)* (Sino-Platonic Papers no. 99) (Philadelphia University of Pennsylvania, 2000), pp. 86–90.

[52] For instance, Kimura suggested that the "Bureau of Royal Kinsmen" (*gongzuliao* 公族寮) constituted an independent segment of the Zhou government, paralleling the Ministry and Grand Secretariat, and assigned the office of Superintendent (*zai*) as its head. Thus, Kimura proposed a "tripartite" structure of the Zhou central government. See Kimura, "Sei Shū kansei," 55–56. Other scholars consider that through the entire Western Zhou, the Zhou central government maintained a "bipartite" structure that was composed of the two large segments: the Ministry (*qingshi liao* 卿事寮) and Grand Secretariat (*taishi liao* 太史寮). See Yang Kuan, "Xi Zhou zhongyang zhengquan," 82–85; Zhang Yachu and Liu Yu, *Xi Zhou jinwen guanzhi yanjiu*, pp. 102–10. However, as I have noted above, there is no solid evidence for the existence of either an independent Grand Secretariat or an independent "Bureau of Royal Kinsmen" during the early Western Zhou.

individuals but not a government organ. As far as the mid-Western Zhou period is concerned, it is possible that the affairs of the royal lineage were managed by a separate structure, but it was by no means fully developed. We actually only know two individuals who are mentioned in the inscriptions as *gongzu*.[53] Their role may be similar to the "Director of the Imperial Clan" (*zongzheng* 宗正) of the Former Han time.[54]

Growth of household administration

The most significant organizational development in the Western Zhou government was the growth of autonomy of the Royal Household (see figure 6). The term "Royal Household" (*wangjia* 王家), which refers to the king's personal family (exclusive of his brothers, who would found their own lineages) and the royal properties necessary for its maintenance, must be first differentiated from the "Royal government," that was the ruling apparatus of the Western Zhou state. Therefore, the term "Household administration" in this context and throughout the whole book refers strictly to the management of the Royal Household. This differentiation is certainly not a matter of interpretational convenience, but reflects an actual historical process that was taking place during much of the Western Zhou.

The concept of the "King's property" being separate from the general possession of the Western Zhou state controlled by the Zhou central government can be traced back to an early Western Zhou inscription, the Yihou Ze *gui* 宜侯夨簋 (JC: 4320; translated in Chapter 6, figure 28), cast in the time of King Kang, on which the "King's people" (*wangren* 王人), counted seven lineages in total, were clearly differentiated from other types of servants given together to the new ruler of the state of Yi. Certainly, the impact of the concept continued to be seen in the expression of "King's officials" (*zhen zhishi* 朕執事), differing from other officials of the royal government, in the inscription of the Maogong *ding* 毛公鼎 (JC: 2841), cast during the long reign of King Xuan.[55] Abundant inscriptional evidence shows that, by the mid-Western Zhou, the concept of "Royal Household" as an autonomous body of administration had been

---

[53] The Royal Kinsman X Li 公族凍釐 appears in the Shi You *gui* 師酉簋 (JC: 4288) and Royal Kinsman X 公族眒 appears in the Mu *gui* 牧簋 (JC: 4343), both as prestigious *youzhe* in the court ceremony of official appointment. On the identity of *gongzu*, see Zhang Yachu and Liu Yu, *Xi Zhou jinwen guanzhi yanjiu*, pp. 39–40. *Youzhe* was the role normally performed by high officials who introduced the appointees to the Zhou king during the appointment ceremonies. Since they customarily stood to the right of the appointees, scholars conventionally called them *youzhe*. The role of the *youzhe* will be discussed again in Chapter 3 in relation to the appointment procedure.

[54] For the function of the "Director of the Imperial Clan," see Bielenstein, *The Bureaucracy of Han Times*, pp. 41–43.

[55] In the Maogong *ding*, the "King's officials" are mentioned after the many court officials as a category of those who were apparently in the direct service of the Zhou king.

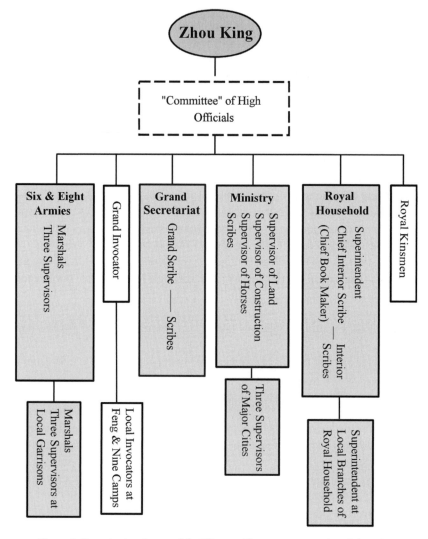

Figure 6. Organizational map of the Western Zhou government (royal domain:
mid-Western Zhou)

firmly established, and this point can be seen also in the appointment
process to be discussed in the next chapter.[56] The inscription of the Cai *gui*
蔡簋 (JC: 4340) states:[57]

[56] It will be shown there that in the appointment ceremonies regularly taking place in the Zhou court,
those officials commanded to work in the Royal Household were customarily introduced to the
king by the head of Royal Household administration. They together formed a self-identified group
of officials.

[57] This important inscription was discovered in the Song dynasty (AD 960–1247) and was recorded
in Xue Shanggong, *Lidai zhong ding yiqi kuanzhi* (Shenyang: Liaoshen shushe, 1985), pp. 264–65.
Although no image of the vessel was transmitted, based on Cai's co-service with Superintendent Hu
and the appearance of Scribe Nian, who announced the royal command to Cai, a fairly accurate

It was the first year, after the full moon, on the *dinghai* day (no. 24), the king was in Yu 淢 Residence. At dawn, the king entered the temple and assumed position. Superintendent Hu 宰智 entered and accompanied Cai 蔡 to his right, standing at the center of the courtyard. The king called on Scribe Nian 史年 to command Cai with a written document. The king said to the effect: "Cai! In the past, the previous king has already commanded you to be Superintendent, and to take charge of the Royal Household. Now, I am to extend your mission and command you and Hu to mutually assist each other as a pair, exerting your utmost effort (*sisi* 死嗣) to supervise the outside and inside of the Royal Household, of which you do not dare not to hear about. Be in charge of the hundred craftsmen, sending out and taking in the orders of Queen Jiang 姜. When someone wants to meet with or to take orders [from the queen], without reporting to Cai in advance, [he] should not dare to hastily enter and report. You do not dare to be not good, following [the example of] Queen Jiang's people, and do not let them be hastily involved in trials (commit offenses). [I] award you a black jacket, and red shoes. Be respectful morning and night, and do not waste my command . . .

This is such an explicit job description for the office of Superintendent as the head of the Royal Household. The duty includes general responsibilities for the internal and external affairs of the Royal Household and supervising the various craftsmen who worked in the Royal Household. In particular, Cai was commanded to send out and take in the commands of the Zhou queen, who apparently had her own possessions and servants. It is also clear from the inscription that access to the Zhou queen, with clearly defined procedures, was tightly and bureaucratically controlled by the official Cai, who was appointed by the king. In the inscription of the Zai Shou *gui* 宰獸簋 (JL: 490), another Superintendent, Shou, was commanded to take charge of a group of people who are described as "Servants and retainers of the Royal Household in Kang Temple" (*Kang Gong wangjia chenqie fuyong* 康宮王家臣妾附庸). In the Yi *gui* 伊簋 (JC: 4287), the expression "Servants of the king in Kang Temple" (*Kang Gong wang chenqie* 康宮王臣妾) is used. Given the fact that the royal Kang Temple certainly belonged to the Royal Household, which would be clear to everyone at the time, the careful wording in these inscriptions indicates the clear definition of "Royal property." In another inscription, the Wang *gui* 望簋 (JC: 4272), Wang was commanded to control the "Royal Household" in the city of Bi (*Bi wangjia* 畢王家), located somewhere to the southeast of the Zhou capital Hao (see Chapter 4).[58]

dating is possible and points to the reign of King Xiao, as suggested by Ma Chengyuan, or slightly earlier to the reign of King Yih, as suggested by Shaughnessy. See Ma Chengyuan, *Shang Zhou qingtongqi mingwen xuan*, 3, p. 264; Shaughnessy, *Sources of Western Zhou History*, p. 119.

[58] Given the limitations of space, detailed notes on the discovery and date of the inscriptions mentioned, except for those whose contents are discussed at length, are generally avoided. For such background information on the inscriptions, the reader should consult Appendix II.

In the mid-Western Zhou inscriptions, we know of more than ten individuals who served as superintendents of the Royal Household; some of them might have worked at the same time as Cai and Hu. Whereas the Royal Household is described as a system of properties belonging directly to the Zhou king, the inscriptions suggest strongly that its administration had become separate from the Zhou government. It had its own officials, servants, craftsmen and retainers, and certainly its own system of operation. The inscriptions further show that the household administration was segmented and the household officials were appointed to manage the various royal possessions with relation to particular locales, as in the case of Wang. However, it is not likely that particular titles were developed for the segmentary offices, which were assigned to the officials more as responsibilities and not as clearly defined positions. In all likelihood, a hierarchy might have been developed in the household administration, but this point will need to be backed up by further evidence.[59]

The conceptual separation of the king's possession and the Household administration from that of the Western Zhou state and its government has important implications. It certainly gave many Zhou officials, especially those who were not affiliated with the Royal Household, a sense of their role not so much as the personal servants of the king (for there were people clearly marked as "King's officials"), but as the functionaries of the Western Zhou state, which was embodied in the divine roles of King Wen and King Wu. And in this sense the reigning king was merely the agent of the Zhou founding kings.[60] In his analysis of ancient Egyptian bureaucracy, Eugene Kamenka considers the separation of the Royal Household from the administration of the royal state as an important step towards permanent bureaucracy.[61] By such separation, the official body of the central government, excluding those who served in the Royal Household, gained its character as a self-determined operational system. Although the system operated on behalf of the king, it was in principle not for the king. It is very likely that the fact that the mid-Western Zhou government was undergoing such a process of separation provided the initial impulse for the bureaucratization of the Zhou government.

Development of ministerial roles

The "Ministry" (*qingshiliao* 卿事寮) is explicitly mentioned in the inscription of the Fansheng *gui* 番生簋 (JC: 4326) from the mid-Western Zhou

---

[59] For a recent discussion of the condition of the Royal Household and the related position of the Superintendent, see also Matsumoto Yoshinori, *Shūdai kokusei no kenkyū* (Tokyo: Kyūko shoin, 2002), pp. 94–121.

[60] On this Zhou mentality, see Li Feng, "'Feudalism' and Western Zhou China," 117–20.

[61] See Kamenka, *Bureaucracy*, pp. 17–18. For a discussion of this separation, see also Finer, *The History of Government*, p. 189.

period, and we have much better information about its internal organization as well as its administrative functions during the mid-Western Zhou than before or after.

The office of Supervisor of Land (*situ* 嗣土) is mentioned in many inscriptions, including a few in which individuals are commanded *to be* Supervisor of Land (*zuo situ* 作嗣土) with their administrative duties specified, which certainly provides us with a solid basis for determining the responsibilities of the office. In the inscription of the Mian *fu* 免簠 (JC: 4626), Mian is appointed Supervisor of Land with responsibility over the forest, marshes, and pastoral land in the district of the city Zheng, located in the western part of the Wei River valley. In the inscription of the Shi Ying *gui* 師穎簋 (JC: 4312), Supervisor of Land Shi Ying was probably put in charge of a floodgate on a river.[62] If we can bring a late Western Zhou case into this context, the Zai *gui* 訇簋(JC: 4255) states that Supervisor of Land Zai was put in charge of the Spring Plowing Ritual.[63] These job descriptions effectively suggest that the work of Supervisor of Land was ultimately land-related civil administration. While the sphere of his service can be reasonably defined on the basis of these inscriptions, some flexibility should also be allowed, since his activities might not have been limited to the specific task of land-related administration. A job description is also available for the Supervisor of Construction with respect to a person named Yang, who cast the inscription of the Yang *gui* 楊簋 # 1 (JC: 4294). According to the inscription, Yang was commanded *to be* Supervisor of Construction (*zuo sigong* 作嗣工) and to take charge of affairs of farming, residential houses, forage grass, law suits, and construction (*gongshi* 工事) of the field of Liang 量.[64] While this entails overall responsibilities in a local area called Liang, duties related to construction are particularly mentioned in the description. Perhaps a Supervisor of Construction in a local area could be charged with duties in addition to those required by his office when the area was not covered by other civil administrative officials. Even in modern bureaucratic governments, under mutual agreement and under special circumstances, an official could be charged with duties that are not in his job description.

In fact, we have a number of lists of the Three Supervisors (*sanyousi* 三有嗣), and a comparison of them tells us more about their administrative functions:

---

[62] For an interpretation of this point, see Li Feng, "'Offices' in Bronze Inscriptions," 33.

[63] The Spring Plowing usually took place before the beginning of the spring season, when the king would arrive in the district and symbolically till the soil himself; his action would be multiplied by his officials down the bureaucratic ranks, reaching eventually to the commoners. For a discussion of the Spring Plowing Ritual, see Yang Kuan, *Xi Zhou shi*, pp. 268–82.

[64] *Gongshi* 工事 is written in Yang *gui* no. 1 (JC: 4294) as *gongsi* 工寺, and in no. 2 (JC: 4295) as *gongshi* 工史. But most scholars read these terms as *gongshi* 工事, "construction." See Ma Chengyuan, *Shang Zhou qingtongqi mingwen xuan*, p. 3.184; Shirakawa Shizuka, "Kinbun tsūshaku," 23.131:85.

Fifth Year Qiu Wei *ding*: 五年裘衛鼎	嗣土邑人逮；嗣馬頙人邦；嗣工陶矩 Supervisor of Land, native of Yi, Pu; Supervisor of Horses, native of Qi, Bang; Supervisor of Construction, Tao Ju.
Qiu Wei *he*: 裘衛盉	嗣土微邑；嗣馬單旗；嗣工邑人服 Supervisor of Land, Wei Yi; Supervisor of Horses, Shan Qi; Supervisor of Construction, native of Yi, Fu.

In both the Fifth Year Qiu Wei *ding* 五年裘衛鼎 (JC: 2832) and the Qiu Wei *he* 裘衛盉 (JC: 9456), the Three Supervisors receive orders from the court magnates and execute the orders of transaction of fields to Qiu Wei from their original owners by actually demarcating their boundaries. The context of the inscriptions fully suggests the civil administrative nature of their offices. Such a role of the Three Supervisors can also be seen in the Yong *yu* 永盂 (JC: 10322), cast very close in time to the Qiu Wei bronzes, which were cast in the reign of King Gong,[65] and even in a newly discovered late Western Zhou bronze, the Wu Hu *ding* 吳虎鼎 (JL: 364), dated to the reign of King Xuan.[66] These inscriptions suggest that, besides serving in their particular functions in particular locations as in the cases of Mian and Yang, the Three Supervisors sometime teamed up in matters that concerned the authority of the Ministry as the executive branch of the central government.

However, the interesting point is: although the Qiu Wei *he* and Fifth Year Qiu Wei *ding* were cast only two years apart within the same reign, the names of the Three Supervisors in the two inscriptions are completely different. Since this cannot be explained by the routine replacement of officials, it seems likely that several individuals might have simultaneously served the function of each of the Three Supervisors. In fact, we already know of such an arrangement from the inscription of the Cai *gui* with regard to a different part of the Zhou government, the Royal Household: according to the Cai *gui* translated above, both Cai and Hu served simultaneously as Superintendents; the Zhou king actually literally commanded them to serve as a pair. Such an arrangement of two or more officials sharing the same government role seems to have been deliberate, and it certainly left an institutional legacy in the long Chinese political tradition,

---

[65] The Fifth Year Qiu Wei *ding* and Qiu Wei *he* are commonly dated to the reign of King Gong based on the mention in the *ding* of the irrigation work commissioned by the king. While the *ding* is self-dated to the fifth year, the *he* is dated two years earlier, to the third year of King Gong. The Yong *yu* does not itself offer a year number, but it mentions the same group of high officials who were also mentioned in the Qiu Wei bronzes, including Jingbo 井伯, Rongbo 榮伯, and Bo Sufu 伯俗父. For the date of the Qiu Wei bronzes, see Tang Lan, *Tang Lan xiansheng jinwen lunji* (Beijing: Zijingcheng, 1995), p. 194; Ma Chengyuan, *Shang Zhou qingtongqi mingwen xuan*, 3, pp. 127, 131; Shaughnessy, *Sources of Western Zhou History*, pp. 110–11.

[66] The Wu Hu *ding* mentions the deceased King Li and is self-dated to the eighteenth year, doubtless in the reign of King Xuan; see *Kaogu yu wenwu* 1998.3, 69–71.

for instance, in the Han government, where some prominent offices were divided and shared between two officials, the Right and the Left.[67] The situation revealed by the Western Zhou inscriptions seems to suggest just the same tendency in the actual appointment of officials to government offices. In other words, in the Western Zhou government, offices were conceived more as "roles" that could be co-played by multiple persons, rather than "posts" that had to be filled by the corresponding number of officials, as is the case in most modern bureaucracies.

As this is probably the case, we can also see the vertical expansion of such "roles" along an administrative hierarchy. Itō Michiharu has pointed out that the Three Supervisors mentioned in the Qiu Wei bronzes were bureaucrats of the central court because they, together with the people of the Royal Household, received direct commands from a group of high officials headed by Jingbo in the central government.[68] And the case of Yiren Pu 邑人逋 mentioned in the first list above provides strong support for this point.[69] On the other hand, we know of individuals like Supervisor of Construction Shi 眉 of the Zhou 周 people, Supervisor of Multitudes Hanfu 凶父 of Zheng 鄭 (Yong *yu*), and Supervisor of Land Si 寺 of Rui 芮 (Wu Hu *ding*); as I have noted in another study, these were officials from the local administration of the cities that will be discussed in detail in Chapter 4.[70] Lower than them in status, in a late Western Zhou inscription, there were also people like Supervisor of Construction Hu 虎 of Huai 淮 and Supervisor of Construction Jing Jun 騬君 of the Bang 邦 people (Sanshi *pan* 散氏盤; JC: 10176), who were minor officials in the rural areas belonging to the polities of San 散 or Ze 夨 in the west end of the Wei River valley. While these inscriptions suggest that the roles of the Three Supervisors existed at every level of Zhou administration, there is no evidence that they themselves formed an independent system of command and operation. Instead, they belonged to the administrative body of Zhou officials at different levels. However, their frequent occurrences in the inscriptions indicate in general that the civil administrative function of the Zhou government was well developed during the mid-Western Zhou.

However, the really tricky issues about the civil administrative function of the Zhou government are those which concern the roles of the Supervisor

---

[67] Such as the office of "Chancellor"; this structure of chancellorship has come back a number of times later in Chinese history. See Bielenstein, *The Bureaucracy of Han Times*, p. 7; Loewe, *The Government of Qin and Han*, p. 20.

[68] See Itō Michihara, *Chūgoku kodai kokka*, p. 261.

[69] Pu 逋 can be confidently identified with the caster of the Pu *yu* 逋盂 (JC: 10321), another mid-Western Zhou bronze already mentioned above. The inscription says that Pu, ordered by the Zhou queen, went to *suitu* 遂土, the far district of the capital, to recruit "female and male servants" for the *liao* 寮 "bureau," which likely refers to the "Ministry." This indicates that Pu was an official in the central bureaucracy: he took orders directly from the Zhou queen and worked for the "bureau." See Shirakawa Shizuka, "Kinbun tsūshaku," 49.*ho*3:311–20; Ma Chengyuan, *Shang Zhou qingtongqi mingwen xuan*, 3, p. 3.

[70] See Li Feng, "'Offices' in Bronze Inscriptions," 25.

of Multitudes (*situ* 嗣徒) and what might have been represented by the term *sikou* 嗣寇. The title "Supervisor of Multitudes" does not appear in the Fifth Year Qiu Wei *ding* and the Qiu Wei *he* (where the office appears as *situ* 嗣土), but appears in the Yong *yu* and is there treated the same as the title "Supervisor of Land" (*situ* 嗣土) by many scholars. Since the former term "Supervisor of Multitudes" did not appear in the early Western Zhou and the latter term "Supervisor of Land" continued to be used during the late Western Zhou, previous scholars have quite often treated them as equivalent to each other.[71] However, the rise of the term *situ* 嗣徒 as a part of the official title, even though it could stand for *situ* 嗣土, may also imply an institutional transition that gradually took place in the government body of the Western Zhou.[72] However, whether the two titles can or cannot be differentiated during the mid-Western Zhou, when the "Three Supervisors" are mentioned in the inscriptions, it is the "Supervisor of Land," but not the "Supervisor of Multitudes," that is counted. The term *sikou* 嗣寇 is a more critical question because it concerns whether the judicial function of the Zhou government constituted a legal office and whether such a role had become separated from other ministerial functions of the Zhou government. The term *sikou* 嗣寇 appears in two mid-Western Zhou inscriptions, the Nanji *ding* 南季 鼎 (JC: 2781), and the Yang *gui* 楊簋 no. 1 (JC: 4294), which are considered by some scholars as evidence for the existence of the office of "Supervisor of Lawsuits" during the mid-Western Zhou.[73] While the office of "Supervisor of Lawsuits" is frequently documented in Eastern Zhou inscriptions and texts as one of the prominent officials of the states, it is so explicit that in both inscriptions named above the term entails official responsibilities but not administrative "offices": in the first inscription, Nan Ji was commanded to assist Shi Sufu 師俗父 to supervise matters of *kou*; in the second inscription, Yang was appointed Supervisor of Construction, and the supervision of matters of *kou* was merely one of the several duties entrusted to him.

---

[71] For instance, Ma Chengyuan treated *situ* 嗣土 in both the Fifth Year Qiu Wei *ding* and the Qiu Wei *he* as equivalent to *situ* 嗣徒. See Ma Chengyuan, *Shang Zhou qingtongqi mingwen xuan*, 3, pp. 127, 131. For such a treatment, see also Guo Moruo, *Jinwen congkao*, revised 2nd edition (Beijing: Renmin, 1954), pp. 63–65; Zhou Fagao, *Jinwen gulin*, pp. 7425–29; Zhang Yachu and Liu Yu, *Xi Zhou jinwen guanzhi yanjiu*, pp. 8–9. But it was *situ* 嗣徒 that was carried down to later time and made its way into the textual tradition. See *Zhouli*, 10, pp. 702–11, 715. For an analysis of the title in the *Zuozhuan*, see Gu Donggao, "Chunqiu lieguo guanzhi biao," in *Chunqiu dashi biao* (Beijing: Zhonghua Press, 1993), pp. 1039–40.

[72] Itō Michiharu has suggested that this might have been a transition from the state's control of people through controlling the land to the control of land through controlling the population, which, by the late Western Zhou, had become considerably mobile. Itō's view is on the mark. See Itō Michiharu, *Chūgoku kodai kokka*, p. 217.

[73] See Guo Moruo, *Jinwen congkao*, p. 66; Zhang Yachu and Liu Yu, *Xi Zhou jinwen guanzhi yanjiu*, pp. 24–25. In her study of the legal tradition of the Western Zhou, Laura Skosey accepts *sikou* as a legal office. But she thinks that the status of *sikou* was not very high – they assisted high officials at the Zhou court in their legal duties. Skosey suggests that the term should be translated as "Supervisor of Criminals." See Skosey, *The Legal System and Legal Tradition of the Western Zhou*, pp. 176–78.

The only other place the character *kou* 寇 appears is the Hu *ding* 曶鼎 (JC: 2838), where it describes a robbery incurred in the caster's fields. Therefore, the character *kou* in the above two inscriptions could simply mean "matters of robbery." If this is the case, the inscriptions are instead evidence that at least during the mid-Western Zhou the judicial function was charged to the civil administrators but did not constitute a separate government role.

Differentiation of secretarial roles

However, it is in the organization of secretarial offices that the mid-Western Zhou government exhibits its most salient feature. The development of the secretarial functions seems to have taken two steps of differentiation of offices during the mid-Western Zhou. The first is the differentiation between Scribe (*shi* 史) and Interior Scribe (*neishi* 内史), and the second is a process of hierarchization of the institution of the Interior Scribes that gave rise to the new office "Chief Interior Scribe" (*neishi yin* 内史尹). Both of these steps are significant in the development of the Western Zhou government into a bureaucratic organization.

In addition to a large number of individuals referred to as Scribes such as Shi Wu 史戍, Shi Quecao 史趞曹, Shi Mao 史懋, Shi Mian 史免, and Shi Qiang 史墙 in the mid-Western Zhou inscriptions, many inscriptions also mention the role of individuals who had the title "Interior Scribes." The best-known person is Interior Scribe Wu 吳, who appears in the inscriptions of the Shi Hu *gui* 師虎簋 (JC: 4316), Shi Yun *gui* 師
癲簋 (JC: 4284), and the Mu *gui* 牧簋 (JC: 4343), suggesting that his service was approximately in the time of late King Gong to early King Xiao. In all three inscriptions, Wu was the one to announce a royal command. The same role was performed by Interior Scribe Nian 年, who served a little later, in the time of King Xiao to King Yi, appearing in the Jian *gui* 諫簋 (JC: 4285), Yang *gui* 楊簋 (JC: 4294), and Wang Chen *gui* 王臣簋 (JC: 4268). These inscriptions suggest that Interior Scribe was quite active in the mid-Western Zhou court as the Zhou king's spokesman in the appointment ceremony.[74] The inscription of the X *ding* 乑鼎 (JC: 2696) suggests that some Interior Scribes might have also served the Zhou queen in particular. Although it is quite clear that the Interior Scribe constantly served in the Zhou king's presence, in one inscription, the Fifth Year Qiu Wei *ding* 五年裘衛鼎 (JC: 2832), the Interior Scribe also participated in the land transaction to Qiu Wei, probably as the king's representative, along with the Three Supervisors from the Ministry. In all, the status and function of the Interior Scribe is very clear in the inscriptions.

Hsu and Linduff have taken the appearance of the office of Interior Scribe as evidence of an institutional reform by which an "inner court"

---

[74] Details of the appointment ceremony will be discussed in Chapter 3, pp. 103–11.

of the Zhou king was formed to exercise the king's authority in a more secular and bureaucratic way.[75] While this observation can be agreed upon with respect to the close association of the Interior Scribe with the Royal Household personnel, the change should probably be explained in light of the growth of autonomy of the Royal Household during the mid-Western Zhou period, already analyzed above. It is only from this perspective that we can understand the development of the interior secretarial body outside of the structure of the Grand Secretariat (*taishi liao* 太史寮), clearly documented by the Fansheng *gui* 番生簋 (JC: 4326) for the second half of the mid-Western Zhou period; this was probably the structure to which many if not all of the ordinary Scribes belonged. While the secretarial function was topped by the office of Grand Scribe during the early Western Zhou, by the middle period, due likely to the growth of household administration, such a function was probably divided into two parts along the lines that segregated the Royal Household from the outer government. Probably also because of this separation, the inner secretarial function was able to develop gradually into a new institution with its own hierarchy. This is evident in the emergence during the mid-Western Zhou of the office of Chief Interior Scribe (*neishi yin* 內史尹), who is mentioned as the king's close assistant in a large number of inscriptions including the Yang *gui* 養簋 (JC: 4243), Chu *gui* 楚簋 (JC: 4246), and Shi Ji *gui* 師籍簋 (JC: 4257), etc. Given the frequent appearance of the Interior Scribes in the mid-Western Zhou inscriptions, they must have been a large crowd headed by the Chief Interior Scribe, whom the inscriptions never mention by name.[76]

In contrast to the large number of Document Makers (*zuoce* 作冊) who were active during the early Western Zhou, we know of only one person for the mid-Western Zhou period, Document Maker Wu 吳 in the Wu *fangyi* 吳方彝 (JC: 9898), whom most scholars identify with Interior Scribe Wu mentioned above. On the other hand, two other inscriptions, the Shi Yu *gui* 師俗簋 (JC: 4277) and Mian *pan* 免盤 (JC: 10161), mention the combined office of "Document Maker and Interior Scribe" (*zuoce neishi* 作冊內史). This does seem to have been the result of an institutional change by which the role of Document Maker might have been absorbed into the role of the Interior Scribe. Although the office of the ordinary Document Makers was largely abandoned during the mid-Western Zhou, nearly ten inscriptions, including the Shi Chen *ding* 師晨鼎 (JC: 2817) and Mian *gui* 免簋 (JC: 4240), actually mention the role of Chief Document Maker (*zuoce yin* 作冊尹), who was very active at the

---

[75] See Hsu and Linduff, *Western Chou Civilization*, p. 247.

[76] This may be an indication of the high prestige of the Chief Interior Scribe as the head of the Zhou king's inner secretarial staff, the person who was most likely to influence the king. Since the inscriptions were all cast by subordinate officials, understandably they would reserve the personal name of the Chief as a courtesy, supposing the name was known to everyone. By the same token, Jingbo 井伯, Rongbo 榮伯, and Yigong 益公, which appear frequently in the inscriptions of the same period, were respectable titles and not personal names.

time, serving as the announcer of royal commands. Again, it is possible that the Chief Document Maker, without subordinate Document Makers working under him, was the same as the Chief Interior Scribe, as has already been suggested by some scholars.[77] While this issue should be left open here, there seems no doubt that when the "Chief" (*yin* 尹 or *yinshi* 尹氏) is mentioned in a simplistic way in the inscriptions such as the Shen *gui* 申簋 (JC: 4267) and Mishu *gui* 弭叔簋 (JC: 4253), it actually refers to the Chief Interior Scribe or Chief Document Maker, or both.[78] All of these bronzes were cast during the mid-Western Zhou and in the times of Kings Yih, Xiao, and Yi. If the suggested identification is in fact true, we must expect a change to have taken place: while during the early Western Zhou some of the Document Makers had worked in the Ministry as evidenced by the Ling *fangyi*, suggesting that, if the Document Makers were indeed composers of administrative orders, the Ministry might have issued orders in its own name, by the second half of the mid-Western Zhou such power might have been discharged by the Ministry or, given the unity of the Document Maker and the Interior Scribe, it might have been monopolized by the king's "inner court." If this was indeed the case, it might be an indication of the king's attempt to concentrate power in his hand. Whether this is true, this change seems to correspond well with the fact that the Zhou king was the only person to make appointments over the whole government, with orders announced and even composed exclusively by his interior secretaries. This might have been one of the critical forces that contributed to the general trend that I have called the "Mid-Western Zhou Transition" (Chapter 1).

The same trend of development is also evident in another government role – the religious office "Invocator" (*zhu* 祝). As mentioned above, the office of "Grand Invocator" already existed in the early period, and it continued to function during the mid-Western Zhou. Even though we only have a limited number of officials who held the title "Invocator," their inscriptions suggest some interesting differentiations in their role. In the Chang Xing *he* 長甶盉 (JC: 9455), a vessel self-dated to the reign of King Mu, the Grand Invocator, along with the prestigious Jingbo 井伯, assisted King Mu in a court ceremony that probably involved feasting, sacrificial offerings, and archery. In another inscription, the Shen *gui* 申簋 (JC: 4267), Shen was appointed as assistant to the Grand Invocator and was assigned to serve in particular as Invocator for the people of the capital Feng and the nine military camps in the capital area (see below). In the inscription of the Qian *gui* 鄜簋 (JC: 4296), Qian is commanded *to be* Invocator in the Five Cities in the Wei River

---

[77] See Wu Zhenfeng, *Jinwen renming huibian* (Beijing: Zhonghua 1987), p. 110.
[78] In the Ke *xu* 克盨 (JC: 4465), Scribe Zhao is described as a fellow of the *yinshi* 尹氏, indicating that the Chief was indeed the head of the Scribes.

valley.[79] While there seems little doubt that the term "Invocator" (*zhu* 祝) in these two inscriptions represents a formal "office," not merely duties, these inscriptions suggest that, since these local Invocators were explicitly acknowledged as assistants (or subordinates) to the Grand Invocator, a process of systemization of the religious offices was probably taking place during the mid-Western Zhou. The situation may well be that the Grand Invocator was the high priest who had his office; under him, there were many subordinate invocators whom he would dispatch to work in particular locations with respect to particular administrative units. The result of this might have been a religious bureaucracy consisting of invocators at different levels of Zhou administration with the Grand Invocator at the central court as their arch-authority.

Development of military administration

It is well known that the main military forces of the Western Zhou were composed of the Eight Armies (*bashi* 八師) and the Six Armies (*liushi* 六師). The Eight Armies were called "Eight Armies of Yin" (*Yin bashi* 殷八師) or "Eight Armies of Chengzhou" (*Chengzhou bashi* 成周八師) and were located first in the former Shang capital area and then relocated in the eastern Zhou capital Chengzhou. The Six Armies were called "Six Armies of the West" (*xi liushi* 西六師) and were stationed on the Wei River plain, probably near the Zhou capitals.[80] While the Six Armies of the West stationed on the Wei River plain were the standing field army that was frequently sent on military campaigns far from their base, the security of the capital region was probably the responsibility of the praetorian troops, known as the Left and Right camps (*zuoyouxi* 左右戲) in the inscription of the Shi Hu *gui* 師虎簋 (JC: 4316), cast at the accession of King Yih.[81] Although we do not know about the number of the soldiers that belonged to these two military camps, they clearly included charioteers as well as foot-soldiers commanded by the Marshals (*shi shi* 師氏). In the First Year Shi Shi *gui* 元年師事簋 (JC: 4279), cast slightly later in the next reign, the Left camp is referred to as the "Great Left" (*dazuo* 大左), where Shi Shi is commanded to work with additional general

[79] The "Five Cities" are the five major royal centers located on the Wei River plain, including the Zhou capitals Feng and Hao and others. For the composition and administrative status of the Five Cities, see discussion in Chapter 4, pp. 165–67.

[80] For discussions of the Zhou military, see Li Xueqin, "Lun Xi Zhou jinwen zhong de liushi bashi," *Huaxia kaogu* 1987.2, 207–10; Kimura Hideumi, "Rokushi no kankōsei ni tsuite: Rei hōson meibun o chūshin ni shite," *Tōhōgaku* 69 (1985), 3–4. See also Yang Kuan, "Zailun Xi Zhou jinwen zhong liushi he bashi de xingzhi," *Kaogu* 1965.10, 525–28.

[81] The Shi Hu *gui* will be considered in detail in Chapter 5 with respect to official service in the Zhou government. The bronze is commonly thought datable to the first year of King Yih, based on its relation to the solar eclipse of 899 BC and on the appearance of multiple individuals who also appear in other datable bronzes. See Shaughnessy, *Sources of Western Zhou History*, pp. 256–58; Ma Chengyuan, *Shang Zhou qingtongqi mingwen xuan*, 3, pp. 167–68; *Xia Shang Zhou duandai gongcheng*, pp. 25–26.

responsibilities over the Marshals in the district of the capital Feng, suggesting that the two camps were probably located in the vicinity of the capital Feng 豐. Another inscription, the Shen *gui* 申簋 (JC: 4267), mentions Nine Camps (*jiuxi* 九戲), the organization of which is unknown, but it is possible that the term refers to the total of the Left and Right Camps and the camps of the Six Armies, and probably something else, to which Shen was appointed Invocator. This can be seen as a summary of the main military forces on the Wei River plain during the Western Zhou. In addition to these centrally directed troops, there were clearly also local military units stationed in each of the five major cities, known as the "Masters of Horses and Charioteers of the Five Cites" (*wuyi zuoma yuren* 五邑走馬馭人) appearing in the inscriptions of the Hu *gui* 虎簋 (JL: 491) and in a late Western Zhou inscription, the First Year Shi Dui *gui* 元年師兌簋 (JC: 4274). The three types of troops formed the basic structure of the Zhou military forces, fully evident in the Western Zhou bronze inscriptions.

In his most extensive study of ancient governments, S. E. Finer expressed the strong view that standing armies could not exist without a civil bureaucracy in place, although there are cases where states equipped with civil bureaucracy did not have a standing army. This is because the men, money, and materials on which the standing army depended had to be raised through a bureaucracy.[82] Be this as it may, what is clear in the Zhou case is that, while the development of civil bureaucracy with regard to the central government was certainly evident, even the military organization itself had come to gain some civil features. During the mid-Western Zhou the Eight Armies and Six Armies had apparently developed into large organizations that not only performed military tasks in foreign warfare but themselves were also charged with some civil functions. The key to understanding this situation lies in the inscription of the Li *fangzun* 盠方尊 (JC: 6013) (see figure 7) and Li *fangyi* 盠方彝 (JC: 9900), which present the identical text:[83]

It was the eighth month, first auspiciousness; the king entered Zhou Temple. Duke Mu (Mugong 穆公) accompanied Li to his right, standing

---

[82] See Finer, *The History of Government*, pp. 36, 59.

[83] Discovered in 1956 at Lijiacun in Meixian, Shaanxi, the Li bronzes were previously dated by most scholars to the second half of the mid-Western Zhou, either in the reign of King Yih or that of King Xiao. See Guo Moruo, "Li qi ming kaoshi," *Kaogu xuebao* 1957.2, 1–6; Li Xueqin, "Meixian Lijiacun tongqi kao," *Wenwu caokao ziliao* 1957.7, 58–59. However, the appearance of Mugong 穆公 as a main figure on the Li bronzes, identified with the caster of the Mugong *guigai* 穆公簋蓋 (JC: 4191), which bears a great-bird ornament, would guarantee a date in the early phase of the mid-Western Zhou, most suitably in the reign of King Mu. This point has been proven by the recent discovery of the Lai 逨 bronzes from the same site, on which the same person Li 盠 (also called Lifu 盠父) is said to have served both King Zhao and King Mu. See *Wenwu* 2003.6, 59. For the Mugong *guigai* 穆公簋蓋, see *Kaogu yu wenwu* 1981.4, 27–28. For the inscription of the Li *fangzun*, see also Ma Chengyuan, *Shang Zhou qingtongqi mingwen xuan*, 3, pp. 228–29; Shirakawa Shizuka, "Kinbun tsūshaku," 19.101:312–23. The *Yin Zhou jinwen jicheng* gives a wrong rubbing under no. 6013; see *Wenwu cankao ziliao* 1957.4, 8.

Figure 7. The Li *fangzun* and its inscription (photograph provided by Cao Wei, Shaanxi Institute of Archeology; inscription from *Wenwu cankao ziliao* 1957.4, 8)

at the center of the courtyard and facing north. The king commanded Li with a written document and ordered the Chief to award Li red knee-pads, a black girdle-pendant, and a bridle, saying: "Herewith take charge of the King's Legion (*wangxing* 王行) and the Three Supervisors (*sanyousi* 三有嗣) of the Six Armies: Supervisor of Land, Supervisor of Horses, and Supervisor of Construction." The king commanded Li and said: "Specially supervise the king's camps in the Six Armies and Eight Armies." Li bowed with his head touching the ground, daring in response to extol the king's beneficence, herewith making [for] my cultured grandfather Duke Yi [this] treasured sacrificial vessel. Li said: "The Son of Heaven is unspoiled and solid in his foundation; for ten thousand years he will protect our ten thousand states." Li dares to bow with his head touching the ground and says: "Valorous and valorous is my body; [it] will replace my predecessors' treasured service."

It is important to read this inscription correctly, but it has caused some confusion among the scholars in the past. For instance, Guo Moruo considered the management of the "King's Legion" (*wanghang* 王行) and the Three Supervisors (*sanyousi* 參有嗣) to be two parallel parts of Li's responsibility.[84] Itō Michiharu, on the other hand, treated the Six Armies, the King's Legion, and the Three Supervisors as three independent units, suggesting that Li had authority over both the Zhou military and the government. This is not only highly unlikely, but causes a problem in the general configuration of the Zhou government.[85] Apparently, both readings identify the Three Supervisors as officials in the Zhou central government, seen also in the inscriptions of the Fifth Year Qiu Wei *ding* 五年裘衛鼎 (JC: 2832) and Qiu Wei *he* 裘衛盉 (JC: 9456) as "Three Supervisors: Supervisor of Land, Supervisor of Horses, and Supervisor of Construction." The reading presented above in the translation agrees with what was suggested by Kimura Hideumi, who considered both the King's Legion and the Three Supervisors to be internal organizations of the Six Armies.[86] This reading suggests that the institution of the "Three Supervisors" also existed in the military organization of the Six Armies, paralleling the Three Supervisors, main offices of the Ministry, in the central government. And given the roles of these offices, the military had apparently assumed some civil administrative functions.

This reading further agrees with, and is supported by, other mid-Western Zhou inscriptions that also suggest the performance of civil administrative functions by the military personnel. The inscription of the Hu *hu* 曶壺 (JC: 9728) records that Hu was appointed Grand Supervisor

<hr />

[84] See Guo Moruo, "Li qi ming kaoshi," 1–6.

[85] See Itō Michiharu, *Chūgoku kodai kokka*, pp. 236–41.

[86] See Kimura Hideumi, "Rokushi no kankōsei ni tsuite," 3–4. For an analysis of the different readings of this key sentence of the Li *fangzun*, see also Li Feng, "'Offices' in Bronze Inscriptions," 34–35.

of Land (*zhong situ* 冢嗣土), to perform his duty in the Eight Armies stationed in Chengzhou.[87] This is clearly a civil administrative office that belonged to the internal organization of the Eight Armies. In the Qi *gui* 趞簋 (JC: 4266), Qi was appointed Supervisor of Horses in the Bin 豳 Garrison with authority over not only the retainers and archers, but also the neighboring residents of the garrison. These inscriptions suggest strongly that there were lands as well as residential sites in the areas where the armies were stationed that were attached to the military and were administered by officers of the military personnel. This point is most explicitly expressed in a late Western Zhou inscription, the Nangong Liu *ding* 南宮柳鼎 (JC: 2805), stating that Liu was commanded to supervise the pastoral lands, orchards, marshes, and even farming affairs belonging to the Six Armies. Although this is a late Western Zhou inscription cast in about the time of King Li, it has a bearing on the possible situation suggested by the Hu *hu* and Qi *gui* cast during the mid-Western Zhou.

While the situation where there were civil administrative functions discharged by military personnel has been recognized previously by modern scholars, the argument has focused on the form in which these lands were held. One view holds that these lands provided the Zhou military with necessary logistics and were managed by the civil officers in the military, like the military cultivation that was practiced also later in the Han dynasty.[88] The opposing view, based on later ritual texts such as the *Zhouli*, suggests that the organization of Six Armies corresponds to the organization of the Six Districts (*liuxiang* 六鄉) surrounding the royal capital. This view argues for an organization that combined both civil and military functions: the Six Armies were composed of the residents of the Six Districts, who were farmers and at the same time soldiers, as the civil officials of the Six Districts were simultaneously military commanders of the Six Armies.[89] While using the *Zhouli* to recover a Western Zhou institution

---

[87] Many scholars identify it with the *da situ* 大嗣徒 "Grand Minister of Land" in the *Zhouli*, described as one of the highest officials at the royal court. See Guo Moruo, *Liang Zhou jinwen ci daxi tulu kaoshi*, p. 100; Si Weizhi, "Xi Zhou jinwen suojian guanming kao," *Zhongguo wenhua yanjiu huikan* 7 (1947), 6. Some also consider that it is "Supervisor of Land" in local areas. See Itō Michiharu, *Chūgoku kodai kokka*, p. 255. Given the recent discovery of the Lu *gui* 親簋, which records the initial appointment of Jingbo 井伯 as *Zhong sima* 冢嗣馬 in the central court, the title certainly was not limited to officials serving in the local areas. It is quite possible that, considering the general operational features of the Zhou government, whereby multiple individuals might have served simultaneously in a single position, *Zhong situ* might have been the head of the ordinary *situ* in an administrative unit. For the Lu *gui*, see *Zhongguo lishi wenwu* 2006.3, 4–6.

[88] See Yu Xingwu, "Luelun Xi Zhou jinwen zhong de liushi he bashi jiqi tuntian zhi," *Kaogu* 1964.3, 152–55; "Guanyu 'Lun Xi Zhou jinwen zhong liu shi bashi he xiangsui zhidu de guanxi' yiwen de yijian," *Kaogu* 1965.3, 131–33.

[89] See Yang Kuan, "Lun Xi Zhou jinwen zhong liushi bashi he xiangsui zhidu de guanxi," *Kaogu* 1964.8, 414–19; "Zailun Xi Zhou jinwen zhong liushi bashi de xingzhi," 525–28. The same view is stated again recently in Yang Kuan, *Xi Zhou shi*, pp. 395–425. Yang's view was adopted by Itō Michiharu, who then suggested that the Six Armies or Eight Armies appearing in inscriptions were essentially geographic units, and only when warfare rose were they moved to function as military organizations. See Itō Michiharu, *Chōgoku kodai kokka*, 154–62.

is a very dangerous game, so far the connection of such an institution to the Western Zhou is almost solely based on the circumstantial "evidence" that in the inscriptions some officials with the title Marshal (*shi* 師) served civil administrative duties. But on this last point, I have recently suggested that civil officials with the title *shi* in the inscriptions were ex-military commanders and not officials who performed both civil and military duties.[90] In other words, there is no real basis for relating the system of Six Districts in the late texts to the Six Armies of the Western Zhou.

Systematization of the Zhou government: an assessment

The above discussion has highlighted some major changes that occurred in the mid-Western Zhou government and are evident in the contemporaneous bronze inscriptions. Although there are still some unclear points, the current evidence suggests strongly that the Zhou government was undergoing a decisive process of expansion and systemization during the mid-Western Zhou. The development took two main directions: (1) the compartmentalization of the Zhou central government; (2) the development of hierarchies within the different segments of the Zhou government. The first trend is most evident in the development of a Royal Household administration that became separate from the central government and formed its own system of authority and management of the various royal properties, servants, artisans, and retainers at various locales in or out of the capitals. Accompanying this development was the rise in prominence of the office of Superintendent as the head of royal administration. It is also evident in the separation of the more specialized body of the interior secretarial staff composed of a large number of Interior Scribes from the ordinary secretarial officials of the government, managed through the structure of the Grand Secretariat. Certainly, the expansion of the Ministry to employ a large number of functionaries to serve the role of each of the Three Supervisors is another indication. Furthermore, the military, or the organization of the Six and Eight Armies, developed from simply a body of the armed forces into a complex system of administration that not only performed military functions, but was also charged with complex civil functions. It is clear that the Six Armies and Eight Armies possessed their own landed properties for which civil administrative management was set up. However, rather than putting this under the temporary authority of the field commanders, the offices of Three Supervisors were established to handle the matter; this is certainly an important step toward bureaucratic management (see figure 6).

The development of hierarchy was another characteristic of the mid-Western Zhou government. This is first of all evident in the differentiation

---

[90] See Li Feng, "Succession and Promotion," 20–25.

of levels of administration embodied in the role of the Three Supervisors; while some were court bureaucrats officiating in the Ministry, others were officials in the local administration of the major cities. The role of the Three Supervisors even existed in the more rural communities in the Zhou royal domain, as I will further discuss in Chapter 4. However, proper terminologies had not been developed to differentiate these officials at different levels, and there is a general lack of evidence that the Three Supervisors at the local level were subordinates to (or directly took orders from) the Three Supervisors at the central court. Although the Three Supervisors might not themselves have formed a separate system of operation and authority, they belonged to the different administrative units that were organized into a ladder of civil administration connected to the Ministry in the central government. Furthermore, such a superior–subordinate relationship is explicitly tested with regard to the religious offices, as the Invocators at different local levels were described as assistants to the Grant Invocator at the central court as their highest authority. In the same way, it is significant that the secretarial function of the Zhou government, while apparently segmented, was also carried out through a hierarchy, with the Chief Interior Scribe or Chief Document Maker as the head of the various Interior Scribes working at the court and at the various royal properties, including the queen's residence.

These developments gave the mid-Western Zhou government the clear organizational characteristics of a bureaucracy. Although we have no statistics of any kind available to test the number of civil officials, given the existence of the various offices and the way they were organized, their number must be quite large. Superimposed on this bureaucratic body was a group of influential court dignitaries who acted as a "committee" that transmitted orders from the king to the executive officials, the Three Supervisors; at the same time, they also acted as judges in important civil matters. Three inscriptions mention this "committee," and despite the different composition of the three lists, the order in which they appear remains very constant: Yigong 益公, Jingbo 井伯, Bo Yifu 伯邑夫, Rongbo 榮伯, Dingbo 定伯, Qiongbo 琼伯, Shanbo 單伯, and Bo Sufu 伯俗父 (Shi Su 師俗).[91] Clearly, Duke Yi was the head of this "committee." It is very likely, given our current evidence, that this "committee" replaced or displaced the role of the Protector (*bao* 保) or Grand Protector (*taibao* 太保) that figured so prominently during the early Western Zhou but was never again mentioned during the mid-Western Zhou. While the implication of this transition will be explored further later in this book, it will suffice here

---

[91] The Fifth Year Qiu Wei *ding* (JC: 2832) mentions: Jingbo, Bo Yifu 伯邑父, Dingbo 定伯, Qiongbo 琼伯, Bo Sufu 伯俗父; the Qiu Wei *he* (JC: 9456) mentions: Bo Yifu, Rongbo, Dingbo, Qiongbo, Shanbo 單伯; and the Yong *yu* (JC: 10322) lists Yigong, Jingbo, Rongbo, Shi Su. For a clear reading of these inscriptions, consult Ma Chengyuan, *Shang Zhou qingtongqi mingwen xuan*, 3, pp. 127, 131, 141; Shirakawa Shizuka, "Kinbun tsūshaku," 49.*ho*3:191–200; 49.*ho*11:257–62.

just to note that the emergence of such structure, instead of the family rule evident in the early Western Zhou, reflects a move to a more open government with relatively non-autocratic authority and impersonal rule. The "committee" served as a buffer between royal authority and the administrative body of the government; because of its appearance during the mid-Western Zhou, the hierarchy of authority in the Zhou government was significantly institutionalized or at least stabilized.

THE LATE WESTERN ZHOU GOVERNMENT

The late Western Zhou period began with a troubled reign in Western Zhou history – that of King Li, who eventually failed to cope with the internal and external pressures and had to spend the rest of his life in exile away from the capital. Although the Zhou also experienced a number of foreign invasions in the middle period, the threat from the outside world had become constant during the late period mainly from two directions: the northwest, where the Xianyun launched repeated attacks on the royal domain in Shaanxi, and the southeast, where the Huaiyi tested the Zhou's ability to hold distant frontiers. Given the current condition of our sources, it is difficult to determine the extent to which outside pressures influenced institutional changes in the Zhou government, but it is possible to identify a number of significant changes in the power structure of the Zhou court as the result of the intensified foreign warfare. As far as the structure of the Zhou government is concerned, it is likely that the trend of compartmentalization continued to develop during the late Western Zhou, as did the vicissitude of offices.

Organizational development

For the late Western Zhou government, we have an explicit statement of its overall organization. From the reign of King Xuan, we have the longest inscription ever (479 characters) – on the Maogong *ding* 毛公鼎 (JC: 2841), currently hosted in the special gallery of the Palace Museum in Taipei (see figures 8 and 9). In fact, the inscription reproduces a long speech made by King Xuan that entrusts Maogong with full responsibilities for the Zhou government, with only the last two lines announcing the Duke of Mao as the caster and owner of the monumental bronze *ding*-vessel. The beginning and middle portions of the inscription read as the following:[92]

---

[92] Guo Moruo dated the bronze to the long reign of King Xuan, a date accepted by most scholars; but there is no internal evidence in the inscription that can definitively link it to any particularly royal reign. Nevertheless, the late Western Zhou date is guaranteed by the bronze's bulging hemispherical design and the double-ring ornament under its rim, which are very similar to other bronzes from the late Western Zhou period such as the Song *ding* 頌鼎 (JC: 2829; see figure 12) and Guo Wengong *ding* 虢文公鼎 (JC: 2636). On the date of the Maogong *ding*, see Guo Moruo, *Liang Zhou jinwen ci daxi tulu kaoshi*, p. 136; Ma Chengyuan, *Shang Zhou qingtongqi mingwen xuan*, 3, p. 316–19; Shirakawa Shizuka, "Kinbun tsūshaku," 30.181:637–87.

Figure 8. The Maogong *ding* in the Palace Museum, Taipei (courtesy of the National Palace Museum, Taipei, reproduced with permission)

The king said to the effect: "Father An! Greatly illustrious were King Wen and King Wu. August Heaven has extended and made fuller their virtue – to be the mates of our Zhou state. [They] chest-carried the Great Mandate, guiding in goodwill the borderland peoples who did not come to the court, but who would then look up to the upright light of King Wen and King Wu…

The king said: "Father An! Now I am only to follow the order of the former kings, commanding you to govern one quarter, expanding our great state and family. Do not be sluggish in government, do not block the XX

Figure 9. Inscription of the Maogong *ding* (from *Yin Zhou jinwen jicheng*, no. 2841.1–2)

of the common people, and do not accept bribery. If you do accept bribery the widowers and widows will be oppressed. Well follow your colleagues and officials, and do not indulge in drinking alcohol...

The king said: "Father An! As said already, as for the Ministry (*qingshi liao* 卿事寮) and the Grand Secretariat (*taishi liao* 太史寮), father, you are their governor. [I] command you to take charge of the Royal Kinsmen (*gongzu* 公族), the Three Supervisors (*sanyousi* 三有嗣), young boys (*xiaozi* 小子), Marshals (*shishi* 師氏), Tiger Servants (*huchen* 虎臣), and my officials (*zhen zhishi* 朕執事). With your kinsmen you shall protect my royal body. Extricate thirty *lue* of *zhuan*-metal ingots. [I] award you one *you*-container of fragrant wine...

The above lines from the inscription make it perfectly clear that the Zhou king is entrusting the Duke of Mao with the entire Zhou regime and specifically with the personnel that included both those who are in the government and those in Royal Household administration. The importance of such "bureaus" as the Ministry and the Grand Secretariat as collective administrative or secretarial bodies but not individual offices has already been discussed above with relation to the early Western Zhou government. The issue is the position and actual role of the Grand Secretariat because the secretarial function had already been divided during the mid-Western Zhou between the outer government and the Royal Household administration whose secretarial officials seem to have played a much bigger role. I believe that the key to understanding the working of this structural division is found in the inscription of the Guo Cong *xu* 虢從盨 (JC: 4466), cast most likely in the time of King Li (translated in Chapter 4, figures 20–21). While the inscription itself describes the transfer of thirteen rural settlements to the caster of the bronze, the royal command was *announced jointly*, and quite uniquely, by two secretarial officials: Interior Scribe Wuqi (*neishi wuqi* 內史無睍) and Grand Scribe X (*taishi qi* 太史䕼). Thus, it is very likely that the juxtaposition of the two secretarial officials in the context of this inscription was a deliberate arrangement at the Zhou court, and this suggests strongly that the Grand Secretariat and the Interior Scribes' group functioned as two independent bodies of officials and had authorities of their own. Certainly, this development reflects the specialization of the secretarial roles and the further bureaucratization of the Zhou government during the late Western Zhou period (see figure 10).

Interestingly, the inscription mentions the structural division between the Ministry and the Grand Secretariat as two main sectors of the Zhou government first in a separate line before presenting a long list of officials that can be read as a summary of the politically notable figures active in the late Western Zhou royal court. These include the *gongzu* or the collective body of the many royal kinsmen, the Three Supervisors, who represented

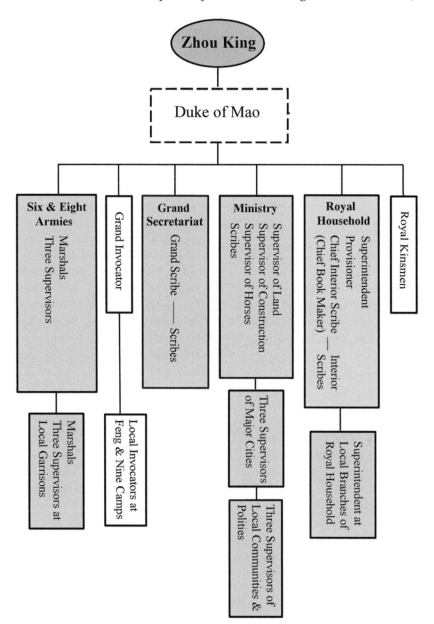

Figure 10: Organizational map of the Western Zhou government (royal domain: late Western Zhou)

the executive officials affiliated with the Ministry, the royal princes, the Marshals, who were probably the security forces of the capital area, and the Tiger Servants, who were the king's body guards. Finally, and most notably, there are officials referred to by the Zhou king as "my officials" (*zhen zhishi* 朕執事), designating undoubtedly those officials affiliated with the Royal Household administration who directly served the king, including presumably also the Interior Scribes.

The vicissitude of official roles

An interesting poem, "Shiyue zhi jiao" 十月之交 (Mao # 193) in the "Minor Odes" section of the *Book of Poetry*, already mentioned above, names a number of dignitaries who had served at one time in the Zhou government under King You before 777 BC: the "August Father" (Huangfu 皇父) was the Prime Minister (*qingshi* 卿士), Fan 番 was Supervisor of Multitudes (*situ* 司徒), Jiabo 家伯 was Superintendent (*zai* 宰), Zhongyun 仲允 was Food Provider (*shanfu* 膳夫), Zouzi 聚子 was Interior Scribe (*neishi* 內史), Jue 蹶 was Master of Horses (*quema* 趣馬=*zouma* 走馬), and Yu 楀 was Marshal (*shishi* 師氏). As I have argued in another place, the year 777 BC marked a major political split in the Zhou court between the part of senior officials led by the "August Father" and the newly rising King You and his supporters. Thus, these were the officials who had once occupied the most important positions in the Zhou central government and who might have followed the August Father in retirement upon the latter's political defeat, a major turning point in late Western Zhou history.[93] Incidentally, the offices listed here coincide exceptionally well with those for which we have better information from the late Western Zhou bronze inscriptions. In this regard, we may be able to view the list as a summary of the most influential official roles in the late Western Zhou government. The August Father himself, according to the *Current Bamboo Annals*, held the positions of both "Grand Marshal" (*taishi* 太師) and "Chief" (*yinshi* 尹氏; presumably the "Chief Interior Scribe") as the head of both Zhou's military forces and the Royal Household administration, and was the caster of a group of important inscribed bronzes discovered in Zhouyuan.[94]

The office of Supervisor of Multitudes (*sutu* 嗣徒) is mentioned in the inscription of the Wuhui *ding* 無惠鼎 (JC: 2814), which suggests that Nanzhong 南仲 was in the position sometime during the long reign

---

[93] See *Shijing*, 12.2, p. 446 (Waley, *The Book of Songs*, p. 171; note that some of the terms here are translated differently by Waley, according to the current scholarship). For the historical significance of the poem, see Li Feng, *Landscape and Power in Early China*, p. 209.

[94] This group includes the two Han Huangfu *ding* 函皇父鼎 (JC: 2548), four Han Huangfu *gui* 函皇父簋 (JC: 4141), and the Han Huangfu *pan* 函皇父盤 (JC: 10164). Unfortunately, the content of the inscriptions on these bronzes is very simple. See *Qingtongqi tushi*, pp. 20–21, pl. 61–6.

of King Xuan. Nan Zhong was a historically known person who had commanded military defense on the northwestern frontier against the Xianyun.[95] Instead, two other late Western Zhou inscriptions, the Zai *gui* 載簋 (JC: 4255) and Ci *ding* 此鼎 (JC: 2821), mention the office of Supervisor of Land (situ 嗣土); the former records that Zai was appointed "Supervisor of Land" with responsibility for the Spring Plowing ritual, explicating that the responsibility of the Supervisor of Land was land-related. Recently discovered bronzes have brought to light information on the other two officials who served as the Three Supervisors: the Jinhou Su *zhong* 晉侯蘇鐘 (JL: 35–50) mentions the Supervisor of Construction, Yangfu 楊父; the Forty-second Year Lai *ding* 四十二年逨鼎 mentions the Supervisor of Construction Bin 枡; and the Forty-third Year Lai *ding* 四十三年逨鼎 mentions the Supervisor of Horses, Shou 壽.[96] In all three inscriptions, they played the role of *youzhe* in the court ceremony of appointment. These inscriptions suggest that the Ministry continued to play a pivotal role in the Zhou government during the late period.

A major change seems to have occurred in the administration of the Royal Household under the direction of the Superintendent (*zai* 宰), who serves as *youzhe* in a number of late Western Zhou inscriptions such as the Song *ding* 頌鼎 (JC: 2829), Shi Li *gui* 師𩰱簋 (JC: 4324), and Yuan *pan* 袁盤 (JC: 10172). But the most active role had shifted onto another official: the Food Provider or Provisioner (*shanfu* 膳夫). As previous scholarship has shown, the Provisioner was originally the person in charge of food provision for the king and his family;[97] but later on the role might have evolved into one that was responsible for the personal wellbeing of the king in general. Probably because of this, beginning from the late part of the mid-Western Zhou, the Provisioner gradually began to exercise important influence on the Zhou government. However, while the Superintendent constantly served as *youzhe* in the court ceremony, which can be explained by his role as the head of administration of the Royal Household (see Chapter 3, 130–31), the Provisioner *never served as youzhe* in any appointment ceremonies, a very meaningful point that seems to suggest that his standing in the Household administration might not have been officially consolidated. However, it is evident that the king tended to rely more and more on the Provisioner, who acted as his personal attendant or representative. It seems likely that the political role of the Provisioner

---

[95] See *Shijing*, 9.4, pp. 415–16 (Waley, *The Book of Songs*, pp. 141–42).

[96] For the Jinhou Su *zhong*, see Ma Chengyuan, "Jinhou Su bianzhong," *Shanghai bowuguan jikan* 1996.7, 1–17. For the Forty-second and Forty-third Year Lai *ding*, see *Shengshi jijin: Shaanxi Baoji Meixian qingtongqi jiaocang* (Beijing: Beijing chubanshe, 2003), pp. 55–73; *Wenwu* 2003.6, 5–22.

[97] See Zhang Yachu and Liu Yu, *Xi Zhou jinwen guanzhi yanjiu*, pp. 42–43; Hsu and Linduff, *Western Chou Civilization*, pp. 231–32. In fact, there is one inscription, the Shanfu Shan *ding* 膳夫山鼎 (JC: 2825), which mentions that Provisioner Shan was put in charge of a group of beverage contributors, that seems to support this function of the Provisioner.

began even before the arrival of the late Western Zhou, for the Da Ke *ding* 大克鼎 (JC: 2836), most likely cast in the late part of the mid-Western Zhou period, describes it as the responsibility of Provisioner Ke to send out and take in the command of the king; such responsibility normally would be assigned to the Superintendent, as evidenced in the Cai *gui* 蔡簋 (JC: 4340).[98] In the Jinhou Su *zhong* mentioned above, the Provisioner was the one who called the ruler of Jin into the royal chamber to receive awards for his military collaboration. Again in the Da *ding* 大鼎 (JC: 2806), Provisioner Geng 駩 called Da and his fellows into the royal quarters to guard the king, for which he received the award of thirty-two fine horses. These inscriptions all suggest that the Provisioner was in a close relationship with the king as his domestic service man. More importantly, we find that during the late Western Zhou period the Provisioner sometimes also carried his mission beyond the court, interfering in the business of the government. For instance, in the Da *gui* 大簋 (JC: 4299), cast three years earlier for the same Da, Provisioner Shi 豕 announced the transfer of land to Da on behalf of the king and then apparently took Da to the field, where the latter received the land from its previous owner and presented the Provisioner with lavish gifts. In a newly discovered inscription, the Wu Hu *ding* 吳虎鼎 (JL: 364), Provisioner Fengsheng 豐生 was on a similar mission, together with the Supervisor of Construction, Yongyi 雍毅, announcing and actually supervising a land transfer to Wu Hu.[99] These inscriptions fully testify to the active role of the Provisioner during the late Western Zhou. Despite the important political role the Provisioner played during the late Western Zhou, his official status in the Royal Household administration could still be much lower than that of the Superintendent.

The importance of the Grand Secretariat is seen not only in the role played by the Grand Scribe in the Guo Cong *xu*, together with the Interior Scribe, but also in the appearance of many Scribes such as Scribe Miao 繆 (Wuhui *ding* 無惠鼎: JC: 2814), Scribe Guosheng 虢生 (Song *ding* 頌鼎; JC: 2829), Scribe Yu 減 (Forty-second Year Lai *ding* 四十二年逨鼎), Scribe Song 頌 (Shi Song *gui* 史頌簋; JC: 4232), and Scribe Hui 莽 (Wu Hu *ding*). The first three are cases where the Scribes read the royal commands to the officials in the court ceremony of appointment; in the fourth

---

[98] The Da Ke *ding* used to be dated by scholars to the reign of King Xiao or King Yi, or even King Li. See Ma Chengyuan, *Shang Zhou qingtongqi mingwen xuan*, 3, pp. 216–17; Shirakara Shizuka, "Kinbun tsūshaku," 28.167:494; Guo Moruo, *Liang Zhou jinwen ci daxi tulu kaoshi*, pp. 121–22. The Da Ke *ding* mentions Ke's grandfather, Shi Huafu 師華父, as having served King Gong, and this provides a basis for dating Ke sometime in the later part of the mid-Western Zhou, but probably not as late as King Li. This time range is corroborated by the date of another person, Shenji 醽季, whom the Da Ke *ding* mentions as *youzhe* but who started his career under King Gong, according to the Fifth Year Qiu Wei *ding* 五年裘衛鼎 (JC: 2832). For more discussion of the dates of Shenji and Ke, see Chapter 5, note 30 on p. 220.

[99] For the Wu Hu *ding*, see *Kaogu yu wenwu* 1998.3, 69–71.

case Scribe Song was sent on a mission to inspect some local areas near the eastern capital, Chengzhou. In the fifth, Scribe Hui performed a secretarial role in a land transaction supervised by the Provisioner and the Supervisor of Construction.

On the other hand, the interior secretarial officials continued to be active in the late Western Zhou government. In the court ceremony of appointment, the interior chief secretary played a more significant role than the Scribes, who were probably affiliated with the Grand Secretariat. We have nearly ten inscriptions from the late Western Zhou period that mention the interior chiefs as the announcers of royal command, calling them Chief Interior Scribe (*neishi yin* 內史尹; e.g. First Year Shi Dui *gui* 元年師兌簋; JC: 4274), or Chief Document Maker (*zuoce yin* 作冊尹; e.g. Nangong Liu *ding* 南宮柳鼎; JC: 2805), or simply the Chief (*yinshi* 尹氏; e.g. Wu *gui* 敔簋; JC: 4323). These inscriptions are the best testimony of the juxtaposition of the interior and outer secretarial bureaucracies in the late Western Zhou government.

Two inscriptions previously dated to the late Western Zhou period offer examples in which *sikou* 嗣寇 precedes personal names, hence, according to the standards set forth in the beginning of this chapter, stands as an official title. The first example is the Sikou Liangfu *hu* 嗣寇良父壺 (JC: 9641). The bronze was cast by Liangfu for his wife from the state of Wey 衛 in northern Henan. There is no guarantee that the *hu* was not cast by a royal official in Shannxi, but it is more likely it was from a regional state that inter-married with the state of Wey, and hence it may not reflect actual changes in the Zhou central government.[100] The second example is the Yu Sikou *hu* 虞嗣寇壺 (JC: 9694), clearly cast in the state of Yu located on the north bank of the Yellow River in Southern Shanxi.[101]

CONCLUSION

About thirty-five years ago, the historian Herrlee G. Creel wrote, with considerable frustration:

It is doubtful that any amount of research could produce a reliable 'table of organization' for the Western Chou government, from the materials that we have or even from any that might be found in the future. The problem is not merely – though this is formidable enough – the scantiness of our

---

[100] See *Huaimi shanfang jijin tu* (Waxian: Caoshi, 1839; Japanese edition, Kyoto: Bunsekidō, 1882), 2.14. The date of this bronze can be confirmed with the depiction of the vessel in *Huaimi* that is decorated with the simple "cross-pattern" of bends often seen on middle to late Western Zhou bronzes such as a *hu*-vessel excavated at Zhangjiapo, which is slightly earlier; see *Kaogu* 1965.9, pl. 2.

[101] For an interpretation of this inscription, see Shirakawa Shizuka, "Kinbun tsūshaku," 34.200:69

sources. There is a very real question as to whether such a tidily organized system of offices existed at all – and whether, if it did, anyone paid very much attention to it. [102]

It was certainly, first of all, a problem of sources. In that regard, Creel's book was published too early to see the tremendous amount of new information that has become available gradually from the 1970s to the 1990s, not to mention the continuous surfacing of long inscriptions in the new century. At the same time, it is not merely a source issue, because the expansion of inscriptional data enables us to develop new analytical methods, such as new standards of dating that in turn allow us to view the Western Zhou government not as a single block as it might have once appeared to Creel, but as a succession of developments over time. Seeing the Western Zhou government in a chronological framework allows us to capture the logic behind the changes of offices as well as the way in which they were integrated into a macro-structure. It is certainly possible to tabulate these changes, as I have suggested above. Although the organization presented in these tables is much smaller than suggested by some scholars,[103] I believe that they reflect quite realistically the current condition of our inscriptional evidence.

In his survey of historical bureaucracies, Weber had the clear idea that the process of bureaucratization was related not to the external expansion of a state, but to the qualitative improvement of its internal administration.[104] While this point will be discussed at some length in later chapters, it will suffice here to note that the Western Zhou government seems to exhibit the same trend of development. The Western Zhou government was the product of the two conquests. Although the consolidation of the conquests was mainly achieved through the establishment of the regional states, the need to sustain continuous expansion and to support the royal Six and Eight Armies did probably provide causes for the development of the Zhou government into one that was oriented towards civil and military administration. With the closing of the early Western Zhou expansion, as a part of the wide-ranging social transition that took place during the mid-Western Zhou, the Zhou government was rapidly systematized.

It is quite possible that the change occurred first in the Royal Household administration, which became separate from the administration of the Zhou government during the mid-Western Zhou. The independence of the Royal Household provided conditions for the rise of an interior secretarial body headed by the Chief Interior Scribe that, by at least the late phase of the mid-Western Zhou, had become the counterpart of the official body of the Grand Secretariat. A parallel development might

---

[102] See Creel, *The Origins of Statecraft in China*, p. 114.
[103] See Zhang Yachu and Liu Yu, *Xi Zhou jinwen guanzhi*, pp. 105–10.
[104] See Weber, "Bureaucracy," pp. 209–14.

have taken place in the civil administration of the government, where the roles of the Three Supervisors of the Ministry were multiplied and stratified. Even the organization of the Zhou military expanded to acquire some civil functions. Thus, what happened during the mid-Western Zhou seems to have been related to a common process of reorganization of the Western Zhou state to better manage the resources it already had and to provide for the better life of its social elites, particularly the family of the Zhou king. Bureaucratization came as an internal process of gradual refinement of the existing structure of the Zhou government after the end of the great early Western Zhou expansion, rather than as a new structure imposed by external challenges. Furthermore, this process seems to have been related also to other aspects of Zhou society, such as changes in bronze art and burial customs. This trend of refinement continued into the late Western Zhou, adding more government offices to the structure that was established during the mid-Western Zhou.

CHAPTER 3

The administrative process of the Zhou central government

The preceding chapter focused on exploring the organizational character-istics of the Western Zhou government and the changes that took place gradually in that system. The present chapter addresses the issue of how the administrative tasks were carried out and through what procedures such goals were fulfilled. The central concern of this chapter is, there-fore, the actual administrative process of the Western Zhou government, understood as the operation or the workings of the Zhou government. The patterns of working that this chapter aims to clarify concern the en-tire Western Zhou period, but more specifically reflect the situation from the mid-Western Zhou onward, when we have a relatively large base of information to test certain regularities. Given the non-systematic nature of our sources, it is considerably difficult at present to study the opera-tional characteristics of the early Western Zhou government. Nevertheless, temporal factors such as the date of the inscriptions will always be consid-ered as necessary to reveal the development of procedures in this and the following chapters.

In modern discussions of government, a number of factors are consid-ered characteristic of the operation of bureaucracy. A government set up as such must deal with administrative matters on a continual basis and in a "regular, routine, and efficient" manner such that it can always respond to future administrative needs.[1] The operation of such government is guided by rules and regulations that can be learned by officials as part of their training for their offices. The use of written documents is extensive, for the production and preservation of which there is a staff of subaltern officials and scribes.[2] It has also been emphasized by Weber and other scholars that the orders of administration are given from a higher authority and pass down through a hierarchy, to be performed by the subordinate officials.[3] These four points summarize the fundamental operational characteristics

---

The content of this chapter is partially based on Li Feng, "'Offices' in Bronzes Inscriptions." I thank the journal *Early China* for granting permission.

[1] See Kamenka, *Bureaucracy*, p. 157; Albrow, *Bureaucracy*, p. 43.

[2] See Weber, "Bureaucracy," pp. 197–98.

[3] See *ibid.*, p. 197; Nickinovich, "Bureaucracy," p. 230; Hall, "The Concept of Bureaucracy: An Empirical Assessment," 33–34.

of bureaucratic government, though in practice the extent to which any government achieves these qualifications may vary.

In the following, I first discuss the general working habits of the Western Zhou government as reflected in the contemporary bronze inscriptions for mainly the middle and late Western Zhou periods. This will give us some basic ideas about the social-political context of the Western Zhou government and the general patterns of its management. Then I will focus on the complex personal network manifest particularly in the "appointment inscriptions," which offer us keys to understanding the rules and regulations in operation in the Zhou government. Finally, I will discuss the forms and sources of authority commanding the Western Zhou central bureaucracy, and the complex factors that might have influenced their operational tendency and efficiency. In this connection, I will also examine the roles played by the Zhou king's person in the government and the possible patterns in his administrative involvement. These discussions will together contribute to a general understanding of the operation of the Western Zhou government.

GENERAL CHARACTERISTICS OF ZHOU ADMINISTRATION

Any government exhibits certain working habits that suit the special temporal and geographical context in which it is constructed and operates. As a Bronze-Age government in China, the Western Zhou government certainly displays some characteristics that would set it apart from many contemporary governments in the world, and from what Balazs calls, quite correctly, the "bureaucratic state centralism" of imperial China that emerged around the time of Qin unification.[4] Defining these general operational habits can provide us with a new basis for understanding the nature and function of the Western Zhou government.

The geographical sphere of administration

In Chapter 2 we discussed how the Western Zhou state was structured according to the principle of bifurcation, by which the royally administered area, mainly located in the west and centering on the Wei River valley of Shaanxi, was separated from the regional states in the east, which constituted a series of zones of delegated administration under the regional rulers. It was also demonstrated that this distinction gave rise to a set of institutional differentiations evident in the bronze inscriptions and the Western Zhou texts. This is an issue not merely of the political theory embraced by the Western Zhou state and entertained by the Zhou elites, but of the actual administrative conduct of the Zhou government.

---

[4] See Balazs, *Chinese Civilization and Bureaucracy*, p. 31.

However, the practice of the "Fengjian" institution, by which the vast eastern territory was put under the control of the regional rulers, does not imply that the Zhou king and the Zhou court were unconcerned with the delegated zones in the east. It would be wrong to assume that, because of the practice of the "Fengjian" system, the Zhou king's political authority was limited to only the royal domain in the west. Quite the contrary: through the entire Western Zhou dynasty, the Zhou court conceived the entire Western Zhou state as the sphere of its responsibility and was making decisions that would affect areas even beyond the circle of the regional states. This point must be emphasized, because it concerns the nature and objectives of the Western Zhou state. An early Western Zhou inscription from the state of Xing, the Chen Jian *gui* 臣諫簋 (JC: 4237), suggests that the royal army was clearly active in the Hebei area fighting the Rong people alongside the troops from the local state of Xing 邢.[5] There are many middle and late Western Zhou inscriptions that record Zhou's military actions in the distant east even when approaching the last decades of the dynasty. While these inscriptions will be discussed in Chapter 6 with respect to the obligations of the regional rulers to the Western Zhou state, it should be mentioned here that a recent discovery has again made this point perfectly clear.[6] By the same token, the inscriptions also tell us that the way in which the central court and the regional states engaged with each other was mainly military, in the form of protection of the regional states from potential threats by the royal armies and military assistance provided by the regional states in campaigns organized by the central court, very often with an official from the royal domain as the chief commander of the operation. There is no evidence that the Zhou king ever interfered in the internal civil administration of the regional states, nor is there evidence that civil administration of the royal domain ever reached out to the regional states. Instead, we have every reason to believe that the civil administrative network constructed by the Zhou court did not go far beyond the Zhou core

---

[5] The Chen Jian *gui* was discovered in 1978 together with a group of nine bronze vessels from a tomb in Yuanshi 元氏, about 70 km to the north of the capital of the state of Xing in present-day Xingtai, Hebei. The inscription mentions a military campaign the ruler of Xing conducted in response to an attack by the Rong people, during which Jian was dispatched by the ruler to deploy his troops in a place called Di 軧, very probably near the place where the bronzes were buried, under the command of the Zhou king. See *Wenwu* 1979.1, 23–26. For an early analysis of the bronzes, see Li Xueqin, who dates the burial to the reign of King Zhao and the Chen Jian *gui* to King Kang; see *Xinchu qingtongqi yanjiu*, pp. 60–67. I have previously dated the group slightly later, to roughly the beginning of the mid-Western Zhou, but the Chen Jian *gui* may be earlier than the date; see Li Feng, "Huanghe liuyu Xi Zhou muzang chutu qingtong liqi de fenqi yu niandai," *Kaogu xuebao* 1988.4, 389.

[6] The Zhabo *ding* 柞伯鼎 mentions a campaign in the south, probably the Huai River region, involving the ruler of the state of Cai 蔡 who fought under the supreme command of Guozhong 虢仲, an official sent from the Zhou royal court in Shaanxi. Guozhong is known in the received texts as a minister of King Li who led a campaign against the Huaiyi in the south and is probably the caster of the Guozhong *xu* 虢仲盨 (JC: 4435), also mentioning Guozhong's southern campaign, together with the king. This date seems to match the design and decorative patterns of the bronze. See Zhu Fenghan, "Zhabo ding yu Zhougong nanzheng," *Wenwu* 2006.5, 67–73.

region.[7] This separation of civil administrative authority from the exercise of royal sovereign power was an important feature of the Western Zhou political system, and this will be discussed in more detail in Chapter 7.

It was noted by Musha Akira many years ago that discoveries of the appointment inscriptions, mainly from the middle and late Western Zhou, have been confined to the area of present-day Shaanxi province.[8] The recent archeological discoveries of court-related appointment inscriptions have not changed this situation. Since these appointment inscriptions are direct testimony to Zhou administrative control, it seems appropriate to take their distribution as an indication that the administrative sphere of the Zhou central government was confined mainly to the Wei River valley of Shaanxi, extending probably also to the small area surrounding the eastern center Chengzhou.

In fact, we have much better information than this that can help us define the actual geography of the central court's direct administrative control. This information comes from those inscriptions that actually describe the specific geographical areas where the officials who cast the bronzes were commanded to perform their duties. In this regard, an interesting example is the Shi Song *gui* 史頌簋 (JC: 4232) from the late Western Zhou period. Apparently, Scribe Song was sent on a trip by the Zhou king to inspect a place called Su 蘇, which scholars unanimously agree was located in present-day Wenxian 溫縣, about 60 kilometers to the north of Luoyang and on the north bank of the Yellow River (see figure 11).[9] The royal inspector was greeted by a crowd of local officials and dignitaries who had come from

---

[7] Creel once gave the Shi Qi *ding* 師旂鼎 (JC: 2809) as an example of royal officers administrating justice "within the feudal lord's domain." As will be discussed later in Chapter 7, Creel's concept of "feudal lord" has serious problems; in this particular case, Shi Qi was certainly not a "feudal lord" or regional ruler, but was a military officer from the Zhou royal domain. See Creel, *The Origins of Statecraft*, p. 70. On this point, our ground is solid: among the numerous appointment inscriptions, no one offers a record that a civil official of a regional state in the east was ever appointed by the Zhou king in the central court. The office of "Inspector" (*jian* 監), as the royal watchman stationed in the regional states, was a different issue; in all likelihood, the "Inspector" was appointed once and for all when his host state was granted, and the office was passed down strictly along hereditary lines. On the other hand, we have cases where the Zhou king interfered in the succession of some regional rulers. But as far as the domestic administrative affairs of the regional states were concerned, the regional rulers were autonomous. On the institution of "Inspector", see details in Chapter 6, pp. 251–52.

[8] See Musha Akira, "Sei Shū satsumei kinbun bunrui no kokoromi," pp. 313–24.

[9] The Scribe Song bronzes, five in all, used to be placed by Guo Moruo in the mid-Western Zhou, but now most scholars date them to the late Western Zhou period, although there is a disagreement on their specific regnal dating. Su was the main base of the Su 蘇 family, whose members held high positions in the royal court during the early Eastern Zhou period (eighth–seventh centuries). According to a record in the *Zuozhuan*, in 712 BC, twelve settlements of the Su family centered on the Wenxian area were seized by the Zhou king and given in exchange for four settlements from the state of Zheng 鄭. This event suggests that even by the early Eastern Zhou the area was still a part of the Zhou royal domain, with settlements held either by the royal house or aristocratic officials in the royal court. See *Zuozhuan*, 4, p. 1737. For a discussion of Su with respect to the discovery of the Su bronzes in western Henan, see *Shangcunling Guo guo mudi* (Beijing: Kexue Press, 1959), pp. 51–52. For the date and content of the Shi Song *gui*, see Guo Moruo, *Liang Zhou jinwen ci daxi tulu kaoshi*, 72; Ma Chengyuan, *Shang Zhou qingtongqi mingwen xuan*, 3, p. 300; Shirakawa Shizuka, "Kinbun tsūshaku," 24.138:174–84.

Figure 11. Inscription of the Shi Song *gui* (from *Yin Zhou jinwen jicheng*, no. 4232)

the Su area to Chengzhou, the eastern administrative center in Luoyang, and presented with luxury gifts of jades, four horses, and metals. The inscription is a lively demonstration of the Zhou administrative thread that weaved the remote local areas together with the central government. It also shows Chengzhou (or Luoyi) as the center of Zhou administration in the east to which local officials paid frequent visits to greet royal commissioners arriving from the west. Three other inscriptions also provide information on Zhou civil administrative initiatives in the Chengzhou area in the east: a mid-Western Zhou inscription, the Xun *gui* 詢簋 (JC: 4321), describes the supervision of four foreign communities including the Xiangren 降人 Suyi 夙夷, located in the Chengzhou area as a part of Xun's official responsibility. The Song *ding* 頌鼎 (JC: 2829), cast most likely by the same royal inspector Scribe Song mentioned above, says that Song was put in charge of the royal warehouses in Chengzhou. The Xijia *pan* 兮甲盤 (JC: 10174) says that after a battle against the Xianyun in the fifth year of King Xuan (823 BC), Xijia was put in charge of the Chengzhou inventory, where the contributions from the regional states as well as foreign lands were stored.[10] These inscriptions portray Chengzhou as an administrative hub in the east during the middle and late Western Zhou, as it was during the early time, as we are informed by the Ling *fangyi* 令方彝 discussed in Chapter 2, from which the Zhou administrative network extended further to surrounding localities like Su and other rural settlements.

Our evidence for Zhou administrative conduct in the Wei River valley is more specific and compelling, allowing us to actually delimit the geography of Zhou royal administrative control (see map 2). For instance, the Tong *gui* 同簋 (JC: 4271), cast during the mid-Western Zhou, describes that the caster was assigned responsibilities over the forests, marshes, and pastoral lands located in the triangular area to the west of the Yellow River, east of the Hu 滹 River, and south of the Xuan 玄 River. Despite the two unidentifiable river-names, given the explicit mention of the Yellow River, there seems little doubt that the area concerned was on the west bank of the Yellow River, roughly in the present-day Heyang 合陽 to Hancheng 韓城 area in the east part of the Wei River valley.[11] Slightly to the west, according to the Yong *yu* 永盂 (JC: 10322), a group of officials was sent by a royal command to transfer some tracts of land that were located on the south and north banks of the Luo 洛 River (*yinyang Luo* 陰陽洛) to a person called Shi Yong 師永. To the north, the Provisioner Ke 克 was sent on an inspection trip along the east of the Jing River all the way to a place called Jingshi 京師, located in the present-day Binxian 彬縣 to Xunyi 旬邑 area (Ke *zhong* 克鐘; JC: 204). To the west, according to the Yang *gui* 楊簋 (JC: 4294), Yang was appointed local administrator in a place named Liang 量; the same place is mentioned also in the Da Ke *ding* 大克鼎 (JC: 2836) as a neighboring

---

[10] It is to be noted again that for inscriptions mentioned here without further discussion of their discovery and date, the reader should consult Appendix II for details.

[11] The inscription mentions the famous official Rongbo 榮伯, who appears in a number of mid-Western Zhou inscriptions. For an interpretation of this inscription, see Ma Chengyuan, *Shang Zhou qingtongqi mingwen xuan*, 3, pp. 162–63.

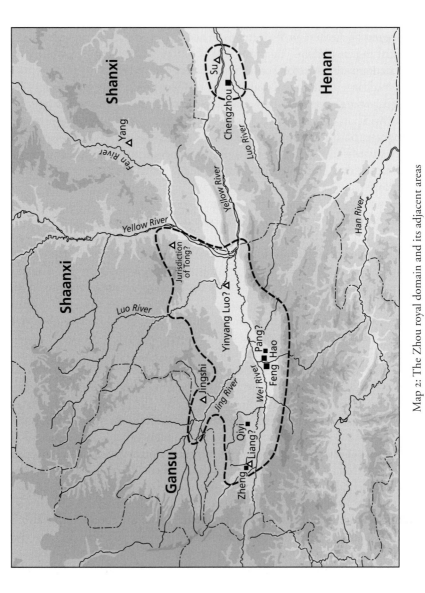

Map 2: The Zhou royal domain and its adjacent areas

area of the lineage of Jing 井 in present-day Fengxiang 鳳翔, near the western end of the middle Wei River valley.[12]

While the above inscriptions offer us information on Zhou administrative conduct in the rural areas distant from the Zhou capitals, there are many more inscriptions describing the activities of Zhou administrators in the more centrally located areas that I will discuss in connection with local administration in Chapter 4. These inscriptions together offer us some solid ideas about the spatial extent of the Zhou central administration that covered central Shaanxi and the small area surrounding Luoyang during the middle and late periods when the bronzes were cast. It is above all important to point out that these inscribed bronzes were not transported here from other areas, but are themselves products of the administrative network extending over the Wei River valleys where they were found. They are reliable sources for reconstructing the Zhou administration in the central region. While the administrative conduct of the Zhou central government was essentially confined to the Wei River valley (plus the upper Jing River valley) and the small area surrounding Chengzhou, under special circumstances civil administrators could also be sent from the central court to perform particular tasks beyond the royal domain. For instance, in the newly discovered Forty-second Year Lai *ding* 四十二年逨鼎, a royal commissioner of marshes and forests was sent to settle the ruler of the newly granted state of Yang 楊 in the Fen River valley of Shanxi.[13] But this is evidence of the central administration taking an active role in installing regional states as an action of the Western Zhou state, and should not be taken as evidence that central power interfered in the internal affairs of the regional states. During the middle and late Western Zhou, such special missions must have happened very irregularly.

The appointment procedure and appointment inscriptions

Government is run by officials, and there are scholars who think that in essentiality Weber's "bureaucracy" means "an administrative body of appointed officials."[14] Therefore, the appointment of officials is not only the key to successful administration, but, when conducted on a regular and institutionalized basis through predetermined procedures, is itself a defining feature of bureaucratic government. While the special implications

---

[12] Most of these inscriptions were cast quite close in time, from roughly the reign of King Gong to that of King Yih during the mid-Western Zhou; the Ke bronzes might have been later, in the later phase of the mid-Western Zhou. On the location of Jingshi, see Li Feng, "Tayūtei meibun o meguru rekishi chiri teki mondai no kaiketsu: Shū ōchō no seihoku keiryaku o kaimei suru tameni, sono ichi," in *Chūgoku kodai no moji to bunka* (Tokyo: Kyūko shoin, 1999), pp. 179–206; see also Li Feng, *Landscape and Power in Early China*, pp. 160–61. On the location of the Jing lineage, see Wang Hui, "Xi Zhou jinei diming xiaoji," 26–28; Lu Liangcheng, "Xi Zhou Ze guo shiji kaolue jiqi xiangguan wenti," in *Xi Zhou shi yanjiu* (Monograph of *Renwen zazhi* 2) (Xi'an: 1984), p. 236.
[13] For the inscription, see *Wenwu* 2003.6, 6–15.   [14] See Albrow, *Bureaucracy*, p. 42.

of appointment for understanding the nature of official service and official careers during the Western Zhou will be discussed at length in Chapter 5, here I will focus only on the institutional aspect of the appointment procedure as a way to uncover the general characteristics of Western Zhou administration.

The procedure of appointment is called *ceming* 冊命, literally "to appoint an official with a written document," in the Western Zhou bronze inscriptions. Among the many early Western Zhou bronzes there is only one, the Da Yu *ding* 大盂鼎 (JC: 2837), that was cast for the purpose of commemorating the receipt of an official appointment, in contrast to the majority of bronzes from the same period that were cast to commemorate the receipt of material gifts from the king or other superiors, or more frequently to celebrate military merits. However, from the early phase of the mid-Western Zhou on, suddenly a large number of bronzes began to emerge as documentation of official appointments, making "appointment" the most dominant theme in the entire corpus of the Western Zhou bronze inscriptions.[15] If what appears in the inscriptions is what the Zhou elites considered important to their lives, then, there must have been a dramatic change in the attitude of the Zhou elites towards government service as well as the social value attached to it. During the early Western Zhou, appointments by the king himself either were infrequent or perhaps were taken for granted, not considered as significant as, for instance, the material awards from the king for military merits.[16] From the mid-Western Zhou on, by the same token, such royal appointments to offices had apparently become an institutionalized procedure that commanded high social prestige, which a great number of economic resources were extended to commemorate. This change, while possibly reflecting the tightening control of the Zhou king over the government in response to the demise of dominance of the prominent dukes over the court as described in Chapter 2, also indicates a tendency to institutionalize government service, and

---

[15] According to a multi-faceted survey conducted by Musha Akira, ninety-one appointment inscriptions were known by the end of 1970s. However, this number was reduced to forty by Yoshimoto Michimasa, who relies solely on the occurrence of the term *ceming* as a standard for appointment inscriptions; this is unnecessary, and there are inscriptions that clearly record the scenario of appointment ceremony without employing the term *ceming*, for instance, the Ji *gui* 即簋 (JC: 4250) and the Tong *gui* 同簋 (JC: 4271). An accurate account of appointment inscriptions discovered since the 1980s does not exist, but even the most conservative estimate would suggest that the total number of appointment inscriptions is over 100 pieces. See Musha Akira, "Sei Shū satsumei kinbun bunrui no kokoromi," pp. 248–49; Yoshimoto Michimasa, "Sei Shū satsumei kinbun kō," *Shirin* 74.5 (1991), 38–66. Two most recent cases of the discovery of the appointment inscriptions are the Shi You *ding* 師酉鼎 and the Jingbo Lu *gui* 井伯𣪘簋, reported in 2004 and 2006, respectively. See *Zhongguo lishi wenwu* 2004.1, 4–10, 35; *Zhongguo lishi wenwu* 2006.3, cover.

[16] Since we do have many other types of inscriptions from the same period, this is certainly not a problem of insufficient data. If the lack of appointment inscriptions reflects the actual lack of such appointments, one possible reason might be the adherence to the strict rule of hereditary succession to government offices during the early Western Zhou. Under such condition, official appointment by the king might not always be necessary and, when it was done by the king, might not be sufficiently appreciated.

perhaps the two processes were closely related, as the Zhou king might have strengthened his control over the government through institutionalizing the official appointments.[17] In a more general sense, the closing of the great early Western Zhou expansion meant decreasing opportunities for military honor for the Western Zhou elites, who would in turn place more emphasis on government service as a way to achieve social prestige.

What is truly important here is not the fact that the appointments were recorded on the bronzes, but the way in which they were recorded. While an early Western Zhou inscription would simply mention the command by a Zhou king to an official to perform a certain duty, and in the best cases, such as the Da Yu *ding*, it would reproduce the Zhou king's speech, accounts of the court ceremony itself appear only in the context where a regional state was granted.[18] However, from the mid-Western Zhou on we find a large number of bronzes cast not only to detail the contents of the official appointments, normally in the king's own words, but also to describe in a highly stylistic language, repeatedly and almost tirelessly, the actual procedures of the court ceremony in which the appointment was announced. A typical description of the appointment ceremony is found on the Song *ding* 頌鼎 (JC: 2829), cast during the late Western Zhou period (see Figure 12):[19]

It was the third year, fifth month, after the dying brightness, *jiaxu* (no. 11). The king was in Kang Shao Gong 康邵宮 in Zhou. At dawn, the king entered the grand chamber and assumed his position. Superintendent Hong 宰弘 accompanied Song 頌 to his right, entering the gate and standing in the center of the courtyard. The Chief (Interior Scribe) received the document of royal command, and the king called out to Scribe Guosheng 虢生 to command Song with the written document. The king said: "Song! [I] command you to take office in charge of the storage of twenty households in Chengzhou, and to inspect and supervise the newly constructed storage house, using palace attendants. [I] award you a black jacket with brocaded hem, red kneepads, a scarlet semi-circlet, a jingle-bell pennant, a bridle with bit and cheek-pieces, with which to serve!" Song bowed with his head touching the ground and received the bamboo document of royal

---

[17] In all likelihood this important change happened during the reign of King Mu, to which the earliest such inscriptions are dated, for instance, the Li *fangzun* 盠方尊 (JC: 6013) and the Li *fangyi* 盠 方彝 (JC: 9900). This time context also paralleled the structural development in the Zhou central government leading to the independence of the Royal Household administration and the separation of the Interior Scribes from the general secretarial body of the Zhou government. On the date of the Li 盠 bronzes, see discussion in Chapter 2, note 83 on p. 79.

[18] See, for instance, the Yihou Ze *gui* 宜侯夨簋 (JC: 4320), which describes the time, the place, and the king's posture as the pre-context of the king's speech establishing Ze as the ruler of the state of Yi. For an interpretation of the inscription, see Guo Moruo, "Ze *gui* ming kaoshi," *Kaogu xuebao* 1956.1, 7–9; Tang Lan, *Tang Lan xiansheng*, pp. 66–71.

[19] For the date of the Song *ding*, see Ma Chengyuan, *Shang Zhou qingtongqi mingwen xuan*, 3, pp. 302–4; Shaughnessy, *Sources of Western Zhou History*, 285.

Figure 12. The Song *ding* and its inscription (Chen Peifen, *Xia Shang Zhou qingtongqi yanjiu*, 6 vols. [Shanghai: Shanghai Guji, 2004], 4, pp. 410, 412)

command, hanging it [on his body] and coming out [of the courtyard]. He then returned and brought in a jade tablet. Song dares in response to extol the Son of Heaven's illustriously fine beneficence, herewith making [for] my august deceased-father Gongshu and august mother Gong Si 龏姒 [this] treasured sacrificial *ding*-vessel, using which to pursue filial piety, to pray for peaceful harmony, pure blessings, long-lasting wealth, and eternal mandate. May Song for ten thousand years enjoy abundant longevity, to serve the Son of Heaven, with no end. [May Song's] sons' sons and grand-sons' grandsons treasure and use [it]!

Such a full account of the appointment process is now found also on the Forty-second Year Lai *ding* 四十二年逨鼎 and Forty-third Year Lai *ding* 四十三年逨鼎.[20] In fact, these bronzes were all cast quite close in time during the late Western Zhou, probably all during the reign of King Xuan, and should reflect the appointment process in its most developed form. Based on these accounts and with reference to other shorter and incomplete accounts on other bronzes, we can offer a general outline of the procedure of the appointment ritual, using the newly excavated temple foundation in Yutang 雲塘, Zhouyuan, as its stage (see figure 13):[21]

Step 1: Arrival of the king
The ritual normally took place at sunrise, as described by the graph *dan* 🝚, when the king would first come into a building called *gong*. In cases of royal temples such as the Kang Gong and Mu Gong, temples for King Kang and King Gong respectively, the king would presumably first make offerings to the deceased Zhou kings worshipped in the Grand Chamber in the temple, but the inscriptions *never* mention this.[22] Then the king would stand on the platform outside the Grand Chamber, facing south.

Step 2: Entering of the appointee
At this point, the appointee enters the gate of the building complex and ar-rives in the open courtyard south of the main hall. He stands at the center of the courtyard, customarily facing north, the direction of the king. Some inscriptions describe that a higher official would accompany the appointee as he entered the gate, while others seem to suggest that the companion

---

[20] See *Wenwu* 2003.6, 6–22.
[21] As noted in the introduction, "ritual" has multiple meanings and various forms. The "appointment ritual" is itself a process designed for political and administrative purposes, and it must first be differentiated from the religious ritual of ancestral worship that had the communication with the supernatural spirits as its purpose, based on an underlying belief system. Although the two processes may sometimes follow each other and even enforce each other, they are different in nature.
[22] In later Confucian ritual books, for instance the *Liji*, it is said that when the ancient rulers granted ranks and awards to their officials, they would necessarily do so in the grand temples, to demon-strate that they did not intend to monopolize the process, but wanted it to be witnessed by the ancestors. The same text also describes that the rulers would descend from the platform and stand in the courtyard close to the host stairs. See *Liji*, 49, p. 1605.

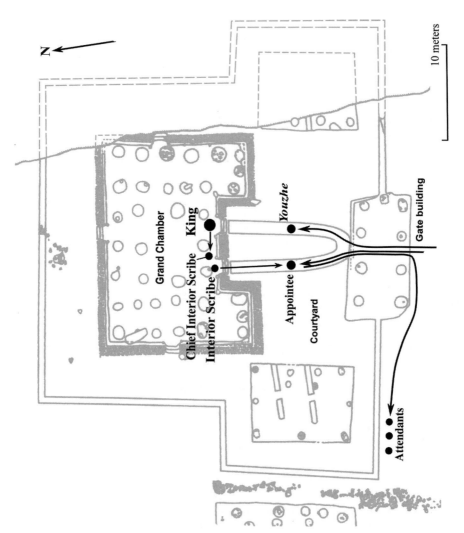

Figure 13. Illustration of the appointment ritual with respect to the Yuntang temple structure (architectural plan adopted from *Kaogu* 2002.9, 5 with modification of details)

would enter the gate after the appointee was already there and assume his position.[23] In any event, the higher official would customarily stand to the right of the appointee, the superior position, and scholars normally refer to his role as *youzhe* 右者, the "Right-person."[24]

Step 3: Utterance of the command

It is very possible that the *youzhe* would introduce the appointee to the king, but this is not clear in the inscriptions. When all people were in position, the utterance of the royal command began. In many cases, the inscriptions would record that the king commanded a single official, whether the Interior Scribe or the Chief Interior Scribe, to read out loud the appointment described on the written document, which was certainly pre-prepared and perhaps written on bamboo strips.[25] In other cases, the king would first hand over the written document to an official, normally the Chief Interior Scribe, who would presumably hold it in his hands; then the king would call on another official, normally an Interior Scribe, to pronounce the command to the appointee. Since the latter situation is described only on some late Western Zhou bronzes, it is likely that this was a new development in the appointment procedure.[26]

This written command, which is in all likelihood pre-prepared and perhaps written on bamboo strips prior to the appointment ritual, describes sometimes in detail the official title granted and the actual administrative responsibilities charged to the appointee. In most cases, the document would detail, certainly as part of the announcer's oral expression, a long list of gifts, including fragrant wine, official garments, jade objects, chariots,

---

[23] Examples of the first situation are the Wu *fangyi* 吳方彝 (JC: 9898), Shi Chen *ding* 師晨鼎 (JC: 2817), and Yuan *pan* 袁盤 (JC: 10172); examples of the second situation are the Shi Hu *gui* 師虎簋 (JC: 4316), Doubi *gui* 豆閉簋 (JC: 4276), and Yang *gui* 楊簋 (JC: 4294). This distinction was first noted by Musha Akira, "Sei Shū satsumei kinbun bunrui no kokoromi," pp. 270–76.

[24] Shaughnessy translated this term *youzhe* as "Guarantor"; see Shaughnessy, *Sources of Western Zhou History*, pp. 116, 262. Another possible translation of the term is "Guardian," but that term conveys a very "personal" relationship, which is not always the case in the inscriptions. While these are useable translations, they only explain certain aspects of the complex role of the *youzhe*, which was quite "bureaucratic" in Zhou administration, as will be clarified below. Here I maintain the original expression in Chinese, which can be explained according to whoever plays the role. In fact, since the king (as host) would stand above the right stair by which he ascends or descends according to later ritual regulations (called *zuojie* 阼階), standing to the right would appropriately put the *youzhe*, as superior to the appointee, right in front of the king (see figure 13).

[25] There was previously a misunderstanding that the document was written during the session in front of the king and the appointee after the command was pronounced. See Huang Ranwei, *Yin Zhou qingtongqi shangci mingwen yanjiu* (Hong Kong: Lungmen Bookstore, 1978), pp. 90, 95. In an earlier study, I have carefully compared the relevant accounts of this procedure in the inscriptions and suggested that the character *shu* 書 in this context must read as a noun and that the document of royal command was already written before the ritual session. For details, see Li Feng, "'Offices' in Bronze Inscriptions," 50.

[26] Typical of this more elaborate procedure are the aforementioned Song *ding*, Yuan *pan*, and Forty-second Year Lai *ding*. The latter two bronzes were doubtless cast during the reign of King Xuan, and the Song *ding*, as already noted, is also from the late Western Zhou. This certainly indicates further bureaucratization of the appointment procedure. See below for more details on the handling of written documents in the appointment ceremony.

and sometimes even land, in varying combinations. A curious aspect of the appointment ritual is that these gifts were rarely handed over to the appointees during the ritual session, but most likely the appointee would pick up such items from the royal inventory afterwards; hence they are not described in the inscriptions.

Step 4: Expression of gratitude

All inscriptions that record appointments by the king mention that as a standard response the appointee would bow to the king and then crouch with his head touching the ground. Although the inscriptions normally offer only a statement that he extols the beneficence and kindness of the king, there seems little doubt that in the actual ritual performance this would involve an oral expression of gratitude.

Step 5: Handover of the document

When this is done, the bamboo document would be handed over by the Interior Scribe or Chief Interior Scribe to the appointee, signifying perhaps the physical transfer of the royal command from the royal secretary to the appointee. The appointee would then hang it on his body and withdraw from the courtyard.

Step 6: Return to the court

Immediately, he would come back into the courtyard again with a jade tablet to present to the king. Presumably, he would have met with his own attendants waiting outside the court during the session and would deposit with them the bamboo document, in exchange for the jade tablet, which he would take back to the courtyard to present to the king.[27]

Afterwards

After the session, the appointee would cast a bronze to commemorate the royal favor; this is the origin of all of the hundred-plus appointment inscriptions which record in more or less detail the same court ritual. It is very likely that many appointment inscriptions contained portions copied directly from the original royal edicts that the casters of the inscriptions received during the appointment ceremony and that were thereafter kept in the family archives of the casters.[28] As such, the appointment inscriptions are stylistically and structurally highly standardized and indeed very bureaucratic.[29]

[27] For an early study of the appointment ritual based on correlating the inscriptions with later ritual texts, see Qi Sihe, "Zhou dai ximing li kao," *Yanjing xuebao* 32 (1947), 197–226.

[28] On the transfer of written documents onto bronze media, see Falkenhausen, "Issues in Western Zhou Studies," 145–46, 161–67; Li Feng, "Ancient Reproductions and Calligraphic Variations," 40–41.

[29] The appointment inscription itself, besides the account of the appointment ritual, would add to it, in most cases: (1) a section introducing the date and place of the ceremony in the opening of the

Despite the varying details in the inscriptional accounts of the appointment ritual, which seem to reflect literary variations in the recounting of the performance in a textual environment – the inscriptions – rather than differences in the actual conduct of the ritual, the appointment procedure was indeed remarkably consistent, with specific rules determining its proper etiquette. Considering that the hundred-plus appointment inscriptions we have today are probably only a fragment of the total number of bronzes cast to document such official procedure, this would imply that the same procedure with the filling (or confirming) of official positions as its sole purpose must have been carried out by the Zhou king in various places hundreds of times during the middle and late Western Zhou, forming the highlight of elite political life in the Zhou central area. More importantly, the pattern of dividing the personnel into two classes, with the king and his secretarial officials on the one side and the appointee and his affiliated administrative authorities on the other, remained constant throughout all the appointment ceremonies; even the spatial positions of the king and the officials of different roles in the session remained constant. Such determinations and the frequency of the ceremony suggest strongly that this was a very bureaucratic procedure. And perhaps even the very basic fact that an appointment had to go through such officially conducted procedure is itself a good indication of the bureaucratic operation of government. Furthermore, the fact that a hundred-plus bronzes were cast to record such procedure suggests strongly that, from the mid-Western Zhou on, formulaic recognition of services in the Zhou government had become highly desirable, and the opportunities granted for such recognition bestowed on the officials what Weber called with regard to modern bureaucrats "a distinct *social esteem.*"[30]

The use of written records

One impressive aspect of the appointment ceremony was the extensive use of written documents that characterized the administrative process of the Western Zhou government. Creel once analyzed, mainly based on the received textual records, the ability of the Western Zhou government to produce and maintain written records and regarded it as an important means of achieving organizational stability.[31] Literally, the "appointment" (*ceming*) involves the use of a "written document" (*ce* 冊), vertical bamboo strips woven together with strings as a medium of writing, suggesting

inscription; (2) a section of dedication that follows the account of the ritual describing to whom the vessel was dedicated; (3) finally, a line that promises the use of the vessel by the future generations of the appointee. For a general discussion of the content of the appointment inscriptions, see also Virginia C. Kane, "Aspects of Western Chou Appointment Inscriptions: The Charge, the Gifts, and the Response," *Early China* 8 (1982–83), 14–28.

[30] See Weber, "Bureaucracy," 199.
[31] See Creel, *The Origins of Statecraft in China*, pp. 123–29.

that most if not all appointments in the middle and late Western Zhou government were actually done in "writing." Certainly, the use of written documents in the appointment ceremonies is also related to the rise to power of the interior secretarial staff headed by the Chief Interior Scribe or Chief Document Maker, analyzed already in Chapter 2. In fact, they were the officials responsible for producing such written documents.

There are actually a number of inscriptions including the Song *ding* translated above suggesting that the pre-prepared written documents were handed over to the appointees during the appointment ceremony, but these inscriptions were previously misinterpreted. For example, in the Song *ding* the king handed a "document of royal command" (*wang ming shu* 王命書) over to the Chief Interior Scribe and commanded Scribe Guosheng 史虢生 to read it to Song; afterwards the written document was given to Song, who brought it out of the courtyard and gave it to his own attendants. The recent discovery of inscriptions has added a few more cases to what is already known: in the Forty-second Year Lai *ding* 四十二年逨鼎, the Chief received the written document (*shu* 書) and Scribe Yu 史減 was called upon to read it; in the Forty-third Year Lai *ding* 四十三年逨鼎, the two officials switched their positions, with the Chief serving as the reader.[32] However, an earlier inscription, the Mian *gui* 免簋 (JC: 4240), has a slightly different wording: "The king gave the Chief Document Maker the document and let him command Mian."[33] The use of the term *shu* 書 in all of these inscriptions, definitely differentiated from the term *ce* 冊, is especially meaningful. While *ce* refers to a document in its physical form, *shu* entails a document as a literary composition and should be rendered more precisely as an "article" or an official "enactment." In any event, we should not overlook the official and bureaucratic value encoded in the term *shu*, which is clearly differentiated from *ce* in the context of the appointment inscriptions.

New evidence suggests that official written records were produced and used not only at the Zhou court, but also beyond it. The Wu Hu *ding* 吳虎鼎 (JL: 364) records a land transaction to Wu Hu ordered by the king, most likely King Xuan. The court official Provisioner Fengsheng 豐生 and Supervisor of Construction Yongyi 雍毅, after announcing the royal command, actually took the beneficiary to the field to demarcate the borders of the land with the assistance of a groups of local officials. When this was done, the transaction was officially concluded with the handover of *shu* 書 to the recipient of the land by a Scribe who was described as a colleague of

---

[32] For the two inscriptions, see *Wenwu* 2003.6, 6–17.

[33] There has been some misreading of these inscriptions by previous scholars. Huang Ranwei treated the word *shu* as a verb and read the context as if an official, Chief Scribe in the Song *ding* and Scribe X 史▨ in the Yuan *pan* 裒盤 (JC: 10172), wrote the document in front of the king during the ceremony. See Huang Ranwei, *Yin Zhou qingtongqi shangci mingwen yanjiu*, pp. 90, 95. For a comparison of different patterns of such a description and corrections of the mistake, see Li Feng, "'Offices' in Bronze Inscriptions," 50.

the Chief (Interior Scribe), for which he received a gift from the beneficiary. This new inscription shows that affairs such as the transfer of land were actually conducted through the use of written documents in Zhou society. In this particular case, since the land to be transferred previously belonged to an individual named Wu Wu 吳盠 and was already under the court's control, and the transfer was to fulfill the will of King Li, the document was issued by the royal court and was handed over to the recipient by a royal Scribe. The inscription gives us a lively sense of just how bureaucratic the civil administrative process had become during the late Western Zhou and what role writing played in the Zhou government. A similar procedure of land transaction is also recorded in a number of other inscriptions, often involving the role of the scribes. A well-known case is the Pengsheng *gui* 倗生簋 (JC: 4262), already translated in the introduction, which describes a land transaction from Gebo to Pengsheng 倗生 in exchange for a horse received by the former. When this was done, the contract, presumably in written form, was split between the seller and the buyer, and the Scribes actually cast the bronze to document (*dian* 典) the transaction, entailing undoubtedly the composition of the inscription. Writing used in legal administration can be seen in the Sanshi *pan* 散氏盤 (JC: 10176), which records the demarcation of borders between the state of Ze 夨 and the San 散 lineage in the present-day Baoji area. In concluding the procedure, a map was officially made, probably as an attachment to the new treaty, which was obviously in writing, and that was signed by a Scribe.[34] The above inscriptions fully demonstrate the crucial role that writing played in the Zhou administration as well as the extensive social use of writing in general.

It is not clear, indeed it is doubtful, whether there were written *manuals* available to regulate official conduct in the Zhou government, a factor that some modern political scientists use to define modern bureaucratic governments.[35] But the undeniable fact is that writing was used in official communications and in recording what was going on in the Zhou administrative body. This extensive administrative use of writing must be understood as a part of the expanding literary culture of the Western Zhou. As I have noted in another study, while the Shang oracle-bone inscriptions were found almost exclusively in one place – the Shang capital Anyang – as strictly divinatory records, the Zhou inscriptions have been found all over the Zhou world, marking the Western Zhou as the most important period in the proliferation of literacy in China.[36] It is evident that writing was not

---

[34] For the use of writing in Zhou legal administration, see Laura Skosey, *The Legal System and Legal Tradition of the Western Zhou*, pp. 126–27.

[35] See Pugh *et al.*, "Dimensions of Organization Structure," 75–76. In the Zhou case, instructions were given by the king orally to the officials receiving the appointments in the form of royal "wishes" for good quality of service.

[36] See Li Feng, *Landscape and Power in Early China*, p. 19.

only used in the central areas and the Zhou regional states, but was even used in some of the peripheral communities that might have had a very different cultural tradition from that of the Zhou.[37] Writing apparently played a crucial role in the management of the Zhou state.

Identifying the official working place

Having discussed some general features of the workings of the Zhou government, we should now ask a more fundamental question: What was the official workplace like during the Western Zhou? Or, where did the Zhou officials conduct their business of government administration? In Chapter 2, I discussed the significance of the Ministry (*qingshiliao* 卿事寮) as a defined government bureau. It was certainly not only a collective body of civil officials (as some may want to read the character as *liao* 僚), but entailed a physical space that had an associated body of secretarial staff and most likely also a crowd of male and female servants needed for logistical purposes. As already noted there, the graph *liao* actually suggests a *gong* 宮-type of architecture, which had the additional feature that in such structures fire was maintained overnight.[38] The graph certainly conveys a strong sense of routine and continuous activity that took place in the inferred physical space. While such a public space can probably be regarded as a "general office," where officials with various civil administrative duties might have gathered to discuss their business, we found that the character *gong* 宮 itself referred to various buildings, including places where the Zhou king and his officials actually performed their administrative duties.

In the past, the meaning of this term *gong* has caused some major debate among authoritative scholars of bronze inscriptions. While some considered *gong* as residential buildings of the Zhou king, as opposed to the *miao* 廟 as temples for ancestral worship, others determined that the various *gong* starting with the Kang Gong 康宮 were all ancestral temples.[39] To clarify the different natures of the building structures referred to by the word *gong*, a systematic control of the sources is required. According to my earlier statistics, there are ninety-nine Western Zhou bronze inscriptions that mention forty-five different names of *gong*, including apparently buildings

---

[37] See Li Feng, "Literacy Crossing Cultural Borders," 210–421.

[38] See Zhou Fagao, *Jinwen gulin*, pp. 4813–14.

[39] Representative of the first view were Guo Moruo and Chen Mengjia. See Guo Moruo, *Liang Zhou jinwen ci daxi tulu kaoshi*, p. 7; Chen Mengjia, "Xi Zhou tongqi duandai," 2.87–91. The opposing view was put forth by Tang Lan. See Tang Lan, "Zuoce Ling zun ji Zuoce Ling yi ming kaoshi," *Guoli Beijing daxue guoxue jikan* 4.1 (1934), 22–25; "Xi Zhou jinwen duandai zhong de Kang Gong wenti," 15–48 (esp. 31–32). For the debate surrounding the meaning of Kang Gong, see also Shaughnessy, *Sources of Western Zhou History*, pp. 199–201; Leon Vandermeersch, *Wangdao ou la Voie Royale*, vol. 1 (Paris: École Française d'Extrême-Orient, 1977), pp. 74–118.

of various functions.[40] Although these buildings were all called by the generic name *gong* (in a few cases, *miao*), the ways in which they appear in the inscriptions can be clearly differentiated according to certain rules. Thus, based on the contexts of the inscriptional language in which they appear, a typology of the *gong*-buildings is indeed possible. For instance, the most common type is the *gong* that is prefixed with royal titles such as *kang* 康, *zhao* 昭, or *mu* 穆. Tang Lan's influential article published in 1962 established that these were the temples of the deceased Zhou kings.[41] Another type of buildings is composed of *gong* prefixed with generic terms such as Shi Gong 濕宮 and Hua Gong 華宮, which, although they might have been named for various reasons, obviously constituted an order different from the royal temples.[42] In fact, Tang admits that some of these *gong* bearing generic terms were residential palaces of the Zhou kings.[43] The third type, which is most meaningful for our study of Zhou administration, consists of many *gong*-buildings that are prefixed with an official title or a personal name, such as Shi Lu Gong 師彔宮 or Situ Hu Gong 嗣土虎宮; more than ten such buildings appear in the bronze inscriptions.[44] For a long time, even these buildings were treated as temples for deceased Zhou officials or non-office-holders, but this seems problematic with regard to the contents of the inscriptions.[45]

The archeological excavations in Zhouyuan have actually uncovered multiple building foundations that might have been called *gong* in their time of occupation. In fact, the excavations show a high degree of contrast in the structural composition of these building compounds, just as the inscriptions show their different names. For instance, the building compound recently excavated in Yuntang 云塘 consisted of a main hall with two smaller buildings in an inverted "U" formation that was enclosed

---

[40] On the meaning of *gong* in Western Zhou bronze inscriptions, see also Li Feng, "'Offices' in Bronze Inscriptions," 4, 65–71.

[41] See Tang Lan, "Xi Zhou jinwen duandai zhong de Kang Gong wenti," 30.

[42] Others in the same category are Ban Gong 般宮, Xue Gong 學宮, and Ju Gong 駒宮, all appearing in middle-late Western Zhou bronze inscriptions.

[43] From the inscriptions, we know for sure that Ju Gong (Mare Palace) was a special facility where the Zhou kings conducted the "Catching Mare" ritual; Xue Gong (Learning Palace) was evidently a royal school where the noble youths learned the art of archery. Hua Gong and Ban Gong appear in late texts as the residences of King Mu. Shi Gong, which literarily means "Lower Palace," was named so probably because it was located on a lower terrain.

[44] Others include Shi Sima Gong 師嗣馬宮, Shi Liang Gong 師量宮, Shi Qin Gong 師秦宮, Shi Tian Gong 師田宮, Shi Zifu Gong 師汈父宮 (Shi Tangfu Gong 師湯父宮?), Taishi Gong 太師宮, Xi Gong 屖宮, Mai Gong 麥宮, Zhai Gong 濂宮, and Geng Ying Gong 庚嬴宮. Shi Zifu Gong appears in the inscription of the Mu *gui* 牧簋 (JC: 4343), discovered during the Northern Song dynasty. In a recent article, I have suggested that the Shi Zifu Gong is probably a miscopy of Shi Tangfu Gong 師湯父宮 by the Song scholar who transcribed the inscription. See Li Feng, "Textual Criticism and Western Zhou Bronze Inscriptions," pp. 280–97.

[45] For instance, Shirakawa Shizuka interpreted most of these *gong* as temples of the Zhou officials: see "Kinbun tsūshaku," 14.37:818, 19.104:364, 20.109:402, 22.124:11; Wu Zhenfeng, *Jinwen renming huibian* (Beijing: Zhonghua, 1987), pp. 73, 195–96; "Xi Zhou jinwen duandai zhong de Kang Gong wenti," 31.

immediately by a wall circle, showing strong resemblance with the ancestral temple of Qin during the Warring States period (see figure 13).[46] It is not impossible, though conjectural at present, that the Yuntang building compound as well as that found in nearby Qizhen 齊鎮 might have been among the royal temples mentioned in the inscriptions, all known to have been located in Zhou, that is, Zhouyuan. By sharp contrast, the building compounds previously found in Fengchu 鳳雛 and Shaochen 召陳, which are structurally different from each other and both dramatically more complex than and different from the Yuntang-Qizhen architectures, might have accommodated a much broader range of social and political activities, including residential occupation by the Zhou kings or their officials.[47] Although it is not possible or even feasible to apply the typology of *gong* in the inscription to the building foundation actually found, the two types of evidence combined should fully alert us to the structural as well as functional differences of the building compounds during the Western Zhou.

In a recent study I suggested that many of the *gong*-buildings in the third category mentioned above actually functioned as government "offices," where the Western Zhou officials conducted their business, and some of them might have simultaneously served as their residences.[48] The reason for this new identification lies in the very fact that in many cases the name by which the building is called in the inscription can be properly identified with the individual official or non-office-holder whom the inscription also records as having played an active role in the named building. This strong link between the building and its associated personnel can be best detected in cases such as Geng Ying Gong 庚嬴宮, Mai Gong 麥宮, Shi Sima Gong 師嗣馬宮, Xi Gong 屖宮, and Zhai Gong 濂宮.[49] In three

---

[46] *Kaogu* 2002.9, 3–26. On the religious functions of the Yuntang and Qizhen architectural compounds, see Xu Lianggao and Wang Wei, "Shaanxi Fufeng Yuntang Xi Zhou jianzhu jizhi de chubu yanjiu," *Kaogu* 2002.9, 27–35.

[47] On the Fengchu building compound, see *Wenwu* 1979.10, 27–34. On the Shaochen building compound, see *Wenwu* 1981.3, 10–22. See also Hsu and Linduff, *Western Chou Civilization*, pp. 289–302. There has been considerable debate about the nature of these building compounds. While some scholars regarded them, particularly the one in Fengchu, as temples for religious activities, others considered that they were probably residential units of the Western Zhou aristocratic families. The new findings in Yuntang and Qizhen, by clear structural contrast, seem to throw doubts on any exclusive religious function previously attributed to these buildings. For the first position, see *Wenwu* 1979.10, 33–34; Yin Shengping, *Zhouyuan wenhua yu Xi Zhou wenming* (Nanjing: Jiangsu jiaoyu, 2005), pp. 447–65. For the second position, see Ding Yi, "Zhouyuan de jianzhu yicun he tongqi jiaocang," *Kaogu* 1982.4, 398–401.

[48] See Li Feng, "'Offices' in Bronze Inscriptions," 1–72.

[49] For instance, the Geng Ying *you* 庚嬴卣 (JC: 5426) records the noble lady Geng Ying's receipt of a gift from the king, most likely King Mu, and this took place in Geng Ying Gong 庚嬴宮, a building structure occupied by Geng Ying. Similarly, a group of inscriptions including the Mai *he* 麥盉 (JC: 9451), Mai *fangyi* 麥方彝 (JC: 9893), and Mai *fangding* 麥方鼎 (JC: 2706) cast by Mai 麥, a high-ranking official of the state of Xing in Hebei, records the ruler of Xing's visit to Mai Gong 麥宮, where he rewarded the official Mai 麥 with fine metals. These are explicit examples of *gong* building compounds being called after the names of their occupants.

other cases, although individuals by such names are not mentioned in the particular inscription that names these buildings,[50] they are mentioned in other inscriptions as high officials active in approximately the same period. The evidence, presented in detail in my previous article and not repeated here,[51] is quite compelling that when a *gong*-building is given the name or official designation of an individual in the inscriptions, it was actually under the authority or jurisdiction of that named individual. Moreover, these types of *gong*-buildings contrast sharply with the royal temples in terms of these geographical locations: whereas the royal temples were exclusively located in one place – Zhou 周 (or Zhouyuan) – the *gong*-buildings of the third type under discussion were located in a number of different cities distant from one another.[52]

What are the implications of all this for Western Zhou government administration? The important fact is that, while these buildings were evidently under the personal authority of individual officials, the inscriptions show quite clearly that most of them were the workplaces where the officials conducted their regular government duties. In other words, these were places where government functions were carried out, resembling administrative "offices" in the modern sense. This naturally brings out the question of whether an official's private life had already been separated from his public activities during the Western Zhou, a separation that was considered by Weber as necessary in defining the *ideal type* of bureaucracy.[53] In this case, it is quite possible that these building compounds were also private homes for their named officials. Thus, we have a very interesting situation here regarding the working patterns of the Zhou government. On the one hand, there were general offices such as the Ministry, where officials probably spent working hours away from their own living quarters; at the latest during the middle and late Western Zhou, the Grand Secretariat was probably also a public government space that accommodated the official activities of a large number of Scribes. In the military context, for instance, the Duoyou *ding* 多友鼎 (JC: 2835) mentions the "Contribution Hall" (Xian Gong 獻宮), which seems to have being a special *gong*-building where field commanders presented war captives; the Jinhou Su *zhong* 晉侯蘇鐘 (JL: 35–50) mentions the "Military Hall" (Shi Gong 師宮) located in the eastern capital Chengzhou that was apparently the headquarters of the Eight Armies of Chengzhou. On the other hand, below the level of such general offices, there is a good possibility that government business was conducted in a more or less "private" manner; that is, particular

---

[50] See Shi Xi Taishi 師戲太室, Situ Hu Gong 嗣上淲宮, and Shi Zifu Gong 師汙父宮.

[51] See Li Feng, "'Offices' in Bronze Inscriptions," 3–14.

[52] For instance, Shi Sima Gong, Shi Lu Gong, and Shi Zifu Gong were located in Zhou, Taishi Gong in Zongzhou 宗周 (capital Hao 鎬), Situ Hu Gong in Chengzhou in the east, and Shi Tian Gong at Yong 永.

[53] See Weber, "Bureaucracy," 197.

government functions were focused on the *gong*-buildings that were occupied by individual officials and would travel when such roles shifted between the officials, but not on function-specific buildings in which different officials could be put from time to time. In other words, rather than putting officials into a designated space for particular functions, it is more likely that such spaces were designated based on who actually held the office. Although this assessment seems to be very speculative, based mainly on the names that were associated with the *gong*-buildings, it seems to be the most logical reading of our current evidence. Furthermore, this assessment is consistent with the fact that the inscriptions make little mention of specialized offices for such roles as Supervisor of Land or Supervisor of Construction (as, hypothetically, Situ Gong 嗣土宮 and Sigong Gong 嗣工宮, without mentioning the name of a particular official), although officials with such titles appear frequently in the inscriptions. We do have one case, Shi Sima Gong 師嗣馬宮, "Office of Supervisor of Horses of the Army," which we know can be identified with Supervisor of Horses Jingbo 井伯, who played an active role in the building. This case may be special because it belonged to the organization of the Six and Eight Armies and may not reflect the situation in civil administration.

However, this does not mean that the Western Zhou officials conducted their business only in the *gong*-buildings discussed above; the royal temples were also places where the appointment ritual took place, perhaps following a religious session involving offerings to the ancestors. By the same token, religious activities could also take place in the *gong*-buildings discussed above. But the very existence of such *gong*-buildings bearing personal names is meaningful to Western Zhou government administration and does suggest a strong personal role in the allocation of governmental functions. Of particular interest is the fact that the Zhou king made frequent visits to, and hosted appointment ceremonies in, these building compounds under the authority of individual officials, just as the officials also attended the king in his palaces. But this will be discussed in some detail later in this chapter.

THE WORKINGS OF THE ZHOU CENTRAL BUREAUCRACY

By virtue of their relatively large number, the "appointment inscriptions" also inform us in a unique way of the actual conduct of the Zhou central bureaucracy. In the present section, I will examine further their implications for Zhou administration by taking a closer look into the content of the inscriptions in relation with each other. The regularities that we can detect in the information offered by these inscriptions enable us to explore a number of important issues concerning the nature of Zhou administration and the level of its bureaucratic development. These issues include, for instance, the arrangement of the appointment ceremonies, the specialization of government roles, personal relationships in the Zhou government, and the hierarchy of administrative order. These issues, when put together, will contribute to a general understanding of how the Western Zhou government actually operated.

The arrangement of the appointments

Attention must be first paid to the appointment ceremonies that were conducted in the same location because they may show some important connections. The places where such ceremonies were most frequently held were the royal temples such as Kang Gong, which hosted the appointments of about fifteen officials, and Grand Temple (*taimiao*), where the appointments of nine officials were announced.[54] However, since the royal temples by their very nature as the ancestral sanctuary might have accommodated all kinds of activities, such cases might not be as informative as the appointments that took place in the building compounds under the supervision of individual officials, the third type of *gong*-building discussed above. The latter inscriptions may provide us with important information about the logic behind the arrangement of official appointments. In fact, we have two groups of such inscriptions that can be examined in this connection.

The first group is composed of five inscriptions including the Shi Yu *gui* 師艅簋 (JC: 4277), Shi Chen *ding* 師晨鼎 (JC: 2817), Xing *xu* 癭盨 (JC: 4462), Jian *gui* 諫簋 (JC: 4285), and Zai Shou *gui* 宰獸簋 (JL: 490).[55] Not only did the five appointment ceremonies take place in a single location – Shi Lu Gong 師彔宮 – but it was the same official – Supervisor of Horses Gong 司馬共 – who played the role of *youzhe* in four of the sessions. The cross-references in these inscriptions to Supervisor of Horses Gong and Interior Scribe Nian 內史年, and the mentions of such officials as Shi Su 師俗, Xing 癭, and Rongbo 榮伯, help date them very close to each other in time during the mid-Western Zhou.[56] Let us examine two of these five inscriptions:

Shi Yu *gui* 師艅簋 (JC: 4277):
It was the third year, third month, first auspiciousness, *jiaxu* day (no. 11); the king was in Shi Lu Gong 師彔宮 in Zhou. At dawn, the king entered

[54] For these figures, see Li Feng, "'Offices' in Bronze Inscriptions," 65.

[55] For the later discovery of the Zai Shou *gui*, see also Luo Xizhang, "Zai Shou *gui* ming luekao," *Wenwu* 1998.8, 83–87.

[56] For the chronological positions of Supervisor of Horses Gong and Interior Scribe Nian in the Kings Yih–Xiao period, see Shaughnessy, *Sources of Western Zhou History*, pp. 119–20. The chronology of the Wei 微 family would date the Xing *xu* 癭盨 some time around the time of King Xiao. See Li Xueqin, *Xinchu qingtongqi yanjiu*, pp. 85, 90–93. Shi Su 師俗 also appears as Shi Sufu 師俗父 in the Yong *yu* 永盂 (JC: 10322) and Bo Sufu 伯俗父 in the Fifth Year Qiu Wei *ding* 五年裘衛鼎 (JC: 2832); the dating of the two bronzes to the Gong–Yih period is generally agreed on. In short, these five bronzes were cast very close in time during the mid-Western Zhou, roughly in the time of King Yih to King Xiao.

the grand chamber and assumed his position. Supervisor of Horses Gong 嗣馬共, accompanying Shi Yu 師舣 to his right, entered the gate and stood in the center of the courtyard. The king called out to the Document Maker and Interior Scribe to command Shi Yu with a written document: "Take charge (釢嗣) of the people of Zhou 侚人.[57] [I] award [you] red kneepads, a scarlet demi-circlet, and a pennant." Yu bowed with his head touching the ground. May the Son of Heaven for ten thousand years enjoy a beautiful long-life and yellowing age, sufficiently being on the throne; may Yu have his merit acknowledged (*mieli* 蔑歷),[58] daily being awarded felicitous beneficence! Yu dares in response to extol the Son of Heaven's illustrious beneficence, and herewith makes this treasured *gui*-vessel. May Yu for ten thousand years be eternally secure, being the servant of the Son of Heaven!

Shi Chen *ding* 師晨鼎 (JC: 2817):

It was the third year, third month, first auspiciousness, *jiaxu* day (no. 11); the king was in Shi Lu Gong in Zhou. At dawn, the king approached the grand chamber and assumed position. Supervisor of Horses Gong, accompanying Shi Chen 師晨 to his right, entered the gate and stood in the center of the courtyard. The king called out to the Chief Document Maker to command Shi Chen with a written document: "Assist (*pi* 疋) Shi Su 師俗 in administering the people of Yi:[59] those Little Servants, Food Providers, keepers of X, and official dog-keepers; and the people of Zheng: Food Providers and official keeper friends. [I] award [you] red slippers." Chen bowed with his head touching the ground. He dares in response to extol the Son of Heaven's illustrious and beneficent command, herewith making [for] my cultured grandfather, Xingong 辛公, [this] sacrificial *ding*-vessel. May Chen for…generations, sons' sons and grandsons' grandsons, eternally treasure and use [it].

It is very interesting to note first that the appointments of Shi Yu and Shi Chen were announced on the same morning of *jiaxu* day (no. 11) of the third month of the third year, and there is a distinct possibility that

---

[57] The graph ▓ (釢) is an unsolved question in the inscriptions. The old fashion was to read it as *bing* 併 or *jian* 兼, meaning "to concurrently serve as." However, these readings make little connection to the graphs, and no inscription that uses the word seems to suggest a secondary duty. In 1957, Guo Moruo proposed to read it as *she* 攝, "to take control" or "to take charge," and this reading has since been followed by many scholars. See Guo Moruo, "Li qi ming kaoshi," 5–6. The graphical "proof" for this reading was supplied by Wu Kuang and Cai Zhemao in a long article published in 1993. Reading the left half of the character as *hui* 彗, "broom," which was read in archaic Chinese as *xi* 習, and since the character *she* 慴 based on *xi* 習 is used in some texts as the phonetic loan word for *she* 攝, the two scholars suggested that the character is indeed the archaic form of 攝. See Wu Kuang and Cai Zhemao, 'Shi X,' *Gugong xueshu jikan*, 11.3 (1993-94), 92–93. While this reading seems to explain most cases and hence is followed here, it is my understanding that the graphic link is still quite uncertain.

[58] The meaning of *mieli* 蔑歷 will be discussed in detail in Chapter 5, pp. 226–29.

[59] *Pi* 疋 is a key term for the Western Zhou government with respect particularly to official service. The meaning and implications of *pi* are discussed fully in Chapter 5, pp. 119–201.

the two officials received their appointments in the same ritual session. Shi Yu was entrusted with the mission of "taking charge of the people of Zhou" 倗人, while Shi Chen was appointed assistant to a higher official, Shi Su 師俗, to supervise the people of Yi 邑 and the people of Zheng 鄭, each composed of a large number of low-status civil officials.[60] Apparently, both Shi Yu and Shi Chen were appointed civil administrators in the major cities, and their appointments were announced in the same ritual session. This case of related appointments suggests that the appointment ceremony was probably not a procedure in which the Zhou king randomly assigned official responsibilities, but was probably conducted according to some rules. They indicate at least some kind of tendency to group officials of the same category in the same ceremony that might have been arranged for some special purpose.

Further reading into the inscription of the Jian *gui* 諫簋 and the recently discovered Zai Shou *gui* 宰獸簋 suggests that the two appointments were also civil administrative in nature: while Jian was commanded to manage the "royal park" (*wangyou* 王囿), Zai Shou was commanded to supervise the servants and retainers in the royal temple Kang Gong. But the two appointments are separated by at least a year, if the two bronzes were indeed cast in the same reign of a mid-Western Zhou king. Also different from Shi Yu and Shi Chen, who were appointed civil administrator, Jian and Superintendent Shu were to work in the Royal Household. The Xing *xu* 瘨盨, on the other hand, records only an award to Xing, but not an official appointment. Since these five appointments were all announced in the Shi Lu Gong, this certainly brings out the question regarding the administrative function of the particular building compound. However, since the building compound was under the authority of an official, in this case, Shi Lu, understandably the administrative function of it was dependent on the role of the official in the Zhou government; and as I have noted recently, an official's governmental role could change over time.[61] Nevertheless, the Shi Lu Gong seems to show very strong characteristics of civil administration, and this contrasts sharply with the functions associated with another building compound – Shi Sima Gong 師嗣馬宮.

The building compound Shi Sima Gong appears in two appointment inscriptions: the Shi Yun *gui* 師瘨簋 (JC: 4283) and the Yang *gui* 養簋 (JC: 4243). The occurrence of Jingbo 井伯 in the Shi Yun *gui* and Yang *gui* would date them slightly earlier than the preceding five inscriptions, to the reign of King Mu or King Gong.[62] According to the first, Shi Yun was commanded by the former king to supervise the "marshals" (*shishi* 師氏) among the people of Yi, and the present king confirmed his mission.

---

[60] For a more detailed interpretation of the two inscriptions, see Li Feng, "'Offices' in Bronze Inscriptions," 20–22.

[61] See Li Feng, "Succession and Promotion," 1–35.

[62] For the time range of Jingbo, see Shaughnessy, *Sources of Western Zhou History*, pp. 118–20.

Clearly, Shi Yun was appointed to officiate over a group of local military men, probably stationed within the territory of Yi. In the second inscription, Yang was commanded by the king with the mission to protect "dikes" (*yan* 堰) in the Five Cities, and the job was also considered to be military in nature.[63] Attention must be paid to the term Shi Sima Gong 師嗣馬宮, which was probably under the authority of Supervisor of Horses Jingbo 嗣馬井伯, who played the role of *youzhe* in the two appointment ceremonies. It is very likely that the term *shi* 師 in this case has a special meaning, identifying Sima Jingbo as the Supervisor of Horses in the Six Armies, to which this particular office was attached, but not the Supervisor of Horses as one of the three supervisors of the Ministry; such a role was probably played by Supervisor of Horses Gong 嗣馬共, who frequently took part in the ceremonies appointing civil administrators.

This phenomenon of the arrangement of appointments in view of the functions of offices certainly needs the support of more evidence, which might come to light in the future and lead to in-depth research on the specialization of government offices during the middle and late Western Zhou. With the concern not to overweigh our current evidence, it would seem reasonable to suggest that some kind of definition of individual administrative offices had already been developed during the mid-Western Zhou that allowed the candidates for similar administrative roles to be grouped to receive royal appointments in the same building compound, and perhaps, as most typically exemplified by the Shi Yu *gui* and Shi Chen *ding*, even in the same session of appointment ritual. It is above all possible that such a divide was first developed between offices of civil administrative nature and military functions. Thus, although the physical location of an office could change according to the tenure of the official who held it, as discussed above, as long as it stayed with an official, that is, under the administrative jurisdiction of the official after whom the particular building compound was named, the governmental conduct that took place in it seems to have been well defined with a focus on specialization.

Interpersonal relations in the central government

A special role in the appointment ceremony was the *youzhe*, the person who leads the candidate into the courtyard and probably introduces him to the king. Because such officials appear so frequently in the appointment inscriptions, their political positions, and especially their administrative roles, have perplexed many scholars in the past. For instance, Yang Kuan suggested that the *youzhe* in the bronze inscriptions were prominent court officials ranking as "Dukes" (*gong* 公) and "Ministers" (*qing* 卿), generally superior to the officials they introduced to the king in the appointment

---

[63] For this reading, see Zhang Yachu and Liu Yu, *Xi Zhou jinwen guanzhi yanjiu*, p. 22.

ceremony.[64] Wang Zhongwen, on the other hand, attempted to establish a rational relationship between the *youzhe* and the appointees, but Wang focussed entirely on the relationship between the *youzhe*'s official titles or ranks and the appointees' official titles, and he further made the error of regarding the term *shi* 師 as a single and specific official title. Finally, Wang failed to discern any constant relationship between the *youzhe* and appointees whom they accompanied, and he concluded that they were randomly grouped.[65] In short, the importance of the *youzhe* was recognized in previous scholarship, but his role in Western Zhou government administration was not fully understood.

Apparently, the relationship between the *youzhe* and the appointees reflected in the appointment process is the key to understanding the workings of the Zhou central bureaucracy. If regularities can be detected, or if rules existed in the selection of *youzhe* for officials in the appointment ritual, it would certainly suggest that in the actual operation of the Zhou government there existed such workgroups. That is, officials with similar responsibilities tended to co-work in a common and independent process, and the administrative conduct of the Zhou government might have combined a number of such conceptually segregated processes. If this is the case, then the question is: How were such processes related, at least from the mid-Western Zhou onwards, when we have a good base of information, to the overall structural divisions of the Zhou central government discussed in Chapter 2? Since any study of regularities would have to be based on a full coverage of data, systematic research to compare the governmental roles of the *youzhe* and those of the officials whom they accompanied in the appointment ceremonies is likewise necessary in this case.

There is a total of forty-one *youzhe* who accompanied sixty-five officials in the appointment rituals or in ritual sessions in which they received royal awards recorded in seventy-one Western Zhou bronze inscriptions available by December 2006 (see table 1). There are twenty cases where the government roles of the *youzhe* cannot be determined (nos. 51–70), and two special cases (nos. 24, 26), where regional rulers from the east received gifts from the king and were accompanied by ministers at the central court,[66]

---

[64] See Yang Kuan, "Xi Zhou wangchao gong qing de guanjue zhidu," in *Xi Zhou shi yanjiu* (monograph of *Renwen zazhi congkan*, no. 2 (Xi'an: 1984), pp. 100–13.

[65] See Wang Zhongwen, *Liang Zhou guanzhi lungao* (Gaoxiong: Fuwen, 1993), pp. 46–48, 58–62. Treating *shi* as a specific official title, Wang finds that *shi* was accompanied in the appointment ritual by *youzhe* who had various government roles. As will be discussed in Chapter 5, *shi* was not an official title, but was a status that suggested an official's previous military career.

[66] The first case is the Yinghou *zhong* 應侯鐘 (JC: 107–108), which records the ruler of Ying's 應 audience with the Zhou king in the Zhou capital Zongzhou (Hao) in Shaanxi; in the audience, he was accompanied by a prominent minister, probably Supervisor of Land-Rongbo. The second case is the Jinhou Su *zhong* 晉侯蘇編鐘 (JL: 35–50), which records the ruler of Jin's 晉 audience with the king that took place in the eastern capital Chengzhou, upon returning from a joint campaign in the farther east; in the ceremony he was accompanied by Supervisor of Construction Yangfu 揚父. Since these are audiences between the Zhou king and the regional rulers, it would seem logical for a prominent official of any role representing the central bureaucracy to serve as their *youzhe*.

Table 1. *Relations between the youzhe and appointees/awardees*

Youzhe	Appointee/ Inscription	Official Duties of Appointee
1 Superintendent Hu 宰智	Cai 蔡 Cai *gui* 蔡簋	昔先王既令汝作宰，嗣王家。今余…令汝眔智觏乩對各，死嗣王家外内…嗣百工，出入姜氏命。厥有見有即命，厥非先告蔡，毋敢侯有入告 In the past, the previous king already commanded you to be Superintendent, in charge of the royal household. Now I…commend you and Hu to mutually assist each other, exerting your utmost effort to be in charge of the outside and inside of the royal household…in charge of the hundred craftsmen, sending out and taking in the orders of Queen Jiang. When someone wants to meet with or to take orders (from the queen), without reporting to Cai in advance, (he) would not dare to hastily enter and report.
2 Superintendent Pengfu 宰倗父	Wang 望 Wang *gui* 望簋	死嗣畢王家 Do your utmost to be in charge of the royal household at Bi.
3 Zhong Pengfu 仲倗父（宰）	Chu 楚 Chu *gui* 楚簋	嗣莽圖官内師舟 In charge of the boats within the government of the territory of (the capital) Pang.
4 Superintendent Xifu 宰犀父	Hai 害 Hai *gui* 害簋	用養乃祖考事，官嗣夷僕小射 With which to nurture your grandfather and father's affairs, officiating in charge of the barbarian servants and the small archers.
5 Xifu 犀父(宰)	Xing 癏 Thirteenth Year Xing *hu* 十三年癏壺	
6 Superintendent Hong 宰弘	Song 頌 (史) Song *ding* 頌鼎	官嗣成周貯二十家，監嗣新造貯，用宮御 Officiate in charge of the warehouse of twelve households at Chengzhou, and supervise the newly constructed warehouse, using palace attendants.
7 Superintendent Fei 宰朏	Document Maker Wu 作冊吳 Wu *fangyi* 吳方彝	嗣旃眔叔金 In charge of the "white flag" and fine silk.
8 Superintendent Zhousheng 宰琱生	Shi Li 師釐 Shi Li *gui* 師釐簋	在昔…先王既命汝更乃祖考嗣小輔。今余…命汝眔乃祖考舊官小輔眔鐘鼓 In the past…the previous king already commanded you to replace your grandfather and father in charge of the musicians of vertically-hanging bells. Now I…command you to take over your grandfather's and father's old post, (in charge) of the musicians of vertically-hanging bells and the musicians of obliquely-hanging bells and drums.

Youzhe	Appointee/ Inscription	Official Duties of Appointee
9 Superintendent Xian (?) 宰頵	Yuan 裛 Yuan *pan* 裛盤	
10 Supervisor of Land Shu 嗣土戍	Yin 殷 Yin *gui* 殷簋	更乃祖考友（又）眔東鄙五邑 Replace your grandfather and father, again in charge of the five towns in the eastern district.
11 Supervisor of Multitudes Shanbo 嗣徒單伯	Yang 揚 Yang *gui* 揚簋	作嗣工，官眔 量田甸，眔居，眔芻，眔寇 眔工事 Be the Supervisor of Construction, officiating in charge of farming, in charge of the residential houses, in charge of the forage grass, in charge of lawsuits, and in charge of the construction of the field of Liang.
12 Supervisor of Land Maoshu 嗣土毛叔	Ci 此 Ci *gui* 此簋	旅邑人善夫 In charge of the food providers of the people of Yi.
13 Nangong Hu (Supervisor of Land) 南宮呼(嗣土)	Food Provider Shan 善夫山 Shanfu Shan *ding* 善夫山鼎	令汝官嗣 飲獻人于竸，用作憲司盯 Command you to officiate in charge of the contributors of drinks at Ke, with which to supply the stores of *xiansi* (?).
14 Supervisor of Construction Yebo 嗣工液伯	Shi Ying 師穎 Shi Ying *gui* 師穎簋	先王既令汝作嗣土，官嗣冰闔 The previous king already commanded you to be Supervisor of Land, officiating in charge of the floodgate (?) of the Fang River (?).
15 Supervisor of Construction San 嗣工散	Supervisor of Marshes Lai 吳逨 Forty-second Year Lai *ding* 四十二年逨鼎 (Retrospectively known from Forty-third Year Lai *ding*)	疌榮兌靯嗣四方虞林，用宮御 Assist Rong Dui to take charge of the marshes and forests in the four directions, using palace attendants.
16 Bo Sufu 伯俗父	Nan Ji 南季 Nan Ji *gui* 南季鼎	左右俗父嗣寇 Assist Sufu in charge of lawsuits.
17 Supervisor of Land Rongbo 嗣土榮伯	Superintendent Shou 宰獸 Zai Shou *gui* 宰獸簋	靯嗣康宮王家臣妾庸 Diligently being in charge of the royal servants, retainers in Kang Gong.
18 Rongbo 榮伯	Tong 同 Tong *gui* 同簋	差右吳太伯嗣場林虞牧，自淲東至于河，厥逆至于玄水 Assist Wu Taibo in charge of the orchards, forests, marshes, and pastoral land, from the Hu River east to the Yellow River, and north to the Xuan River.
19 Rongbo 榮伯	Shi Xun 師詢 Shi Xun *gui* 師詢簋	令汝惠雝我邦大小酋 Command you to beneficially harmonize the great and small chiefs of our state.

(continued)

Table 1. *Relations between the youzhe and appointees/awardees (continued)*

Youzhe	Appointee/Inscription	Official Duties of Appointee
21 Rongbo 榮伯	Musician Shi Li 輔師釐 Fu Shi Li *gui* 輔師釐簋	更乃祖考嗣輔 Replace your grandfather and father in charge of the musicians of vertically-hanging bells.
22 Rongbo 榮伯	Wei 衛 Wei *gui* 衛簋	
23 Rongbo 榮伯	Mibo Shi Ji 弭伯師籍 Shi Ji *gui* 師籍簋	
24 Rongbo 榮伯	Yinghou 應侯 Yinghou *zhong* 應侯鐘	
25 Supervisor of Multitudes Nanzhong 嗣徒南仲	Wuhui 無惠 Wuhui *ding* 無惠鼎	官嗣𧊒王復側虎臣 Officiate in charge of the tiger servants at the body side of X king.
26 Supervisor of Construction Yangfu 嗣工揚父	Jinhou Su 晉侯蘇 Jinhou Su *bianzhong* 晉侯蘇編鐘	伐東國 (Attacked the eastern states.)
27 Supervisor of Constructions X 嗣工 XX	Lu 覭 Jingbo Lu *gui* 井伯覭簋	更乃祖服，作家嗣馬 Replace your grandfather's service; to be Grand Supervisor of Horses
28 Supervisor of Horses Gong 嗣馬共	Shi Yu 師舲 Shi Yu *gui* 師舲簋	死嗣偋人 Do you utmost to be in charge of the people of Zhou.
29 Supervisor of Horses Gong 嗣馬共	Shi Chen 師晨 Shi Chen *ding* 師晨鼎	疋師俗父嗣邑人：唯小臣，善夫，守口，官犬；眔鄭人：善夫，官守友。 Assist Shi Sufu in charge of the people of Yi: they are the little servants, food providers, x-guards, care takers of official dogs; and the people of Zheng: food providers, and the friends of the official guard (?).
30 Supervisor of Horses Gong 嗣馬共	Jian 諫 Jian *gui* 諫簋	先王既令汝龢嗣王囿 The previous king already commanded you to be in charge of the royal park.
31 Supervisor of Horses Gong 嗣馬共	Xing 㷼 Xing *xu* 㷼盨	
32 Supervisor of Horses Shou 嗣馬壽	Supervisor of Marshes Lai 吳逨 Forty-third Year Lai *ding* 四十三年逨鼎	官嗣歷人 Officiate in charge of the people of Li.

Youzhe	Appointee/ Inscription	Official Duties of Appointee
33 Wugong 武公	Nangong Liu 南宮柳 Nangong Liu *ding* 南宮柳鼎	嗣六師牧，場，虞口；嗣義夷陽佃事 In charge of the pastoral land, orchards, marshes, and X of the Six Armies; in charge of the affairs of farming of *Xiyi yang* (?).
34 Wugong 武公	Wu 敄 Wu *gui* 敄簋	追伐南淮夷 Pursued the Southern Huai Barbarians.
35 Mugong (military rule) 穆公	Li 盠 Li *fangzun* 盠方尊	嗣六師王行參有嗣：嗣土，嗣馬，嗣工。 颮 嗣 六師眾八師埶 In charge of the Three Supervisors – Supervisor of Land, Supervisor of Horses, and Supervisor of Construction – of the royal guard legion in the Six Armies; in charge of the camping affairs of the Six Armies and the Eight Armies.
36 Beizhong 備中	Lü Fuyu 呂服余 Lü Fuyu *pan* 呂服余盤	令汝更乃祖考事，疋備中嗣 六師服 Command you to take over your grandfather and father's affairs, assisting Beizhong in charge of the affairs of the Six Armies.
37 Supervisor of Horses Jingbo 嗣馬井伯	Shi Yun 師瘨 Shi Yun *gui* 師瘨簋	官嗣邑人師氏 Take office in charge of the marshals of the people of Yi.
38 Supervisor of Horses Jingbo 嗣馬井伯	Zou 走 Zou *gui* 走簋	颮疋口 Assist X.
39 Supervisor of Horses Jingbo 嗣馬井伯	Shi Kuifu 師奎父(師氏) Shi Kuifu *ding* 師奎父鼎	用嗣乃父官友 With which to be in charge of the friends of your father in the government.
40 Jingbo 井伯	Yang 養 Yang *gui* 養簋	用大備于五邑守堰（?） With which to greatly accomplish the protection of dikes (?) in the Five Cities.
41 Jingbo 井伯	Dou Bi 豆閉 Dou Bi *gui* 豆閉簋	用口 乃祖考事，嗣爰餘邦君嗣馬，弓矢 With which to take over (?) your grandfather and father's affairs, to serve as Supervisor of Horses under the *bangjun* of Youyu, (in charge of) bows and arrows.
42 Jingbo 井伯	Shi Hu 師虎 Shi Hu *gui* 師虎簋	令汝更乃祖考，啻嗣左右戲繁荊 Command you to replace your grandfather and father in charge of the horses in the Left and Right Camps.
43 Jingbo 井伯	Shi Maofu 師毛父 Shi Maofu *gui* 師毛父簋	(Ban *gui* 班簋: Maofu led troops to attack the eastern states)

(continued)

Table 1. *Relations between the youzhe and appointees/awardees (continued)*

Youzhe	Appointee/ Inscription	Official Duties of Appointee
45 Jingbo 井伯	Quecao (Scribe) 趞曹(史) Seventh Year Quecao *ding* 七年趞曹鼎	
46 Mishu 密叔	Qi 趞 Qi *gui* 趞簋	作豳師 冢嗣馬，啻官僕，射士，訊小大又鄰 Be the Grand Supervisor of Horses in the Bin Garrison, officiating in charge of the chariot guides, archers, prisoners, and to question minor and great among the neighbors.
47 Mishu 密叔	Hu 虎 Hu *gui* 虎簋	疋師戲嗣走馬馭人，衆五邑走馬馭人 Assist Shi Xi in charge of the Masters of Horses and Charioteers, and the Masters of Horses and Charioteers in the Five Cities.
48 Yigong 益公	Shen 申 Shen *gui* 申簋	更乃祖考，疋大祝官嗣 豐人衆九戲祝 Replace your grandfather and father, assisting the Grand Invocator to officiate as Invocator for the people of Feng and the nine-garrison-camps.
49 Yigong 益公	Xun 詢 Xun *gui* 詢簋	啻官嗣邑人先虎臣，後庸，西門夷，秦夷，京夷，𩰀夷；師苓側新□華夷，弊□夷𩰀人；成周走亞□，秦人，降人，服夷 Take office in charge first of the tiger servants, and then of the retainers, the barbarians of Ximeng, barbarians of Qin, barbarians of Jing, and the barbarians of Quan, all of the people of Yi; (in charge of) those on the side of Shi Qin, including the barbarians of X-hua, barbarians of Biren (?), and the people of X; (in charge of) those in Chengzhou including *zouya*-X, the people of Qin, people of Xiang, and the barbarians of Fu.
50 Yigong 益公	Master of Horses Xiu 走馬休 Xiu *pan* 休盤	
51 Zhong Taishi 中太師	Zha 柞 Zha *zhong* 柞鍾	嗣五邑佃人事 In charge of the affairs of the farmers of the Five Cities.
52 Jinggong 井公	Hu 曶 Hu *hu* 曶壺	更乃祖考作冢嗣土于成周八師 Replace your grandfather and father and be the Grand Supervisor of Land in the Eight Armies of Chengzhou.
53 Jingshu 井叔	Mian 免 Mian *gui* 免簋	令汝疋周師嗣𢿸 Command you to assist Zhou Shi in charge of the forest.
54 Jingshu 井叔	Mian 免 Mian *zun* 免尊	作嗣工 Be Supervisor of Construction.

	Youzhe	Appointee/ Inscription	Official Duties of Appointee
55	Jingshu 井叔	Yi 趩 Yi *zhi* 趩觶	更厥祖考服 Replace his grandfather's and father's service.
56	Jingshu 井叔	Mishu Shi Qiu 弭叔師求 Mishu *gui* 弭叔簋	
57	Mugong 穆公	Zai 𧦝 Zai *gui* 𧦝 簋	令汝作嗣土，官嗣 籍田 Command you to be Supervisor of Land, officiating in charge of the Spring Plowing Ritual.
58	Dingbo 定伯	Ji 即 Ji *gui* 即簋	嗣 琱宮人虢稻 In charge of the people of the Zhou Palace, *baodao*.
59	Nanbo 南伯	Qiu Wei 裘衛 Qiu Wei *gui* 裘衛簋	
60	Shenji 讎季	Yi 伊 Yi *gui* 伊簋	䎛官嗣康宮王臣妾百工 Officiate in charge of the royal servants, the female slaves, and the hundred craftsmen in Kang Gong.
61	Shenji 讎季	Food Provider Ke 善夫克 Da Ke *ding*大克鼎	昔余既令汝出內王命 In the past, I already commanded you to send out and take in the royal command.
62	Xigong 遲公	Shi Shi 師事 First Year Shi Shi *gui* 元年師事簋	備于大左，官嗣豐還左右師氏 To supplement the Great Left, officiating in charge of the Marshals of the Left and Right of the District of Feng.
63	Tong Zhong 同仲	Shi Dui 師兌 First Year Shi Dui *gui* 元年師兌簋	疋師和父嗣左右走馬，五邑走馬 Assist Shi Hefu in charge of the Masters of Horses of the Left and Right, and the Masters of Horses of the Five Cities.
64	Huibo 毀伯(師毀)	Shi Dui 師兌 Third Year Shi Dui *gui* 三年師兌簋	余既令汝疋師和父嗣左右走馬，今余-- 命汝䎛嗣走馬 I already commanded you to assist Shi Hefu in charge of the Masters of Horses of the Left and Right; Now, I…command you to be in charge of the Masters of Horses.
65	Maobo毛伯	Qian 鄦 Qian *gui* 鄦簋	䎛五邑祝 Serve as the Invocator of the Five Cities.
66	Kanggong 康公	He Yuan 郃兇 He Yuan *gui* 郃兇簋	用嗣乃祖考事，作嗣土 With which to succeed your grandfather's and father's affairs; be the Supervisor of Land.
67	Guozhong 虢仲	He 何 He *gui* 何簋	

(continued)

Table 1. *Relations between the youzhe and appointees/awardees (continued)*

Youzhe	Appointee/ Inscription	Official Duties of Appointee
69 Royal kinsman X Li 公族㻋釐	Shi You 師酉 Shi You *gui* 師酉簋	嗣乃祖啻官邑人虎臣，西門夷，𡔽夷，秦夷，京夷，畀人夷 Succeed your grandfather officiating in charge of the people of Yi, who are the Tiger Servants, the barbarians of Ximeng, barbarians of Quan, barbarians of Qin, barbarians of Jing, and the Biren barbarians.
70 Royal kinsman X 公族𪉷	Mu 牧 Mu *gui* 牧簋	昔先王既令汝作嗣士，今余唯或㲃改令汝辟百僚 In the past, the previous king already commanded you be the Supervisor of Land; now, I am to change the order and command you to discipline the hundred bureaus.
71 Daoren 道人(?)	Wu Hu 吳虎 Wu Hu *gui* 吳虎簋	□吳盨舊疆 X the previous territory of Wu Xu.

(Inscriptions discovered by December 2006)

but the remaining forty-nine cases still constitute a sizable database to determine whether there was a regularity in the relationship between the *youzhe* and the appointees. In the first group (nos. 1–9), we have eight Superintendents of the Royal Household who served as *youzhe* in nine inscriptions. Among the nine individuals whom they accompanied, six – Wang 望, Cai 蔡, Hai 害, Wu 吳, Song 頌, Shi Li 師𩛥 – were given palace-related duties. In particular, Wang was appointed director of the Royal Household at Bi (as Bi Wangjia 畢王家; Wang *gui*; JC: 4272), and Cai was accompanied by Superintendent Hu 宰曶 in the ceremony and was himself appointed "Superintendent" with the responsibility to handle the outer and inner affairs of the Royal Household (Cai *gui*; JC: 4340).[67] In the remaining three cases, two were simply records of the granting of gifts by the Zhou king, and in the last case, Chu 楚 was assigned a duty that might or might not have been related to palace service.[68] Thus, the situation is clear: in cases that are certain, the Superintendents of the Royal Household accompanied officials who were exclusively appointed to work in the Royal Household.

[67] In the other four inscriptions, Hai 害 was commanded to supervise "barbarian servants" and "small archers" (Hai *gui*; JC: 4259); Wu 吳 was commanded to be in charge of the "white flag" and a kind of silk (Wu *fangyi*; JC: 9898) (in this case, we actually know that Wu was Interior Scribe and Book Maker and was a member of the Royal Household administration, discussed in Chapter 2); Song 頌 was commanded to be in charge of the royal warehouse, using palace attendants (Song *ding*; JC: 2829); and Shi Li 師𩛥 was to be in charge of the royal musicians, a post that was held by his family for generations (Shi Li *gui* 簋; JC: 4324). On the dates of these bronzes, all from the middle–late Western Zhou period, please consult Appendix II.

[68] The two cases of awards are Xing 癲 and Yuan 寰. Chu 楚 was commissioned to be in charge of the official boats inside the area of the capital Pang (Chu *gui* 楚簋; JC: 4246).

The relationship between the royal officials and the Superintendents was overwhelmingly constant and self-contained. In these cases, the *youzhe* was actually the future supervisor of the officials appointed to the Royal Household administration.

We have eleven officials whose titles were Supervisor of Land, Supervisor of Multitudes, or Supervisor of Construction (nos. 10–27), all civil administrators from the central government whom served as *youzhe* in the appointment ritual. Among the eighteen individuals whom they had accompanied, nine of them, Nanji 南季, Shi Ying 師穎, Lai 逨, Yin 殷, Yang 楊, Ci 此, Shan 山, Tong 同, and Shi Xun 師詢 (nos. 10–16, 18, 19), were appointed civil administrators. They were either commanded with civil responsibilities in particular locations in the rural areas or were put in charge of certain groups of the civil population in or around the major cities.[69] There are cases in which a Supervisor of Construction such as Yang 楊 was accompanied by a Supervisor of Multitudes such as Shanbo 單伯, or a Supervisor of Land such as Shi Ying 師穎 was accompanied by a Supervisor of Construction such as Yebo 淲伯. But overall, the above officials formed an interesting professional group of civil administrators whose jobs were evidently different from the first group – the Royal Household officials. They were accompanied in the appointment ceremonies by officials whose governmental roles were also civil administrative in nature. The remaining eight cases in this category involve mostly Rongbo, who was an eminent official in the mid-Western Zhou court (see below).

After the civil administrators, there are six *youzhe* of military character, most notably Mugong 穆公 and Wugong 武公 (see table 1, nos. 28–47). Duke Mu was an eminent military leader in the reign of King Mu, and he accompanied Li 盠, who was commanded to supervise the civil administrative matters in the Six Armies and was particularly responsible for "the king's legions" (Li *fangzun*, JC: 6013). Duke Wu's central role in the military defense against foreign invasions in the late Western Zhou is seen in a number of inscriptions. He accompanied Wu 敔, who was rewarded for his military contribution in pursuit of the southern Huaiyi (Wu *gui*; JC: 4323), and Nangong Liu 南宮柳, who was commanded to be in charge of the pastoral land, orchards, and marshes that belonged to the Six Armies (Nangong Liu *ding*; JC: 2805). Another important military authority was Supervisor of Horses Jingbo 井伯, who accompanied nine officials (see

---

69 Nanji 南季 (accompanied by Bo Sufu) was commanded to assist the latter with lawsuits (Nanji *ding*, JC: 2781); Shi Ying 師穎 was appointed Supervisor of Land (Shi Ying *gui*, JC: 4312); Lai 逨 was to take charge of the marshes and forest in the four directions (Forty-second Year Lai *ding*, *Wenwu* 2003.6, 6); Yin 殷 was to govern the five towns in the eastern district (Yin *gui*, JL: 487–88); Yang 楊 was commissioned as governor of the land of Liang 量 with authority over farming, residential housing, foraging, lawsuits, and construction (Yang *gui*, JC: 4294); Ci 此 was to supervise the people of Yi who were "food providers" (Ci *ding*, JC: 2821); Provisioner Shan 善夫山 was to supervise the "drink contributors" in Ke 宽, with the purpose of replenishing the stores of *xiansi* 憲司 (Shanfu Shan *ding*, JC: 2825); Tong 同 was to assist Wu Taibo 吳太伯 and to be in charge of forest and marshes (Tong *gui*, JC: 4271); and Shi Xun 師詢 was to govern some ethnic groups in the Zhou capital areas (Shi Xun *gui*, JC: 4342).

table 1, nos. 37–45); four of them – Shi Yun 師瘨, Yang 養, Dou Bi 豆閉, and Shi Hu 師虎 – were appointed to military posts.[70] Two more individuals – Shi Kuifu 師奎父 and Shi Maofu 師毛父 – accompanied by Supervisor of Horses Jingbo are known from other inscriptions to have played military roles.[71] Another military figure, Beizhong 備仲, accompanied Lü Fuyu 呂服余, who in this case was appointed to serve as the assistant to Beizhong in the Six Armies (Lü Fuyu *pan*; JC: 10169).

Based on table 1, there are ten cases (20.4 percent of all forty-nine cases) involving only six *youzhe* whose government roles appear to be inconsistent with the duties of the appointees they accompanied. But considering factors that may alter the regular pattern of conduct of the government, some of these irregular cases can be well explained by the special status of the *youzhe* or appointees involved.[72] Despite the existence of these irregular cases, we do have a much larger margin suggesting that there is a general pattern in the team-up of the *youzhe* with the appointees: the Western Zhou officials were usually accompanied by people from the same administrative sectors of the central government. This is particularly so in cases involving the Superintendent, who exclusively accompanied officials who were appointed by the Zhou king to work in the Royal Household. Furthermore, in most cases the *youzhe* were superior in status to the appointees. The superior–subordinate relation is most explicitly expressed in the Nanji *ding* and the Lü Fuyu *pan*,

---

[70] Shi Yun 師瘨 was commanded to supervise the military men in Yi (Shi Yun *gui*; JC: 4283); Yang 養 was commanded to be in charge of the protection of dikes in the Five Cities (Yang *gui*; JC: 4243); Dou Bi 豆閉 was appointed Supervisor of Horses under the *bangjun* 邦君 of Youyu 夋 (Dou Bi *gui*; JC: 4276); Shi Hu 師虎 was commanded to be in charge of the "fine horses" in the two military camps (Shi Hu *gui*; JC: 4316).

[71] Shi Kuifu 師奎父 was a service Marshal (Yong *yu* 永盂; JC: 10322) and Shi Maofu 師毛父 may be identified with Maofu Ban 毛父班 (Ban *gui* 班簋; JC: 4341), who led troops to attack the eastern states. Jingbo also accompanied Superintendent Li 利 (Li *ding* 利鼎; JC: 2804) and Scribe Quecao 趞曹 (Seventh Year Quecao *ding*; JC: 2783), making two occasions when the appointment was not to a military post.

[72] These ten cases are nos. 17, 20, 21, 25, 27, 28, 29, 30, 32, and 45. Supervisor of Horses Gong 共 accompanied three civil administrators (Shi Yu, Shi Chen, Jian; nos. 28, 29, 30); and Supervisor of Horses Shou 壽 accompanied Lai, who was appointed administrator of the people of Li (no. 32); and Supervisor of Multitudes Nanzhong 南仲 accompanied Wuhui 無惠, who was appointed leader of the royal body guards – the "tiger servants" (no. 25). And other five irregular cases involve Jingbo or Rongbo, who were eminent officials in the mid-Western Zhou court and might have played provisional roles across departments at the top level of the bureaucracy. For instance, Jingbo was in charge of the Zhou military, but he accompanied Quecao, who was a Scribe (no. 45). Rongbo is known from the Zai Shou *gui* as the Supervisor of Land at the central court, but he apparently also had major influence over the Royal Household, and he accompanied Kang (no. 20) and Shi Li (no. 21) as officials to work in the Royal Household. When the top officials were themselves appointed, it is even more conceivable that they would be accompanied by officials of comparable or higher status, but such officials would sometimes have to come from a different department. For instance, Supervisor of Construction X accompanied Jingbo in his initial appointment as the Grand Supervisor of Horses (no. 27); Rongbo accompanied Zai Shou, who was appointed Superintendent as the head of Royal Household administration (no. 17). Two other factors could also have contributed irregular cases: (1) the regular working pattern of the government could be interrupted in a national crisis such as enemy invasions or fierce political struggle in the court; (2) an official could have served as *youzhe* in different periods of his career, which could change significantly over time, as I have demonstrated before. See Li Feng, "Succession and Promotion," 1–35.

where the appointees were commanded to work under the officials who actually accompanied them in their appointment ceremonies. Needless to say, the Superintendents were superior to all officials whom they accompanied to work in the Royal Household.

In addition to the above statistics, which suggest possible separations of the administrative process into "professional groups," we do have information on how such groups were actually formed and worked during the middle and late Western Zhou. In this regard, a personal network centered on a military official named Hu 虎 (Hu *gui* 虎簋; JL: 491) will best reveal the operation of the military personnel (figure 14). Hu can be safely identified with Shi Hu 師虎, who was accompanied by Jingbo in the Shi Hu *gui* 師虎簋 already mentioned above.[73] In the Hu *gui* that was cast some twenty years earlier he was also given a military post as an assistant to a military commander, Shi Xi 師戲, who was in charge of the Masters of Horses and Charioteers. The mention of Shi Xi is above all significant, for Dou Bi 豆閉, accompanied by the same Jingbo who also accompanied Shi Hu in the Shi Hu *gui*, was appointed Supervisor of Horses at Youyu in the Shi Xi Taishi 師戲太室, a building structure that was clearly under Shi Xi's administrative jurisdiction. Moreover, in the Hu *gui*, Hu was accompanied by Mishu 密叔; the same Mishu also accompanied Qi 趞 in the Qi *gui* 趞簋 (JC: 4266). According to the latter inscription, Qi was commanded to be a Supervisor of Horses in the Bin 斌 military garrison.

This is a chain of personal relations that can be reconstructed based on information available in the bronze inscriptions regarding military personnel. The network can be traced even further through the link of Jingbo, who also accompanied other officials who had served military functions at approximately the same time. It suggests that in the Zhou government, from the mid-Western Zhou on, officials with similar administrative responsibilities had a much better chance to come across each other by either the link of their common *youzhe* or their association with common offices than by crossing administrative divisions. Such professional groups are marks of a government that divided administrative tasks along professional lines and conducted business on a long-term basis.

Assessment of the working patterns

The above discussion has demonstrated how work relations were constructed in the central government of the Western Zhou. As suggested by the personnel network centered on Hu or Shi Hu, officials with similar

---

[73] Most scholars date the Shi Hu *gui* to the first year of King Yih; see Shaughnessy, *Sources of Western Zhou History*, pp. 257, 284; Ma Chengyuan, *Shang Zhou qingtongqi mingwen xuan*, 3, p. 168; *Xia Shang Zhou duandai gongcheng*, p. 31. Since the Hu *gui* records the thirtieth year, this would necessarily put the vessel in the reign of King Mu, for no other mid-Western Zhou kings ruled that long. In other words, the Shi Hu *gui* and Hu *gui* represent a personal network formed by officials whose covered time of careers was from late King Mu to King Yih. For more discussion on this point, see Chapter 5, pp. 192–96.

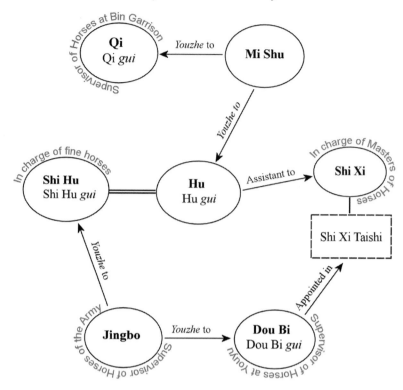

Figure 14. Military personnel surrounding Hu (Shi Hu)

government roles formed "professional groups" through links provided by their common *youzhe* as well as by the common ritual context of appointment ceremonies taking place in particular locations, where they received such appointments. This is certainly not limited to the military personnel: such groups can also be reconstructed among the civil administrative officials. The reason behind the emergence of such professional groups was primarily the separation of administrative processes according to their objectives.

The overall regularities in the grouping of the *youzhe* and appointees indicate that there were definable borders in Zhou administration first between the workings of the Royal Household and those of outer government, and then, to a less definite extent, between civil administration and the military administration. And these borders correspond well with the structural divisions of the Zhou central government that were examined in Chapter 2. In other words, each of the structural divisions seems to have operated relatively independently, and the appointment process, though involving the king, was very much the internal affair of the divisions. This is particularly true with regard to the Royal Household administration: the above analysis has shown that the officials who were accompanied by the Superintendent were almost exclusively commanded to work in the Royal Household. Although it is also true that appointees to the Royal Household could be accompanied by some court magnates such as Rongbo, who also accompanied appointees to other government divisions, there is *never* a case where the Superintendent accompanied someone whose duty was clearly unrelated to works of the Royal Household. This situation corresponds very well with what we have learned about the growth of the Royal Household during the mid-Western Zhou. In short, the evidence shows not only that the Royal Household was an organization that was structurally differentiated from the central government as discussed in Chapter 2, but that its operation was also separated from the central administrative process.

While the civil administrators and military officials constituted largely separate working groups, there was also an overlap between the two sides that contributed to many of the inconsistencies in the arrangement of the *youzhe* for the appointees in table 1. Beside the factors noted above that might have contributed to this overlap, this may also be explained by the sharing of military functions between the two sectors, as the office of Supervisor of Horses existed in both the Ministry and the Six and Eight Armies. In fact, such functional overlaps can be seen even in many modern bureaucratic states. In this regard, it is extremely suggestive that Jingbo 井伯 was called "Supervisor of Horses of the Army" (*shi sima* 師嗣馬), or "Grand Supervisor of Horses" (*zhong sima* 冢嗣马), as known from the most recently discovered Jingbo Lu *gui* 井伯覕簋, differing from the ordinary Supervisor of Horses in the central bureaucracy. It is not impossible that officials like Supervisor of Horses Gong (see table 1, nos. 28–31), or even Supervisor of Horses Shou (see table 1, no. 32), were affiliated with the Ministry and therefore accompanied civil administrators, although we do not have clear confirmation on this point.

However, the workings of the Grand Secretariat (*taishiliao* 太史寮) are insufficiently represented in the appointment inscriptions. As noted in Chapter 2, evidence for the existence of the Grand Secretariat (Fansheng *gui* 番生簋) is only from the second part of the mid-Western Zhou, and by the late Western Zhou it seems to have become a well-established government organ. A very interesting phenomenon in the bronze inscriptions is that, despite the over 100 inscriptions documenting appointments to various offices, there *has never been* a case where an official was appointed to a secretarial position, although there are cases in which people already in such positions were given awards by the Zhou king. Given the relatively large number of appointments we know of and the large number of bronzes cast by the Scribes we have, this does not seem to be accidental. There could be two possibilities: First, the secretarial offices might have been exclusively hereditary, placing them outside the circulation of government offices during the Western Zhou, and therefore, no such official appointment was necessary. Second, such appointments might have been done by the king in a more private manner, and not in the regular government protocol, as such officials were considered by the king as his domestic servants (*zhen zhishi* 朕執事).[74] Whatever the case might be, it seems evident that the secretarial offices were excluded from the institution of regular royal appointment during the middle–late Western Zhou. However, we have evidence that the head of the Royal Household administration, the Superintendent, was officially appointed during the Western Zhou.[75] Three secretarial officials who were already serving in their positions were accompanied by the Superintendent, and two of them were assigned tasks in the Royal Household.[76] This indicates that the duties of these officials were closely associated with the Royal Household administration.

The hierarchy of working order

The appointment inscriptions also suggest a relatively stable working relationship between the superior officials and their subordinates in the Zhou administration, as officials were regularly accompanied in their appointment ceremonies by higher authorities. As will be shown later in Chapter 5, it was quite common that young officials were first appointed as assistants to senior officials and then were promoted to offices of full capacity after some years of service; there are also cases of the young officials being promoted to take up their superiors' offices after the departure of the latter from their posts. This certainly suggests a structure of authority. In order to understand how such a structure worked, we need to investigate the process by which administrative orders were passed down and were executed during Western Zhou. In this regard, a very interesting mid-Western Zhou inscription, the Yong *yu* 永盂 (JC: 10322), gives us a vivid insight into the working hierarchy of the Western Zhou government:

It was the twelfth year, first auspiciousness, *dingmao* day (no. 4), Duke Yi 益公 entered to take orders from the Son of Heaven. The duke thus sent out his command, awarding and giving Shi Yong 師永 his fields on the south and north banks of the Luo River (*yinyang Luo* 陰陽洛), its territory reaching to the fields of Shi Sufu 師俗父. Those together with the duke in sending out the command are: Jingbo 井伯, Rongbo 榮伯, the Chief 尹氏, Shi Sufu 師俗父, Qianzhong 遣仲. The duke thereupon commanded Hanfu 㽙父, Supervisor of Multitudes of Zheng 鄭, Shi 眉, the Supervisor of Construction of the Zhou 周 people, the Minor Scribe

---

[74] This notion clearly appears in the inscription of the Maogong ding 毛公鼎 (JC: 2841).

[75] For instance, the Cai *gui* 蔡簋 (JC: 4340) records the appointment of Superintendent Cai, and the Zai Shou *gui* 宰獸簋 (JL: 490) records the appointment of Superintendent Shou; in the appointment ritual, Shou was accompanied by Rongbo (see table 1, nos. 1, 17).

[76] These are Scribe Song (Song *ding* 頌鼎; JC: 2829), Xing (Thirteenth Year Xing *hu* 十三年癲壺; JC: 9723), and Document Maker Wu (Wu *fangyi* 吳方彝; JC: 9898) (see table 1, nos. 5, 6, 7).

敔史, Marshal Kuifu 奎父 from Yi 邑, and (Marshal) Shi Tong 師同 from Bi 畢, to hand over to Yong his fields. The person who led to demarcate its territory was Song Ju 宋句. Yong bowed with his head touching the ground, in response extolling the beneficial command of the Son of Heaven. Yong takes it to make [for] my cultured deceased father Yi Bo 乙伯 [this] sacrificial *yu*. May Yong for ten thousand years grandsons' grandsons and sons' sons eternally follow in treasuring and using [it].[77]

Although this is not a very long inscription, taking out the reference to Yong, it would appear to be a pure description of the Western Zhou bureaucracy. And indeed, the composer of the inscription took great caution to list officials at each level of the bureaucratic ladder along which the royal order was carried down (Figure 15). While the highest authority was the Zhou king, the initiator of the royal command, it was Duke Yi, representing the next level of authority, who first entered the king's inner quarters and received the order. When the duke came out from the king's chamber, he was joined by the "committee" of five high officials at the court, including Jingbo 井伯, Rongbo 榮伯, the Chief 尹氏, Shi Sufu 師俗父, and Qianzhong 遣仲, each probably representing an important aspect of Zhou administration,[78] to promulgate the royal command. Whether the role of these officials in the process was ceremonial, or they constituted a solitary level of authority below Duke Yi, who was certainly higher than them in status, their participation in the process certainly made the order less personal and more institutional, hence enforcing its bureaucratic character. The order was then given to a group of executive officers at the next level, including the Supervisor of Multitudes, Supervisor of Construction,[79] and the Minor Scribe, who was probably a subordinate of the Chief Interior Scribe. These officials with practical roles, together with two local Marshals, thus took the order to the field and performed the actual transfer of land to Yong. However, the actual marking of the boundaries was done through the office of Song Ju, most likely

---

[77] Since the inscription mentions multiple names that co-appear in King Gong-period inscriptions such as the Fifth Year Qiu Wei *ding* 五年裘衛鼎 (JC: 2832), it must have been cast during or not far off the reign of King Gong. In fact, most authorities date it to the twelfth year of King Gong; see Tang Lan, *Tang Lan xiansheng*, pp. 171, 175; Ma Chengyuan, *Shang Zhou qingtongqi mingwen xuan*, 3, p. 141–42; Shaughnessy, *Sources of Western Zhou History*, pp. 109, 258. Only Shirakawa Shizuka dates it to the reign of King Yi based the incompatibility of the date recorded in the Yong *yu* with the calendar of King Gong established on the basis of other inscriptions, but clearly some of the inscriptions that Shirakawa used to reconstruct the calendar of King Gong are misdated by him. See Shirakawa Shizuka, "Kinbun tsūshaku," 48.*ho*3:197–98. Therefore, it is safe to say that the Yong *yu* reflects the situation in the Zhou government during the early phase of the mid-Western Zhou.

[78] As already noted above, Jingbo was a high official of the Zhou military, Rongbo had authority over the royal property, the "Chief Interior Scribe" (*yinshi*), who was never mentioned by his name in the inscriptions, was the head of interior secretarial staff, and Shi Sufu was the head of local administration, as known from the Shi Chen *ding* 師晨鼎 (JC: 2817).

[79] It should be noted that, in this case, the Supervisor of Multitudes and Supervisor of Construction are not officials at the central court, but were called in from the major cities Zhou and Zheng.

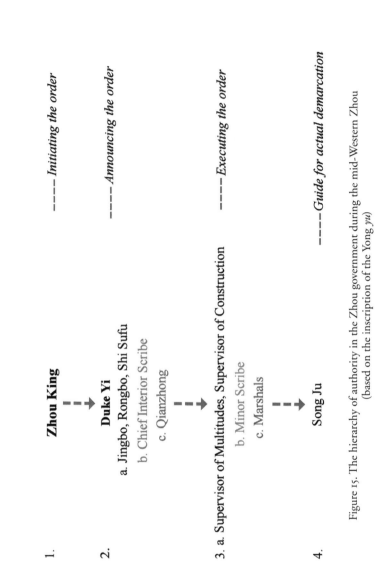

Figure 15. The hierarchy of authority in the Zhou government during the mid-Western Zhou (based on the inscription of the Yong *yu*)

a local official in the area of the land in the Luo River valley, representing the bottom level of Zhou administration.

Through the inscription, we can discern at least four and probably five levels of authority, and the royal order was carried step by step down from the top of the Zhou central government to the bottom of the Zhou administrative ladder. Moreover, we find an interesting correspondence in the composition of personnel that acted at the second and third levels in the relations of 2.*a*–3.*a*, 2.*b*–3.*b*, 2.*c*–3.*c*. (*a* represents civil administrative officials, *b* secretarial officials, *c* persons in military roles or responsible for local security).[80] This suggests quite evidently that the Zhou had a good understanding about what social spheres an incident like land transaction would involve, and what government functions at each level of administration needed to be mobilized to fulfill the task. As such, the Zhou officials appeared as a well-organized workforce with officials at each level performing only the task appropriate to their own level as expected by their corresponding higher authority. The case of the Yong *yu* indicates clearly strongly that a hierarchy of authority was fully developed in the administrative process of the Zhou government. Such a hierarchy could work only when the officials at different levels of the Zhou administration were fully aware of the authority and limit of their own institutional roles as well as the direction of administrative orders. The inscription of the Yong *yu* certainly offers us a vivid idea of how things were actually worked out in the Zhou government.

This situation was certainly not limited to matters of civil administration, but was pertinent also to military matters, as best illustrated by the inscription of the Duoyou *ding* 多友鼎 (JC: 2835):[81]

It was in the tenth month, because the Xianyun 玁狁 greatly arose and broadly attacked Jingshi 京師, [it] was reported to the king. The king commanded Duke Wu 武公: "Dispatch your most capable men and pursue at Jingshi!" Duke Wu commanded Duoyou 多友: "Lead the ducal chariots and pursue at Jingshi!" . . . Duoyou contributed the captured, the heads, and the prisoners to the duke, and Duke Wu then contributed [them] to the king. [The king] therefore addressed Duke Wu and said: "You have pacified Jingshi; [I] enrich you and award you lands." . . . The duke personally

---

[80] The official roles of most individuals mentioned in the inscription are self-evident or have been fully discussed before. The Meng *gui* 孟簋 (JC: 4162) documents Qianzhong's 遣仲 role as a military commander on campaign in the east, alongside the Duke of Mao. At the time when the Yong *yu* was cast, Qianzhong was the head of security forces at the central court.

[81] This important inscription has been dated either to King Li or to King Xuan. For the first view, see Li Xueqin, *Xinchu qingtongqi yanjiu*, pp. 126–33; Ma Chengyuan, *Shang Zhou qingtongqi mingwen xuan*, 3, pp. 283–85; for the second view, see Liu Yu, "Duoyou ding de shidai yu diming kaoding," *Kaogu* 1983.2, 152–57; Edward Shaughnessy, "The Date of the 'Duo You *Ding*' and Its Significance," *Early China* 9–10 (1983–85), 55–69. I have analyzed in detail reasons for dating the bronze to the reign of King Li, a time that I think is most appropriate for the Duoyou *ding*. See Li Feng, *Landscape and Power in Early China*, pp. 131–32.

addressed Duoyou and said: "I initially assigned [you the task], and you have done well! [you] have not disobeyed, and have accomplished [the deed and] have taken many captives. You have pacified Jingshi. [I] award you one *gui*-XX, one set of bells made in finest bronzes, and one-hundred-*jun* of the *jiaoyou*-copper."

This is a unique inscription that gives details of a battle between the Zhou and the Xianyun, a northwestern people who frequently invaded Zhou during the late part of the dynasty. But the more important point for us here is that it shows an interesting hierarchy in carrying out the royal order to go to war. The whole operation was a response to an attack by the Xianyun on the frontier settlement Jingshi, located in the upper Jing River valley, not very far from the Zhou capital.[82] The message instantly reached the king, and in this case the decision was a simple one because a counter-attack by the Zhou forces would seem inevitable. Thus, the royal order of campaign was given to Duke Wu. But Duke Wu was not the official commanding troops in the field; instead, he commanded Duoyou to go to the field. Certainly in this case we can imagine that Duoyou must have had his own subordinates fighting under his command. When the war was concluded after a series of battles along the Jing River to the northwest of the Zhou capital, Duoyou contributed his captives to the duke, and the duke in turn contributed them to the king. However, the royal award only reached the duke, who had never been to the battleground but had earned the reputation as one who brought peace to the frontier. While the duke received the royal gift of landed property, Duoyou, the commander who had fought the actual combat, was rewarded by the duke with a ritual jade, a set of bronze bells, and some metal.

The inscription presents a very cautious description of the hierarchy through which the royal order was first passed down, the war spoils were then sent up, and finally the royal awards were passed down. Other inscriptions, such as the Yu *ding* 禹鼎 (JC: 2833) and the Wu *gui* (JC: 4323), suggest that Duke Wu was in a very prominent position at the Zhou court probably during the reign of King Li,[83] presenting a crucial layer of authority that separated the Zhou king, the highest authority of the Zhou state, and his many military commanders, who could not easily contact each other. Certainly, this role resembles closely that which

---

[82] On the geography of the Zhou–Xianyun war, see Li Feng, *Landscape and Power in Early China*, pp. 160–65.

[83] In the Yu *ding*, he was the central figure at the Zhou court who organized the military operation confronting the rebellion of Ehou the Border Protector 鄂侯馭方 that almost pushed the Western Zhou dynasty to the edge of collapse. In the Wu *gui*, after a successful campaign against the invading Southern Huaiyi, Duke Wu guided the field commander Wu to enter the Grand Temple in the eastern capital Chengzhou and reported the victory to the Zhou ancestors, witnessed by the Zhou king. For a clear reading of these two inscriptions, see Ma Chengyuan, *Shang Zhou qingtongqi mingwen xuan*, 3, pp. 282–87. See also Shirakawa Shizuka, "Kinbun tsūshaku," 27.162: 442–63, 27.164: 469–76.

was played by Duke Yi in Zhou civil administration in the time of King Gong and King Yih. It is very likely that, as in the civil administration, military tasks were also conducted in a stratified way through a well-developed hierarchy of authority. It was probably even more crucial for the Zhou military than for the civil government to develop a clearly de-fined hierarchy of orders to meet the urgent requirements of defending the Zhou state and because of the need to operate over a much broader geographical area.

THE KING'S ROLE IN ZHOU ADMINISTRATION

One question concerning the operation of the Zhou government is the role the Zhou king played and the way in which he entered a relation-ship with his government. The question has important implications for understanding the source of authority in the Zhou government and the way in which the royal authority was carried through in a bureaucratic governmental structure. Weber used to be thought as having come closest to a "definition" of bureaucracy when he said that bureaucracy was a "body of appointed officials." Thereafter, political scientists regarded the "rule by officials" as one of the most defining characteristics of bureaucracy.[84] If the Western Zhou government was indeed a bureaucracy, as the evidence analyzed so far indicates, that promoted rules and regulations through the workings of the officials, then to what extent was it still possible for the Zhou king to impose on them his personal will? In what cases, or under what circumstances, could or did he actually do so? Could the Western Zhou bureaucracy be run without the interference of the Zhou king? In order to answer these questions, we need to examine systematically the Zhou king's administrative conduct.

The administrative role of the Zhou king

It should be confirmed first that the Zhou king did have an active role in the administrative process of the Zhou government; that is, he participated personally in the management of the Zhou government. This can be seen in the simple fact that, no matter who the *youzhe* was, the appointment ceremonies were almost exclusively hosted by the king, and the official appointments were essentially perceived as a beneficence or favor that the candidates received from the Zhou king. In the entire corpus of Western Zhou inscriptions, we have only two exceptions, the Mao *gui* 卯簋 (JC: 4327) and the Shi Hui *gui* 師毀簋 (JC: 4311), where the appointments were hosted by the ministers, and in the latter case, the host was probably

---

[84] For instance, see Albrow, *Bureaucracy*, pp. 91–92.

acting in the king's capacity.[85] Therefore, in the middle-late Western Zhou context, almost all government appointments (except a few) recorded in the inscriptions were conceived of as originating from the Zhou king and were hence extolled as royal favors by their recipients. This fact suggests that at least in theory the Zhou king, as the ruler who stood outside and above the Zhou bureaucracy, enjoyed dictatorial power over the administrative personnel. However, what he was expected to do according to his institutional role might be different from what he could actually do, and the success of a Zhou king, as is true for all rulers, had to be conditioned by his personal quality as well as the political circumstances.

The appointment ceremony most regularly took place in the various royal temples such as Kang Gong and Zhao Gong; however, there were other building compounds which the Zhou king frequently visited and in which he hosted appointment ceremonies, and many of these building compounds, as clarified earlier, were actually under the administrative jurisdiction of the individual officials. Since these "offices" were spatially separate from the royal temples and palaces that were the primary base of the king, and indeed many of these official compounds were located in different cities, here we have the unique situation that the Zhou king was actually traveling between the cities and making regular visits to the various "offices." Thus, unlike the later Chinese emperors, who gave orders from deep inside the palace, the Zhou king frequently left his own space and hosted appointment ceremonies in buildings in different locations and controlled by the various officials. In such cases, the appointment process could have been done simply through the delivery by the royal secretaries of an "appointment letter," which was evidently used in the Zhou government, but the Zhou king clearly preferred personal visits and presiding himself over the formally conducted ceremonies. What makes this more peculiar is the fact that, as discussed above, some of the building compounds might have also accommodated the private lives of their entitled officials. The evidence suggests that, rather than presenting himself as the ultimate authority above the government, the Zhou king actively engaged in the administrative process of the Zhou government, "making" decisions, whether in an actual or ceremonial way, over the many administrative details that were brought before him. He actually presented himself as an active manager of the Zhou government.

Furthermore, the Zhou king's involvement can be explained by the partly religious claim that might have underlain some of the appointment

---

[85] In the Mao *gui* 卯簋 (JC: 4327), the appointment ceremony was hosted by Rongbo. Mao, whose father and grandfather had all served the Rong 榮 family, was accompanied by Rongji 榮季, clearly one of Rongbo's kinsmen, and was commanded to supervise the Pang Palace 莽宮 and the Pang people 莽人. In the Shi Hui *gui* 師毀簋 (JC: 4311), Shi Hui was commanded by Shi Hefu 師和父 to supervise the servants of Shi Hefu's family. Shi Hefu is identified with Gongbo He 共伯和, who ruled in King Li's stead after the king went into exile in 842 BC. For the status of Shi Hefu, see Shaughnessy, *Sources of Western Zhou History*, p. 272.

ceremony. This is more likely in many appointment ceremonies that took place in the royal temples and possibly followed a religious session in which the Zhou king made sacrificial offerings to the former kings. There were also appointment ceremonies that took place in the Grand Temple (*taimiao* 太廟), where the pre-dynastic Zhou ancestors were worshipped. The religious context of such ceremonies and the role the Zhou king played in them can be inferred from an excerpt found in the "Jitong" 祭統 chapter of the *Liji* 禮記 (Records of Rite):

When the ancient brilliant ruler ranked those who had virtue and rewarded those who had merit, he necessarily granted the rank and award in the grand temple, so that he could demonstrate that he did not intend to monopolize (*bugan zhuan* 不敢專) [the process]. Therefore, on the day of sacrifice, once the offerings are made, the ruler descends and stands to the south of the stairways, facing south. The appointee faces north. The scribe holds the written document and commands [him] from the right of the ruler. [The appointee] twice bows with his head touching the ground, receiving the document, with which he returns home, and worships it at his own family temple. This is how the rank and award were granted.[86]

The above paragraph, though probably a late Warring States account that purports to speak retrospectively about the "ancient brilliant ruler," is remarkable for its close parallels with the description of the appointment ceremony in the Western Zhou bronze inscriptions.[87] It is above all significant that the paragraph suggests a direct link between the administrative ritual of appointment and the religious-ritual offerings the Zhou king made to his ancestors. According to this account, the ceremony appears to have been performed immediately following the presentation of offerings in the Grand Temple. The implication of this is probably that, by conducting the appointment session in front of the spirits of the ancestors, the appointment itself gained legitimacy and was literally sanctioned by the royal ancestors, who, as will be discussed in Chapter 7, were the true bearers of sovereignty of the Western Zhou state.[88] But the message needed to be presented to the appointee by the reigning king, who, as agent of the Zhou ancestors, ruled with the sovereign power delegated to him by the ancestors. Thus, the appointment ceremony was as much an administrative process as a political process through which a new political relation between the Zhou king and the appointees was constructed.

---

[86] *Liji*, 49, p. 1605.

[87] For instance, the directions the king and the appointees faced and the role played by the Scribe who took the written document in his hand and read it to the appointees coincide well with the inscriptions. More significantly, it describes that the appointee, after bowing to the king, received the document and brought it home, a scenario that is clearly seen in the inscription of the Song *ding* translated above. However, the important role of the *youzhe* is not mentioned in this paragraph.

[88] On this point, see also, Li Feng, "'Feudalism' and Western Zhou China," 117–20.

Regularities in the Zhou king's administrative conduct

However, the appointment procedure was itself more bureaucratic than religious, although it might have been conducted in a religious environment
and the king might have been supported by a religious claim for legitimacy
to carry out the ritual. It was rather a bureaucratic process and a routine
designed and conducted to fulfill its own secular and always specifically defined administrative goals. The fact that a particular appointment was held
on a certain day and in a certain place (even an ancestral temple) was not
generated from the need of worship but arose from the actual working situation of Zhou administration. Even in cases where religious offices were
filled by the appointments, such as in the Shen *gui* 申簋 (JC: 4267), the
appointment ritual itself must be understood as an administrative, but not
religious, program. In such appointment rituals, the Zhou king as the representative of the royal ancestors in this world played the role of a secular
administrator or manager of the political Zhou state. As such, it is quite
impressive to see that the Zhou king was actually dealing with, at least in
a ceremonial way, all kinds of details of administration through his unique
role in the appointment procedure.

The question is: as an administrator, on what regular basis did the Zhou
king enter into contact with his officials? Or did the king's administrative
conduct manifest any routine? I have shown previously that there was a
high concentration of the king's visits to the various building compounds
at the beginning and end of the year, paralleled by an overwhelming preference for the first quarter of the month.[89] This study identified the overall
trend in the Zhou king's administrative conduct and the time preference
of his activity. In addition to this overall trend, the inscriptions also show
us a high regularity in the Zhou king's visits to particular building compounds. This is indicated by three groups of inscriptions, each recording
the royal visits to a single building compound that was under the authority
of an individual official (see table 2). For instance, the king appeared in the
Shi Lu Gong over four consecutive years, hosting five events, exclusively
in the second or third month, and four times during the first quarter of
the month. In the Shi Sima Gong, the two royal visits both took place
during the second month and in the first quarter. In the X Chen Gong
燹辰宮, the two royal visits were three years apart in the twelfth and fifteenth years, but both happened in the third month, and even the day
number is the same for both visits. Thus, we have an example of the king
arriving at the same building three years apart to award the same official
in the same month and on exactly the same day number. All this cannot
be accidental.

---

[89] It has been shown there that 48 percent of the king's seventy-five visits to the various *gong* or *miao*
buildings took place in the first through third months of the year, and 55.8 percent of the total of
eighty-six royal visits occurred in the first quarter of the month. See Li Feng, "'Offices' in Bronze
Inscriptions," pp. 45–46.

Certainly, the Zhou king's visits to the royal temples show a much wider time-range. However, the above are the only cases of royal visits to the same building compounds under the authority of the individual officials. The message they deliver is too consistent and overwhelmingly clear to be dismissed as mere coincidence. They suggest that, as some of these buildings might have been located far away from the king's palace, there must have been some administrative rules, or perhaps a certain timetable, available for the Zhou king to consult in making these consistent visits.

Factors behind the royal "decision"

Finally, we need to ask: Since the Zhou king "made" all but two appointments as suggested by the inscriptions, on what basis did he make such decisions? In order to answer this question, we need to look at the content of the appointments. In table 1, we have such cases as nos. 1, 14, 30, and 61, where the Zhou king did not actually make concurrent appointments, but merely reiterated the appointments made by the former kings or previously by himself, indicating the ceremonial nature of the *ad hoc* appointment procedure.[90] While the majority of the appointments were administrative orders issued to effect the actual conduct of the government, there is an undeniable aspect of the appointment ritual that was symbolic and performed to reassert the existing working order. By the same token, it also suggests that the role of the Zhou king in administration could be more ceremonial than actually effective in at least some cases, calling to mind the expression "formality," a term we often use for some *de facto* ineffective bureaucratic procedures of our time.

Furthermore, when we look at the numerous new appointments and alterations of previous appointments, there must also be some doubt about the degree to which these new appointments reflected the royal will. It is commonly held by political scientists that the more developed the bureaucratic rules are, the less possible it would be for an outside power to impose its will on the bureaucracy; bureaucracy normally tends to develop a kind of power to protect itself from outside interference. In the Western Zhou case, although the Zhou king was the nominal initiator of almost all official appointments, the bare fact is that, given the large number of appointments he made, it was probably impossible for the Zhou king to know personally everyone that he put in office. There was a high possibility that the bureaucracy exercised its influence in the decision-making process prior to the appointments; indeed, the relatively stable relationship

---

[90] According to a previous study conducted by Chen Hanping, the appointment inscriptions can be classified into roughly six categories: (1) initial appointment; (2) succession of appointment granted to older generations; (3) confirmation of an appointment by the former king; (4) increasing duties on initial appointment; (5) revision of initial appointment; (6) posthumous appointment. Unfortunately, Chen's classification was not done on a statistical basis. See Chen Hanping, *Xi Zhou ceming*, pp. 29–31.

Table 2. *Regularity of the Zhou king's visits to building compounds under official authority*

	Inscription	Year	Lunar Phase	Month	Day
Shi Lu Gong 師彔宮					
	Shi Yu *gui* 師艅簋	3	A	3	*jiaxu*
	Shi Chen *ding* 師晨鼎	3	A	3	*jiaxu*
	Xing *xu* 興盨	4	B	2	*wuxu*
	Jian *gui* 諫簋	5	A	3	*gengyin*
	Zai Shou *gui* 宰兽簋	6	A	2	*jiaxu*
Shi Sima Gong 師司馬宮					
	Shi Yun *gui* 師癭簋	?	A	2	*wuyin*
	Yang *gui* 養簋	?	A	2	?
X Chen Gong 𤔲夋宮					
	Da *gui* 大簋	12	B	3	*dinghai*
	Da *ding* 大鼎	15	B or D	3	*dinghai*

between the *youzhe* and the appointees in the appointment process as discussed above is itself a good indication of such "bureaucratic autonomy." This point is also supported by the fact that the written documents used in the appointment ceremonies were pre-prepared but were not drafted during the session as the result of immediate decisions. It is not likely that the decision over appointments could have been made without previous consultation of the superior officials in the respective government units before the Zhou king actually met the appointees.

However, this aspect of the royal appointment has been overshadowed by the overwhelming appraisal that was directed to the Zhou king in the appointment inscriptions. Nevertheless, in one inscription, the Zha *zhong* 柞鐘 (JC: 134), we actually learn that this was, at least sometimes, probably the case:[91]

It was the king's third year, fourth month, first auspiciousness, *jiayin* (# 51). Zhong Taishi 仲太師 accompanied Zha 柞 to his right, and Zha was awarded purple [kneepads], a red demi-circlet, and jingle-bells, [and was commanded] to be in charge of the affairs of peasants in the five cities. Zha

[91] The Zha *zhong* 柞鐘 (JC: 134), seven in total, were found at Qijiacun 齊家村 in 1960. Guo Moruo, who wrote the brief introduction to the original report, dated them to the period of King Yi or King Li; the same view was also held by Chen Gongruo. See *Fufeng Qijiacun qingtongi qun*, p. 4–5; Chen Gongruo, "Ji Jifu hu Zha zhong jiqi tongchu de tongqi," *Kaogu* 1962.2, 88–101. However, other scholars date them to the third year of King You (779 BC), based on the calendrical information in the inscription. See Ma Chengyuan, *Shang Zhou qingtongqi mingwen xuan*, p. 323; Shaughnessy, *Sources of Western Zhou History*, p. 285; Shirakawa Shizuka, "Kinbun tsūshaku," 33.198:898–901. Besides this, there does not seem to have been any solid ground to date the bells. But it is safe to say that they were from the late Western Zhou period.

bowed and in response extols the beneficence of Zhong Taishi, herewith making the grand *lin*-chimes. May my son's sons and grandson's grandsons eternally treasure it.

First of all, this is an appointment inscription in which the etiquette of appointment ceremony is mentioned. Since the highest authority recorded here, Zhong Taishi, is only the *youzhe* in the ceremony, and since most Western Zhou appointment inscriptions record the Zhou king as the host of the appointment ceremonies, it is most likely that Zha's appointment was also presided over by the Zhou king. However, in this inscription the appointee Zha does not express his gratitude to the Zhou king, as is typical for all other appointees, but instead extols the beneficence that he received from Zhong Taishi, who was only the *youzhe* in his appointment ritual. Furthermore, the section that typically appears in an appointment inscription describing the king's behavior preceding the appointment ritual was apparently omitted from this inscription, and the Zhou king is not even mentioned in the inscription. In all likelihood, it was Zhong Taishi who was the real initiator of Zha's appointment. If the Zha *zhong* bells were indeed cast in the third year of King You, putting them into historical context, I would suspect that Zhong Taishi was the same as the "August Father" (Huangfu 皇父) who held the position of "Taishi" and was at this point in a political struggle with the king, a struggle that eventually forced Huangfu out of the capital in 777 BC.[92] This identification may serve to explain one of the circumstances under which the royal will could be altered by powerful ministers. But this link cannot be confirmed until the date of the bells can be ascertained.

Given the uneven personal quality of the Zhou kings, especially during the mid-Western Zhou, when a number of weak kings ruled, there must have been opportunities for the powerful court officials to influence royal decisions. This implies that, despite his regular involvement in administrative matters, the actual relation between the king and the government could have been mediated by the influential officials at the Zhou court. And this point is also supported by the existence of a hierarchy of order in the Zhou administration, as indicated by the inscriptions of the Yong *yu* and the Duoyou *ding*. A strong king could control the administrative process of the government through his active but sometimes ceremonial role in the appointment procedure, but a weak or minor king could be manipulated by his powerful officials in the same system.

CONCLUSION

In the present chapter, I have discussed at length the workings of the Western Zhou government as reflected mainly in the middle and late Western

---

[92] For the historical role of the "August Father" and his struggle with King You, see Li Feng, *Landscape and Power in Early China*, pp. 203–15.

Zhou bronze inscriptions. It is first of all significant that some divisions developed in the administration of the Zhou government, corresponding roughly to the structural divides analyzed in Chapter 2. This is most evident in the workings of the Royal Household, which became separate from tasks handled by the Zhou central government; a similar divide was also visible between the civil administration and the management of the Zhou military. It has been shown that there were "professional groups" among the officials who shared similar administrative responsibilities as well as the same personal network. The study also shows that there was a well-defined hierarchy of orders in the carrying out and execution of administrative orders in both civil and military matters. Especially in civil administration, a well-constructed ladder with defined administrative levels is fully evident in the inscription of the Yong *yu*.

Creel once characterized the workings of the Western Zhou government as a "Mad Hatter's Tea Party."[93] Our current evidence shows that this is clearly not true. On the contrary, there were rules and regularities in the administrative conduct of the Zhou government that can now be established on the basis of a much larger database of inscriptions. In particular, the appointment ceremony was itself a very bureaucratic procedure in which the Zhou king and the officials of different status strictly performed their own institutionalized roles. In the appointment ceremonies, those who played the role of *youzhe* were usually superior in status to the candidates, and in some cases actual superior–subordinate relationships can be detected. Clearly, the government was an organized body of appointed officials. Administrative rules and regularities can also be found in the conduct of the Zhou king, whose visits to some building compounds seem to have followed a strict routine. Through his visits to the various buildings, the Zhou king maintained his active role as the head of the government.

The chapter further clarifies that written documents were used and written records were kept extensively both in the central court and beyond in local administrations. And some of the written documents were evidently transferred onto the bronze vessels. This agrees closely with the existence of a large number of secretarial offices analyzed in Chapter 2. In the study of the spatial configuration of the Zhou government, it is suggested that some of the building compounds to which the Zhou king made frequent visits were both government headquarters and private spaces for their entitled officials. However, it has also been shown that some general offices, such as the Ministry, the Grand Secretariat, and the "Contribution Hall," did exist as spaces separate from the officials' private lives. The chapter also defines the spatial dimension of the Zhou administration, which is linked by the bronze inscriptions to the Wei River valley of central Shaanxi and the small area surrounding the eastern capital Chengzhou.

---

[93] See Creel, *The Origins of Statecraft*, p. 420.

CHAPTER 4

Managing the core: local society and local administration in the royal domain

There are certain obstacles to any attempt to provide a basic outline of Zhou local administration. It has been sufficiently clarified in the beginning of Chapter 2 that the Western Zhou state was composed of two large zones: the royally managed west and the regional states in the east. This division was not merely as a geographical divide, but a separation of two systems of administration or two different approaches to royal control. "Local administration" here does not mean the overall administration of the eastern region, which was "local" in some way *vis-à-vis* the Zhou royal domain as the focus of Zhou central power. Rather, it means the ways in which state control was constructed on, and linked to, the locally based communities, whether in the west or east. It is ultimately a manner of state control and management of the population and the natural resources available to it, or the way in which social integration was achieved through an administrative structure. Taking this line of investigation, we found that information on local administration in the eastern states is almost totally lacking until the arrival of the Spring and Autumn period, when the received textual records offer insight into the internal situation of these states. In the royal domain in the west, however, we have many bronze inscriptions from the Western Zhou period that were cast by the local civil administrators or involve local matters, providing us with first-hand information.

The purpose of this chapter is to present a close reading of the currently available inscriptional evidence and to arrive at a coherent understanding of the ways in which the Zhou royal domain, the core of the Western Zhou state, was formed and managed at the local level. There are certain gaps in our information, but for the same reason this study serves to identify these gaps so that we can be aware of new evidence that may be brought to light by future archeological discoveries. I believe, however, that it is possible and indeed important at present to connect those known points to recover the overall framework and dimensions of Zhou local administration and to explore the rationales behind it. To do so, I will first clarify the overall social structure of the Zhou royal domain in the Wei River valley of Shaanxi. Then I will discuss the administration of the cities, which by themselves formed a network on which the royal power rested. Finally,

I will discuss the administration of the rural communities, which were linked to the cities by their political and economic ties.

To offer an account of local administration, we must first make an effort to understand the macro-structural divisions of the Wei River society across which the administrative network was constructed. Here, we need to introduce the concept of "landed property," the way in which the land, on which all social relations were constructed, was owned and managed. In ancient China, as in other ancient agricultural societies, the way in which the land was split and owned determined the way in which the population was organized. Therefore, clarifying the condition of landed property will help us to delineate the boundaries between mutually exclusive social divisions and to understand the dynamics that underlay their relationships. The condition of landed properties further provides the basic environment in which suitable administrative machines were set up, for the simply reason that land was the ultimate source of wealth of the royal Zhou state.

It should be noted that land ownership has been a central debate in modern Chinese historiography, relating necessarily to the much larger question about the periodization of Chinese history according to the Marxist theory of social development.[1] With no intention to replicate the complications

---

[1] The debate had its origin in the "Social History Controversy" in the 1930s and has since generated a massive volume of literature. See Arif Dirlik, *Revolution and History: Origins of Marxist Historiography in China, 1919–1937* (Berkeley: University of California Press, 1978), pp. 95–179. In general, scholars who advocate that the Western Zhou was in the "feudal" stage of social development usually advocate the existence of private land ownership in the form of the "Well-Field" (*jingtian* 井田) described by Mencius (the partition of a square area into one "public" piece surrounded by eight "private" pieces). Scholars who regard the Western Zhou as a "slave-owning" society, on the other hand, often advocate a total state control of land, or, in a modified position, community ownership of land (in their interpretation of the "Well-Field"), which was worked by a forced labor force. For a preliminary reading of the relevant arguments, see Guo Moruo, *Nulizhi shidai* (Beijing: Renmin, 1973), pp. 26–31; Zhao Guangxian, "Cong Qiu Wei zhuqi ming kan Xi Zhou de tudi jiaoyi," *Beijing shifan daxue xuebao* 1979.6, 16–23; Chen Changyuan, "Zhou dai jingtian zhidu jianlun," in *Xian Qin shi lunwenji* (Xi'an: Renwen zazhi, 1982), pp. 141–53; Chen Fudeng and Wang Hui, "Jijian tongqi mingwen zhong fanying de Xi Zhou zhongye de tudi jiaoyi," *Liaohai wenwu xuekan* 1986.2, 77–85; Zhou Ziqiang, "Chonglun Xi Zhou shiqi de gongtian he sitian," *Shilin* 1987.1, 1–10. Although the main concern of the debate is the relationship between the landowner and the farmers and hence the mode of exploitation, it has been argued by some, particularly those who took the second position, that the Zhou king was the sole owner of land during the Western Zhou, and a recent analysis by Li Chaoyan suggests that the *zhuhou* 諸侯 (a term that makes no distinction in Chinese historiography between the regional rulers in the east and the aristocratic families in the royal domain of Shaanxi) only had recipient rights (*lingyou quan* 領有權) over their lands. See, Guo Moruo, *Nulizhi shidai*, pp. 28–29; Han Lianqi, "Xi Zhou de tudi suoyouzhi he boxue xingtai," *Zhonghua wenshi luncong* 1 (1979), 81–102; Li Chaoyuan, *Xi Zhou tudi guanxi lun* (Shanghai: Renmin, 1997), pp. 99–155. However, the majority opinion, which has been strengthened by the discovery of land-sale inscriptions, is that the aristocrats, whether as individuals or lineages or heads of communities, actually owned the land they occupied. See He Ziquan, "Zhou dai tudi zhidu he tade yanbian," *Lishi yanjiu* 1964.3,

here, but cautioned by problems arising from this debate among the Marxist historians, we raise two points that are relevant to the methodological basis for the present consideration of landed properties during the Western Zhou. First, the regional states in the east, as explicated in Chapter 2, constituted a very different context and should be segregated from consideration of land ownership in the royal domain. Second, as far as the royal domain in Shaanxi is concerned, a more complex approach must be adopted to allow for the co-existence of different types of land ownership in the same period and perhaps the same area. With regard to the second point, I believe that in the Western Zhou bronze inscriptions we can actually discern roughly three different types of landed properties and hence three different types of land ownership *per se* – that is to say, three different ways in which the land was owned and managed by the Zhou social elite. This includes the royal properties, the aristocratic lineage estates, and the state-maintained land and estates. The combination of the three types of landed properties formed the entirety of the Zhou royal domain. State control, however, was achieved not through the division but through the integration of the divided social parts into an organic socioeconomic system structured according to a royally directed hierarchy. In this hierarchy, the rural communities were firmly connected to the cities and to the royal capitals.

The royal properties

It has been shown in the preceding chapters that by the mid-Western Zhou the concept of "Royal Household" (*wangjia* 王家) had been firmly established. It was also shown there that in the appointment ceremonies the Superintendent (*zai* 宰), the head of royal administration, constantly accompanied officials who were assigned works in the Royal Household, suggesting that the management of the Royal Household had become an autonomous sphere. What actually constituted the royal property? The royal property was composed of the various palaces and temples located in the major cities as well as gardens and estates scattered in their suburbs; these elements were managed by the officials that the Zhou king called "My Officials" (*zhen zhishi* 朕執事).[2] Sometimes the royal property was

---

145–62; Wang Yuzhe, "Xi Zhou jinwen zhong de zhu he tudi guanxi," *Nankai xuebao* 1983.3, 47–53; Li Xueqin, "Xi Zhou jinwen zhong de tudi zhuanrang," in *Shixue lunwen xuan* (Beijing: Guangming ribao, 1984), pp. 69–74; Zou Junmeng and Du Shaoshun, "Xi Zhou tudi suoyouzhi wenti qianjian," *Huanan shifan daxue xuebao* 1987.3, 53–59; Du Jianmin, "Xi Zhou tudi zhidu xintan," *Shixue yuekan* 1992.2, 15–27.

2 In the Maogong *ding* 毛公鼎 (JC: 2841), King Xuan counts "My Officials" (*zhen zhishi* 朕執事) after the "Three Supervisors" (*sanyousi* 三有嗣), "Young Boys" (*xiaozi* 小子), "Marshals" (*shishi* 師氏), and "Tiger Servants" (*huchen* 虎臣), who were all put under the authority of the Duke of Mao. Clearly "My Officials," as the domestic officials of the Zhou king, constituted an order different from all groups mentioned here that represented the jurisdiction of the Zhou central government. For a reading of this list, see Ma Chengyuan, *Shang Zhou qingtongqi mingwen xuan*, 3, p. 317; Shirakawa Shizuka, "Kinbun tsūshaku," 30.181:680.

prefixed with a place-name such as Bi Wangjia 畢王家, referring particularly to the whole royal possession located in Bi, located probably to the
southeast of the Zhou capital Hao, which is said in the texts to have been
the burial ground for King Wen, King Wu, and the Duke of Zhou.[3] In
this case, the place-name Bi actually served as the branch title of the Royal
Household, and the existence of such branch titles suggests strongly the
multiplicity of the royal possessions scattered over the Wei River plain.

We have no account about the total size of royal property either as
building compounds or as land estates. Although a quantitative estimate
is unrealistic here, a qualitative approach based on the bronze inscriptions
may provide us with a good sense of what kind of facilities might have
actually formed the royal possessions. Let us take as an example the royal
possessions located in the capital Pang 莽, a city frequently mentioned in
the bronze inscriptions, which thus offers us a chance to capture the essential compositional features of the Western Zhou city.[4] There was, first
of all, a royal palace named "Lower Palace," or more precisely the "Wet
Palace" (Shi Gong 濕宮), which, from the semantics of the word, must
have been a royal facility near water in a lowland.[5] Correspondingly, two
other inscriptions mention the "Bi Pond" (Biyong 璧癰 or Bichi 璧池) in
the capital Pang, almost certainly a small lake in the shape of the *bi*-jade
disk with water surrounding the hill at the center.[6] These inscriptions are
important because they offer what was apparently the prototype of a type
of ritual architecture that had long been revered in the Confucian tradition

---

[3] For Bi as the burial-ground of the Zhou founders, the earliest record is found in the "Zuoluo" 作洛
chapter of the *Yizhou shu*; see Zhu Youzeng, *Yi Zhou shu jixun jiaoshi* (Hubei: Chongwen shuju,
1877), 5, p. 7. The location of the Zhou royal cemetery is one of the unsolved mysteries in Western
Zhou archeology, but some archeologists believe that it was located not far to the southeast of the
capital Hao, at an unknown place in present-day Chang'an county 長安縣 that was called Biyuan
畢原 during the Tang dynasty. On this point, see Lu Liancheng, "Xi Zhou Feng Hao liangjing kao,"
paper presented in the conference for the 30th anniversary of the establishment of the Shaanxi Provincial Institute of Archaeology and the Banpo Museum (Xi'an: 1988), pp. 41–48.
[4] New evidence from the Wuhu *ding* 吳虎鼎 (JL: 364) suggests that Pang might have been somewhere to the southeast of the capital Hao and northwest of Bi. The inscription mentions Pang as
the western limit of the land granted to Wuhu, while the southern limit is mentioned as Bi, most
likely in present-day Chang'an. In fact, the bronze was found in Chang'an in 1992. See *Kaogu yu
wenwu* 1998.3, 69–71.
[5] The "Lower Palace" is mentioned in the inscriptions of the Shi Mao *hu* 史懋壺 (JC: 9714) and Bo
Jiang *ding* 伯姜鼎 (JC: 2791) as a building complex where the Zhou king rewarded his domestic
officials and aristocratic ladies. The translation "Lower Palace" is based on the inscription of one of
the stone drums of Qin, the "Fenci," which offers the phrase "Yuanshi yingyang" 邍(原)濕陰陽, in
which *shi* has the opposite meaning of *yuan* 邍 (high plateau). See Guo Moruo, "Shiguwen yanjiu,"
in *Guo Moruo quanji: Kaogu bian 9* (Beijing: Kexue, 1982), p. 66.
[6] See Mai *fangzun* 麥方尊 (JC: 6015) and Bo Tangfu *ding* 伯唐父鼎 (JL: 356). In the ritual institution
transmitted by the Confucian tradition, the Bi Pond is depicted as a circular water system surrounding a multi-story central hall called "Bright Hall" (*mingtang* 明堂), where the king met with regional
rulers and also where noble youths were educated. See *Liji*, 31, p. 1487. In fact, the Han model of
the Bi Pond and Bright Hall reconstructed under Wang Mang (r. AD 9–24), according to the ritual
books, was excavated to the south of the Han capital Chang'an. See illustrations in *Kaogu* 1960.7, 37;
see also Wang Shiren, "Han Chang'an Cheng nanjiao lizhi jianzhu (Datumencun yizhi) yuanzhuang
de tuice," *Kaogu* 1963.9, 506.

as the focal point of the royal or imperial state. In fact, both inscriptions that mention the Bi Pond record occasions when the Zhou king performed an archery ritual with his officials and even regional rulers from the distant east; during the ritual, they shot beasts and birds from the boats. Interestingly, the same pond was probably also a part of a facility named "Learning Hall" (Xue Gong 學宮), where, according to the Jing *gui* 靜簋 (JC: 4273), professional archers like the official Jing 靜 taught noble youth the art of archery.[7] In addition, in the case of the Zhou capital Pang, an inscription also mentions the "Upper Palace" (Shang Gong 上宮), which, in contrast to the "Lower Palace," must have been a building complex located on higher ground in the capital Pang.[8] Although we are far from being able to construct a complete picture of royal possessions in the capital Pang, which has not been discovered by archeologists, the currently available inscriptions do provide us with a good sense of the complexity of royal activities that the royal properties might have accommodated.

As for the renowned Zhou capitals Feng and Hao, although frequently mentioned in the inscriptions, no particular building structures are recorded except for the Taimiao 太廟 "Grand Temple" in Hao, which was the political center of the Western Zhou state. The Western Zhou inscriptions also mention ancestral temples for individual Zhou kings, including Kang Gong 康宮, Zhao Gong 昭宮, Mu Gong 穆宮, and Yi Gong 夷宮; these royal temples were all located in a place called Zhou 周 in present-day Zhouyuan 周原. In the same location, two inscriptions mention Ban Gong 般宮, probably a residential palace of King Mu.[9] And the bone inscriptions from a building foundation in Fengchu 鳳雛 identify the site with royal activity (see below for details of the composition of the city of Zhou). Some other royal facilities probably also existed in a place called An 斥, located by some scholars in present-day Meixian, where the Zhou king performed the ritual of "Catching Foals" (*zhiju* 執駒);[10] in the same area, a bronze *ding* cast by the Zhou king was found, indicating the location of royal occupation in the region.[11]

Some inscriptions also tell us about the internal organization of the royal palace. For instance, the Yi *gui* 伊簋 (JC: 4287) lists the population belonging to Kang Gong, the temple of King Kang, including the "King's

---

[7] In the Han reconstruction, the "Learning Hall" was built on a much larger scale as the "Imperial University" (*Taixue* 太學), located to the west of the Bi Pond. See Huang Zhanyue, "Han Chang'an cheng nanjiao lizhi jiànzhu de weizhi jiqi youguan wenti," *Kaogu* 1960.9, 56.

[8] The "Upper Palace" is mentioned in the Zhen *yi* 朕匜 (JC: 10285).

[9] Ban Gong is mentioned in the Li *ding* 利鼎 (JC: 2804) and the Seventh Year Quecao *ding* 七年趞曹鼎 (JC: 2783), both from the mid-Western Zhou period. Indeed, Li appears in the *Current Bamboo Annals* as an official at King Mu's court. See *Zhushu jinian*, 2, p. 9 (Legge, *The Shoo King*, p. 150).

[10] This is mentioned in the inscription of the Li *juzun* 盠駒尊 (JC: 6011), which was cast on a bronze horse of 23.4 cm, excavated in Lijiacun in Meixian in 1955; see *Qingtongqi tushi*, pp. 54–55. On the location of An, see Lu Liancheng, "An di yu Zhao Wang shijiu nian nanzheng," 75–79.

[11] This huge bronze *ding* was cast by an early Western Zhou king for a lady called Zhong Jiang 仲姜 (JC: 2191); see *Kaogu yu wenwu* 1982.2, 6.

male and female servants and the hundred craftsmen" (*wang chenqie baigong* 王臣妾百工). Certainly this record is not odd; it is confirmed with another inscription, the Zai Shou *gui* 宰獸簋 (JL: 490), that calls the population in Kang Gong "male and female servants and retainers of the Royal Household" (*wangjia chenqie fuyong* 王家臣妾附庸). The explicit uses of the terms *wang* or *wangjia* as possessive pronouns in these inscriptions suggest literally the social position of this group of people as a part of the possession of the king and his household. By an extension of logic, they also suggest that the famous building compound named Kang Gong belonged to the Royal Household and was managed by the royal personnel. Furthermore, the affiliation of the "hundred craftsmen" with the Royal Household is also confirmed with the inscription of the Cai *gui* 蔡簋 (JC: 4340), where Cai was appointed Superintendent of the Royal Household and was put in charge of the hundred craftsmen. The people called *fuyong* 附庸 in the Zai Shou *gui* are often associated with *tutian* 土田 (land and field), referring particularly to agricultural labors, such as in the inscription of the Fifth Year Zhousheng *gui* 琱生簋 (JC: 4292).

The above discussion should have given us some solid ideas of what might have materially constituted the Royal Household during the Western Zhou. Evidently, it was a complex system composed of building complexes of various functions scattered in the major cities and their vicinities, and of a population of diverse roles and occupations. These royal facilities were not merely the spaces of royal entertainment and political activities, but were also the bases of organized production of crafts for royal use. This suggests that there must have been workshops in or outside of these building complexes that belonged to the Royal Household and were managed by minor officers who were the subordinates of the Superintendent. More significantly, there were also fields attached to the royal temples that were cultivated by royal retainers. In fact, another inscription, the Ji *gui* 即簋 (JC: 4250), even seems to talk about food processing in the Zhou Palace.[12]

The aristocratic estates

Unlike the royal property, the aristocratic properties were located mainly in the countryside in the form of land estates. Many of the aristocratic lineages had a very long duration, tracing their origins to the beginning of the Western Zhou dynasty, and their members continued to play political roles in the Zhou court throughout the dynasty. Over generations, the aristocratic lineages developed an interesting pattern of distribution of property:

---

[12] The term that is used in the inscription is *baodao* 糙稻, the meaning of which is unclear, but some scholars believe that it refers to the process of pounding rice in a mortar; see Chen Hanping, *Jinwen bian dingbu* (Beijing: Zhongguo shehui kexue, 1993), pp. 472–73.

for instance, the Jing 井 lineage, which was very active during the mid-Western Zhou, had its main cluster of estates in present-day Fengxiang area; however, Jing also had residences in the capital Feng, where the cemetery of Jingshu 井叔 of four generations was excavated, and probably also in Zheng 鄭, as the inscription of the Kang *ding* 康鼎 (JC: 2786) mentions Kang as a member of the Jing lineage at Zheng.[13] Moreover, the Jing lineage might have also held residences in the city of Zhou.[14] While these residences in the cities were probably originally outposts of their rurally based lineage, at some point in their development, they might have come to constitute new sub-lineages of Jing. The Guo 虢 lineage, on the other hand, had its base in the Baoji area, but a cache containing Guo bronzes was discovered in Zhouyuan, indicating a Guo residence; another lineage, San 散, whose estates were also located in the Baoji area at the west end of the middle Wei River valley, also had its bronzes excavated in Zhouyuan (see figure 16). There seems little doubt that cities were an important locus of aristocratic life during the Western Zhou. The situation of the three lineages mentioned above was probably quite typical of the ecology of the aristocratic lineages that, although they derived their revenues from the rural estates, enjoyed the life of the metropolis. In this way, the city and the countryside were closely linked together (see below).[15]

There are still many unclear aspects of the aristocratic estates. The most important is whether the Zhou king had real power over the estates owned by the aristocratic lineages. The situation might have been quite complex, and the king might have actually had the power to strip a lineage of its property. But this was not typical of the relationship between the king and the lineages. It is very likely that, under normal condition, the estates were privately owned by the lineages, which evidently had the rights to sell or alienate them. Such sales of landed properties are the subject of a number of well-known inscriptions, including the Pengsheng *gui* 倗生簋 (JC: 4262; translated in the introduction) and the Ninth Year Qiu Wei *ding* 九年裘衛鼎 (JC: 2831), which have been discussed by a number of scholars in the past.[16] However, this does not mean that the

---

[13] On the location of Zheng, see Lu Liancheng, "Zhou du Yu Zheng kao," in *Guwenzi lunji* (*Kaogu yu wenwu congkan* no. 2; Xi'an: 1983), pp. 8–11. For Jing property in Zheng, see Li Feng, "Xi Zhou jinwen zhong de Zheng di he Zheng guo dongqian," *Wenwu* 2006.9, 73–74. For a recent discussion of the phenomenon of an aristocratic lineage, for instance Jing, holding multiple residences in different cities, see also Sena, "Reproducing Society: Lineage and Kinship in Western Zhou China," pp. 277–89. Sena seems to view such a process as a strategy the lineage adopted to stay in close contact with the royal court, hence holding on to power. See pp. 277, 285.

[14] This is indicated by the discoveries of the Yu *ding* 禹鼎 (JC: 2833) and another bronze that carries a part of the inscription of the Jingren Ning *zhong* 井人妄鐘 (JC: 112), both evidently cast by members of the Jing lineage during the late Western Zhou. On this point, see Zhu Fenghan, *Shang Zhou jiazu xingtai yanjiu*, pp. 348–50.

[15] On the power of the aristocratic lineages in the Wei River valley of Shaanxi, see Li Feng, *Landscape and Power in Early China*, pp. 126–34.

[16] See particularly, Zhou Yuan, "Jubo Qiu Wei liang jiazu de xiaozhang yu Zhouli de benghuai: Shilun Dongjiacun tongqiqun," *Wenwu* 1976.6, 45–50; Zhao Guangxian, "Cong Qiu Wei zhuqi ming,"

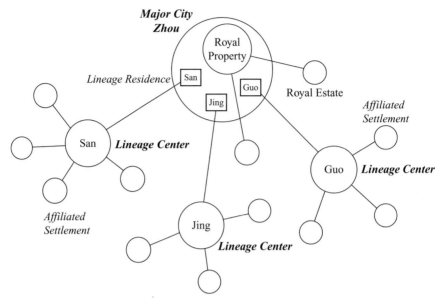

Figure 16: Condition of properties of the aristocratic lineages

lineage lands were placed completely outside the royal jurisdiction despite the fact that they were privately owned; instead, we have a number
of cases where disputes over such ownership were brought to the royal
court for settlement, and even the transaction of land such as in the Qiu
Wei inscriptions was monitored by the royally commissioned officials.
While we have little information about the system of land distribution
within the lineage,[17] particularly because of such sale and exchange of
land between the lineages, it seems likely that from the mid-Western
Zhou on the solidarity of lineage property began to suffer heavily from
fragmentation. Since the land sold from a lineage property could not be
physically transferred to a new location, the frequent sale or exchange of
land must have caused important changes in the way the land was managed by the lineages. Itō Michiharu has demonstrated this change with a
diagram in an important article on land ownership during the Western
Zhou, using the inscription of the Fifth Year Qiu Wei *ding* – the inscription suggests that the new parcel of land acquired by Qiu Wei was actually located in the midst of fields owned by three other lineages and was

16–23; Chen Fudeng and Wang Hui, "Jijian tongqi mingwen zhong," 77-80; Itō Michiharu, "Kyūei
shoki kō: Sei Shū ki tochi shoyū keitai ni kansuru shaken," *Tōyōshi kenkyū* 37.1 (1978), 35–58.

[17] In his recent study, Zhu Fenghan suggests that within the lineage (*zongzu* 宗族), land was separately
occupied by the smaller units – families (*jiazu* 家族) that actually organized agricultural as well as
crafts production. See Zhu Fenghan, *Shang Zhou jiazu zhidu yanjiu*, pp. 300–302, 322–28. However,
whether the families enjoyed any degree of land ownership is still a question.

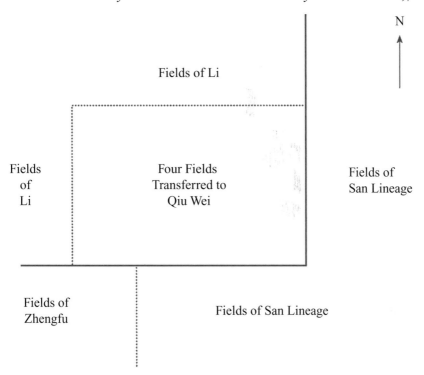

Figure 17: Itō's demonstration of land transaction recorded in the Fifth Year Qiu Wei *ding* (adopted from *Tōyōshi kenkyū* 37.1 [1978], 41. Itō's original diagram put San's fields to the north and Li's field to the east, a mistake that was corrected in his 1987 book; see Itō Michiharu, *Chūgoku kodai kokka no shihai kōzō* [Tokyo: Chūō kōronsha, 1987], p. 193)

disconnected from Qiu Wei's previous properties (see figure 17).[18] On the other hand, we find that, paralleling in time this change in lineage land management, the awards of land by the Zhou king also ceased to come in large pieces; instead, from the mid-Western Zhou on, the granting of piecemeal portions of land by the Zhou king to the aristocratic lineages became the normal pattern of land transfer. The inscription of the Mao *gui* 卯簋 (JC: 4327) says that Mao was given land in four locations, each called by a different place-name. In the inscription of the Da Ke *ding* (JC: 2836), Ke received a royal award of seven pieces of land in seven different locations, each marked by a specific place-name. One has little doubt that most if not all of these seven separate pieces of land must

[18] See Itō Michiharu, "Kyūei shoki kō," 35–58. Another example is the inscription of the Yong *yu* 永盂 (JC: 10322), translated in the preceding chapter, which indicates the same situation. The bronze was found in Lantian 藍田, suggesting that Yong's lineage base might have been in the Ba 灞 River valley. But the land newly given him was located in the Luo River valley to the north, where the land of Shi Sufu, a well-known official at the central court, was also located.

have existed in a condition very similar to that described by Itō for the four fields received by Qiu Wei.[19]

The selling or royal award of land in piecemeal fashion gave rise to a situation whereby an aristocratic lineage could have held estates in multiple locations, and many of the pieces could have been located in the midst of a cluster of fields belonging to other lineages, as in the case of Qiu Wei's new fields. The number of piecemeal land-award inscriptions suggests that such small land holding was probably more often the rule than the exception during the middle and late Western Zhou in the royal domain in Shaanxi, and its spread must have caused important changes in the outlook of the Wei River society. This was an economic process and was simultaneously a social process for the splitting of lineage property, and it might have caused significant changes to the lineage structure itself. When the management of the lineage possessions in certain outlying areas became stabilized and permanently fixed on certain branches of an aristocratic lineage, it provided reasons for the division of the lineage into multiple sub-lineages. Thus, the slicing of land property might have indeed led to the partition of lineages into smaller units and created a general social atmosphere marked by intense competition and conflict among the Wei River aristocracy.

The state-managed property

Beyond the royal properties managed by the "royal officials" and the landed properties possessed and managed by individual lineages, there were lands controlled by the state and managed by the court-appointed civil officials. These lands constituted the main source of revenue of the Western Zhou state and were used to cover the expenses of the central government (and partly probably also of the royal house) and to support the Zhou military. The extensive availability of such lands is fully indicated by the fact that the central court frequently appointed local administrators to manage them; they were inscribed as *yi* 邑 or as *tian* 田, preceded by particular place-names that specified their locations. This was the matrix in which the Zhou local administrative mechanism was developed and through which the strings of state control connected the local communities with the central government. After all, they were also potential sources of royal land grants to the aristocratic lineages. We will discuss the condition of these state-controlled areas in some detail later.

In short, the assemblage of the three types of landed properties discussed above formed the whole of the Zhou royal domain. They not only represented three different ways in which the land in the royal domain was held, but more importantly also constituted three different systems of

---

[19] On this change and its political implications, see Li Feng, *Landscape and Power in Early China*, pp. 122–25.

management. Although the line dividing them is fully discernible in our sources, this line remained quite fluid. As discussed elsewhere, throughout the Western Zhou dynasty, the Zhou king continued to grant his officials land, which, in effect, served to transform the state-managed properties into aristocratic possessions. On the other hand, the Zhou king, under special political circumstances, could also order the transfer of land back to state management or to the possession of the Royal Household. The line between the royal property and state-managed properties was probably also very flexible, but as long as the concept of *wangjia* continued to exist, there was a divide between the two systems of management. After all, the royal properties were mainly concentrated in the cities and their vicinities, while the lands in the remote rural areas were managed by the administrative machine of the state.

THE CITY AND ITS VICINITY

The cities were the focus of elite social life and were also the hubs of Zhou local administration. Therefore, we should first discuss the administration of the cities. Throughout the Western Zhou, there was a cluster of cities located on the Wei River plain, including most importantly the Zhou capitals Hao 鎬 (Zongzhou 宗周) and Feng 豐, located on the two banks of the Feng River, and Zhou 周 (Qiyi 岐邑) in present-day Zhouyuan. In addition to these three sites, which have been undergoing substantial archeological excavations for many decades, the bronze inscriptions also mention two other centers: Zheng 鄭 and Pang 莽. Zheng was located in the western part of the Wei River valley, most likely somewhere in the present-day Fengxiang area,[20] and the capital Pang, according to the recently discovered Wu Hu *ding*, was somewhere to the southeast of the capital Hao (see map 2). These cities formed an important layer of Zhou local administration; they also formed a network through which the Zhou king frequently traveled.

The composition of the Western Zhou city

What constituted a Western Zhou city? What were the functions of the Western Zhou city? How was it integrated with the rural areas economically and culturally? The notion of "ceremonial city" that is found in works such as that by Wheatley thirty years ago tends to over-simplify the complex nature and functions of the city in Shang and Western Zhou China.[21]

---

[20] On the location of Zheng, see Lu Liancheng, "Zhou du Yu Zheng kao," 8–11; Li Feng, "Xi Zhou jinwen zhong de Zheng di," 73–74.

[21] See Paul Wheatley, *The Pivot of the Four Quarters: A Preliminary Enquiry into the Origins and Characteristics of the Ancient Chinese City* (Chicago: Aldine Publishing Company, 1971), pp. 478–80. This view has recently been voiced also by some scholars in China; see Wang Zhengzhong, *Zhongguo wenming qiyuan de bijiao yanjiu* (Xi'an: Shaanxi renmin, 1994), pp. 267–83.

This view was partly a result of the insufficiency of data thirty years ago and also shows a strong influence of the cultural image of the Shang capital An'yang. From the 1970s, archeological excavations have brought to light tremendous new materials from a number of Shang and Western Zhou cities. Furthermore, as far as the Western Zhou period is concerned, archeology is not the only path through which we know the cities; the bronze inscriptions offer us additional information about cities, especially the complex social relations surrounding them, which can be considered together with archeological data. Correlating these two types of evidence, we can now provide a quite realistic sketch of the compositional characteristics of the Western Zhou city. Let us take Zhou in present-day Zhouyuan as an example.

The city of Zhou was located on the loess highlands to the north of the Wei River and in front of the Qishan 岐山 Mountain, and it straddles the current border between the Fufeng 扶風 and Qishan counties (see map 3).[22] Archeological survey has confirmed rich and extensive cultural deposits within a core area of 5 × 5 square kilometers. The excavation in the 1980s exposed two building complexes located in Shaochen 召陳 and Fengchu 風雛 respectively. From a pit dug into the Fengchu earth foundation, a large quantity of Zhou royal divinatory records carved on bones was excavated, suggesting that the building complex was probably under royal occupation. Recent archeological works have again revealed the plans of two other remaining building complexes in the area of Yuntang 雲塘 and Qizhen 齊鎮, showing clear structural parallels to some later religious-ritual architecture.[23] The Western Zhou bronze inscriptions confirm Zhou as first of all the base of the royal ancestral worship, as the temples of the deceased Zhou kings from King Kang to King Yi were all located in Zhou, already mentioned above.[24] The inscriptions

---

[22] This area was traditionally known as the "Plain of Zhou" (Zhouyuan 周原), where the Ancient Duke (Gugong 古公) settled and where the city of Zhou was located. This point was well testified by the discovery of the inscription of the Shi Qiang *pan* 史墻盤 (JC: 10175) in 1976 from the site, which says explicitly that Qiang's family lived in Zhou. See *Wenwu* 1978.3, 1–18. For a presentation of evidence identifying the site as "Zhou," see most recently Yin Shengping, *Zhouyuan wenhua yu Xi Zhou wenming*, pp. 247–65. It should also be noted that there has also been a thread of scholarship that contested this identification; for instance, earlier Chen Mengjia identified the site with "Zongzhou" 宗周; see Chen Mengjia, "Xi Zhou tongqi duandai," 2.141. A recent analysis identified "Zhou" with the capital Feng; see Cao Wei, "Yetan jinwen zhong de Zhou," in *Zhouyuan yizhi yu Xi Zhou qingtongqi* (Beijing: Kexue, 2004), pp. 107–30. However, the overwhelming majority of scholars identify the site Zhouyuan with the city of Zhou frequently mentioned in the bronze inscriptions (as 周 or 珂), and, as far as our current evidence goes, this is still the best-supported identification of the site. See also Li Xueqin, *Xinchu qingtongqi yanjiu*, pp. 227–33; Zong Desheng, "Shilun jinwen zhong de Zhou," *Nankai xuebao* 1985.2, 55–58.

[23] See *Kaogu* 2002.9, 3–26. The structure of the two groups of buildings found in Yuntang and Qizhen is closely paralleled by the temple complex excavated at the Qin capital during the Spring and Autumn period in Fengxiang, particularly located in Majiazhuang 馬家莊; see *Wenwu* 1985.2, 1–8. For a discussion of the latter building complex, see Lothar von Falkenhausen, "The Waning of the Bronze Age," in *The Cambridge History of Ancient China*, pp. 459–63.

[24] When these temples are mentioned in the bronze inscriptions, they are always preceded by the location "Zhou" 周.

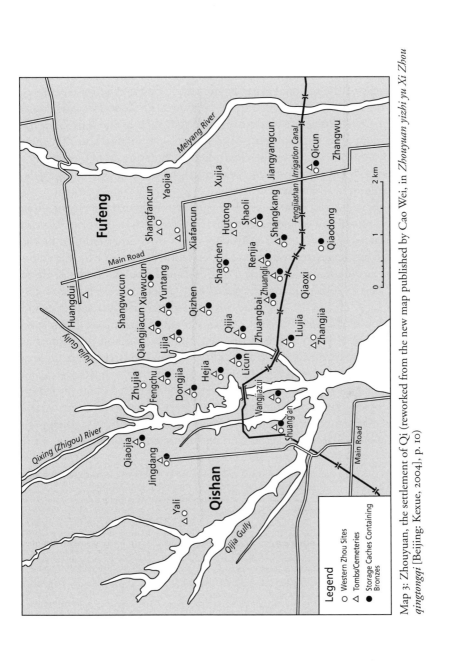

Map 3: Zhouyuan, the settlement of Qi (reworked from the new map published by Cao Wei, in *Zhouyuan yizhi yu Xi Zhou qingtongqi* [Beijing: Kexue, 2004], p. 10)

also mention the "Zhou Temple" (Zhou Miao 周廟) or more generally the "Grand Temple" (Tai Miao 太廟) located in the city of Zhou, which was evidently the temple-complex of the Zhou founders; according to Tang Lan's theory, those pre-dynastic ancestors were worshipped separately from dynastic Zhou kings after King Kang and constituted a different order in Zhou religion.[25] The bronze inscriptions suggest that such a temple or temple-complex also existed in other major cities or even in the capitals of the regional states in the east.[26] Besides the royal temples, which might have occupied a quite large area in Zhou, we also know that some royal palaces were located in Zhou, such as the Ban Gong 般宮 mentioned on two bronzes.[27] The inscriptions suggest also that there were royal facilities such as the "Foal Palace" (Ju Gong 駒宮), probably a royal park, where the Zhou king performed the ritual of "Catching Foals" that was located in Zhou.[28]

The above inscriptional evidence suggests strongly that the city of Zhou probably served as a religious center in the political system of the Western Zhou state; at least, it stakes a stronger claim than other cities to be the center of royal ancestral worship. This certainly has to do with the status of Zhou as the pre-dynastic capital of Zhou and hence the origin of Zhou power. The discovery of the Hu *gui* 㝅簋 (JC: 4317), a huge bronze vessel cast by King Li, also provided strong evidence of royal activities and occupation of the site. However, this is only one of the many interrelated aspects of social-political life of the city. The city of Zhou functioned as much as an aristocratic town as a royal base. Zhouyuan is known as the area where, since the early twentieth century, more than sixteen storage caches containing bronze vessels have been discovered, most of them buried by the aristocratic families at the end of the Western Zhou.[29] The aristocratic families represented by these bronzes include: Wei 微, Qiu 裘, Zhong 中, San 散, Guo 虢, Rong 榮, Han 函, Liang Qi 梁其, and probably also the

---

[25] According to Tang Lan, this constituted a different order in the Zhou ancestral cult, including shrines of the Grand King (or Ancient Duke), King Ji, King Wen, King Wu, and King Cheng, all worshipped in the Grand Temple in Zhou, while kings from/after King Kang were worshipped in the Kang Gong 康宮, which included temples for individual Zhou kings. See Tang Lan, "Xi Zhou jinwen duandai zhong de Kang Gong wenti," 24–26. There seems little doubt that the Zhou Miao mentioned in the Ran *fangding* 𡐅方鼎 (JC: 2739) and Xiao Yu *ding* 小盂鼎 (JC: 2837) or the Tai Miao mentioned in Third Year Shi Dui *gui* 三年師兌簋 (JC: 4318) were located in Zhou. The Ran *fangding* was cast in the early years of King Cheng, and the Xiao Yu *ding* is generally dated to King Kang, suggesting undoubtedly that this is a temple or temple-complex of the Zhou founders.

[26] For instance, the Qi *gui* 趞簋 (JC: 4266) and the Tong *gui* 同簋 (JC: 4271) mention the Tai Miao, which was located in Zongzhou 宗周 or the capital Hao; the Wu *gui* 敔簋 (JC: 4323) mentions the Tai Miao, which was located in Chengzhou 成周, the eastern capital. These temples belonged to the same order of ancestral cult kept by the Zhou people in all major cities.

[27] Ban Gong is mentioned in the Li *ding* 利鼎 (JC: 2804) and the Seventh Year Quecao *ding* 七年𪚩曹鼎 (JC: 2783).

[28] The "Foal Palace" is mentioned in the Ninth Year Qiu Wei *ding* 九年裘衛鼎 (JC: 2831).

[29] For the discovery of bronze-yielding caches in Zhouyuan, see Luo Xizhang, "Zhouyuan qingtongqi jiaocang jiqi youguan wenti de tantao," *Kaogu yu wenwu* 1988.2, 40–47. For another list of caches in Zhouyuan, see Yin Shengping, *Zhouyuan wenhua yu Xi Zhou wenming*, pp. 251–54.

Jing 井 lineage.[30] There seems little doubt that these bronzes were buried on the properties of these families, who, while maintaining residences in the city, had their bases in the more rural areas in the Wei River valley. Because of the large number of their remains in Zhouyuan, some scholars have defined the city as mainly a town of various aristocratic properties.[31] Although this view may not be accurate, considering the evidence of royal occupations given above, it does suggest the diversified social life of Zhou. Some of the families such as Wei had been settled there by royal order since the beginning of the Western Zou and were long-standing residents of the city. Some of the old families, such as the Rong 榮 family, might have had their estates in the vicinity of the city, but perhaps it is more common that the families lived on revenues derived from estates located far from the city.

We should also not forget the fact that some government headquarters were evidently located in the city of Zhou. The bronze inscriptions mention three such headquarters and clearly mark them as having been located in the city of Zhou: Shi Sima Gong 師司馬宮, Shu Lu Gong 師彔宮, and Shi Zifu (Tangfu) Gong 師湯父宮. As already noted in Chapter 3, these were building compounds under the supervision of individual officials and had probably functioned as government "offices." Since it was the Zhou king who announced appointments of officials in these building compounds, they seem to have belonged to the central government and were not local administrative offices. Besides the above facilities known from the Western Zhou inscriptions, the archeological work has recovered more complex phenomena of the city of Zhou, including the remains of large-scale workshops such as the bone-object workshop in Yuntang 雲塘 and the many pottery kilns scattered over the site.[32] Recent excavations in Zhouyuan have also exposed a large quantity of clay moulds associated with a bronze-casting foundry located in Qijiacun 齊家村.[33] Since the inscriptions mention crafts-production associated with the royal temples, these workshops might have belonged to the royal house. But families in Zhou like that of Qiu Wei 裘衛, which evidently engaged in crafts-production of chariots and fabrics, must have had their own factories in the city of Zhou; the family of Qiu Wei certainly also had its own landed properties located away from the city.[34] In addition, there were probably also areas where the poor population lived, including those who served the royal and aristocratic houses. In this respect, the recent archaeological excavations

---

[30] For the aristocratic lineages represented by bronzes from Zhouyuan, see also Zhu Fenghan, *Shang Zhou jiazu xingtai yanjiu*, pp. 338–76.

[31] See, for instance, Ding Yi, "Zhouyuan de jianzhu yicun he qingtongqi jiaocang," *Kaogu* 1982.4, 398–401.

[32] See *Wenwu* 1980.4, 27–38.   [33] See *Kaogu nianbao* 2003, 13; *Kaogu* 2004.1, 3–6.

[34] The inscription of the Ninth Year Qiu Wei *ding* 九年裘衛鼎 (JC: 2831) suggests that Qiu Wei once traded jades, fabrics, and chariots for land.

have exposed more than ten subterranean houses which were probably the dwelling sites of the workers in the bronze foundry in Qijiacun. Furthermore, there seems little doubt that the city of Zhou also housed a sizable peasant population that worked on the fields surrounding the city, which either belonged to the Royal Household or the lineages, or was managed by the state. We have clear evidence that officials were appointed to take charge of the peasants in the major cities.[35]

The above analysis particularly of Zhou has revealed the extremely complex nature of the Western Zhou city, which accommodated multiple functions (figure 18). The city was simultaneously the base of royal activity, both religious and secular, and a place of aristocratic residence. In the latter case, the city was closely linked to the rural estates where the power centers of the aristocratic families were located and from which various types of agricultural products were brought into the city for consumption by their members. Considering particularly the economic ties that linked cities and the rural societies, the notion of "consumer city," frequently used by the social historians of the Classical West, was probably quite accurate in describing the real ecology of the Western Zhou city.[36] The city was also the center of administration, where the government headquarters were located and from where officials were sent to manage the distant rural regions. As the city was the center of consumption of agricultural produce, it was also the center of production of luxury goods, from simple items such as jades, bone tools, and fabrics to large and "high-tech" items such as bronze vessels and bronze-fitted chariots. More importantly, the city was also home to a sizable agricultural labor force that cultivated the land in the city's close vicinity.[37] In short, the inscriptional as well as archeological evidence we have today presents the Western Zhou city as very close to what was once described by K. C. Chang as "multi-functional in character."[38]

---

[35] See the inscription of the Zha *zhong* 柞鐘 (JC: 134). In fact, the eight bells were excavated together with thirty-one other bronzes at Qijiacun 齊家村 in 1980. See *Fufeng Qijiacun qingtongqi qun*, pl. 24–31.

[36] The model of "Consumer City" or "Consumption City" is conceived not on the basis that the city did not produce, but that it derived maintenance from the countryside without giving it anything in return. In the Zhou case, this can probably be contested, given the delivery to the rurally based lineages of bronze vessels presumably manufactured in the central cities. But the model may still be valid because these items were used only by the elites who held residency also in the cities, hence such consumption can be considered an extension of the city's function. See, for instance, M. I. Finley, *The Ancient Economy* (updated edition with foreword by Ian Morris; Berkeley: University of California Press, 1999), pp. 138–39. The model is discussed in length in Garnsey and Saller, *The Roman Empire*, pp. 48-51.

[37] See *Kaogu nianbao* 2003, 13.

[38] See Kwang-chih Chang, *Early Chinese Civilization: Anthropological Perspectives* (Cambridge, MA: Harvard University Press, 1976), p. 64. It must be noted that Chang considered walls as an essential feature of the ancient Chinese cities, which included, in Chang's account, the new cities that arose during the Eastern Zhou time. None of the major Western Zhou cities in the central region was encircled by a city wall, at least as the present state of Western Zhou archeology shows.

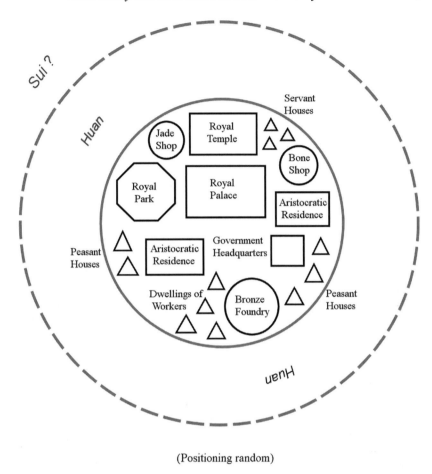

(Positioning random)

Figure 18: Idealized compositional model of the city of Zhou

The administration of cities

With the above understanding of the multiple functions of the Western Zhou city as background, we can now discuss the ways in which the city was managed during the Western Zhou. One of the important features of the local administration of the Western Zhou is that the Zhou king frequently appointed officials with responsibility for the "Five Cities" (*wuyi* 五邑), suggesting that the cities constituted a unique and clearly defined category in Zhou local administration. It has been suggested by Cho-yun Hsu and Katheryn Linduff that the Five Cities might have been counted among Qi 岐, Cheng 程, Feng 豐, Hao 鎬, Xizheng 西鄭, and Huaili 槐里, all mentioned in the chapter on the Zhou dynasty in the *Shiji*.[39] While

---

[39] See Hsu and Linduff, *Western Chou Civilization*, p. 247.

some of these places such as Cheng and Huaili appear only in later texts for which there is no contemporary inscriptional evidence, I consider that the cities frequently mentioned in the inscriptions such as the capital Pang 莽, Bi 畢, or even Zheng 鄭 would have been logically included among the Five Cities. While a definite account of the Five Cities cannot be given at present, there seems no doubt that they were the five most prominent cities on the Wei River plain.

The known administrative responsibilities assigned to officials of the Five Cities included public security, religion, and probably also agricultural management. In the inscription of the Hu *gui* 虎簋 (JL: 491), cast probably in the twenty-eighth year of King Mu, Hu was appointed assistant to Shi Xi, who was in charge of the "masters of horses and charioteers" of an unspecified unit and the "masters of horses and charioteers" in the Five Cities. Interestingly, the two parts of Hu's duty run a close parallel to the responsibility recorded in the First Year Shi Dui *gui* 元年師兌簋 (JC: 4274), cast nearly a century later during the late Western Zhou, where Shi Dui 師兌 was appointed assistant to Shi Hefu 師龢父, who was in charge of the "masters of horses" in the Left and Right Camps and the "masters of horses" in the Five Cities. Furthermore, in the Third Year Shi Dui *gui* 三年師兌簋 (JC: 4318), we find that the responsibility for "masters of horses" was officially conferred on Shi Dui, perhaps after the departure of Shi Hefu from the post. In this case, although the inscription does not mention the Five Cities, since this is a reconfirmation of Shi Dui's appointment in the first year, there seems little doubt that he was to continue to perform, now as an official in full capacity, the same duties in the two camps and the Five Cities.[40] The office assigned to Hu was the collective management of such military units that were stationed in each of the five large cities, different from the royal Six Armies. It is most likely that these were the security forces of the major cities. Correlating the three inscriptions, it becomes clear also that the configuration of these security forces in the Five Cities as a collective responsibility remained constant in the hundred and more years from the middle to the late Western Zhou. At the same time, the combination of the command of these forces with that of the similar units in the two major military camps into a single office suggests that authority over the security of the Five Cities was centralized and unified with the command of the praetorian army units.

In mid-Western Zhou inscriptions, we find another official, Yang, who was once put in charge probably of the protection of dikes in the Five Cities (Yang *gui* 養簋; JC: 4243). In another inscription, the Qian *gui* 鄩簋 (JC: 4296), the official Qian was appointed Invocator of the Five Cities. While both of these two inscriptions were cast during the mid-Western Zhou

---

[40] The transfer of duties from Shi Hefu to Shi Dui will be discussed again in the broad context of official career in Chapter 5.

Table 3. *Officials with responsibilities for the Five Cities*

Official	Responsibility	Inscription
Hu 虎	Assist Shi Xi in charge of the Masters of Horses and Charioteers, and the Masters of Horses and Charioteers in the Five Cities.	Hu *gui* 虎簋 (Mid-W. Zhou)
Shi Dui 師兌	Assist Shi Hefu in charge of the Masters of Horses on the Left and Right, and the Masters of Horses in the Five Cities.	First Year Shi Dui *gui* 元年師兌簋 (Late W. Zhou)
Shi Dui 師兌	In charge of the Masters of Horses.	Third Year Shi Dui *gui* 三年師兌簋 (Late W. Zhou)
Yang 養	In charge of the protection of dikes (?) in the Five Cites.	Yang *gui* 養簋 (Mid-W. Zhou)
Qian 鄠	Be Invocator of the Five Cities.	Qian *gui* 鄠簋 (Mid-W. Zhou)
Zha 柞	In charge of the affairs of farmers in the Five Cities.	Zha *zhong* 柞鐘 (Late W. Zhou)

period, another late Western Zhou inscription, the Zha *zhong* 柞鐘 (JC: 134) already mentioned above, records that a civil administrator named Zha was put in charge of the affairs of the peasants in the Five Cities (see table 3). The message expressed by these inscriptions – especially the last two, which record civil administrative matters – is very clear: although these cities might have been located some distance from each other, the Zhou had conceived of them as essentially an interconnected unit for which collective responsibilities were designed and assigned to the officials. In other words, rather than being an independent social entity, each city constituted only a part of a widely cast administrative network through which multiple strings of administrative control were running. Furthermore, this situation in the Zhou local administration coincides well with the way political power was configured in the Western Zhou state: as I have noted in another place, in contrast to the late Shang state, the power of which was concentrated on the capital Anyang, the Zhou royal power rested on a network of cities through which the Zhou king frequently traveled.[41] In this sense, the Western Zhou cities were very different from the autonomous cities of the Greco-Roman civilization, which were basically self-governing entities.[42] Instead, the Zhou had inaugurated a tradition that was to persist in China for the next 2000 years – that cities were essentially focuses of the political and administrative power of the royal or imperial state.

[41] See Li Feng, *Landscape and Power in Early China*, pp. 56–57.
[42] On the political status of cities in the Mediterranean world, see Garnsey and Saller, *The Roman Empire*, pp. 26–34.

However, the extension of centralized administrative control over the Five Cities did not prevent the existence of administrative staffs affiliated with the individual cities. Quite the contrary, the inscriptions actually tell us that each of the Five Cities seems to have had its own management body of officials. In this regard, an interesting list can be found in the inscription of the Yong *yu* 永盂 (JC: 10322), translated already in Chapter 3 in relation to the administrative process; in that inscription, the land transferred to Yong under royal order was finally demarcated by a group of officials including the Supervisor of Multitudes of the city of Zheng and the Supervisor of Construction in the city of Zhou. These are good indications that the three supervisors existed at the city level, different from the Three Supervisors of the Ministry in the central government. Particularly for the city of Zheng, this point can be fully confirmed with another group of inscriptions relating to a few more official roles. In the inscription of the Mian *fu* 免簠 (JC: 4626), Mian 免 was commanded in the third month to take office as Supervisor of Land in Zheng with the specific responsibility for the forest, orchard, and pastoral land in Zhenghuan 鄭還 (see below); the Mian *zun* 免尊 (JC: 6006) cast by the same Mian in the sixth month, probably three months later, records that Mian was reappointed Supervisor of Construction, and this appointment was actually made in Zheng.[43]

Furthermore, in the inscription of the Er *ding* 寽鼎 (JC: 2755), Er was commanded to be in charge of the land attached to the city of Zheng; the inscription of the Shou *gui* 受簋 (JC: 3878) also mentions a person named Shou, who probably had the duty for horses in the city of Zheng. Another important inscription is the Shi Chen *ding* 師晨鼎 (JC: 2817), which states that Shi Chen was appointed assistant to Shi Su with the responsibility for supervising the people of Zheng, who were the "food providers" and "government guarding fellows," and the people of Yi 邑, which I suspect is one of the royal capitals, who were the "little servants," "food providers," and "government dog keepers."[44] It would be wrong to treat all of these terms as official titles; instead, it is very likely that they were servants of low status attached to the government branches in the two cities. Later on, Food Provider (*shanfu* 膳夫) became an official title of high prestige during the later Western Zhou, but that must be differentiated from the "food providers" here. It is important to note that all bronzes mentioned above are very close in time, dating to the second half of the mid-Western Zhou, and the individuals they mention are roughly contemporaries, except for Shou in the Shou *gui*, who lived in the late

---

[43] If the Mian *zun* was indeed cast three months after the Mian *fu*, then we have an interesting case of the Zhou king first appointing an individual to an office in the city of Zheng and then moving him to another office, but still in the same city. While the initial appointment was made in the Zhou capital, upon a personal visit to Zheng, the king factually revised his appointment onsite.

[44] For this reading, see Li Feng, "'Offices' in Bronze Inscriptions," 21–24.

Western Zhou.[45] They, when put together, show quite interestingly how the administrative duties in a city were divided among the local officials.

What we can learn from the currently available inscriptions about the administration of the Western Zhou cities can probably be summarized as follows. First, it is not likely that there was something that can be called "city government" as a body of officials headed by the Mayor representing the "free will" of its residents, whether appointed or elected, with jurisdiction over all matters related to the city. Instead, the bronze inscriptions suggest that some matters of the cities were categorically and collectively handled by administrators appointed at the royal court, suggesting that in such cases city administration was subject to central control. The cities were not self-determining sociopolitical solidarities but were placed within the sphere of Zhou royal authority. Second, this does not mean the cities were in a condition of anarchy; on the contrary, each city had its own management bureaucracy composed of officials, such as the three supervisors who officiated, for instance, in the city of Zheng. The inscription of the Mian *fu* suggests that at least some of the city officials were royally appointed, while other minor functionaries who served under them were probably locally recruited. Third, it is important to point out that there was little overlap between administrative duties charged to the city officials and those charged to officials with authority of some kind over all the Five Cities. It is also important to note that the roles of "Three Supervisors" seem to have been always city-specific – no individual *was ever appointed* "Supervisor of Construction" or "Supervisor of Land" in the Five Cities. This interesting point implies a division between the two administrative bodies, one with city-specified duties and the other with specific duties for all the Five Cities (see figure 19); it also brings up the question about the relationship between the two groups. In the same way, while we know that administrative staff bodies existed in the individual cities, it remains obscure in what structure they were organized, for the very reason that there has never been an inscription that records the appointment of an official as the head of administration of a major city. Such administrative heads did exist for the rural administrative units, but are unknown for the cities.

---

[45] The Shi Chen *ding* belongs to the group of bronzes all mentioning Sima Gong 嗣馬共; the multiple references to individuals in the inscriptions date them certainly to a period from King Yih to King Xiao (see Chapter 3, note 56). The Yong *yu* mentions a number of datable individuals, including Shi Sufu, who is also mentioned in the Shi Chen *ding*. Since it at the same time mentions Jingbo, who was active during the Mu–Gong period, it may be slightly earlier than the Shi Chen *ding*. The Mian *fu* belongs to the Jingshu-related bronzes, mostly from the Yi–Xiao period. The Er *ding* mentions Qian Zhong, who appears also in the Yong *yu*. See Li Feng, "'Offices' in Bronze Inscriptions," 19, note 56; Shaughnessy, *Sources of Western Zhou History*, 119; Chen Mengjia, "Xi Zhou tongqi duandai," 6.111–13; Zhang Changshou, "Lun Jingshu tongqi: 1983-86 nian Fengxi fajue ziliao zhi er," *Wenwu* 1990.7, 32–35. For the relationship between the above individuals, see Tang Lan's table, "Yong yu mingwen jieshi," *Wenwu* 1972.1, 61.

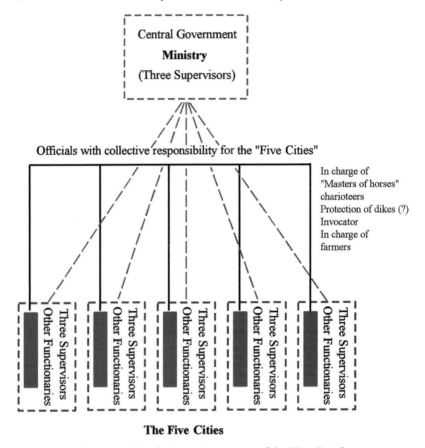

Figure 19: The administrative structure of the "Five Cities"

The vicinity: Huan 還 *and Sui* 遂

Special attention must be paid to the expression of Zhenghuan 鄭還 in the Mian *fu*, which says that Mian was appointed Supervisor of Land with particular responsibility for the forest, marsh, and pastoral land in Zhenghuan. The term *huan* also appears in the inscription of the First Year Shi Shi *gui* 元年師事簋 (JC: 4279), which, actually in a very different context, mentions that Shi Shi was put in charge of the marshals of the Left and Right camps in Fenghuan 豐還, Feng being the Zhou capital on the west bank of the Feng River. In both cases, the term *huan* is used in association with a city name. Apparently, *huan* has a special meaning, and it probably designates a specific geographical as well as administrative area associated with the city.

Some paleographers, for instance Li Jiahao of Beijing University, have proposed that the character *huan* should be read as *xian* 縣 (county), since the character *huan* 還 can be written as *huan* 寰, which in some later texts is also written as *xian* 縣. Therefore, they take the inscription of the Mian *fu* as evidence that the administrative unit "county" had already appeared during the Western Zhou time. However, such a phonological equation without consideration of the history of institutional development is very misleading;[46] and the appearance of counties in the Spring and Autumn period was the beginning of a whole range of institutional changes that eventually led to the formation of empire in China.[47] In recent years, Matsumoto Yoshinori has produced a long discussion providing support to Li's thesis from the standpoint of institutional history.[48] But the attempt is not very successful, and it does not overturn the basic point that *huan* was not an administrative unit, but roughly a geographical area. Nevertheless, the semantic relations between the characters 還, 寰, 環, all rooted in the single graph *huan* 睘 (which appears in the inscriptions, referring to jade circlets), are quite obvious; they all mean something "round" or "circular," and by an extension of logic, the character 還 also means "to return." Thus, it seems evident to me that *huan* refers to the surrounding territory of a city. In fact, this meaning is self-evident in the inscription of the Mian *fu*, which indicates that the *huan* is where the forest, marshes, and pastoral lands that belonged to the city of Zheng over which Mian exercised authority were located. In the Shi Shi *gui*, however, *huan* is also the place where two praetorian military camps were located.

This issue has important implications for our conceptualization of the macro-structure of the Western Zhou city. In this regard, the inscriptions of the Zha *zhong* and Mian *fu* suggest the existence of non-arable and arable lands that were cultivated by peasants housed in and administered by officials based on the city. This was the component layer of the city that was called *huan* in the inscriptions, and this coincides well with the common pattern of *yi* 邑 (settlement) that will be discussed soon below; as a matter of fact, the city is sometimes also called *yi* in the bronze inscriptions.[49] The ambiguity in the language of the bronze inscriptions between

---

[46] See Li Jiahao, "Xian Qin wenzi zhong de xian," *Wenshi* 28 (1987), 49–58. The equation is itself problematic in paleography because the character *xian* 縣 has its own semantic origin representing a human head suspended on a rope, hence meaning "to tie up" or "to suspend" (as *xuan* 懸). After all, the phonetic borrowing of *xian* 縣 for *huan* 寰 or vice versa cannot be used to explain the semantic origin of the term *huan* 還. For the relationship between *xian* 縣 and *xuan* 懸, see Duan Yucai, *Shuowen jiezi zhu* (Shanghai: Shanghai Guji, 1981), p. 423.

[47] On the emergence of *xian* 縣 (county), see also Creel, "The Beginning of Bureaucracy in China: The Origins of the *Hsien*," 155–83; Masubuchi Tatsuo, "Sen Shin jidai no hōken to gunken," *Hitotsubashi daigaku kenkyū nenpō: Keizaigaku kenkyū* 12 (1958), 175–298. On the origin of *xian* in the perspective of sociopolitical changes in the Spring and Autumn period, see also Yan Zhu, "Junxian zhi de youlai," *Beijing shiyuan xuebao* 1978.3–4, 53–59. For a recent analysis, see Wan Changhua, "Junxian zhi qiyuan lilun de lishi kaocha," *Qi Lu xuekan* 2000.5, 77–80.

[48] See Matsumoto Yoshinori, *Shūdai kokusei no kenkyū*, pp. 256–72.

[49] For instance, the "New Settlement" (Xinyi 新邑) or "New Capital" (Xinjing 新京, as in the Chen Wei *zun* 臣衛尊 [JC: 5987]) that appears frequently on early Western Zhou bronzes refers to the Zhou eastern capital Luoyi 洛邑 in Zhou literature. On Xinyi, see Chen Gongrou, "Xi Zhou jinwen zhong de Xinyi Chengzhou yu Wangcheng," in *Qingzhu Su Binqi xiansheng kaogu wushiwu nian lunwenji* (Beijing: Wenwu, 1989), pp. 386–97. In the poem "Wen Wang yousheng" 文王有

the *yi*-city and the rural *yi* settlement suggests that they shared conceptually the same pattern of spatial existence. Further enhancing this configuration of the Western Zhou city is the fact that so far no city wall has been discovered in any of the major cities in the Wei River valley.[50] Instead, the spatial transition from the residential core of the city to its outlying farming lands was just as natural as continuing. Reading the inscriptions from this perspective, it is actually significant to note that such farming lands, peripheral forest, and pastoral land were considered parts of the city's jurisdiction, which naturally extended over these land features.

Another important term is *sui* 遂, appearing in the inscription of the Pu *yu* 逋盂 (JC: 10321), which says that the caster was commanded by the Zhou queen to go to the "Land of *sui*" (*suitu* 遂土) to recruit male and female servants for the government bureau.[51] It is certainly possible that *sui* is a particular place-name, but it is also possible that it refers to certain areas in a special geopolitical relation with the city. In 1964, Yang Kuan proposed an influential theory that the institution of "District and Suburb" (*xiangsui* 鄉遂 or *liuxiang* 六鄉), described in later ritual texts such as the *Zhouli*, can be traced back to the Western Zhou period. In Yang's interpretation, the residential area outside the royal residence was divided into "Six Districts" (*liuxiang* 六鄉), the population of which was called "Townspeople" (*guoren* 國人), in contrast to the "Country people" (*yeren* 野人) who lived in the "Suburb" (*sui* 遂) lying outside of the city. The organization of the "Six Districts" corresponded to the military organization of the "Six Armies," which were formed by the people of the "Six Districts."[52] Yang's theory was accepted by Itō Michiharu and was reiterated recently by Yang himself and others after the discovery of the Shi Mi *gui* 史密簋 (JL: 489) mentioning a group of people called *suiren* 遂人 commanded by Shi Mi on a campaign in the east.[53] However, Yang's thesis was strongly rejected

聲 in the *Book of Poetry*, the Zhou capital Feng is also referred to as *yi* 邑; see *Shijing*, 16.5, p. 526 (Waley, *The Book of Songs*, pp. 241–42).

[50] A note has to be made about some of the recent findings in the Zhou cultural sphere. A wall-enclosure has been found surrounding the possible cemetery of the Duke of Zhou's family on the slopes of Zhougongmiao 周公廟 in Qishan, Shaanxi. The wall was constructed to protect the cemetery and not the main residential area that is located close by to its south. About 20 km to the west of Zhougongmiao, another wall-enclosure of "possible" Western Zhou date has been found on a hilltop of the site referred to as Shuigou 水溝 in the present-day Fengxiang area. See Xu Tianjin, "Zhougongmiao yizhi de kaogu suohuo ji suosi," *Wenwu* 2006.8, 55–62. In the periphery of the Zhou world, the remaining section of a wall-enclosure of certain Western Zhou date was found in Liulihe 琉璃河, Beijing, belonging to the state of Yan, and two other consecutive wall circles of "possible" Western Zhou date were found in Guicheng 歸城, Shandong. See *Liulihe Xi Zhou yan guo mudi*, pp. 4–5; *Kaogu* 1991.10, 910–12.

[51] For this reading, see Shirakawa Shizuka, "Kinbun tsūshaku," 49.*ho*13:314–19. See also Huang Shengzhang, "Pu yu xinkao," 98–102.

[52] See Yang Kuan, "Lun Xi Zhou jinwen zhong liushi bashi he xiangsui zhidu de guanxi," 414–18.

[53] See Itō Michiharu, *Chūgoku kodai kokka*, pp. 154–62; Yang Kuan, *Xi Zhou shi*, pp. 395–425. For a recent analysis that argues that the institution of "District and Suburb" originated in the state of Qi during the Western Zhou, see Zhang Maorong, *Guwenzi yu qingtongqi lunji* (Beijing: Kexue, 2002), pp. 34–41. Both Yang and Zhang take the appearance of *suiren* in the Shi Mi *gui* as a proof

by Yu Xingwu, who thought that the "District and Suburb" system was a practice only of some states during the Spring and Autumn period, and it was not a Western Zhou institution.[54]

It seems to me that although the reading of the graph as *sui* 遂 is guaranteed in the context of the inscriptions, as the same graph sometimes also stands for the character *zhui* 墜 (Da Yu *ding* 大盂鼎 [JC: 2837]), which was phonetically related to *sui* 遂, there is really no hard evidence for the existence of the regulated "District and Suburb" system described in the *Zhouli* as a way to manage the city and its suburbs during the Western Zhou. All we can say in this matter is that the term *sui* clearly had a Western Zhou origin and its semantics seem to have been passed down to the later time, referring to areas some distance from the cities. The inscription of the Shi Mi *gui* suggests that some people who lived in the *sui* suburb might have been moved into war by the Zhou government. Then the question is about the relationship between the *sui* and the *huan*. While the question has to be left open here, it is likely that *sui* referred to the more remote areas, in contrast to *huan*, which was in the immediate vicinity of the city (see figure 18). As for the "Six Districts" system described in the *Zhouli* as the organization of the "Townspeople" (*guoren*), it seems more likely a reflection of the Warring States idea that a free and to some extent self-governing plebeian population was available in the cities for military service.

RURAL ADMINISTRATION

How was the large area beyond the city managed? The Western Zhou state with its bureaucracy and large military body could not have lived on the produce of the limited size of land surrounding the five major cities. Instead, it derived its revenue from the farming land along all branches of the Wei River and on the high plain in front of the Northern Mountain system. As noted above, there were numerous aristocratic estates scattered over the Wei River plain, but we have every reason to believe that a much larger proportion of land, at least during the early and much of the mid-Western Zhou, belonged to the state, which extended its lines of administrative control to the rurally located communities centered on the structure of the *yi* 邑 settlement.

The rural community: Yi 邑 *and Tian* 田

It must be noted first that the *yi* settlement formed the basic unit of land in the agricultural areas. In Matsumaru's conceptualization of the *yi* unit,

that the *xiangsui* system existed in the Western Zhou. But none of them mentions the inscription of the Pu *yu*.

[54] See Yu Xingwu, "Guanyu 'Lun Xi Zhou jinwen zhong liu shi bashi he xiangsui zhidu de guanxi' yiwen de yijian," 131–33.

which is mentioned so frequently in both the Shang oracle-bone and Western Zhou bronze inscriptions, a rural *yi* settlement naturally included the arable land surrounding its residential core and the non-arable land occupied by forests and marshes on its periphery; these natural resources were controlled by the *yi* and provided the *yi* population with necessary supplies. The hierarchical relationships among the *yi*, manifested as the dominance of the smaller "affiliated settlements" (*shuyi* 屬邑) by the "lineage settlements" (*zuyi* 族邑), where the aristocrats of the lineage lived, and the lineage settlements by the "great settlement" (*dayi* 大邑), formed the fundamental social structure of the Shang and Western Zhou states.[55] This issue relates to the theoretical debate about "city-state" and "settlement state" as alternative models of the ancient Chinese state, which I will review in some detail in Chapter 7 of this book. The bronze inscriptions suggest that the normal pattern of existence of land during the Western Zhou was indeed *yi*, which was composed of essentially the residential core and the farming land surrounding it. *Yi* existed both as aristocratic estates and as landed properties controlled directly by the state. Originally, people who lived in the same *yi* settlement were naturally a kin-descended group, but this situation became less and less true, as mentioned above, following the passage of time, because of the transaction of land among the aristocratic families or from the state possession into aristocratic possessions. Since the transaction of land entails not a change of the location of the land to be transferred, but a spatial extension of a family's management and the movement of people needed for the land's maintenance, the frequent sale of land during the middle and late Western Zhou must have had some major impact on the diversity of population associated with the *yi*.

The bronze inscriptions provide us with first-hand information on the condition of existence of these rural *yi* settlements during the Western Zhou. It is stated clearly on the Yihou Ze *gui* 宜侯夨簋 (JC: 4320) that thirty-five such *yi* settlements were granted to the ruler of the new state of Yi 宜. When the Yin *gui* 殷簋 (JL: 487–88) states that Yin was commanded to govern the "Five Settlements" *wuyi* 五邑 in the eastern suburbs, since the term *wuyi* is prefixed by the term *dongbi* 東鄙, it was such rural settlements that were implied, not the "Five Cities," as in other cases. The term *tian* 田 (fields) in most cases, particularly those of land transaction or granting, refers to pieces of land of a certain size (see below), normally under cultivation, but in some other cases it is also used as a generic term meaning "land." The most explicit expression of this relationship between *tian* and *yi* is found in the inscription of the Guo Cong *xu* 虢從 盨 (JC: 4466) (see figures 20, 21).[56]

---

[55] See Matsumaru Michio, "In Shū kokka no kōzō," pp. 72–79.

[56] Guo Cong also cast another vessel, the Guo Cong *ding* 虢從鼎 (JC: 2818), dating to the thirty-first year. The date of the latter vessel to the reign of King Li can be established on the basis of its

Figure 20: The Guo Cong *xu* (from *Gugong qingtongqi* [Beijing: Zijincheng, 1999], p. 206)

Figure 21: Inscription of the Guo Cong *xu* (from *Yin Zhou jinwen jicheng*, no. 4466)

It was the king's twenty-fifth year, seventh month, after . . . [the king] was at Shi Tian Gong 師田宮 in Yong 永. (He) commanded Little Servant Chengyou 成友 to greet . . . Interior Scribe Wuqi 無踥 and the Grand Scribe X 膚 announced: "Award Guo Cong 爾從 the land (*tian*) that was taken by his official (Hufu), the *yi* settlements of which are Shen 姉, Zi 兹, X 羉; also present Guo Cong with land, the *yi* settlements of which are Fuci 復嚳, Yan 言, two settlements. Reward Guo Cong and return Guo Cong's land that was taken by his official (*xiaogong*), the *yi* settlements of which are Ji 彶, Jushang'er 句商兒, Chou Zai 雔戈. Again, delimit and give Guo Cong land, the *yi* settlements of which are Jin 競, Shi 楙, Jia 甲, three settlements; and Zhou 州, Lu 瀘, two settlements. In all, return and give Guo Cong land of thirteen *yi* settlements." The person who accompanied Guo Cong to his right was Provisioner X. Guo Cong makes for my august grandfather Dinggong 丁公 and cultured father Huigong 惠公 [this] *xu*-vessel. May my sons' sons and grandsons' grandsons eternally treasure and use [it].

This inscription documents a rather unusual situation of land transaction where large clusters of land were relinquished from their previous occupants to the caster of the bronze together with pieces perhaps newly granted by the king. The order was announced jointly by the Grand Scribe, head of the Grand Secretariat, and the Interior Scribe, indicating the high level of the transaction. Although we still have difficulty comprehending the relationships in the inscription between the previous occupants of these lands and the new recipient, Guo Cong, the vivid sense in which the inscription describes "Land the *yi* settlements of which . . ." (田，其邑 . . .) suggests that such *yi* settlements must have been surrounded by the lands. Therefore, the lands in question can actually be defined and counted by the number of *yi* settlements as their units. In fact, towards the end, very interestingly, the inscription self-summarizes that the sum of the land transferred to Guo Cong was "thirteen *yi* settlements," an account that meets the number of individual *yi* settlements mentioned by name in the inscription. This makes sense only when the land is conceived as appending to the individual *yi* settlements, so that it could be indicated by the name of the respective *yi* settlements. This condition of the *yi* settlements corroborates the structural configuration of *yi* suggested by Matsumaru, as mentioned above.

However, in the narrow sense, the term *tian* 田 referred to a unit of land, and it was indicated by a number, such as in the inscriptions of the

mention of the temple of King Yi and the name of Guo Lü 虢旅 (also as Guoshu Lü 虢叔旅), caster of many other inscriptions commonly dated to the Yi–Li period. In fact, the design and ornament of both the *ding* and the *xu* vessels would undoubtedly put them in the late Western Zhou period. For the date for the Guo Cong *ding*, see Tang Lan, *Tang Lan xiansheng*, pp. 125–26; Ma Chengyuan, *Shang Zhou qingtongqi mingwen xuan*, 3, p. 194. See also Shirakawa Shizuka, "Kinbun tsūshaku," 29.180:627–36.

Wu *gui* 敔簋, which mentions that fifty fields were given to Wu, and the Mao *gui* 卯簋, which mentions that ten fields were given to Mao. Evidently, in such cases *tian*, which I propose to translate as "field," refers to a regulated piece of land that was even smaller than *yi*. In fact, such small parcels were the most common types of land to be transferred between the aristocratic lineages or granted by the king as royal gifts during the middle and late Western Zhou. By contract, the lands relinquished to Guo Cong recorded in his *xu* vessel must have constituted a considerably large geographical land-space that allowed a total of thirteen *yi* settlements to exist. The actual transaction of such small pieces of *tian*-fields has been convincingly demonstrated by Itō Michiharu based on the inscription of the Fifth-year Qiu Wei *ding* 五年裘衛鼎 (JC: 2832) (see figure 17). If we put Itō's diagram in the larger context of *yi* settlements, we can acquire a spatial composition somewhat similar to the situation mapped out in figure 22. Scholars have long been puzzled by the fact that, whereas

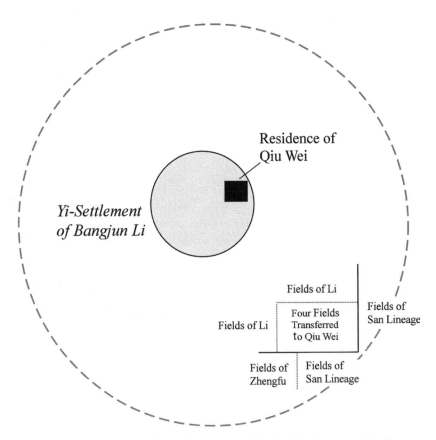

Figure 22: The composition of *Yi* and transaction of land (with reference to Itō's diagram in *Tōyōshi kenkyū* 37.1 [1978], 41)

the inscription mentions that five such fields were to be transferred from Bangjun Li to Qiu Wei, in the actual demarcation of the land, only four fields were handed over to Qiu Wei, bordering on the fields belonging to the San 散 lineage and Zhengfu 政父, and the large tract of land of Li himself from which the four fields were sliced off.[57] In addition, Qiu Wei was given a residence (*yu* 寓) in the *yi* settlement of Bangjun Li. In the configuration of the spatial relationship between the *yi* and *tian* suggested above, this point can be easily explained. Since the *tian*-fields transferred cannot be physically relocated to the *yi* settlement of those who acquired the fields, land transfer usually meant an extension of management from the recipient's base to the new fields, sometimes accompanied also by the transfer of farmers from the recipient's base to the new location if the recipient's base was too distant to allow his farmers to travel to the new fields on a daily basis. Therefore, in the case of the Qiu Wei *ding*, it is very possible that, in order to allow the fields to be productive to their new owner, Bangjun Li had to yield a part of his *yi*, the residential core, to allow Qiu Wei to construct houses to accommodate the latter's management personnel and perhaps also farmers. In other words, this small piece of residential land in Li's *yi* actually offset the one missing field that was to be transferred to Qiu Wei. The Qiu Wei case of land transaction illustrates the inseparable relationship between the land and *yi* settlements, in Western Zhou society.

In short, the *yi* settlement was the basic unit of the rural community and the cell of Western Zhou society. The settlement provided the fundamental structure for organizing the arable land as well as the agricultural population to support the Western Zhou state and its social elite. Therefore, the way in which the *yi* settlements were organized reflects the basic sociopolitical relationship of the Western Zhou state, which, as will be argued in Chapter 7, was a gigantic system for organizing and redistributing the thousands of *yi* settlements on the northern China plains and valleys. As mentioned above, many of the *yi* were the properties of the aristocratic lineages that managed them, but the state's control of the *yi* on the state-managed land was its essential task with regard to local administration. Unfortunately, current evidence is quite inadequate to make a generalization about this. However, we do have two inscriptions that tell us how the state might have controlled these rural *yi* settlements. The first is the Yin *gui* 殷簋 (JL: 487–88), discovered in 1985 in Yaoxian 耀縣, which mentions that Yin was commanded by the Zhou king to administer the "Five Settlements" in the "eastern periphery" (*dongbi wuyi* 東鄙五 邑) with no duties specified.[58] It is not clear whether the *dongbi* refers to

---

[57] For instance, Itō explained that the field-investigation of the damages Qiu Wei incurred and of the condition of the land had probably resulted in the deduction of "one field" from the original "five" as promised by Bangjun Li to Qiu Wei; see Itō Michiharu, "Kyūei shoki kō," 36–42.

[58] For the discovery of the Yin *gui*, see *Kaogu yu wenwu* 1986.4, 4–5. There is little information in the inscription that can provide a basis for dating. However, the vessel resembles the Fifth Year Shi Shi

the area in the eastern part of the Wei River plain where the bronze was discovered, or merely the eastern suburb of Zhou, where the appointment was made. But the modification "eastern periphery" suggests that it must be differentiated from the *wuyi* 五邑 mentioned in other inscriptions that referred to the Five Cities as royal centers on the Wei River plain. The inscription seems to be good evidence that the Zhou central court appointed local administrators to take charge collectively of a certain number of rural settlements.

The second inscription, the Yang *gui* 揚簋 (JC: 4294), says that Yang was appointed Supervisor of Construction with responsibilities over matters of farming, residential houses, forage grass, law suits, and constructions in Liangtian 量田.[59] The problem is that we don't know whether Liang is the name of a settlement or the name of an area that embraces multiple *yi* settlements. But considering the fact that the appointment was made by the Zhou king at the central court, Liang was probably a rather larger area composed of multiple *yi* (that is, *tian* is used in the generic sense), and in this case it can hardly be mistaken that Yang was given overall administrative authority over Liang. In any event, the existence of such all-in-one roles suggests that the state administrative control of the rural settlements remained quite underdeveloped in contrast to the many functions charged by the city bureaucracy, as discussed earlier. Rather than regular "offices," in the sense that they represented a certain bureaucratic level and could be replicated in other areas, these roles were conceived more like responsibilities with respect to particular areas at particular times. Perhaps the reason for this underdevelopment of rural administration was the relatively independent and self-governing nature of the *yi* settlements.

In addition, we know that the Zhou court also appointed officials with special responsibilities for large areas that were covered essentially by forest and had less arable land. According to the Tong *gui* 同簋 (JC: 4271), cast not far off the time when the above Yang *gui* was cast, an official named Tong was once appointed assistant to Wu Dafu 吳 (虞) 大父, seemingly a high-ranking official at the court with overall responsibility for forests and marshes in the royal domain, to oversee forests, marshes, hunting grounds, and pastoral land in a triangular area on the western bank of the Yellow River. What we do not know in this case is whether this meant only

---

gui 五年師事簋 (JC: 4216) very closely in terms of both its body-design and ornament. We have good reason to believe that the latter bronze was case in the time of King Yi and relates to the Zhou campaign against the state of Qi in Shandong. Henceforth, it is safe to say that the Yin *gui* was cast sometime during the late phase of the mid-Western Zhou. For the design and date of the Fifth Year Shi Shi *gui*, see Zhang Changshou *et al.*, *Xi Zhou qingtongqi fenqi duandai yanjiu* (Beijing: Wenwu, 1999), pp. 99–101; Shaughnessy, *Sources of Western Zhou History*, pp. 266–71.

59 Since the Yang *gui* mentions Supervisor of Multitudes Shanbo 單伯 as Yang's *youzhe*, who was included in the "committee of high officials" appearing in the Qiu Wei bronzes, it is not difficult to anchor it to the network of the mid-Western Zhou personnel, active in the time of King Gong to King Yih. In fact, Ma Chengyuan dates the bronze to King Yih; see Ma Chengyuan, *Shang Zhou qingtongqi mingwen xuan*, 3, p. 183.

as a responsibility, as Tong was appointed assistant to another official, or whether a particular administrative position existed for this area.

Local control: Li 里 and Lijun 里君

What was probably a regular local administrative office was the "district administrator" (*lijun* 里君), the official in charge of the administrative unit *li*. In order to understand the significance of this office, we must first discuss the organization of *li*. It has been previously argued by some scholars that a *li* was a district in the residential area of the city and that it served at the same time as the organization of the "Townspeople" (*guoren*); the existence of such an organized population was further seen as an indication of the city-state in China.[60] As will be demonstrated in Chapter 7, the "city-state" model is largely misconceived in the time context of the Western Zhou, as the interpretation of *li* to support the application of such model to the period certainly cannot stand the test of the bronze inscriptions, which indicate that *li* existed mainly in the rural area. After all, *guoren* is an Eastern Zhou term appearing only in the texts and there is no evidence in the Western Zhou bronze inscriptions for the existence of such groups. Western Zhou society was not marked by such oppositions between the *guoren* and the "wild people" (*yeren* 野人) so much as it was marked by the integration of the cities with the rurally located communities.

Attention must be first paid to the inscription of the Shao *huanqi* 鹽圓器 (JC: 10360), which records Shao's receipt of a royal award of land in Bi 畢 that was measured "fifty *li* square" (*fang wushi li* 方五十里).[61] There has been an attempt to calculate the actual size of fifty *li* but without much success.[62] But perhaps the important point is the simple fact that here *li* is used as a unit to measure the area of land granted to Shao, and such usage is also seen frequently in the *Book of Poetry*. In this regard, *li* was probably similar to the *tian*-field, both being a piece of land of a fixed size, but the former is likely to have been much larger than the latter. Perhaps because the *li* has a fixed square area, hence a fixed length on each side, the *li* as a length unit was derived and was used throughout the historical period in China. Although there is no solid basis on which we can actually measure

---

[60] See Du Zhengsheng, *Zhou dai chengbang* (Taipei: Lianjing, 1979), pp. 29–41.

[61] The Shao *huanqi* belongs to the group of bronzes cast probably on the eve of King Zhao's southern campaign in his nineteenth year. See Li Feng, *Landscape and Power in Early China*, pp. 94–95.

[62] Certainly, the Western Zhou sources provide no basis for any reliable calculation of the actual size of a square *li*. Tang Lan calculated the area of a *li* by the standard for the *jing* 井 unit of land recorded in the *Zhouli* and *Mencius* and came to the result that 900 *mu* constituted a *li*. In the same system, 100 *mu* is the area assigned to a single farmer for cultivation which is called *tian* 田. See Tang Lan, *Tang Lan xiansheng*, pp. 196, 293, 494–95. For the sources for this calculation, see *Zhouli*, 11, p. 711; *Mencius*, pp. 87–88. The latter calculation of *tian* as 100 *mu* is also adopted by some other scholars; see, for instance, Ma Chengyuan, *Shang Zhou qingtongqi mingwen xuan*, 3, p. 131. However, given the spurious nature of these records in the Confucian texts, there is little basis for calculating the areas of units of land in the Western Zhou inscriptions.

the size of the *li*, it is likely that a *li* was a territory somewhat bigger than the rural *yi* settlement. But we do not have hard evidence on the relation between the *yi* and the *li*. Neither do we know whether the *li* was a widely existent administrative unit, or only existed in territories near the major cities. What we do know for sure is that, during the Western Zhou, *li* were managed by a regular office – the "District Administrator" (*lijun* 里君). *Lijun* is mentioned in the inscription of the Ling *fangyi* 令方彝 (JC: 9901) after the Many Officials (*zhuyin* 諸尹) and before the Hundred Craftsmen (*baigong* 百工) in a list of officials inspected by Duke Ming in the eastern capital.[63] The order in which the district administrators are mentioned suggests that they were lower in status than the many court officials but higher than the small officials who were directly responsible for the various professions of craft production. In the Shi Song *gui* 史頌簋 (JC: 4232), *lijun* was among the group of officials from the local area, Su, to greet the royal inspector Song in Chengzhou. This status of *lijun* as local administrator fits well with the position of the *li* in the Zhou administrative structure.

Two inscriptions are particularly informative about the condition of *li* and their administrative apparatus. The first inscription on the Da *gui* 大簋 (JC: 4298) describes the transaction of a *li* district to Da 大, the caster of the bronze.[64] It was the Provisioner Shi 豕, a court official, who announced the order to Ci Kui 詛冟 on behalf of the Zhou king: "I have awarded Da your *li*." Ci Kui, under whose name the *li* was listed, accepted the royal order and presented Shi with a jade tablet and a roll of silk. Thereafter, the Provisioner Shi took Ci Kui to inspect the *li*, where they presumably met with Da, the new owner of the district. Da thus presented Shi with a jade tablet and two horses, and presented Ci Kui with a jade tablet and a roll of silk. The interesting point is Da's treatment of Ci Kui. The items Ci Kui received from Da are exactly the same as what he himself presented to the court official Shi. In other words, Ci Kui, under whose name the land was listed, got nothing from the transaction.[65] In contrast to the modest gifts Ci Kui received, the royal Provisioner received gifts from both ends of the transaction.

The second inscription, the Ninth Year Qiu Wei *ding* 九年裘衛鼎, describes a much more complex scenario where a *li* by the name of "Linzi" 林酉 was sold by Ju 矩 to Qui Wei 裘衛 together with the Yan 顏 Forest that was located on it. Before the actual transaction took place, Qiu Wei

---

[63] See discussions of this inscription in Chapter 2, p. 45.

[64] Da is responsible also for the three Da *ding* 大鼎 (JC: 2806–2808), the inscription of which suggests that Da and his colleagues kept guard for a Zhou king at a banquet. Hence Da might have been a close associate of the Zhou king, who rewarded him with land. The Da *ding* vessels are of typical late Western Zhou deep hemispherical body design, and there is a possibility that they were cast during the reign of King Li; on this date, see Shaughnessy, *Sources of Western Zhou History*, pp. 278–80.

[65] Li Chaoyuan explains this by the possibility that the minister-level officials did not have actual ownership over the land they occupied, and the Zhou king could legitimately take their land away. See Li Chaoyuan, *Xi Zhou tudi guanxi lun*, pp. 149–50.

furnished Yan Chen 顏陳 and his wife Yan Si 顏姒 with horses. Besides, Qiu Wei also honored Yan's officials Shou Shang 壽商 and Li 螽 with gifts. Thus, Zhai Lin 濂粦, an official of Ju, the actual owner, carried Ju's order to Yan's officials Shou Shang and Chi 啻 to walk through and demarcate the *li* by making four *feng* 封, a customary practice in which a tree is planted to define the border (see Chapter 2, pp. 47–48). A young son of the Yans also participated in the demarcation of the borders of Linzi district. When the transaction was completed, a new range of gifts was handed to all involved officials, both of Ju and of the Yans, who were greeted by a young son and an official of Qiu Wei, the new owner. The most puzzling point of the inscription is the relationship between Ju, the previous owner who relinquished the land, and the Yan family, whose officials accomplished the transaction of the Linzi district from the Ju family to the Qiu Wei family. The Yan family was apparently in a closer relationship with the land than the Jus, its owner, and indeed the surname "Yan" is clearly identified with the Yan Forest, suggesting that the Yans were probably indigenous residents of the Linzi district. Itō Michiharu's analysis suggests that, while Ju was the undisputed owner of Linzi district, the Yan family actually represented the bureaucracy that managed Linzi district, and that the transaction of the district meant also the transfer of the bureaucracy attached to it from Ju to Qiu Wei. Therefore, the modest gifts from Qiu Wei to the Yans and their officials were not meant as payment for the land but symbolized the establishment of a new relationship between the Yan family and its new master.[66] This is probably the most logical explanation of the complex personal relationships reflected in the inscription.

Although these inscriptions are evidence of the *li* district privately owned by the aristocratic families and transferred among them as a commodity, they are important in showing how the districts were managed. They suggest that the ownership and the management of the *li* were probably two different things, and the relationship between the management body and the *li* remained unchanged despite the changes in ownership. Although such a relationship may not be directly projected onto the *li* managed by the state, it is by all means possible that something similar to the management of *li* districts by the locally rooted families also existed in the state-controlled areas. In other words, the Yan family in the Qiu Wei inscription was probably in a similar position as the District Administrators who, according to the Ling *fangyi* and the Shi Song *gui*, formed a special stratum in the administrative structure of the Western Zhou state. There is no evidence that the District Administrators were ever appointed by the central government, although we know for sure that the court appointed local administrators for some areas. The *li* district as an administrative unit existed both in the state-controlled areas and on the aristocratic properties.

---

[66] See Itō Michiharu, *Chūgoku kodai kokka*, pp. 165–66.

Bang 邦 *and Bangjun* 邦君

Besides *lijun*, there is a similar term, *bangjun* 邦君, which is mentioned in two inscriptions. The first is the inscription of the Fifth Year Qiu Wei *ding* 五年裘衛鼎 (JC: 2832), which mentions Bangjun Li 邦君厲 relinquishing five fields to the above-mentioned Qiu Wei; the inscription also mentions a group of officials serving under Bangjun Li. The second is the inscription of the Dou Bi *gui* 豆閉簋 (JC: 4276), which mentions an individual named Dou Bi, who was appointed the Supervisor of Horses of the *bangjun* of Youyu 窓舒 (meaning unclear).[67] Therefore, the question is not simply who the *bangjun* were, but what the *bang*-polity was as an important unit of organization and how it was incorporated into the general administrative structure of the Western Zhou state.

In Chapter 2, I discussed the distinction between *guo* 國, a term used to refer to the regional Zhou states in the east, and *bang* 邦, referring to the aristocratic lineages in the royal domain in Shaanxi. The bronze inscriptions suggest that some of the lineages were actually called *bang*, for instance, the Jing 井 lineage is referred to as the "Polity of Jing" (Jingbang 井邦) in the inscription of the Yu *ding* 禹鼎 (JC: 2833).[68] In such a case, we must admit that the person referred to as *bangjun* was probably the head of the lineage. But it is difficult to explain why the Zhou king had to appoint officials to serve under the *bangjun*, which seems to belong to the domestic affairs of the lineage. It remains to be asked whether all aristocratic lineages, no matter how small they were, could be called *bang*, or only those which had reached certain size and complexity. While there is no definite evidence for this, the use of such a term for the lineages is rather rare in the inscriptions, suggesting that the latter might have been the case. It is likely, however, that a *bang* had a political status somewhere between the regional states and the self-governing lineage organizations in the royal domain.

The administration of Bang and Yi

Both *li* and *bang* were necessarily composed of multiple *yi* settlements. This leads us finally to the question of how at least some of the large lineages in the royal domain were managed and whether there was an administrative structure embedded in the lineage system. These questions offer us a

---

[67] Dou Bi, with Jingbo as the *youzhe* in his appointment ceremony, belonged to the network of military personnel centered on Hu (Shi Hu), active during the mid-Western Zhou, already discussed in Chapter 3, p. 133; see also figure 15 on p. 134.

[68] The inscription on the Yu *ding* 禹鼎 (JC: 2833) is a critical document on Zhou's struggle with the state of E 鄂, a former Zhou ally that rebelled against Zhou during the reign of King Li. However, the inscription starts off with a personal announcement by Yu in which he extols his ancestors and declares himself the new head of *Jingbang* 井邦. This Yu also cast the Shu Xiangfu Yu *gui* 叔向父禹簋 (JC: 4242). See Ma Chengyuan, *Shang Zhou qingtongqi*, 3, pp. 281–85; Shirakawa Shizuka, "Kinbun tsūshaku," 27.161:433–41; 27.162:442–63.

Figure 23: The Sanshi *pan* in the Palace Museum, Taipei (courtesy of the National Palace Museum, Taipei, reproduced with permission)

chance to further look into the administration of the *yi* as the basic unit of the Western Zhou society and into the way in which they were integrated with the lineage centers and, further, the major cities on the Wei River plain. In this regard, the inscription of the Sanshi *pan* 散氏盤 (JC: 10176) provides us with a unique pool of information.[69] The inscription records a treaty by which a new borderline was fixed and actually marked up between the state of Ze 夨, located in the area from Baoji to Longxian along the Qian River, and the lineage of San 散 to its south, in the southern part of present-day Baoji City (see figures 23 and 24).[70] Although this inscription

[69] The Sanshi *pan* was previously alternatively referred to as the Zeren *pan* 夨人盤, depending on the perceived state (polity) that cast the bronze. It is clearly now that the bronze was cast in the polity of San and it should be correctly called Sanshi *pan*. The dating of the bronze to the late Western Zhou, cast probably during the reign of King Li, is based on the inscription's mention of an officer named You Cong Guo 攸從鬲, who can be reasonably identified with Guo You Cong 鬲攸從, the caster of the Guo You Cong *ding* 鬲攸從鼎 and the Guo Cong *xu* 鬲從盨, bronzes commonly dated to the reign of King Li. For the inscription, see Ma Chengyuan, *Shang Zhou qingtongqi mingwen xuan*, 3, pp. 297–99; Shirakawa Shizuka, "Kinbun tsūshaku," 24.139:191–227.

[70] While San was one of the well-known lineages during the Western Zhou, Ze had a special political status. Since the ruler of Ze was referred to as "king," being equal to the Zhou king, but had the same surname, Ji, as the Zhou royal family, it is very likely that Ze was independent from the Zhou political system. For the location and historical background of San and Ze, see Li Feng, *Landscape and Power in Early China*, pp. 186–87. There has been an effort among the scholars to locate the new border between San and Ze in the Qian River valley to the north of Baoji. See Lu Liancheng, "Xi Zhou Ze guo shiji kaolue jiqi xiangguan wenti," pp. 240–42. See also Qu Yingjie, "San *pan* tushuo," in *Xi Zhou shi yanjiu* (Monograph of *Renwen zazhi* 2) (Xi'an: 1984), pp. 325–333.

Figure 24: Inscription of the Sanshi *pan* (from *Yin Zhou jinwer jicheng*, no. 10176)

informs us more about the management of *yi* as lineage properties, it has important implications for understanding the administrative control of the *yi* settlements in general. The most impressive aspect of the inscription is, besides the detailed information on the demarcation of land between the lineage of San and the state of Ze, the two lists of a total of twenty-five officials who took part in the event, representing either Ze or San:

Officials from Ze:

1 Xian 鮮, Qie 且, Wei 微, Wufu 武父, Xigong Xiang 西宮襄;
2 a. Dou 豆 people: Supervisor of Marshes Gai 丂, Lu Zhen 彔貞, Marshal You Sheng 右眚, Little Gate Official Yao 繇;
 b. Yuan 原 people: Supervisor of Marshes Nai 荐;
 c. Huai 淮: Supervisor of Construction Hu 虎, Zi Lun 孜冊, Fengfu 豐父;
 d. Wei 堆 people: Officials Jing 井, Gai 丂.

[15 officials]

Officials from San:

1 Supervisor of Land Ni Yin 逆軍, Supervisor of Horse Shan Kun 單堒;
2 a. Bang 邦 people: Supervisor of Construction Jing Jun 騬 君, Superintendent Defu 德父;
   b. San 散 people: Young Boy Rong 戎, Weifu 微父, Yao Qufu 效叟 父;
   c. Xiang 襄 people: Official Tuo 橐, Zhou Jing 州景, You Cong Guo
   攸從喬.

[10 officials]

The above reconstruction of the two lists of officials from the Sanshi *pan*
provides us with an important opportunity to look into the administrative
structure in the rural areas in the western part of the Wei River valley,
particularly in areas controlled by the aristocratic lineages. It is first of
all significant that both lists are composed of two parts. In the first part,
officials are listed, either by their personal names or official titles, but no
specific place-names prefixing them besides the fact that they were officials
of either Ze (as in the cases of Xian 鮮, Qie 且, Wei 微, Wufu 武父, Xigong
Xiang 西宮襄), or San (as in the cases of Ni Yin 逆軍 and Shan Kun 單
堒). But in the second parts of the two lists, the officials are mentioned,
either by personal name and official title, under specific place-names (such
as Huai 淮) or place-specified community names (such as Dou 豆 people,
Yuan 原 people). This difference between the two parts of the lists is the
key to understanding the administrative hierarchy in the rural areas. The
structural parallel between the two lists implies that this might have been
the general pattern of the administrative body of the prominent lineages
on the Wei River plain.

The lineage of San is called *Sanyi* 散邑 in the inscription, which clearly
refers to the totality of San as a social and political entity, but not the
individual physical settlements, as in the inscription of the Guo Cong *xu*
analyzed above. Itō has correctly pointed out that place-names such as
Yuan 原 and Wei 堆 that appear in the lists prefixing the officials actually
appear earlier in the same inscription as places where border marks were
made to define the territory to be transferred from Ze to San. In other
words, most of these place-names represent individual *yi* settlements that
were either affected by the new treaty or belonged to Ze or San, as the officials bearing these place-names were actually administrators of these rural
settlements. On the other hand, the *bangren* 邦人 on the San side were
probably the people of the central settlement of San, since the bronze was
cast in San, suggesting San was referred to as a *bang*. The officials mentioned in the first parts of the two lists were probably officials from the
central administrative body of the state of Ze and the polity of San. This
point becomes even clearer later in the inscription when the officials from
Ze are put under oath. It was only the officials mentioned in the first part
of the Ze list (line 1), including Xian, Qie, Wufu, and Xigong Xiang, who

took the oath representing the state of Ze; none of the officials mentioned in the second part of the Ze list was asked to do so because they, as local functionaries, were probably not qualified to sign the treaty for which the representation of the state power of Ze is required.

This analysis of the Sanshi *pan* suggests that, during the late Western Zhou when the bronze was cast, different levels of administration had already been developed in the political structure of the *bang* lineages located in the rural areas distant from the Zhou royal capital in the Wei River valley. This hierarchy demonstrates a separation between the central management with overall responsibility for a polity and the administration of the individual *yi* settlements. The official hierarchy corresponded with the hierarchy of settlements divided into the "Lineage settlements" (*zuyi* or *zongyi*, where the lineage was located) and the "Affiliated settlements" (*shuyi*; small settlements controlled by the lineage) and is the testimony of the relationship between the two levels of settlements. In the case of San, the central management included functionaries such as Supervisor of Land and Supervisor of Horses, and probably other offices such as Supervisor of Construction, although the inscription does not mention them. We found these administrative roles in both the royal court (Ministry) and the city administration. Although each aristocratic polity was a closed system, its internal administration was evidently centrally directed, and its authority extended over the small settlements. However, we are not sure when such a rural administrative structure emerged during the Western Zhou since the Sanshi *pan* was cast in the late part of the period and may represent a new development.

Furthermore, the inscription of the Sanshi *pan* also informs us about the way in which the small rural *yi* settlements were managed. Apparently, there were officials who managed the affairs of these settlements and their relations to the surrounding regions. One of the regular functionaries in the management of such *yi* settlement was probably the "Supervisor of Marshes" (*yu* 虞), appearing for both Dou and Yuan, two settlements located on the new border. Since the duty of *yu* was to supervise the marshes and forest surrounding the farmland of a *yi* settlement, this must have been a widely existing office in the rural areas of the Wei River valley. There was also the office of "Supervisor of Construction" attached to the settlement Huai. In addition, the role of the "Little Gateman" (*xiao men ren* 小門人) is mentioned for the settlement Dou, and such a person was probably responsible for the gates of an *yi* settlement. Whether these roles were regular offices or temporary responsibilities, they show quite clearly that a rudimentary administrative body did exist for many of the *yi* settlements during the Western Zhou. This evidence further strengthens the position of the *yi* as a self-managing social entity, whether when it was the constituting element of an aristocratic property or when it was a part of the administrative unit – the *li* district.

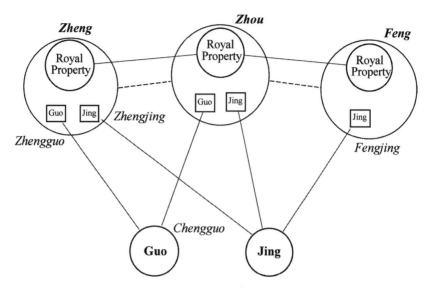

Figure 25: Social structure of the royal domain

Thus, we have a situation where numerous lineage settlements (*zongyi*) were scattered over the Wei River plain as the residential and political centers of the aristocratic lineages mentioned in the bronze inscriptions of the contemporary time. Each of the central settlements such as those of San and Ze had under its control tens or hundreds of smaller settlements such as those mentioned in the Guo Cong *xu* – the affiliated settlements (*shuyi*) – where agricultural production was carried out, providing the main revenue for their lineages. The lineage centers as the focus of the local society were further connected to the major cities through their links – whether in material or social terms – to their residences located in the major cities, which they owned and supported with portions of their revenue derived from their affiliated settlements. As mentioned earlier, not only the lineage of San but also the inscriptional evidence suggests that the lineages of Jing and Guo, located in the Baoji-Fengxiang area, also had their residences in the Zhou major cities (see figure 25). In this way, social integration in the Wei River valley was actually achieved through the structure of lineage administration. However, it should also be noted that outside of this structure there were still numerous *yi* settlements that constituted parts of the royally owned estates or existed as state-managed properties in the royal domain, as suggested earlier in this chapter.

CONCLUSION

Despite the existence of some gaps in our current knowledge, the following can be concluded with regard to the social and political structure of the Zhou royal domain in central Shaanxi and its corresponding administrative system. The bronze inscriptions suggest that there were three types of properties, or three ways in which the land was held, including the royal property, the aristocratic estates, and the state-managed land. This division of the royal domain into three conceptual parts also represented three largely independent systems of administration. While the royal properties were managed by the royal officials from the Royal Household, the local administration of the Zhou government was most developed at the major city level. It has been suggested that there were five cities that formed a network on the Wei River plain for which officials with collective responsibilities were appointed by the Zhou king. While such responsibilities could have changed over time, the inscriptions suggest that the appointments were made at least for matters of local security and religious affairs. Therefore, although each city accommodated multiple social and economic functions, it did not constitute an independent political entity. However, despite the centralized control of the cities, there was an administrative staff body existing in each of the cities, composed of roles such as the "Supervisor of Land," "Supervisor of Multitudes," and "Supervisor of Construction."

In rural areas, the *yi* settlement formed the basic social units, the cell of Western Zhou society; it offered a way of marking the land and territory. A *yi* was composed of a residential core and arable land extending from it and the marshes and forests on its edges. It shared the same structure, and certainly also the same word *yi*, with the city, which was but an enlarged and more complex settlement. The *yi* settlement existed extensively in both the state-managed areas and on the aristocratic properties. The inscriptions suggest that by the late Western Zhou the roles of the Three Supervisors had developed as the management staff of the *yi* in at least the western part of the Wei River valley. In the state-managed areas, the administrative structure of *li*, possibly composed of multiple *yi* settlements in a given area, was established on the basis of *yi*. The "District Administrator" played an important mediating role between the Zhou central government and the numerous small local communities. The central government, on the other hand, seems to have appointed officials with overall responsibilities for some rural areas, perhaps in charge of several *li*. In the aristocratic lineages, at least the more prominent polities called *bang*, building on the foundation of the *yi* settlements was the superstructure of the lineage administration, composed also of the roles of the Three Supervisors. This stratification in the local administration of the aristocratic lineages is fully indicated by the inscription of the Sanshi *pan*.

CHAPTER 5

Official service and career development during the Western Zhou

A government is a body of officials that exercises authority over a certain population in a defined territory on the basis of granted or constitutional legitimacy, and a bureaucracy is a body of officials that is organized and operates in certain ways when exercising such authority. In the preceding chapters I have discussed the structural as well as operational characteristics of the Western Zhou government that had come to bear by the mid-Western Zhou important features of a bureaucracy. I have further examined, focusing on the Zhou royal domain in Shaanxi of which we are better informed by the bronze inscriptions, the ways in which local administration was constructed and local society was integrated with the Zhou royal capitals. In the present chapter I will turn to explore another important aspect of the Western Zhou government – the nature and terms of government service. What was official service like during the Western Zhou? Were there rules that regulated the recruitment process and government service? Was there a track of career development in the Western Zhou government as in most modern bureaucratic governments? These questions will relate us to the fundamental characteristics of the Western Zhou government and provide yet another way to assess the level to which it was bureaucratized.

Although most of the contemporary discussion on bureaucracy consists of studies of the organizational complexity as well as the operational procedures of bureaucratic government, in the classical casting of bureaucracy by Weber the life of the officials figured very heavily. Bureaucracy cannot run without bureaucrats, and their lifestyle comes to bear important marks of the system in which they work. According to Weber, bureaucratic officials are those who are: (1) appointed but not elected; (2) hold the office as their "vocation," or at least as their primary occupation; (3) presuppose a *tenure* for life; (4) are paid with a fixed salary; (5) are set for a "career" within the hierarchical order; and (6) work in a public space separate from their private quarters.[1] We cannot expect the Western Zhou officials to

The content of this chapter is partly published in, "Succession and Promotion." I thank *Monumenta Serica* for permission to use it.
[1] See Weber, "Bureaucracy," pp. 198–204.

have matched all of these standards for modern bureaucrats, for two obvious reasons: first, they did not have that kind of democratic freedom based on constitutional rights that would set their appointments on a completely free contract that can be terminated by their free will; second, they were not paid with a fixed salary determined by the importance of the position in which they served. Nevertheless, the bronze inscriptional evidence suggests that there are certain areas where the lifestyle of the Western Zhou officials ran closely parallel to that of the modern bureaucrats and, to a higher degree, that of the officials of most historical bureaucracies. Demarcating these areas will enable us to understand the fundamental principles of the Zhou government as well as the dynamics of the Zhou elite society.

Below, I first discuss the sources of Western Zhou officials and their paths to government service. This discussion throws meaningful doubts on the traditional belief that the Western Zhou government practiced strict hereditary succession to office. Then, I discuss the possibility for promotion and the patterns of career development of the Western Zhou officials. In the last section, I further examine the relationship between military service and civil administrative offices. A part of the discussion will focus on the meaning and status of *shi* 師 in bronze inscriptions, and this provides another important clue to understanding the nature of government service during the Western Zhou. The evidence shows that there was a certain degree of bureaucratic freedom in the Zhou government, as officials were regularly promoted to higher offices and sometimes transferred across administrative borders.

PATHS TO GOVERNMENT SERVICE

Traditional historical records describe the Western Zhou dynasty as a period when aristocratic officials were placed in government offices by the right of their birth, in contrast to the meritocracy that did not appear in China until the Warring States period. With minor modifications, this view is still strongly held by many scholars in China writing about the Western Zhou state and its government.[2] Western scholars, for instance, Herrlee Creel, favored a more flexible position, considering that hereditary service was practiced only partially in a short period of fifty years during the mid-Western Zhou and then was abandoned in preference for selecting officials on the basis of merit.[3] On the other hand, Hsu

---

[2] For instance, Yang Kuan emphasized that main offices in the Western Zhou government were hereditarily held, but, based on information from the inscriptions, that succession to office required royal sanction; see Yang Kuan, *Xi Zhou shi*, pp. 364–66. Chu Ren argued that hereditary succession was dominant, while qualification was considered only for low-ranking officials; see "Xi Zhou meiyou shiqing shilu zhidu ma?" *Jinyang xuekan* 1985.5, 30, 86–87. Wang Yiliang suggested that hereditary offices were predominant, and appointments based on qualifications were only marginal and decorative; see "Yelun Xi Zhou renguan zhidu," *Huadong shifa daxue xuebao* 1989.1, 90–96.

[3] See Creel, *The Origins of Statecraft in China*, pp. 396–400.

and Linduff regarded hereditary succession to office as the normal pattern but considered that during the late phase of the mid-Western Zhou flexibility began to appear, allowing selective appointments based on qualifications.[4]

It is quite obvious that in practice hereditary succession could not work alone and could not account for all cases of appointments because it had to meet the challenge of the law of nature when current office holders produced no offspring to succeed them or their sons were denied access to office by political circumstances. There must have been a complementary system in place to ensure that offices were filled with qualified candidates. Therefore, at least, there is a margin that we need to define in order to capture the reality of government service in a society. At a more fundamental level, we must be mindful of a more delicate but very meaningful difference between the hereditary family qualification that would allow young people to enter government service and the exclusive family right to occupy particular offices. This is not simply a matter of different levels of rights, but relates to different mechanisms that were built into the system of government and potentially led the government to develop in different directions in the future. The inscriptional evidence shows that even in cases where hereditary family rights were taken into full consideration as a basis for official appointment, the situation in the Western Zhou government could be very flexible and indeed complicated, rather than exclusive. Therefore, we need to analyze actual examples and see what the general patterns were or could have been.

The flexibility in hereditary succession

In many appointment inscriptions, it is clearly stated that the appointee was ordered to perform official duties as the successor to his father and grandfather. In such cases, the appointment can be considered as an hereditary succession. A typical case is the Shi Hu *gui* 師虎簋 (JC: 4316) (figure 26):

It was the first year, sixth month, after the full moon, *jiaxu* (no. 11), the king was in the Du 杜 House. [He] arrived in the grand chamber, and Jingbo 井伯 entered and accompanied Shi Hu 師虎 on the right, standing in the center of the courtyard and facing north. The king called out to Interior Scribe Wu 吳 and said: "Command Hu with a document." The king spoke to the effect: "Hu! In the time of the former king, he already assigned your grandfather and father affairs, only taking office in charge (*shi si* 啻嗣) of the fine horses (*fanjing* 繁荊) in the Left and Right Camps.[5]

---

[4] See Hsu and Linduff, *Western Chou Civilization*, pp. 249–51.

[5] The meaning of *chi* 啻 has caused some confusion in previous studies. According to Chen Mengjia, who read the character as *di* 嫡, whoever commanded to "*di guan* 嫡官" was actually to inherit

Figure 26: The Shi Hu *gui* and its inscription (from Chen Peifen, *Xia Shang Zhou qing-tongqi yanjiu*, 3, pp. 282, 284)

Now, I am to follow the model of the former king, commanding you to replace your grandfather and father, only taking office in charge of the horses in the Left and Right Camps. Be respectful morning and night, and do not neglect my command! I award you red shoes with which to conduct your affairs." Hu dares to bow with his head touching the ground, in response extolling the Son of Heaven's greatly felicitous beneficence, with which to make for my valorous father Ri Geng 日庚 [this] sacrificial *gui*-vessel. May my sons' sons and grandsons' grandsons eternally treasure and use it.

his father's service. See Chen Mengjia, "Xi Zhou tongqi duandai," 6.93. The Shi You *gui* 師酉簋 (JC: 4288) says: 嗣（嗣）乃祖啻官邑人虎臣… Here, since the meaning of "to inherit" is already expressed by *si* 嗣 (standing for *si* 嗣), it is very likely that *chi* 啻 has a different meaning. Another reading of the character is *shi* 適 "to adapt to." See Ma Chengyuan, *Shang Zhou qingtongqi, mingwen xuan* 3, p. 168. I suggest reading the character *chi* 啻 as it is, meaning "only," or "strictly." The word is used in the "Duoshi" 多士 chapter of the *Shangshu*: 爾不啻不有爾土 (You not only would not have your land). Another chapter, "Wuyi" 無逸, says: 不啻不敢含怒 (not only would you not dare to have anger). In both cases, the term *bu chi* 不啻 is used in a negative sense "not only." See *Shangshu*, 16, pp. 220–21 (Legge, *The Shoo King*, pp. 462–63); 16, p. 223 (Legge, *The Shoo King*, 472–73). Therefore, when *chi guan* 啻官 appears in the appointment inscriptions, it conveys a sense that the appointee was commanded to work specially or strictly in a particular office. Guo Moruo reads *fanjing* 繁荊 in the inscription as "Fine horses" (*jingfan* 旌繁); see Guo Moruo, *Liang Zhou jinwen ci daxi tulu kaoshi*, p. 74.

Most scholars believe that this bronze was cast in the first year of King Yih of Zhou. As the appointment took place in the first year, Hu was clearly among the officials who received their appointments upon the accession of the new king.[6] However, it is stated in the king's own words that Hu's grandfather and father had previously served under the former king as commanders of the *fanjing* 繁荊, interpreted as fine horses, in the *zuoyou xi* 左右戲, the two military camps located in the vicinity of the Zhou capital. It is Hu who is now commanded by the new king to take charge of the *fanjing* in the two military camps. In making this appointment, the new king insisted, he had followed the way of the former king, transferring the office from the father to the son. Hu, thereupon, received the appointment and cast this bronze dedicated to his father, Ri Geng 日庚, who had apparently died before the accession of the new king. Thus, the inscription of the Shi Hu *gui* provides strong evidence for hereditary succession to government office, and is indeed a good example that a son was put in exactly the same office as the successor of his grandfather and father.

While this is certainly true in the context of the Shi Hu *gui* inscription, when we put it in connection with other inscriptions, the situation then becomes much more complicated. The most important connection is with the later-discovered Hu *gui* 虎簋 (JL: 491):[7]

It was the thirtieth year, fourth month, first auspiciousness, *jiaxu* (no. 11), the king was in the New Palace in Zhou, and he arrived in the grand chamber. Mishu 密叔 entered and accompanied Hu 虎 to his right, assuming position. The king called out to the Interior Scribe and said: "Command Hu with a document." [He] said: "In the time of your grandfather and father, they served the former king and were in charge of the Tiger Servants. Now, (I) command you and say: replace your grandfather and father and assist (*pi* 𤰇) Shi Xi in charge of Masters of Horses and Charioteers, and the Masters of Horses and Charioteers in the Five Cities.[8] Do not dare not to be good at your affairs. I award you a pair of dark kneepads, a scarlet demi-circlet, a black jacket with *jing*-hem, and jingle-bells and pennant with five suns, with which to conduct your affairs." Hu dares to bow with his head touching the ground, in response extolling the Son of Heaven's greatly felicitous beneficence. Hu said: "Shining and bright are my greatly illustrious and valorous grandfather and father, who ably served the former king.

---

[6] The reason for this dating is based on the date notation of the Shi Hu *gui*, which is incompatible with the calendar of King Gong derived from the clearly datable inscriptions from the reign, such as the Qiu Wei bronzes, but the Shi Hu *gui* is among the group of inscriptions all mentioning Jingbo who had been active since the time of King Mu and could not have lived much later than King Yih. This date is widely agreed among the scholars; see Edward Shaughnessy, *Sources of Western Zhou History*, pp. 257–58, 284; Ma Chengyuan, *Shang Zhou qingtongqi mingwen xuan*, 3, p. 168; Xia Shang Zhou duandai gongcheng, p. 31.

[7] The Hu *gui* was found in 1996 in Danfeng 丹鳳 county in southern Shaanxi. See Wang Hanzhang, "Hu gui gai min kaoshi," *Kaogu yu wenwu* 1997.3, 78–80.

[8] On the term *pi* 𤰇, see the discussion of assistantship below, pp. 199–201.

It is the Son of Heaven who does not forget their grandson and son, and gives him their superior office (*shangguan* 尚官). May the Son of Heaven for ten thousand years extend this command!" [He] makes for [his] cultured father Ri Geng日庚 [this] sacrificial *gui*-vessel. May my sons' sons and grandsons' grandsons eternally treasure and use it, morning and evening offering in the ancestral temple!

All scholars agree that this inscription was cast by the same Hu 虎 who also cast the Shi Hu *gui*. This identification is not only based on the same name of casters of the two bronzes, but also on the fact that the two bronzes were dedicated to the same deceased father, Ri Geng 日庚.[9] Since the appointment of Hu in this inscription was made in the thirtieth year, it is almost certain that the bronze was cast during the reign of King Mu because none of the other mid-Western Zhou kings probably ruled that long. Therefore, the Hu *gui* was most likely to have been cast some twenty-five years earlier than the Shi Hu *gui* mentioned above if King Mu had indeed ruled thirty-eight years and King Gong seventeen (or fifteen) years.[10] Despite its strong connections with the Shi Hu *gui*, the Hu *gui* seems to record an appointment that was significantly different from that which was recorded on the Shi Hu *gui*. Correlating the two inscriptions, we can clarify the following points.

First, according to the Hu *gui*, Hu's grandfather and father served the former kings by commanding the "Tiger Servants" (*huchen* 虎臣); but Hu himself was now ordered to assist Shi Xi 師戲, who was in charge of the Masters of Horses and Charioteers, which were probably a combat unit stationed in the capital region, and the Masters of Horses and Charioteers stationed in the Five Cities, the five royal centers in the Wei River valley, already discussed in the preceding chapter. According to the military organization analyzed in Chapter 2, Shi Xi was probably the head of the locally based military forces and security units in the Wei River valley, and Hu was to serve as his assistant (see below for more discussion on assistantship). "Tiger Servants" also appears in some other inscriptions and refers to warriors of possibly foreign background who served as the king's praetorian guards.[11] By all definitions, the people who are referred to as Masters of

---

9 Moreover, both inscriptions contain the same patterns of wording such as 曰冊命虎曰 (Said: 'Command Hu with a document.' Said …) and 不㐬休 (Greatly felicitous beneficence). These expressions, though not entirely unseen, are by no means common in other inscriptions; they strengthen the identification of Hu with Shi Hu.

10 For the dates of the Western Zhou kings, see Shaughnessy, *Sources of Western Zhou History*, xix. Shaughnessy has also recently argued, based on the newly discovered Jingbo Lu *gui* 井伯盠簋, that King Mu could not have reigned for as long as forty years. See Xia Hanyi, "Cong Lu gui kan Zhou Muwang zaiwei nianshu ji niandai wenti," *Zhongguo lishi wenwu* 2006.3, 9–10. In fact, traditional records give fifty-five years for King Mu, a date adopted by the Xia-Shang-Zhou Chronology Project; see *Xia Shang Zhou duandai gongcheng*, p. 88.

11 For instance, the inscriptions of the Shi You *gui* 師酉簋 (JC: 4288), Shi Ke *xu* 師克盨 (JC: 4467), Wuhui *ding* 無惠鼎 (JC: 2814). For a detailed discussion of the role of the "Tiger Servants," see Zhang Yachu and Liu Yu, *Xi Zhou jinwen guanzhi yanjiu*, pp. 14–15.

Horses and Charioteers under Shi Xi's jurisdiction under whom Hu served are different from the Tiger Servants, ones commanded previously by Hu's grandfather and father according to the Hu *gui*, although they may all have served military functions. In other words, Hu was not put in the same office once served by his father and grandfather.

Second, this new office that Hu received in King Mu's thirtieth year is also different from his reappointment some twenty-five years later, in the first year of King Yih, recorded in the Shi Hu *gui*. According to the Shi Hu *gui*, only by then was Hu put in charge of the fine horses in the two military camps, serving exactly the same function as did his father and grandfather.

Third, the government role of his father and grandfather is recorded differently in the two bronzes: in the Hu *gui*, their position was described as the supervisor of the Tiger Servants, and in the Shi Hu *gui*, they are described as being in charge of the fine horses in the two military camps, a position that was taken over by Hu himself. Thus, even Hu's father or grandfather might have served in different government positions in their lives.

Fourth, the very fact that the inscription was cast on a bronze dedicated to Hu's father provides us with an additional piece of information: it can thus be deduced that, since in the thirtieth year of King Mu, when Hu received his first appointment as assistant to Shi Xi, he had already cast a sacrificial vessel (the Hu *gui*) for his father, his father must have already been dead. Since he was not put in his father and grandfather's office as supervisor of fine horses in the two military camps (Shi Hu *gui*) left by his father, someone else must have been appointed to occupy the position during the next twenty-five years or so before Hu was appointed to the position, as recorded in the Shi Hu *gui*.

Fifth, what complicates the situation even more is a unique part of the inscription of the Hu *gui* that rarely appears in other inscriptions: Hu is himself quoted as saying that the new appointment was indeed to give him the "superior office" (*shangguan* 尚官) of his grandfather and father.[12] But the inscription indicates clearly that he was assigned to a different office.

Here, I believe we can see what was actually going on in the system of hereditary succession to government offices during the Western Zhou, and the situation is much more complicated than simply a son following in his father's footsteps into office. At the very general level, there was no one-to-one correspondence between the offices available and the families of office-holders, and therefore, there was room for the king (or high officials) to manipulate the appointment process. By the same token, not only

---

[12] Another possible reading of the term is "Normal office" (*changguan* 常官); if right, it would convey an even stronger sense that the office was exclusively occupied by Hu's family. See "Hu gui gai ming zuotan jiyao," *Kaogu yu wenwu* 1997.3, 81.

young officials were candidates for their fathers' offices, but new opportunities could open in front of them for service in other posts, depending on the judgment of the king. Even so, they still considered themselves successors to their fathers' and grandfathers' offices. This situation leads us to rethink the nature of government service during the Western Zhou as well as what hereditary rights might enable one to do in that system. It is very likely that the hereditary principle only entailed a qualification that would enable one to enter government service, not the exclusive right to occupy exactly the same office previously held by one's father or grandfather, at least not in the beginning of one's career. Government service in the Western Zhou state, as in many other ancient societies, was a profession of opportunity as well as challenge, and it promised the young members of the social elites better political and economic futures, and what Weber called "a distinct *social esteem.*"[13]

Furthermore, there are also inscriptions that show that, although perhaps the same office was passed on from father to son, sanctioned by royal appointment, the actual duty might increase or decrease across different generations. For instance, a late Western Zhou bronze, the Shi Li *gui* 師釐簋 (JC: 4324), mentions that the king assigned Shi Li his father's old office, putting him in charge of the players of the vertically-hanging-bells and the musicians of the drums. But the inscription also mentions that on a previous occasion when the former king appointed Shi Li he was only put in charge of the bell-players as the successor of his father. This is certainly not a matter of abbreviation because the latter duty is also confirmed with the Fu Shi Li *gui* 輔師釐簋 (JC: 4286), on which Shi Li is actually called by his official title *fu* 輔 (one in charge of the bell-players).[14] This suggests that previously as *fu* he had responsibility only for the bell-players, but in his reappointment, recorded by the Shi Li *gui*, the players of drums were also put under his supervision.

[13] See Weber, "Bureaucracy," p. 199.

[14] The Shi Li *gui* 師釐簋, from its mention of the death of Shi Hefu 師龢父 (historically known as Gongbo He 共伯龢) and its relation with some other late Western Zhou bronzes, can be certainly dated to the late Western Zhou, specifically perhaps the eleventh year of King Xuan. For a detailed discussion of this point, see Li Feng, *Landscape and Power in Early China*, p. 107. The date of the Fu Shi Li *gui* 輔師釐簋, which was discovered later, is a major problem in bronze scholarship. The content of the inscription is closely linked to the Shi Li *gui*–both mention Shi Li's appointment to be in charge of *fu* (bell-players), although the Shi Li *gui* refers to it as an earlier appointment to be reconfirmed by the king. This would necessarily date the Fu Shi Li *gui* earlier than the Shi Li *gui*, but perhaps it could not be much earlier than King Li's reign (in fact, the Rongbo mentioned by the Fu Shi Li *gui* also appears with the same role in other inscriptions from the period, different from the Rongbo who was active during the mid-Western Zhou). On the other hand, the Fu Shi Li *gui* was cast in a nearly straight body decorated with long-tail-bird patterns that would necessarily put it in the early phase of the mid-Western Zhou, not too far off the reign of King Mu. Although this conflict between the inscription and the artistic features of the Fu Shi Li *gui* cannot be resolved at present, it is quite possible that the Fu Shi Li *gui* is a later bronze cast in an early design, as we also have other bronzes of archaistic designs from approximately the same period. On the discovery of the Fu Shi Li *gui* and its relation with the Shi Li *gui*, see Guo Moruo, "Fu Shi Li gui kaoshi," *Kaogu xuebao* 1958.2, 1–3.

Further evidence of flexibility in appointments to the same office comes from a pair of mid-Western Zhou inscriptions, the Xun *gui* 詢簋 (JC: 4321) and Shi You *gui* 師酉簋 (JC: 4288), which have been often taken as evidence of hereditary succession:[15]

Shi You *gui* 師酉簋 (JC: 4288):
Succeed your grandfather in officiating specially in charge of the people of Yi who are the Tiger Servants, the barbarians of Ximeng, barbarians of Quan, barbarians of Qin, barbarians of Jing, and the Biren barbarians.

Xun *gui* 詢簋 (JC: 4321):
Take office specially in charge first of the Tiger Servants, and then of the retainers, the barbarians of Ximeng, barbarians of Qin, barbarians of Jing, and the barbarians of Quan, all of the people of Yi; [in charge of] those on the side of Shi Qin, including the barbarians of X-hua, barbarians of Biren (?), and the people of X; [in charge of] those in Chengzhou including *zouya*-X, the people of Qin, people of Xiang, and the barbarians of Fu.

The inscription of the Xun *gui* states that Xun was given authority over three communities of resident aliens including those of Yi 邑 (probably the Zhou capital), those in the area administered by Shi Qin 師芩, and those in the eastern capital Chengzhou. However, in the Shi You *gui*, only those of Yi were given under the authority of Shi You. Many scholars have believed that Shi You was the father of Xun because the former dedicated the vessel to "Father Yibo 乙伯" and the latter to "Grandfather Yibo," but Professor Shaughnessy has recently shown that their relation could be reversed.[16] The government duties charged to the father and son are clearly of the same nature, but their responsibilities are different. If Shi You was Xun's father, from Shi You to Xun, although the job remained the same, the actual responsibilities increased three times. But if Shi You was Xun's son, he would have succeeded to only a third of the official responsibilities of his father Xun, a significant decrease involved in the transfer of service from a father to a son. In either case, the other two-thirds of the

---

[15] The body part of the Xun *gui* 詢簋 is designed exactly the same as the Shi Hu *gui*, commonly dated to the first year of King Yih, already noted above. The design of the Shi You *gui* 師酉簋 lasted over a long period and is not helpful for dating, but the newly discovered Shi You *ding* 師酉鼎, apparently cast by the same individual, comes very close to the Fifteenth Year Quecao *ding* 十五年趞曹 鼎; self-dating to the time of King Gong. Moreover, the Xun *gui* mentions Duke Yi 益, and the Shi You *gui* mentions Scribe Qiang 墙. These connections provide a solid ground to anchor the two bronzes to the period of King Gong to King Yih during the mid-Western Zhou. For an interpretation of the two inscriptions, see Ma Chengyuan, *Shang Zhou qingtongqi mingwen xuan*, 3, p. 125–27, 150–51; Shirakawa Shizuka, "Kinbun tsūshaku," 31.182:702; 29.173:555. On the discovery of the Shi You *ding*, see Zhu Fenghan and Yao Qingfang, "Shi You ding yu Shi You gui," *Zhongguo lishi wenwu* 2004.1, 4–10, 35.

[16] See Guo Moruo, "Mishu gui ji Xun gui kaoshi," *Wenwu* 1960.2, 5; Ma Chengyuan, *Shang Zhou qingtongqi mingwen xuan*, 3, p. 151. See Xia Hanyi, "Fu bu fu, zi bu zi: Shilun Xi Zhou zhongqi Xun gui he Shi You gui de duandai," *Zhongguo guwenzi yu guwenxian* 1 (1999), pp. 62–64.

responsibilities would have to be taken by another official, probably from a different family.

The above cases show clearly that the actual assignment of responsibilities to family members or even the same individual serving in the same office could change significantly over time. There were hereditary appointments to offices, but the actual fulfillment of the appointments could adjust to circumstances that involved different arrangement of tasks and partitions of responsibilities.

The issue of assistantship

In fact, the inscription of the Hu *gui* brings up another important question regarding government service during the Western Zhou – the issue of assistantship. Did the Zhou make a distinction between appointments that conferred the full responsibility of an office on certain officials and those that mandated officials with only assistant roles affiliated with certain offices? In other words, did the Zhou conceive all government appointments as "prominent," or did they see at least some of the positions as probationary, to which young officials were appointed on the presumption of future promotion, with proven credentials, to roles of full capacity? This is certainly a key issue in understanding the dynamics of government service as well as the career pattern of the Western Zhou officials. In the Hu *gui*, Hu was appointed by the Zhou king to take over his father's and grandfather's service and to assist Shi Xi, who was an official with full responsibility in charge of Masters of Horses and Charioteers, and the Masters of Horses and Charioteers in the Five Cities. As will be mentioned later in the chapter, there is a significant number of mid- to later Western Zhou inscriptions that describe the same circumstance.

The term for "to assist" is *pi* 正, written as in the inscriptions. This graph used to be read *zu* 足 and was taken to mean "to go after" or "to succeed" by most early experts of inscriptions.[17] According to this reading, when a person is commanded to *zu* someone, he was indeed appointed successor to him in the same government office with the same responsibility. However, this reading fails to explain a number of important cases of appointment where the official who was the object of the verbal term continued to serve in the same capacity after another was allegedly appointed "successor" to his government role.[18] The opposing reading of it as

---

[17] See, for instance, Wu Shifen, *Jungu lu jinwen* (China: Wushi, 1895), 1, p. 56. In fact, Guo Moruo once even read the character as *shi* 世, commanding a strict sense of hereditary succession to government offices, but he abandoned this reading in favor of reading the graph as *zu* 足, "to succeed," or "to continue." See Guo Moruo, *Liang Zhou jinwen ci daxi tulu kaoshi*, p. 115. In Rong Geng's dictionary of inscriptions, all cases of the graph are read as *zu* 足. See Rong Geng, *Jinwen bian*, re-edited and enlarged (Beijing: Zhonghua, 1985), p. 123.

[18] For instance, in the Cai *gui* 蔡簋 (JC: 4340), the term is used in a statement that clearly describes that Cai was appointed Superintendent of the Royal Household, pairing up with Hu (正對各) who

pi 疋, "to assist," was proposed by Chen Mengjia in 1956. Chen compared all cases of [graph] in the inscriptions and argued that the character *pi* 疋 is written as *zu* 足 in the Han Dynasty dictionary *Shuowen jiezi* 說文解字; indeed, *pi* 疋 is the varied form of the character *xu* 胥, which is glossed in other texts as "to assist" or "to help."[19] Although the reading is largely based on philological works produced in the Han dynasty, it is indeed strongly supported by inscriptional evidence from the Western Zhou time. A number of inscriptions suggest circumstances in comparison where the graph in question must be read *pi* 疋, "to assist,"[20] while in other cases the officials who were commanded "to assist" clearly served in a subordinate function in comparison to the officials to be "assisted".[21] These inscriptions make clear that the [graph] appearing in the inscriptions must be correctly read as *pi* 疋 (=*xu* 胥), meaning "to assist."[22]

This suggests that in the construction of appointments in the Western Zhou government, there were probationary roles that were conceived as "tentative" in the sense that they only constituted a single "step" in an official's history of government service and would necessarily lead to the promotion sooner or later in his life to a full official role. Although these roles were "tentative," it is important to note that they were an "official step" in the service structure of the Western Zhou government for which royal sanctions announced through regular appointment ritual was necessary, hence bronzes vessels were cast to commemorate them. A government that was able to

---

was also a Superintendent of Royal Household; certainly Cai was not the successor of Hu. The inscription of the Shan *ding* 善鼎 (JC: 2820) records a previous appointment of Shan to [graph] (verbal term) Quanhou, but in the confirmation of this earlier appointment, which presumably took place after some time, Shan was commanded to do the same. This suggests Shan was never to replace Quanhou in his government capacity.

19 See Chen Mengjia, "Xi Zhou tongqi duandai," 6.96–97. See also *Shuowen jiezi* (Beijing: Zhonghua, 1963) pp. 48.

20 In the Shan *ding* 善鼎 (JC: 2820) mentioned above, the term appears in the phrase "佐疋彙侯" which stands in exactly parallel to the phrase "差（左）右吳太伯" that appears in the inscription of the Tong *gui* 同簋 (JC: 4271). There can be no doubt that *zuopi* 佐疋 here conveys the same meaning as *zuoyou* 左右, "to assist." On the Xing *zhong* 撰鐘 (no. 4; JC: 248), three ancestors of Xing are said to have assisted (*pi* 疋) the Chief Interior Scribe in upholding his dignity. It cannot mean that three generations of Xing's ancestors had all "succeeded" the Chief Interior Scribe. "To assist" is a necessary reading in this context.

21 For instance, Shi Chen 師晨 in the Shi Chen *ding* 師晨鼎 (JC: 2817) was commanded to assist Shi Sufu 師俗父, a high official at the central court, to administer the people in two local cities, while another person, Nanji 南季 in the Nanji *ding* 南季鼎 (JC: 2781), assisted (here the term *zuoyou* 左右 is used) the same Shi Sufu in legal matters. Evidently, both Shi Chen and Nanji assisted Shi Sufu in subdivided functions.

22 Further support for this reading of the graph [graph] as *pi* 疋 (hence, *xu* 胥) comes from bamboo strips discovered at Guodian 郭店. In the article titled "Qiongda yishi" 窮達以時, the name Zixu 子胥 (minister of the state of Wu) is actually written as 子 [graph], similar to the inscription form. See *Guodian Chu mu zhujian* (Beijing: Wenwu, 1998), pp. 27, 145. For reading the graph as "to assist," see also Ma Chengyuan, *Shang Zhou qingtongqi mingwen xuan*, 3, p. 161; Shirakawa Shizuka, "Kinbun tsūshaku," 22.125:19.

differentiate between roles of full capacity and probationary roles must have been a government that had conceived at least two fundamental points: (1) official service is a process along a certain "track" leading to higher positions; (2) service in full government roles requires certain qualifications that one might not naturally have and must learn through service in assistant positions. The implications of these two points for the Western Zhou government will be fully explored below with actual examples.

Balance of appointments

More importantly, the above analysis reveals the fact that in the government system of the Western Zhou state, hereditary rights probably only offered the young elites a better chance to enter the government and to compete, starting perhaps with an assistantship, with others whose families did not have such prestigious history of service in the central government. But was government service in the Western Zhou competitive at all? If so, at what level? It must have been; at any given time the number of aristocratic families in the royal domain in Shaanxi who had the chance to serve in the central government could be fairly low. The real question is: To what extent was the government service dominated by people whose father and grandfather had served in the government, or did hereditary succession constitute the rule? In order to answer this question, we must evaluate the hereditary appointments against the overall situation of appointment and service, and determine whether a significant margin did exist in the system.

For this purpose, table 4 presents sixty-three appointments recorded in bronze inscriptions that clearly mention the government roles or responsibilities assigned to their casters, and it is complete in that regard as of December 2006. It suggests that the rate of hereditary appointments was not impressively high. Indeed, only about twenty-four cases constitute appointments that can be evidently judged as such based on the appointees' family history of service (see table 5.1). The inscriptional expression of such a context varies quite significantly. The largest group of inscriptions is those that state the candidates were commanded to "take over (or nurture) your grandfather's and father's affairs" (更/養乃祖考事), or "to replace your grandfather and father" (更乃祖考). There are also inscriptions that mention that the candidates were commanded "to take over your grandfather's and/or father's service" (更厥祖考服). These inscriptions provide clear cases where younger officials were assigned government responsibilities as successors of their grandfathers and fathers. However, such clear cases of hereditary appointments count for 38.10 percent of all appointments analyzed. The other thirty-nine appointments (61.90 percent) are recorded to have been made without references to the candidates' fathers and grandfathers, and the dominant majority of these cases are new appointments (47.62 percent), along with several confirmations of previous

Table 4: *Official appointments in Western Zhou bronze inscriptions*

I: Appointment as successor of grandfather and father
II: Confirmation of appointment made by a former king
III: New appointment
IV: Alteration of previous appointment

No.	Officials	Appointment	Dedication	Bronzes
I.1	殷 Yin	更乃祖考菁，嗣東鄙五邑 Replace your grandfather, father, and their friends in charge of the five towns in the eastern district.	X	殷簋 Yin *gui*
2	呂服余 Lü Fuyu	令汝更乃祖考事，疋備中嗣六師服 Command you to take over your grandfather's and father's affairs, assisting Beizhong in charge of the affairs of the Six Armies.	X	呂服余盤 Lü Fuyu *pan*
3	師奎父 Shi Kuifu	用嗣乃父官友 With which to be in charge of your father's office and the friends.	烈仲 Lie Zhong	師奎父鼎 Shi Kuifu *ding*
4	豆閉 Dou Bi	用俾乃祖考事，嗣爰豁邦君 嗣馬，弓矢 With which to take over (?) your grandfather's and father's affairs, serving as the Supervisor of Horses under the Area Minister of Youyu (?), (in charge of) bows and arrows.	文考豁叔 Cultured father Li Shu	豆閉簋 Dou Bi *gui*
5	師虎 Shi Hu	虎，龡先王既命乃祖考，龡宮龡左右戲緐荊。今余惟帅型 先王，命汝更乃祖考，龡宮龡左右戲緐荊 In the time of the former king, he already assigned your grandfather and father affairs, only taking office in charge of fine horses in the Left and Right Camps. Now, I am to model on the former king, commanding you to replace your grandfather and father, only taking office in charge of the horses in the Left and Right camps.	烈考日庚 Valorous father Ri Geng	師虎簋 Shi Hu *gui*

	Name	Text	Father	Vessel
6	虎 Hu	觏乃祖考事先王，嗣虎臣。今命汝曰：更乃祖考，疋師戲嗣走馬馭人眾五邑走馬馭人嗣走馬嗣人眾五邑走馬駿人。汝毋敢不善于乃政。 In the time of your grandfather and father, they served the former king and were in charge of the Tiger Servants. Now, (I) command you and say: replace your grandfather and father and assist Shi Xi in charge of Masters of Horses and Charioteers, and the Masters of Horses and Charioteers in the Five Cities.	文考日庚 Cultured father Ri Geng	虎簋 Hu *gui*
7	輔師氂 Musician Shi Li	更乃祖考嗣輔 Replace your grandfather and father in charge of the musicians of vertically-hanging-bells.	X	輔師氂簋 Fu Shi Li *gui*
8	師氂 Shi Li	在昔一先王既命汝更乃祖考嗣小輔一今余一命汝嗣乃祖考舊官小輔眔鼓鐘鼓 In the past . . . the previous king already commanded you to replace your grandfather and father in charge of the musicians of vertically-hanging-bells. Now I . . . command you to take over your grandfather's and father's old post, (in charge) of the musicians of vertically-hanging bells and the musicians of obliquely-hanging bells and drums.	文考輔伯 Cultured father Fubo	師氂簋 Shi Li *gui*
9	申 Shen	更乃祖考，疋大祝官，嗣豐人眾九戲祝 Replace your grandfather and father, assisting the Grand Invocator to serve as invocator of the people of Feng and the nine-garrison-camps.	皇考季孟 August father Ji Meng	申簋 Shen *gui*
10	曶 Hu	更乃祖考作塚嗣土于成周八師 Replace your grandfather and father and be the Grand Supervisor of Land in the Eight Armies of Chengzhou.	文考氂公 Cultured father Ligong	曶壺 Hu *hu*
11	曶 Hu	更乃祖考，嗣卜事 Replace your grandfather and father in charge of the affairs of divination.	文考宰伯 Cultured father X Bo	曶鼎 Hu *ding*

(*continued*)

Table 4: *Official appointments in Western Zhou bronze inscriptions (Continued)*

No.	Officials	Appointment	Dedication	Bronzes
12	師詢 Shi Xun	乃聖祖考克左右先王，作厥肱股……今余唯醽肇乃命，命汝惠雝我邦小大猶 Command you to beneficially harmonize the great and small chiefs of our state.	烈祖乙伯咸姬 Valorous grandfather Yibo, Xian Ji	師詢簋 Shi Xun *gui*
13	詢 Xun	丕顯文武受命，則乃祖奠周邦。今余命汝啻官□邑人先虎臣、後庸，西門夷、秦夷京夷、□夷師芩側新□華夷，異□夷朆走亞□，秦人、降人、服夷 The greatly illustrious King Wen and King Wu received the mandate; so your ancestors consolidated the Zhou state. Now I command you to take office in charge first of the Tiger Servants, and then of the retainers, the barbarians of Ximeng, barbarians of Qin, barbarians of Jing, and the barbarians of Yi; (in charge of) those on the side of Shi Qin, including the barbarians of X-hua, barbarians of Biren (?), and the people of X; (in charge of) those in Chengzhou including *zouya*-X, the people of Qin, people of Xiang, and the barbarians of Fu.	文祖乙伯同姬 Cultured grandfather Yibo, Tongji	詢簋 Xun *gui*
14	師酉 Shi You	嗣乃祖啻官邑人虎臣，西門夷、薰夷、秦夷、京夷、畀人夷 Succeed your grandfather officiating in charge of the people of Yi who are the Tiger Servants, the barbarians of Ximeng, barbarians of Quan, barbarians of Qin, barbarians of Jing, and the barbarians of Biren.	文考乙伯 Cultured father Yibo	師酉簋 Shi You *gui*
15	縲 Yi	更厥祖考服 Replace his grandfather's and father's service.	X	縲觶 Yi *zhi*
16	郘兟 He Yuan	用嗣乃祖考事，作嗣土 With which to succeed your grandfather's and father's affairs; be the Supervisor of Land.	X	郘兟簋 He Yuan *gui*

17	宰獸 Zai Shou	昔先王既命汝，今余唯或鬹纂乃命，更乃祖考事，䤨嗣嗣康宮王家臣妾庸，外內勿敢舞矤智 In the past, the former king already commanded you. Now, I am also to extend your mission, replacing your grandfather's and father's service, diligently in charge of the royal servants, retainers in Kang Gong palace; external and internal affairs, you don't dare not to listen and know.	烈祖幽仲益姜 Valorous grandfather Youzhong, Yi Jiang	宰獸簋 Zai Shou gui
18	害 Hai	用養乃祖考事，官嗣夷僕小射 With which to nurture your grandfather's and father's affairs, officiating in charge of the barbarian servants and the small archers.	文考 Cultured father	害簋 Hai gui
19	單伯 Shanbo	王呼內史冊命單伯，錫 … 用養乃祖考事，官嗣夷僕小射 The king called out to the Interior Scribe to command Shan Bo and reward him … With which to nurture your grandfather's and father's affairs, officiating in charge of the barbarian servants and the small archers.	文考 Cultured father	單伯鼎 Shanbo ding
20	伯晨 Bo Chen	嗣乃祖考侯于胄 Replace your grandfather and father to be the ruler of Huan.	文考瀕公 Cultured father Pingong	伯晨鼎 Bo Chen ding
21	師克 Shi Ke	則唯乃先祖考有勳于周邦，干害王身，作爪牙。王曰：克，余唯經乃先祖考，克釐臣先王。昔余既命汝，命汝更乃祖考䤨嗣蒙乃命 It was your grandfather and father who had their merit in the Zhou state, protecting the king from harm and being his claws and	X	師克盨 Shi Ke xu

(continued)

Table 4: *Official appointments in Western Zhou bronze inscriptions (Continued)*

No.	Officials	Appointment	Dedication	Bronzes
		teeth. The king said: Ke! I am to follow your grandfather and father who ably assisted and served the former king. In the past, I already commanded you; now, I am to extend your mission, commanding you to replace your grandfather and father to diligently be in charge of the Left and Right Tiger Servants.		
22	逨 Lai	今余惟巠乃厥乃聖祖考、龗褱乃命，命汝疋榮兌胷嗣四方虞林，用宫御 Now I am to follow your sagely former grandfather and and father, reiterate your command, and order you to assist Rong Dui to take charge of the marshes and forests in the four directions, using palace attendants.	皇祖考 August grandfather and father	逨盤 Lai *pan*
23	逨 Lai	今余惟巠乃先祖考有勛于周邦，龗褱乃命，命汝官嗣歷人 Now I am to follow your deceased grandfather and father, who had merits in the Zhou state, and reiterate your command, ordering you to officiate in charge of the people of Li.	皇考龏叔 August father Gongshu	四十三年逨鼎 Forty-third Year Lai *ding*
24	逯 Lu	更乃祖服，作冢嗣馬 Replace your grandfather's service; to be Grand Supervisor of Horses.	文祖幽伯 Cultured Grandfather Youbo	井伯逯簋 Jingbo Lu *gui*

		X	
II. 25 蔡 Cai	昔先王既令汝作宰，嗣王家，嗣王家外內——嗣百工，今余一令汝眾胥辪乃對各，死嗣王家，出入姜氏命。厥有見有即命。厥非先告蔡，毋敢有入告 In the past, the previous king already commanded you to be Steward, in charge of the royal household. Now I … command you and Hu to mutually assist each other, ultimately being in charge of the outside and inside of the Royal Household … in charge of the hundred craftsmen, sending out and taking in the orders of Queen Jiang. When there is someone who wants to meet or to report, without reporting to Cai in advance, (he) dares not to enter and report.		蔡簋 Cai *gui*
26 師穎 Shi Ying	先王既令汝作嗣土，官嗣涵嗣 The previous king already commanded you to be Supervisor of Land, officiating in charge of the floodgate (?) of the Fang River (?).	文考尹伯 Cultured father Yinbo	師穎簋 Shi Ying *gui*
27 諫 Jian	先王既令汝辪嗣王宥 The previous king already commanded you to be in charge of the royal park.	文考惠伯 Cultured father Huibo	諫簋 Jian *gui*
28 師觻 Shi Yun	先王既令命汝，今余惟餼釐爨先王，命汝宮嗣邑人師氏 The former king already commanded you; now I am to reiterate the former king's (command), ordering you to take office in charge of the marshals of the people of Yi.	文考外季 Cultured father Waiji	師觻簋 Shi Yun *gui*
29 善夫克 Food Provider Ke	昔余既令汝出內王命 In the past, I already commanded you to send out and take in the orders of the king.	文祖師華父 Cultured Grandfather Shi Huafu	大克鼎 Da Ke *ding*

(continued)

Table 4: *Official appointments in Western Zhou bronze inscriptions (Continued)*

No.	Officials	Appointment	Dedication	Bronzes
30	鄴 Qian	昔先王既命汝作邑，䚅五邑祝。今余唯䌛覉景乃命 In the past, the former king already commanded you to make settlements, diligently serving as the Invocator of the Five Settlements. Now, I am to extend your command.	文考龔伯 Cultured father Gongbo	鄴簋 Qian *gui*
31	善 Shan	昔先王既命汝佐正覉侯。今余唯肇覉先王命，命汝佐正覉侯，盬戲師戍。賜汝祖考旃，用事。 In the past, the former king already commanded you to assist Quanhou. Now, I am to reiterate the command of the former king, commanding you to supervise the garrison at X. I grant you your grandfather's and father's flag with which to conduct affairs.	X	善鼎 Shan *ding*
III. 32	望 Wang	死戲畢王家 Ultimately being in charge of the royal household at Bi.	皇祖伯囧父 August grandfather Bo X-Fu	望簋 Wang *gui*
33	楚 Chu	戲夆圖宮内師舟 In charge of the boats within the government of the territory of (the capital) Pang,	X	楚簋 Chu *gui*
34	頌 Song	官戲成周貯二十家，監嗣新造貯，用宮御 Officiate in charge of the warehouse of twenty households at Chengzhou, and supervise the newly constructed warehouse, using palace attendants.	皇考龔叔 皇母龔姒 August father Gongshu, August mother Gongsi	頌鼎 Song *ding*

35	作冊吳 Document Maker Wu	嗣旛釆叔金 In charge of the "white flag" and silk.	青尹 Qing Yin	吳方彝 Wu fangyi
36	揚 Yang	作嗣工、官嗣量田甸、嗣居、嗣芻、嗣寇、嗣工事 Be the Supervisor of Construction, officiating in charge of farming, in charge of the residential houses, in charge of the forage grass, in charge of lawsuits, and in charge of the construction of the field of Liang.	烈考憲伯 Valorous father Xianbo	揚簋 Yang gui
37	此 Ci	旅邑人善夫 In charge of the food providers of the people of Yi.	皇考癸公 August father Guigong	此簋 Ci gui
38	善夫山 Food	令汝官嗣飲獻人于𫑛、用作憲嗣貯 Command you to officiate in charge of the contributors of drinks at Ke, with which to supply the storage of xiansi (?).	皇考碩父 August father Shuofu	善夫山鼎 Shanfu Shan ding
39	南季 Nanji	左右俗父嗣寇 Assist Sufu in charge of lawsuits.	X	南季鼎 Nanji ding
40	無惠 Wuhui	官嗣𦈢王復側虎臣 Officiate in charge of the Tiger Servants at the body side of X king.	烈考 Valorous father	無惠鼎 Wuhui ding
41	師𩫋 Shi Yu	死嗣周人 Ultimately being in charge of the people of Zhou.	X	師𩫋簋 Shi Yu gui
42	師晨 Shi Chen	疋師俗父嗣邑人:唯小臣、善夫、守口、官犬、官守友。 Assist Shi Sufu in charge of the people of Yi: they are the little servants, food providers, x-guards, caretakers of official dogs; and the people of Zheng; food providers, and the friends of the official guard (?).	文祖辛公 Cultured grandfather Xingong	師晨鼎 Shi Chen ding

(continued)

Table 4: *Official appointments in Western Zhou bronze inscriptions (Continued)*

No.	Officials	Appointment	Dedication	Bronzes
43	南宮柳 Nangong Liu	嗣六師牧、場,虞□; 嗣羲夷陽佃事 In charge of the pastoral land, orchards, marshes, and X of the Six Armies; in charge of the affairs of farming of *Xiyi yang* (?).	烈考 Valorous father	南宮柳鼎 Nangong Liu *ding*
44	盠 Li	嗣六師王行參有嗣: 嗣土、嗣馬、嗣工。耤嗣六師眾八師藝 In charge of the Three Supervisors – Supervisor of Land, Supervisor of Horses, and Supervisor of Construction – of the royal guard legion in the Six Armies; in charge of the camping affairs of the Six Armies and the Eight Armies.	文祖益公 Cultured grandfater Yigong	盠方尊 Li *fangzun*
45	走 Zou	耤定□ Diligently assist X.	X	走簋 Zou *gui*
46	養 Yang	用大備于五邑守堰（？） With which to greatly accomplish the protection of dams (?) in the Five Cities.	X	養簋 Yang *gui*
47	趞 Qi	作冢嗣家嗣馬、啻官僕、射士、訊、小大又鄰 Be the Grand Supervisor of Horses in the Bin garrison, officiating in charge of the chariot guides, archers, prisoners, and those minor and great among the neighbors.	季姜 Ji Jiang	趞簋 Qi *gui*
48	同 Tong	差右吳大伯嗣場林虞牧,自流東至于河,厥逆至于玄水。世孫孫子子差右吳大伯,毋汝有閑 Assist Taibo of Wu in charge of the orchards, forests, marshes, and pastoral land, from the Hu River east to the Yellow River, and north to the Xuan River.	文考惠仲 Cultured father Huizhong	同簋 Tong *gui*

No.	Name	Command	Ancestor	Vessel
49	康 Kang	王令死嗣王家 The king commanded (Kang) to ultimately be in charge of the Royal Household.	文考釐伯 Cultured father Libo	康鼎 Kang *ding*
50	柞 Zha	嗣五邑佃人事 In charge of the affairs of the farmers of the Five Cities.	X	柞鍾 Zha *zhong*
51	免 Mian	令汝疋周師嗣林 Command you to assist Zhou Shi in charge of the forest.	X	免簋 Mian *gui*
52	免 Mian	令免作嗣土，嗣鄭還林、眔吳眔牧，錫… Command Mian to be Supervisor of Land, in charge of the forest of Zhenghuan, marshes and hunting.	X	免簠 Mian *fu*
53	免 Mian	作嗣工 Be Supervisor of Construction.	X	免尊 Mian *zun*
54	裁 Zai	令汝作嗣土、官嗣籍田 Command you to be Supervisor of Land, officiating in charge of the Spring Plowing Ritual.	文考 Cultured father	裁簋 Zai *gui*
55	即 Ji	嗣琱宮人虦稻、用事 In charge of the people of the Zhou palace.	文考幽叔 Cultured father Youshu	即簋 Ji *gui*
56	伊 Yi	瓤官嗣康宮王臣妾百工 Officiate in charge of the royal servants, the female slaves, and the hundred craftsmen in Kang Gong.	文祖皇考㺪叔 Cultured grandfather, August father Yishu	伊簋 Yi *gui*
57	師事 Shi Shi	備于大左、官嗣豐還左右師氏 To supplement the Great Left, officiating in charge of the Marshals of the Left and Right of the Feng district.	文祖益仲 Cultured grandfather Yizhong	元年師事簋 First Year Shi Shi *gui*

(continued)

Table 4: *Official appointments in Western Zhou bronze inscriptions (Continued)*

No.	Officials	Appointment	Dedication	Bronzes
58	師兌 Shi Dui	疋師龢父嗣左右走馬，五邑走馬 Assist Shi Hefu in charge of the Masters of Horses of the Left and Right, and the Masters of Horses of the Five Cities	皇祖城公 August grandfather Chenggong	元年師兌簋 First Year Shi Dui *gui*
59	恒 Heng	命汝更黃，兌嗣亯郬 Command you to replace Jing to be ably in charge of the immediate suburbs.	文考公叔 Cultured father Gongshu	恒簋 Heng *gui*
60	瀞 Fu	命汝嗣成周里人及諸侯大亞，訊訟罰 Command you to be in charge of the district people and the *Daya*-generals of the Many Rulers in Chengzhou.	X	瀞簋 Fu *gui*
61	微緣 Wei Man	王命微緣嗣九陂 The king commanded Wei Man to be in charge of the Nine Reservoirs.	皇考 August father	微緣鼎 Wei Man *ding*
IV. 62	牧 Mu	昔先王既令汝作嗣土，今余唯或窳改令汝辟百僚 In the past, the previous king already commanded you be the Supervisor of Land; now, I ... change it and command you to rule the hundred departments.	文考益伯 Cultured father Yibo	牧簋 Mu *gui*
63	師兌 Shi Dui	余既令汝疋師龢父嗣左右走馬，今余唯豪離乃令，命汝 亂嗣走馬 I already commanded you to assist Shi Hefu in charge of the Masters of Horses of the Left and Right. Now, I am to extend your mission and command you to be in charge of the Masters of Horses.	皇考聾公 August father Ligong	三年師兌簋 Third Year Shi Dui *gui*

(Inscriptions published by December 2006)

Table 5: *Percentage of official appointments (based on table 4)*

(5.1: Classified)

Appointments	Number	Percentage
I Hereditary appointment	24	38.10
"Take over grandfather's and father's affairs":	7	
"Replace grandfather and father":	10	
"Take over grandfather's and father's service":	2	
Other expressions of hereditary appointment	5	
A. As assistant to senior officials:	4	
B. In charge of:	15	
C. Official titles conferred:	3	
D. Others	2	
II Verification of previous appointment	7	11.11
A. As assistant to senior officials:	1	
B. In charge of:	4	
C. Official titles conferred:	2	
III New appointment	30	47.62
A. As assistant to senior officials:	6	
B. In charge of:	18	
C. Official titles conferred:	5	
IV Alteration of previous appointment	2	3.17
Total	63	100

appointments. Thus, the situation reflected in the bronzes inscriptions is very different from what the traditional historical records would have us believe. The study shows that, although hereditary succession to government offices was clearly practiced and yielded opportunities to a significant number of officials to enter government service, the Zhou king actually made many more appointments without reference to the family history of the candidates.

Is this merely the bias of our sources? Probably not. New office-holding families may have opted to cast more bronzes to commemorate such important events in their family histories, but this can be offset by another consideration – that perhaps the traditional office-holding families might have had more economic power to do so. It is also possible that some appointments were made with reference to the services performed by the candidates' fathers and grandfathers, but the inscriptions failed to mention them. While this possibility cannot be excluded, there is no proof that it must be so; nor is there any logical reason why it should be so.[23] In fact, the nature of the appointment inscriptions as documents actually copied from the official edicts used in the court ceremony of appointment, as clarified in the introduction, seems to require accurate recording of the circumstances surrounding the appointments. In fact, the mention of family history of service normally appears in the quotation of "royal words," which could not be carelessly omitted. After all, the margin is quite large (38.10 percent *vs.* 61.90 percent) as present in the bronze inscriptions, and it seems difficult for some serendipitous cases to overturn the overall balance of the picture. It is, therefore, very unlikely that hereditary succession ever played an overwhelmingly dominant role in the appointments of Western Zhou officials, much less that it was the exclusive way to enter government service. It is safe to say that the Zhou king, in consideration of his own power base and the political circumstances at the central court, made a larger number of appointments, if not the majority of all appointments, without reference to the candidates' family history of service. This situation is quite consistent with the practice of the promotion of officials, which I will discuss soon below.

The statistics also show that hereditary appointment declined over time, while appointment from non-hereditary sources was on the rise (see table 5.2). As noted in Chapter 3, we have no appointment inscriptions from the early Western Zhou period. Therefore, how far the pattern of appointments described above goes back in time is still open to question.[24] From the mid-Western Zhou to the late Western Zhou, the rate of hereditary appointments dropped significantly. Among the forty-six cases from the mid-Western Zhou period, nineteen (41.3 percent) were appointments that were made with references to the candidates' grandfather and/or father, in contrast to twenty-seven cases (58.69 percent) of appointments that were made without such references. Among the seventeen late Western Zhou appointments, five (29.41 percent) were hereditary in nature, while other twelve (70.58 percent) were probably not – entailing a decrease of hereditary appointments by 28.78 percent from the mid-Western Zhou base. If we examine the contents of the late Western Zhou cases of hereditary appointments, we find that the five cases actually involve only three individuals: two of the cases (nos. 7, 8) involve the single person, Shi Li 師釐, already discussed above; another

---

[23] On the contrary, given the fact that some of the bronzes carrying such inscriptions were actually (though not exclusively) used in contexts of ancestral worship, and if the king indeed mentioned the caster's father and/or grandfather during the appointment ritual, casting a statement by the king on the vessel would be an ideal way to honor the appointee's father and grandfather.

[24] Only one early Western Zhou inscription, the Da Yu *ding* 大盂鼎 (JC: 2837), records a royal appointment, but it does not record the appointment ritual; therefore, it is not strictly an appointment inscription. In fact, one of the reasons for the lack of appointment inscriptions during the early Western Zhou might have been the adherence to hereditary rules that, since service is a presumed family right, would have made royal appointment unnecessary; or, even if it was necessarily done by the king, it might not have carried a high enough sociopolitical value to require commemoration on the bronze vessels.

(5.2: Periodized)

Category	Mid-Western Zhou	Late Western Zhou	Total
I	Nos. 1, 2, 3, 4, 5, 6, 9, 10, 11 12, 13, 14, 15, 16, 17, 18, 19 21, 24	Nos. 7, 8, 20, 22, 23	24
II	Nos. 25, 27, 28, 29, 31	Nos. 26, 30	7
III	Nos. 32, 33, 35, 36, 39, 41, 42 44, 45, 46, 47, 48, 51, 52, 53 54, 55, 56, 57, 59, 61	Nos. 34, 37, 38, 40 43, 49, 50, 58, 60	30
IV	No. 62	No. 63	2
Total	46	17	63

two new cases (nos. 22, 23) involve the person Lai 逨, whose appointments were indeed made with reference to his higher rather than immediate grandfather and father. The third individual, Bo Chen 伯晨 (no. 20), as will be examined soon below, was actually set up as a regional ruler by the Zhou, and such rulership was necessarily hereditary in the Zhou political system, hence different from regular official appointments in the Zhou central court. This small number of individual officials who came to office along a hereditary line during the late Western Zhou makes the drop of such appointments from the mid-Western Zhou even sharper. The fact is that appointments of officials as immediate successors of their grandfathers and fathers in government service were rarely made during the late Western Zhou.

Patterns of recruitment

The above discussion suggests that rather than a system that allowed only a limited number of prominent families to monopolize most of the offices, the Western Zhou government seems to have been open to a wide group of social elites. As the Zhou king could probably decide on a large number of new appointments (which in some cases might actually reflect the wills of his advisors, as noted in Chapter 3), the system actually fostered competition in which personal qualifications could have been an important factor.[25] While having a glorious grandfather and father could probably

---

[25] Certainly such competition might not always be based on personal excellence. In a society like the Western Zhou, social ties outsides one's own family line, particularly ties with powerful figures at the Zhou court and with the king's regular attendants, could be an important factor determining one's future, and whatever advantages were granted by such patronage (or even by financial standing) could be an important part of one's qualification for a new appointment. Certainly too, even modern democratic bureaucracies are not free of influence by such elements.

get one an easy toll to enter the service over elite competitors, getting a
desired appointment and being able to stay in the royally granted position
required probably not just a good birth, but more importantly a great deal
of personal effort. Certainly, this is not to argue that family background
was not important. Candidacy for government service in an aristocratic
society like the Western Zhou would probably have required some basic
social qualifications such as elite membership and an education that only
an aristocratic family could afford to provide. After all, it is not impossible
that the new appointees might have come from families that, although
they had not produced office-holders in recent generations, might have
had a family history of government service in the distant past; in that strict
sense they were not "new men" to the government. However, the fact that,
in their family history, particular "recent" service was not considered by
the Zhou king as a basis for new appointment is still very significant. It
reflects how the Zhou king (or his advisors) actually thought about what
the power structure of the Western Zhou government was and should be,
and how this bureaucratic machine should be operated. With consideration of all these factors, the present inscriptional evidence is compelling
in suggesting that by the mid-Western Zhou the Zhou central government
was based on the presumed participation of all elite families that had a
residence in the royal domain in Shaanxi, but not limited to a small group
of elites. In fact, the large number of officials with diverse lineage names
appearing in the middle and late Western Zhou inscriptions is itself a support to this point.[26]

Based on the above discussion, we can reach the following preliminary conclusions on the patterns of official selection during the middle–
late Western Zhou. (1) Hereditary succession was an important avenue
to government office as the Zhou king appointed many officials to carry
on their grandfathers' and fathers' service in the Zhou government. (2) It is
not likely that hereditary succession ever became a rule in selecting officials
for service, for the Zhou king appointed at least an equally large number
of officials with no demonstrable family history of service. Clearly there
were multiple paths to government offices. (3) In the time context suggested by our current inscriptions, hereditary appointments seem to have
been largely concentrated in the mid-Western Zhou period; as time went
on, the Zhou king appointed more and more officials from non-hereditary
sources. By the late Western Zhou, immediate hereditary succession seems
to have been mainly applied to offices that required professional skills. (4)
Even if an official's family history of service got him an appointment, there
was no guarantee that he would serve in the same office once occupied by
his grandfather and father. The inscriptional evidence suggests that the situation was rather the opposite. (5) Since one's family heritage meant only

---

[26] On this point, see again, Zhu Fenghan, *Shang Zhou jiazu xingtai yanjiu*, pp. 338–84.

a "qualification," or perhaps only a "better chance," the official had much to do himself to climb the bureaucratic ladder. The evidence provided in the next section of this chapter on the promotions of individual officials demonstrates that this was certainly the case.

PROMOTION AND OFFICIAL CAREER

One of the most characteristic aspects of the modern bureaucrats is that their lives are tied to a "career track" that carries with it expectations for status promotion, a rise in salary, and certainly a rise in prestige. This is not about their right or opportunity to enter government service, as discussed above, but about what they can do to make their life prosper after they have completed the first step and entered the system. In analyses by modern political scientists, the existence of such a "career track" has been taken as an important indication of a bureaucratic government. Weber states clearly that the "ideal-bureaucratic" official "is set for a *career* within the hierarchical order of the public service," and this is in a system where " *tenure* for life is presupposed, even where the giving of notice or periodic reappointment occurs."[27] After Weber, modern scholars continued to describe promotion along a career ladder as one of the most defining futures of bureaucracy.[28] Could Western Zhou officials be promoted? In other words, was there a career structure in the government service of the Western Zhou state? If such a career structure did exist, even at a rudimentary level, then the government service in the Western Zhou could not be one in which officials, once they were granted entrance, had their welfare secured no matter how poorly they performed, but one in which they had to work hard for a better life and higher position. In such case, an official career could well have included challenges and dangers as well as possibilities.

The promotion of officials

Let us first review the case of Hu. In the thirtieth year of King Mu, Hu was first appointed assistant to Shi Xi, with responsibilities for the Masters of Horses and Charioteers in the Zhou capital area and in the Five Cities on the Wei River plain; this appointment is said to have been the replacement of his grandfather's and father's service as previous supervisors of the Tiger Servants, the praetorian guards of the Zhou king. After serving at the post for some twenty-five years (he might have held other offices before his current appointment), when King Yih was established, and perhaps in conjunction with the inauguration of his new government, Hu was eventually given the office of Supervisor of Fine Horses in the two military camps.

---

[27] See Weber, "Bureaucracy," 202–3.
[28] See Albrow, *Bureaucracy*, p. 45; Hall, "The Concept of Bureaucracy – An Empirical Assessment," 33.

This time, it is clearly said in the inscription that Hu was granted the position held previously by his grandfather and father. Since his first appointment was only as an assistant to a higher military official, and his second appointment was evidently to an office of full capacity, the change probably included a major progression in Hu's official career. This certainly opens the possibility that when he first came into the government he was perhaps too young and inexperienced to be able to serve in his father's office.

We do not know how typical the case of Hu is due to the fact that few bronzes display the interesting relationship that we see between the Shi Hu *gui* and the Hu *gui*. After all, Hu was a person with a family history of service, and he might have entered the government at a much younger age than people who were the first in their family lines to enter the central government. But the case of Hu shows at least that officials were clearly not fixed to a particular office, but could be promoted and transferred from office to office. In fact, if officials were not appointed on the basis of their grandfathers' and fathers' government service as shown above, then it would seem natural that Western Zhou officials (many of them actually freshmen), once in the system, would make their way up the bureaucratic ladder. While this is certainly significant in itself, it means that opportunities and therefore expectations for new and better positions were characteristics of the system of the Western Zhou government. This point, I believe, is strongly suggested by actual cases of career development that we can learn from the bronze inscriptions we currently have.

Corroborating the pattern of official recruitment discussed above, the bronze inscriptions show that promotion of officials was rather regularly practiced in the Zhou government, forming one of the basic principles of government service during the Western Zhou. This can be learned from a series of important inscriptions that were cast by, or mention, individual officials at different stages in their lives during the mid- and late Western Zhou. Certainly, the key to the success of such analysis lies in the accurate dating of the relevant bronze vessels that carry such records, and fortunately, given the knowledge base we possess today about Western Zhou bronzes and their inscriptions, this is indeed possible by employing multiple standards of dating based on the internal links of these inscriptions to each other and to other inscribed bronzes of their contemporary periods, and on archeological-art historical observations of their body designs and decorative patterns (evidence for dating will be presented mainly in the footnotes below). In fact, particularly for the purpose of this analysis, relative dating of the inscriptions cast by, or mentioning, a single individual is more important, and indeed much easier, than the accurate regnal dating of each individual bronze. Therefore, there is a solid basis to support this analysis.

Below, I will first discuss the career development of four officials. Their life experience tells us that there were bureaucratic ladders by means of which a person, as a member of the social elite, could make his way to the top of the Zhou bureaucracy:

The first official is Shi Chen 師晨, who appears in the inscriptions of the Shi Chen *ding* 師晨鼎 (JC: 2817) and Taishi Cuo *gui* 太師虘簋 (JC: 4251). He is probably also the same person as Bo Chen 伯晨 in the Bo Chen *ding* 伯晨鼎 (JC: 2816). Chronological studies suggest that the Taishi Cuo *gui* is later than the Shi Chen *ding* and the Bo Chen *ding* is later than the Taishi Cuo *gui*.[29] According to the Shi Chen *ding*, Shi Chen previously served as an assistant under Shi Su 師俗, who was in a leading position in the civil administration of the major cities in the Wei River valley in the time of King Gong through King Yih. The position, though not insignificant, was not one of high prestige because it was not an office of full capacity. However, by the time when the Taishi Cuo *gui* was cast, Shi Chen was the person in the royal court who took the king's order to summon the candidate into audience with the king; normally the role was played by royal attendants such as the Chief Interior Scribe or the Document Maker. This indicates that Shi Chen made his way from the local administration of the cities into the king's direct service, a significant progression in his career. The inscription of the Bo Chen *ding* records a ceremony in which the Zhou king commanded Bo Chen 伯晨 (= Shi Chen) to succeed his grandfather and father to be the ruler of the state of Huan 𣏄. This suggests that Shi Chen might have been a young prince from a small regional state ruled by his father. After serving many years in the local administration of the royal domain and then at the royal court attending the Zhou king, he was eventually appointed as the next ruler of his father's state by the Zhou king, who by this time must have known him personally very well.

The second case is Shenji 龗季, who is mentioned in the famous Fifth Year Qiu Wei *ding* 五年裘衛鼎 (JC: 2832) as a minor officer in the small

---

[29] As mentioned in Chapter 3, note 56, the Shi Chen *ding* is among the group of bronzes all mentioning Supervisor of Horses Gong 共 as the *youzhe* in appointment ceremonies that took place in the Shi Lu Gong 師彔宮, dating to the period of King Yih and King Xiao. The Taishi Cuo *gui*, on the other hand, records Superintendent Hu 曶 as the announcer of a royal command; this suggests that the Taishi Cuo *gui* might have been cast very close in time to the Cai *gui* 蔡簋 (JC: 4340), which also records Superintendent Hu of the Royal Household, active sometime later in the reign of King Xiao or early King Yi. Indeed, Ma Chengyuan dates the Cai *gui* to the first year of King Yi and the Taishi Cuo *gui* in the twelfth year of the king; see Ma Chengyuan, *Shang Zhou qingtongqi mingwen xuan*, 3, pp. 263–64. So, it is very likely that the Shi Chen *ding* is earlier than the Taishi Cuo *gui*. Even if the two bronzes were from the same reign, the Taishi Cuo *gui* is necessarily later because it was cast in the twelfth year, while the Shi Chen *ding* was cast in the third year. On this sequence, see also Shaughnessy, *Sources of Western Zhou History*, pp. 262–63. As for the Bo Chen *ding*, there is little inscriptional evidence to link it to other bronzes. However, archeological study of the vessel would leave us little doubt that it is later than both the Shi Chen *ding* and the Taishi Cuo *gui*. The vessel has long been lost, but the *Huaimi shanfang jijin lu* 懷米山房吉金錄 depicts it as a deep-bellied hemispherical *ding* sitting on horse-hoof legs with ear-handles turning up straight from under the rim. Such hemispherical *ding* vessels are normally dated to the late Western Zhou. Therefore, the Bo Chen *ding* could not be much earlier than the time of King Li. See *Huaimi shanfang jijin lu* (Cao Zaikui)(Kyoto: Bunsekidō, 1882), p. 2.7; see also Shirakawa Shizuka, "Kinbun tsūshaku," 22.12528–37.

bureaucracy under Bangjun Li 邦君厲, who was actually sued by Qiu Wei at the Zhou court. However, in the Yi *gui* 伊簋 (JC: 4287) and the Da Ke *ding* 大克鼎 (JC: 2836), both evidently cast later than the Fifth Year Qiu Wei *ding*,[30] he played the important role of *youzhe*, usually played by eminent officials at the court. Both Yi and Ke were commanded to work in the royal household, and Ke was given the mission of taking in and sending out the royal command. There is clearly a dramatic gap between Shenji's earlier status as reflected in the Qiu Wei *ding* and his later standing at the royal court. By the time of Ke's appointment, he might have already served more than one king and must have been an eminent senior official at the Zhou court, holding a position somewhat similar to the Superintendent.[31]

The third case is Shi Dui 師兌, the caster of the First Year Shi Dui *gui* 元年師兌簋 (JC: 4274) and the Third Year Shi Dui *gui* 三年師兌簋 (JC: 4318).[32] In the first year of probably King Li, Shi Dui was appointed assistant to Shi Hefu 師龢父 in charge of the Masters of Horses in the Left and Right Camps and the Masters of Horses in the Five Cities; thus Shi Dui held a first position very similar to Hu's about a hundred years previously. The Third Year *gui* cast by Shi Dui is above all illuminating. The inscription records the Zhou king actually recounting Shi Dui's initial appointment as assistant two years previously (recorded in the first year *gui*), and then, the king commanding Shi Dui to take over the office left behind by Shi Hefu as commander of the Masters of Horses in the two camps and the Five Cities.[33] As the Third Year Shi Dui *gui* is necessarily

---

[30] It is generally agreed that the Fifth Year Qiu Wei *ding* was cast in the fifth year of King Gong; see Shaughnessy, *Sources of Western Zhou History*, 254–55; Ma Chengyuan, *Shang Zhou qingtongqi mingwen xuan*, 3, p. 131. The Yi *gui* and Da Ke *ding*, by their designs, are necessarily later than the time of King Gong during the mid-Western Zhou, but not too late to have been cast during Shenji's lifetime. As already mentioned in Chapter 2, the Da Ke *ding* mentions that Ke's grandfather, Shi Huafu 師華父, had served King Gong; with one reign in between during which Ke's father might have served King Yih, Ke himself might have lived in the time of King Xiao to King Yi. Therefore, the Da Ke *ding* has been dated by scholars to the reign of King Xiao or King Yi. Of course, because of the uneven length of the reigns, this date can be moved a bit up or down. But since Ke's grandfather lived in the reign of King Gong, when the Fifth Year Qiu Wei *ding* was cast, it is reasonable that Ke himself cast bronzes in a later time. If Shenji started his service under Bangjun Li as a young minor officer when Ke's grandfather was in office, it is quite possible for him to see Ke entering the government; by that time, Shenji was probably a senior official with thirty–forty years of experience, and the inscriptions of the Yi *gui* and Da Ke *ding* indeed suggest that this is the case. On the date of the Da Ke *ding*, see Ma Chengyuan, *Shang Zhou qingtongqi mingwen xuan*, 3, pp. 215–17. The Yi *gui*, with its bold-line decorative patterns and the two exaggerated handles, certainly assures a date later than the time of King Gong.

[31] Judging from Shenji's name, he might have come from the state of Shen, probably located in the upper Jing River valley. This indicates that Shenji might have followed the same path into Zhou government as did Shi Chen. On the state of Shen, see Li Feng, *Landscape and Power in Early China*, pp. 221–28.

[32] This case was noted about forty years ago by Professor Cho-yun Hsu in "Some Working Notes on the Western Chou Government," 523.

[33] Most scholars agree that Shi Hefu, also mentioned in the Shi Hui *gui* 師毀簋 (JC:4311) (as Bo Hefu 伯龢父) and Shi Li *gui* 師𩰚簋 (JC: 4324), was the historical Gongbo He 共伯龢, who stepped in to rule after King Li went into exile in 842 BC. It seems likely that Shi Hefu previously served as the head of the locally based military forces in the Zhou capital region. When he left the office,

later than the First Year Shi Dui *gui* as self evident in their inscriptions, this presents an excellent example that a person was promoted to an office of full capacity after the departure of his superior under whom he had served previously as an assistant. By the same token, by the mention of Shi Dui's earlier assistantship to Shi Hefu, the Third Year inscription naturally confirms the early date of the First Year inscription.

The fourth case is recorded by the recently discovered Meixian 眉縣 bronzes. The main body of the long text on the Lai *pan* 逨盤 celebrates the family history of Lai, juxtaposed with the genealogy of the Zhou kings whom the ancestors of Lai are reported to have served in their lives. The inscription records that Lai 逨 was himself recruited for government service following his ancestors and was appointed assistant to a higher official named Rong Dui 榮兌 in managing the marshes and forests in the Four Directions. The Forty-second Year Lai *ding* 四十二年逨鼎 from the same cache, cast apparently by the same Lai, records a battle with the invading Xianyun in which Lai made a significant military contribution.[34] It so happened that war broke out just at the point when Lai was sent to settle Changfu, newly established by King Xuan as the ruler of the state of Yang 楊, in the Fen River valley in southern Shanxi, probably performing his duty as assistant to the Rong Dui responsible for marshes and forests. Lai's career continued to develop in the forty-third year of King Xuan when the Forty-third Year Lai *ding* 四十三年逨鼎 was cast. The inscription presents one of the most detailed accounts of the appointment ritual, in which King Xuan first retrospectively recounted Lai's initial appointment as assistant to Rong Dui. Thereupon, the king reappointed Lai to serve as the administrator of the people of Li 歷, apparently an office of full capacity in controlling the population in a local area. One may speculate that what is recorded on the Forty-second Year *ding* might have contributed at least partly to Lai's promotion in the forty-third year of King Xuan.

The above are explicit examples of officials who started their careers in a minor office and were then promoted to higher positions after a certain period of service (see table 6). The two Shi Dui *gui* suggest that assistantship in an office could lead directly to full appointment to the same office. The cases of Shi Chen and Shenji demonstrate that people who started as minor local civil administrators had chances to move up into the direct service of the Zhou king and thus exercise important influence in the royal

---

his former assistant, Shi Dui, filled in his position. For Shi Hefu, see also Shaughnessy, *Sources of Western Zhou History*, pp. 272–73.

34 The high year numbers on the Forty-second and Forty-third Year *ding* suggest that the Lai bronzes were certainly cast in the later years of the reign of King Xuan, the only late Western Zhou king who ruled that long. This date is also corroborated by the royal genealogy recorded on the Lai *pan* that runs down uninterruptedly from King Wen to King Li, leaving out only the last two kings of the Western Zhou. For the discovery of the Meixian bronzes, see *Shengshi jijin*, pp. 55–57; see also, *Wenwu* 2003.6, 16–27.

Table 6: *Career development of seven Western Zhou officials (dates approximate)*

Kings	Mu	Gong	Yih	Xiao	Yi	Li	Xuan
Hu 虎		Assistant to Shi Xi (Masters of Horses and Charioteers)					
膳季 Shenji		Minor official under Bangjun Li	In charge of fine horses in the Left and Right Camps		*Youzhe* in appointment ceremony		
曶 Hu			Royal Diviner (or Supervisor of Land in the Eight Armies of Chengzhou) ------	Superintendent of Royal Household			
師晨 Shi Chen				Assistant to Shi Su ------	Important court official ------	Ruler of Huan	
免 Mian					Assistant to Zhou Shi (sup. forest) ----- Supervisor of Land --	Supervisor of Construction?	
師兌 Shi Dui						Assistant to Shi Hefu (Masters of Horses) -- In full charge	
逨 Lai						Assistant to Rong Dui of Li ---	In full charge of people of Li

court. The following two cases, though involving uncertainties in the identification of the casters and the chronological sequence of their bronzes, also suggest changes of position in an official's career.

The first case is Hu 曶, who appears in the Hu *hu* 曶壺 (JC: 9728), Hu *ding* 曶鼎 (JC: 2838), Cai *gui* 蔡簋 (JC: 4340), and the Taishi Cuo *gui* 太師虘簋 (JC: 4251). The Hu *hu* states that Hu was appointed "Grand Supervisor of Land" (*zhong situ* 塚司土), belonging to the military organization of the Eight Armies stationed in the eastern capital Chengzhou. The Hu *ding* inscription is a complex one composed of three parts, the last of which records that Hu was appointed royal diviner to replace his father. However, since the two vessels were dedicated to different fathers, they might not have been cast by the same person.[35] The Cai *gui* then records Hu's role as one of the Superintendents, the leading figures of the Royal Household officials, and this position of Hu is further confirmed by the inscription of the Taishi Cuo *gui*. Guo Moruo suggested that the Superintendent Hu was the same as the diviner Hu;[36] since both roles belonged to the administration of the Royal Household, Guo is probably right in suggesting this identification. Since most scholars agree that the Cai *gui* was cast later than the Hu *ding*, this suggests that Hu might have started his career as a royal diviner and gradually reached the top of the bureaucracy of the Royal Household.

The second example is Mian 免, who cast the Mian *gui* 免簋 (JC: 4240), Mian *fu* 免簠 (JC: 4626), and Mian *zun* 免尊 (JC: 6006).[37] The Mian *gui* says that in the twelfth month, Mian was appointed assistant to a civil administrator named Zhou Shi 周師 in charge of the forests. According to

---

[35] The Hu *hu* is dedicated to "Cultured Deceased Father Ligong" 文考釐公, while the Hu *ding* is dedicated to "Cultured Deceased Father Gongbo" 文考弈伯; for this view, see *Shanzhai yiqi tulu* (by Rong Geng; Beiping: Harvard-Yenching Institute 1936), p. 28; Ma Chengyuan, *Shang Zhou qingtongqi mingwen xuan*, 3, p. 213. However, there are also scholars who think that the Hu *ding* and Hu *hu* were cast by the same person; see Guo Moruo, *Liang Zhou jinwen ci daxi tulu kaoshi*, p. 100. As for the date of the Hu bronzes, Shaughnessy dates the Hu *ding* to the first year of King Yih, in the same year as the Shi Hu *gui* 師虎簋, based on its mention of the names of Jingbo and Kuang 匡; the latter person cast another inscription, the Kuang *you* 匡卣 (JC: 5423), clearly mentioning King Yih. See Shaughnessy, *Sources of Western Zhou History*, pp. 119, 257; Ma Chengyuan, *Shang Zhou qingtongqi mingwen xuan*, 3, pp. 169–72. The shape of the surviving cover of the Hu *hu* suggests a square-bodied *hu*-vessel, which did not appear until the very late phase of the mid-Western Zhou. Considering the different dedications of the two bronzes, it would be better to treat them as two people. In any event, the Hu *ding* would necessarily date earlier than the Cai *gui* and Taishi Cuo *gui*, cast during the Xiao–Yi period as already discussed above.

[36] Guo also pointed out that since both the Hu *ding* and the Cai *gui* were cast in the first year but mention different offices of Hu, the Cai *gui* must have been cast in a later reign. See Guo Moruo, *Liang Zhou jinwen ci daxi tulu kaoshi*, pp. 103–4. See also Chen Mengjia, "Xi Zhou tongqi duandai," 6.122.

[37] The Mian bronzes belong to the group of bronzes centering on Jingshu 井叔, whose time of activity in the Zhou court was evidently the late phase of the mid-Western Zhou, spanning roughly across the reigns of King Xiao and King Yi, and whose tomb is probably among the group of large tombs excavated at Zhangjiapo 張家坡. See Chen Mengjia, "Xi Zhou tongqi duandai," 6.106–113; see also Zhang Changshou. "Lun Jingshu tongqi: 1983–86 nian Fengxi fajue ziliao zhi er," *Wenwu* 1990.7, 32–35.

the Mian *fu*, in the third month, Mian was appointed Supervisor of Land with jurisdiction over the forest, hunting affairs, and animal breeding in the suburb of the city Zheng 鄭. Then the Mian *zun* says that, in the sixth month, the king reappointed Mian as the Supervisor of Construction. The chronological sequence of these three bronzes cannot be determined. But they show us at least how a single official could be transferred between offices.

General trends in career development

Although the above cases may not be sufficient to suggest a general rule about the promotion of Western Zhou officials, they are enough to make the point that Western Zhou officials could elevate their status through promotion. Clearly, there were multiple channels to government office and opportunities for people with less prestigious origins to move up to the top level of the bureaucracy. There were also opportunities for people in the small local states to move into service in the central government and become influential bureaucrats at the central court. Furthermore, the examples analyzed above seem to suggest two possible trends in the mechanism of official promotion in the Western Zhou government.

First, three officials we have discussed, Shi Chen, Shi Dui, and Lai, were first appointed as assistants to senior officials; only after a period of service were they promoted to offices of full capacity. This is also true of Hu 虎, discussed earlier, who entered military service along a hereditary line. These individual cases suggest that it must have been quite common, if not always, that an official started his service at the assistant level and then, after a period of service, was promoted to an office of full capacity. If this had been the regular pattern of promotion, experience and personal merit would have been considered very important factors in the government service of the Western Zhou. And, as discussed earlier regarding assistant-ship, government service during the Western Zhou would have been based on the expectation that the officials would improve their status through continuing effort and good performance. Second, in the cases of Shi Chen and Shenji, the promotion clearly involved transference from local civil administration to the central court and then into direct service of the king. This is probably because direct service to the king was the most prestigious category of jobs in the whole Western Zhou state. By the late Western Zhou the Superintendent had become one of the most important political figures at the Zhou court.[38]

The first trend is strongly supported by the statistics. Tables 4–5 show that a total number of eleven individuals in our current corpus of

---

[38] On the importance of the office of Superintendent, see Zhang Yachu and Liu Yu, *Xi Zhou jinwen guanzhi yanjiu*, p. 41. See also discussions in Chapter 2, pp. 68–70.

inscriptions were appointed assistants to senior officials, as compared to thirty-seven individuals who were put in full charge of some duties and ten officials who were granted official titles, with or without administrative duties specified. We found that among the eleven people who were appointed assistants, four (36.36 percent) cast vessels for their fathers, in contrast to the twenty-two (59.46 percent) full-capacity office holders who cast vessels for their deceased fathers. Among the ten people who obtained official titles, five (50 percent) cast vessels for their fathers. These figures have significant implications. They suggest that almost twice as many officials charged with full responsibilities had fathers who had died by the time of their appointments as officials whose fathers had died by the time of their first assistantship. This strongly suggests that the people who were appointed assistants were a much younger group of officials than those who were charged with full responsibilities. The percentage 59.46 percent is meaningful in itself: by the time when Western Zhou official got his full appointment, there was a 59.46 percent chance that his father had already died. In other words, in the government service of the Western Zhou, one probably had to wait until a relatively old age to get a full appointment. By the same token, the relatively low percentage (36.36 percent) of the people whose fathers died before their first appointment as assistants suggests that officials did not have to wait to enter government service until the death of their fathers, and there are examples of a son and his father serving in the same period of time in the Western Zhou government.[39] This again argues that there was no rule determining that a son must succeed to the same office previously held by his father. Evidently, official service during the Western Zhou was neither a deadlock in the sense that everyone was fixed in a particular position, nor was it a random process in which only good luck could bring people a better future. Instead, our inscriptions suggest

---

[39] In fact, the bronze inscriptions offer circumstances where father and son appeared in the same scene of government. For instance, the Li *ding* 利鼎 (JC: 2804) records Li's 利 appointment to government office; incidentally, in the appointment ritual Li was accompanied by Jingbo 井伯, the well-known head of the Jing 井 lineage during the King Mu–Gong period. The name Li 利 matches closely Jing Li 井利 listed in the *Mu Tianzi zhuan* for King Mu's reign (which I suspect is wrongly transmitted as Gonggong Li 共公利 in the *Current Bamboo Annals*). Thus, most probably, Li was a son of Jingbo. See *Mu Tianzi zhuan*, 1, pp. 1–2; *Zhushu jinian*, 2, p. 9 (Legge, *The Shoo King*, Prolegomena, p. 150); on the identification of Li, see also Ma Chengyuan, *Shang Zhou qingtongqi mingwen xuan*, 3, p. 133. In the Mao *gui* 卯簋 (JC: 4327), another mid-Western Zhou inscription, we find that Rongji 榮季 was playing the role of *youzhe* in an appointment ceremony hosted by Rongbo 榮伯, probably his elder brother. In a military context, for instance, the Ban *gui* 班簋 (JC: 4341) suggests that Qi 遣 was commanded to assist his father, the Duke of Mao 毛, Ban 班, on a campaign in the east. Both figures are mentioned in the *Zhushu jinian* as Maobo Qian 毛伯遷 and Maogong Ban 毛公班. On this relationship see Edward L. Shaughnessy, "On the Authenticity of the *Bamboo Annals*," *Harvard Journal of Asiatic Studies* 46.1 (1986), 152–55; Ma Chengyuan, *Shang Zhou qingtongqi mingwen xuan*, 3, pp. 108–110. Even in an early Western Zhou inscription, the Qin *gui* 禽簋 (JC: 4041), Qin 禽 (later Ruler of the state of Lu) is mentioned as serving as Invocator on a campaign during which his father, the Duke of Zhou, was the royal advisor. Although the issue needs to be studied more systematically, it seems evident that the Western Zhou government provided opportunities for the sharing of administrative responsibilities between family members, particularly father and son.

that there were rules that the officials could and were expected to follow and a career track in which personal effort could make a difference.

Criteria for promotion

This is an area that we know very little about. But this is an important subject, so perhaps we should lay out what we do know now and what we should expect to know in the future. Logically, in a government that allowed regular promotions, personal merit must have served as an important base. However, our current evidence for this is inadequate, and the actual circumstances that led to a person's promotion in the government system of the Western Zhou could be just as complex as in the bureaucracies of the modern world; it could hardly always be a fair competition even in the most bureaucratized system. Besides family background, which has already been discussed fully above, even in the channel of personal competition, social distinctions, social ties with particularly influential ministers at the court, and economic standing could all play an important part, resulting in numerous contingencies. But this does not mean that there could not have been basic standards or conventions of personal excellence required for promotion. In fact, there was an institution that seems to have been closely related to the process of promotion in the Western Zhou government.

For a long time, scholars have debated about the meaning of *mie-li* 蔑歷, a term that frequently appears in the Western Zhou bronze inscriptions (蔑歷) and possibly designates the practice of merit-recounting. The term is used in the following contexts:

Lu Dong *you* 彔致卣 (JC: 5419):
Bo Yongfu 伯雍父 recounted Lu's merits (蔑彔歷) and awarded [him] ten strings of cowries …

Jing *you* 競卣 (JC: 5425):
Bo Xifu 伯犀父 honored Jing and arrived at his office. Jing was recounted [his] merits (競蔑歷). [Bo Xifu] awarded Jing a jade tablet …

Shi Wang *ding* 師望鼎 (JC: 2812):
The king therefore will not forget the offspring of the sagely person and will abundantly recount merits and award beneficence (多蔑歷賜休) …

The Lu Zhong *you* and the Jing *you* emerge from military contexts of campaigns led by Bo Yongfu and Bo Xifu against the invasion by the Huaiyi (or Southern Yi) evidently during the reign of King Mu, where Lu Zhong and Jing as subordinate officers received *mieli* performed by their respective superior commanders.[40] The Shi Wang *ding*, on the other hand,

---

[40] The Lu Zhong *you* belongs to the group of inscribed bronzes that have common reference to the prominent figure Bo Yongfu 伯雍父; the Jing *you* belongs to the group of bronzes centered on Bo

carries a pronouncement by Shi Wang, a Royal Household official who sent out and took in the king's command, in which the caster prayed for the benefice of abundant performance of *mieli* by the king.[41] Tang Lan suggested that *mieli* means "to praise or to acknowledge merit," and this interpretation has been widely followed by other scholars.[42] In an earlier study, Yan Yiping identified *mieli* with the term *fayue* 伐閱, appearing in the *Hanshu*, referring to the process of "recounting one's *curriculum vitae*."[43] There are a total of more than thirty inscriptions that mention the performance of *mieli*, making such records one of the most frequently recurrent genres among the bronze inscriptions.[44] The inscriptions suggest that *mieli* was regularly performed by the Zhou king for the officials or by the superior officials for their subordinates. In general, it can be said that *mieli* was an action that a person with superior authority performed to/for his subordinates or subjects, associated with which was a deep sense of recognition and appreciation, and that it was itself considered by the recipients as an honor worth recording in the bronze inscriptions. This point can be further confirmed by the fact that such a performance was often followed by material rewards to the officials for whom the ritual of *mieli* was conducted. It is likely that the action involved the oral expression and the recording in writing of what the authorities considered meritorious. Although we still do not know in detail what was actually done, its function can nevertheless be largely ascertained.

While this interpretation seems largely acceptable, the real problem is that we cannot detect a constant way in which *mieli* was related to government appointments. If a consistency between the two rituals can be found, we would be able to suggest that recounting one's merit was a foundation for government appointments. But the condition of our sources is apparently

---

Xifu伯犀父. Ma Chengyuan dates both groups to King Mu, with the Bo Yongfu-group preceding the Bo Xifu-group, while Chen Mengjia places them in the time of King Kang, which is now clearly impossible. See Ma Chengyuan, *Shang Zhou qingtongqi mingwen xuan*, 3, pp. 113–24; Chen Mengjia, "Xi Zhou tongqi duandai," 5.107–12. I believe that stylistic consideration would suggest that the Bo Xifu-group bronzes might be slightly earlier than the Bo Yongfu-group of bronzes.

[41] The Shi Wang *ding*, recently purchased by the Art Institute of Chicago, was clearly related to a group of bronzes cast by the members of the Guo 虢 lineage, excavated in Qiangjiacun 強家村 in Zhouyuan, the family genealogy of which can date it with little doubt to the time of King Yih to King Xiao. See Li Xueqin, *Xinchu qingtongqi yanjiu*, pp. 85–87.

[42] Tang Lan argued that 蔑 depicts the action of cutting off one's leg or foot, hence coming close to the meaning of *fa* 伐; in cases where the character *mie* 蔑 is used alone, it can be substituted with *fa*. Furthermore, the character *fa*伐 has the meaning of *mei*美, in both its adjectival senses (fine, beautiful) and its verbal senses (to praise, to honor), supported by textual examples. As for *li*歷, it has been read to mean "experience" or "merit" by scholars since the Qing dynasty. See Tang Lan, *Tang Lan xiansheng*, pp. 224–35. See also Ma Chengyuan, *Shang Zhou qingtongqi mingwen xuan*, 3, pp. 3–4.

[43] Yan offered many examples from the *Hanshu* and *Houhan shu* where officials were inspected for their *fayue* 伐閱; the context of the texts suggests a type of written statement similar to modern-day *lüli* 履歷 (*curriculum vitae*). See Yan Yiping, "Mieli guyi," *Zhongguo wenzi* 10 (1962), 1–13.

[44] An early list drawn up by Yan Yiping gives thirty-five inscriptions by 1962. Zhang Yachu's new index to bronze inscriptional terms lists thirty-one clear cases of *mieli*. See Yan Yiping, "Mieli guyi," 1–5; Zhang Yachu, *Yin Zhou jinwen jicheng yinde* (Beijing: Zhonghua, 2001), p. 1086.

disappointing in this regard. There is only one inscription, the Mian *zun*
免尊 (JC: 6006), that records an appointment announced following the
ritual of *mieli*:

It was the sixth month, first auspiciousness, the king was in Zheng 鄭. On
day *dinghai* (no. 24), the king entered the grand chamber. Jingshu 井叔
accompanied Mian 免 to his right. The king recounted Mian's merit (*mieli*
蔑歷) and commanded Scribe Mao to award Mian dark kneepads and a
jade circlet; [Mian] to be Supervisor of Construction. In response [Mian]
extols the king's beneficence, herewith makes [this] sacrificial vessel. May
Mian for ten thousand years eternally treasure and use it.

   This is among a group of inscriptions cast by an official called Mian in
the late part of the mid-Western Zhou period. Mian also served as Supervisor of Land in the vicinity of the city of Zheng, as recorded in the Mian *fu*
免簠 (JC: 4626). The current inscription records the king's visit to the city
of Zheng, where he had an audience with Mian. In the audience, the king
first performed the ritual of *mieli* for Mian and then furnished him with
royal gifts and reappointed him Supervisor of Construction. Although we
cannot be sure that the two bronzes were cast in the same year, if they were,
the Mian *zun*, cast in the sixth month, would be necessarily later than the
Mian *fu*, cast in the third month of the year. The link between the two
inscriptions suggests that Mian's successful performance as the Supervisor
of Land in Zheng might have been responded to by the king with the offer
of the ritual of *mieli*, resulting directly in his new appointment as Supervisor of Construction in the same city.
   Among the more than thirty inscriptions that record the performance
of the *mieli*-ritual, the majority (more than twenty) are from the mid-
Western Zhou period. But *mieli* seems to have had a much longer history
than the appointment ritual, having its origin in the late Shang Dynasty,
as suggested by the inscription of the Xiaozi X *you* 小子𣄤卣 (JC: 5417);[45]
during the early Western Zhou period, *mieli* was often conducted, mostly
relating to the promotion of military merits. After perhaps the first two
kings of the mid-Western Zhou, performances of the ritual of *mieli* began
to decline in number, and there are only two late Western Zhou inscriptions, including the Liang Qi *zhong* 梁其鐘 (JC: 187–188) and Wu *gui*
敔簋 (JC: 4323), that mention the performance of the *mieli* ritual. This
marked decline in the popularity of the *mieli* ritual coincided with the

---

[45] The content of the inscription is apparently related to a Shang campaign against the Renfang
人方 in the Shandong region during which the caster of the bronze was rewarded with two strings
of shells by a Shang prince, and the *mieli* ritual was conducted for him by the latter. For a reading of this inscription, see Ma Chengyuan, *Shang Zhou qingtongqi mingwen xuan*, 3, pp. 3–4. For
a discussion of the inscription and others in the context of Shang campaign against Renfang, see
Akatsuka Kiyoshi, "In kinbun," in *Chūgoku kodai no shūkyō to bunka* (Tokyo: Kadokawa shoten,
1977), pp. 675–79.

rise of the appointment ritual, which did not gain its full popularity in Zhou governmental practice until after the reign of King Mu. This may in some way explain why the two rituals are largely isolated from each other, but still the gap in our inscriptional records is difficult to fill. Perhaps the tradition of *mieli* was so broadly and loosely conceived that its performance was not limited to administrative merits; in fact, we do know that the ritual was conducted also for some aristocratic ladies, such as in the case recorded in the Geng Ying *you* 庚嬴卣 (JC: 5426). Certainly the initiator of the ritual did not have to be the Zhou king, but could be any one in a superior position *vis-à-vis* his subordinate who was to receive the benefit of the ritual. It suited a government system that was largely unbureaucratic and operated for the most part on personal rules; it certainly had not developed the kind of institutional features associated with the Han Dynasty practice of *fayue* 伐閱. As the bureaucratic trend of the Zhou government was gradually intensified during the middle and late Western Zhou as indicated by the emergence of the appointment ritual, which required the interaction of multiple official roles including the king in a highly regularized process, the *mieli* ritual, though might still be performed, ceased to attract enough of the attention of the Zhou aristocratic officials to warrant pouring in their resources to record it on their bronzes. But again, much of this speculation needs to be confirmed with evidence that may become available in the future.

MILITARY SERVICE AS QUALIFICATION FOR CIVIL OFFICE

One of the most fundamental functions of the government was to conduct warfare. The Western Zhou government was no exception, and military affairs remained one of its most important businesses throughout the dynasty. However, as noted in Chapter 2, even in the early Western Zhou the civil offices, though they could be temporarily or even prominently held by men of military background, were well developed. By the mid-Western Zhou, the Six and Eight Armies had together developed into a complex system with its own structure of civil and military administration, largely separate from the civil administration of the Zhou central government. Therefore, the question is: As a government institution, how militant was the Western Zhou government in the sense that military officials were put in charge of most if not all civil functions? Or, from the perspective of individual officials, how important was one's military background as a qualification for service in the central government?

Shi 師 *as ex-military officers*

In the Western Zhou bronze inscriptions, particularly the appointment inscriptions, the most common style of names is those prefixed with the character *shi* 師, for instance, Shi Hu 師虎, Shi Xun 師詢, Shi Ke 師克, etc. According to a list offered by Wu Zhenfeng, fifty-three Western Zhou officials are referred to as *shi* in the bronze inscriptions.[46] The number far exceeds other official titles we find in the inscriptional records, except probably only for the designation *shi* 史 (Scribe). This term *shi* 師 has long been treated as a military title, the same as the title *Shishi* 師氏 (Marshal) that designated service military generals.[47] However, the inscriptional evidence shows that many people who bore this title were actually officials with civil administrative responsibilities. This created a problem in the interpretation of the Western Zhou government, and contributed to the impression that civil offices were freely occupied by military commanders who gave the Zhou government a strong military character. This impression somehow conflicts with our understanding of the Zhou government in other aspects that show a well-developed system of civil administration by, at the latest, the mid-Western Zhou.

A systematic analysis conducted by Zhang Yachu and Liu Yu on the meaning of *shi* concluded that the responsibilities of *shi* covered both military and civil administrative and even educational affairs.[48] Treating *shi* as a specific official title, the analysis failed to suggest a consistent interpretation of *shi* but instead made it an omnipresent figure in the Western Zhou government. In order to understand the various roles of *shi* recorded in the bronze inscriptions, a more complex approach must be adopted. The important point here is that, as already pointed out in Chapter 2, not all titles mentioned in the inscriptions were official titles; some titles might have been designations of status or even merely personal names. An "official title" is the title of a government office to which defined administrative jurisdictions were attached. With this new understanding, I believe that the problem can now be explained quite logically, and the answer actually provides us with the key to understand the relationship between military service and civil administration in the Western Zhou.

In fact, a number of inscriptions actually suggest that men with the title *shi* had actually served military functions. For instance, in the Dong *gui* 㝬簋 (JC: 4322), *shishi* were sent to attack the invading enemies. In two other inscriptions, the First Year Shi Shi *gui* 元年師事簋 (JC: 4279) and Fifth Year Shi Shi *gui* 五年師事簋 (JC: 4216), the term *shishi* apparently designates military units stationed near the Zhou capital Feng.[49] However,

---

[46] See Wu Zhenfeng, *jinwen renming huibian* (Beijing: Zhonghua, 1987), pp. 195–201.

[47] See Guo Moruo, "Zhouguan zhiyi," pp. 85–86. It is worth noting that Shirakawa Shizuka wrote a long article to explain the origin of *shi*. Arguing in a tortuous way that the left component of the graph

represents the meat offered by the ancient communities on the eve of their members departing for hunting or military activities (a very problematic argument), Shirakawa eventually returned to the basic point that the term referred to troops and commanders of an army. See Shirakawa Shizuka, "Shaku shi," in *Kōkotsu kinbungaku ronshū* (Kyoto: Hōyū Shoten, 1974), pp. 207–305.

[48] See Zhang Yachu and Liu Yu, *Xi Zhou jinwen guanzhi yanjiu*, pp. 3–6.

[49] The First Year Shi Shi *gui* mentions that Shi Shi 師事 was commanded to supervise the *shishi*

a direct link between the term *shishi* and the title *shi* can be found in the inscription of the Shi Ju *gui* 師遽簋 (JC: 4214):[50]

It was the king's third year, fourth month, after the growing brightness of the moon, *xinyou*-day (no. 58); the king arrived at the New Temple (*xin-gong* 新宮). The king extended to inspect the marshals (*shishi* 師氏). The king called on Shi Zhen 師朕 to reward Shi Ju 師遽 with ten strings of shells. Ju bowed with his head reaching the ground, and he dares to extol the felicitous beneficence of the Son of Heaven, with which [he] makes for his deceased father Maoshu 旄叔 [this] sacrificial *gui* vessel. May [his] grandsons and sons for generations eternally treasure [it].

The inscription says that the Zhou king inspected a group of marshals (*shishi*) and commanded an individual named Shi Zhen 師朕 to give an award to another person, Shi Ju 師遽, both evidently belonging to the group of *shishi*. Hence, it is very likely that *shi*, when used alone, was the abbreviated form used for the Marshals (*shishi*). Another inscription, the Yong *yu* 永盂 (JC: 10322), also provides support to this identification. In this inscription, both Shi Tong 師同 and Kuifu 奎父 are listed as *shishi*. Although in this inscription Kuifu is not called by the title *shi*, there is little doubt that he is the same person as Shi Kuifu 師奎父, caster of the Shi Kuifu *ding* 師奎父鼎 (JC: 2813). Evidently, both Shi Tong and Shi Kuifu actually had the status of *shishi*.

The strong link demonstrated by the inscriptions suggests that officials referred to as "Shi X" probably had all served military functions at some point in their life, either as *shishi* or as commanders of the field army. If a person's current role was civil administrative and he was referred to as *shi* (with the title *shi* prefixed to his personal name), the title must have been used to designate his past service as a "marshal" or "general." In modern days, retired military generals continue to be referred to as "general" as ex-presidents continue to be referred to as "president"–the titles are honorary. In a society like the Western Zhou, it must have been quite common for noble youths to fight in wars and then to find their way into the

---

associated with the Left Camp in the district of the capital Feng. The Fifth Year Shi Shi *gui* mentions that the same Shi Shi 師事 was sent to attack the state of Qi in the far east. As noted earlier, the two bronzes were probably cast in the late phase of the mid-Western Zhou, most likely related to King Yi's campaign against Qi. On this point, see again Shaughnessy, *Sources of Western Zhou History*, pp. 266–71.

[50] The date of the Shi Ju 師遽 bronzes, including the Shi Ju *gui* 師遽簋 (JC: 4214) and Shi Ju *fangyi* 師遽方彝 (JC: 9897), currently housed in the Shanghai Museum, has been fully discussed by Shaughnessy with relation to the Li *fangyi* 盠方彝 (JC: 9900), cast in the reign of King Mu. While the two *fangyi* vessels closely resemble each other, the name Shi Ju 師遽 is also mentioned in another bronze cast by Li, the Li *juzun* 盠駒尊 (JC: 6011); these connections suggest that the two officials were very close in time. See Shaughnessy, *Sources of Western Zhou History*, p. 249. The uncertain point is the mention of "New Temple" (*xingong* 新宮) in the Shu Ju *gui* that appears on other bronzes with an indisputable King Gong date. Therefore, the Shi Ju *gui* could be from the next reign, that of King Gong. See Tang Lan, *Tang Lan xiansheng*, pp. 162–65; Ma Chengyuan, *Shang Zhou qingtongqi mingwen xuan*, 3, p. 130.

government, either by their hereditary rights or by their personal qualification. This, I believe, is the reason why so many people mentioned in the bronze inscriptions bear the title *shi* 師 "ex-military-officer." It is not an official title but a designation of past experience and hence probably also personal qualification.

The flow into civil service

This new explanation of *shi* as ex-military officers helps us to identify an important current of officials who served in the Western Zhou government. In table 4, twelve individuals with the title *shi* were appointed to government posts, including probably eight as civil administrators or Royal Household officials, about 20 percent of all officials in the same categories. If this was the normal percentage of civil administrators who were ex-military officers, then they might have constituted an important flow of officials from the military service into the civil administration, numbering more than a fifth of the civil offices at any given time. The actual number of people who had any military experience might have been even bigger than this, but it seems to be a reasonable figure for military officers who had risen to significant positions in the Zhou government that qualified them for the receipt of royal appointment. We might also expect that the figure could be bigger for the early Western Zhou during the great Zhou expansion than for the middle and later Western Zhou, when bureaucratization of the Zhou government was well under way.

These ex-military officers might have constituted an important order in the Zhou officialdom. They could have formed an influential group of men who had a similar background and mentality and perhaps also similar interests. But when they were appointed civil administrative roles, they were basically civil administrators. Many of these people performed important civil administrative roles. For instance, the well–known figure Shi Su 師俗 had commanded troops from the state of Qi on a campaign in the east in the time of King Mu to King Gong, recorded on a *gui* vessel, the Shi Mi *gui* 史密簋, cast by a scribe who had accompanied him on his major military operation.[51] Shi Su was also called Shi Sufu 師俗父 or Bo Sufu 伯俗父 in a number of contemporaneous or slightly later inscriptions, such as the Fifth Year Qiu Wei *ding* 五年裘衛鼎 (JC: 2832), Yong *yu* 永盂 (JC: 10322), and Shi Chen *ding* 師晨鼎 (JC: 2817). These inscriptions suggest that Shi Su held estates in the Luo River region in the east part of the Wei River valley and had clearly served as the head of civil administration of the major cities at the Zhou court. Under his direction, Shi Chen 師晨 had served as an assistant with responsibilities particularly for the city of Yi and the city of Zheng. Shi Su was also included in the "Committee of

---

[51] See *Kaogu yu wenwu* 1989.3, 7–9.

High Officials" at the courts of King Gong and King Yih that acted on a number of occasions commanding the whole government.

CONCLUSION

The evidence presented in this chapter suggests that, contrary to the traditional belief that the Western Zhou government featured the principle of hereditary offices, there were actually different paths for young social elites to enter government service of the Zhou state. At the time of the mid-Western Zhou, for which we have better information, the Zhou king seems to have appointed more officials from non-hereditary sources than from hereditary sources. And as time went by the rate of hereditary appointments seems to have continuously declined. Even hereditary officials had no guarantee that they could serve in their father's office; on the contrary, they might first be put in a more minor position than that once held by their fathers. The inscriptional evidence suggests that the Western Zhou government was an institution established on the idea of the presumed participation of all social elites, and, as such, it offered opportunities for the relatively weaker groups of the elite society to compete with their prestigious peers.

This situation of different avenues to government service corresponds well with what the officials might do once they entered office. The evidence suggests that the promotion of officials was regularly practiced by the Zhou government, hence offering the expectation of better jobs and higher status. It is above all significant that certain procedures were developed by which the young officials were first appointed assistants to senior officials and were then after some years of service promoted to offices of full capacity, showing evidently the existence of a career track. In a government system that allowed promotion, the personal merit of the officials could be an important factor that would lead to such opportunity, and the way up the bureaucratic ladder was often by one's own efforts. As promotion was practiced, officials could also be transferred across administrative divisions, mainly in two directions of flow: from local civil administration to the direct service of the Zhou king, and from military service to civil administration.

The evidence suggests that the lives and careers of the Western Zhou officials had gained clear bureaucratic features by the middle of the dynasty, as the government system in which they served had evidently become a bureaucracy. The Western Zhou officials, like the officials of all ancient bureaucracies, were a body of professional men who took government service as their lifelong enterprise from which they derived great honor and with which they fulfilled their personal dreams and expectations for a better future. They did not need to wait after the deaths of their fathers to enter the government, but their service could turn out to be a long journey that would take many years to bring them a full appointment. By that time, it is more likely than not that their fathers had already died. Also like other bureaucratic officials, they were subject to certain rules and procedures that governed their conduct in the government and were on a career track that, if they performed well, would surely bring them progress through promotion. Their service might not always be placed away from their home-base, as is the case for most modern bureaucrats, but they clearly had a public capacity of which they were fully aware and through which they entered contacts with other officials. This was the official body on which the Zhou king relied and by which the Western Zhou state was governed.

CHAPTER 6

The regional states and their governments

The preceding chapters have provided both an overview of the structural evolution of the Zhou central government and an in-depth analysis of its operational logic and working conventions. However, the most defining characteristics that separate the Western Zhou state and its government from political systems that existed before or after it in China lie instead in the way it accommodated the existence of the numerous regional states. Although the relationship between the Zhou central government and these outlying regional states was hardly ever administrative, much less bureaucratic, these regional segments constituted an important part of the operation of the Western Zhou state at large. It would be wrong to assume that these regional territories were placed outside the perceived perimeters of the Western Zhou state, or were unaffected by the policies made in the central court. The present chapter will fully explore this unique and complex relationship between the central court and the many regional states. Certainly, it was these regional segments that survived even after the fall of the Western Zhou and provided an important link between the royal state of Western Zhou and the imperial bureaucratic states rising from competitions that were soon to storm its ruin.

There are a set of questions that we must ask and should examine: What constituted a regional state? What were the alternatives for the Zhou to achieve royal control without installing these regional states far from home in an age when the bureaucratic system of administration was still not a part of the political knowledge of the state? While these questions must be addressed with respect to the historical circumstances and whatever answers we can draw must be based on the currently available evidence, the inquiry actually points to the basic historical mission of the Zhou regional states. We should also ask: Were there basic premises under which the regional states operated? What were their rights and obligations in the large political organization that was the Western Zhou state? Besides considering their political status, we must also examine their internal operation, and therefore a further question is: What was the level of development of their governments? The answer or answers to these questions will not only clarify the nature of the Zhou regional states, but also contribute to a deep understanding of the political logic as well as the historical legacy of the Western Zhou state as a whole.

In the last decades of the past century, archeological excavations threw important light on the cultural and political environment of these regional states. This is marked by the excavation of half a dozen cemeteries belonging to the states of Guo 虢, Ying 應, Xing 邢, Yan 燕, Lu 魯, and Qin 秦, and the rich material remains from these distant states demonstrate the Western Zhou as a period of great cultural and literacy expansion.[1] The excavations have also given us a vivid sense about how culturally these regional segments were linked to (and at the same time differentiated from) the Zhou core area, and how they responded to the royal requests politically and militarily as shown in their bronze inscriptions. The time has come for an informed assessment of the nature and functions of these regional states, although there is still a significant lack of information about the organization and operation of the regional governments. This gap in our information is due mainly to the absence of a type of inscriptions like the "appointment inscriptions" from the Zhou royal court. By the same token, the lack of such inscriptions could itself be an indication of the underdevelopment of the regional governments, which might have provided no political circumstances necessitating such a bureaucratized procedure of official appointments. Let us begin by addressing the issue of what the regional state was.

WHAT CONSTITUTED A REGIONAL STATE?

As clarified in Chapter 2, the regional states were mostly located in the river valleys and plains in the east, being geographically separate from the Zhou royal domain in Shaanxi. These states formed a special system and served as an important protection for the Zhou center (see map 1). However, what was the level of their political organization, and does it make any sense to call them "states"?

The concept of "regional state"

Before we can answer the question of what constituted a "regional state," we must first clarify the meaning of "state" as it is used in this book. "State" is one of the most diversely defined terms in sociology and political science, and different scholars tend to emphasize different aspects of it. Quentin Skinner in his study of the history of European political thought has shown how the concept of "state" was transformed from one that referred to the condition or standing of communities, peoples, or princes to one that, after the fifteenth century, referred to the apparatus of government

---

[1] For the geography of these regions, see Li Feng, *Landscape and Power*, pp. 68–70, 256–58, 265–67, 314–15, 335–38.

or the bearer of sovereign power.[2] Thus, modern definitions of the "state," whether in the Hobbesian sense of a necessary means for men to avoid the miserable condition of war against each other,[3] or in the Marxist sense of an inevitable institution for containing and suppressing class struggles,[4] stressed its status as an institution *versus* its individual citizens. There are also scholars who treat the "state" as a structural repository of the authority (or monopoly, in the Weberian terminology) to use legitimate force in a legal-political sense.[5] In the contemporarily popular construct of the "nation state" as the fundamental political expression of nationalism we see the concept extended to gain cultural and ethnic dimensions.[6] However, there are certain elements that most scholars would agree constitute part of the modern concept of the "state," gathered in the following definition proposed by the pioneering Scottish-American sociologist Robert M. MacIver: "The state is an association which, acting through law as promulgated by a government endowed to this end with coercive power, maintains within a community territorially demarcated the universal external conditions of social order."[7] Thus, the "state" is distinguished from other human associations by its purpose to establish order and security, its method of promulgating law and employing coercive power to enforce it, and its territory, based on sovereign powers originating either from an actual "sovereign" or the "people."[8] Moreover, as the "state" varies both in size and complexity in a historical sense, it certainly does not demand unity in culture and tradition within its boundaries; instead, it achieves as its mission political unity imposed on (or shared by) diverse cultural and ethnic groups, as was most often the case in the ancient world. Therefore, the "state," as the term is used in the present book, is understood as a social-political organization "materialized" in its very geographical existence, which one can actually see, and the order and security it provides, which one can actually feel.

I expect that the reader has by now become familiar with the use of the expression of the "Western Zhou state" in the previous chapters of this

---

[2] See Quentin Skinner, "The State," in *Political Innovation and Conceptual Change*, ed. Terence Ball, James Farr, and Russell L. Hanson (Cambridge: Cambridge University Press, 1989), pp. 90–131; "How We Acquired the Concept of the State (and What Concept[s] We Acquired)?" paper presented at the Columbia Conference on the "State," April 2005, Columbia University, New York.

[3] See Thomas Hobbes, *Leviathan*, ed. and intro. C. B. Macpherson (New York: Penguin Books, 1968), pp. 223–31.

[4] See Frederick Engels, *The Origin of the Family, Private Property and the State*, ed. and intro. Eleanor Burke Leacock (New York: International Publishers, 1972), pp. 228–29.

[5] See, for instance, Martin Sicker, *The Genesis of the State* (New York: Praeger, 1991), 7–10; Elman Service, *Origins of the State and Civilization: The Process of Cultural Evolution* (New York: W. W. Norton & Company, 1975), pp. 14–15.

[6] See Subhakanta Behera, *Nation-State: Problems and Perspectives* (New Delhi: Sanchar Publishing House, 1995), pp. 15–17.

[7] See R. M. MacIver, *The Modern State* (London: Oxford University Press, 1955), p. 22.

[8] On the concept of the "state," see also, "State," *Encyclopaedia Britannica* from *Encyclopaedia Britannica Online*, www.search.eb.com/article?eu=1297 (accessed July 15, 2004).

book. Not only did the Western Zhou state possess all of the elements of the "state" outlined above, the Zhou also, as will be detailed in the next chapter, fostered a mature theory of the origin of their state and a profound understanding of its historical as well as divine roles. The reason that a "regional state" is called a "state" is because it was charged with all the functions and roles performed by the Western Zhou state and possessed most of the qualifications required for a "state" apart from "sovereignty," which resided with the Zhou king. Of course, law, which is clearly the responsibility of the regional ruler, could be codified or customary; territory could be defined by borders or by the distribution of settlements – the Zhou case is a typical settlement-based state (see Chapter 7) – and the purpose of establishing order and security, which was clearly the *raison d'être*, can be both for the wellbeing of its local residents and in the interest of the Western Zhou state. It is "regional" because it is local, situated in an environment that embraced strong indigenous traditions and a largely locally based population, and because it was an active participant, as will be shown below, in the larger social-political organization that is called the "Western Zhou state."

However, even though the "regional states" performed the same functions and even possessed a similar governmental structure to that of the Western Zhou state, albeit to a lesser degree of complexity, the regional ruler was not a real "sovereign ruler"; instead, he ruled with a political power delegated to him by the Zhou king. The concept of "regional state" provides us with sufficient flexibility to represent the structural as well as operational similarities between the Western Zhou state and its various regional segments and at the same time not to blur the dimensional differences between them. The "regional state" was a human association that replicated the Western Zhou state in very fundamental ways. There is a certain degree of ambiguity caused by the use of "state" at both levels, but it is this ambiguity that indeed characterized the Western Zhou institution.

Land and population

A few inscriptional accounts on the establishment of the regional states provide us with some true sense about what might have materially constituted a regional state during the Western Zhou. The most informative is that on the Yihou Ze *gui* 宜侯夨簋 (JC: 4320), discovered in Dantu, Jiangsu Province, in 1955 (see figures 27 and 28).[9]

It was the fourth month; the time was the *dingwei* day (no. 44). [The king] observed the map of King Wu and King Cheng's campaigns against Shang and thereupon inspected the map of the eastern states. The king stood in

---

[9] For the discovery of the Yihou Ze *gui*, see *Wenwu cankao ziliao* 1955.5, 58–62.

Figure 27: The Yihou Ze *gui* (from Li Xueqin, *Zhongguo qingtongqi gaishuo*
[Beijing: Foreign Language Publisher, 1995], p. 123)

the ancestral temple of Yi 宜, facing south. The king commanded the Ruler
of Yu, Ze 虞侯矢 and said: "Transfer and be the ruler (*hou* 侯) at Yi 宜.
[I] award you X-fragrant wine of one *yu*-jar, and award one *zan*-jade, one
red-lacquered bow and one hundred red-lacquered arrows, ten black bows
and one thousand black arrows. [I] award you land, the *zhen*-fields (叫川=圳)
of which are three hundred and ...; the ... of which are one hundred and
...; the residential settlements (宅邑) of which are thirty-five; and the ...
of which are one hundred and forty. [I] award you ... and seven clans of
the king's men (王人) at Yi, and award the seven Elders (*bo* 伯) of Zheng
鄭 whose X-retainers are ... and fifty men. [I] award you commoners of Yi
numbering six hundred and ... six men." Yihou Ze extols the king's beneficence, making [for] Yugong 虞公, Father Ding, [this] sacrificial vessel.

This long inscription is interesting in many ways, and it generated considerable discussion immediately after its discovery.[10] It is interesting first

---

[10] The main debate has focused on the historical-geography of the new state of Yi, which closely concerns the issue of fixing the geopolitical perimeters of the Western Zhou state. It so happened that
the bronze was discovered in the traditional territory of the state of Wu 吳 in the Yangzi delta during
the Spring and Autumn period. Since the words Yi 宜 and Wu 吳 were presumably interchangeable
in archaic Chinese, the bronze was thus taken by some scholars as evidence on the establishment of
the state of Wu in the Yangzi Delta. See Guo Moruo, "Ze gui ming kaoshi," *Kaogu xuebao* 1956.1,
7–10; Tang Lan, "Yihou Ze gui kaoshi," *Kaogu xuebao* 1956.2, 79–83. However, the opposing view
holds that the bronze was probably imported from the north and hence constitutes no evidence to
support any Zhou connections to the Yangzi Delta. See Huang Shengzhang, "Tongqi mingwen Yi
Yu Ze de diwang jiqi yu Wuguo de guanxi," *Kaogu xuebao* 1983.3, 295–305; Edward L. Shaughnessy,

Figure 28: Inscription of the Yihou Ze *gui* (from *Yin Zhou jinwen jicheng*, no. 4320)

of all in the way the inscription begins: the observation of the war and territorial maps by the hosting king, almost certainly King Kang, because the inscription explicitly mentions his predecessors Kings Wu and Cheng. This action of observing a map indicates that, when establishing a regional state, a "territory" of a certain size in an appropriate location would be of the first royal concern. As will be detailed in Chapter 7, the conditions of such small "territories" could vary, and in the formation of the Western Zhou state it did not have to be a single block, but could have embraced

"Historical Geography and the Extent of the Earliest Chinese Kingdoms," *Asia Major* 2.2 (1989), 13–18. In fact, the second view is well supported by the archeological context, which shows clearly that the bronze was buried as an "exotic" item among local-style bronzes accompanied by ceramics characteristic of the southern culture. There seems little doubt that the state of Yi was located somewhere in the north, probably in the Henan-Shanxi region, although the specific location of Yi cannot be determined.

multiple parcels of land. As a matter of fact, Ze was given a "territory" that was not demarcated by a linear border (as in some cases of land awards in the royal domain discussed in Chapter 4), but was measured as more than three hundred *zhen*-fields, a type of arable land most likely to have been surrounded by irrigation trenches,[11] along with thirty-five natural villages, the "residential settlements" (*zhaiyi* 宅邑). Besides land, a population was granted to the state of Yi, and the interesting point of all this is that the population was mentioned in a way that suggests a multi-layered structure of social groups. This grant included first of all the "king's people" (*wangren* 王人), who, by the administrative divisions we have discussed in the previous chapters, clearly belonged to the king's personal possession, and who are mentioned as having already been in the "territory" of Yi. Secondly, seven Elders (*bo* 伯) with their servants, most likely the indigenous residents of the later city Zheng 鄭 in the west part of the Wei River valley, were given over to the new state Yi.[12] Finally, the commoners of Yi, obviously the native population of the destination settlements, were legally put under the authority of the state of Yi. In short, the inscription informs us in a unique way of the geopolitical as well as anthropological composition of the region state. If the Yihou Ze *gui* is to be used as a model of the regional state, this state must have been composed of a ranked population with the Zhou immigrants (who were further differentiated into the king's people and those of the Zhou state) from the Wei River valley superimposed on a larger base of indigenous people in a "territory" marked by a certain number of residential settlements and the land surrounding them. Here again, we see the type of *yi* settlement already discussed in detail in Chapter 4.

In a more simplistic way, however, we learn about the nature of the regional states from the inscription on the Ke *lei* 克罍 (JL: 987), which was discovered in the cemetery of the state of Yan 燕 in Liulihe 琉璃河, Beijing, probably from the tomb of the state's first ruler (see figure 29):[13]

The king said: "The Grand Protector (*taibo* 太保), you have brightened your fragrant wine and offered it to your monarch. I greatly respond to your offering, commanding Ke 克 to be ruler (*hou* 侯) in Yan 燕, to govern

---

[11] See Tang Lan, "Yihou Ze gui kaoshi," 80; Ma Chengyuan, *Shang Zhou qingtongqi mingwen xuan*, 3, p. 35.

[12] On the location and condition of Zheng, see Li Feng, "Xi Zhou jinwen zhong de Zheng di," 70–78.

[13] Yan was one of the prominent states recorded in the *Shiji* as having been granted by King Wu to the Duke of Shao 召. However, while the prominent political role of the Duke of Shao is fully documented in the early Western Zhou bronze inscriptions, the Ke *lei* inscription here makes it clear that the state was indeed granted to Ke 克, probably a son of the Duke of Shao, in honor of the Duke. See *Shiji*, 34, p. 1549. On the discovery of the Ke *lei*, see *Kaogu* 1990.1, 20–31. For a discussion of the historical background of casting the Ke *lei*, see Li Feng: "Ancient Reproductions and Calligraphic Variations," 4–8. For the political role of the Duke of Shao, see Shaughnessy, "The Role of Grand Protector Shi," 51–77.

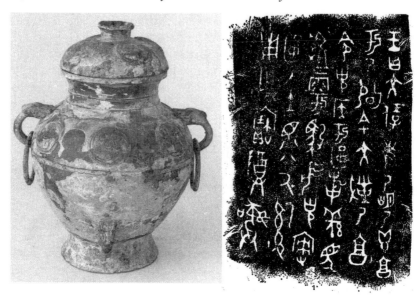

Figure 29: The Ke *lei* and its inscription recording the establishment of Yan (from *Kaogu* 1990.1, 25, fig. 4, pl. 2.2)

the Qiang 羌, Ma 馬, Zha 斸, Yu 雩, Yu 馭, and Chang 長." Ke arrived at Yan, took in land and its officials, and herewith makes [this] treasured sacrificial vessel.

The inscription, undoubtedly a fresh record on the establishment of the state, says that six ethnic groups of people were granted by the Zhou king to the state of Yan, and when Ke, the new ruler, arrived at the site, the first thing he did was to take in the land and its officials, implying the incorporation of the preexisting administrative structure into the new state Yan. As for the six groups of people granted to the Yan ruler, apparently at least some of them were not the indigenous population of the Yan region, but were immigrants that Ke received from the Zhou court and brought to his new state, as in the case of the ruler of Yi discussed above. For instance, the Qiang 羌 group was the most frequent target of military attacks by the Shang and was considered by oracle-bone scholars to have been located somewhere in southern Shanxi and eastern Shaanxi (probably even farther to the west); the Ma 馬 group was probably in southern Hebei; the Chang 長 in the mountains of eastern Shanxi; and the Zha 斸 group probably somewhere near Shang.[14]

---

[14] On the location of these ethnic groups, see variously, Chen Mengjia, *Yinxu buci zongshi*, pp. 282–84; Zheng Jiexiang, *Shang dai dili gailun*, pp. 207, 303, 314; Ding Shan, "Zha yi kao," *Zhongyang yanjiuyuan lishi yuyan yanjiusuo jikan* 2.4 (1932), 419–22. See also Zhang Yachu, "Lun Lutaishan Xi Zhou mu de niandai he zushu," *Jianghan kaogu* 1984.2, 23–28. It should be noted that, although there is no doubt that these terms designated ethnic groups active during the late Shang period, there is a degree of uncertainty about their specific locations suggested by the oracle-bone scholars.

In addition to these inscriptions, an earlier analysis conducted by Itō Michiharu of textual records on the establishment of three other states including Wey 衛, Lu 魯, and Jin 晉 concluded that the granting of groups of people from their previous locations of residence, whether temporary or permanent, constituted an essential part of the Zhou state's political-ritual strategy by which a regional state came into existence.[15]

A brief description of the regional state can be given here on the basis of the above discussion. A regional state was represented first of all by the land it occupied and by the population it possessed. In space, a regional state was defined by a cluster of *yi* settlements, each of which was surrounded by a certain area of arable land, located at a distance from a central site, where the residence of the ruler and his family temple and burial ground were located. The population of a regional state was diversified and typically stratified. In principle, it was composed of first of all a small group of conquerors, the Zhou and their close affiliates, the social elite that was organized around the ruler's family. Under them, there were immigrants of all ethnic and cultural backgrounds, brought into the new state by the Zhou elite, with whom they had complex social relationships; some of them might have been long-time allies of the Zhou, while others might have been Zhou's enemies, such as the seven clans of the Shang people reportedly to have been offered by the Zhou court to the new state Lu in Shandong. At the bottom of this social hierarchy was the mass of the native commoners, new subjects of the regional state (see figure 30). The archeological evidence shows that the conquered masses maintained their own culture for a very long time on the eastern plains distinct from the elite culture, which was closely linked to the Zhou.[16] However, this does not

---

[15] These textual records seem to describe the same scenario of the political ritual of establishing regional states seen in the contemporary bronze inscriptions. For instance, the *Zuozhuan* suggests that when the state of Lu was established, the ruler of Lu was given six groups of the Shang people who were to be translocated to the new state in Shandong; in the same text, the ruler of Jin in Shanxi received from the Zhou court nine lineages of the Huai 懷-surnamed people, most likely ethnically related to the Guifang 鬼方 active in northern Shanxi and Shaanxi during the late Shang. See *Zuozhuan*, 54, pp. 2134–35. For Itō's study, see Itō Michiharu, *Chūgoku kodai kokka*, pp. 78–83, 98–105.

[16] For a discussion of archeological evidence on this point, see Li Feng, *Landscape and Power in Early China*, pp. 78–82. However, it is always difficult to demonstrate ethnic distinctions based on archeological evidence from a single regional state. A forcibly argued case in archeology is the state of Lu in Shandong, where multiple burial segments as well as residential sites excavated in Qufu were classified by the reporter into Group A, representing the Zhou elite, Group B, representing the Shang population that the ruler of Lu received from the Zhou court. The two groups are largely contemporaneous in the system of dating developed by the reporter, although Group B is supposed to have lasted longer into the Warring States period. See *Qufu Lu guo gucheng*, pp. 80–85, 114–15, 183–86. As already pointed by a number of scholars, the difference between the ceramics of the two groups reflects more a change in time but not ethnic identity, and the rest of the criteria deduced by the reporter to differentiate the two groups reflect rather gaps in the wealth and social status of the tomb occupants. After all, if the historical tradition regarding the composition of the population of Lu is reliable, the Shang groups in Lu should have belonged to the order of immigrants, but not the native masses. See Cui Lequan, "Shandong diqu Dong Zhou kaoguxue wenhua de xulie," *Huaxia Kaogu* 1992.4, 73–97; Iijima Taketsugu, *Chūgoku Shū bunka kōkogaku kenkyū* (Tokyo: Dōseisha, 1998), pp. 219–28. For a recent criticism of this argument, see Falkenhausen, *Chinese Society in the Age of Confucius*, pp. 186–200.

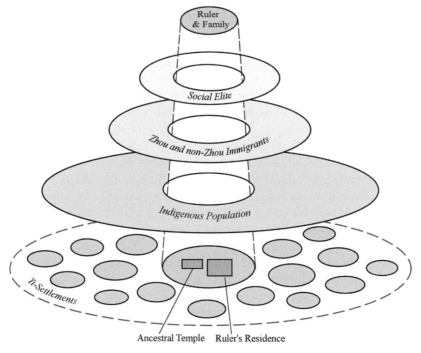

Figure 30: Model of the regional states

mean that people in each category kept exactly the same social status throughout the 400 years after the time of the Zhou conquest, when the lineage remained the essential organizing power within the perimeter of the ethnic unit. Such social distinctions are fully evident in the inscription of the Yihou Ze *gui*, particularly in the fact that the seven families of possibly the original residents of Zheng that were commanded to move into the new state Yi all brought with them their own retainers; needless to say, each of these families was headed by an Elder (*bo* 伯), who was doubtless the primary authority of the family. Sometimes, even the preexisting local administrative structure, no matter how rudimentary it was, would make its way into the new order of the regional state, as is evident in the case of Yan, which clearly recruited the local administrative officers into its new government.

It is fair to say that there was a population, if not an ethnic structure, within the regional state for the maintenance of which the regional government was instituted and through which the regional state realized itself.[17] Ethnic and social distinctions were two strings that intersected

---

[17] Even in the Zhou central areas we sometimes still see the existence of such ethnic units, which are clearly differentiated from the local Zhou population in the language of the bronze inscriptions. For instance, as mentioned in Chapter 5, Xun and Shi You each had several groups of such peoples under their control in different locations during their time in office. See Ma Chengyuan, *Shang Zhou*

each other. But in the main, the regional state was constructed along an ethnic hierarchy that was determined by the circumstances of its founding, the Zhou conquests. However, as time went on, the line demarcating ethnic groups within a regional state gradually lost its weight as the line dividing the rich and the poor gradually gained importance, resulting from the Zhou elite increasingly gaining a local root. While this process requires much more study, it seems likely that the change in significance of the two types of social distinctions was further intensified and made permanent after the sixth century by a general decline of the status of the social elites, both Zhou and non-Zhou, when one's welfare owed more to one's personal quality than to one's ethnic or social origin.

Rights and obligations

What gave this diverse population an "arch-authority" was the presence of the regional ruler, to whom they carried all claims and whose will they all served. The rights and obligations of a regional ruler were those of his state. Within his state, he exercised full administrative as well as military power, but the right to do so resided in the royal Zhou state that granted the regional state both its legitimacy and its basic social structure. Even in a time long after the waning of the Zhou royal power, relationship to the royal genealogy through a common ancestral cult still remained a legitimizing power in the political discourses of the Spring and Autumn period. However, for a very long time, the rights and obligations of the regional ruler and hence of his state were interpreted largely in the framework of "feudalism."[18] In a recent study, I have made an effort to invalidate such interpretation and to redefine the role of the regional states and their rulers.[19]

The issue must be viewed in two ways. First, the Zhou regional states enjoyed the full rights of government over the subjects in their territories. The function of the government was carried out first of all through the implementation of legal punishment, which is required for the "establishment of order and security" as a political state. In this regard, and quite different from the medieval European fiefs, which constituted a separate institution from the legal system, the right to mete out punishment was granted to a regional ruler when he received his state. Although the inscriptions on the establishment of the regional states do not explicate this point, the received textual records speak very strongly about this situation. In the

---

qingtongqi mingwen xuan, 3, pp. 125–26, 150–51; Shirakawa Shizuka, "Kinbun tsūshaku," 29.173, 553–60; 31.182, 701–9.

[18] See, for instance, Creel, *The Origins of Statecraft*, pp. 317–87; Hsu and Linduff, *Western Chou Civilization*, pp. 151–58. See also, Bodde, "Feudalism in China," in *Essays on Chinese Civilization* (Princeton: Princeton University Press, 1981), pp. 85–131.

[19] See Li Feng, "'Feudalism' and Western Zhou China," 115–44. See also the discussion in Chapter 7, pp. 288–90.

"Kanggao" 康誥 chapter of the *Shangshu*, the regent Duke of Zhou concerned himself almost entirely with instructing Kangshu 康叔, the new regional ruler of the state of Wey, in the principles of government, centering on the proper application of punishment to the subjugated Shang people.[20] In this way, the Zhou had started a tradition that was to stand in China for the next 3000 years – that political authority and legal authority were viewed as one.

What is even more is that, in the Western Zhou context, legal authority as well as the whole idea of "regional government" were not regarded together as just a right granted to a regional ruler; in a more precise sense, they were charged to the regional ruler, who, as an agent of the "Western Zhou state," was rather responsible and morally obligated to take charge of such authority. The *Shangshu* chapters including the "Kanggao" and "Jiugao" 酒誥 convey a deep sense of fear that a regional ruler might fail to guard such responsibilities, hence failing to help the Zhou king to create a New People (*xinmin* 新民).[21] The inscriptions also suggest that not only was the right to exercise government granted to a regional ruler, but also the right to organize military forces and the right to extract economic resources from the territory. In short, a regional state was a small but complete social-political entity that enjoyed the combined rights of civil administration, justice, finance, and military authority over an accumulated area of land and a diverse and stratified population. The government of a regional state performed the full range of functions carried out by the Zhou central government, though on a much smaller scale.

However, the regional state also had obligations, not only to its people, but to the larger organization – the Western Zhou state and its king. The regional ruler was a ruler because he was the subject of a higher ruler – the Zhou king. The power of the regional ruler was delegatory in nature and was installed in him by the king and resided in him tentatively in the sense that there was a possibility that it could be confiscated by the king, as happened in a number of actual cases; after all, it was confined to a certain area specially sanctioned by a royal order, the content of which could be altered later.[22] The punishment of a disobedient regional ruler by the Zhou king was normally inflicted only on the ruler himself, and in such cases it carried the royal will that the regional state would continue to prosper under a different ruler, normally related to the punished one in blood. Very rarely, the punishment

---

[20] In particular, for instance, the Duke of Zhou pronounced Kangshu the sole person who had the authority to punish and execute people in his state, the capital crime being harsh treatment of one's parents, higher than the crimes of banditry and robbery. See *Shangshu*, 14, pp. 202–5 (Legge, *The Shoo King*, pp. 381–98).

[21] See *Shangshu*, 14, p. 203 (Legge, *The Shoo King*, pp. 382–84).

[22] A typical case is the state of Shen 申, which was translocated by King Xuan from the upper Jing River valley in eastern Gansu to the Nanyang basin in southern Henan; the move is commemorated in the poem "Songgao" 崧高 (# 259) in the *Book of Poetry*, which offers a lot of details; see *Shijing*, 18.3, pp. 565–66 (Waley, *The Book of Songs*, pp. 272–74).

would go deeper to the level that even the statehood of the regional state could be called into question. This does not mean that the Zhou king could always do so, certainly not for the most part of the middle and late Western Zhou when the royal power declined in the face of a rising regionalism. But he could legitimately do so when he was strong. The obligation of the regional state was conceived in a number of ways. At the fundamental level, a regional ruler was responsible for keeping order on his lands, which he held against foreign invasions not only for the wellbeing of his own subjects, but in the interests of the Western Zhou state. As the regional states were established for the purpose of defending the Zhou central area, they had to recognize, and act in accordance with, the grand strategy of the Western Zhou state. This obligation was most often materialized in the military assistance the regional state provided to the Zhou king. A proof of such military assistance as obligation lies in the fact that, as repeatedly shown by the inscriptions, the regional troops not only assisted the royal armies fighting enemies among their immediate neighbors, but sometimes such service could draw them to fight enemies far away from their own lands alongside the Zhou royal armies. The last point has been repeatedly shown by the bronze inscriptions, including some that have only recently been discovered.[23]

Such service provided by the regional states to the Zhou king seems to have been unconditional and non-contractual. It is the service performed by a subject for his ruler, and the Zhou king was certainly the ruler of all regional rulers. As such, besides the military service he provided for the Zhou king, a regional ruler was also obligated, at least in common practice, to report back to the Zhou capital in Shaanxi, particularly at the site of Zongzhou. This was necessary especially when a new ruler was established, and a number of bronze inscriptions, as we will show below, were cast to commemorate the regional ruler's first visit to the Zhou capital.[24] Such a visit was clearly designed to obtain royal sanction of a transfer of the right to rule from a previous ruler to a new ruler. It was the Zhou king's right not to sanction such transfer from a previous ruler to a new ruler whom the king did not like. When the obligation of the regional ruler was conceived in terms of the rights of the Zhou king, we find that the Zhou king had authority to interfere in the succession of power in the regional states. Although the local administration was completely the

---

[23] For instance, in the Shi Yuan *gui* 師袁簋 (JC: 4313), troops from regional states in Shandong were enlisted to fight the Huaiyi 淮夷 in the south, along with the Zhou royal army. The Jinhou Su *bianzhong* 晉侯蘇編鐘 (JL: 35–50) records a military campaign conducted by the Zhou king, assisted by the ruler of Jin, whose own state was in the Fen River valley of Shanxi, against indigenous groups possibly in the northern Jiangsu or southern Shandong region; see Ma Chengyuan, "Jihou Su bianzhong," 1–17. Another recently discovered late Western Zhou bronze inscription, the Zhabo *ding* 柞伯鼎, documents a military operation in the south led by a Zhou official from the central court and participated in by the regional rulers in the east. See Zhu Fenghan, "Zhabo ding yu Zhougong nanzheng," 67–73. For more details, see discussions below, pp. 267–68.

[24] One of the most typical cases is the Mai *fangzun* (JC: 6015), which records the ruler of Xing's visit to the Zhou king in the Zhou capital in Shaanxi. This point will be discussed in detail later in the chapter.

"domestic" affair of a regional ruler, as will be shown below, the Zhou king in practice placed inspectors in the regional states.

Besides the obligation of a regional ruler as a subject to the Zhou king, the Zhou institution was characteristic in prescribing a separate obligation to the Zhou king as the common patriarch of the regional rulers. This relationship was built in the process by which the Western Zhou state was formed, as most of the regional rulers were factually descendants of the Zhou royal family; in fact, the power to rule was delegated through such a lineage structure with the Zhou king at the top. According to Zhou family practice of primogeniture, which is termed "Lineage Law" (*zongfa* 宗法) by many scholars,[25] the Zhou king, who was normally succeeded by his eldest son by his primary wife, was called the "primary line" (*dazong* 大宗), while the regional rulers, who descended from the minor sons of the Zhou kings, constituted the group of "minor lines" (*xiaozong* 小宗). The minor lines were required to submit to the great line in the Zhou capital, represented by the Zhou king. The essence of the system of lineage segmentation was to regulate inheritance of power and property through a kinship structure. The Western Zhou inscriptions suggest that such a system was probably practiced during the Western Zhou.[26] Whether the Lineage Law had the effect of law is very hard to determine, for there is no mention in the inscriptions of a person being sued for disobeying members of his primary line. But the Lineage Law did carry a set of values and was meaningful in that regard. The system certainly provided a moral power in regulating the obedience and obligation of the distant relatives to the main branch of the Zhou royal family through a common cult of ancestral worship. Such a personal relationship between the Zhou king and the regional rulers served to ensure the fulfillment of the obligation of the regional rulers as subjects to the Zhou king as the head of the Western Zhou state.

THE REGIONAL GOVERNMENT

The above discussion has clarified the social-structural characteristics of the regional states and their positions in the larger political organization of the

---

[25] This is a Warring States term to describe the Zhou system of lineage that was adopted by many modern scholars. Just to list a few, Zhao Guangxian, *Zhou dai shehui bianxi* (Beijing: Renmin, 1982), pp. 99–110; Jin Jingfang, *Gushi lunji* (Jinan: Qilu, 1982), pp. 111–40. On the general rule of *zongfa*, see Barry Blakeley, "Regional Aspects of Chinese Socio-Political Development in the Spring and Autumn Period (722–464 BC): Clan Power in a Segmentary State," unpublished PhD thesis: University of Michigan (1970), pp. 16–21; Hsu and Linduff, *Western Chou Civilization*, pp. 163–71. For a recent discussion of the rule of lineage segmentation and the possible ways it works in bronze inscriptions, see Falkenhausen, *Chinese Society in the Age of Confucius*, pp. 66–68; Sena, "Reproducing Society: Lineage and Kinship in Western Zhou China," pp. 89–95.

[26] The bronze inscriptions actually mention such terms as "First son of the primary line" (*zongzi* 宗子) (Shan *ding* 善鼎; JC: 2820) and "Head of the primary line" (*zongjun* 宗君) (Sixth Year Zhousheng *gui* 六年琱生簋; JC: 4293), which clearly suggest a differentiation between the primary line and the minor lines of a family.

Western Zhou state. Based on the above delineation, we should now look carefully into how a regional state was managed from inside. As already noted in the beginning of the chapter, this is the area where our current inscriptional evidence is most inadequate, and we are not in a position to reconstruct the governmental practice of any single regional state during the Western Zhou in any reliable way. Nonetheless, the inscriptions gathered from the various states across a large area do allow us to make a general assessment of the overall structural features of the regional governments. While running the risk that such a generalization imposes an unwarranted uniformity on the governments of the many regional states that could well have fostered regional political cultures through the 276 years of the Western Zhou period, it is significant, I think, to lay out what has already become known at present as a basis for generating questions for the future.

Organization reflected in the bronze inscriptions

The offices we know from the inscriptional sources are indeed many, and the problem is that they are not systematic. There is no divisional statement such as the ones we find for the Zhou central government, the Ling *fangyi* for the early Western Zhou, Fansheng *gui* for the mid-Western Zhou, and Maogong *ding* for the late Western Zhou, all having been discussed in Chapter 2. There is even rarely an inscription that would mention "multiple officials" from a single regional state. The office of Supervisor of Land (*situ* 嗣土) appears in the inscription of the Ta Situ *gui* 康侯簋 (JC: 4059), which records the Zhou king's attack on Shang, whereby he established Kanghou Tu 康侯圖 as ruler of Wey 衛. At this point, the Supervisor of Land of Mu 沐, probably a place in the Shang capital area now under Zhou occupation, cast the bronze to commemorate the event.[27] While the content of the inscription corroborates the historical account presented in the "Kanggao" chapter of the *Shangshu* on the founding of the state of Wey, it suggests that the institution of the Three Supervisors was transplanted into the eastern states soon after the Zhou conquest. The office of Supervisor of Multitudes appears in a number of late Western Zhou inscriptions from the regional states: a bronze *ding* was cast by the Supervisor of Multitudes of Jin 晉, Bo Kefu 伯都父 (JC: 2597); a bronze *xu* was cast by the Supervisor of Multitudes of Lu 魯, Bo Wufu 伯吳父 (JC: 4415); and a group of six bronzes cast by another Supervisor of Multitudes of Lu 魯, Zhong Qi 仲齊, was excavated from tomb no. 48 in the Lu capital Qufu, probably the burial of this Lu minister.[28] Of a slightly later date, a bronze *fu* was cast by the Grand Supervisor of Construction (*da sigong* 大司工) of Zhengbo

---

[27] Chen Mengjia identified this Supervisor of Land with Mubo 沐伯, who was the caster of a number of bronzes. See Chen Mengjia, "Xi Zhou tongqi duandai," 1.163–65.

[28] See *Qufu Lu guo gucheng*, pp. 147–50.

鄭伯 in the state of Zheng during the early Spring and Autumn period (Shaoshu Shanfu *fu* 召叔山父簋; JC: 4602).

Besides the civil administrators, secretarial offices are also present in the regional bronze inscriptions. The most important case is Document Maker Mai 作冊麥 of the state of Xing in present-day Hebei province, who cast four bronzes that we know of. Three of them commemorate the receipt of metal as award from the Xing ruler and mention Mai himself as "official" (*li* 吏) or "principal official" (*zhengli* 正吏) of the state of Xing.[29] The long inscription on the Mai *fangzun* 麥方尊 (JC: 6015) records the Xing ruler's visit to the Zhou capital in Shaanxi, where he was treated by the Zhou king with great courtesy; upon his return to Xing, he awarded Document Maker Mai metal. Given the detail of the visit that Mai was able to describe in the inscription (see below), it is possible that he had actually accompanied the ruler on his trip to the Zhou capital in Shaanxi; but the inscription itself does not provide clear reference to this point.[30] In addition, certainly the more general clerical office Scribe (*shi* 史) also existed in many regional states, appearing, for instance, on a bronze *zhi*-cup from tomb no. 253 in the cemetery of the state of Yan in Beijing.[31] We also know two other bronzes cast by a Scribe from the state of Qi (JC: 3740).

Another office known for the state of Xing in southern Hebei is the Grand Superintendent (*taizai* 太宰); a late Western Zhou bronze *fu* cast by the Grand Superintendent of Xing Jiang 邢姜, probably the consort of the ruler of Xing, was found in Inner Mongolia, possibly brought there by a northern tribe during the raid on Xing around 662 BC.[32] We know that such an office existed also in other states such as Southern Shen 南申 in Henan, for a bronze cast by the Grand Superintendent of Southern Shen (Zhong Chengfu *gui* 仲再父簋; JC: 4188) was discovered in Nanyang in 1981.[33] As sufficiently shown in the previous chapters, the Superintendent was the head of the Royal Household and played an important role in the middle and later Western Zhou court. It is likely that the office was replicated in the regional states, where it played a more central role in the regional

---

[29] On the Mai bronzes, see Li Feng, "'Offices' in Bronze Inscriptions," 6–8. See also Shirakawa Shizuka, "Kinbun tsūshaku," 11.60:618–24.

[30] On the Mai bronzes as products of a regional state, see Matsumaru Michio, *Sei Shū seidōki to sono kokka*, pp. 137–66. See also Shirakawa Shizuka, "Kinbun tsūshaku," 11.60:629.

[31] See *Liulihe Xi Zhou Yan guo mudi* (Beijing: Wenwu Press, 1995), p. 173. This *shi* 史 must be differentiated from the *shi* 史 as a family emblem on many late Shang and early Western Zhou bronzes, most numerously being excavated from Qianzhangda 前掌大 in Tengzhou 滕州, Shandong, in recent years; see *Tengzhou Qianzhangda mudi* (Beijing: Wenwu, 2005), pp. 210–305.

[32] See *Neimenggu wenwu kaogu* 1982.2, 5–7. On the raid on Xing, see Jaroslav Průšek, *Chinese State-lets and the Northern Barbarians in the Period 1400–300 BC* (New York: Humanities Press, 1971), pp. 142–46.

[33] See *Zhongyuan wenwu* 1984.4, 13–16, pl. 5. From the same tomb, a total of four bronzes were excavated. The *ding* and two *gui* vessels are of typical late Western Zhou design, but the *pan* basin may be later, possibly cast during the early Spring and Autumn period.

governments.[34] Another official whose service might have been related to the Superintendent is the Provisioner (*shanfu* 膳夫), an office that is also found on the regional bronzes; a bronze *fu* cast by the Grand Provisioner of the state of Cai 蔡 in southern Henan was found in Hubei in 1987, dating to the early Spring and Autumn period.[35]

Besides these official roles that replicated those which existed in the Zhou central government, the really unique office in the regional states was the Inspector (*jian* 監), evident in a number of inscriptions. The most important one is the inscription of the Yingjian *yan* 應監甗 (JC: 883), discovered in Jiangxi province. The bronze was apparently cast during the early Western Zhou in the state of Ying in present-day Pingdingshan 平顶山, Henan, and in a study of this bronze soon after its discovery, Guo Moruo pointed out the possibility that it was cast by a royal inspector stationed in the state of Ying.[36] Another early Western Zhou bronze *ding* discovered in Longkou 龍口, Shandong, in 1964 was cast by an individual named *X-jian* 回監, most likely an inspector of an unidentified local state.[37] It has been traditionally known that such royally sanctioned officials existed in the state of Qi, where they occupied prestigious offices on a hereditary basis.[38] It is likely that this office was not limited to the non-Ji-surnamed states such as Qi, but was widely present also in many regional states of Zhou royal descent, and if so, it must have been an institutionalized royal attempt at tight control over the regional states because they were watchdogs for the Zhou king. A critical piece of evidence for the institution of Inspectors as a royal method of political control comes from the inscription of the Zhong Jifu *gui* 仲幾父簋 (JC: 3954), cast probably during the late phase of the mid-Western Zhou,[39] from the Zhou royal domain in Shaanxi that records that Scribe Ji 幾, a royal official in the capital, was sent as an envoy to the "Many Inspectors of the Many Regional Rulers" (*zhuhou zhujian* 諸侯諸監).[40] The inscription suggests clearly a mission to gather information about the regional states from the many Inspectors stationed there by the king. It also implies that the Inspector was a widely existing office in the many regional states.

---

34 On the other hand, the "Superintendent" at the Zhou royal court was never prefixed with the honorable term "Grand." See discussion in Chapter 2, pp. 68–70.

35 See *Kaogu* 1989.11, 1041–44.

36 See Guo Moruo, "Shi Ying Jian yan," *Kaogu xuebao* 1960.1, 7–8.

37 See *Wenwu* 1991.5, 84–85.

38 The inspecting families in the state of Qi were the Guo 國 family and Gao 高 family that hereditarily held the highest official positions in the state of Qi. See Melvin P. Thatcher, "A Structural Comparison of the Central Government of Ch'u, Ch'i, and Chin," *Monumenta Serica* 33 (1977–78), 147–53.

39 Zhong Jifu can be reasonably identified with Jifu 幾父, caster of the Jifu *hu* 幾父壺 discovered in Qijiacun 齊家村 in 1960 and dated by scholars to the Yi–Li period. See Chen Gongrou, "Ji Jifu hu Zha zhong jiqi tongchu de tongqi," 88–101.

40 Certainly an alternative and still valid reading could be "Many Rulers and Many Inspectors," but this does not overturn the fact that the Many Inspectors were royal officials stationed in the regional states ruled by the Many Rulers.

The Zhong Chengfu *gui* 仲再父簋 (JC: 4188), discovered in Nanyang, suggests that even during the late Western Zhou the Zhou court continued to station inspecting officials in some newly founded regional states, in accordance with the early practice:

The Grand Superintendent (*taizai* 太宰) of the ruler of Southern Shen 南申伯, Zhong Chengfu, who was his official, makes [for] his august grandfather and father King Yi 夷王 and Jianbo 監伯 [this] sacrificial *gui* vessel. With it he will make offerings, be filial, and be awarded abundant longevity, pure blessing, peace and harmony for ten thousand years without limit. [His] sons' sons and grandsons' grandsons eternally use it in offering.

There are a number of interesting points in this inscription. But it should be mentioned first, as I have explicated in another study, that the state of Southern Shen 南申 was established in the time of King Xuan as a branch of the Northern Shen, a non-Ji polity and longtime ally of the Zhou, possibly located in the upper Jing River region in eastern Gansu. The relocation of Southern Shen, probably together with some other states such as Lü 呂 in the Nanyang basin, was a part of King Xuan's strategy to regain control over the distant regions.[41] Interestingly, the caster of the bronze claims to be a grandson of King Yi of Zhou and son of the "Inspector Elder" (*Jianbo* 監伯). Beyond this genealogy, I believe that the inscription actually evidences an important fact that a Zhou noble who was probably a son of King Yi was stationed in the new state Southern Shen as an inspecting official, and founder of a family from which the caster of this bronze descended. The inscription is an excellent example of how the political power of a regional state was interwoven with that of the Zhou court.

Textual records and their implications for early eastern Zhou regional governments

Summarized above is what we know at present from the contemporaneous bronze inscriptions about the establishment of offices in the regional states during the Western Zhou. Although the inscriptions give us a good sense of what functionaries might have once played political and administrative roles in these regional states, there is no structural description of governmental divisions in the available inscriptions. On the other hand, most regional state and their governments endured longer than did the Western Zhou state and the Zhou central government. Indeed, many were still politically active at a time when relatively detailed textual accounts became available; except for the seven conquering states, all the regional states had

---

[41] On the founding and political circumstances of the translocation of the state of Shen, see Li Feng, *Landscape and Power in Early China*, pp. 225–27. On the relocation of Shen and Lü, see also Xu Shaohua, *Zhou dai nantu lishi dili yu wenhua* (Wuhan: Wuhan daxue, 1994), pp. 28–44.

been annexed by the end of the fourth century BC.[42] These textual records, most systematically found in the *Spring and Autumn Annals* and
in the *Zuozhuan* commentary, were produced in the post-Western Zhou
era and therefore are methodologically questionable as sources for Western Zhou regional governments without demonstrable links to the governmental institutions reflected in the bronze inscriptions of the Western
Zhou time. However, they are valid sources for the regional governments
during the Spring and Autumn period that were part of the common legacy left behind by the Western Zhou state. In this regard, as reflections
of that common legacy originating in the Western Zhou, they can, when
properly analyzed, help us recover some main trends of structural as well
as operational transitions of the regional governments from the Western
to the Eastern Zhou. These textual records are used below only for this
purpose.

According to Melvin Thatcher's interpretation based on the fundamental work by the Qing dynasty historian Gu Donggao 顧棟高 on the
Spring and Autumn Annals, regional government in the more traditional
states such as Jin during the early Spring and Autumn period remained
structurally similar to the central government of the Western Zhou. But
subsequent reforms in these states had created the prominent office of
"Chief Minister" (*xiang* 相), which added a significant new element to
the overall structure of government in these states.[43] In the mid-Western
Zhou period, as clarified in Chapter 3, there was a "Committee of high
officials" that was charged with overall responsibilities for the entire government. So the role might have been reinstitutionalized in the office of
"Chief Minister" in the regional states as a way of concentrating power.
According to Gu's table,[44] it is quite clear that the government in the major northern states (the southern state Chu had its own distinctive system
of administration) of the Spring and Autumn period, including Lu 魯,
Song 宋, Jin 晉, Zheng 鄭, and Wey 衛, was conventionally centered
on the roles of the three ministerial officials: Supervisor of Multitudes,
Supervisor of Construction, and Supervisor of Horses; officials with such
titles from the various states are frequently mentioned in the records of
the *Zuozhuan.* As mentioned above, these roles can be largely confirmed
with the regional inscriptions for the Western Zhou period. Besides the
more traditional "Three Supervisors," the role of Supervisor of Lawsuits (*sikou* 司寇) is frequently mentioned in the records. As mentioned
in the previous chapters, we are not sure whether the legal function of

---

[42] For the dates of the termination of the regional states, see Chen Mengjia, *Xi Zhou niandai kao*
(Shanghai: Shangwu, 1945), pp. 53–55.

[43] See Melvin P. Thatcher, "A Structural Comparison of the Central Government of Ch'u, Ch'i, and
Chin," 140–61.

[44] See Gu Donggao, "Chunqiu lieguo guanzhi biao," pp. 1033–1123. For a short analysis of the offices
in the major states, see also Gu Derong and Zhu Shunlong, *Chunqiu shi* (Shanghai: Shiji Press,
2001), pp. 290–97.

the Western Zhou government had become separate from the role of the ministerial officials.[45] The frequent mention of the office of Supervisor of Lawsuits probably suggests a new development in the civil administration of the Spring and Autumn period. Certainly this is a reflection of the general trend that gradually took place in the Spring and Autumn period to enforce the legal system of the state as a number of states began to promulgate written legal codes cast on bronze vessels.[46] There were also some irregular ministerial offices such as the Supervisor of Cities (*sicheng* 司城) in the state of Song, but the four Supervisors mentioned above were the more prominent and most common by far.

Another prominent role in the governments of the early Spring and Autumn period was the Superintendent or Grand Superintendent, which is actually mentioned in the inscription of the Zhong Chengfu *gui* from the late Western Zhou period, already translated above. The Superintendent was frequently sent on diplomatic missions between the many states, representing their rulers. In some states, such as Song, the role of Superintendent was further divided between the Grand Superintendent (*taizai* 太宰) and Minor Superintendent (*shaozai* 少宰), while in other states, such as Wey, it was divided between Right and Left. It is likely that the Superintendent played a more central role in the regional states during the Spring and the Autumn period than did the same official in the central court of the Western Zhou. As the inscription of the Zhong Chengfu *gui* tells us, the Grand Superintendent of Southern Shen was probably a royal descendant from the family of an Inspector; a Grand Superintendent with such a prestigious family background must have played a very important political role in his state.

Other offices that are commonly mentioned for the many regional states in the textual records included the Grand Scribe (*taishi* 太史), Manager of the Lineage (*zongren* 宗人), and Grand Invocator (*taizhu* 太祝), etc. As analyzed in Chapter 2, the "Grand Scribe" had been an important office since the early Western Zhou; by the mid-Western Zhou the Grand Scribe had come to represent an important government bureau, the "Grand Secretariat," paralleling that of the Ministry and the Royal Household, where the bureaucracy of the Interior Scribes was placed. As also clarified in Chapter 2, the office of Grand Invocator was well developed by the mid-Western Zhou, with its subordinates serving such functions in the local areas. The office of "Manager of the Lineage" does not seem to be a Western Zhou name, although a similar function might have been carried out by the officials who were responsible for the Royal Kinsmen (*gongzu* 公族) in the Zhou court. But the office of "Document Maker" that was

---

[45] The term *sikou* 嗣寇 is mentioned on two mid-Western Zhou bronzes: the Nanji *ding* 南季鼎 (JC: 2781) and the Yang *gui* 楊簋 (JC: 4294). However, in both cases, the term is used to describe the administrative responsibilities charged to the appointees, but is not an official title.

[46] See Gu Derong and Zhu Shunlong, *Chunqiu shi*, pp. 298–305.

confirmed for the regional states during the early Western Zhou does not seem to have survived into the Spring and Autumn period.

Assessment of the structure and operation

When we compare this general composition of offices in the regional states during the Spring and Autumn period based on the textual records with what is known from the bronze inscriptions about the regional governments during the Western Zhou, we find close links in the information derived from the two types of sources. Except for the Document Maker, which was mainly an early to mid-Western Zhou office, other roles mentioned in the inscriptions from the regional states continued to be mentioned in the textual records for the Spring and Autumn period. This suggests a basic structural continuity in the government practice of the regional states from the Western Zhou to the early Spring and Autumn period. This structure is characterized by the central role of the Three Supervisors plus the Superintendent, assisted by other officials such as the Grand Scribe and Grand Invocator. Of course, outside of this structure was the office of Inspector, who by origin was not an official of the regional states, but one responsible to the Zhou king. Although there were distinctive offices in some of the states, especially at a lower level, and the actual power structure in each state was conditioned by the political reality of the state, we can be sure that the structural features recovered from the two types of sources above represent the normal pattern of regional governments during the middle and late Western Zhou through the early Spring and Autumn period.

Thus, we have a situation whereby the regional governments ran in a close structural parallel to the Zhou central government, especially the early Western Zhou government (although the office of Superintendent was not prominent in the central government during the early Western Zhou), which was larger in size and more complex in organization and operation. The regional governments not only performed the political and administrative functions performed by the Zhou central government as already noted above, but also replicated its structural features. Such a strong structural similarity between the central government and the regional segments did not appear again under the imperial system, which assigned the local governments very different functions from the central government. The similarity analyzed here provides strong support to the argument that has already been laid out earlier in the chapter: the regional states were smaller political organizations that were fully equipped with all the functions of a state.

However, the level of development was different between the Zhou central government and the regional Zhou states. In this regard, the regional governments do not seem to have gone through the process of bureaucratization that from the mid-Western Zhou on moved the Zhou central government to a new level of complexity; instead, the regional governments resembled more closely the early Western Zhou government. While the proof of this assessment has to wait until more evidence is brought to light in the future, it can at least be said that even by the early Spring and Autumn period that kind of organized structural divisions fully testified for the Zhou central government during the middle and late Western Zhou did not appear in the regional states. Thatcher has tried to evaluate the working patterns of the Qin government during the early Spring and Autumn period and concluded that it was highly personal and was dominated by autocratic rulers, with few bureaucratic roles to follow.[47] The situation is obviously very different from that which I have analyzed for the middle and late Western Zhou central government. Thatcher's analysis focused on the role of a group of officials who served Duke Mu of Qin 秦穆公 (659–621 BC), for which period the historical records in *Zuozhuan* provide appropriate information for such a study. However, Thatcher's study should be accepted with caution because the state of Qin, owing to its late date of founding and longtime isolation in the Gansu region before the fall of the Western Zhou, might have been one of the most underdeveloped governments among the many regional states. Other more traditional states such as Jin, Qi, and Lu might have long since developed a formal governmental structure through which state affairs were managed. And the Spring and Autumn period in these eastern states has been seen in general by other scholars as a period of steady bureaucratic expansion following economic and military developments.[48] Nevertheless, as far as the Western Zhou period (and even the early Spring and Autumn period) is concerned, we have every reason to believe that the regional governments were likely to have been more personal and unbureaucratic when compared with the Zhou central government.

RELATIONSHIP WITH THE ZHOU CENTRAL COURT

How did the relationship between the numerous regional states and the Zhou central court actually work out? In this final section, I will take a close look at the *de facto* operation of the relationship between the Zhou court and the regional states as reflected in the Western Zhou bronze inscriptions. In this regard, controlled archeological excavations in the past twenty years have brought to light tremendous new information, particularly inscribed bronzes found in archeologically analyzed field-contexts that enable us to use such information in sure spatial and chronological orders. In general, in the current corpus of Western Zhou inscriptions, we can identify three

---

[47] See Melvin P. Thatcher, "Central Government of the State of Ch'in in the Spring and Autumn Period," *Journal of Oriental Studies* (Hong Kong) 23.1 (1985), 38.
[48] See Cho-yun Hsu, "The Spring and Autumn Period," in *The Cambridge History of Ancient China*, pp. 570–76.

ways in which the regional states entered contact with and hence participated in the Western Zhou state: (1) the participation of the personnel of the regional states in the political, especially ritual ceremonies conducted by the Zhou central court, often centering on the Zhou king; (2) the purposely arranged personal interaction between the Zhou king and the regional rulers through the regional rulers' visits to the Zhou capital; and (3) the military assistance the regional states provided for the Zhou royal army, fighting enemies chosen by the royal court. In these three ways, the regional states fulfilled their responsibilities and maintained their membership in the Western Zhou state.

Political participation in the Western Zhou state

Let us first look at the inscription of the Shu Ze *fangding* 叔夨方鼎, which has been very recently excavated in the cemetery of the state of Jin in Shanxi (see figure 31):[49]

It was the fourteenth month, the king performed the wine-offering ritual (*rong* 肜), and greatly entreated (*hui* 祭) with [pronouncing] the written document (*ce* 冊), in Chengzhou. Upon completing the ritual, the king called to assemble [in audience] his officials (*jueshi* 厥士), and awarded Shu Ze 叔夨 a cap, a jacket, a chariot with horses, and thirty strands of cowries. [Shu Ze] dares to extol the king's beneficence, herewith makes [this] treasured sacrificial vessel. May [Shu Ze] for ten thousand years extol the king's glorifying of his officials.

There is nothing surprising in the inscription itself, for both the award to officials and the recorded ritual procedure have been seen many times before. Even when the two factors are combined, we already know of three individuals who received royal awards after a similar ritual session either in the capital Zongzhou or in the eastern capital Chengzhou.[50] However, it is the archeological context that provides the most important point in this case – the bronze was excavated in 2000 from one of the burials (tomb no. 114) that clearly belonged to the rulers of the state of Jin in Beizhao 北趙, Shanxi.[51] Indeed, based on the dating of the tomb to the early Western

---

[49] For the discovery of the Shu Ze *fangding*, see *Wenwu* 2001.8, 9.

[50] The ritual is recorded in three inscriptions including the Xianhou *ding* 獻侯鼎 (JC: 2626), Yu *jue* 盂爵 (JC: 9104), and Shi Shu *gui* 史叔簋 (JC: 4132). The Xianhou *ding* states that when the Zhou king performed the grant *hui*-ritual in Zongzhou, Xianhou was awarded cowries by the king; the Yu *jue* documents an occasion when the king performed the *hui*-ritual for the first time in the eastern center Chengzhou, and the official Yu was sent to convey royal wishes to Dengbo 鄧伯, probably the ruler of Deng 鄧 located in the Nanyang basin, and subsequently received gifts from the latter; the Shi Shu *gui* records a similar occasion of *hui*-ritual performance when a scribe of Queen Jiang was sent to see the Grand Protector (the Duke of Shao). All three bronzes are of early Western Zhou design, close in time to the Shu Ze *fangding* under discussion here.

[51] The Beizhao cemetery hosted a total of nineteen large tombs arranged in pairs in three rows from the east to the west. Each pair of burial pits hosted a Jin ruler and his consort, and the whole

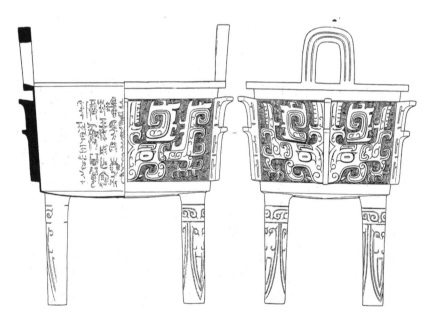

Figure 31: The recently excavated Shu Ze *fangding* and its inscription (provided by the excavator)

Zhou as clearly indicated by the artifacts from it, some scholars have identified Shu Ze, the caster of the bronze with Shu Yu 叔虞, the historically
known founder of the state of Jin, since the two characters *ze* 夨 and *yu*
虞 were phonetically interchangeable in the ancient time.[52] While this
identification is pending, given the context of the burial and the caster's
direct access to the Zhou king, Shu Ze is indeed very probably one of the
early rulers of the state of Jin. This provides us with an important basis
for reconsidering the significance of the inscription. Thus the inscription
actually records the participation of a regional ruler, whose base was in
the Fen River valley of Shanxi, in the state ritual conducted by the Zhou
king in the eastern capital Chengzhou in present-day Luoyang. In such a
context, it is very interesting to read the last line of the inscription, where
Ze referred to himself as the king's official (*jueshi* 厥士), as he was likely
to have been treated as such, just a few lines above. The inscription speaks
literally about the political relationship between the Zhou king and the
regional rulers who, in the Zhou mentality, were evidently conceived as
the agents of the Zhou king.

It was probably in a similar if not the same ritual session in Chengzhou
that some officials from Yan, the most remote regional state in present-
day Beijing, were also present. An individual named Yu 圉 cast a number
of bronzes that were excavated together in tomb no. 253 in the cemetery
in Yan in Liulihe 琉璃河. The inscriptional texts on these bronzes commemorate his receipt of the award of cowries granted by the Zhou king
in Chengzhou at the time of an entreating (*hui* 祓) ritual session.[53] From
the same tomb, another very interesting bronze *ding* cast by Jin 堇 was
discovered. The inscription on the bronze records Jin's personal visit from
the state of Yan to the Zhou capital Zongzhou (Hao) in Shaanxi for the
purpose of presenting the Grand Protector, father of the first ruler of Yan,
with some special food or candy. The Grand Protector was thus pleased
and in turn furnished the messenger from his son's state with cowries.[54]
Besides, from tomb no. 251 in Liulihe, a pair of bronze *zhi* bears inscriptions that describe Gong Zhong's 公仲 gift of cowries to an individual;[55] a
previously known inscription, the Gong *qi* 玕器 (JC: 10581), records Gong
Zhong's gift of cowries to another person, and the gift was made clearly in
Zongzhou in Shaanxi. The two vessels are close to each other in time, both
having been cast during the early Western Zhou.

cemetery was indeed the burial-ground of nine generations of the Jin rulers. The pair M113–M114
is located in the easternmost point of the central row. For the contents and general layout of the
Beizhao cemetery, see *Wenwu* 1993.3, 11–30; 1994.1, 4–28; 1994.8, 1–21; 1994.8, 22–23; 1995.7, 4–38;
2001.8, 4–21.

[52] For the identification of Shu Ze, see Li Boqian, "Shu Ze fangding mingwen kaoshi," *Wenwu* 2001.8,
39–41.

[53] Tomb no. 253 yielded a total of twenty-two bronze vessels, all with characteristic designs belonging
to the early phase of the early Western Zhou. The reporters suggest that the tomb was buried sometime in the Cheng–Kang period; see *Liulihe Xi Zhou Yan guo mudi*, pp. 36, 187.

[54] See *ibid.*, p. 106.   [55] See *ibid.*, p. 173.

As I have noted in another study, these newly discovered inscriptions suggest a close link of communication of people and ideas between the Zhou central court and the remote regional states such as Yan during the early Western Zhou, motivated either by political obligations or by personal connections.[56] It seems likely that the major events that happened in Chengzhou, the political and administrative center of Zhou in the east, were occasions that would bring together rulers and their officials from the various regional states. This certainly takes us back to the inscription on the Ling *fangyi* 令方彝 (JC: 9901), which has been translated and examined in Chapter 2. In this famous inscription, the "Many Rulers" (*zhuhou* 諸侯) were listed as counterparts of the many court officials to be inspected and addressed by the new minister, Duke Ming 明公, upon the latter's arrival in Chengzhou from the Zhou capital in Shaanxi. Although we do not know what institution was there to regulate the participation of the regional rulers in such major state ceremonies, it seems likely that they had obligations to do so. The point is: when the regional states were granted, they were not simply left alone or forgotten; instead, they were actively involved in the political scene in the Zhou capitals during the early Western Zhou. However, during the middle and late Western Zhou, such visits by regional officials to the Zhou capitals seem to have clearly declined. And among the many middle and late Western Zhou inscriptions, there is rarely a mention of state ritual that was held in Chengzhou. Of course, communication could also take the other direction – from the royal court to the regional states. For instance, the inscription of the Cai *zun* 蔡尊 (JC: 5974) indicates clearly that the Zhou king was once present in the state of Lu in Shandong, where he rewarded Cai, the caster of the bronze. This again took place during the early Western Zhou or the early phase of the mid-Western Zhou.[57]

Personal visit of the regional rulers to the Zhou king

However, there seems to have been one type of visit that was arranged for the regional rulers, especially newly established ones, to meet with the Zhou king in person, and such meetings seem to have been considered valid only when they happened onsite in the Zhou capital Zongzhou in Shaanxi. Three inscriptions – the Mai *fangzun* 麥尊 (JC: 6015), the Yanhou Zhi *ding* 匽侯旨鼎 (JC: 2628), and the X *zun* 𡥏尊 (JC: 5986) – record such visits by the regional rulers of Wei, Yan, and Xing to the Zhou king in Shaanxi; two of these visits, that of the Yanhou Zhi *ding* and the Mai *fang-zun*, seem to have taken place immediately after the establishment of the new rulers. These inscriptional records of the visits by the regional rulers

---

[56] See Li Feng, *Landscape and Power in Early China*, pp. 114–15.

[57] The bronze was discovered late in the Qing dynasty, and only an ink-rubbing has survived to the present day. The approximate date adopted here is based entirely on the calligraphic features of the inscription.

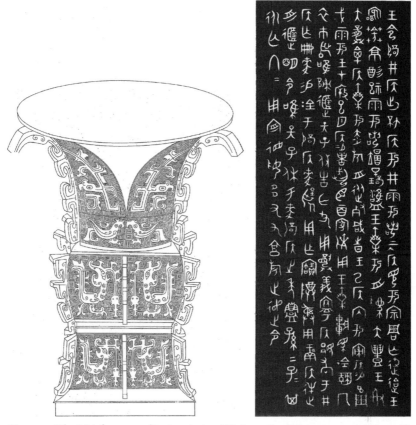

Figure 32: The Mai *fangzun* and its inscription (*Xiqing gujian* [Qing court, 1755], 8.33a–b)

to the Zhou king in Zongzhou offer us a special opportunity to investigate the political meaning of such meetings in the general political life of the Western Zhou state.

Above all, the Mai *fangzun* provides us with the most detailed account of such a visit as well as the royal reception accorded to the prestigious visitors (see figure 32):[58]

The king commanded [my] ruler Xinghou 邢侯 to go out from Pei 杊, *hou* 侯-ing in Xing 邢. Coming to the second month, the ruler presented himself in Zongzhou 宗周, with no problems.

It was when the king took residence in Pangjing 莽京, making the *rong* 肜 -sacrificial offering. Coming to the next day, and in the *biyong* 璧灉 -circular

---

[58] The Mai-group bronzes include, besides the Mai *fangzun*, the Mai *fangyi* 麥方彞 (JC: 9893), the Mai *fangding* 麥方鼎 (JC: 2706), and the Mai *he* 麥盉 (JC: 9451), most probably cast during the Cheng–Kang period of the early Western Zhou. See Shirakawa Shizuka, "Kinbun tsūshaku," 11.60:618–46; Ma Chengyuan, *Shang Zhou qingtongqi mingwen xuan*, 3, pp. 46–50.

pool, the king rode in the boat and performed the great ritual. The king shot the great bird. The ruler [of Xing] rode in the boat with red flags and followed [the king]. All was well done. In the day, the king took the ruler into his sleeping chamber. The ruler was awarded a decorated black *ge*-dagger by the king. At An 芹, in the evening, the ruler was awarded two hundred households of brown-clothed and barefoot slaves. He was rewarded with the use of royal chariot, metal bridles, cap, jacket, kneepads, and shoes. Upon return, [he] upheld the beneficence of the Son of Heaven, and reported [to the ancestors] that there was no trouble [during the visit].

For [Mai] has comforted the ruler with respect and good manners, and demonstrated his filial heart to the ruler of Xing, Mai was awarded metal by his ruler. Mai extols and herewith makes [this] treasured sacrificial vessel with which to assist the ruler in receiving and upholding the bright command. It was in the year when the Son of Heaven rewarded Mai's ruler with beneficence that it was cast. May [Mai's] grandsons' grandsons and sons' sons forever have no ending; with it they receive virtue, peace, and many friends, making offerings and running in service to the command.

The ruler of Xing, after at least two months of journey from his home state Xing in present-day Xingtai 邢臺, Hebei, arrived in the Zhou capital at a time when the Zhou king was offsite performing a sacrificial ritual in the capital Pang, located not far from the capital Hao. Apparently, the ruler went on to see the king in the capital Pang, where he was greeted by the king with the ritual of archery that they together performed in the great pool. Clearly, the king treated the regional ruler with great courtesy. Subsequently, the regional ruler was taken by the king into his sleeping quarters, probably in the inner palace, and was permitted the *right of riding in the royal chariot*, which by ritual sumptuary rules was not normally permitted to the court officials. In addition to this special courtesy, the ruler was also furnished with rich material gifts, most significantly in the form of 200 households of barefoot slaves.

The symbolism of this special royal treatment lies in the recognition of the ruler of Xing's rulership, which was conceived in that capacity as being functionally equal to the Zhou king himself. He manifestly had a status that was meaningfully different from, and much higher than, that of the court officials, and hence deserved special treatment by the Zhou king. This certainly was not merely because the ruler of Xing was a guest from afar, but because he was politically more prominent than the court officials. On the other hand, the ruler was granted, besides the right to ride in royal chariot, a set of official paraphernalia that later became regularly associated with official appointments during the mid-Western Zhou. Thus, although the regional ruler was recognized for his rulership, in the political philosophy of the Zhou, his role was still conceived as an "official" of the Western Zhou state, and the right to furnish him with various material as well as human gifts was itself a declaration of the king's sovereign power over his subject.

The inscription of the Yanhou Zhi *ding* records probably the same circumstance, but it says clearly that it was cast when the ruler of Yan, from an even more distant state, first visited the Zhou capital, where the ruler was awarded cowries by the Zhou king.[59] However, the inscription is too brief to convey any more information. The X *zun* records the caster's receipt of cowries from the ruler of Wey on a trip that the ruler took to the Zhou capital in Shaanxi from northern Henan.[60] The personal visits by the regional rulers to the Zhou king were important events through which the relationship between the regional states and the Western Zhou state was reconfirmed and reiterated. Especially in case of the first visit to the king, the occasion certainly did serve to verify the status of the rulers as such in their home states.

All of the inscriptions discussed above are from the early Western Zhou period; for the long period from King Gong to King Li, we have only one such inscription – the Yinghou *zhong* 應侯鐘 (JC: 107–108), discovered in Lantian 藍田, Shaanxi, in 1974.[61] The inscription records the ruler of Ying's meeting with the Zhou king in Zongzhou, immediately upon the king's return from Chengzhou in the east. The interesting point is that the home state of the ruler of Ying was located in Pingdingshan 平頂山, southern Henan, where recent archeological excavations have exposed the cemetery of Ying; hence, it would have been more convenient for the ruler to meet with the king in Chengzhou, only about 125 kilometers from Ying (see map 1). However, the inscription suggests that he had to traverse some 500 kilometers across the difficult mountains in western Henan to meet with the Zhou king in Zongzhou in the Wei River valley in the west immediately upon the latter's return from Chengzhou in the east, which was more convenient for the regional ruler to visit. The political geography of the ruler of Xing's visit suggests strongly that the meeting with the Zhou king at the prime powerbase of the Western Zhou state in Shaanxi, rather than any of its administrative or ritual substitute locations, had a special

---

[59] The Yanhou Zhi *ding* (JC: 2628) has a tripartite shallow basin decorated with bold-line *taotie* masks, and a flat rim, typical of the early Western Zhou. Zhi must have been a ruler after Ke, the first ruler of Yan, who cast the Ke *lei* 克罍 excavated in Liulihe. See Shirakawa Shizuka, "Kinbun tsūshaku," 8.38:413.

[60] The bronze was found in tomb no. 60 together with other five vessels, all typical of the Cheng–Kang period of the early Western Zhou. See *Xunxian Xincun* (Beijing: Kexue, 1964), pl. 9–16.

[61] For the discovery of the Yinghou *zhong*, see *Wenwu* 1975.10, 68–69. The inscription of this *zhong* is incomplete; the second half of the inscription is found on a *zhong* in the Museum of Calligraphy (Shodō Hakubutsukan), Tokyo; see *Wenwu* 1977.8, 27–28; Shirakawa Shizuka, "Kinbun tsūshaku," 48.*ho*9:230–36. For an English translation of the inscription, see Lothar von Falkenhausen, *Suspended Music: Chime-Bells in the Culture of Bronze Age China* (Berkeley: University of California Press, 1993), pp. 58–59.

and profound symbolic meaning. Correspondingly, in all other cases mentioned above, the regional rulers all had to see the Zhou king in Zongzhou in the Wei River valley in Shaanxi. This situation, besides testifying to the paramount importance of the visits by the regional rulers in the relationship between the Zhou central court and the regional states, also serves to verify the special status of the Zhou capital Zongzhou as the "Prime Root" (*zong* 宗) of the Western Zhou state in the political-cosmological thinking of the Zhou elite.

Military assistance to the Zhou royal armies

Another way in which the regional states entered into contact with the Western Zhou state was through the military assistance they provided to the Zhou royal armies. However, a political organization's military conduct on the borders depends on the perceived objectives of the organization and also reflects the work of its internal political structures. For the period of the great early Western Zhou expansion, when warfare was the most normal pattern of conduct of the Western Zhou state, it is probably difficult and indeed of little meaning to try to differentiate military operations conducted by the central court from those that were initiated by the regional states. Very often, military expansion was followed by the establishment of the regional states to consolidate the conquered space, and the survival of the regional states in the new environment in turn depended on the military backup involving first of all the Zhou royal forces. It was a unified program of expansion and colonization that the Zhou court pursued through much of the early part of the dynasty. It was only during the mid-Western Zhou, when large-scale expansion gave way to smaller border conflicts and when the granting of states had become exceptional rather than regular policy, that we see a separation between the two types of military action.

The complex involvement of the regional states with the central forces is seen first of all in the case of Bo Maofu 伯懋父, the supreme commander of the royal Eight Armies on campaign against the Dongyi 東夷, indigenous groups in the present-day Shandong region. Bo Maofu is mentioned in a number of inscriptions cast by his subordinate military personnel, including the Xiaochen Lai *gui* 小臣逨簋 (JC: 4238), Shi Qi *ding* 師旂鼎 (JC: 2809), Lüxing *hu* 呂行壺 (JC: 9689), etc. Guo Moruo proposed the identification of him with Kangbo Mao 康伯髦, the second ruler of the state of Wey in northern Henan, and the identification has won wide support.[62] In fact, for some time during the early Western Zhou, the royal Eight Armies were actually stationed in the Anyang region, where the state

---

[62] Most of these bronzes are from the late phase of the early Western Zhou or early phase of the mid-Western Zhou, corresponding to the reigns of King Zhao and King Mu. See Guo Moruo, *Liang Zhou jinwen ci daxi tulu kaoshi*, p. 23; Chen Mengjia, "Xi Zhou tongqi duandai," 1.171; Ma Chengyuan, *Shang Zhou qingtongqi mingwen xuan*, 3, pp. 50, 59–60.

of Wey was located, and therefore were called the "Eight Armies of Yin" (*Yin bashi* 殷八師).[63] Another interesting case is the Chen Jian *gui* 臣諫簋 (JC: 4237), discovered in 1978 together with nine other vessels in Yuanshi 元氏, Hebei, to the north of the state of Xing in Xingtai.[64] The bronze was cast slightly later than the Mai bronzes, which mention the ruler of Xing's visit to the Zhou capital. This inscription describes a battle between the troops of Xing and the Rong 戎 people that took place on the northern fringe of the state of Xing, involving the Xing troops commanded by the ruler of Xing. However, interestingly, in the battle Chen Jian, caster of the inscription, clearly a Xing official, fought under the command of the Zhou king, who probably led a Zhou royal army. The inscription suggests that during the early Western Zhou even some localized battles near the regional states might have required the joint operation of the royal forces and the regional troops.

During the mid-Western Zhou, when communication by official visits from the regional states to the central court apparently declined, we found that some remote regional states continued to provide military assistance to the central forces sent from Shaanxi. A recently discovered inscription, the Shi Mi *gui* 史密簋 (JL: 489), provides us with a unique way to look at how the royal forces and regional forces acted together under unified command.[65] The inscription records a complex military operation in the Shandong region commanded by two officials sent directly from the central court in response to a joint attack on the eastern Zhou regional states by five indigenous groups of people apparently from the south. In this operation, under the command of the official Shi Su 師俗, there were troops from the state of Qi; under command of the official Shi Mi 史密, there were troops led by the ruler of the state of Lai 萊, located near Longkou to the east of Qi in Shandong.[66] The battle shows what the normal pattern of military collaboration probably was between the Zhou central court and

---

[63] An interesting point is that, according to the Xiaochen Lai *gui*, after the campaign against the Dongyi, the "Eight Armies of Yin" commanded by Bo Maofu returned to Mushi 牧𠂤, that is Muye 牧野, located near Anyang and Wey. See Ma Chengyuan, *Shang Zhou qingtongqi mingwen xuan*, 3, p. 50.

[64] See *Wenwu* 1979.1, 23–26. Some scholars date most of the bronzes from the tomb to the reign of King Kang or early King Zhao. But I think most of them meet more closely the stylistic features of the early mid-Western Zhou. See Li Xueqin, *Xinchu qingtongqi yanjiu*, p. 64; Li Feng, "Huanghe liuyu Xi Zhou muzang chutu qingtong liqi," 389, 403.

[65] The bronze was found in Ankang 安康, southern Shaanxi. See *Kaogu yu wenwu* 1989.3, 7–9. Since it mentions Shi Su 師俗 as one of the commanders, known also from other mid-Western Zhou bronzes such as the Shi Chen *ding* 師晨鼎, the bronze must have been cast some time during the mid-Western Zhou, most likely in the Yih–Xiao period.

[66] Lai is traditionally identified with a walled city called Guicheng 歸城, located about 6.5 km to the southeast of present-day Longkou 龍口 City (previously Huangxian 黃縣). According to a survey conducted in the late 1980s, the central area of the site is encircled by two concentric walls. See Chen Pan, *Chunqiu dashi biao lieguo juexing ji cunmie biao zhuanyi*, pp. 391–93; *Kaogu* 1991.10, 910–18; Li Feng, *Landscape and Power in Early China*, pp. 309–10. Collaborative efforts by Columbia University, the Institute of Archaeology of CASS, and the Shandong Institute of Archaeology in recent years have confirmed the specific location of the city walls.

those regional states whose security was threatened by foreign attacks. In such cases, the central court was able to organize a united front against the common enemy not of any particular regional states, but of the Western Zhou state.

Two other inscriptions suggest that Zhou court could do probably even more than just this – that is, mobilize forces from the regional states to conduct military operations in regions far beyond their homelands, in cases where the security of their regional home states was not threatened. In such cases, the regional forces were clearly fighting the enemies not for their immediate interests but rather because of their obligations to the Western Zhou state. This is precisely what the inscription of the Shi Yuan *gui* 師衰簋 (JC: 4313) tells us (see figure 33):[67]

The king said as such: "Shi Yuan, hey! The Huaiyi 淮夷 have long been our obscure tributary subjects. Now they force their people in indolence (in matters of sending in tributes), rebel against their officials (*gongli* 工吏), and will not follow our eastern states. Now I initiate by commanding you to lead the Qi Army (*Qishi* 齊師), [that of] Ji 異 (=紀), Lai 贅 (=萊), X 杕, X 尻, as well as the Tiger Servants to campaign against the Huaiyi. Quickly cut off the "beasts" (rebel chiefs) of their polities – named Ran 冉, X 豩, Ling 鈴, and Da 達!" Shi Yuan was cautious and did not fail [the mission]; morning and night he was faithful to his military duty. It was good that he has had accomplishments, cutting off heads and taking in prisoners. [His] fearless foot-soldiers and charioteers wounded and captured men, women, sheep, and cows, [and they] captured auspicious metal. Now, I have no leisure to go there [again]. I herewith make [for] my son (*hounan* 後男) X 鼠 [this] sacrificial *gui* vessel. May [my] sons' sons and grandsons' grandsons for ten thousand years eternally treasure and use [it] in offering!

The inscription records a punitive attack organized by the Zhou central court during the reign of King Xuan against the Huaiyi 淮夷, an indigenous people in the Huai River region, who had allegedly disobeyed their Zhou masters. However, this war was fought mainly by the troops from the states of Qi, Ji, Lai, and others, all regional states located in the Shandong region, under the chief command of Shi Yuan, who had brought from the Zhou capital some praetorian troops including the renowned "Tiger Servants." The campaign is recorded as a success with the allied Zhou troops capturing men, women, and domestic animals, as well as metal.

---

[67] The Shi Yuan *gui* is mostly likely to have been cast by the same person who also cast the Yuan *pan* 衰盤 (JC: 10172); the latter bronze used to be dated earlier to King Li, but its close link to the newly discovered Lai bronzes suggests that it must have been cast in the twenty-eighth year of King Xuan. For the inscription and date of the Shi Yuan *gui*, see Ma Chengyuan, *Shang Zhou qingtongqi mingwen xuan*, 3, pp. 307–8; Shirakawa Shizuka, "Kinbun tsūshaku," 29.178:600–612. For the date of the Yuan *pan*, see most recently, Li Feng, "Xi Zhou jinwen zhong de Zheng di," 70–71.

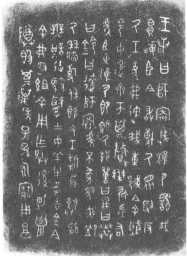

Figure 33: Inscription of the Shi Yuan *gui* (Chen Peifen, *Xia Shang Zhou qingtongqi yanjiu*, 4, pp. 465, 467)

Another recently discovered inscription, the Jinhou Su *zhong* 晉侯蘇鐘 (JL: 35–50), speaks even more explicitly about the military assistance a regional ruler was able to offer to the Zhou king.[68] The inscription describes a military campaign carried out by the Zhou king himself against the Suyi 夙夷 in the Shandong region. In this operation, the ruler of Jin from Shanxi was called on to assist the royal campaign. The ruler of Jin, with Jin troops under his personal command, served as the vanguard of the Zhou forces, breaking first into the enemy fortress from the direction ordered by the Zhou king. Upon return to the eastern capital Chengzhou, the king twice personally received the ruler of Jin, and each time he furnished him with royal gifts of four horses. Although the gifts seem to be modest, compared with what a previous king had given to the ruler of Xing during the early Western Zhou, they symbolized the relationship between the king and the ruler.

Another recently discovered inscription, the Zhabo *ding* 柞伯鼎, also from the late Western Zhou, again provides special insights into the military collaboration between the royal power and the regional states. The inscription records a military campaign led by the famous commander Guozhong 虢仲, sent by the Zhou court, assisted by Zhabo 柞伯, most probably also from the royal domain in Shaanxi. In the campaign Zhabo led the ruler of the regional state Cai 蔡, located in southern Henan and probably not far from the Zhou frontier, to attack the Hun 昏 settlement. When the

[68] See Ma Chengyuan, "Jinhou Su bianzhong," 1–17; Jaehoon Shim, "The 'Jinhou Su Bianzhong' Inscription and Its Significance," *Early China* 22 (1997), 43–75.

encirclement was completed, the ruler of Cai made a report to the supreme commander Guozhong on behalf of Zhabo.[69] Guozhong subsequently arrived on the scene and launched the attack. The context of the inscription suggests that clearly the regional ruler of Cai served a subordinate function in the military campaign organized by officials sent from the central court in Shaanxi.

These inscriptions reflect a profound political relationship between the Zhou king and the various regional rulers that was evidently different from that which bound temporary and negotiable military allies such as those we see frequently in the *Zuozhuan* commentary, and this relationship was characterized by positive instructions and unconditional obedience, fitting into an existing political system that was the Western Zhou state. They suggest that even during the late Western Zhou, more than 200 years after the founding of the Zhou state, the Zhou central court was still able to organize military operations involving the regional states in regions far beyond their lands. More importantly, for instance, the inscription of the Shi Mi *gui* actually gives us a vivid sense that the regional troops were not fighting the enemies as allied forces of the Zhou in the sense that they were commanded by their own rulers, as in the many joint military expeditions during the Spring and Autumn period, but as the king's soldiers under centrally appointed military commanders. Even when the regional ruler was in command of his own troops, as in the inscription of the Jinhou Su *zhong*, he acted more like an official of the Zhou king than his counterpart, receiving orders from the king without dispute, and was rewarded for doing the job well. Of course, not all middle and late Zhou kings were able to command the regional troops as King Xuan probably did. Indeed, in the case of King Yi, not only was he probably unable to command the regional troops, he was actually compelled to send the royal troops to attack the state of Qi in Shandong, as recorded probably in the inscription of the Fifth Year Shi Shi *gui* 五年師事簋 (JC: 4216). But such failure can only be attributed to the weakening of political influence of the royal power during the mid-Western Zhou period, particularly in the time of King Yi. The institution of regional states, as it stood, granted the Zhou king the authority and expected legitimacy to command the regional forces; all he needed was to be strong enough to take up the authority.

CONCLUSION

The regional states are one of the most defining features of the Western Zhou political system. The above discussion has clarified that the regional states were political organizations comparable to the Western Zhou state

---

[69] See Zhu Fenghan, "Zhabo ding yu Zhougong nanzheng," 67–73.

as a whole and performed the same set of functions as the latter did. This was reflected in the authority of the regional rulers over both civil and military affairs in their states and in their possession of the power of legal punishment. A regional state was formed physically by a cluster of *yi* settlements scattered around a central site as the residence of the ruler and the location of his ancestral temples and by a population that was typically stratified based on ethnic principles. The population of a typical regional state was composed of the Zhou elite and the various Zhou or non-Zhou immigrants superimposed on a much larger base of the indigenous masses. The regional states not only had their rights as states, but also obligations as active participants in the larger Western Zhou state. At the fundamental level, the regional rulers were responsible for holding their settlements in defense of the Zhou state against foreign enemies. But such obligation also extended to the military assistance the regional rulers provided the Zhou king and to the highly symbolic personal visits to the Zhou capital Zongzhou in Shaanxi. Certainly the regional states were not independent "kingdoms"; instead, they were the active agents of the Western Zhou state.

The regional governments by and large replicated the Zhou central government. The bronze inscriptions suggest that, in addition to the Three Supervisors, offices such as the Grand Scribe and Grand Invocator also existed in the regional states. However, the office of Grand Superintendent, though evolving probably from the role of Superintendent, seems to have been more prominent in the regional states. Moreover, research into the textual records on the composition of the regional governments in the Spring and Autumn period reveals a strong continuity from what we know about these governments during the Western Zhou period. However, despite the initial similarities in the composition of offices between regional and central governments, the regional governments do not seem to have undergone the process of bureaucratization that took place in the Zhou central government leading to the creation of large structural divisions as well as operational rules during the middle and late Western Zhou. Therefore, even in the early Spring and Autumn period, the regional governments still remained largely personal and non-bureaucratic in nature.

The relationship between the regional states and the central court is well documented in the contemporaneous bronze inscriptions. During the early Western Zhou, communication between the regional states and the central court was frequent, as most evident in the participation of the regional rulers and their officials in state rituals held by the Zhou king. However, the most critical kind of communication was the personal visits of the regional rulers to the Zhou capital in Shaanxi. Such visits provided important occasions on which the political relationship between the Zhou king and the regional rulers was reiterated and reinforced. The inscriptions suggest that, while their status as rulers was fully acknowledged, the regional rulers were at the same time considered the agents of the Western Zhou state and the subordinates of the Zhou king. As such, we find that the regional rulers not only provided military assistance to the Zhou royal armies in wars that took place in their neighborhood, but sometimes also assisted the Zhou king in military operations far away from their home states.

CHAPTER 7

Reconceptualizing the Western Zhou state: reflections on previous theories and models

The preceding chapters have together presented a new and integrated account of the political system and government practice of the Western Zhou state as informed by the contemporaneous bronze inscriptions. On the basis of this new knowledge, in this final chapter, I plan to review a number of sociopolitical models that have been previously applied by scholars to the Western Zhou state. Through this review, I hope also to define a way in which the Western Zhou state and its government can be properly characterized in theoretical terms. By characterizing it in sociopolitical and even anthropological terms, we actually suggest a comparison with other ancient states, or a contextualization in which by virtue of such comparison the nature and significance of the Western Zhou system can be further excavated and fully appreciated. In this way, I hope too that the appropriate theoretical reframing of the Western Zhou state and its government can contribute to our general understanding of the development of political organizations in the ancient world.

However, as soon as we take up this task, we find ourselves confronting a long tradition that started with the beginning of modern historiography and had many divided roots extending into the common soil of scholarly attempts to characterize the "ancient Chinese state." Therefore, the clarification of the issue requires a review of such scholarship in at least the last 100 years. As a matter of fact, the "ancient Chinese state" has been variously called a "city-state," "territorial state," "feudal state," "segmentary state," and "settlement state." All of these models have problems in their internal theoretical formation and also conflict with the historical reality and archeological evidence when applied to China. The clear point is that, whatever model one is to use, it must be based on a correct reading and understanding of the political system as well as the social conditions of the Western Zhou period. It must also, needless to say, be consistent with the situation of the society that served as the prototype of the model. I suggest that, on the new basis established through the present book, the Western Zhou state would be best described as a "delegatory kin-ordered settlement state."

MODELS AND THEIR APPLICATIONS

Below, I will first discuss mainly the five models: "city-state," "territorial state," "feudal state," "segmentary state," and "settlement state." Each model can be seen to represent a specific way in which political power was constructed in a given geographical space. For each model, I will first discuss briefly its historical origin and theoretical background, and then I will discuss its relevance to the Western Zhou state, as intended by the earlier scholars.

City-state

Among the models that have been applied to ancient China, the best defined and least ambiguous is the "city-state" model. The concept of "city-state" was developed in Hellenistic studies with the Greek *polis* as its reference and has a history that goes back to the Renaissance, when the Italian city-states drew on ancient precedent to justify their own secular political systems.[1] After the two "Classical" examples of "city-states," Greek and Italian, the model was applied to other civilizations, most noticeably the Sumerian city-states and the Maya city-states.[2] A recent study of city-states worldwide identifies thirty-four such incidences.[3] A study that aims at uncovering the cultural settings of city-states explicates a salient feature of the city-state that has often been overlooked: a city-state cannot exist by itself, but must exist in a cluster with other city-states as its neighbors.[4] Or, in Trigger's terms, city-state systems took the form of a network of adjacent city-states, the elites of which tended to compete with one another.[5] This is certainly not a simple singular-plural question, but calls attention to the nature of the city-state as one in a network of multiple small and self-determining entities with a common cultural and linguistic background. And in order to be called "state," it must also satisfy the condition of "state" discussed in Chapter 6, that is, a minimum degree of political independence.[6] Thus, according to Griffeth

---

[1] See Thomas H. Charlton and Deborah L. Nichols, "The City-State Concept: Development and Applications," in *The Archaeology of City-States: Cross-Cultural Approaches* (Washington: Smithsonian Institution Press, 1997), pp. 2–4.

[2] See, for instance, Song Nai Rhee, "Sumerian City-States," *The City-State in Five Cultures*, ed. Robert Griffeth and Carol G. Thomas (Santa Barbara: ABC-Clio, 1981), ch. 1, pp. 1–30; Bruce Trigger, *Early Civilization* (Cairo: American University in Cairo Press, 1993), p. 9.

[3] See Mogens Herman Hansen, ed., *A Comparative Study of Thirty City-State Cultures: An Investigation Conducted by the Copenhagen Polis Centre* (Copenhagen: The Royal Danish Academy of Sciences and Letters, 2000).

[4] See *ibid.*, pp. 16–17.   [5] See Trigger, *Early Civilization*, pp. 8–9.

[6] While Griffeth and Thomas and Trigger describe political independence as the most important characteristic of the city-state, Hansen notes that a self-governing city-state was not necessarily independent. See Griffeth and Thomas, *The City-State in Five Cultures*, pp. xiii–xx; Bruce Trigger, "The Evolution of Pre-Industrial Cities: A Multilinear Perspective," in *Mélanges offerts à Jean*

and Thomas, a city-state was a polity that was small in territorial size and citizen population, characterized by four things: a well-defined core – the city – defended by wall or surrounded by water; targeted economic sufficiency supported through the acquisition of an immediate productive hinterland; a fundamental sense of shared language, culture, and history with other city-states in the same region; and political independence and *de facto* sovereignty, although its actual autonomy could be interrupted by a strong authority.[7] The width of the city-state is estimated at approximately the distance one could walk from the center to the frontier in one day, about 30 kilometers, and its population typically ranged from four digits to five digits. Its citizens were stratified and its government highly centralized.[8]

The "city-state" model seems to have only recently begun to attract scholarly attention in Western Sinological circles, where two relevant articles have been written by respected scholars of Early China. In the first of these, Robin Yates systematically refutes a number of the preexisting paradigms that describe the Shang and Zhou states as shamanistic, feudal, or imperial. The city-state model was suggested by Yates as an alternative on the basis in part of the correspondence between the "city-state" and the ancient Chinese conception of their *yi* 邑 settlement as a cosmological whole incorporating both human and divine elements. This is further supported, in Yates' view, by a terminological correspondence between the physical walled town (*guo* 國) and the political state (also called *guo* 國).[9] In the second study, while identifying the many competing states in Spring and Autumn China as city-states, Mark Lewis traces the history of the so-called "city-state culture" to a much earlier time, during the Shang dynasty. In that regard, building on Keightley's notion of the Shang state as a thin network of pathways and encampments along which the king moved or sent his commands, Lewis advocated that the Shang state was a "city-state kingdom," a league of towns allied by kinship or shared religious practice, and the king's authority.[10] Furthermore, the Shang model of the state was inherited by the Western Zhou state, which continued to be a cluster of state-cities that owed their common

---

Vercoutter, ed. Francis Geus and Florence Thill (Paris: Editions Recherche sur les Civilisations, 1985), pp. 343–47; Hansen, *A Comparative Study of Thirty City-State Cultures*, p. 18. The situation is that, although the city-states could be organized into a hierarchy in which the strong dominated the weak through tributary relationships, none of them had the presumed institutional right to rule over the others.

[7] See Griffeth and Thomas, *The City-State in Five Cultures*, pp. xiii, 194.

[8] Hansen, *A Comparative Study of Thirty City-State Cultures*, pp. 17–19.

[9] See Robin D. S. Yates, "The City-State in Ancient China," in *The Archeology of City-States: Cross-Cultural Approaches* (Washington, DC: Smithsonian Institution Press, 1997), pp. 71–90.

[10] See Mark Lewis, "The City-State in Spring-and-Autumn China," in *A Comparative Study of Thirty City-State Cultures: An Investigation Conducted by the Copenhagen Polis Centre*, ed., Mogens Herman Hansen (Copenhagen: The Royal Danish Academy of Sciences and Letters, 2000), pp. 359–73.

allegiance to the Zhou king.[11] In this way, Lewis actually sees continuity in the fundamental pattern of the early Chinese states from Shang to the Spring and Autumn period, with only the hegemonic power of the king changing hands and eventually disappearing.

In Japan, the "city-state" model (*toshi kokka* 都市国家) was used, mainly by the successive scholars of the *Kansai* School, to interpret the ancient Chinese states in a much earlier time and has since served as one of the two competing pillars that supported Japanese scholarship on Early China. This can be seen in the explicit statement by Kaizuka Shigeki and Miyazaki Ichisada.[12] Miyazaki in particular, quite typical of the evolutionist view that was popular during the early twentieth century, saw the "city-states" as a common stage in the development of civilization, sandwiched between the "clan system" that preceded it and the large "territorial state" that followed it. Even after half a century, the *toshi kokka* model is still exercising major influence on the young generation of Japanese scholars. In an article included in an important volume that aims at bringing together the two Japanese Sinological traditions, Emura Haruki reasserts the central position of the walled cities in the social life of ancient China. Basing his view on archeological evidence and Kaizuka's theory, Emura suggests that the Shang and Western Zhou cities demonstrate the basic pattern that excluded the production and living sites of the ordinary citizens from its walled inner space and that shows ostensible political, military, and religious characters. Such cities formed the axis of the political and social life of the Shang and Zhou states.[13] In China, roughly about the same time that the Japanese scholars began to apply the "city-state" model, Hou Wailu argued quite systematically for the model of "city-state" as a way to interpret the Zhou dynasty. Starting by arguing that the term *fengjian* means the founding of cities (which is inaccurate), and not the granting of territories as was transmitted in traditional historiography, Hou traced the origin of the Chinese "city-states" to later Shang, when some large cities began to be built, a process that was then accelerated by the Zhou conquest and the subsequent construction of numerous local cities all over the North China plain. This process was likened by Hou to the establishment of cities during the Greek and Roman expansions.[14] Despite Hou's forceful argument for the "city-state," there was no continuation of

---

[11] In his recent publication, Lewis has redefined the timeframe of the "city-state" with the following line: "The Spring-and-Autumn period (771–481 BC) was the age of the city-state in China. The city-states emerged from the collapse of the Zhou state, which had itself been a league of cities." It would seem to me that Lewis no longer thinks that the Zhou (Western) state was a city-state, although it might have been a "league of cities." See Lewis, *The Construction of Space in Early China*, p. 138.

[12] See Kaizuka Shigeki, *Chūgoku no kodai kokka* (Kōbundō, 1952), pp. 1–63; Miyazaki Ichisada, *Chūgoku kodaishi gairon* (Kyoto: Toshisha daigaku, 1954), pp. 1–35; Miyazaki Ichisada, "Chūgoku jōdai ha hōkensei ka toshi kokka ka," *Shirin* 33.2 (1958), 1–20.

[13] See for instance, Emura Haruki, "Kodai toshi shakai," in *In Shū Shin Kan jidaishi no kihon mondai*, ed. Matsumaru Michio *et al.* (Tokyo: Kyūko shoin, 2001), pp. 28–38, 52.

[14] See Hou Wailu, *Zhongguo gudai shehui shi lun* (Beijing: Renmin, 1955), pp. 143–205.

this line of study in China; the main camp of the Chinese scholars continued to rely on Marxist theory, seeking the model of the early Chinese state in Marx's understanding of slave and feudal society. However, in Taiwan the "city-state" model was enthusiastically endorsed by Du Zhengsheng, who similarly traces the origin of the Chinese "city-states" to the military colonization following the Zhou conquest, but sees the similarity between China and the Greek states to lie in the fact that both had a self-determining pro-democratic body of citizens.[15]

Territorial state

According to Hansen, the concept of "territorial state" goes back to the Treaty of Westphalia of 1648, which confirmed the territorial rights of a number of modern European states as well as that of the many German princes.[16] In that context, a territorial state is marked by a clearly defined territory in which the state exercised full territorial rights in contrast to the so-called "feudal" form of state. However, the "territorial state" model has been further developed by Bruce Trigger in opposition to the "city-state," and in Trigger's terminology it is indeed often equated to "empire." In Trigger's system, the "territorial state" and "city-state" are described as the two alternative trajectories of development of state in early civilizations. While the "city-state" was represented by the civilizations of Sumer, Aztec, Maya, and Yoruba, the "territorial state" form of development was exemplified by the civilizations of Egypt, Inca, and Shang and Western Zhou China. The "territorial state" was a large organization with a rather small center (sometimes two), the capital, which, unlike the city of the "city-state," was inhabited only by the ruling class, the administrators, and people who were in their immediate service. On the other hand, the "territorial states" developed large administrative networks that were managed by large bureaucracies. Also unlike the "city-state," which was inherently integrated with its hinterland, the only significant economic link between rural and urban centers in the "territorial state" tended to be the payment of rents and taxes and the performance of *corvées* by peasants. Trigger further compares the treatment inflicted by the two types of states on their conquered enemies: while the "city-state" normally required its enemies to pay tribute and left their political institutions intact, inside the "territorial state" tribute was replaced by taxation and no semi-autonomous state was permitted.[17]

Drawing on K. C. Chang's work, Trigger applied this model to Shang and the Western Zhou, which he thinks were two successive territorial

---

[15] See Du Zhengsheng, *Zhou dai chengbang*, pp. 21–46.
[16] See Hansen, *A Comparative Study of Thirty City-State Cultures*, p. 16.
[17] See Trigger, "The Evolution of Pre-Industrial Cities," 347–49; Trigger, *Early Civilization*, pp. 10–12.

states, but not networks of city-states, contrary to what Mark Lewis suggested.[18] A recent important example of work using the "territorial state" model is Li Liu and Xingcan Chen's new study of the formation of the state in Early China. The two authors note a possible structural change in the Shang state dating probably to the Erligang–Anyang transition, and suggest that prior to it the Erlitou (1900–1500 BC) and Erligang (1500–1400 BC) states largely fitted the description of the "territorial" type of state proposed by Trigger, who himself actually applied the concept to the Anyang period. In any event, Liu and Chen view the "territorial state" in pre-Anyang China as the result of continued political expansion of the state to control material resources, especially salt, copper, and tin in the peripheral mountainous regions, hence forming a fundamental center–periphery political structure. The driving power of this formation was the bronze industry, which had been developed to the highest level in the world in terms of size and technical sophistication. The raw materials were transported to these central sites where bronze vessels and weapons were produced and were then distributed down to the regional centers to be used by the local elites. The whole system shows a high degree of centralization of political control and administration by the centers over the large territories of these early states. However, according to Liu and Chen, such a "territorial state" might have given way at the end of the Erligang period to a more regionally based power structure.[19]

In Japanese scholarship, there has been a general agreement that the "territorial state" (*ryōdo kokka* 領土国家 or *ryōiki kokka* 領域国家) emerged at a much later time, during the late Spring and Autumn period. Whether it was the "city-state" (*toshi kokka*) or the "settlement state" (see below) that preceded it has long been debated.[20] As the traditional texts clearly record borders and custom houses between the states in this period, the states of the Warring States period were clearly territorial powers. The new state of the Warring States period is described as a centralized bureaucracy centered on the rule of the despotic king and ruling over a clearly marked territory through the implementation of universal taxation and military service. Thus, the new state represented the direct domination by the state of the peasants through the new administrative structure – "county" (*xian* 縣). At the same time, it also displayed a form of military presence that was characterized by the huge central standing armies whose soldiers were no longer aristocrats but were ordinary peasants commanded

---

[18] See Trigger, "The Evolution of Pre-Industrial Cities," 347–49; Trigger, *Early Civilization*, p. 10. See also Bruce Trigger, "Shang Political Organization: A Comparative Approach," *Journal of East Asian Archaeology* 1 (1999), 43–62.

[19] See Li Liu and Xingcan Chen, *State Formation in Early China*, pp. 24, 131–48.

[20] See Kaitsuka, *Chūgoku no kodai kokka*, pp. 61–63; Miyazaki, *Chūgoku kodaishi gairon*, pp. 22–27; Nishijima Sadao, *Chūgoku kodai no shakai to keizai* (Tokyo: Tokyo University Press, 1981), pp. 41–42; Matsumaru Michio and Nagata Hidemasa, *Chūgoku bunmei no seiritsu* (Tokyo: Kōdansha, 1985), pp. 106–9.

by professional military generals. This type of "territorial state" has been seen as the transition to empire in China.

Feudal state

In Western Sinology, the "feudal" model of the state has had a much longer history than both the "city-state" and "territorial state" models. With particular relation to the Western Zhou, the "feudal state" model seems to have dominated the theoretical interpretation since the early twentieth century and until very recently. The "feudal state" model was developed in Medieval Studies and had its origin in the French words *feu, feud,* or *feudum* (fief). The adjective "feudal" was coined by French and English lawyers during the seventeenth century to characterize this type of landholding, which then gave rise to the concept of "feudalism."[21] Different from the "city-state," which is defined by at least some visible physical features, the "feudal state" refers rather to a set of social relations in and by which it existed; therefore, it is considerably difficult to define it. One of the well-known definitions of "feudalism" is: "A body of institutions creating and regulating the obligations of obedience and service – mainly military service – on the part of a free man (the vassal) towards another free man (the lord), and the obligations of protection and maintenance on the part of the lord with regard to his vassal. The obligation of maintenance had usually as one of its effects the granting by the lord to his vassal of a unit of real property known as a fief."[22] In this definition, two essential features of "feudalism" are vassalage, by which a contracted lord–vassal relationship was established, and fief, for which the vassal who received it provided military service to the lord.[23] However, there were also scholars who saw "feudalism" as a type of society, or a form of government characterized by the fragmentation of political authority.[24]

Since the mid-twentieth century, the "feudal" model of the state has been systematically applied to the Western Zhou, first by French scholars in a time when Japanese scholars began to talk about the "city-states" of Zhou,[25] and then by American Sinologists such as Herrlee Creel.[26] Creel particularly considered that the entire Zhou realm from the central

---

[21] See Elizabeth A. R. Brown, "The Tyranny of a Construct: Feudalism and Historians of Medieval Europe," *The American Historical Review* 79.4 (1974), 1063–88.
[22] See F. L. Ganshof, *Feudalism*, trans. Philip Grierson (1st edn, 1950; New York: Harper & Row, 1964), p. xvi.
[23] On the "contract of vassalage," see Ganshof, *Feudalism*, pp. 70–72.
[24] See Marc Bloch, *Feudal Society*, trans. L. A. Manyon (French edition, 1949; London: Routledge & Kegan Paul Ltd., 1961), p. 446. See also Joseph R. Strayer, "Feudalism in Western Europe," in *Feudalism in History*, ed. Ruthton Coulbourn (Princeton: Princeton University Press, 1956).
[25] See Henri Maspero, "Le Régime féodal et la propriété foncière dans la Chine antique," *Mélanges posthumes sur les religions et l'histoire de la Chine, III. Études historiques* (Paris, 1950), pp. 111–46; Marcel Granet, *La Féodalité chinoise* (Paris: H. Aschehoug & Co., 1952), pp. 1–32, 187–96.
[26] See Creel, *The Origins of Statecraft in China*, pp. 317–87.

government to the local administration was based on the principle of "feudalism," which he regarded as a form of government, and suggested a whole range of characterizations of Zhou China. Thus, the regional Zhou states were called "feudal states" or "vassal states," their rulers "feudal lords," the Western Zhou state a "feudal regime," and the Zhou government a "feudal system." According to this "feudal" model of interpretation, the Western Zhou state was a cluster of proto-independent political entities loosely bound together by contracted obligations. The Zhou king had little power beyond the small area of his own domain, and the Zhou government was staffed by hereditary officials who were little more than the king's personal servants.[27] After Creel, the second general history of the Western Zhou period in the English language also adopted "feudalism" as its theoretical framework to interpret the Western Zhou state.[28] Thereafter, "feudalism" or "feudal system" became the most frequently used terms in the vocabulary of the scholars writing about both Western and Eastern Zhou China.

Segmentary state

The "segmentary state" model was originally a purely anthropological construct, but it has by now become a much broader sociopolitical argument. The Alur society, the raw model indicated by the theory, by either the definition of the state accepted in the present study or by Nadel's largely comparable definition of the state that Southall adopted, was not even a state.[29] Instead, it was a "proto-state," as Marshall Sahlins once called it.[30] Clearly social differentiation had already taken place in the areas conceived as Alur territory (the present-day Congo) largely through the incorporation of the native populations into Alur society in the peaceful process of Alur migration from the Nile region. A general structure of power to achieve political dominance was developed through the segmentary lineage system that held together the many chiefs and chieflets. However, there was nothing like an organized government, no planned system of administration and regular offices, no military organization, not even a theory of the "state." In fact, as Southall described it, "the society was not a political unity, and no authority within it could regard its interests as a whole, plan for its

---

[27] It should also be noted that this "feudal model" is different from the Marxist "feudal model" (translated by the traditional term *fengjian* 封建), which was already popular in China and Japan from the early decades of the twentieth century. The Marxist "feudal model" basically supposes a mode of production through the exploitation of landless farmers by landowners through tenancy. It formed an important part of the "social history" debate under the Republic and is still dominant in PRC historiography. See Dirlik, *Revolution and History*, pp. 57–136.

[28] See also Hsu and Linduff, *Western Chou Civilization*, pp. 150–85.

[29] See Aidan Southall, *Alur Society: A Study in Processes and Types of Domination* (Cambridge: W. Heffer & Sons Limited, 1956), pp. 247–48; Aidan Southall, "The Segmentary State in Africa and Asia," *Comparative Studies in Society and History* 30.1 (1988), 52–82.

[30] See Marshall Sahlins, "The Segmentary Lineage: An Organization of Predatory Expansion," *American Anthropologist* 63.2, Part 1 (1961), 322.

future, or take stock of the present in the light of its own policies pursued in the past."[31] Political relations between the central domain and the local clans were achieved through occasional tribute and the kidnapping of the chief's sons to live among the local units. There is no tradition that a chief would ever use physical means to enforce his authority outside his small domain. The chief's authority was dependent on his mystical power to control rain and the continuation of chiefship.[32]

Since the publication of Southall's book in 1956, the "segmentary state" model has been applied to a number of apparently more advanced societies,[33] and this has forced Southall to subsequently revise his model to fit the various new examples. Thus, the "segmentary state" is redefined as: "One in which the sphere of ritual suzerainty and political sovereignty do not coincide. The former extends widely towards a flexible, changing periphery. The latter is confined to the central core domain."[34] Simply speaking, the "segmentary state" is redefined as a "core" over which the ruler exercised sovereignty and a periphery over which the ruler claimed ritual suzerainty. Thus, in his later articles, Southall began to speak about the Alur "kingship" embodied in the institution of the "Kingdom of Atyak" (which he did not speak about in 1956) and the king's punitive power to carry out raids against disobedient units. Through this theoretical reworking, the Alur society began to reemerge as a coherent political state.[35]

In the more recent writings by Southall, the "segmentary state" model has become entangled with the Marxist concept of the "Asiatic mode of production,"[36] and because of this, he has come to believe that the "segmentary state" model is even applicable to China. He first identified the Shang state as Creel and Keightley described it as a "segmentary state," and hence one with an Asiatic mode of production, in contrast to the "feudal mode of production" of the Western Zhou. Then the entire Chinese history down to the twelfth century is regarded as a swing between two poles: political "unity" representing the "segmentary state" based on the "Asiatic mode of production," and "disunity" based on the "feudal mode of production." In Southall's theory, even the Han and Tang Empires were the expressions of "Asiatic mode of production" and, by the extension of the same logic, "segmentary states."[37] Among Sinologists Barry B. Blakeley was the first to have discussed the "segmentary state."

---

[31] See Southall, *Alur Society*, pp. 238–40; quote from p. 239.   [32] See, *ibid.*, pp. 188–90.

[33] These include the Rajput state and Cola state in northern and southern India, the Indian Vijayanagara Empire, and the Maya state in Central America. See John W. Fox, Garrett W. Cook, Arlen F. Chase, and Diane Z. Chase, "Questions of Political and Economic Integration: Segmentary versus Centralized States among the Ancient Maya," *Current Anthropology* 37.5 (1996), 795–801.

[34] See Southall, "The Segmentary State in Africa and Asia," 52.   [35] See *ibid.*, 57–65.

[36] See Aidan Southall, "The Segmentary State: From the Imaginary to the Material Means of Production," in *Early State Economy*, ed. Henri Claessen and Pieter Van De Velde (New Brunswick: Transaction Publishers, 1991), pp. 75–96.

[37] See Aidan Southall, "Urban Theory and the Chinese City," in *Urban Anthropology in China*, ed., Greg Guldin and Aidan Southall (Leiden: E. J. Brill, 1993), p. 33–37.

He saw the "segmentary state" as a theoretical alternative to the "feudal state" with the flexibility to take into account many sociopolitical systems that are similar to European "feudalism" but cannot be labeled "feudal." Blakeley thought that Zhou China was such a system.[38] In his early writings, Keightley used to call the Shang state an "incipient dynastic state."[39] But after some years of research, he has now decided that Shang was a "segmentary state." Keightley does not actually analyze the features of the Shang state in the light of the "segmentary state" model, but says in a note in a judgmental manner that "the model, I believe, is probably as appropriate for the Late Shang." Then, he quotes at length Southall's characterization of the "segmentary state," which suggests certainly that he thinks that these features are pertinent to Shang:

Territorial sovereignty is recognized but limited and essentially relative, forming a series of zones in which authority is most absolute near the centre and increasingly restricted towards the periphery, often shading off into a ritual hegemony; there is centralised government, yet there are also numerous peripheral foci of administration over which the centre exercises only a limited control... monopoly of the use of force is successfully claimed to a limited extent and within a limited range by the central authority, but legitimate force of a more restricted order inheres at all the peripheral foci.[40]

These are the terms that Southall used to characterize his "segmentary state" model in 1956 and that Southall himself has abandoned as "awkward and cumbersome" in favor of a more straightforward and indeed very loose definition of the model in 1988.[41] One must point out that, even if the terms could be descriptive of the Late Shang state, they suggest a situation, especially in the expressions of "centralised government" and "monopoly of the use of force," very far removed from the Alur reality as Southall himself described it.

Settlement state

The "settlement state" (*yūsei kokka* 邑制国家) model has been developed, mainly in the Japanese scholarship, through struggles with the "city-state" model. While the latter model considers China as composed essentially of numerous independent polities standing equal to each other, the former argues that there was a hierarchy, a layered structure, and a relationship of dominance and subjugation among them. This point was made first

---

[38] See Blakeley, "Regional Aspects of Chinese Socio-Political Development in the Spring and Autumn Period," pp. 59–62.
[39] See Keightley, "The Late Shang State."
[40] See Keightley, *The Ancestral Landscape*, p. 56; quote from Southall, *Alur Society*, p. 248.
[41] See Southall, "The Segmentary State in Africa and Asia," 52.

by Matsumoto Mitsuo,[42] and was developed by a number of other scholars who took such hierarchical relationships among the *yi* settlement communities as the main feature of pre-Qin China.[43] The idea was further developed into a sociopolitical model of the state by Matsumaru Michio and has since been widely accepted by scholars, especially those who are based in eastern Japan.[44] As a scholar of oracle-bone and bronze inscriptions, Matsumaru started by investigating the meaning of *yi* in the contemporary sources and was able to isolate three types of settlements all referred to as *yi*. The first is the capital *yi*, such as the Shang capital Anyang, which is referred to on the oracle bones as "great settlement" (*dayi* 大邑), or "celestial settlement" (*tianyi* 天邑).[45] Larger in number were the secondary settlements that were occupied by the individual lineage communities; these were called "lineage settlement" (*zuyi* 族邑). Furthermore, both the "great settlement" and "lineage settlement" had their attached settlements, which he called "affiliated settlement" (*shuyi* 屬邑), where most activities of subsistence production took place. Matsumaru thinks that such stratification of the settlements at three levels was the fundamental structure of the Shang and Zhou states, and the lack of differentiation of these settlements in the inscriptional language suggests that they all accommodated similar socioeconomic functions.

Matsumaru sees the "lineage settlements" as the essential units of Shang and Zhou societies and speaks of them as "settlement states" in the plural. These *yi* communities or "settlement states" were basically autonomous entities; and the Shang and Zhou states were each a coalition of multiple "settlement states."[46] But when he speaks of the three-level stratification (*dayi-zuyi-shuyi*) as the fundamental structure of the Shang and Zhou states, he suggests that the whole political organization of the Shang or Zhou state can be spoken of also as a "settlement state" (*yūsei kokka* 邑制国家).[47] In fact, it is in the construct of the relationship among the settlements through a hierarchy, but not that of the "lineage settlements" as individual units, that the "settlement state" model can be best differentiated from the "city-state" model. Matsumaru further studied the ways in which these large groups of "settlement states" that had the same cultural and historical background were organized into larger political organizations, the Shang or Zhou state. Accordingly, the coalition of Shang was established through

---

[42] See Matsumoto Mitsuo, "Chūgoku kodai no yū to min, jin to no kankei," *Yamanashi daigaku gakugei gakubu kenkyū hōkoku* 3 (1952), 91.
[43] See Utsunomiya Kiyoyoshi, *Kandai shakai keizaishi kankyū* (Tokyo: Kōbundō, 1955), pp. 16–18; Masubuchi Tatsuo, *Chūgoku kodai no shakai to kokka* (Tokyo: Kōbundō, 1960), pp. 279–92.
[44] See Matsumaru Michio, "In Shū kokka no kōzō," pp. 49–100.
[45] On this point, see also Keightley, *The Ancestral Landscape*, pp. 57–60.
[46] Matsumaru made this clear in Matsumaru Michio and Nagata Hidemasa, *Chūgoku bunmei no seiritsu* (Tokyo: Kōdansha, 1985), pp. 61–63.
[47] See Matsumaru, "In Shū kokka no kōzō," p. 59; Matsumaru and Nagata, *Chūgoku bunmei no seiritsu*, p. 62.

a system of "fictional kinship," where the chiefs of the various "settlement states" were regarded as nominal sons of the Shang ancestors and as brothers of the Shang king, from whom they received occasional gifts and whose fathers and grandfathers they worshipped as their own. The Zhou, on the other hand, implemented an actual kinship through the preexisting structure of the "settlement states" by sending royal kinsmen to control these locally based "states."[48]

In recent Japanese historical scholarship, the "settlement state" model continues to be employed as a main framework to interpret Shang and Zhou societies and has been redefined with reference to the "city-state" model. For instance, Ogata Isamu reasserted that the key feature of the "settlement state" is a network that connects the numerous *yi* settlements in a "point-line" relationship of obedience of settlement to settlement and lineage to lineage.[49] On the other hand, Matsui Yoshinori discussed the theoretical basis for both the "city-state" and "settlement state" models. While recognizing the importance of the relationship of obedience among the settlements, Matsui pointed out that the key to the "settlement state" model lies in its internal lineage system, instead of a free citizenry, as required by the "city-state" model.[50]

However, the "settlement state" model has not attracted much attention in the West. Instead, a somewhat similar model, the "village-state," was proposed by Charles Maisels, also in opposition to the "city-state" model. These two types of state, first of all, represented two forms of spatial configuration: the "city-state" (Mesopotamia) were densely distributed centers in a relatively small area, while the "village-state" (China) saw the capital site dominating a larger area in which the numerous lineage-organized villages were located.[51] In socioeconomic terms, they are described as the "Asiatic mode of production" and the "city-state mode of production," and represented two trajectories of the emergence of states: the "city-state mode" had independent households as the building blocks of its society based on a highly productive agriculture, while the lineages inhabiting the villages were basic

---

[48] See Matsumaru, "In Shū kokka no kōzō," pp. 72–99. In recent years, Matsumaru further modified this hierarchy into four levels, with the "lineage settlement" divided into "greater lineage settlement" and "minor lineage settlement." See Matsumaru Michio, "In Shū Shunjū shi sōsetsu," in *In Shū Shin Kan jidaishi no kihon mondai*, ed. Matsumaru Michio *et al.* (Tokyo: Kyūko shoin, 2001), pp. 3–26.

[49] As such, the Shang and Zhou states were relatively loosely bound congregations of settlements that leave gaps among them. See Ogata Isamu and Kishimoto Mio, eds. *Chūgoku shi*, Chapter 2: "Kōtei shihai no seiritsu" (Tokyo: Yamakawa, 1998), pp. 61–67. In the same book, Hirase Takao titled his chapter on pre-Qin China "Ancient Civilization and Settlement States," but he does not address the issue. See *ibid.*, Chapter 1: "Kodai bunmei to yūsei kokka," pp. 24–60.

[50] While Matsui was himself suspicious about the integrity of Zhou lineage system, hence about the "settlement state" model, he refrained from making choices between the two. See Matsui Yoshinori, *Shūdai kokusei no kenkyū*, pp. 11–13.

[51] See Charles Maisels, "Models of Social Evolution: Trajectories from the Neolithic to the State," *Man* 22.2 (1987), 340–43.

units of the "village-state" society based on a less productive agriculture.[52] Although the "village-state" model also emphasizes the lineage structure in the rural communities as does the "settlement state" model, the "village-state" model says little about the relationship between the villages and the way in which they were grouped into a large state.

EVALUATION AND CRITICISM

Above, I have reviewed the five sociopolitical and anthropological models and their applications to Early China, particularly the Western Zhou, as advocated by previous scholars. It must be noted that the attempts to use these models have not yielded great success, and there was the danger that the adoption of a wrong model could lead to serious misunderstandings of the sociopolitical system of the early Chinese states. In general, there are two kinds of problems that hinder the application of the models. The first are problems with the models themselves – whether they are logically consistent and well enough defined to allow a good balance between historical particularities and general principles when applied to actual cases. In this regard, we must first ask a very simple and perhaps philosophical question: What is a model, and why do we need it? To most historians, the great advantage offered by models lies in their comparative value. A model is a theoretical construct or a framework with carefully selected and defined variables. Therefore, models invoke theoretical analyses at a level expressed in abstract terms that would allow the possibility of comparison of cultures developed in different historical contexts. Another advantage of models lies in their interpretive value; that is, through contextualization using a proposed model, historical facts that emerge from their particular cultural environment can be better understood as a part of the common human experience, and, as such, their implications can be fully explored. However, it is my conviction that models do not and should not exist by themselves as empty constructs. A model, no matter how abstract it becomes, must be capable of returning to, and therefore forming an inherent relationship with, the "mould," the society or culture from which it was derived.

Secondly, the eventual success of a model depends on the accurate control of data derived from analyses of the target society to which the model is applied. This has become a particularly important issue as the base of our information has been constantly changed and indeed revolutionized by archeology in China during the past fifty years. In this regard, as Liu and Chen recently pointed out, many attempts to apply these models were based on analyses of data produced in China many decades ago, and as a result, the conclusions drawn to fit China into the respective models must

---

[52] *Ibid.*, 331–37, 54–55; Charles Maisels, *Early Civilizations of the Old World: The Formative Histories of Egypt, the Levant, Mesopotamia, India and China* (London: Routledge, 1999), pp. 354–56.

be reevaluated against new archeological evidence.[53] In this connection, it is especially worth noting that the "Pre-Qin China" or "Ancient China" as a temporal whole to which the models were often applied has been collapsing in the face of the more specialized analyses such as the present book addressing particular historical issues in particular time periods. The plainest fact is that in the 2000 years before the unification by Qin, the societies in China underwent tremendous changes in terms both of their material foundation and the ways in which they were organized. Therefore, the Western Zhou must be differentiated from the Spring and Autumn period and certainly also from the Shang dynasty, particularly the late Shang. With these considerations in mind, I will now examine each of the five models introduced above.

The "city-state" model

The "city-state" model is itself probably the least problematic, and the question is whether it fits the situation of ancient China, or to what period it should be applied. As mentioned above, the most important feature of "city-states" is that they have to exist in a cluster or network that implies a relatively, at least theoretically, equal relationship among its participants. A single city cannot form a "city-state" unless it is one among many others. Therefore, the important point is not to have a city (even if the city has a wall-enclosure), but to have neighboring cities with which the city coexists and stands in equal relation. It is probably acceptable, as suggested by Mark Lewis, to apply the "city-state" model to the Spring and Autumn period of China,[54] but any effort to apply the concept before that period has to meet strong challenges. In this regard, we have to take serious account of the evidence brought to light by recent archeology and synthesized by Liu and Chen, who suggested on such a basis that the pre-Shang and Shang central sites such as Erlitou, Zhengzhou, and Anyang far exceeded in size and power any secondary sites on the East China plain in their respective times. And temporally, these three central sites overlap each other very little. Consequently, we are clearly not in a situation in which there were many competing small polities coexisting in a small area, but one in which there was a settlement hierarchy and perhaps dominance by the central sites over the smaller ones. For instance, in Zhengzhou, Shang cultural remains covered an area of 2500 ha in contrast to the secondary centers in the region, which had an area of 8–18 ha (except the second center, Yanshi, which had an area of 200 ha), and to even those outlying regions under Shang influence, such

---

[53] See Liu and Chen, *State Formation in Early China*, pp. 23–24.
[54] For the social and political condition of city-states in Spring and Autumn China, see Mark Lewis' recent discussion: Lewis, *The Construction of Space*, pp. 138–50.

as southern Shanxi, eastern Shaanxi, and northern Hubei, where contemporary sites were all under 200 ha.[55] It is clear that Zhengzhou was the greatest metropolis on the eastern China plain during 1500–1400 BC, and it existed in a hierarchical structure of settlements, but not in a network of roughly comparable polities such as those in Mesopotamia or ancient Greece. This situation did not change during the late Shang, where the biggest sites on the eastern plain were only a fraction of the size of Anyang, not to mention the gap between the cultural contents exposed in these sites. Therefore, it seems quite problematic to try to look for the origin of "city-states" in the Shang period.

Only when we come to the Western Zhou period do we begin to see a cluster of cities of comparable size developed in the central and western parts of the Wei River plain within about 200 kilometers. However, the bronze inscriptions analyzed in Chapter 4 suggest that these cities, such as Feng, Hao, and Zhou, and even Pang and Zheng, instead of being a group of independent polities, formed a network of royal activities and were controlled by the same administrative machine. The analysis in Chapter 4 has shown also that in a considerably stable way some of the functions of these cities were handled collectively by officials appointed in the central court with responsibility for the Five Cities. Certainly, they were not "states." On the eastern China plain, following the establishment of the many regional states, a regional pattern similar to the "city-states" began to emerge and certainly provided the foundation for the "city-state" culture of the subsequent Spring and Autumn period. But they were not yet "city-states" during the Western Zhou period because they were not independent, but were under watch by the royal power, which stationed a huge army in Chengzhou in present-day Luoyang. The bronze inscriptions suggest that at least during the early Western Zhou the regional states were active participants in the Western Zhou state, but were not in a condition of free competition. The inscriptional evidence shows very clearly that the political system in which they participated was much larger than that of the "city-states." The situation during the middle and late Western Zhou when the royal power was weakened might be slightly different from this, but that has to be regarded as a later modification of the system, and not what the system was intended to be.[56] Even during the Spring and Autumn period, when such conditions emerged with the removal of royal authority, not all the states active in the time can be called "city-states." The concept is suitable probably only to the cluster of smaller states on the eastern China plain, whereas those larger states in the periphery such as Qin, Jin, Chu, and Qi had moved very

---

[55] See Liu and Chen, *State Formation in Early China*, pp. 85–113.

[56] But even during the late Western Zhou, there was a period, e.g. the early decades of King Xuan, when Zhou royal power exercised considerable influence over the eastern plain, as shown by the bronze inscriptions.

swiftly to establish their territorial rule.[57] There is really no need to force all of them into a single "city-state" model.

It has been argued that the ancient Chinese notion of city expressed in the term *yi* 邑, representing a walled settlement as an organic whole of space accommodating both human and divine uses, corresponds well with the concept of "city-state."[58] However, paleographical studies have shown that the situation was much more complicated. The etymology certainly does not support its correspondence to the city of the "city-states," as the small circle in the graph *guo* 國 does not necessarily represent a wall enclosure, but simply and probably marks the residential core of a *yi* settlement that conceptually, as clarified in Chapter 4, also embraces the outlying fields surrounding it; the outer circle was not often present in the graph until the Spring and Autumn period. In fact, none of the Western Zhou central sites has been confirmed as having such a wall enclosure. What is more important is the social context in which the various *yi* settlements as large as the capitals Feng and Hao, and as small as hamlets occupied by a couple of residential houses, existed. These settlements were interwoven into larger networks organized along a lineage structure. That is, many of the *yi*, like those mentioned in the Guo Cong *xu* 聯從盨 (JC: 4466), were owned and managed by the aristocratic lineages located elsewhere, and most settlements called *yi* did not have the function of city except for a few large central settlements (see Figure 16). The indistinguishability in the language of the bronze inscriptions between the *yi* settlements of various sizes suggests that they were fundamentally different from the cities of the "city-states." Even those large cities, as demonstrable from the bronze inscriptions, served probably as the gatherings of the outposts of the aristocratic families who had their lineage bases in the rural areas with which they were identified, not the city. So, whereas the Sumerian and Greek cities stood opposing the rural societies, the Western Zhou *yi* was integrated with rural communities by complex sociopolitical ties. Therefore, the distinction between *guo* 國 as cities occupied by the nobles and *ye* 野 inhabited by the agricultural population was probably a social change that did not occur until the Eastern Zhou period. Nowhere in the Western Zhou bronze inscriptions is a city called *guo* 國 and its people *guoren* 國人; instead, *yi* 邑 and *yiren* 邑人 are terms to express such concepts.

In this regard, Maisels' comparative model can probably help highlight another major characteristic of the regional states in contrast to the "city-states." In Maisels' view, in the transition from kinship-ordered egalitarian society to state-ordered stratified society, the "city-state," as exemplified by

---

[57] Mark Lewis recognizes this difference between the so-called "city-states" and the peripheral larger states, which he calls "congeries of semi-independent city-states." However, this expression is conceptually problematic, and it is likely that these larger states during their expansion continued to replicate a lineage-based structures and not internal "city-states." See Lewis, *The Construction of Space*, pp. 140–41.

[58] See Yates, "The City-State in Ancient China," pp. 82–83.

the Sumerian cities, represented one of two possible trajectories, the other being China. In Mesopotamia, irrigation and "mechanized" agriculture enabled the growth of "households" into the basic organizational unit of reproduction, and hence the building blocks of the "city-state" society. While stratification could take place within the households, all households were linked through conciliar structures, "circles of the people," led by elders who were also senior householders. According to Maisels, this process did not happen in China, where the land was less productive and the descent group, the lineage, always remained strong.[59] Looking from this perspective, the "city-states" and the early Chinese states were two societies organized on very different socioeconomic bases. And in a society where lineages are strong powers, there is probably no chance for the development of the free citizenry that was so characteristic of the Greek city-states.[60] Therefore, the *guoren* 國人 that is frequently mentioned in the written records for the Spring and Autumn period as a politically active, self-identifying, and self-determining citizenry was almost certainly the result of the collapse of lineage bonds.[61] Any attempt to try to look for such social groups in a typical lineage-dominated society such as the Western Zhou and, based on it, to determine the Western Zhou as "city-states," would seem to have taken a wrong trajectory from the very beginning.[62] In the Western Zhou sources, there is no evidence for the existence of a free citizen body outside the structure of lineages.

The "territorial state" model

However, "territorial state" is not our choice of term to call the Western Zhou for the very reason that the entire Zhou proper was not managed in an administrative way, that is to say, through a planned administrative network that was directed by the central court. Certainly there was a high degree of territorial control attempted by the Western Zhou state, but *it was different from territorial administration*. The "territorial state," as Trigger describes it, involves centralized administration through a layered and compartmented bureaucracy set up for, and was supported by, the collecting of taxes throughout the state.[63] Due to the lack of written evidence, this is perhaps something we will never know about for the early and pre-Shang states. But from the evidence on bronzes, we can be sure that the Western Zhou state was not managed in this way. In the Western Zhou case, territorial control was clearly attempted by the Zhou central

---

[59] See Maisels, "Models of Social Evolution," 334, 42–43, 54–55.
[60] This lack of free citizen body has been recognized by some writers on the "city-states" in China; see Yates, "The City-State in Ancient China," p. 76.
[61] For the composition and political role of the *guoren* and their active assemblies, see Mark Lewis' recent discussion; *The Construction of Space*, pp. 144–47.
[62] For such views, see Du Zhengsheng, *Zhou dai chengbang*, pp. 21–46.
[63] See Trigger, *Early Civilization*, pp. 10–11; Trigger, "The Evolution of Pre-Industrial Cities," 347–48.

court and was achieved mainly through installing the many locally based and administratively autonomous agents – the regional states. But, there was certainly no centralized "territorial administration" that is essential to the "territorial state" model. As it is generally agreed among the Japanese scholars, the territorial state was a new phenomenon that appeared in the late Spring and Autumn period as the result of expansion by the original regional states newly equipped with the centralized bureaucratic machine. So, if the "territorial state" did exist in the pre-Shang or Shang period, it must have been quite different and may require a different set of theoretical terms to describe it.

As evident in such expressions as "our eastern states" (*wo dongguo* 我東國) and "our southern states" (*wo nanguo* 我南國), the outlying regional states distant from the Zhou royal domain were clearly perceived as Zhou "territories," and attacks on them would be ideally met with royal actions. On the other hand, administrative decision over these "territories" was completely put in the hands of the regional rulers. The Zhou had actually parceled their state out into many small jurisdictions in that regard, and the state-wide administration was essentially localized. Furthermore, the Western Zhou state was actually not defined by its territorial size with a linear border; instead, it was defined by the distribution of the numerous regional states, and each of the regional states was in turn defined as a cluster of integrated settlements. Beyond the territorial core, the royal domain in Shaanxi, there was probably no "territory" that we can call Zhou, but there were thousands of settlements that were linked by roads to the many regional centers that formed the Zhou state. In between and beyond these settlements, there were forests, virgin lands, and probably also settlements, especially in the east and north, inhabited by some non-Zhou communities. Moreover, the settlements belonging to a regional state might not necessarily all be located close to the central site where the ruling lineage was located. There could well be a situation in which a settlement belonging to state A was located closer to the central site of state B and was surrounded by the settlements of the latter state (see figure 34 below). This situation must be understood from the perspective of lineage politics and was probably the result of the land exchange that is frequently mentioned in the bronze inscriptions. Such a pattern of settlement integration could hardly be called "territorial."

The "feudal state" model

The failure of the "feudal state" model owes as much to the inherited problems in the construct of "feudalism" itself as to the misinterpretation of the social and political system of the Western Zhou state. It should be noted first that in recent years the concept of "feudalism" has come under severe and increasing attack by the Medievalists. For instance, Elizabeth

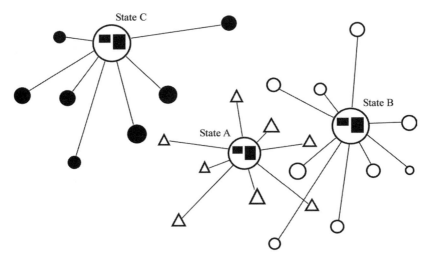

Figure 34: Pattern of settlement organization of the regional states

Brown pointed out that "feudalism" had its origin in a special form of landholding (fief), and it takes this one aspect to generalize for a characterization of the whole medieval society. The term "feudalism" is not only hard to define, but, however defined, also impossible to apply to every part of Europe because it over-simplifies a much more complex situation.[64] Therefore, Brown suggested that the best way to deal with "feudalism" is to abandon it. A massive attack on the concept of "feudalism" was launched by Susan Reynolds in her 1994 book that completely repainted the image of medieval Europe and thoroughly undermined the foundation of "feudalism."[65] Reynolds rejected all "feudal" terms and instead looked directly into a much larger set of social and political relations to demonstrate how and to what degree vassalage and fief (two key elements of "feudalism") constituted institutions in medieval society. In her interpretation, vassalage as "a freely contracted relation" was but one of the many important social relations as fief was only one of the numerous forms of landholding in the medieval period, and as such, they were not institutionalized until the eleventh century.[66] In other words, for about a half of the medieval period, there is no basis for talking about the "feudo-vassalic institutions" (her term to replace "feudalism"). After a century and a half of dominance, the concept "feudalism" has now been discarded by most, if not all, historians of medieval Europe.

---

[64] See Elizabeth A. R. Brown, "The Tyranny of a Construct," 1074–75.
[65] Susan Reynolds, *Fiefs and Vassals: The Medieval Evidence Reinterpreted* (Oxford: Clarendon Press, 1994).
[66] See Reynolds, *Fiefs and Vassals*, 18, 84–86, 117–19.

The collapse of the "feudalism" doctrine in Medieval Studies certainly calls into question the application of the concept to other societies based on the misinformed comparison with medieval Europe. In a previous study, I have systematically discussed the invalidity of the concept when applied to Western Zhou China, and perhaps a summary of the points should suffice here.[67] First, vassalage was an entirely personal contract between two free men and was an exclusive "marriage" between the two men in their private capacity. Because of its contractual nature, the fundamental features of the lord–vassal relationship were the equality it implied and mutual obligations it demanded. The relationship between the Zhou king and the various regional rulers had a clear "public" nature, and as such it was a "ruler–subject relationship" that demanded the unconditional submission of the latter to the former. Second, the medieval fief was fundamentally different from the Zhou regional state. The former was a form of stipend and was a property with limited rights but more contracted obligations. The Zhou regional state was essentially a form of government which had responsibility for civil administration, justice, and the military, and was considered necessary by the Zhou central court in accordance with the grand strategy of the Western Zhou state. Third, the comparison of the system of "Five Ranks" with the medieval European ranking system was misplaced because the "Five Ranks" was not a Western Zhou institution, and because even the medieval European ranking system was not an element of so-called "feudalism." Fourth, the contrast in military organization is even more obvious. The essence of the feudo-vassalic institutions was to free the lord from the burden of equipping his warriors by granting them the fiefs so that the warriors could furnish themselves with weapons and horses to serve the lord when needed (the maximum period of service was forty days). Therefore, there was no standing army at the medieval king's disposal. The Zhou king had a huge central standing force at his disposal, and service in the royal army does not seem to have had any fixed time limits. Finally, as for Creel's characterization of the Western Zhou government as a "feudal" institution, it should be clarified that the "feudo-vassalic institutions" were simply not a form of government; instead, they introduced personal ties to maintain and ensure the proper operation of the government. For the above reasons, the application of the "feudal" model to the Western Zhou state was clearly misconceived, and it is even doubtful that the "feudal state" itself can still exist as a model.

The "segmentary state" model

Like the "feudal state" model that was challenged by the ongoing research on medieval Europe, the "segmentary state" model also has some serious

[67] See Li Feng, "Feudalism and Western Zhou China," 115–44.

problems in itself. An early objection to the model was raised by the eminent anthropologist Marshall Sahlins as early as 1961.[68] Sahlins first confirmed the by now most widely used scheme of progress of social organizations from band to tribe, to chiefdom, and to state. According to Sahlins, the "segmentary lineage system" typically characterized the tribal-level society, but cannot be used to characterize societies like Alur, which he called "proto-states," skipping the chiefdom level of development. In other words, the concept of "segmentary state" was conceived wrongly in the first place, and when you have a "state," you cannot at the same time have a "segmentary lineage system." In Sahlins' interpretation, the "segmentary lineage system" means much more than just having the segments. Segments exist in many societies from primitive to modern, even in the University of Michigan, where Sahlins used to teach. The segmentary lineage is really a system that is connected to territory through *local-genealogical segmentation,* in which the lineage segmentation corresponds well to the local territorial segmentation. "It is not simply that each territorial entity is identified with a lineage segment, but also that contiguous segments of the same inclusive territorial entity are identified with equivalent branches of the same inclusive lineage."[69] The segments are all the same and equal, lacking internal political structures, and those closer in genealogical relations are also located closer to each other on the ground. Furthermore, the segmentary lineage manifests the principle of *structural relativity,* which is in some way a system of reference in which a member of a segment refers to himself to outsiders according to the latter's relationship to his segment and lineage branch.[70] These are the defining features of the segmentary lineage system that Southall has not demonstrated for the Alur society, nor for any other societies to which the "segmentary state" model was applied, including the Western Zhou.

A recent and more severe criticism of the "segmentary state" model was raised by a group of archeologists writing about archaic states. They thought that the "segmentary state" model had seriously misled scholars to believe that the societies referred to by it were of state level while the Alur were no more than a rank society at best. They lamented the use of such terms as "king," "kingdom," and "state" for what were actually rank societies without real social distinctions, kingship, or central government.[71] It seems to me that these scholars have pointed out the main contradictions in the "segmentary state" model, and if a model has anything to do with reality, it must first account for the features of the society of

---

[68] See Marshall Sahlins, "The Segmentary Lineage," 322–45.

[69] See *ibid.*, 331.

[70] For instance, a person speaks of himself as a member of group *a* relative to those of group *b*. But the same person is a member of 1 in reference to *c* and *d* (which are 2) and of *A* (composed of 1 and 2) in reference to those of *B*. See Sahlins, "The Segmentary Lineage," 333–34.

[71] See Gary M. Feinman and Joyce Marcus, eds., *Archaic States* (Santa Fe: School of American Research Press, 1998), pp. 7–8.

its origin. However, reading through Southall's book, one doubts strongly that the definitions of "segmentary state" that Southall proposed and Keightley adopted have much to do with the Alur society that the former described, as Southall admitted himself that the Alur political system stands near the bottom of the range of segmentary states.[72] The "segementary state" model came into existence as a solution to the debate of the "segmentary lineage system" *versus* "unitary state" that characterized early African Studies. But it seems to have been a mistake corrected in a mistaken way.[73] If Southall had started from the world context, where, e.g. particularly in China, segmentary organizations coexisted with and in fact supported the political system of the unitary state, he would not have invented the "segmentary state" as a form of political organization in opposition to the unitary state. Therefore, without careful consideration of the unique theoretical environment in which the "segmentary state" model was conceived and the complex debates that have occurred since its birth, the use of it to describe China could lead to serious and unnecessary misinterpretations.

Perhaps we do not need Sahlins' definition of "segmentary lineage system" to invalidate the application of the "segmentary state" model to the Western Zhou; and perhaps we should just compare the Western Zhou to the Alur society from which the "segmentary state" model was derived. The Alur society was a loosely bound society with no central government or other machineries of the state, although the chief did have a small group of embryonic administrative staff.[74] Although the superiority of the central lineages was recognized by distant groups, there was no central coercive power, a standing military force that is essential to any "state"-level societies. The only thing the chief could do in order to keep the distant groups in line was to call on the help of some other groups to carry out a raid on the disobedient ones, and thereupon to establish his residence there and eat up all their grain.[75] The Western Zhou had a well-constructed form of state with a bureaucracy running the central government at least from the mid-Western Zhou and a strong central standing armed force, the Six and Eight Armies, to enforce political order throughout the Zhou realm. Even in local government, as demonstrated in the preceding chapters, regular offices were established and routine administrative control was planned and maintained. More importantly, the Zhou had a well-formulated theory of their state based on the concept of the Mandate of Heaven, which provided legitimate authority for the king to eliminate any potential threats from outside and within. The Western Zhou state was not even a "pristine" state in North China, where the hegemonic religion-focused Shang state had ruled before it. Overall, although

---

[72] See Southall, *Alur Society*, p. 252.   [73] See *ibid.*, pp. 241–44.   [74] See *ibid.*, p. 240.
[75] See *ibid.*, p. 237; Southall, "The Segmentary State in Africa and Asia," 64.

there are structural similarities between the Western Zhou state and the Alur society in the way that both embraced lineage segments, besides this, there is little if anything that can possibly suggest a sensible comparison between the two systems, which were clearly at different stages of social development. Therefore, the "segmentary state" model has very limited value for the Western Zhou.

The "settlement state" model

Among the many models, the "settlement state" model best reflects the internal organizational principle of the Western Zhou state. In particular, its structural configuration of layered settlement entities, when applied to the Western Zhou, has potentially very significant interpretive values. Moreover, it is certainly superior to the "city-state" model or even the "village-state" model because it does not need to confront the difficult definitional distinction between the "city" and the "village," which does not exist in the language of the contemporary bronze inscriptions. Naturally, the "settlement state" model embraces in its theoretical framework both large and small settlements, which are all called *yi* in the inscriptions. The value of the model lies particularly in its configuration of the relationship between the large cities and smaller settlements through the role of the lineage centered on the "lineage settlement." More importantly, the model perceives the *yi* settlement as the basic unit of social production utilizing whatever natural resources that were available within its reach, and such production, though independently carried out, was integrated into the whole economy through the lineage as its organizing power.

The problem with the "settlement state" model lies in its insufficient consideration of the political power of the state, which was not only present, but clearly superimposed on the organizing structure of the *yi* settlements. Due to the lack of consideration of state power, the model itself suggests little distinction between the Western Zhou state and the Shang state, although they were most likely to have been organized in very different ways. It further fails to account for the possible differences in the way the settlement hierarchy was organized in the areas where the regional Zhou states exercised power compared to the areas where they did not exist, for instance, in the royal domain in Shaanxi. It is not clear, moreover, when the regional states did exist, how the power of the state was connected to the "lineage settlements" or the "affiliated settlements." The "settlement state" model explains well the vertical relationship in Western Zhou society, but is insufficient in interpreting its horizontal spatial relationship, that is, how the different parts of the Western Zhou state were integrated into a political whole. The model apparently lacks a delicate political dimension.

THE WESTERN ZHOU AS A "DELEGATORY KIN-ORDERED SETTLEMENT STATE"

It has been shown above that none of the models employed previously by scholars to characterize the Western Zhou state can still serve such purpose without serious modification. On the other hand, the study of the Western Zhou government presented in the present book, on the basis of the contemporaneous bronze inscriptions, has given us a new basis for reframing the Western Zhou state in sociopolitical terms. As the result of this study, and having considered all theoretical alternatives, I think that the Western Zhou state can be best characterized as a "delegatory kin-ordered settlement state." I believe that the integration of a political power structure constructed according to delegative rules with the socioeconomic system of the "settlements" can best reveal the organizational and operational logic of the Western Zhou state. However, it is not my purpose here to suggest yet another model, but to reconceptualize the Western Zhou state and to capture its most salient features.

The expression "delegatory" is used in the sense that the exercisers of political authority did not actually possess the source of the political authority but ruled with a power that was delegated to them by the true bearer of sovereignty, which could not be partitioned. It was "delegated" in the sense that the authority was not permanently granted (or given away), but could be withdrawn by the bearer of sovereign power, in this case, the Zhou king. The Western Zhou state was politically "delegatory" in two ways: (1) the reigning Zhou king delegated his power to the regional rulers; (2) the reigning Zhou king ruled with a power that was conceived in Zhou political philosophy as originating in the dynastic founders, particularly King Wen. Therefore, the key political relationship in the Western Zhou state was constructed according to the principle of "delegacy" that had its deep roots in the Zhou theory of the origin of the state. The clarification of the nature of this relationship not only is important for revealing the ultimate source of power and the ways in which political authority was achieved, but can also help overcome the contradiction in Creel's interpretation of the Western Zhou state as both an aggregation of proto-independent "feudal states" and a system of centralized administration.[76] As I have shown earlier, neither were there "feudal states," nor was there a system of centralized administration involving the whole of the Western Zhou state.

The Zhou had a clear political theory on which the Western Zhou state was founded. According to this theory, the ultimate legitimacy of the state was granted by Heaven to, in particular, King Wen as its recipient. This is clearly stated in early Western Zhou inscriptions such as the Xiao Yu

---

[76] See Creel, *The Origins of Statecraft*, pp. 423–24.

ding 小盂鼎 (JC: 2839) and is transmitted in early Western Zhou texts such as the "Kanggao" chapter of the *Shangshu*. Although, from the mid-Western Zhou, King Wu, who actually achieved the conquest, was added, and thereafter the expression of King Wen and King Wu receiving Heaven's Mandate became formulaic in the bronze inscriptions,[77] absolutely no other kings who came to reign after King Wu are said in any inscription to have received the mandate from Heaven. So, the situation was clearly that, in the Zhou theory of the state, King Wen (and King Wu, from mid-Western Zhou) was the sole bearer of the sovereignty of the Zhou state from which all authority originated. As already noted in Chapter 2, this Zhou reverence for the divine role of King Wen and King Wu as the sole bearers of sovereignty might have provided a favorable condition for the development of the concept of "state" and bureaucracy, as separate from the secular role of the reigning Zhou kings.

However, what is even more is that in Zhou cosmology King Wen and King Wu were not theoretically dead when they physically faded. As is quite characteristic of early Chinese religion centering on the ancestral cult, the Zhou had the clearest notion that after their physical disintegration (or perhaps concealment from the secular world), King Wen and King Wu actually ascended to the court of High God (*shangdi* 上帝), where they continued to "live." They not only attended High God in his court above, but occasionally also traveled to the secular realm, where they received ritual offerings from the descendant kings.[78] This pattern of behavior is described in a number of inscriptions but most explicitly in the inscription of the Hu *gui* 㝬簋 (JC: 4317), cast by King Li during the late Western Zhou. In this cosmological configuration of the Western Zhou state, the reigning Zhou king ruled on behalf of King Wen and King Wu with a sovereign power delegated to him. As such, he had a constant fear that the power might someday be withdrawn, a point that can be confirmed by a number of Zhou documents such as the inscriptions of the Xun *gui* 詢簋 (JC: 4321) and the Maogong *ding* 毛公鼎 (JC: 2841) and a number of poems in the *Book of Poetry*.[79] Only when we understand the delegative and tentative nature of the Zhou kingship can we really understand the source of this over-expressed fear manifestly appearing in the bronze inscriptions.

---

[77] This appears in numerous inscriptions such as the Xun *gui* 詢簋 (JC: 4321), Guaibo *gui* 乖伯簋 (JC: 4331), Maogong *ding* 毛公鼎 (JC: 2841), and the Lai *pan* 逨盤.

[78] In his analysis of the poem of "Chuci" 楚茨, Martin Kern carefully reconstructed the circumstances of ancestral worship in which ancestral spirits that descended from Heaven to the temple were entertained with a whole range of food and alcohol offerings accompanied by musical performances and ritual prayers. See Martin Kern, "Shi Jing Songs as Performance Texts: A Case Study of 'Chu Ci' (Thorny Caltrop)," *Early China* 25 (2000), 49–111.

[79] For instance, the poem "Wenwang" (Mao, no. 235) describes the Mandate of Heaven as not constant; and the poems "Sangrou" (Mao, no. 257), "Yunhan" (Mao, no. 258), "Zhaohao" (Mao, no. 265) all talk about the destructive power of Heaven. See *Shijing*, Sz, 16.1, p. 504; 18.2, p. 559; 18.2, p. 561; 18.5, p. 579 (Waley, *The Book of Songs*, pp. 228, 268, 270–71, 285–86).

The status of the regional states and the political role of their rulers have been discussed fully in Chapter 6. As was clarified there, a regional ruler by his very status, *hou* 侯, had full authority over the internal affairs of his state and the right to decide its foreign policy exclusive of cases in which the interests of the Western Zhou state were involved. The bronze inscriptions show that the regional rulers formed a specially privileged stratum in the Zhou political system, being higher in status than the court officials, and were sometimes permitted to use royal insignias as suggested by the Mai *fangzun* 麥方尊 (JC: 6015). Their right as rulers was fully recognized by the Zhou court and the Zhou king. However, the bronze inscriptions also show that the regional rulers were not independent "sovereign" rulers; instead, they ruled on behalf of the Zhou king with a power delegated to them by the king. As such, they were active participants in the Western Zhou state and sometimes also attended the Zhou king in the central court. To some extent, this relationship resembles that between the Roman emperor and the client kings in the east, whose autonomy was fully recognized but who had surrendered their sovereignty to the empire. But they had different origins as most of the Zhou regional states were actually established by the Zhou royal court.

Thus, when the Zhou king delegated his power, he did it through a kinship structure, and this gave the Western Zhou state yet another important dimension. It was the kinship structure of the royal lineage that provided the main roads along which political power was distributed from the king to his regional delegates (by extension, it also reached some marriage partners of the royal lineage). Thus, the regional rulers were by and large the heads of the new lineages as sub-branches of the Zhou royal lineage. In this way, the social organization of the lineages was transferred into the political organization of the Western Zhou state. It was also the lineages, when transferred into focal points of the widely extending political network as a result of the delegation of power, that provided the crucial link between the state and its subject population that lived on the *yi* settlements. In this regard, the Western Zhou state can be seen as an association of thousands of settlements that were organized by the political power of the state through the kinship structure of the lineages. This is the "settlement state," and it is "kin-ordered." The control of such settlements through the kinship structure of the lineages was the fundamental mission of the Western Zhou state that provided them with a unitary political order and also the means (i.e., coercive power) to enforce that order.

The "settlement state" means two things in the geopolitical configuration of the Western Zhou state: (1) The "settlements," indistinguishably called *yi* 邑 in the bronze inscriptions, were the basic social entities as well as geographic units that the power of the "state" reached. Thus, the Western

Zhou state did not exist as an integral geographic whole clearly demarcated by linear borders, but was marked by the location of the thousands
of *yi* settlements in which the "state" existed. As such, the Western Zhou
state in geographic terms was an aggregation of thousands of pieces of land
woven together (in a layered structure) by its political power. (2) Because
the Western Zhou state *existed as* "settlements," there were empty spaces
existing within the state's conceived "territory"; there were also overlaps
between the perceived "territories" of the regional states as the constituent
parts of the Western Zhou state as the settlements controlled by a state
might have been located closer to the core of another (see figure 34). This
condition of existence of the regional states, fully clarified in Chapter 6,
provided an important starting point for a whole range of social changes
that were to occur when the political power of the Western Zhou state
eventually waned. It is critical to understand this starting point in order
to understand the subsequent transition to territorial states and further to
empire in Chinese history.

As far as the structure of political control of the *yi* settlements is concerned, there was a difference between the east, where the Zhou king delegated his power, and the royal domain, where he did not. In the east, the
capital sites of the regional states formed the "great settlements," the loci
of state power. Beyond these capital sites were located the "lineage settlements," which were occupied mainly by the various indigenous lineages
whose history can be traced back to before the Zhou conquest. Surrounding them, there were the numerous small and "affiliated settlements" that
were controlled by the lineages (see figure 35). The regional rulers, with
the power delegated to them by the Zhou king, commanded these lineages and hence through them controlled the numerous rural settlements.
The establishment of the regional states was in essence to provide the
numerous local settlements in eastern China with a political structure that
would bring them into the possession of the Western Zhou state. In the
royal domain in Shaanxi, where the king did not delegate his power, a
three-tier settlement hierarchy was also present. The royal cities such as
Feng, Hao, and Zhou served as the great settlements; they accommodated
royal activities and also embraced residences of the aristocratic lineages.
However, the powerbase of the aristocratic lineages was located in the
lineage settlements that were located far from the royal centers and were
connected with (indeed supported) the aristocratic residences in the major royal centers. Surrounding the lineage settlements were the numerous
affiliated settlements that were controlled by the lineages. This formation
is fully evident in the bronze inscriptions discussed in Chapter 4. However, in the royal domain, there were also numerous settlements controlled
directly by the state, hence located outside of the lineage structure. These
settlements were managed by officials dispatched directly from the central
government.

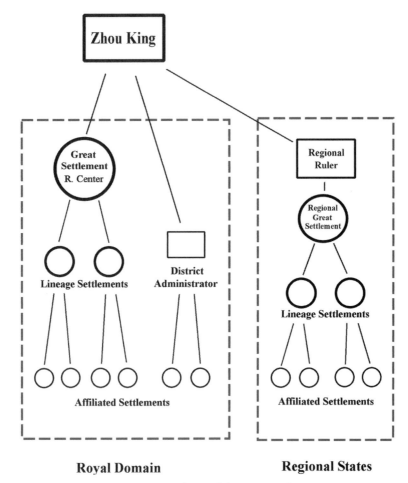

Royal Domain   **Regional States**

Figure 35: Conceptual map of the Western Zhou state

The above characterization would best explain the situation of the West-ern Zhou state during the early part of the dynasty, when the system was created. As time went on, some modifications certainly occurred to move the system in new directions. One of these modifications took place in the power structure, whereby the power delegated by the Zhou king tended to reside permanently with the regional rulers. On the other hand, new sub-lineages were established by the sons of the regional rulers, leading to the creation of new lineage settlements in the regional states. In the royal do-main, as land transactions between lineages were frequently documented by bronze inscriptions, some of the affiliated settlements might have ac-quired multiple affiliations. However, these can all be seen as later develop-ments and are different from what the system was designed to achieve and intended to bring.

CONCLUSION

In this chapter, I first examined the origins of five theoretical models hitherto employed by scholars to define the early Chinese states, particularly the Western Zhou. Based on the latest archeological and inscriptional evidence, I have discussed problems with each of these models when applied to the Western Zhou. In brief, the "city-state" model fails mainly because it entails a cluster of mutually independent political entities that did not exist in the Western Zhou, when the regional states were participants in a much larger political system and the major cities on the Wei River plain were organized into a single administrative network. The "territorial state" is unsuitable because the Western Zhou state was not defined by "territory" (but by the *yi* settlements), and because, although territorial control was attempted, territorial administration was limited to the royal domain. The "feudal" model fails because it oversimplifies the situation in medieval Europe and because it misinterprets the situation of the Western Zhou state. The "segmentary state" model is also hindered by problems in itself; but more importantly, it provides very little comparative value for the Western Zhou state in reference to the Alur society from which the model was derived. Finally, the "settlement state" model best explains the way in which the Zhou society was organized, but it falls short in explaining the real political power configuration in the Western Zhou state.

The Western Zhou state, instead, is here defined as a "delegatory kin-ordered settlement state." It is conceived first of all as a gigantic congregation of clusters of *yi* settlements organized into a layered network by the political power of the state. In this network, the rural and affiliated settlements were connected by roads to the lineage settlement, which were further linked by roads to the regional capitals, where the minor branches of the Zhou royal lineage were located. At the top layer, the royal centers – the Five Cities on the Wei River plain and Chengzhou in the east – formed a power network through which the Zhou king traveled. By the principle of delegacy, the power of the state reached out from the royal centers to the regional capitals through the kinship structure of the royal lineage, and it further reached the various indigenous lineages through the political structure provided by the regional states. In the royal domain in the west, it reached directly from the royal centers to the lineage centers that were in control of the numerous affiliated rural settlements. This was the political and socioeconomic structure of the Western Zhou state that emerged as the result of the two conquests and from the continuing expansion that followed them.

Conclusion

All conquering powers had something to rely on to overcome their enemies. Although there is no reliable figure for the Shang troops in comparison to that of the Zhou, which is also unknown, at the point of the Zhou conquest, the Zhou seem to have had little if any material wealth that can be compared with what has been demonstrated by the huge size of the Shang capital and the immense volume of its bronze industry. However, the Zhou defeated the Shang superpower and were able to prosper in the next two centuries; they must have had something that enabled them to do so.

One of the factors that might have contributed to the Zhou's strength lay in their better organization. As mentioned in Chapter 1, the divinatory officials did play a central role in the Shang government. The Shang king consulted the deities about a wide range of topics that concerned him and the Shang state, and yet he showed very little interest in the establishment of administrative offices and the conduct of his officials. The Zhou might have been as religious as the Shang, and the Zhou king might have consulted his ancestors on many decisions in a context different from what the appointment inscriptions would indicate. However, despite being religious themselves, the Zhou government from the early time seems to have had a clear civil character. As clarified in Chapter 2, the early Western Zhou government was centered on the roles of the Three Supervisors, who were organized into the general bureau of the Ministry. These executive officials were further assisted by a large number of Document Makers and Scribes, who produced and kept written records for the Zhou government. If the religious officials had been active in the court and received frequent awards from the Zhou king, we would expect them to have cast as many inscriptions as did the administrative and secretarial officials. This is certainly the case with the Invocators, who cast a number of inscriptions, and we actually do know that the Diviner Hu cast the famous Hu *ding* 曶鼎 (JC: 2838). But the religious officers are nowhere near as significant as the administrative and secretarial officials. This suggests that the Zhou probably had a different approach to the management of their state and to the way in which political authority could be achieved. On the other hand, one may speculate that the peripatetic nature of the Shang kingship, as David Keightley calls it, might have in some way hindered the development of a stable and routine bureaucracy.[1] And the relatively loose and underdeveloped political structure of the Shang state, brought together by the hegemonic power of the Shang king, could collapse quickly when confronting a firm and well-organized attack.

The Zhou might have also been better organized in another way. It is likely that the Zhou should be accredited with the creation of the institution of "surnames" (*xing* 姓) that has survived through to modern-day China. The system of surnames served as the basis for another institution – the practice of exogamy – which regulated marriage groups among the elites of the Western Zhou state, and prohibited marriages between close relatives within the Zhou royal Ji clan.[2] The Shang, in all likelihood, married internally among the ten branches that formed the royal Zi clan.[3] The Zhou preference for distant kin groups outside the royal clan probably had over time provided a very powerful drive to expand the Zhou kinship network. Within the lineage, the practice of "Lineage Law" (*zongfa* 宗法) normally regulated succession to power and wealth.[4] These are all likely signs that the Zhou elites were probably better organized.

Therefore, with their historical conquests, the Zhou probably introduced a new form of government and also a new political culture that was to endure in China for many centuries thereafter. They installed an initial condition that would allow the growth of the first bureaucracy in China and one of the oldest bureaucracies in the world. With the Mandate of Heaven as the foundation of their state, hence a vision of their historical mission very different from that of the Shang, the Zhou elites were committed to practical if not pragmatic management of their affairs through careful civil and military administrations employing a large number of executive and secretarial officials. This was probably the tradition that Confucius praised as so "civil,"[5] rather than, perhaps, mysterious!

The early Western Zhou government seems to have managed the Zhou state well through the period of great expansion, which seems to have benefited from the strong leadership of such figures like the Duke of Zhou and the Duke of Shao. The bureaucratization of the Zhou government did not come as the direct result of the expansion but as the fruit of an internal readjustment and reorganization after the great expansion was brought to an end. From the beginning of the mid-Western Zhou, signs began to appear clearly indicating the structural compartmentalization as well as operational systematization of the Zhou government. In his survey of historical

---

[1] See Keightley, *The Ancestral Landscape*, p. 58.

[2] On this point, see the recent discussions in Edwin Pulleyblank, "Ji and Jiang: the Role of Exogamic Clans in the Organization of the Zhou Polity," *Early China* 25 (2000), 1–27.

[3] See Matsumaru Michio, "In jin no kannen sekai," in *Chūgoku no In Shū bunka-Symposium* (Tokyo: Yomiuri shinbun, 1986), pp. 140–42.

[4] See Hsu and Linduff, *Western Chou Civilization*, pp. 163–71.

[5] See *The Analects of Confucius*, trans. Arthur Waley (New York: Vintage Books, 1938), p. 97.

bureaucracies, Weber has delineated the ways in which bureaucratic organizations developed. He had the clear idea that the process of bureaucratization was unrelated to the power of the state to expand. For instance,
the great Roman Empire was created in the absence of bureaucracy and
disintegrated when bureaucracy was at work. The impetus of bureaucratization came from the need of the high social strata to increase the possession of goods and to improve their standard of living, and from the need
of the society for security, welfare, a better postal service, transportation,
and irrigation. Therefore, he saw bureaucratization as an internal process
rather than external expansion.[6]

The bureaucratization of the Zhou government clearly took the trajectory described by Weber. It was the need to improve the management of
the Royal Household by separating it from the central government that
seems to have provided the initial impulse for bureaucratization. Parallel
to this development, the secretarial offices were also divided between an
interior secretarial body in the direct service of the king and a group of
scribes that was organized into the bureau of the Grand Secretariat. The
bronze inscriptions provide clear evidence for the coexistence of different secretarial units. Another important change took place in the military
organization – the Six and Eight Armies were developed into a complex
system that embraced both civil and military administration. Accompanying this trend towards increasing structural complexity, the hierarchy of
order was also created. As vividly shown by the Yong *yu* 永盂 (JC: 10322),
a person with *gong* status received orders from the king; he, assisted by a
group of high officials, gave orders to the executive officials, who would
carry them beyond the royal court. But the final fulfillment of the orders
depended on the local officials. The study of local administration further
shows that, by the late Western Zhou, there were Three Supervisors at each
level of the Zhou administration down to the rural settlement performing
the duties required by their titles.

The bureaucratization of the Zhou government took place also in
other areas. The nearly 100 "appointment inscriptions" are themselves the
best testimony of the standardization of administrative procedures. For
instance, rules were developed that determined the arrangement of the
youzhe for their relevant appointees, and also determined their respective
positions in the general etiquette of the appointment ceremony. It should
also be noted that the appointment was clearly done in writing, which was
used extensively in the management of the Western Zhou state. And the
possible distinction between those who kept the records and those who
wrote the orders is an important mark of specialization. Furthermore, the
government allowed competition among young officials of different family backgrounds, and there was a career track that could be followed from

---

[6] See Weber, "Bureaucracy," pp. 209–14.

assistantship to senior positions through subsequent promotions. These are but some of the most visible features of the middle to late Western Zhou bureaucracy that we know from the bronze inscriptions.

However, the swing of bureaucratization seems to have left the regional governments untouched. During the Western Zhou, probably none of the regional states managed a "territory" that can in anyway be compared to the Zhou royal domain. Therefore, a simple administrative structure would probably have been sufficient to manage their domestic affairs. In speculation, one may also say that the native lineage structure in the regional states remained strong to provide for the need of local administration, which may in turn have restricted the expansion of the regional governments. However, the regional governments were important mechanisms in a "delegatory kin-ordered settlement state" that had the control of local settlements as its mission. The situation began to change significantly during the Spring and Autumn period, when the regional states gradually gave way to the large "territorial states." When bureaucratization took its second turn in China, focusing particularly on the regional states, in a time when the need for more effective administration over an ever expanding territory significantly increased, it provided the key to the future empire.

The Western Zhou state that has emerged from this study of its government and political system is one that diverges significantly from most, if not all, previous models of the ancient state. But beyond doubt it qualifies as a "state" both by its historical mission to establish political order in North China and by its well-tested willingness to use coercive forces to maintain such order, in a "territory" so defined not by a linear border (as in the territorial state), but by the very physical existence of the *yi* settlements. Thus, the Western Zhou can be seen as a gigantic sociopolitical organization that brought the thousands of settlements in North China into (and managed them through) a state structure, built soon after the two conquests by extending the royal lineage to establish locally based regional states. Presiding over the state structure was the sovereign Zhou king, who ruled with a power originating in the Zhou founder, King Wen, whose legitimacy was once confirmed by Heaven. The Zhou king further delegated his power to the regional rulers, who had the full capacity of a ruler but who showed unconditional submission to the Zhou king (very different from the "feudal" vassal). In the bifurcated structure of the Western Zhou state, the royal domain was an accumulation of the *yi* settlements that were stratified and connected to the royal capitals by the socioeconomic ties of the aristocratic lineages. In turn, each regional state can also be seen as a cluster of the *yi* settlements controlled by lineages whose position was determined by the political order of the Western Zhou state. Thus, the Western Zhou state was a huge layered network of the *yi* settlements woven together by the political power of the state through the extension of lineages in accordance with the principle of political delegacy. In this "delegatory kin-ordered settlement state" no settlement was independent (like the city-state), but each was connected to all the others by its allegiance to the Zhou king and by the promise of good life from Heaven that only the institution of the Western Zhou state could fulfill.

The introduction promised that the present study would lay out what we do know and what we do not but wish to know about the Western Zhou state and its government. Through the study, I have identified a number of areas for which we are in particular need of future evidence: we need more inscriptions that will tell us about the material conditions and workings of bureaus with general responsibilities such as the Ministry and the Grand Secretariat. We also need more evidence on the rule of the Provisioner and his relationship with the Superintendent; we need to know the criteria for official promotion and the role played by personal patronage. Regarding local administration, we need more evidence to define the administrative status of the city; we want to know the qualifications of the *bang* polities; more critical information is needed as well for reconstructing the administrative structure of the areas managed directly by the state, with respect particularly to the *li* district. Moving beyond the royal domain, we are in general need of information on the structure and workings of the regional governments; we certainly also need to know how in practice the regional states were connected to the indigenous "lineage settlements" and what obligations the lineages had to their states.

A list of official titles in Western Zhou bronze inscriptions

In composing this list, I am indebted to two scholars, Zhang Yachu and Liu Yu, for their early survey, which brought to light inscriptional evidence for Western Zhou offices down to 1986.[1] The current list draws on a much larger base of information incorporating especially inscriptions that have been discovered in the last twenty years. The inscriptions are carefully screened and, by the standards set forth at the outset of Chapter 2, only those titles (a smaller number than in Zhang and Liu's table) that represented constant offices with definable responsibilities are included in the list. They are interpreted in a government system that has emerged through discussions in the chapters of this book. One important characteristic of the Western Zhou government is that the same title was found at different levels of administration in contrast to the practice of the early empires, where local administration was equipped with a system of titles largely separate from that of the central bureaucracy.[2] On the one hand, this enables us to approach the official titles in a unitary way when they are understood as functional "roles"; on the other hand, we need to carefully consider their positions in the overall administrative hierarchy. Needless to say, we need also to trace changes over time.

SANYOUSI 三有嗣: THREE SUPERVISORS

Central roles of Western Zhou administration, including the Supervisor of Land, Supervisor of Construction, and Supervisor of Horses; existed at different levels of the Zhou government.

As main figures of the Ministry (*Qingshiliao* 卿事寮, Ling *fangyi* 令方彝 [JC: 9901], Fansheng *gui* 番生簋 [JC: 4326], Maogong *ding* 毛公鼎 [JC: 2841]), mentioned in Fifth Year Qiu Wei *ding* 五年裘衛鼎 (JC: 2832) and Qiu Wei *he* 裘衛盉 (JC: 9456) by their collective name "Three Supervisors."

---

[1] See Zhang Yachu and Liu Lu, *Xi Zhou jinwen guanzhi yanjiu.*

[2] See Bielenstein, *The Bureaucracy of Han Times*, pp. 90–113; Loewe, *The Government of the Qin and Han*, pp. 37–55.

As administrative officials of the Zhou military (Six Armies and Eight Armies), mentioned in Li *fangzun* 盠方尊 (JC: 6013) and Li *fangyi* 盠方彝 (JC: 9900).

SITU 嗣土: SUPERVISOR OF LAND

Responsible for land administration and land-related matters; active at different levels and different locations.

As official of the central government, mentioned in He Yuan *gui* 郃尻簋 (JC: 4197; appointed Supervisor of Land), Zai *gui* 訧簋 (JC: 4255; in charge of Spring Plowing Ritual), Ci *ding* 此鼎 (JC: 2821; serves as *youzhe*), Fifth Year Qiu Wei *ding* 五年裘衛鼎 (JC: 2832; witnesses land sale), Qiu Wei *he* 裘衛盉 (JC: 9456; *id.*).

Possibly as Supervisor of Land in the eastern capital Chengzhou, mentioned in Thirteenth Year Xing *hu* 十三年瘨壺 (JC: 9723; as official name prefixing a building structure), Xian *zhong* 鮮鐘 (JC: 143; *id.*).

As administrative official in the Zhou military, mentioned in Li *fangzun* 盠方尊 (JC: 6013), Li *fangyi* 盠方彝 (JC: 9900).

As local administrator of major cities, mentioned in Mian *fu* 免簠 (JC: 4626; appointed as such with responsibilities for forests, marshes, and pastoral lands in the suburb of Zheng).

As local administrator of the local *bang* polity, seen in Sanshi *pan* 散氏盤 (JC: 10176; official from San).

As administrator of local settlements, mentioned in Zhou Situ *zun* 螯嗣土尊 (JC: 5917).

As official of the regional states, mentioned in Ta Situ *gui* 渣嗣土簋 (JC: 4059).

As caster of bronzes, mentioned in Situ Si *gui* 嗣土嗣簋 (JC: 3696), Situ Hu *gui* 嗣土梡簋 (JC: 3671), Nangong Hu *zhong* 南宮乎鐘 (JC: 0181).

RELATED, *SITU* 嗣徒: SUPERVISOR OF MULTITUDES

Same as Supervisor of Land; does not appear until the mid-Western Zhou.[3]

As official of the central court, mentioned in Yang *gui* 楊簋 (JC: 4294; serves as *youzhe*) and Wuhui *ding* 無惠鼎 (JC: 2814; *id.*).

As administrator of major cities, appears in Yong *yu* 永盂 (JC: 10322; witness of land transaction).

As official of the regional states, mentioned in Zhongqi *xu* 仲齊盨 (JC: 4440; from state of Lu in Shandong), Bo Wu *xu* 伯吳盨 (JC: 4415; *id.*), Bo Kefu *ding* 伯郤父鼎 (JC: 2597; from state of Jin in Shanxi).

---

[3] On the relation between Supervisor of Land and Supervisor of Multitudes, see the discussion in Chapter 2, pp. 73–74.

RELATED, *ZHONG SITU* 冢嗣土: GRAND SUPERVISOR OF LAND

Grand Supervisor of Land, or Head Supervisor of Land in an administrative unit.

As chief administrator of the Zhou military in Chengzhou, mentioned in Hu *hu* 曶壺 (JC: 9728; appointed Grand Supervisor of Land in the Eight Armies of Chengzhou).

SIGONG 嗣工: SUPERVISOR OF CONSTRUCTION

Responsible for construction and public works.

As official of the central administration, belonging to the Ministry, mentioned in Shi Ying *gui* 師穎簋 (JC: 4312; serves as *youzhe*), Jinhou Su *zhong* 晉侯蘇鐘 (JL: 35–50; *id.*), Forty-second Year Lai *ding* 四十二年逨鼎 (*Wenwu* 2003.6, 16–27; *id.*), Fifth Year Qiu Wei *ding* 五年裘衛鼎 (JC: 2832; witness of land transaction), Qiu Wei *he* 裘衛盉 (JC: 9456; *id.*).

As administrative official in the Zhou military, mentioned in Li *fangzun* 盠方尊 (JC: 6013), Li *fangyi* 盠方彝 (JC: 9900).

As administrator of the major cities, seen in Mian *zun* 免尊 (JC: 6006; appointed such in Zheng), Yong *yu* 永盂 (JC: 10322; official from Zhou, witness of land transaction).

As administrator of local settlements in royal domain, mentioned in Yang *gui* 揚簋 (JC: 4294; appointed such with responsibilities for farming, residential houses, forage grass, lawsuits, and construction officers in Liangtian).

As official of the local *bang* polity, seen in Sanshi *pan* 散氏盤 (JC: 10176; officials from both San and Ze).

As caster of bronzes, seen in Sigong Ding *jue* 嗣工丁爵 (JC: 8792).

SIMA 嗣馬: SUPERVISOR OF HORSES

Responsible for military affairs, as one of the "Three Supervisors."

As official of the central court, mentioned in Shi Yu *gui* 師艅簋 (JC: 4277; serves as *youzhe*), Shi Chen *ding* 師晨鼎 (JC: 2817; *id.*), Jian *gui* 諫簋 (JC: 4285; *id.*), Xing *xu* 瘨盨 (JC: 4462; *id.*), Forty-third Year Lai *ding* 四十三年逨鼎 (*Wenwu* 2003.6, 16–27; *id.*), Fifth Year Qiu Wei *ding* 五年裘衛鼎 (JC: 2832; witness of land sale), Qiu Wei *he* 裘衛盉 (JC: 9456; *id.*).

As official of the Zhou military, seen in Li *fangzun* 盠方尊 (JC: 6013), Li *fangyi* 盠方彝 (JC: 9900).

As official of the local *bang* polity, mentioned in Dou Bi *gui* 豆閉簋 (JC: 4276; as official of the *bangjun* of Youyu), Sanshi *pan* 散氏盤 (JC: 10176; official from San).

RELATED, *ZHONG SIMA* 冢嗣馬: GRAND SUPERVISOR OF HORSES

As Head Supervisor of Horses at the central court, mentioned in Jingbo Lu *gui* 井伯親簋(*Zhongguo lishi wenwu* 2006.3, 4–13; initial appointment of Jingbo Lu 井伯親 as such); the same Jingbo is more often called simply "Supervisor of Horses" in Shi Yun *gui* 師瘨簋 (JC: 4283; serves as *youzhe*), Zou *gui* 走簋 (JC: 4244; *id.*), Shi Kuifu *ding* 師奎父鼎 (JC: 2813; *id.*).

As Grand Supervisor of Horses in Bin 㣇 military garrison, seen in Qi *gui* 趞簋 (JC: 4266; appointed as such with responsibilities for servants, archers, warriors, and matters related to the neighbors).

RELATED, *SHI SITU* 師嗣馬: SUPERVISOR OF HORSES OF THE ARMY

Mentioned as an official title prefixing a building structure in Shi Yun *gui* 師瘨簋 (JC: 4283; as *Shi sima gong* 師嗣馬宮), Yang *gui* 養簋 (JC: 4243; *id.*).

TAISHI 太史: GRAND SCRIBE

Chief secretarial official at the central court, giving name to the *Taishiliao* 太史寮 "Grand Secretariat" (see Fansheng *gui* 番生簋 [JC: 4326]; Maogong *ding* 毛公鼎 [JC: 2841]).

Mentioned in Zhong *fangding* 中方鼎 no. 1 (JC: 2785; as royal inspector to the south), Guo Cong *xu* 虢從盨 (JC: 4466; announces award of land as counterpart of the Interior Scribe).

As caster of bronzes, mentioned in Taishi You *yan* 太史友甗 (JC: 915).

RELATED, *GONG TAISHI* 公太史: DUKE GRAND SCRIBE

Grand Scribe with the special rank *gong* 公, "Duke"; eminent figure at the central court.

Mentioned in Zuoce Hu *you* 作冊魑卣 (JC: 5432; gives rewards to subordinate officials).

As caster of bronzes, seen in Gong Taishi *ding* 公太史鼎 (*Jianghan kaogu* 1982.2, 45).

NEISHI 內史: INTERIOR SCRIBE

Secretary of the king's inner court and member of the Royal Household bureaucracy, responsible for handling and keeping written documents; important character of middle–late Western Zhou government.

Mentioned in Rong *gui* 榮簋 (JC: 4241; receives royal order regarding the term of service of the ruler of Xing in Hebei), Shi Hu *gui* 師虎簋 (JC: 4316; announces government appointment on behalf of the king), Shi Yun *gui* 師瘨簋 (JC: 4283; *id.*), Mu *gui* 牧簋 (JC: 4343; *id.*), Jian *gui* 諫簋 (JC: 4285; *id.*), Yang *gui* 楊簋 (JC: 4294; *id.*), Shi Kuifu *ding*

師奎父鼎 (JC: 2813; *id.*), Dou Bi *gui* 豆閉簋 (JC: 4276; *id.*), Yi *zhi* 遷觶 (JC: 6516; *id.*), Shi Maofu *gui* 師毛父簋 (JC: 4196; *id.*), Feng *ding* 趩鼎 (JC: 2815; *id.*), Qian *gui* 鄴簋 (JC: 4296; *id.*), Shi Ying *gui* 師穎簋 (JC: 4312; *id.*), Qi *gui* 趞簋 (JC: 4266; receives royal command), Qiu Wei *gui* 裘衛簋 (JC: 4256; gives gifts on behalf of the king), Dong *ding* 尅鼎 (JC: 2789; as representative of the king or queen), Fifth Year Qiu Wei *ding* 五年裘衛鼎 (JC: 2832; witness of land sale), Guo Cong *xu* 虢從盨 (JC: 4466; announces awards of land as counterpart of Grand Scribe).

NEISHI YIN 內史尹: CHIEF INTERIOR SCRIBE

Head of the Interior secretarial body; high prestige and never mentioned by his personal name, but sometimes as Yinshi 尹氏, the "Chief."

Mentioned in Yang *gui* 養簋 (JC: 4243; announces official appointment on behalf of the king), Chu *gui* 楚簋 (JC: 4246; *id.*), Shi Ji *gui* 師籍簋 (JC: 4257; *id.*), First Year Shi Dui *gui* 元年師兌簋 (JC: 4274; *id.*), Third Year Shi Dui *gui* 三年師兌簋 (JC: 4318; *id.*).

SHI 史: SCRIBE

The ordinary scribes, very numerous, playing clerical and secretarial roles at every level of Western Zhou administration.

As officials of the central court, mentioned in Wu *fangyi* 吳方彝 (JC: 9898; announces official appointment on behalf of the king), Wang *gui* 望簋 (JC: 4272; *id.*), Cai *gui* 蔡簋 (JC: 4340; *id.*), Xing *xu* 癲盨 (JC: 4462; *id.*),[4] Song *ding* 頌鼎 (JC: 2829; *id.*), Wuhui *ding* 無惠鼎 (JC: 2814; *id.*), Forty-second Year Lai *ding* 四十二年逨鼎 (*Wenwu* 2003.6, 16–27; *id.*), Chen Chen *he* 臣辰盉 (JC: 9454; as royal envoy), Zhong *yan* 中甗 (JC: 949; *id.*), Shi Song *gui* 史頌簋 (JC: 4232; as royal inspector to the east), Shi Shou *ding* 史獸鼎 (JC: 2778; sent by a chief official to meet with the king in Chengzhou), Wu Hu *ding* 吳虎鼎 (JL: 364; handles documents of land transaction, as subordinate of the Chief Interior Scribe), Shi Tian *gui* 史臨簋 (JC: 4030; recipient of royal gifts), Shi Mao *hu* 史懋壺 (JC: 9714; *id.*), etc.

As secretarial official in the local *bang* polity, mentioned in Sanshi *pan* 散氏盤 (JC: 10176; official from Ze signing on map as attachment to a treaty).

As secretarial official of the regional states, mentioned in Shi *zhi* 史觶 (*Liulihe Xi Zhou Yan guo mudi*, p. 173), Qi Shi Huan *gui* 齊史逭簋 (JC: 3740).

As caster of bronzes, seen in Shi Lai *jiao* 史逨角 (JC: 9063), Shi Mian *fu* 史免簋 (JC: 4579), Shi Qiang *pan* 史墻盤 (JC: 10175), etc.

---

[4] The Scribe Nian 年 mentioned in the Wang *gui*, Cai *gui*, and Xing *xu* here can be identified with the Interior Scribe Xian mentioned in the Jian *gui* (JC: 4285; *id.*) and Yang *gui* (JC: 4294).

RELATED, *YUSHI* 禦史: ATTENDANT SCRIBE[5]

Scribe who attends the king or high officials at royal banquet.

Mentioned in Yushi Jing 御史競簋 (JC: 4134; recipient of award from higher official), Yu *gui* 遹簋 (JC: 4207).

RELATED, *SHENGSHI* 省史: INSPECTING SCRIBE

Scribe with special responsibility for inspection.

Mentioned in Guo Cong *ding* 虢從鼎 (JC: 2818; transmits royal command).

As caster of bronzes, seen in Shengshi *zun* 省史尊 (JC: 5951).

RELATED, *SHUSHI* 書史: BOOK SCRIBE

Scribe who particularly handled written documents.

Mentioned in Pengsheng *gui* 倗生簋 (JC: 4262; marks boundaries and casts bronze to document the transaction of land).

ZUOCE 作冊: DOCUMENT MAKER

Mainly an early Western Zhou office, possibly inherited from Shang (seen in Sixth Year Yiqi *you* 六年琱其卣 [JC: 5414]); responsible for composing royal or government documents).

As secretarial official at the central court, mentioned in Zuoce Zhe *zun* 作冊折尊 (JC: 6002; as royal envoy), Zuoce Huan *you* 作冊睘卣 (JC: 5407; as messenger of the queen); Ling *fangyi* 令方彝 (JC: 9901; as staff of Ministry and recipient of gifts from Duke Ming), Zuoce Zi *you* 作冊䰟卣 (JC: 5400; recipient of gifts from Duke Ming), Zuoce Hu *you* 作冊魕卣 (JC: 5432; subordinate to Duke Grand Scribe), Zuoce Da *fangding* 作冊大方鼎 (JC: 2760; recipient of gifts from Duke of Shao), Wu *fangyi* 吳方彝 (JC: 9898; recipient of royal command), etc.

As secretarial official of the regional states, mentioned in Mai *fangzun* 麥方尊 (JC: 6015; as the "prime official" of ruler of Xing).

As caster of bronzes, seen in Yi *you* 益卣 (JC: 5427), Yu *ding* 寓鼎 (JC: 2756).

RELATED, *ZUOCE NEISHI* 作冊內史: DOCUMENT MAKER AND INTERIOR SCRIBE

Interior Scribe with special responsibility for composing royal commands, seen only during the mid-Western Zhou.[6]

---

[5] Zhang and Liu give more than fifteen such titles representing Scribes of various and specific responsibilities. Some of the terms that prefix *shi* refer probably to a place or person, while in other cases, the character *shi* 史 may be a miswriting of *shi* 事 and hence cannot be read as an official title. But the three listed here are evidently Scribes of special responsibilities. See Zhang Yachu and Liu Yu, *Xi Zhou jinwen guanzhi yanjiu*, pp. 30–34, 81–82.

[6] This is supported by the case of Wu 吳 in the Wu *fangyi* 吳方彝 (JC: 9898), who calls himself Document Maker in his own inscription; but he was referred to by other officials as Interior Scribe.

Mentioned in Mian *pan* 免盤 (JC: 10161; hands gifts to officials on behalf of the king), Shi Yu *gui* 師艅簋 (JC: 4277; announces royal appointment).

ZUOCE YIN 作冊尹: CHIEF DOCUMENT MAKER

Popular during the mid-Western Zhou; supposedly head of the many Document Makers, but might have been an office without many officials (Document Maker had disappeared during the mid-Western Zhou); sometimes simply as Yinshi 尹氏, the "Chief."[7]

Mentioned in Shi Chen *ding* 師晨鼎 (JC: 2817; announces government appointment), First Year Shi Shi *gui* 元年師事簋 (JC: 4279; *id.*), Zou *gui* 走簋 (JC: 4244; *id.*), Fu Shi Li *gui* 輔師釐簋 (JC: 4286; *id.*), Xiu *pan* 休盤 (JC: 10170; *id.*), Nangong Liu *ding* 南宮柳鼎 (JC: 2805; *id.*); Mian *gui* 免簋 (JC: 4240; receives written document from the king and announces official appointment); Thirteenth Year Xing *hu* 十三年癲壺 (JC: 9723 hands out royal gifts).

TAIZHU 太祝: GRAND INVOCATOR

Chief religious official at the Zhou central court; responsible for various state rituals and sacrifices to the Zhou ancestors; head of the many Invocators that might have served the Zhou court.

Mentioned in Qin *gui* 禽簋 (JC: 4041; follows Zhou king on campaign in the east, identified with Qin in Dazhu Qin *ding* 大祝禽鼎 [JC: 1937]), Chang Xing *he* 長甶盉 (JC: 9455; assists King Mu in court ceremony), Shen *gui* 申簋 (JC: 4267; as superior to Invocator Shen).

As caster of bronzes, seen in Dazhu Qin *ding* 大祝禽鼎 (JC: 1937).

ZHU 祝: INVOCATOR

Mentioned in Shen *gui* 申簋 (JC: 4267; as Invocator for the people of the capital Feng and the "Nine Military Camps" in the district of Feng), Qian *gui* 鄘簋 (JC: 4296; as Invocator in the Five Cities in the Wei River valley).

ZAI 宰: SUPERINTENDENT

Head official of the Royal Household administration with general responsibilities; prominent role at the Zhou court from the mid-Western Zhou on. By origin the title was inherited from Shang (e.g. Zai Hao *jiao* 宰椃角 [JC: 9105]).

Mentioned in Cai *gui* 蔡簋 (JC: 4340; with responsibility for the inside and outside of the Royal Household, and in control of access to Queen

---

7 This simple designation *Yinshi* 尹氏 (the "Chief") appears in many inscriptions, seemingly referring to the combined office of the Chief Document Maker and Chief Interior Scribe. This is discussed in Chapter 2, pp. 76–77.

Jiang), Wu *fangyi* 吳方彝 (JC: 9898; plays the role of *youzhe* in appointment ritual for subordinate officials of the Royal Household), Wang *gui*
望簋 (JC: 4272; *id.*), Chu *gui* 楚簋 (JC: 4246; *id.*), Hai *gui* 害簋 (JC: 4259;
id.), Thirteenth Year Xing *hu* 十三年癲壺 (JC: 9723; *id.*), Song *ding* 頌鼎
(JC: 2829; *id.*), Shi Li *gui* 師釐簋 (JC: 4324; *id.*), Yuan *pan* 袁盤 (JC:
10172; *id.*).

As official of local *bang* polity, mentioned in Sanshi *pan* 散氏盤 (JC:
10167; official from the polity of San).

TAIZAI 太宰: GRAND SUPERINTENDENT

Prominent official in the regional states, popular during the late Western
Zhou; not seen in the Zhou central court.

Mentioned in Zhong Chengfu *gui* 仲再父簋 (JC: 4188; from the state
of Southern Shen), Xing Jiang Taizai *fu* 邢姜太宰簠 (*Neimenggu wenw
kaogu* 2 (1982), 5–7; from the state of Xing).[8]

SHANFU 膳夫: PROVISIONER

Provisioner responsible for the physical wellbeing of the king including
preparation of meals; played an eminent role during the late Western Zhou.

As eminent official at the central court, belonging to the Royal Household
administration, mentioned in Da *ding* 大鼎 (JC: 2806; attends the king),
Da *gui* 大簋 (JC: 4298; as recipient of royal grant of land; as the one to
complete transaction of land on behalf of the king), Da Ke *ding* 大克鼎
(JC: 2836; assigned responsibility similar to that of Superintendent), Wu
Hu *ding* 吳虎鼎 (JL: 364; supervises the transaction of land ordered by
the king); Jinhou Su *zhong* 晉侯蘇鍾 (JL: 35–50; as the king's attendant,
summoned the ruler of Jin in audience with the king).

As minor officials in the major cities, see Shi Chen *ding* 師晨鼎 (JC:
2817; in Zheng and Yi).

SHISHI 師氏: MARSHALS

Strictly, not an official title, but a designation of men with certain military
roles.[9]

---

[8] During the following Spring and Autumn period, the office of Grand Superintendent was very
popular among the many states, and a number of bronzes from the period were cast by officials with
such a title. See Zhang Yachu and Liu Yu, *Xi Zhou jinwen guanzhi yanjiu*, pp. 40. For textual records
on the office of Grand Superintendent during the Spring and Autumn period, see Gu Donggao,
"Chunqiu lieguo guanzhi biao," pp. 1033–1123.

[9] No Western Zhou inscriptions ever recorded an appointment to the role of *Shishi*; this suggests that
the career of *Shishi* does not follow the normal path as those of court officials. People might have
entered military service at a younger age, and the promotion to the status of *Marshal* might not
have reached the level of the royal court. In addition, Zhang and Liu list a large number of officials
with the title *Shi* 師, and take it as equivalent to *Shishi*. As discussed in Chapter 5, I consider that
most of them are officials with former military roles. See Zhang Yachu and Liu Yu, *Xi Zhou jinwen
guanzhi yanjiu*, pp. 62–67.

As military units located in/near the major cities, mentioned in X *ding* 雩鼎 (JC: 2741; on campaign against the Dongyi), Lu Dong *you* 彔茲卣 (JC: 5419; on defense against the Huaiyi), Dong *gui* 茲簋 (JC: 4322; *id.*), First Year Shi Shi *gui* 元年師事簋 (JC: 4279; on campaign against Qi), Ling *ding* 令鼎 (JC: 2803; performs archery in the company of the king), Shi Ju *gui* 師遽簋 (JC: 4214; inspected by the king), Shi Yun *gui* 師瘨簋 (JC: 4283; as unit belonging to Yi), Ran *xu* 塑盨 (JC: 4469).

As individual officials called by the term, see Yong *yu* 永盂 (JC: 10322; participate in land transaction).

As local military officer in the *bang* polity, mentioned in Sanshi *pan* 散氏盤 (JC: 10176; official of San).

TAISHI 太師: GRAND MARSHAL

Might not be a regular office, but a title conferred on some senior and eminent officials.

As high official at central court, mentioned in Taishi Cuo *gui* 太師虘簋 (JC: 4251; recipient of royal gifts), Zha *zhong* 柞鐘 (JC: 134; plays the role of *youzhe*), Bo Ke *hu* 伯克壺 (JC: 9725; as giver of award of servants), Shi Zai *ding* 師𩱦鼎 (JC: 2830), Shi Wang *ding* 師望鼎 (JC: 2812), Bo Gongfu *fu* 伯公父簠 (JC: 4628; as superior officials or lineage head).

As caster of bronzes, seen in Taishi *gui* 太師簋 (JC: 3633).

YU 虞: SUPERVISOR OF MARSHES[10]

Responsible for management of natural resources.

As official at the central court, see Tong *gui* 同簋 (JC: 4271; as Wu Dafu 吳（虞）大父, with responsibility for forests, pastoral lands, and marshes). Mentioned also in Forty-second Year Lai *ding* 四十二年逨鼎 (*Wenwu* 2003.6, 16–27; helps settle the new state of Yang), Forty-third Year Lai *ding* 四十三年逨鼎 (*Wenwu* 2003.6, 16–27; with responsibilities for marshes and forests in the four directions).

As official of the local *bang* polity, see Sanshi *pan* 散氏盤(JC: 10176; official of Ze).

LIJUN 里君: DISTRICT ADMINISTRATOR

Very probably a regular office in local administration (lower than court officials), responsible for the management of the *li* 里 land-units.

As officials in the royal domain, mentioned in Ling *fangyi* 令方彝 (JC: 9901), Shi Song *gui* 史頌簋 (JC: 4232; as local officials of Su near Chengzhou in the east).

---

[10] It is not very clear whether the "Supervisor of Marshes" constituted a regular office in the central government. Very often such responsibilities were assigned as temporary duties to officials; sometimes such tasks were performed by the Supervisor of Land, as in the case of the Mian *fu* 免簠 (JC: 4626).

JIAN 監: ROYAL INSPECTOR

Stationed in the regional states in the east, with responsibilities to monitor the situation in their resident states and report back to the Zhou king.

Mentioned in Zhong Jifu *gui* 仲幾父簋 (JC: 3954; as the "Many Inspectors" stationed in the regional states), Yingjian *yan* 應監甗 (JC: 883; as Royal Inspector stationed in the state of Ying), Zhong Chengfu *gui* 仲再父簋 (JC: 4188; Royal Inspector, as father of the caster of the bronze).

(Listed above are twenty-nine official titles mentioned in Western Zhou bronze inscriptions discovered by December 2006.)

A bibliographical list and index of inscribed bronzes cited in the book

Compiled by Nicholas Vogt

The following is a compilation of bibliographical data for every inscribed bronze mentioned by name in this book. It has been provided for two reasons: for the convenience of specialists who want to find more information on a particular inscription or its bronze, and in the interest of helping scholars in all fields navigate the sometimes opaque world of pre-Qin Chinese inscriptional studies. In composing this list, I have frequently consulted the online database of inscriptions provided by the *Academia Sinica*, which is in turn based on the *Yin Zhou jinwen jicheng* 殷周金文集成 (Beijing: Zhonghua, 1984–94) (herein abbreviated as JC), and I would like to express my gratitude to the scholars who have made these sources available. Many of the bronzes listed here were discovered after 1994, when the last volume of JC was published, and are thus new additions to the record.

The relevant data appear under the following abbreviations:

Ds.: Year the bronze was discovered (approximate)
Pd.: Place in which the bronze was discovered
Fp.: First registration in a publication
Nc.: Number of characters inscribed
Co.: Current ownership
Dt.: Date (approximate)

Each listing also includes a brief English-language summary of the inscription's contents and an index of its appearances in the book. A complete listing is as follows:

Example:
   Chen Chen *he* 臣辰盂 (JC: 9454): *ds.* 1929; *pd.* Mapo, Luoyang, Henan; *fp. Zhensong* 8.43; *nc.* 50; *co.* Freer Gallery, Washington, DC; *dt.* early Western Zhou.
   Summary: The king dispatches Shi Shang and Scribe Yin to Chengzhou; Shi Shang receives royal gifts.
   Index: 55 n. 26, 309

Available information on the discovery of some bronzes is limited to records of their acquisition – potentially including collection or purchase – and may not correspond to their original locations of deposition. In these cases, the *pd.* entry is enclosed in brackets (e.g., *pd.* [Qishan, Shaanxi]). Similarly, only secondhand information is available on the original locations of some bronzes; *pd.* entries based on such information include a question mark (e.g., *pd.* Qishan, Shaanxi?). When JC lacks information on the time and place of a bronze's discovery, I have taken extra care in checking the first publication of the inscription for such information.

Publications in book format are referred to by abbreviations, a list of which appears at the end of this appendix. Page numbers are given for journals and those books which number front and back pages separately (e.g., *Kaogu* 1989.6, 524–26). For books in folio format and those in which vessels are sequentially ordered, simple numbers are given (e.g., *Xiqing* 13.12). The first number refers to the *juan* 卷 or *ce* 冊 (i.e., volume) in which the vessel is found, and the second number usually indicates the page on which the vessel's record begins; in certain cases, the second number refers to the order of the vessel in the sequence of listings.

The author of the book has updated the record of the current ownership of the bronzes based on the latest available information, with special attention given to those vessels discovered in the last twenty years. Likewise, the author has reviewed the accepted dating of the bronzes. Reign periods are provided only for bronzes the inscriptions of which contain direct internal evidence for such dating. Many other vessels included in the list can be dated more precisely based on formal criteria and connection with other bronzes; for such vessels, dating is restricted to the broad periods of early, middle, and late Western Zhou, as well as early and late Spring and Autumn.

For consistency's sake, the bronzes have been alphabetized based on their full Romanized names as written in this book, including word breaks; thus the Xian *zhong* 鮮鐘 (JC: 143), for example, appears before the Xian-hou *ding* 獻侯鼎 (JC: 2626), since "Xianhou" is treated as a single word. Likewise, the vessels' types have been treated as part of their names, as is the convention in the field, and have been accounted for in determining their order.

LIST OF INSCRIPTIONS

Ban *gui* 班簋 (JC: 4341): *fp. Xiqing* 13.12; *nc.* 195 (1 repetition mark); *co.* Capital Museum, Beijing; *dt.* middle Western Zhou.
   Summary: The king dispatches Maofu Ban to lead a campaign against enemy polities in the east, assisted by Wubo and Lübo.
   Index: 127, 132 n. 71, 225 n. 39

Bo Chen *ding* 伯晨鼎 (JC: 2816): *fp. Huaimi* 3.7; *nc.* 97 (1 repetition mark, 2 compounds); *dt.* late Western Zhou.
   Summary: The king commands Bo Chen to succeed his deceased father as ruler of Huan.
   Index: 205, 219, 219 n. 29

Bo Gongfu *fu* 伯公父簠 (JC: 4628): *ds.* 1977; *pd.* Huangdui, Fufeng county, Shaanxi; *fp. Wenwu* 1982.6, 88, figs. 4–5; *nc.* 59 (2 repetition marks); *co.* Zhouyuan Museum, Shaanxi; *dt.* late Western Zhou.

Summary: Bo Gongfu, son of the Elder Grand Marshal, makes a food vessel.

Index: 313

Bo Jiang *ding* 伯姜鼎 (JC: 2791): *pd.* Puducun, Chang'an county, Shaanxi; *fp. Wenwu* 1986.1, 11, fig. 19, pl. 3.4; *nc.* 64; *co.* Provincial Committee for the Management of Cultural Relics, Shaanxi; *dt.* early Western Zhou.

Summary: At the Lower (Wet) Palace at the capital Pang, the king presents Bo Jiang with cowries.

Index: 152 n. 5

Bo Ke *hu* 伯克壺 (JC: 9725): *pd.* [Qishan, Shaanxi]; *fp. Kaogutu* 4.37; *nc.* 56 (2 repetition marks); *dt.* late Western Zhou.

Summary: Bo Taishi (the "Elder Grand Marshal") gives Bo Ke several servants; Bo Ke casts a vessel commemorating the gift.

Index: 313

Bo Kefu *ding* 伯郜父鼎 (JC: 2597): *fp. Bogu* 3.14; *nc.* 18; *dt.* late Western Zhou.

Summary: The Supervisor of Multitudes of Jin, Bo Kefu, casts a vessel for the lady Zhou Ji.

Index: 249, 306

Bo Tangfu *ding* 伯唐父鼎 (JL: 356): *ds.* 1984; *pd.* Zhangjiapo, Chang'an county, Shaanxi; *fp. Kaogu* 1989.6, 524–26; *nc.* 66; *co.* Institute of Archaeology, CASS, Beijing (Xi'an Research Station); *dt.* middle Western Zhou.

Summary: The Zhou king conducts archery in the Bi Pond in Pangjing; Bo Tangfu is rewarded for his assistance.

Index: 152 n. 6

Bo Wufu *xu* 伯吳父盨 (JC: 4415): *fp. Zhensong* 5.18; *nc.* 15; *co.* National Museum of China, Beijing; *dt.* middle Western Zhou.

Summary: The Supervisor of Multitudes of Lu, Bo Wu, casts a *gui* vessel.

Index: 249, 306

Bo Zhefu *gui* 伯者父簋 (JC: 3748): *fp. Yin and Chou* E40; *nc.* 11; *co.* Freer Gallery, Washington, DC; *dt.* early Western Zhou.

Summary: Bo Zhefu makes a vessel for feasting the king.

Index: 15

Cai Da Shanfu *fu* 蔡大善夫簠: *ds.* 1978; *pd.* Zhushixiang, Yicheng county, Hubei; *fp. Kaogu* 1989.11, 1042–43; *nc.* 31 (2 repetition marks); *co.* Xiangfan Municipal Museum, Hubei; *dt.* early Spring and Autumn.

Summary: The Grand Provisioner of the state of Cai in southern Henan casts a bronze *fu* vessel.

Index: 251

Cai *gui* 蔡簋 (JC: 4340): *ds.* tenth–eleventh centuries; *fp. Lidai* 14.9, 148; *nc.* 157 (1 repetition mark); *dt.* middle Western Zhou.

Summary: The king extends Cai's mission to serve as Superintendent, commanding him to cooperate with Hu, to govern the hundred craftsmen, and to serve as Queen Jiang's liaison with the outside world.

Index: 68–69, 72, 92, 124, 130, 136 n. 75, 154, 199 n. 18, 207, 219 n. 29, 223, 223 n. 35–36, 309, 309 n. 4, 311

Cai *zun* 蔡尊 (JC: 5974): *fp. Lishuo* 1.25; *nc.* 15 (1 compound); *dt.* early–middle Western Zhou.

Summary: At Lu, the king awards Cai ten strings of cowries.

Index: 260

Caihou *zhong* 蔡侯鐘 (JC: 210): *ds.* 1955; *pd.* Ximen, Shou county, Anhui; *fp. Shouxian*, pl. 21:2, 19:2, 52.53, 89:2; *nc.* 79 (2 repetition marks, 1 compound); *co.* Anhui Provincial Museum; *dt.* late Spring and Autumn.

Summary: The ruler of Cai speaks of his will to assist the King of Chu.

Index: 48 n. 12

Chang Xing *he* 長甶盉 (JC: 9455): *ds.* 1954; *pd.* Puducun, Chang'an county, Shaanxi; *fp. Wencan* 1955.2, 128, 130; *nc.* 54 (2 repetition marks); *co.* National Museum of China, Beijing; *dt.* middle Western Zhou (King Mu).

Summary: King Mu holds festivities and acknowledges Chang Xing's merits.

Index: 77, 311

Chen Chen *he* 臣辰盉 (JC: 9454): *ds.* 1929; *pd.* Mapo, Luoyang, Henan; *fp. Zhensong* 8.43; *nc.* 50; *co.* Freer Gallery, Washington, DC; *dt.* early Western Zhou.

Summary: The king dispatches Shi Shang and Scribe Yin to Chengzhou; Shi Shang receives royal gifts.

Index: 55 n. 26, 309

Chen Jian *gui* 臣諫簋 (JC: 4237): *ds.* 1978; *pd.* Xizhangcun, Yuanshi county, Hebei; *fp. Kaogu* 1979.1, 25, fig. 4; pl. 8:4; *nc.* 72; *co.* Hebei Provincial Institute of Cultural Relics; *dt.* middle Western Zhou.

Summary: Chen Jian fights the Rong people alongside the ruler of Xing; Chen Jian calls upon his nephew to serve the state of Xing.

Index: 18, 98, 265

Chen Wei *zun* 臣衛尊 (JC: 5987): *fp. Jianghan* 1985.1, p. 103, figs. 2-3; *nc.* 24; *co.* Wuhan Municipal Cultural Relics Store; *dt.* early Western Zhou.

Summary: At Xin XX, the duke awards cowries to Chen Wei with which Chen Wei casts a bronze for Father Xin.

Index: 171 n. 49

Chenhou *gui* 陳侯簋 (JC: 3815): *ds.* 1976; *pd.* Lingkou, Lintong county, Shaanxi; *fp. Wenwu* 1977.8, 5, fig. 14; pl. 3:2; *nc.* 13; *co.* Lintong County Museum, Shaanxi; *dt.* late Western Zhou.

Summary: The ruler of Chen casts a vessel for Wang Wei.

Index: 44 n. 5

Chu *gui* 楚簋 (JC: 4246): *ds.* 1978; *pd.* Renbeicun, Wugong county, Shaanxi; *fp. Kaogu* 1981.2, 128; *nc.* 69 (2 repetition marks); *co.* Wugong County Museum, Shaanxi; *dt.* middle Western Zhou.

Summary: Chu is commanded to take charge of the boats in the capital Pang.

Index: 76, 124, 130 n. 68, 208, 309, 312

Ci *ding* 此鼎 (JC: 2821): *ds.* 1975; *pd.* Dongjiacun, Qishan county, Shaanxi; *fp. Wenwu* 1976.5, 36, fig. 12; *nc.* 110 (1 repetition mark); *co.* Qishan County Museum, Shaanxi; *dt.* late Western Zhou.

Summary: Ci is appointed to take charge of the provisioners of the people of Yi.

Index: 91, 131 n. 69, 306

Ci *gui* 此簋 (JC: 4303): *ds.* 1975; *pd.* Dongjiacun, Qishan county, Shaanxi; *fp. Wenwu* 1976.5, 35, fig. 9, pl. 3:4; *Shaanxi*, 1.199; *nc.* 110 (2 repetition marks); *co.* Qishan County Museum, Shaanxi; *dt.* late Western Zhou.

Summary: At the Yi Temple of the Kang Temple at Zhou, the king commands Ci to supervise the provisioners of the people of Yi.

Index: 125, 209

Da *ding* 大鼎 (JC: 2806): *fp. Xiqing* 2.19; *nc.* 47 (remaining); *dt.* late Western Zhou.

Summary: Da and his colleagues guard the king during a feast at X Chen Palace; the king calls Da in and grants him gifts.

Index: 92, 146, 181 n. 64, 312

Da *gui* 大簋 (JC: 4298): *fp. Xiqingjia* 12.46; *nc.* 105 (2 repetition marks); *co.* Royal Palace, Stockholm, Sweden; *dt.* late Western Zhou.

Summary: At X Chen Palace, the king awards Da lands previously belonging to Ci Kui; the royal envoy takes Ci Kui to walk through the lands to be transferred.

Index: 92, 146, 181, 312

Da *gui* 大簋 (cover) (JC: 4299): *fp. Yunqing* 3.33; *nc.* 106 (2 repetition marks); *co.* National Museum of China, Beijing; *dt.* late Western Zhou.

Summary: At X Chen Palace, the king awards Da lands previously belonging to Ci Kui; the royal envoy takes Ci Kui to walk through the lands to be transferred.

Index: 92, 146, 181, 312

Da Ke *ding* 大克鼎 (JC: 2836): *ds.* 1890; *pd.* Rencun, Fufeng county, Shaanxi; *fp. Kezhai* 5.1; *nc.* 281 (7 repetition marks, 2 compounds); *co.* Shanghai Museum; *dt.* middle Western Zhou.

Summary: Provisioner Ke praises his deceased grandfather Shi Huafu, who served King Gong as advisor and as tutor to aristocratic sons. The king awards Provisioner Ke a variety of lands and servants.

Index: 37 n. 40, 92, 101, 129, 157–58, 207, 220, 312

Da Yu *ding* 大盂鼎 (JC: 2837): *ds.* 1820; *pd.* Mei county, Shaanxi; *fp.* Hengxuan 9; *nc.* 286 (5 compounds); *co.* National Museum of China, Beijing; *dt.* early Western Zhou (King Kang).
> *Summary*: The king recalls the glories of the past Zhou kings and commands Yu to succeed to his ancestor the Duke of Nan's position, awarding him the Duke of Nan's former flag.
> *Index*: 104–5, 173, 214 n. 24

Dazhu Qin *ding* 大祝禽鼎 (JC: 1937): *fp. Shiliu* 1.15; *nc.* 4; *dt.* early Western Zhou.
> *Summary*: *Ding*-vessel of the Great Invocator Qin.
> *Index*: 58, 311

Dong *gui* 㦪簋 (JC: 4322): *ds.* 1975; *pd.* Baijiacun, Fufeng county, Shaanxi; *fp. Wenwu* 1976.6, 57, fig. 17; 59, fig. 28; pl. 7.1; *nc.* 132 (2 repetition marks); *co.* Fufeng County Museum, Shaanxi; *dt.* middle Western Zhou.
> *Summary*: Dong leads the marshals to counterattack Rong invaders. In thanks for his mother's spiritual protection in the battle, he casts a vessel.
> *Index*: 230, 313

Dou Bi *gui* 豆閉簋 (JC: 4276): *pd.* [Xi'an]; *fp. Kezhai* 10.10; *nc.* 92; *co.* Palace Museum, Beijing; *dt.* middle Western Zhou.
> *Summary*: The king appoints Dou Bi as Supervisor of Horses under the *bangjun* of Youyu.
> *Index*: 109 n. 23, 127, 132-33, 132, n. 70, 183, 202, 307, 309

Duoyou *ding* 多友鼎 (JC: 2835): *ds.* 1980; *pd.* Xiaquancun, Chang'an county, Shaanxi; *fp. Renwen* 1981.4, 115–18; *nc.* 275 (1 repetition mark, 1 compound); *co.* Shaanxi Provincial Museum; *dt.* late Western Zhou.
> *Summary*: On the king's orders, Duke Wu dispatches Duoyou to fight the invading Xianyun and reclaim Zhou settlements in the upper Jing River valley.
> *Index*: 16, 18 n. 69, 117, 139–40, 147

Er *ding* 宯鼎 (JC: 2755): *fp. Kezhai* 6.6; *nc.* 40 (2 repetition marks); *co.* Shanghai Museum; *dt.* middle Western Zhou.
> *Summary*: Qianzhong commands Er to take charge of fields associated with the city of Zheng.
> *Index*: 168

Fan Jusheng *hu* 番菊生壺 (JC: 9705): *fp. Zhensong* 7.32; *nc.* 30 (2 repetition marks); *co.* The Avery Brundage Collection of the Asian Art Museum, San Francisco; *dt.* middle Western Zhou.
> *Summary*: Fan Jusheng casts a vessel for his eldest daughter Ji Guai's dowry.
> *Index*: 64 n. 49

Fansheng *gui* 番生簋 (JC: 4326): *fp. Taozhai* 2.16; *nc.* 131 (1 repetition mark); *co.* Nelson-Atkins Museum, Kansas City; *dt.* middle Western Zhou.

Summary: The king commands Fansheng to supervise the royal kinsmen, the Ministry, and the Grand Secretariat.

Index: *63–67*, 70–1, 76, 135, 249, 305, 308, jacket illustration

Fifteenth Year Quecao *ding* 十五年趩曹鼎 (JC: 2784): *fp. Zhoucun* 2.27; *nc.* 57; *co.* Shanghai Museum; *dt.* middle Western Zhou (King Gong).

Summary: At the Archery House of the New Palace at Zhou, the king conducts archery and awards Quecao various accoutrements, including archery implements.

Index: 198 n. 15

Fifth Year Qiu Wei *ding* 五年裘衛鼎 (JC: 2832): *ds.* 1975; *pd*: Dongjiacun, Qishan county, Shaanxi; *fp. Wenwu* 1976.5, 38, fig. 15; pl. 2:1; *nc.* 201 (5 repetition marks, 1 compound); *co.* Qishan County Museum, Shaanxi; *dt.* middle Western Zhou (King Gong).

Summary: Qiu Wei makes a claim against Bangjun Li. Elders of the Zhou government enforce the claim and order the Three Supervisors and other officials to transfer five fields to Qiu Wei.

Index: 72, 74–75, 81, 84 n. 91, 92 n. 98, 119 n. 56, 137 n. 77, *156–58*, 177, 183, 219–20, 232, 305–7, 309

Fifth Year Shi Shi *gui* 五年師事簋 (JC: 4216): *ds.* 1961; *pd*: Zhangjiapo, Chang'an county, Shaanxi; *fp. Kaogu xuebao* 1962.1, 7, fig. 3; *nc.* 57 (2 repetition marks); *co.* Shaanxi Provincial Museum; *dt.* late Western Zhou.

Summary: The king dispatches Shi Shi to attack the state of Qi, awarding him military accoutrements.

Index: 35 n. 36, 178 n. 58, 230, 268

Fifth Year Zhousheng *gui* 五年琱生簋 (JC: 4292): *fp. Jungu* 3.2.25; *nc.* 104; *co.* Yale University Art Gallery, New Haven; *dt.* late Western Zhou (King Xuan).

Summary: Shaobo Hu visits the Zhou lineage when Zhousheng hosts a major event; Zhousheng delivers a message from Junshi proclaiming Zhou's position on the property dispute between the Zhou and Shao lineages.

Index: 154

First Year Shi Dui *gui* 元年師兌簋 (JC: 4274): *fp. Zhoucun* 3 (supplement) (lid); *Zhensong* 6.18; *nc.* 89 (2 repetition marks); *dt.* late Western Zhou.

Summary: The king commands Shi Dui to assist Shi Hefu in charge of the Masters of Horses of the Right and Left camps and of the Five Cities.

Index: 40 n. 47, 79, 93, 129, 166, 167, 212, 220–21, 309

First Year Shi Shi *gui* 元年師事簋 (JC: 4279): *ds.* 1961; *pd*: Zhangjiapo, Chang'an county, Shaanxi; *fp. Kaogu xuebao* 1962.1, 5, fig. 2; *nc.* 96; *co.* Shaanxi Provincial Museum; *dt.* late Western Zhou.

Summary: The king commands Shi Shi to take charge of the marshals of the Left and Right camps in the *huan* area of the capital Feng.

Index: 78, 129, 170, 211, 230, 311, 313

Forty-second Year Lai *ding* 四十二年逨鼎: *ds*: Jan. 19, 2003; *pd*: Yangjiacun, Mei county, Shaanxi; *fp*. *Shengshi*, 55–73; *Wenwu* 2003.6, 16–27; *nc*. 280 (4 repetition marks); *co*. Baoji Municipal Museum, Shaanxi; *dt*. late Western Zhou (King Xuan).

Summary: Lai settles the new ruler Changfu at Yang and subsequently fights the invading Xianyun.

Index: 37 n. 40, 48, 91–2, 103, 107, 109 n. 26, 112, 125, 131 n. 69, 221, 307, 309, 313

Forty-third Year Lai *ding* 四十三年逨鼎: *ds*: Jan. 19, 2003; *pd*: Yangjiacun, Mei county, Shaanxi; *fp*. *Shengshi*, 55–73; *Wenwu* 2003.6, 16–27; *nc*. 316 (7 repetition marks); *co*. Baoji Municipal Museum, Shaanxi; *dt*. late Western Zhou (King Xuan).

Summary: The king commands Lai to take charge of the people of Li; the inscription mentions his previous appointment as assistant to Rong Dui.

Index: 39, 91, 107, 112, 125–26, 206, 221, 221 n. 34, 307, 313

Fu *gui* 𣪕簋 (JC: 4215): *fp*. *Zhenbu* 27.1-2; *nc*. 56 (2 repetition marks); *co*. Palace Museum, Taipei; *dt*. late Western Zhou.

Summary: Fu is commanded to take charge of the people of the Chengzhou district as well as the *Daya*-generals of the many rulers at Chengzhou.

Index: 212

Fu Shi Li *gui* 輔師嫠簋 (JC: 4286): *ds*. 1957; *pd*. Zhaoyuanpo, Chang'an county, Shaanxi; *fp*. *Kaogu xuebao* 1958.2, 1–3, pl. 2; *nc*. 100 (2 repetition marks); *co*. National Museum of China, Beijing; *dt*. late Western Zhou.

Summary: The king appoints Shi Li to succeed his grandfather and father in taking charge of the musicians of bells.

Index: 126, 197, 203, 311

Geng Ying *you* 庚嬴卣 (JC: 5426): *fp*. *Erbai* 3.1; *nc*. 51 (2 repetition marks); *co*. Fogg Art Museum, Harvard; *dt*. middle Western Zhou.

Summary: The king bestows gifts on the noblewoman Geng Ying at her palace.

Index: 116 n. 49, 229

Gong *qi* 玒器 (JC: 10581): *fp*. *Jungu* 2.3.10.1; *nc*. 21 (1 compound); *dt*. early Western Zhou.

Summary: At Zongzhou, Gong Zhong awards Gong 玒 cowries with which Gong casts a vessel.

Index: 259

Gong Taishi *ding* 公太史鼎: *ds*. 1977–78; *pd*. Lutaishan, Huangpi county, Hubei; *fp*. *Jianghan* 1982.2, 45, fig. 6.3; pl. 2.1; *nc*. 9; *co*. Huangpi County Museum, Hubei; *dt*. early Western Zhou.

Summary: The Duke Grand Scribe makes a sacrificial vessel for Ji Yu.

Index: 308

Gong Zhong *zhi* 公仲觶: *ds.* 1973–7; *pd.* Liulihe, Fangshan county, Beijing; *fp. Liulihe*, pp. 171–3; *nc.* 13; *co.* Beijing Municipal Institute of Cultural Relics; *dt.* early Western Zhou.

Summary: Gong Zhong awards X cowries with which X casts a vessel.

Index: 259

Guaibo *gui* 乖伯簋 (JC: 4331): *fp. Kezhai* 11.22; *nc.* 149 (1 compound); *co.* National Museum of China, Beijing; *dt.* late Western Zhou.

Summary: The king commands Duke Yi to conduct a punitive expedition against Mei'ao; later, Mei'ao renews his relationship with the king and receives fur garments.

Index: 295 n. 77

Guo Cong *ding* 膳從鼎 (JC: 2818): *fp. Jigu* 4.31; *nc.* 98 (4 repetition marks); *co.* Kurokawa Institute of Ancient Cultures, Hyōgo prefecture, Japan; *dt.* late Western Zhou.

Summary: Guo Cong brings a law suit against You Wei Mu before the king. The king's representative, Inspecting Scribe Nan, brings the matter before Guoshu Lü, who settles it in favor of Guo Cong.

Index: 174 n. 56, 310

Guo Cong *xu* 膳從盨 (JC: 4466): *fp. Zhoucun* 3.152; *nc.* 121; *co.* Palace Museum, Beijing; *dt.* late Western Zhou.

Summary: At Yong, Interior Scribe Wuqi and Grand Scribe X jointly announce the king's orders that Guo Cong be awarded a variety of fields and settlements.

Index: 88–90, 92, 174–77 (Figs. 20–21), 184 n. 69, 186, 188, 286, 308–9

Guo Wengong *ding* 虢文公鼎 (JC: 2636): *fp. Huaimi* 2.5; *nc.* 20 (2 repetition marks); *co.* Musée Cernuschi, Paris; *dt.* late Western Zhou.

Summary: Duke Wen of Guo, Zizhi, casts a vessel for Shu Ji.

Index: 85 n. 92

Guozhong *xu* 虢仲盨 (JC: 4435): *fp. Zhensong* 6.41; *nc.* 22; *co.* Institute of Archaeology, CASS; *dt.* late Western Zhou.

Summary: Guozhong accompanies the king on campaigns in the south against the Huaiyi.

Index: 98 n. 6

Hai *gui* 害簋 (JC: 4259): *fp. Bogu* 16.44; *nc.* 72 (2 repetition marks); *dt.* middle Western Zhou.

Summary: At the Xi Palace, the king orders Hai to see to his grandfather's and father's duties, governing the barbarian servants, minor archers, etc.

Index: 124, 130 n. 67, 205, 312

Han Huangfu *ding* 函皇父鼎 (JC: 2548): *ds.* 1933; *pd.* Kangjiacun, Fufeng county, Shaanxi; *fp. Luyi* 82; *nc.* 15 (2 repetition marks); *co.* Shaanxi Provincial Museum; *dt.* late Western Zhou.

Summary: Han Huangfu casts a cauldron for Zhou Yun.

Index: 41 n. 51, 90 n. 94

Han Huangfu *gui* 函皇父簋 (JC: 4141): *ds.* 1870; *pd.* Fufeng county, Shaanxi; *fp. Conggu* 15.26; *nc.* 34; *co.* Tenri Gallery, Tenri, Nara, Japan; *dt.* late Western Zhou.

Summary: Han Huangfu casts a set of vessels for Zhou Yun.

Index: 41 n. 51, 90 n. 94

Han Huangfu *pan* 函皇父盤 (JC: 10164): *ds.* 1933; *pd.* Kangjiacun, Fufeng county, Shaanxi; *fp. Luyi* 497; *nc.* 37 (2 repetition marks); *co.* Shaanxi Provincial Museum; *dt.* late Western Zhou.

Summary: Han Huangfu casts a set of vessels for Zhou Yun.

Index: 41 n. 51, 90 n. 94

He *zun* 砢尊 (JC: 6014): *ds.* 1963; *pd.* Jiacun, Baoji county, Shaanxi; *fp. Wenwu* 1966.1, 4; *nc.* 119 (2 compounds); *co.* Baoji Municipal Museum, Shaanxi; *dt.* early Western Zhou (King Cheng).

Summary: The king addresses royal youth He at Chengzhou; He is rewarded.

Index: 12

He Yuan *gui* 郃夗簋 (JC: 4197): *fp. Luyi* 165; *nc.* 48 (2 repetition marks); *co.* Guangzhou Museum; *dt.* late Western Zhou.

Summary: The king orders He Yuan to succeed his grandfather and father and to serve as Supervisor of Multitudes.

Index: 129, 204, 306

Hu *ding* 曶鼎 (JC: 2838): *pd.* [Xi'an]; *fp. Jigu* 4.35; *nc.* 376 (remaining; 4 repetition marks); *dt.* middle Western Zhou.

Summary: The king commands Hu to succeed his father in taking charge of the affairs of crack-divination. The inscription also documents two separate legal cases that Hu filed at the Zhou court against Xian and Kuangji, respectively, to be judged by Jingshu.

Index: 18, 37 n. 41, 60 n. 41, 75, 203, 223, 300

Hu *gui* 獣簋 (JC: 4317): *ds.* 1978; *pd.* Qicun, Fufeng county, Shaanxi; *fp. Wenwu* 1979.4, 89, fig. 1; 90, fig. 3; pl. 9:1; *nc.* 122 (1 repetition mark, 1 compound); *co.* Fufeng County Museum, Shaanxi; *dt.* late Western Zhou (King Li).

Summary: Hu (i.e., King Li) seeks blessings, long life, and a long reign from his ancestors.

Index: 162, 295

Hu *gui* 虎簋 (JL: 491): *ds.* 1996; *pd.* Shangoucun, Danfeng county, Shaanxi; *fp. Kaogu yu wenwu* 1997.3, 78–9; *nc.* 158 (1 repetition mark); *dt.* middle Western Zhou (King Mu).

Summary: The king orders Hu to succeed his grandfather and father and assist Shi Xi in managing the Masters of Horses and Chariot Drivers, as well as the Masters of Horses and Chariot Drivers in the Five Cities.

Index: 79, 128, 133, 166–67, 194–97, 199, 203, 218

Hu *hu* 曶壺 (JC: 9728): *fp. Zhenbu* 1.39; *nc.* 100 (2 repetition marks); *co.* Palace Museum, Taipei; *dt.* middle Western Zhou.

Summary: The king orders Hu to take up his father's former position as Grand Supervisor of Land for the Eight Armies of Chengzhou.

Index: 81–2, 128, 203, 223, 307

Ji *gui* 即簋 (JC: 4250): *ds.* 1974; *pd.* Qiangjia, Fufeng county, Shaanxi; *fp. Wenwu* 1975.8, 61, fig. 6; pl. 10:2; *nc.* 70 (2 repetition marks); *co.* Shaanxi Provincial Museum; *dt.* middle Western Zhou.

Summary: At the Kang Palace, the king commands Ji to manage the rice-pounders (?) of the Zhou Palace.

Index: 104 n. 15, 129, 154, 211

Jian *gui* 諫簋 (JC: 4285): *pd.* [Fufeng, Shaanxi]; *fp. Taozhai* 2.10; *nc.* 100 (2 repetition marks); 99 (on the vessel); *co.* Palace Museum, Beijing; *dt.* middle Western Zhou.

Summary: The king extends Jian's mission to serve as manager of the royal parks.

Index: 75, 119, 121, 126, 146, 207, 307–8, 309 n. 4

Jin *ding* 堇鼎: *ds.* 1973–7; *pd.* Liulihe, Fangshan county, Beijing; *fp. Liulihe*, pp. 101, 103–6; *nc.* 26; *co.* Beijing Municipal Institute of Cultural Relics; *dt.* early Western Zhou.

Summary: The ruler of Yan orders Jin to present food to the Grand Protector at Zongzhou; the Grand Protector rewards Jin with cowries.

Index: 259

Jing *gui* 靜簋 (JC: 4273): *fp. Xiqing* 27.14; *nc.* 88 (2 repetition marks); *dt.* middle Western Zhou.

Summary: The king commands Jing to take charge of an archery rite at the Learning Hall; Jing is later rewarded for his tireless efforts.

Index: 153

Jing *you* 競卣 (JC: 5425): *fp. Sen'oku* 2.63; *nc.* 51 (vessel and cover); *co.* Sen'oku Museum, Kyoto; *dt.* middle Western Zhou.

Summary: Bo Xifu leads the Chengzhou armies east to defend against the Southern Yi. At Pei, Bo Xifu has Jing's merits recounted and rewards Jing with a jade tablet.

Index: 226

Jingren Ning *zhong* 井人妄鐘 (JC: 112): *ds.* 1966; *pd.* Qizhen, Fufeng county, Shaanxi; *fp. Wenwu* 1972.7, 10; *nc.* 41 (8 repetition marks); *co.* Baoji Municipal Museum; *dt.* late Western Zhou.

Summary: Ning casts a bell for Father He, seeking blessings (inscription incomplete).

Index: 155 n. 14

Jingshu *zhong* 井叔鐘: *ds.* 1984; *pd.* Tomb 163 at Zhangjiapo, Chang'an county, Shaanxi; *fp. Kaogu* 1986.1, 25–26; *nc.* 39 (2 repetition marks); *co.* Institute of Archeology, CASS, Beijing; *dt.* middle Western Zhou.

Summary: Jingshu casts a *zhong* in honor of his deceased father Duke Mu.

Index: 14, 19 n. 70

Jinhou Su *zhong* 晉侯蘇鐘 (JL: 35–50): *ds.* 1991-2; *pd.* Beizhao, Quwu county, Shanxi; *fp. Shanghai jikan* 1996.7, 1-17 (JL: 35–48); *Wenwu* 1994.1, 16, 19 (JL: 49–50); *nc.* 355; *co.* Shanghai Museum (JL: 35–48); Shanxi Provincial Institute of Archeology, Taiyuan (JL: 49–50); *dt.* late Western Zhou.

Summary: A detailed account appears of a military campaign conducted by the Zhou king against the Suyi in the east with the help of the ruler of Jin. After the campaign, the ruler of Jin is furnished with royal gifts in Chengzhou.

Index: 91–92, 117, 123 n. 66, 126, 247 n. 23, 267–68, 307, 312

Kang *ding* 康鼎 (JC: 2786): *fp. Ningshou* 1.17; *nc.* 60 (2 repetition marks); *co.* Palace Museum, Taipei; *dt.* late Western Zhou.

Summary: The king commands Kang to manage the Royal Household.

Index: 155, 211

Ke *lei* 克罍 (JL: 987): *ds.* 1986; *pd.* Liulihe, Fangshan county, Beijing; *fp. Kaogu* 1990.1, 24–25, pl. 2; *nc.* 43; *co.* Capital Museum, Beijing; *dt.* early Western Zhou.

Summary: As a reward for the Grand Protector, the king establishes Ke as ruler of the state of Yan.

Index: 43 n. 3, 48 n. 11, 241–42 (fig. 29), 263 n. 59

Ke *xu* 克盨 (JC: 4465): *ds.* 1890; *pd.* Rencun, Fufeng county, Shaanxi; *fp. Kezhai* 15.18; *nc.* 100 (2 repetition marks); *co.* Art Institute of Chicago; *dt.* middle Western Zhou.

Summary: At the Kang Mu Temple at Zhou, the king commands that Provisioner Ke be given land and people.

Index: 77 n. 78

Ke *zhong* 克鐘 (JC: 204): *ds.* 1890; *pd.* Rencun, Fufeng county, Shaanxi; *fp. Zhuiyi* 1.6; *nc.* 39; *co.* Neiraku Art Museum, Nara, Japan; *dt.* middle Western Zhou.

Summary: The king orders Ke to conduct inspections along the east of the Jing River, reaching Jingshi.

Index: 101

Kuang *you* 匡卣 (JC: 5423): *fp. Jungu* 3.1.32; *nc.* 51; *dt.* middle Western Zhou (King Yih).

Summary: Kuang assists the king at the Archery House.

Index: 223 n. 35

Lai *pan* 逨盤; *ds.* 2003; *pd.* Yangjiacun, Mei county, Shaanxi; *fp. Shengshi*, 55–57; *Wenwu* 2003.6, 16–27; *nc.* 372 (12 repetition marks, 1 compound); *co.* Baoji Municipal Museum, Shaanxi; *dt.* late Western Zhou (King Xuan).

Summary: Lai commemorates the services rendered to eleven Zhou kings by eight generations of his ancestors; the king appoints Lai to assist Rong Dui in supervising the marshes and forests of the four directions.

Index: 34 n. 33, 206, 221, 221 n. 34, 295 n. 77

Li *ding* 利鼎 (JC: 2804); *fp. Zhoucun* 2.26.1; *nc.* 70; *co.* Department of History, Beijing Normal University; *dt.* middle Western Zhou.

Summary: At the Ban Palace, the king rewards Li with accoutrements.

Index: 132 n. 71, 153 n. 9, 162 n. 27, 225 n. 39

Li *fangyi* 盠方彝 (JC: 9900); *ds.* 1955; *pd.* Lijiacun, Mei county, Shaanxi; *fp. Wencan* 1957.4, 9; *nc.* 106 (1 compound); *co.* Shaanxi Provincial Museum; *dt.* middle Western Zhou.

Summary: Li is appointed to oversee the Three Supervisors of the Six Armies and Eight Armies, particularly the royal guard legion.

Index: 36 n. 39, *79–81*, 105 n. 17, 231 n. 50, 306–7

Li *fangzun* 盠方尊 (JC: 6013); *ds.* 1955; *pd.* Lijiacun, Mei county, Shaanxi; *fp. Wencan* 1957.4, 8; *nc.* 105 (2 repetition marks); *co.* Shaanxi Provincial Museum; *dt.* middle Western Zhou.

Summary: Li is appointed to oversee the Three Supervisors of the Six Armies and Eight Armies, particularly the royal guard legion.

Index: 36 n. 39, *79–81* (Fig. 7), 105 n. 17, 127, 131, 210, 306–7

Li *gui* 利簋 (JC: 4131); *ds.* 1976; *pd.* Lingkou, Lintong county, Shaanxi; *fp. Wenwu* 1977.8, 2, fig. 2; pl. 1; *nc.* 32; *co.* National Museum of China, Beijing; *dt.* middle Western Zhou (King Wu).

Summary: After the Zhou conquest of Shang, King Wu rewards Li in the Shang capital area.

Index: 31 n. 28, 44 n. 5

Li *juzun* 盠駒尊 (JC: 6011): *ds.* 1955; *pd.* Lijiacun, Mei county, Shaanxi; *fp. Wencan* 1957.4, pp. 5–6; *nc.* 11 (cover); 92 (2 repetition marks) (vessel); *co.* National Museum of China, Beijing; *dt.* middle Western Zhou.

Summary: The king performs the ritual of catching foals at An and rewards Li with a foal.

Index: 153 n. 10, 231 n. 50

Liang Qi *zhong* 梁其鐘 (JC: 187–88): *ds.* 1940; *pd.* Rencun, Fufeng county, Shaanxi; *fp. Luyi* 3.1–4 (187), *Mingwenxuan* 3, p. 273 (188); *nc.* 70 (4 repetition marks) (187), 67 (7 repetition marks) (188); *co.* Shanghai Museum (188); *dt.* late Western Zhou.

Summary: Liang Qi extols the virtues of his deceased ancestors and casts a set of bells for them, seeking blessings. The king performs the *mieli* (recounting of merits) ritual for Liang Qi.

Index: 228

Ling *ding* 令鼎 (JC: 2803): *pd.* Ruicheng county, Shanxi; *fp. Yunqing* 4.1; *nc.* 70; *dt.* early Western Zhou.

Summary: Ling and Fen guide the horses of the king's chariot on the way back from the Qi field, where the king has conducted the Spring Plowing Ritual and archery. The king rewards them.

Index: 313

Ling *fangyi* 令方彝 (JC: 9901): *ds.* 1922; *pd.* Mapo, Luoyang, Henan; *fp. Zhensong* 4.49; *nc.* 185 (2 repetition marks); *co.* Freer Gallery, Washington, DC; *dt.* early Western Zhou.

Summary: Duke Ming (Ming Bao), son of the Duke of Zhou, is appointed to head the Ministry. Duke Ming addresses his subordinates at Chengzhou. Ming Bao rewards Document Maker Ling (Ze) and Kang.

Index: 45–7 (figs. 1–2), 50–53, 53 n. 20, 58 n. 34, 59–60, 66, 77, 101, 181–82, 249, 260, 305, 310, 313

Ling *fangzun* 令方尊 (JC: 6016): *ds.* 1929; *pd.* Mapo, Luoyang, Henan; *fp. Zhensong* 7.19; *nc.* 184 (2 repetition marks); *co.* Palace Museum, Taipei; *dt.* early Western Zhou.

Summary: Duke Ming (Ming Bao), son of the Duke of Zhou, is appointed to head the Ministry and the Three Affairs. Duke Ming addresses his subordinates at Chengzhou. Ming Bao rewards Document Maker Ling (Ze) and Kang.

Index: 50–2

Ling *gui* 令簋 (JC: 4300): *ds.* 1929; *pd.* Mapo, Luoyang, Henan; *fp. Zhensong* 6.11; *nc.* 107 (2 repetition marks, 1 compound); *co.* Musée Guimet, Paris; *dt.* early Western Zhou.

Summary: Queen Jiang rewards Document Maker Ze Ling during a royal campaign against Chu.

Index: 16

Lu Dong *you* 彔戜卣 (JC: 5419): *fp. Taozhai* 2.39; *nc.* 49; *co.* Palace Museum, Taipei; *dt.* middle Western Zhou.

Summary: After Dong leads a successful retaliatory strike against the invading Huaiyi under the king's orders, Bo Yongfu gives Dong gifts and acknowledges his merit.

Index: 226, 313

Lu *gui* 親簋: *ds.* early Republican period; *pd.* Baoji?; *fp. Zhongguo* 2006.3, 4, cover; *nc.* 110; *co.* National Museum of China, Beijing; *dt.* middle Western Zhou (King Mu).

Summary: Jingbo Lu is appointed as Grand Supervisor of Horses.

Index: 82 n. 87, 104 n. 15, 126, 135, 195 n. 10, 206, 308

Lü Fuyu *pan* 呂服余盤 (JC: 10169): *pd.* [Xi'an]; *fp. Wenwu* 1986.4, 1, pl. 1; *nc.* 65 (2 repetition marks); *co.* Municipal Committee for the Management of Cultural Relics, Xi'an, Shaanxi; *dt.* middle Western Zhou.

Summary: The king commands Lü Fuyu to succeed his grandfather and father in helping Beizhong to manage the Six Armies.

Index: 127, 132–33, 202

Lüxing *hu* 呂行壺 (JC: 9689): *fp. Xiqing* 19.8; *nc.* 21; *dt.* middle Western Zhou.

Summary: Bo Maofu campaigns to the north; Lüxing captures cowries and uses them to cast a vessel.

Index: 264

Mai *fangding* 麥方鼎 (JC: 2706): *ds.* 1896; *pd.* [Yongjia]; *fp. Liangzhou, lu* 21, *kao* 42; *nc.* 27 (1 compound, 1 repetition mark); *co.* Zhejiang Provincial Museum; *dt.* early Western Zhou.

Summary: The ruler of Xing visits the Zhou capital in Shaanxi, rewarding Mai upon his return.

Index: 15, 116 n. 49, 261 n. 58

Mai *fangyi* 麥方彝 (JC: 9893): *fp: Xiqing* 13.10; *nc.* 35 (2 repetition marks); *dt.* early Western Zhou.

Summary: The ruler of Xing rewards his official Mai with metal.

Index: 116 n. 49, 261 n. 58

Mai *fangzun* 麥方尊 (JC: 6015): *fp: Xiqing* 8.33; *nc.* 164 (3 repetition marks); *dt.* early Western Zhou.

Summary: The newly appointed ruler of Xing visits the Zhou king in Zongzhou. He joins the king in an archery ritual and has an audience in the king's private chambers. Later, Mai receives a gift of metal from the ruler of Xing.

Index: 43 n. 3, 152 n. 6, 247 n. 24, 250, 260–63 (fig. 32), 296, 310

Mai *he* 麥盉 (JC: 9451): *fp: Xiqing* 31.31; *nc.* 30; *co.* Sen-oku Museum, Kyoto; *dt.* early Western Zhou.

Summary: The ruler of Xing rewards his official Mai with metal.

Index: 116 n. 49, 261 n. 58

Maogong *ding* 毛公鼎 (JC: 2841): *ds.* 1850; *pd.* Qishan county, Shaanxi; *fp. Conggu* 16.18; *nc.* 479 (9 repetition marks, 9 compounds); *co.* Palace Museum, Taipei; *dt.* late Western Zhou (possibly King Xuan).

Summary: The king gives a long speech commanding the Duke of Mao, An, to supervise the entire Zhou government and the various officials and to assist the king to consolidate the Zhou state. The Duke of Mao is granted a set of gifts.

Index: 18 n. 69, 40 n. 46, 48 n. 10, 53 n. 19, 63 n. 48, 66–67, 85–90 (figs. 8–9), 136 n. 74, 151 n. 2, 249, 295, 295 n. 77, 305, 308

Mao *gui* 卯簋 (JC: 4327): *fp. Jigu* 6.19; *nc.* 148 (1 repetition mark, 1 compound); *dt.* middle Western Zhou.

Summary: Rongbo commands Mao, whose father and grandfather before him served the Rong family, to take charge of the Pang Palace and the people of Pang.

Index: 141–42, 157, 177, 225 n. 39

Meng *gui* 孟簋 (JC: 4162): *ds.* 1961; *pd.* Zhangjiapo, Chang'an county, Shaanxi; *fp. Kaogu xuebao* 1962.1, pls. 1–2; *nc.* 40 (2 repetition marks); *co.* Shaanxi Provincial Museum, Xi'an; *dt.* middle Western Zhou.

Summary: Meng casts a vessel in honor of his deceased father, who campaigned with Maogong and Qianzhong against Wuxu.

Index: 139 n. 80

Mian *fu* 免簠 (JC: 4626): *fp. Jigu* 7.3; *nc.* 44; *dt.* middle Western Zhou.

Summary: The king appoints Mian as Supervisor of Land in charge of forests, marshes, and pastoral land around the city of Zheng.

Index: 42 n. 2, 71, 168–71, 211, 223–24, 228, 306, 313 n. 10

Mian *gui* 免簋 (JC: 4240): *fp. Yunqing* 3.18; *nc.* 64; *co.* Shanghai Museum; *dt.* middle Western Zhou.

Summary: The king commands Mian to assist Zhou Shi in managing forests.

Index: 76, 112, 128, 211, 223, 311

Mian *pan* 免盤 (JC: 10161): *fp. Jigu* 7.17; *nc.* 33; *dt.* middle Western Zhou.

Summary: At Zhou, the king commands the Interior Scribe to offer Mian a set of gifts and to acknowledge his merits.

Index: 76, 311

Mian *zun* 免尊 (JC: 6006): *fp. Ningshou* 3.16; *nc.* 49; *co.* Palace Museum, Beijing; *dt.* middle Western Zhou.

Summary: At Zheng, the king commemorates Mian's merit and appoints him as Supervisor of Construction.

Index: 128, 168, 211, 223–24, 228, 307

Mishu *gui* 弭叔簋 (JC: 4253): *ds.* 1959; *pd.* Sipocun, Lantian county, Shaanxi; *fp. Wenwu* 1960.2, 7, 10; *nc.* 70 (2 repetition marks); *co.* Committee for the Management of Cultural Relics, Lantian county, Shaanxi; *dt.* middle Western Zhou.

Summary: At the capital Pang, the king awards Shi Qiu (Mi Shu) accoutrements upon an appointment.

Index: 77, 129, 198 n. 16

Mu *gui* 牧簋 (JC: 4343): *ds.* 960–1126; *pd.* [Fufeng]; *fp. Kaogutu* 3.24; *nc.* 219 (2 repetition marks); *dt.* middle Western Zhou.

Summary: The king appoints Mu to govern various officials, changing his mandate from the previous king to serve as Supervisor of Land.

Index: 35 n. 35, 53 n. 20, 67 n. 53, 75, 115 n. 44, 130, 212, 308

Mugong *guigai* 穆公簋蓋 (JC: 4191): *fp. Kaogu yu wenwu* 1981.4, 27–28; *nc.* 44 (1 compound); *co.* Qingyang County Museum, Gansu; *dt.* middle Western Zhou.

Summary: Returning from the Shang garrison, the king holds a sacrificial feast at Zhou with which Mugong assists (?); the king rewards Mugong with cowries.

Index: 79 n. 83

Nangong Hu *zhong* 南宮乎鐘 (JC: 0181): *ds.* 1979; *pd.* Baozigou, Fufeng county, Shaanxi; *fp. Kaogu yu wenwu* 1980.4, 20; *nc.* 67; *co.* Fufeng County Museum, Shaanxi; *dt.* late Western Zhou.

Summary: Supervisor of Land Nangong Hu casts bells dedicated to his ancestors the Duke of Nan and Gongzhong.

Index: 306

Nangong Liu *ding* 南宮柳鼎 (JC: 2805): *pd.* Guozhen, Baoji county, Shaanxi; *fp. Luyi* 98; *nc.* 77 (2 repetition marks); *co.* National Museum of China, Beijing; *dt.* late Western Zhou.

Summary: The king commands Nangong Liu to take charge of the pastoral land, orchards, marshes, and X of the Six Armies and of the affairs of farming in Xiyi Yang (?).

Index: 82, 93, 127, 131, 210, 311

Nanji *ding* 南季鼎 (JC: 2781): *fp. Jungu* 3.1.36; *nc.* 53 (2 repetition marks); *co.* Palace Museum, Beijing; *dt.* middle Western Zhou.

Summary: The king appoints Nanji to assist Supervisor of Lawsuits Bo Sufu.

Index: 74, 131 n. 69, 132–33, 200 n. 21, 254 n. 45

Ninth Year Qiu Wei *ding* 九年裘衛鼎 (JC: 2831): *ds.* 1975; *pd.* Dongjia, Qishan county, Shaanxi; *fp. Wenwu* 1976.5, 39, fig. 16; pl. 2:2; *nc.* 191 (1 repetition mark, 3 compounds); *co.* Qishan County Museum, Shaanxi; *dt.* middle Western Zhou.

Summary: Qiu Wei trades a wide range of chariots, fittings, fabrics, and jades to Ju in exchange for the Linzi district; the land is carefully demarcated, and Qiu Wei casts a bronze to record the sale.

Index: 18, 155, 162 n. 28, 163 n. 34, 181–82

Pengsheng *gui* 倗生簋 (JC: 4262): *fp. Yunqing* 3.23; *nc.* 77 (2 repetition marks); *co.* Shanghai Museum; *dt.* middle Western Zhou.

Summary: Gebo purchases horses from Pengsheng in exchange for thirty fields; Pengsheng casts a vessel to record the transaction.

Index: 17, 113, 155, 310

Pu *yu* 逋盂 (JC: 10321): *ds.* 1967; *pd.* Xinwangcun, Chang'an county, Shaanxi; *fp. Kaogu* 1977.1, pls. 9.1–2; *nc.* 49; *co.* Municipal Committee for the Management of Cultural Relics, Xi'an, Shaanxi; *dt.* middle Western Zhou.

Summary: The Zhou queen commands Pu to recruit male and female servants for the Ministry from the remote suburbs.

Index: 53 n. 20, 53–54, 73 n. 69, 172, 173 n. 53

Qi *gui* 趞簋 (JC: 4266): *fp. Kezhai* 5.10; *nc.* 80; *co.* Shodō Museum, Tokyo; *dt.* middle Western Zhou.

Summary: The king commands Qi to serve as the Grand Supervisor of Horses in the Bin garrison, governing a variety of military officials.

Index: 82, 128, 133, 162 n. 26, 210, 308–9

Qian *gui* 鄡簋 (JC: 4296): *pd.* Fufeng, Shaanxi; *fp. Kaogutu* 3.8; *nc.* 104 (2 repetition marks); *dt.* late Western Zhou.

Summary: The king extends Qian's prior mission to serve as the Invoker of the Five Cities.

Index: 77–8, 129, 166–67, 208, 309, 311

Qian *you* 趙卣 (JC: 5402): *fp. Qigu* 5.13; *nc.* 28 (1 compound); *co.* Freer
Gallery, Washington, DC; *dt.* early Western Zhou.
Summary: The king confers land and cowries upon Qian at An dur-
ing the thirteenth month.
Index: 36 n. 40

Qianshi *ding* 猷史鼎 (JC: 2166): *ds.* 1974; *pd.* Liulihe, Fangshan coun-
ty, Beijing; *fp. Kaogu* 1974.5, 313, fig. 9; *nc.* 6; *co.* Capital Museum,
Beijing; *dt.* early Western Zhou.
Summary: Scribe of Qian makes a vessel for his deceased father.
Index: 56 n. 28

Qin *gui* 禽簋 (JC: 4041): *fp. Shiliu* 2.3; *nc.* 23; *co.* National Museum of
China, Beijing; *dt.* early Western Zhou (King Cheng).
Summary: When the king attacks the ruler of Gai (i.e., Yan), the
Duke of Zhou trains Qin as Invocator, and the king rewards Qin for
performing an invocation.
Index: 58, 225 n. 39, 311

Qishi Huan *gui* 齊史逭簋 (JC: 3740): *fp. Zhenbu* 1.24; *nc.* 10; *dt.* middle
Western Zhou.
Summary: Scribe Huan of Qi makes a vessel.
Index: 56 n. 29, 250, 309

Qiu Wei gui 裘衛簋 (JC: 4256): *ds.* 1975; *pd.* Dongjiacun, Qishan county,
Shaanxi; *fp. Wenwu* 1976.5, p. 36, fig. 13; *nc.* 71 (2 repetition marks);
co. Qishan County Museum; *dt.* middle Western Zhou.
Summary: At Zhou, Qiu Wei receives rewards from the king.
Index: 129, 309

Qiu Wei *he* 裘衛盉 (JC: 9456): *ds.* 1975; *pd.* Dongjiacun, Qishan county,
Shaanxi; *fp. Wenwu* 1976.5, 37, fig. 14; 44, fig. 41; pl. 2:4; *nc.* 118 (2 repetition marks, 2 compounds); *co.* Qishan County Museum, Shaanxi;
dt. middle Western Zhou.
Summary: Qiu Wei carries out a land transaction with Ju Bo and
others.
Index: 72, 77 n. 65, 74, 74 n. 71, 81, 84 n. 91, 305–7

Ran *fangding* 塑方鼎 (JC: 2739): *ds.* 1924; *pd.* Fengxiang, Shaanxi; *fp.*
Wenlu 1.11; *nc.* 34 (1 compound); *co.* The Avery Brundage Collection
of the Asian Art Museum, San Francisco; *dt.* early Western Zhou
(King Cheng).
Summary: After returning from his campaigns to the east, the Duke
of Zhou offers sacrifice in the Zhou Temple and rewards Ran with
cowries.
Index: 162 n. 25

Ran *xu* 塑盨 (JC: 4469): *pd.* [Xi'an]; *fp. Kaogutu* 3.34; *nc.* 151 (2 repetition
marks, 1 compound); *dt.* late Western Zhou.
Summary: The king exhorts Ran to serve as an example to his peers,
awarding him various accoutrements.
Index: 313

Rong *gui* 榮簋 (JC: 4241): *fp. Eumorfopolous*, pls. 13–14; *nc.* 67 (1 compound); *co.* British Museum, London; *dt.* early Western Zhou.
Summary: The king commands Rong to deliver slaves as rewards to the ruler of Xing; Rong casts a bronze for the Duke of Zhou to document the royal command.
Index: 17–18, 308

Sanshi *pan* 散氏盤 (JC: 10176): *ds.* [1735]; *pd.* [Fengxiang, Shaanxi]; *fp. Jigu* 8.3; *nc.* 349 (1 compound); *co.* Palace Museum, Taipei; *dt.* late Western Zhou.
Summary: Representatives of the states of Ze and San carry out an exchange of land.
Index: 18, 18 n. 69, 40, 48 n. 10, 73, 113, *184–88 (figs. 23–24)*, 306–7, 309, 313

Seventh Year Quecao *ding* 七年鵲曹鼎 (JC: 2783): *fp. Zhoucun* 2.26.2; *nc.* 56; *co.* Shanghai Museum; *dt.* middle Western Zhou (King Gong).
Summary: At the Ban Palace, King Gong rewards Quecao with accoutrements.
Index: 128, 132 n. 71, 153 n. 9, 162 n. 27

Shan *ding* 善鼎 (JC: 2820): *pd.* [Chang'an]; *fp. Jungu* 3.2.49; *nc.* 110 (1 repetition mark, 1 compound); *co.* Musée Cernuschi, Paris; *dt.* middle Western Zhou.
Summary: The king extends Shan's mission from the former king to assist Quanhou in overseeing the armies at the Bin Garrison. The king grants Shan his grandfather's and father's flag.
Index: 200 n. 18, 200 n. 20, 208, 248 n. 26

Shanfu Shan *ding* 膳夫山鼎 (JC: 2825): *pd.* Near the borders between Linyou, Fufeng, and Yongshou, Shaanxi; *fp. Wenwu* 1965.7, 21, fig. 6; plate 4:2; *nc.* 119 (2 repetition marks); *co.* Shaanxi Provincial Museum; *dt.* late Western Zhou.
Summary: The king commands Provisioner Shan to supervise the "drink contributors" at Ke in replenishing the stores of *xiansi* (?).
Index: 91 n. 97, 125, 131 n. 69, 209

Shao *huanqi* 䚸圜器 (JC: 10360): *fp. Zhoucun* 5 (supplement); *nc.* 44; *co.* National Museum of China, Beijing; *dt.* early Western Zhou.
Summary: The king rewards Shao for his service with fifty *li* of land in Bi.
Index: 36 n. 40, 180

Shaoshu Shanfu *fu* 召叔山父簠 (JC: 4602): *fp. Ningshou* 11.24; *nc.* 26 (2 repetition marks); *co.* Palace Museum, Taipei; *dt.* early Spring and Autumn.
Summary: The Grand Supervisor of Construction of the state of Zheng, Shaoshu Shanfu, casts a vessel.
Index: 249–50

Shen *ding* 申鼎 (JC: 2732): *fp. Kezhai* 6.7; *nc.* 32; *dt.* late Spring and Autumn.

Summary: Shen, Grand Scribe of Ying, makes a vessel for entertaining.

Index: 56 n. 30

Shen *gui* 申簋 (JC: 4267): *fp. Kaogu yu wenwu* 1983.2, 18, fig. 3; *nc.* 82 (2 repetition marks); *co.* Zhenjiang Municipal Museum, Jiangsu; *dt.* middle Western Zhou.

Summary: The king appoints Shen to succeed his deceased father and grandfather, to assist the Great Invoker, and to serve as Invoker for the people of Feng and the nine garrison camps.

Index: 77, 79, 128, 144, 203, 311

Shengshi *zun* 省史尊 (JC: 5951): *fp. Jicheng* 5951; *nc.* 11; *co.* Shanghai Museum; *dt.* early Western Zhou.

Summary: The Inspecting Scribe makes a vessel for Grandfather Ding.

Index: 56 n. 28, 310

Shi Chen *ding* 師晨鼎 (JC: 2817): *fp. Jungu* 3.2.21; *nc.* 97 (2 repetition marks, 1 compound); *dt.* middle Western Zhou.

Summary: The king appoints Shi Chen as assistant to Shi Su in charge of groups of civil officers and servants in the cities of Yi and Zheng.

Index: 76, 109 n. 23, 119–22, 126, 137 n. 78, 146, 168–9, 169 n. 45, 200 n. 21, 210, 219, 232, 265 n. 65, 307, 311–12

Shi Hu *gui* 師虎簋 (JC: 4316): *fp. Jungu* 3.2.58; *nc.* 121 (3 repetition marks); *co.* Shanghai Museum; *dt.* middle Western Zhou.

Summary: The king orders Shi Hu to carry on his grandfather's and father's service, taking charge of the fine horses in the Left and Right camps.

Index: 75, 78, 109 n. 23, 127, 132 n. 70, 133, 192–4 (fig. 26), 195–6, 198 n. 15, 202, 218, 223 n. 35, 308

Shi Hui *gui* 師毀簋 (JC: 4311): *fp. Bogu* 16.30; *nc.* 110 (2 repetition marks); *co.* Committee for the Management of Cultural Relics, Lantian County, Shaanxi; *dt.* late Western Zhou (Gong He).

Summary: Bo Hefu commands Shi Hui to follow in his father's footsteps and serve Bo Hefu's family, overseeing various types of servants.

Index: 40 n. 47, 141–42, 220 n. 33

Shi Ji *gui* 師籍簋 (JC: 4257): *ds.* 1963; *pd.* Wangchuan, Lantian county, Shaanxi; *fp. Wenwu* 1966.1, 5–6; *nc.* 71 (2 repetition marks); *co.* Committee for the Management of Cultural Relics, Lantian County, Shaanxi; *dt.* middle Western Zhou.

Summary: The king awards Shi Ji a variety of valuables for use in his service.

Index: 76, 126, 309

Shi Ju *fangyi* 師遽方彝 (JC: 9897): *fp. Kezhai* 13.9; *nc.* 66; *co.* Shanghai Museum; *dt.* middle Western Zhou.

Summary: At the bedchamber of the Kang Palace at Zhou, Shi Ju receives the *mieli* (recounting of merits) ritual and assists the king; the king rewards him.

Index: 231 n. 50

Shi Ju *gui* 師遽簋 (JC: 4214): *pd.* Qishan, Shaanxi?; *fp. Jigu* 6.15; *nc.* 56 (1 compound); *co.* Shanghai Museum; *dt.* middle Western Zhou.

Summary: At the New Palace at Zhou, the king inspects the Marshals, ordering that Shi Ju be rewarded with ten strings of cowries.

Index: 231, 313

Shi Ke *xu* 師克盨 (JC: 4467): *ds.* 1875–1908; *pd.* Fufeng, Shaanxi; *fp. Wenwu* 1959.3, 64; *nc.* 141 (3 repetition marks); *co.* Palace Museum, Beijing; *dt.* late Western Zhou.

Summary: The king renews Ke's command, ordering him to succeed to his father's and grandfather's post in charge of the Tiger Servants of the Left and Right.

Index: 195 n. 11, 205

Shi Kuifu *ding* 師奎父鼎 (JC: 2813): *pd.* [Guanzhong region]; *fp. Yunqing* 4.20; *nc.* 92 (1 repetition mark); *co.* Shanghai Museum; *dt.* middle Western Zhou.

Summary: The king appoints Shi Kuifu to manage his father's old office and colleagues.

Index: 54 n. 21, 127, 202, 231, 308–9

Shi Lai *jiao* 史逨角 (JC: 9063): *ds.* 1966; *pd.* Hejiacun, Qishan county, Shaanxi; *fp. Wenge,* p. 40 (vessel image); *Shaanxi* 156; *nc.* 6; *co.* Shaanxi Provincial Museum; *dt.* early Western Zhou.

Summary: Scribe Lai makes a vessel.

Index: 55 n. 26, 309

Shi Li *gui* 師𩰫簋 (JC: 4324): *fp. Kezhai* 9.17; *nc.* cover: 121 (4 repetition marks), vessel: 138 (4 repetition marks); *co.* Shanghai Museum; *dt.* late Western Zhou.

Summary: The king extends Shi Li's mission to take charge of the royal musicians of bells and drums.

Index: 40 n. 47, 91, 124, 130 n. 67, 197, 197 n. 14, 203, 220 n. 33, 312

Shi Mao *hu* 史懋壺 (JC: 9714): *fp. Conggu* 1.6; *nc.* 41; *co.* Shanghai Museum; *dt.* middle Western Zhou.

Summary: At the Lower (Wet) Palace at the capital Pang, the king orders Scribe Mao to perform *lu*-divination.

Index: 152 n. 5,

Shi Maofu *gui* 師毛父簋 (JC: 4196): *fp. Bogu* 17.19; *nc.* 46 (2 repetition marks); *dt.* middle Western Zhou.

Summary: Shi Maofu is rewarded with accoutrements.

Index: 127, 309

Shi Mi *gui* 史密簋 (JL: 489): *ds.* 1986; *pd.* Wangjiaba, Ankang county, Shaanxi; *fp. Kaogu yu wenwu* 1989.3, 7–9; also *Wenwu* 1989.7, 64-5; *nc.*

91 (2 repetition marks, 1 compound); *co.* Ankang District Museum, Shaanxi; *dt.* middle Western Zhou.

Summary: The king orders Shi Su and Shi Mi to conduct a punitive campaign to the east against Changbi; they take 100 captives.

Index: 172–73, 265, 268

Shi Mian *fu* 史免簠 (JC: 4579): *fp. Jungu* 2.3.16; *nc.* 20 (2 repetition marks); *co.* Shandong Provincial Museum (lid); *dt.* late Western Zhou.

Summary: Scribe Mian makes a grain vessel to use while on military campaigns with the king.

Index: 309

Shi Qi *ding* 師旂鼎 (JC: 2809): *fp. Congkao* 382; *nc.* 79; *co.* Palace Museum, Beijing; *dt.* middle Western Zhou.

Summary: Shi Qi's many servants fail to join the king's punitive attack against Yufang, for which Bo Maofu punishes them with a fine. The servants are eventually ordered to submit the fine to Shi Qi instead, and a Scribe makes a record of the change.

Index: 99 n. 7, 264

Shi Qiang *pan* 史牆盤 (JC: 10175): *ds.* 1976; *pd.* Zhuangbaicun, Fufeng county, Shaanxi; *fp. Wenwu* 1978.3, p. 14, fig. 21; *nc.* 276 (5 repetition marks, 3 compounds); *co.* Zhouyuan Museum, Shaanxi; *dt.* middle Western Zhou.

Summary: In the first part of the inscription, Scribe Qiang recounts the generations of the Zhou royal line from King Wen to King Mu, highlighting the qualities and accomplishments of the individual kings; in the second part, he describes the services rendered to the royal house by his ancestors.

Index: 160 n. 22, 309

Shi Shou *ding* 史獸鼎 (JC: 2778): *fp. Zhuiyi* 4.5; *nc.* 50; *co.* Palace Museum, Taipei; *dt.* early Western Zhou.

Summary: Scribe Shou announces the completion of his works at Chengzhou to the Chief.

Index: 56–57, 309

Shi Shu *gui* 史叔簋 (JC: 4132): *fp. Duandai*, 3.65, figs. 1–2, pl. 1; *Luyi*, 161a; *nc.* 32; *co.* Palace Museum, Beijing; *dt.* early Western Zhou.

Summary: When the king performs an entreaty rite, Wang Jiang dispatches Shu as an envoy to the Great Protector, awarding Shu various goods.

Index: 257 n. 50

Shi Song *gui* 史頌簋 (JC: 4232): *fp. Jungu* 3.1.54; *nc.* 60 (2 repetition marks, 1 compound); *co.* Shanghai Museum (vessel; location of lid unknown); *dt.* late Western Zhou.

Summary: The king orders Scribe Song to inspect Su. Officials and dignitaries from Su meet Song at Chengzhou and give him gifts.

Index: 40 n. 48, 92–93, *99–101 (fig. 11)*, 181–82, 309, 313

Shi Tian *gui* 史喈簋 (JC: 4030): *ds.* 1966; *pd.* Hejiacun, Qishan county, Shaanxi; *fp. Wenwu* 1972.6, 26; *nc.* 22 (1 compound); *co.* Shaanxi Provincial Museum; *dt.* early Western Zhou.

Summary: While addressing Duke Bi, the king awards Scribe Tian cowries. Scribe Tian records the event on a bronze and promises to observe and record morning and night.

Index: 55 n. 26, 56 n. 27, 309

Shi Tian *gui* 史甜簋 no. 2 (JC: 4031): *fp. Yunqing* 5.11; *nc.* 22 (1 compound); *co.* Palace Museum, Beijing; *dt.* early Western Zhou.

Summary: While addressing Duke Bi, the king awards Scribe Tian cowries. Scribe Tian records the event on a bronze and promises to observe and record morning and night.

Index: 17

Shi Wang *ding* 師望鼎 (JC: 2812): *ds.* late Qing; *fp. Kezhai* 5.7; *nc.* 91 (3 repetition marks); *co.* Art Institute of Chicago; *dt.* middle Western Zhou.

Summary: Shi Wang exalts his ancestor's virtue and recounts his own merits in sending out and taking in royal commands.

Index: 226–27, 313

Shi Xun *gui* 師詢簋 (JC: 4342): *fp. Lidai* 14.14, 153; *nc.* 210 (3 repetition marks); *dt.* middle Western Zhou.

Summary: The king orders Shi Xun to succeed his ancestor Ke in serving the throne, commanding him to harmonize the great and small chiefs of the state.

Index: 125, 131 n. 69, 204

Shi Ying *gui* 師穎簋 (JC: 4312): *fp. Lishuo* 2.1; *nc.* 110 (2 repetition marks); *dt.* middle Western Zhou.

Summary: The king extends Shi Ying's mission to serve as Supervisor of Land and to oversee the floodgate of the Fang River (?).

Index: 71, 125, 131 n. 69, 207, 307, 309

Shi You *ding* 師酉鼎: *ds.* 2004; *fp. Zhongguo* 2004.1, 4–10; *nc.* 92; *co.* Poly Museum, Beijing; *dt.* middle Western Zhou.

Summary: The king addresses Shi You and gives him gifts.

Index: 104 n. 15, 198 n. 15

Shi You *gui* 師酉簋 (JC: 4288): *fp. Jigu* 6.23; *nc.* 104 (2 compounds); *co.* Palace Museum, Beijing; *dt.* middle Western Zhou.

Summary: At Wu, the king commands Shi You to succeed his grandfather, taking charge of the Tiger Servants among the people of Yi and the barbarians of Ximeng, Quan, Qin, Jing, and Biren.

Index: 67 n. 53, 130, 193 n. 5, 195 n. 11, 198, 198 n. 16, 204

Shi Yu *gui* 師艅簋 (JC: 4277): *fp. Jungu* 3.2.15; *nc.* 97; *dt.* middle Western Zhou.

Summary: The king commands Shi Yu to supervise the people of Zhou.

Index: 76, 119–22, 126, 146, 209, 307, 311

Shi Yuan *gui* 師衰簋 (JC: 4313): *fp. Yunqing* 3.35.1–3.36; *nc.* cover: III (2 repetition marks), vessel: II5 (2 repetition mark); *co.* Shanghai Museum; *dt.* late Western Zhou.
Summary: The king dispatches Shi Yuan at the head of a group of Tiger Servants to attack the Huaiyi; Shi Yuan also commands troops from the states of Qi, Ji, Lai, etc.
Index: 247 n. 23, 266–77, (fig. 33)

Shi Yun *gui* 師瘨簋 (JC: 4283): *ds.* 1963; *pd.* Beipocun, Wugong county, Shaanxi; *fp. Wenwu* 1964.7, 27, fig. 15; pls. 5.4–5; *nc.* 100 (3 repetition marks); *co.* Shaanxi Provincial Museum; *dt.* middle Western Zhou.
Summary: The king extends Shi Yun's mandate from the previous king to command the marshals of the people of Yi.
Index: 121–22, 127, 132 n. 70, 146, 207, 308, 313

Shi Yun *gui* 師瘨簋 (JC: 4284): *ds.* 1963; *pd.* Beipocun, Wugong county, Shaanxi; *fp. Wenwu* 1964.7, 26, fig. 14; pls. 5.2–3; *nc.* 100 (3 repetition marks); *co.* Shaanxi Provincial Museum; *dt.* middle Western Zhou.
Summary: The king extends Shi Yun's mandate from the previous king to command the marshals of the people of Yi.
Index: 75

Shi Zai *ding* 師𪊨鼎 (JC: 2830): *ds.* 1974; *pd.* Qiangjiacun, Fufeng county, Shaanxi; *fp. Wenwu* 1975.8, 61, figs. 3–4; pl. 9.1; *nc.* 190 (1 repetition mark, 9 compounds); *co.* Shaanxi Provincial Museum; *dt.* middle Western Zhou (King Gong).
Summary: Shi Zai, who served King Mu as well as King Gong, receives gifts from King Gong. In return, he praises both the king and the Elder Grand Marshal.
Index: 313

Shi *zhi* 史觶: *ds.* 1973-7; *pd.* Liulihe, Fangshan county, Beijing; *fp. Liulihe*, p. 173; *nc.* 8; *co.* Shaanxi Provincial Museum; *co.* Beijing Municipal Institute of Cultural Relics; *dt.* early Western Zhou.
Summary: The Scribe casts a vessel for Grandfather Ji.
Index: 250, 309

Shou *gui* 受簋 (JC: 3878): *fp. Luyi* 150; *nc.* 15 (2 repetition marks); *co.* National Museum of China, Beijing; *dt.* late Western Zhou.
Summary: Groom Shou of Zheng casts a precious *gui*-vessel.
Index: 168–69

Shoushu Huanfu *xu* 獸叔奐父盨: *ds.* 1990; *pd.* Tomb M2006 of the Guo 虢 state cemetery at Sanmenxia, Henan; *fp. Wenwu* 2004.4, 90; *nc.* 33 (2 repetition marks); *co.* Guo State Museum, Sanmenxia, Henan; *dt.* late Western Zhou.
Summary: Shoushu Huanfu makes a vessel for Maiden Meng to use in entertaining guests.
Index: 15

Shu Xiangfu Yu *gui* 叔向父禹簋 (JC: 4242): *fp. Jungu* 3.1.59; *nc.* 65 remaining; *co.* Shanghai Museum; *dt.* late Western Zhou.

Summary: Shu Xiangfu Yu casts a vessel for and seeks blessings from his deceased grandfather, You Taishu.

Index: 183 n. 68

Shu Ze *fangding* 叔矢方鼎: *ds.* 2000; *pd.* Beizhao, Quwu county, Shanxi; *fp. Wenwu* 2001.8, 9; *nc.* 48; *co.* Shanxi Provincial Institute of Archeology, Taiyuan (Houma Archeological Station); *dt.* early Western Zhou.

Summary: The Zhou king conducts a great entreating rite in Chengzhou; Shu Ze receives royal gifts of a chariot, horses, etc.

Index: 257–59 (fig. 31)

Shu *zhi* 庶觶: *ds.* 1973–7; *pd.* Liulihe, Fangshan county, Beijing; *fp. Liulihe*, pp. 172–73; *nc.* 15; *co.* Beijing Municipal Institute of Cultural Relics; *dt.* early Western Zhou.

Summary: Gong Zhong rewards Shu with cowries.

Index: 259

Sigong Ding *jue* 嗣工丁爵 (JC: 8792): *pd.* [Jun County, Henan]; *fp. Zhenbu* 2.27; *nc.* 3; *dt.* Shang.

Summary: Supervisor of Works Ding is mentioned.

Index: 54, 307

Sikou Liangfu *hu* 嗣寇良父壺 (JC: 9641): *fp. Huaimi* 2.14; *nc.* 14 (2 repetition marks); *dt.* late Western Zhou.

Summary: Sikou Liangfu casts a bronze for his wife, who is from the state of Wey.

Index: 93

Situ Hu *gui* 嗣土虎簋 (JC: 3671): *fp. Yunqing* 3.51; *nc.* 8; *dt.* early Western Zhou.

Summary: Supervisor of Land Hu makes a treasured vessel.

Index: 306

Situ Si *gui* 嗣土嗣簋 (JC: 3696): *fp. Xiqingjia* 6.22; *nc.* 9; *co.* Palace Museum, Beijing; *dt.* early Western Zhou.

Summary: Supervisor of Land Si casts a vessel for his deceased father.

Index: 54, 306

Sixth Year Yiqi *you* 六年𠨘其卣 (JC: 5414): *pd.* [Anyang, Henan]; *fp. Luyi* 273; *nc.* 27; *co.* Palace Museum, Beijing; *dt.* Shang.

Summary: Document Maker X casts a vessel for his ancestor Gui upon receiving rewards from Yiqi.

Index: 28 n. 18, 61 n. 43, 310

Sixth Year Zhousheng *gui* 六年琱生簋 (JC: 4293): *fp. Jigu* 6.17; *nc.* 104; *co.* National Museum of China, Beijing; *dt.* late Western Zhou (King Xuan).

Summary: Shaobo Hu reports to Zhousheng on the result of a dispute over land properties.

Index: 48 n. 10, 248 n. 26

Song *ding* 頌鼎 (JC: 2829): *fp. Jungu* 3.3.3; *nc.* 149 (2 repetition marks); *co.* Shanghai Museum; *dt.* late Western Zhou.

Summary: The king commands Song to take charge of twenty households at Chengzhou and to oversee the newly constructed warehouse using palace attendants.

Index: 85 n. 92, 91–92, 101, 105–7 (fig. 13), 109 n. 26, 112, 112 n. 33, 124, 130 n. 67, 136 n. 76, 143 n. 87, 208, 309, 312

Ta Situ *gui* 渣嗣土簋 (Kanghou gui 康侯簋) (JC: 4059): *pd.* Ji county or Jun County, Henan; *fp. London*, pl. XI, p. 250; *nc.* 24; *co.* British Museum, London; *dt.* early Western Zhou (King Cheng).

Summary: After the Zhou attack on the Shang capital, the king commands the ruler Kang to establish the state of Wei; the Supervisor of Land for Ta casts a bronze.

Index: 43 n. 3, 54 n. 23, 249, 306

Taibao *gui* 太保簋 (JC: 4140): *ds.* 1821–61; *pd.* [one of seven vessels discovered near Mt. Liang, Shouzhang county, Shandong]; *fp. Jungu* 2.3.82; *nc.* 34; *co.* Freer Gallery, Washington, DC; *dt.* early Western Zhou.

Summary: The Grand Protector puts down a rebellion in the east and receives land in Yu as a reward.

Index: 18

Taishi Cuo *gui* 太師盧簋 (JC: 4251): *ds.* 1941; *pd.* [Xi'an]; *fp. Duandai* 6.119; *nc.* 70; *co.* Palace Museum, Beijing; *dt.* middle Western Zhou.

Summary: At the Shi Liang Palace at Zhou, the king confers tiger furs on Grand Marshal Cuo.

Index: 219, 223, 223 n. 35, 313

Taishi *gui* 太師簋 (JC: 3633): *ds.* 1972; *pd.* Zhouzhi county, Shaanxi; *fp. Kaogu yu wenwu* 1981.1, pl. 5.5; *nc.* 7; Zhouzhi County Department of Culture, Shaanxi; *dt.* late Western Zhou.

Summary: The Grand Marshal makes a vessel for Meng Jiang.

Index: 313

Taishi You *yan* 太史友瓻 (JC: 915): *ds.* [late eighteenth century]; *pd.* [One of seven vessels discovered near Mt. Liang, Shouzhang county, Shandong]; *fp. Jungu* 2.1.42; *nc.* 9; *co.* Sen-oku Museum, Kyoto, Japan; *dt.* early Western Zhou.

Summary: Grand Scribe You makes a vessel for the Duke of Shao.

Index: 55, 308

Third Year Shi Dui *gui* 三年師兌簋 (JC: 4318): *fp. Zhoucun* 3.15 (front and back); *nc.* 124 (3 repetition marks, 1 compound); *co.* Shanghai Museum; *dt.* late Western Zhou.

Summary: The king commands Shi Dui to take full charge of the Masters of Horses of the Left and Right camps.

Index: 40 n. 47, 129, 162 n. 25, 166–67, 212, 220–21, 309

Third Year Xing *hu* 三年㝬壺 (JC: 9726): *ds.* 1976; *pd.* Zhuangbaicun, Fufeng county, Shaanxi; *fp. Wenwu* 1978.3, p. 11, fig. 16; p. 17, figs. 26–7; plate 5.3; *nc.* 60; *co.* Zhouyuan Museum, Shaanxi; *dt.* middle Western Zhou.

Summary: At Zheng, the king awards sacrificial lamb meat to Xing during a feast; later, at Gouling, the king awards Xing sacrificial pig meat. Xing casts a vessel for his deceased father.

Index: 64 n. 49

Thirteenth Year Xing *hu* 十三年㝬壺 (JC: 9723): *ds.* 1976; *pd.* Zhuangbai, Fufeng county, Shaanxi; *fp. Wenwu* 1978.3, 10, fig. 13; *nc.* 56; *co.* Zhouyuan Museum, Shaanxi; *dt.* middle Western Zhou.

Summary: At the Palace of Supervisor of Multitudes Hu at Chengzhou, the king presents accoutrements to Xing.

Index: 124, 136 n. 76, 306, 311–12

Tong *gui* 同簋 (JC: 4271): *fp. Zhoucun* 3 (supplement); *nc.* 87 (4 repetition marks); *co.* Palace Museum, Beijing; *dt.* middle Western Zhou.

Summary: The king orders Tong to assist Wu Taibo in managing orchards, forests, marshes, and pastoral lands west of the Yellow River, east of the Hu River, and south of the Xuan River.

Index: 101, 104 n. 15, 125, 131 n. 69, 162 n. 26, 179–80, 200 n. 20, 210, 313

Wang Chen *gui* 王臣簋 (JC: 4268): *ds.* 1977; *pd.* Nanchuanye, Chengcheng county, Shaanxi; *fp. Wenwu* 1980.5, 64; *nc.* 85; *co.* Institute for the Management of Cultural Relics, Chengcheng County, Shaanxi; *dt.* middle Western Zhou.

Summary: The king awards Wang Chen various valuables.

Index: 75

Wang *gui* 望簋 (JC: 4272): *fp. Yunqing* 3.48; *nc.* lid: 87 (4 repetition marks), vessel: 81 (1 repetition mark); *dt.* middle Western Zhou.

Summary: The king appoints Wang to oversee the Royal Household at the city of Bi.

Index: 69, 124, 130, 208, 309, 309 n. 4, 312

Wei *gui* 衛簋 (JC: 4209): *ds.* 1973; *pd.* Mawangcun, Chang'an county, Shaanxi; *fp. Kaogu* 1974.1, 3, fig. 4, pl. 3.3; *nc.* 55; *co.* Municipal Committee for the Management of Cultural Relics, Xi'an; *dt.* middle Western Zhou.

Summary: The king commands and rewards Wei.

Index: 126

Wei Man *ding* 微鸞鼎 (JC: 2790): *ds.* ca. 1102; *pd.* Shangzhou, South Shaanxi; *fp. Lidai* 10.8; 110; *nc.* 63 (1 repetition mark); *dt.* late Western Zhou.

Summary: The king orders Wei Man to take charge of the Nine Reservoirs.

Index: 212

Wu *fangyi* 吳方彝 (JC: 9898): *fp. Jigu* 5.34; *nc.* 101 (1 compound); *co.* Shanghai Museum; *dt.* middle Western Zhou.

Summary: The king places Document Maker Wu in charge of the white banner and fine silk.

Index: 76, 109 n. 23, 124, 130 n. 67, 136 n. 76, 208, 309–10, 310 n. 6, 312

Wu *gui* 敔簋 (JC: 3827): *fp. Wenlu* 3.32; *nc.* 14; *co.* Capital Museum, Beijing; *dt.* early Western Zhou.

Summary: Wu makes a vessel for serving food to his sons and grandsons.

Index: 15

Wu *gui* 敔簋 (JC: 4323): *fp. Bogu* 16.38; *nc.* 134 (3 repetition marks, 4 compounds); *dt.* late Western Zhou.

Summary: The king orders Wu to counterattack the invading Huaiyi; afterwards, the king rewards Wu for his success in the campaign.

Index: 93, 127, 131, 140, 162 n. 26, 176–7, 228

Wu Hu *ding* 吳虎鼎 (JL: 364): *ds.* 1992; *pd.* Xujiazhai, Chang'an county, Shaanxi; *fp. Kaogu yu wenwu* 1998.3, 69–71; *nc.* 163 (2 repetition marks); *co.* Committee for the Management of Cultural Relics, Chang'an county, Shaanxi; *dt.* late Western Zhou (King Xuan).

Summary: At the Yi Hall of the Kang Palace at Zhou, King Xuan announces King Li's will to transfer land to Wu Hu.

Index: 40 n. 48, 72–73, 92–3, 112–13, 152 n. 4, 159, 309, 312

Wuhui *ding* 無惠鼎 (JC: 2814): *fp. Jigu* 4.28; *nc.* 93 (1 compound); *co.* Zhenjiang Municipal Museum, Jiangsu; *dt.* late Western Zhou.

Summary: The king appoints Wuhui to command the praetorian Tiger Servants attending the king.

Index: 90–2, 126, 195 n. 11, 209, 306, 309

X *ding* 冢鼎 (JC: 2696): *fp. Zhenbu* 1.11; *nc.* 26; *co.* Palace Museum, Beijing; *dt.* middle Western Zhou.

Summary: The Interion Scribe issues an order for service and confers a gift of metal.

Index: 75

X *ding* 筍鼎 (JC: 2741): *fp. Zhenbu* 1.12; *nc.* 35; *dt.* early Western Zhou.

Summary: During the king's campaigns against the Dongyi, the Duke of Zhai orders X and Scribe Qi to lead the Marshals and officials in an attack. They capture cowries with which X has a vessel made.

Index: 313

X *zun* 隩尊 (JC: 5986): *ds.* 1933; *pd.* Xincun, Jun county, Henan; *fp. Junxian*, pp. 12–3; *nc.* 24; *co.* Academia Sinica, Taipei; *dt.* early Western Zhou.

Summary: X accompanies the ruler of Wei to visit Zongzhou and is awarded cowries.

Index: 260, 263

Xian *zhong* 鮮鐘 (JC: 143): *ds.* 1952; *fp. Tushi* 126; *nc.* 52 (2 repetition marks); *co.* Shaanxi Provincial Museum; *dt.* late Western Zhou.

Summary: At the palace of Supervisor of Land Hu 滹, the king presents Xian with metal.

Index: 306

Xianhou *ding* 獻侯鼎 (JC: 2626): *fp. Xiqingyi* 1.6; *nc.* 20 (several unclear); *co.* Palace Museum, Taipei; *dt.* early Western Zhou (King Cheng).

Summary: When King Cheng performs a great entreaty at Zongzhou, (he) awards cowries to the ruler of Xian.

Index: 257 n.

Xiao Yu *ding* 小盂鼎 (JC: 2839): *pd.* Qishan, Shaanxi; *fp. Jungu* 3.3.42; *nc.* 390; *dt.* early Western Zhou.

Summary: At Zhou Temple, Yu announces his great victory in major campaigns against the Guifang people; the Zhou king rewards Yu with a large number of households together with their slaves.

Index: 162 n. 25, 294–95

Xiaochen Lai *gui* 小臣逨簋 (JC: 4238): *ds.* 1931; *pd.* Jun county?; *fp. Zhensong* 6.6; *Zhenbu*, 1.28–29; *nc.* 64; *co.* Palace Museum, Taipei; *dt.* early Western Zhou.

Summary: Bo Maofu leads the Eight Armies of Yin to attack the Dongyi; after the campaign, Xiaochen Lai is honored and receives a reward.

Index: 264, 265 n. 63

Xiaochen X *ding* 小臣𧊒鼎 (JC: 2556): *fp. Duandai* 2.94–95; *nc.* 16 (1 compound); *dt.* early Western Zhou.

Summary: Setting up the state of Yan, the Duke of Shao rewards Petty Servant X with cowries.

Index: 48

Xiaozi X *you* 小子𥷑卣 (JC: 5417): *fp. Zhuiyi* 6.18; *nc.* 48 (cover: 45, vessel: 3); *co.* Hakutsuru Fine Art Museum, Kobe, Japan; *dt.* Shang.

Summary: During a campaign against the Renfang, Zi performs the *mieli* (recounting of merits) ritual for Xiaochen X.

Index: 228

Xijia *pan* 兮甲盤 (JC: 10174): *fp. Jungu* 3.2.67; *nc.* 129 (4 repetition marks); *dt.* late Western Zhou.

Summary: After Xi Jia distinguishes himself fighting against the Xianyun, the king appoints him to oversee the collection of tribute at Chengzhou.

Index: 101

Xing Jiang Taizai *fu* 邢姜太宰簠: *ds.* 1975; *pd.* Bayaertuhushuo, Zhelimu district, Inner Mongolia; *fp. Neimenggu* 1982.2, 5–7, pl. 2; *nc.* 15 (2 repetition marks); *co.* Zhelimumeng Museum, Inner Mongolia; *dt.* late Western Zhou.

Summary: The Grand Superintendent of the consort of the ruler of Xing casts a bronze.

Index: 250, 312

Xing *xu* 癲盨 (JC: 4462): *ds.* 1976; *pd.* Zhuangbai, Fufeng county, Shaanxi;
    fp. Wenwu 1978.3, 5, fig. 3; 18, fig. 43; pl. 6:1; *nc.* 62 (2 repetition marks);
    co. Zhouyuan Museum, Fufeng, Shaanxi; *dt.* middle Western Zhou.
    Summary: The king rewards Xing.
    Index: 119, 119 n. 56, 121, 126, 146, 307, 309

Xing *zhong* 癲鐘 (JC: 248): *ds.* 1976; *pd.* Zhuangbai, Fufeng county,
    Shaanxi; *fp. Wenwu* 1978.3, 13, fig. 20; pl. 8:1; *nc.* 100 (4 repetition
    marks); *co.* Zhouyuan Museum, Fufeng, Shaanxi; *dt.* middle Western
    Zhou.
    Summary: Xing, whose ancestors served under the Chief Interior
    Scribe, casts a vessel to commemorate the king's generosity.
    Index: 200 n. 20

Xiu *pan* 休盤 (JC: 10170): *fp. Zhoucun* 3.27; *nc.* 89 (2 repetition marks); *co.*
    Nanjing Museum; *dt.* middle Western Zhou.
    Summary: The king awards Xiu accoutrements.
    Index: 128, 311

Xun *gui* 詢簋 (JC: 4321): *ds.* 1959; *pd.* Sipocun, Lantian county, Shaanxi;
    fp. Wenwu 1960.2, 8; *nc.* 131 (2 repetition marks); *co.* Committee for
    the Management of Cultural Relics, Lantian County, Shaanxi; *dt.*
    middle Western Zhou.
    Summary: The King appoints Xun to take charge of the Tiger Ser-
    vants, the retainers, and several communities of aliens in the Zhou
    capital region.
    Index: 29 n. 20, 101, 128, 198–99, 198 n. 16, 204, 295, 295 n.77

Xunhou *pan* 荀侯盤 (JC: 10096): *ds.* 1961; *pd.* Zhangjiapo, Chang'an
    county, Shaanxi; *fp. Kaogu xuebao* 1962.1, 11, pl. 17.2; *nc.* 12; *co.* Shaanxi
    Provincial Museum; *dt.* late Western Zhou.
    Summary: The ruler of Xun casts a vessel for Shu Ji.
    Index: 44 n. 5

Yang *gui* 養簋 (JC: 4243): *fp. Wenwu* 1979.2, 94; *nc.* 67 (2 repetition
    marks); *co.* Municipal Office for the Management of Cultural Relics,
    Tianjin; *dt.* middle Western Zhou.
    Summary: Yang is commanded to protect dams in the Five Cities.
    Index: 76, 121–22, 127, 132 n. 70, 146, 166–67, 210, 308–9

Yang *gui* 楊簋 no. 1 (JC: 4294): *fp. Jungu* 3.2.33; *nc.* 104 (3 repetition
    marks); *dt.* middle Western Zhou.
    Summary: The king appoints Yang as Supervisor of Construction and
    puts him in charge of affairs of farming, residential housing, pasture,
    lawsuits, and construction at a place called Liang.
    Index: 71, 74–75, 101, 109 n. 23, 125, 131 n. 69, 179, 209, 254 n. 45,
    306–8, 309 n. 4

Yang *gui* 楊簋 no. 2 (JC: 4295): *fp. Kezhai* 11.16; *nc.* 104 (3 repetition
    marks); *co.* Palace Museum, Beijing; *dt.* middle Western Zhou.

Summary: The king appoints Yang as Supervisor of Construction and orders him to take charge of affairs of farming, residential housing, pasture, lawsuits, and construction at a place called Liang.

Index: 71 n. 64, 125, 209

Yanhou *gui* 燕侯簋 (3614): *fp. Jicheng* 3614; *nc.* 7; *co.* Jinan Municipal Museum, Shandong; *dt.* early Western Zhou.

Summary: The ruler of Yan casts a vessel for Ji.

Index: 44 n. 4

Yanhou Zhi *ding* 匽侯旨鼎 (JC: 2628): *fp. Zhoucun* 2 (supplement); *nc.* 20 (1 compound); *co.* Sen-oku Museum, Kyoto; *dt.* early Western Zhou.

Summary: The ruler of Yan, Zhi, visits the Zhou king at Zongzhou for the first time; the king awards him twenty strings of cowries.

Index: 260, 263

Yangshi *zun* 羕史尊 (JC: 5811): *fp. Yunqing* 2.21; *nc.* 5; *dt.* early Western Zhou.

Summary: A Scribe of Yang makes a vessel.

Index: 56 n. 28

Yi *gui* 伊簋 (JC: 4287): *fp. Zhoucun* 3.23; *nc.* 102 (2 repetition marks); *dt.* middle Western Zhou.

Summary: The king appoints Yi to oversee the royal servants, female slaves, and craftsmen of the Kang Temple.

Index: 69, 129, 153–54, 211, 220

Yi *you* 益卣 (JC: 5427): *fp. Pangu* 2.18; *nc.* 61; *co.* Shanghai Museum; *dt.* middle Western Zhou.

Summary: Document Maker Yi casts a vessel in honor of his deceased parents.

Index: 310

Yi *zhi* 趩觶 (JC: 6516): *fp. Hengxuan* 1.50; *nc.* 67 (1 compound); *dt.* middle Western Zhou.

Summary: Yi is commanded to succeed his grandfather and father in service.

Index: 129, 204, 309

Yihou Ze *gui* 宜侯夨簋 (JC: 4320): *ds.* 1954; *pd.* Mt. Yandunshan, Dantun county, Jiangsu; *fp. Wencan* 1955.5, 59–60, pls. 1–3; *nc.* 126 (2 compounds); *co.* National Museum of China, Beijing; *dt.* early Western Zhou (King Kang).

Summary: The king commands the ruler of Yu, Ze, to serve as the ruler of Yi. Ze receives gifts of land and people with this new state.

Index: 43 n. 3, 67, 105 n. 18, 174, 238–41 (figs. 27–28), 244

Yin *gui* 殷簋 (JL: 487–88): *ds.* 1984; *pd.* Dingjiagou, Yao county, Shaanxi; *fp. Kaogu yu wenwu* 1986.4, 4–5; *nc.* 80 (2 repetition marks); *co.* Tongchuan Municipal Museum, Shaanxi; *dt.* middle Western Zhou.

Summary: Yin is commanded to succeed his grandfather, his father, and their friends in managing the five towns in the eastern district.

Index: 125, 131 n. 69, 174, 178–79, 202

Yinghou *zhong* 應侯鐘 (JC: 107–8): *ds.* 1974 (JC: 107); *pd.* Hongxing,
Lantian county, Shaanxi (JC: 107); *fp. Wenwu* 1975.10, 68–69 (JC:
107); *Wenwu* 1977.8, 27 (JC: 108); *nc.* 39 (2 compounds) (107); 30
(2 repetition marks, 1 compound) (108); *co.* Lantian County Museum,
Shaanxi (107); Shodō Museum, Tokyo (108); *dt.* middle–late Western
Zhou.

Summary: When the king returns from Chengzhou, the ruler of Ying
has an audience with him at Zongzhou.

Index: 123 n. 66, 126, 263–64

Yingjian *yan* 應監甗 (JC: 883): *ds.* 1958; *pd.* Huangjinbu, Yugan county,
Jiangxi; *fp. Kaogu* 1960.2, 44; *Kaogu xuebao* 1960.1,7, pls. 1–2; *nc.* 6; *co.*
Jiangxi Provincial History Museum; *dt.* early Western Zhou.

Summary: The Royal Inspector of Ying casts a yan vessel.

Index: 251, 314

Yong *yu* 永盂 (JC: 10322): *ds.* 1969; *pd.* Hubin, Lantian county, Shaanxi;
fp. Wenwu 1972.1, 62; *nc.* 121 (2 repetition marks); *co.* Municipal
Committee for the Management of Cultural Relics, Xi'an; *dt.* middle
Western Zhou.

Summary: Duke Yi, together with a group of high officials, announces
a royal order to award Shi Yong land. A description of the hierarchy of
administrative authority is included.

Index: 72–74, 84 n. 91, 101, 119 n. 56, 132 n. 71, 136–39 (fig. 15), 139 n.
80, 147–48, 157 n. 18, 168, 169 n. 45, 231–32, 302, 306–7, 313

Yu *ding* 寓鼎 (JC: 2756): *fp. Zhoucun* 2 (supplement); *nc.* 40 (1 compound);
co. Shanghai Museum; *dt.* early–middle Western Zhou.

Summary: The king commemorates Yu's deeds and rewards him.

Index: 310

Yu *ding* 禹鼎 (JC: 2833): *ds.* 1942; *pd.* Renjiacun, Fufeng county, Shaanxi;
fp. Luyi 99; *nc.* 204 (3 repetition marks); *co.* National Museum of
China, Beijing; *dt.* late Western Zhou.

Summary: Under Duke Wu's orders, Yu puts down a rebellion led by
the "Border Protector," the ruler of E.

Index: 18 n. 69, 47–48, 48 n. 10, 140, 155 n. 14, 183

Yu *fangding* 圉方鼎: *ds.* 1973–7; *pd.* Liulihe, Fangshan county, Beijing;
fp. Liulihe, pp. 101–2, 110; *nc.* 14; *co.* Beijing Municipal Institute of
Cultural Relics; *dt.* early Western Zhou.

Summary: The ruler of Yan awards Yu cowries.

Index: 259

Yu *gui* 遹簋 (JC: 4207): *ds.* 1910; *pd.* Shaanxi; *fp. Zhoucun* 3.40; *nc.* 53
(5 repetition marks); *co.* Palace Museum, Taipei; *dt.* middle Western
Zhou (King Mu).

Summary: King Mu conducts fishing at the Great Pond at Pangjing;
the king personally bestows a reward upon Yu.

Index: 56 n. 30, 310

Yu *gui* 圉簋: *ds.* 1973–7; *pd.* Liulihe, Fangshan county, Beijing; *fp. Liulihe,*
pp. 134–35, 148–51; *nc.* 14 (cover), 6 (vessel); *co.* Beijing Municipal
Institute of Cultural Relics; *dt.* early Western Zhou.

Summary: When the king conducts the *hui*-entreaty rite at Chengzhou,
he awards Yu cowries (cover); Bo Yu casts a precious vessel (vessel).

Index: 259

Yu *jue* 盂爵 (JC: 9104): *fp. Jungu* 2.3.3; *nc.* 21; *dt.* early Western Zhou.

Summary: When the king first performs the entreaty rite, he commands Yu to pacify Dengbo, awarding him cowries.

Index: 257 n. 50

Yu Sikou hu 虞嗣寇壺 (JC: 9694): *fp. Jungu* 2.3.30–31; *nc.* 22 (2 repetition
marks); *co.* Palace Museum, Beijing (cover); *dt.* late Western Zhou.

Summary: Bo Chui, Supervisor of Lawsuits of the state of Yu, casts a
hu-vessel.

Index: 93

Yu *yan* 圉甗: *ds.* 1973–7; *pd.* Liulihe, Fangshan county, Beijing; *fp. Liulihe,*
pp. 147, 165–66; *nc.* 14; *co.* Beijing Municipal Institute of Cultural
Relics; *dt.* early Western Zhou.

Summary: When the king conducts the *hui*-entreaty rite at Chengzhou, he awards Yu cowries.

Index: 259

Yu *you* 圉卣: *ds.* 1973–7; *pd.* Liulihe, Fangshan county, Beijing; *fp. Liulihe,*
pp. 183, 186–89; *nc.* 14; *co.* Beijing Municipal Institute of Cultural
Relics; *dt.* early Western Zhou.

Summary: When the king conducts the *hui*-entreaty rite at Chengzhou,
he awards Yu cowries (cover); Bo Yu casts a precious vessel (vessel).

Index: 259

Yuan *pan* 寰盤 (JC: 10172): *fp. Jigu* 8.9; *nc.* 101 (2 repetition marks); *co.*
Palace Museum, Beijing; *dt.* late Western Zhou.

Summary: The king commands that Yuan be awarded various valuable accoutrements.

Index: 91, 109 n. 23, 109 n. 26, 112 n. 33, 125, 266 n. 67, 312

Yushi Jing *gui* 御史競簋 (JC: 4134): *ds.* 1925 or 1926; *pd.* Miaoguo, Luoyang, Henan; *fp. Zhensong* 5.40; *nc.* 32; *co.* Royal Ontario Museum,
Toronto; *dt.* early Western Zhou.

Summary: Bo Xifu acknowledges Scribe Jing's merits and rewards him
with bronze.

Index: 56 n. 28, 310

Zai Chen *ding* 宰僕鼎 (JC: 2010): *fp. Qing'ai* 13; *nc.* 5; *dt.* early Western
Zhou.

Summary: Superintendent Chen makes a *ding*-vessel for Father Ding.

Index: 59

Zai *gui* 䣄簋 (JC: 4255): *pd.* Fufeng; *fp. Kaogutu* 3.22; *nc.* 70 (2 repetition marks); *dt.* late Western Zhou.

Summary: The king appoints Zai as Supervisor of Land and commands him to oversee the Spring Plowing Ritual.

Index: 71, 91, 129, 211, 306

Zai Hao *jiao* 宰槵角 (JC: 9105): *ds.* 1997; *fp. Shiliu* 1.9; *nc.* 29 (1 compound); *co.* Senoku Museum, Kyoto; *dt.* Shang.

Summary: Superintendent Hao receives cowries from the Shang king and casts a vessel for Father Ding.

Index: 28 n. 18, 59 n. 38, 311

Zai Shou *gui* 宰獸簋 (JL: 490): *ds.* 1997; *pd.* Datongcun, Fufeng county, Shaanxi; *fp. Wenwu* 1998.8, 83; *nc.* 128 (1 repetition mark); *co.* Zhouyuan Museum, Shaanxi; *dt.* middle Western Zhou.

Summary: The current king extends Zai Shou's mission, commanding him to succeed his grandfather and father and to take charge of the royal servants and retainers in the Kang Palace.

Index: 69, 119, 121, 125, 132 n. 72, 136 n. 75, 146, 154, 205

Zha *zhong* 柞鐘 (JC: 134): *ds.* 1960; *pd.* Qijia, Fufeng county, Shaanxi; *fp. Wenwu* 1961.7, 59; *nc.* 45 (3 repetition marks); *co.* Shaanxi Provincial Museum; *dt.* late Western Zhou.

Summary: Zha is appointed to govern affairs of farmers in the Five Cities; Zhong Taishi presides as *youzhe*.

Index: 128, 146–47, 164 n. 35, 167, 171, 211, 251 n. 39, 313

Zhabo *ding* 柞伯鼎: *ds.* 2005; *fp. Zhongguo* 2006.6, 67–73; *nc.* 112 (2 compounds); *co.* National Museum of China, Beijing; *dt.* late Western Zhou.

Summary: Guozhong, assisted by Zhabo, leads a military campaign against the settlement of Hun in the south; the ruler of Cai takes part in the operation.

Index: 98 n. 6, 247 n. 23, 267–68

Zhen *yi* 朕匜 (JC: 10285): *ds.* 1975; *pd.* Dongjiacun, Qishan county, Shaanxi; *fp. Wenwu* 1976.5, 42, fig. 24; 43, fig. 30; plate 3:3; *nc.* 154 (3 compounds); *co.* Qishan County Museum, Shaanxi; *dt.* middle Western Zhou.

Summary: In a legal case, Bo Yangfu passes judgment against Muniu in Zhen's favor.

Index: 37 n. 41, 153 n. 8

Zhong Cheng *gui* 仲再簋 (JC: 3747): *fp. Zhensong* 4.45; *nc.* 11; *co.* Art Institute of Chicago; *dt.* early Western Zhou.

Summary: Zhong Cheng makes a vessel for feasting the king.

Index: 15

Zhong Chengfu *gui* 仲再父簋 (JC: 4188): *ds.* 1981; *pd.* Nanyang, Henan; *fp. Zhongyuan* 1984.4, 15; *nc.* 42 (2 repetition marks); *co.* Nanyang Municipal Museum, Henan; *dt.* late Western Zhou.

Summary: Zhong Chengfu, who served the ruler of Southern Shen as Grand Superintendent, casts a vessel in honor of his grandfather, King Yi, and his father, "Inspector Elder."

Index: 250, 252, 254, 312, 314

Zhong *fangding* 中方鼎 no. 1 (JC: 2785): *ds.* 1118; *pd.* Xiaogan county, Hubei; *fp. Bogu* 2.19; *nc.* 57; *dt.* early Western Zhou.

Summary: Zhong receives a royal award of land, administered by the Grand Scribe.

Index: 55, 308

Zhong Jiang ding 仲姜鼎 (JC: 2191): *ds.* 1981; *pd.* Youfangbao, Mei county, Shaanxi; *fp. Kaogu yu wenwu* 1982.2, p. 6, fig. 4; *nc.* 6; *co.* Baoji Municipal Museum; *dt.* middle Western Zhou.

Summary: The king casts a *ding*-vessel for Zhong Jiang.

Index: 153, 153 n. 11

Zhong Jifu *gui* 仲幾父簋 (JC: 3954): *fp. Jungu* 2.2.62; *nc.* 18; *dt.* late Western Zhou.

Summary: Scribe Ji of Zhong Jifu is sent as an envoy from the royal court to the "Many Inspectors of the Many Regional Rulers."

Index: 251, 314

Zhong *yan* 中甗 (JC: 949): *ds.* 1118; *pd.* Xiaogan county, Hubei; *fp. Lidai* 16.2, 172; *nc.* 100; *dt.* early Western Zhou.

Summary: Zhong inspects the Zhou military encampment in the south. The king sends Scribe Er with further orders requiring Zhong to visit various states.

Index: 56, 309

Zhongqi *xu* 仲齊盨 (JC: 4440): *ds.* 1977; *pd.* Qufu county, Shandong; *fp. Qufu*, p. 149, figs. 95.1–2; *nc.* 26 (2 repetition marks); *co.* Qufu County Committee for the Management of Cultural Relics, Shandong; *dt.* Spring and Autumn.

Summary: Zhongqi, Supervisor of Land for the state of Lu, casts a vessel for his deceased father Bo Zoufu.

Index: 249, 306

Zhou Situ *zun* 盩司土尊 (JC: 5917): *fp. Zhensong* 7.15; *nc.* 9; *co.* Palace Museum, Beijing; *dt.* early or middle Western Zhou.

Summary: You, Supervisor of Land for Zhou 盩, makes a vessel for Grandfather Xin.

Index: 54 n. 23, 306

Zou *gui* 走簋 (JC: 4244): *fp. Xiqingjia* 12.44; *nc.* 67 (2 repetition marks); *dt.* middle Western Zhou.

Summary: The king commands Zou to assist X.

Index: 127, 210, 308, 311

Zuoce Ban *yuan* 作冊般黿: *ds.* 2005; *fp. Zhongguo* 2005.1, 6–10; *nc.* 32; *co.* National Museum of China, Beijing; *dt.* late Shang.

Summary: The Shang king shoots turtles on the Huan River; Document Maker Ban casts a bronze turtle to commemorate the event.

Index: 28 n. 18

Zuoce Da *fangding* 作冊大方鼎 (JC: 2760): *ds.* 1929; *pd.* Mapo, Luoyang, Henan; *fp. Zhensong* 3.25.2/3.26.1; *nc.* 41; *co.* Palace Museum, Taipei; *dt.* early Western Zhou (King Kang).

Summary: The Duke and Great Protector, who has cast a great *ding* vessel dedicated to Kings Wu and Cheng, awards Document Maker Da a white horse.

Index: 57 n. 32, 310

Zuoce Hu *you* 作冊魅卣 (JC: 5432): *pd.* [near Luoyang, Henan]; *fp.* *Duandai* 2. III; pl. 9, fig. 15; *nc.* 63; *co.* Palace Museum, Beijing; *dt.* early Western Zhou.

Summary: The Duke Grand Scribe inspects various officials at Zongzhou. The king sends him on a new assignment, and he rewards Document Maker Hu with horses at Feng.

Index: 56, 57 n. 32, 308, 310

Zuoce Huan *you* 作冊睘卣 (JC: 5407): *fp.* *Yunqing* 2.44; *nc.* 33 (2 repetition marks); *dt.* early Western Zhou.

Summary: Queen Jiang commands Huan to pacify the Elder of Yi.

Index: 12, 57, 310

Zuoce Huan *zun* 作冊睘尊 (JC: 5989): *fp.* *Jungu* 2.3.50; *nc.* 25 (2 repetition marks); *co.* Palace Museum, Taipei; *dt.* early Western Zhou.

Summary: Queen Jiang commands Huan to pacify the Elder of Yi.

Index: 12

Zuoce Zhe *zun* 作冊折尊 (JC: 6002): *ds.* 1976; *pd.* Zhuangbai, Fufeng county, Shaanxi; *fp.* *Wenwu* 1978.3, pl. 3:1; *nc.* 42; *co.* Zhouyuan Museum, Shaanxi; *dt.* early Western Zhou.

Summary: The king commands Document Maker Zhe to confer the land of Wang upon the ruler of Xiang.

Index: 57, 310

Zuoce Zi *you* 作冊䚄卣 (JC: 5400): *ds.* 1929; *pd.* Mapo, Luoyang, Henan; *fp.* *Zhensong* 8.29; *nc.* 26; *co.* Shanghai Museum; *dt.* early Western Zhou.

Summary: When Mingbao has an audience with the king at Chengzhou, he rewards Document Maker Zi.

Index: 57 n. 32, 310

ABBREVIATIONS

Bogu: *Xuanhe bogu tu* 宣和博古圖 (or *Bogu tulu* 博古圖錄) (ed. Wang Fu 王黼 *et al.*), 30 *juan*, ca. 1110 (preface after 1123; Jiang Yang edition, 1528).

Conggu: *Conggu tang kuanzhi xue* 從古堂款識學 (Xu Tongbai 徐同柏), 16 *juan*, Shanghai: Tongwen shuju, 1886 (preface by Ruan Yuan 阮元, 1839).

Congkao: *Jinwen congkao* 金文叢考 (Guo Moruo 郭沫若), 3 vols., Tokyo: Bunkyūdō, 1932 (revised, 1954).

Duandai: "Xi Zhou tongqi duandai I–VI" 西周銅器斷代 (Chen Mengjia 陳夢家), *Kaogu xuebao* 考古學報 9 (1955), 137–75; 10 (1955), 69–142; 1956.1, 65–114; 1956.2, 85–94; 1956.3, 105–278; 1956.4, 85–122.

Erbai: *Erbai lanting zhai suocang jinshi ji* 二百蘭亭齋收藏金石記 (Wu Yun 吳雲), 4 vols., Wushi, 1856.

Eumorfopolous: *The George Eumorfopoulos Collection: Catalogue of the Chinese and Corean Bronzes, Sculpture, Jades, Jewellery and Miscellaneous Objects* (W. Perceval Yetts), London: E. Benn, 1929.

Fufeng: *Fufeng Qijiacun qingtongqi qun* 扶風齊家村青銅器羣 (Shaanxi sheng bowuguan 陝西省博物館), Beijing: Wenwu, 1963.

Guzhou: *Guzhou shiyi* 古籀拾遺 (Sun Yirang 孫詒讓), 3 *juan*, 1888.

Haiwai: *Haiwai jijin tulu* 海外吉金圖錄 (Rong Geng 容庚), 3 vols., Beiping: Yanjing daxue kaoguxue she, 1935.

Haitong: *Haiwai Zhongguo tongqi tulu* 海外中國銅器圖錄 (Chen Mengjia 陳夢家), 2 vols., Beiping: Beiping tushuguan, 1946.

Hengxuan: *Hengxuan suojian suocang jijin lu* 恆軒所見所藏吉金錄 (Wu Dacheng 吳大澂), 2 vols., 1885.

Huaimi: *Huaimi shanfang jijin tu* 懷米山房吉金圖 (Cao Zaikui 曹載奎), 2 *juan*, Wuxian, Caoshi, 1839 (Japanese edition, Kyoto: Bunsekidō, 1882).

Jianghan: *Jianghan kaogu* 江漢考古.

Jicheng: *Yin Zhou jinwen jicheng* 殷周金文集成, 18 vols. (Institute of Archeology, CASS), Beijing: Zhonghua, 1984–94.

Jigu: *Jigu zhai zhongding yiqi kuanzhi* 積古齋鐘鼎彞器欵識 (Ruan Yuan 阮元), 10 *juan*, 1804 (reprint, Wuchang: Chongwen shuju, 1879).

Jiwei: *Jiweiju jinwen shuo* 積微居金文說 (Yang Shuda 楊樹達), Beijing: Kexue, 1952 (supplemented, Beijing: Zhonghua 1997).

Jungu: *Jungu lu jinwen* 攈古錄金文 (Wu Shifen 吳式芬), 9 vols., Haifeng: Wushi, 1895 (completed before 1956).

Junxian: *Junxian yiqi* 濬縣彞器 (Sun Haibo 孫海波), Henan: Tongzhiguan, 1937.

Kanka: *Kankarō kikin zu* 冠斝樓吉金圖 (ed. Umehara Sueji 梅原末治), Kyoto: Kobayashi shuppanbu, 1947.

Kaogu: *Kaogu* 考古.

Kaogu xuebao: *Kaogu xuebao* 考古学报.

Kaogu yu wenwu: *Kaogu yu wenwu* 考古與文物.

Kaogutu: *Kaogu tu* 考古圖 (Lü Dalin 呂大臨), 10 *juan*, 1092 (Dade edition, 1299; Boruzhai edition, 1368).

Kezhai: *Kezhai jigu lu* 愙齋集古錄 (Wu Dacheng 吳大澂), 26 vols., Shanghai: Hanfenlou, 1918 (preface 1896).

Liangzhou: *Liang Zhou jinwen ci daxi tulu kaoshi* 兩周金文辭大系圖錄考釋 (Guo Moruo 郭沫若), 8 vols., Tokyo: Bunkyūdō, 1935 (reprint, Beijing: Kexue, 1958).

Lidai: *Lidai zhongding yiqi kuanzhi fatie* 歷代鐘鼎彞器款識法帖 (Xue Shanggong 薛尚功), 20 *juan*, stone edition, 1144 (Wanyue shanren edition, 1588).

Lishuo: *Jinwen lishuo shuzheng* 金文歷朔疏証 (Wu Qichang 吳其昌), 2 vols., Shanghai: Shangwu, 1936.

Liulihe: *Liulihe Xi Zhou yan guo mudi* 琉璃河西周燕國墓地 (Beijing shi wenwu yanjiusuo 北京市文物研究所), Beijing: Wenwu Press, 1995.

London: The Chinese Exhibition: A Commemorative Catalogue of the International Exhibition of Chinese Art, Royal Academy of Arts, November 1935–March 1936. London: Faber and Faber, 1936.

Luyi: Shang Zhou jinwen luyi 商周金文錄遺 (Yu Xingwu 于省吾), 1 vol., Beijing: Kexue, 1957.

Mingwenxuan: Shang Zhou qingtongqi mingwen xuan 商周青銅器銘文選 (Ma Chengyuan 馬承源) 4 vols., Beijing: Wenwu, 1986–90.

Neimenggu: Neimenggu wenwu kaogu 內蒙古文物考古.

Ningshou: Ningshou jiangu 寧壽鑑古 (Qianlong Emperor), 16 *juan*, Shanghai: Hanfenlou, 1913 (completed before 1779).

Qigu: Qigu shi jijin wenshu 奇觚室吉金文述 (Liu Xinyuan 劉心源), 20 *juan*, China: 1902.

Pangu: Pangu lou yiqi kuanzhi 攀古廔彝器款識 (Pan Zuyin 潘祖蔭), 2 vols., Beijing: Pangxi zhai, 1872.

Qing'ai: Qing'ai tang jiacang zhongding yiqi kuanzhi fatie 清愛堂家藏鐘鼎彝器款識法帖 (Liu Xihai 劉喜海), 1 *juan*, 1838.

Qufu: Qufu Lu guo gucheng 曲阜魯國故城 (Shandong sheng wenwu kaogu yanjiusuo 山東省文物考古研究所 *et al*), Jinan: Qilu, 1982.

Renwen: Renwen zazhi 人文雜誌.

Sandai: Sandai jijin wencun 三代吉金文存 (Luo Zhenyu 羅振玉), 20 *juan*, Baijuezhai, 1936.

Sen'oku: Sen'oku seishō 泉屋清賞 (Hamada Kōsaku 浜田耕作) 6 vols., Japan, 1919.

Shaanxi: Shaanxi chutu Shang Zhou qingtongqi 陝西出土商周青銅器, 4 vols. (Shaanxi sheng kaogu yanjiusuo 陝西省考古研究所 *et al.*), Beijing: Wenwu, 1979–84.

Shanghai: Shanghai bowuguan cang qingtongqi 上海博物館藏青銅器 (Shanghai bowuguan 上海博物館), 2 vols., Shanghai: Renmin, 1964.

Shanghai jikan: Shanghai bowuguan jikan 上海博物館集刊.

Shanzhai: Shanzhai yiqi tulu 善齋彝器圖錄 (Rong Geng 容庚), Beiping: Harvard-Yenching Institute, 1936.

Shengshi: Shengshi jijin: Shaanxi Baoji Meixian qingtongqi jiaocang 盛世吉金: 陝西寶鷄眉縣青銅器窖藏 (Shaanxi sheng wenwuju 陝西省文物局), Beijing: Beijing chubanshe, 2003.

Shiliu: Shiliu changle tang guqi kuanzhi kao 十六長樂堂古器款試考 (Qian Dian 錢坫), 4 *juan*, 2 vols., 1796 (reprint, Shanghai: Kaiming shuju, 1933).

Shouxian: Shouxian Caihou mu chutu yiwu 壽縣蔡侯墓出土遺物 (Anhui sheng wenwu guanli weiyuanhui 安徽省文物管理委員會 *et al.*), Beijing: Kexue, 1956.

Taozhai: Taozhai jijin lu 陶齋吉金錄 (Duan Fang 端方), 8 *juan*, Shanghai: Youzheng shuju, 1908.

Tongkao: Shang Zhou yiqi tongkao 商周彝器通考 (Rong Geng 容庚), 2 vols., Beiping: Harvard-Yenching Institute, 1940.

Tsūshaku: "Kinbun tsūshaku" 金文通釈 (Shirakawa Shizuka 白川静), *Hakutsuru bijutsukanshi* 白鶴美術館誌, 56 vols., Kobe, 1966–83.

Tushi: *Qingtongqi tushi* 青銅器圖釋 (Shaanxi sheng bowuguan 陝西省博物館 and Shaanxi sheng wenwu guanli weiyuanhui 陝西省文物管理委員會), Beijing: Wenwu, 1960.

Weihua: *Weihua ge jigu lu bawei* 韡華閣集古錄跋尾 (Ke Changji 柯昌濟), 15 *juan*, 1935 (compiled 1916).

Wencan: *Wenwu cankao ziliao* 文物參考資料.

Wenge: *Wenhua dageming qijian chutu wenwu* 文化大革命期間出土文物 (Zhanlan gongzuozu 展覽工作組), vol. 1, Beijing: Wenwu, 1972.

Wenlu: *Jijin wenlu* 吉金文錄 (Wu Kaisheng 吳闓生), 1932.

Wenxuan: *Shuangjian chi jijin wenxuan* 雙劍誃吉金文選 (Yu Xingwu 于省吾), Beijing: 1933.

Wenwu: *Wenwu* 文物.

Xiqing: *Xiqing gujian* 西清古鑒 (ed. Liang Shizheng 梁詩正 *et al.*), 40 *juan*, Beijing: Qing Court (Wuyingdian), 1755 (reprint, Shanghai: Hongwen shuju, 1888).

Xiqingjia: *Xiqing xujian jia bian* 西清續鑑甲編 (ed. Wang Jie 王傑 *et al.*), 20 *juan* (supplement: 1 *juan*), Shanghai: Hanfenlou, 1910 (completed 1793).

Xiqingyi: *Xiqing xujian yi bian* 西清續鑑乙編 (ed. Wang Jie 王傑 *et al.*), 20 *juan*, Beiping: Beiping guwu chenliesuo 1931 (completed 1793).

Yin and Chou: Karlgren, Bernhard, "Yin and Chou in Chinese Bronzes," *Bulletin of the Museum of Far Eastern Antiquities* 8 (1936).

Yunqing: *Yunqing guan jinwen* 筠清舘金文 (Wu Rongguang 吳榮光), 5 *juan*, Yunqing guan, 1842.

Zhenbu: *Zhensong tang jigu yiwen buyi* 貞松堂集古遺文補遺 (Luo Zhenyu 羅振玉), 3 juan, 1931.

Zhensong: *Zhensong tang jigu yiwen* 貞松堂集古遺文 (Luo Zhenyu 羅振玉), 16 *juan*, 1930.

Zhongguo: *Zhongguo lishi wenwu* 中國歷史文物.

Zhongyuan: *Zhongyuan wenwu* 中原文物, Zhengzhou: Zhongyuan wenwu bianji bu.

Zhoucun: *Zhou jinwen cun* 周金文存 (Zou An 鄒安), 6 *juan*, Shanghai: Cangsheng mingzhi daxue, 1916.

Zhuigao: *Zhuiyi zhai yiqi kuanzhi kaoshi gaoben* 綴遺齋彝器款識考釋稿本 (Rong Geng 容庚), manuscript.

Zhuiyi: *Zhuiyi zhai yiqi kuanzhi kaoshi* 綴遺齋彝器款識考釋 (Fang Junyi 方濬益), 30 *juan*, Shanghai: Hanfenlou, 1935 (completed 1894).

Zungu: *Zungu zhai suojian jijin tu chuji* 尊古齋所見吉金圖初集 (Huang Jun), 4 *juan*, Beijing: Zunguzhai, 1936.

Bibliography

Albrow, Martin, *Bureaucracy*, New York: Praeger Publishers, 1970.

The Analects of Confucius, trans. Arthur Waley, New York: Vintage Books, 1938.

Akatsuka, Kiyoshi 赤塚忠, "In kinbun" 殷金文, in *Chūgoku kodai no shūkyō to bunka* 中國古代の宗教と文化, Tokyo: Kadokawa shoten, 1977, pp. 615–835.

Aylmer, G. E., "Review: *The History of Government from the Earliest Times. Vol. I: Ancient Monarchies and Empires. Vol. II: The Intermediate Ages. Vol. III: Empires, Monarchies and the Modern State* (by S. E. Finer)," *The English Historical Review* 113.453 (1998), 953–55.

Bagley, Robert, "Shang Archaeology," in *The Cambridge History of Ancient China: From the Origins of Civilization to 221 BC,* ed. Michael Loewe and Edward L. Shaughnessy, Cambridge: Cambridge University Press, 1999, pp. 124–25.

 ed., *Ancient Sichuan: Treasures from a Lost Civilization,* Princeton: Princeton University Press, 2001.

Bailey, Donald A., "Review: *The History of Government from the Earliest Times* (by S. E. Finer)," *Sixteenth Century Journal* 30.2 (1999), 601–3.

Balazs, Etienne, *Chinese Civilization and Bureaucracy: Variations on a Theme,* New Haven: Yale University Press, 1964.

Barbieri-Low, Anthony J., *Wheeled Vehicles in the Chinese Bronze-Age (c. 2000-741 BC)* (Sino-Platonic Papers no. 99), Philadelphia: University of Pennsylvania, 2000.

Beetham, David, *Bureaucracy,* 2nd edn, Minneapolis: University of Minnesota, 1996.

Behera, Subhakanta, *Nation-State: Problems and Perspectives,* New Delhi: Sanchar Publishing House, 1995.

Bendix, Richard, "Bureaucracy," in *International Encyclopedia of the Social Sciences,* ed. David Sills, New York: Crowell and Macmillan, 1968, pp. 206–7.

Bielenstein, Hans, *The Bureaucracy of Han Times,* New York: Cambridge University Press, 1980.

Blakeley, Barry, "Regional Aspects of Chinese Socio-Political Development in the Spring and Autumn Period (722–464 BC): Clan Power in a Segmentary State," unpublished PhD thesis, University of Michigan, 1970.

 "On the 'Feudal' Interpretation of Chou China," *Early China* 2 (1976), 35–37.

 "King, Clan, and Courtier in Ancient Ch'u," *Asia Major* 3.5.2 (1992), 1–39.

Bloch, Marc, *Feudal Society,* trans. L. A. Manyon, London: Routledge & Kegan Paul, 1961.

Bodde, Derk, "Feudalism in China," in *Essays on Chinese Civilization,* Princeton: Princeton University Press, 1981, pp. 85–131.

Brown, Elizabeth A. R., "The Tyranny of a Construct: Feudalism and Historians of Medieval Europe," *The American Historical Review* 79.4 (1974), 1063–88.

Cao, Wei 曹瑋, *Zhouyuan jiaguwen* 周原甲骨文, Beijing: Shijie tushu, 2002.

"Yetan jinwen zhong de Zhou" 也談金文中的周, in *Zhouyuan yizhi yu Xi Zhou qingtongqi* 周原遺址與西周青銅器, Beijing: Kexue, 2004, pp. 107–30.

Zhouyuan yizhi yu Xi Zhou qingtongqi 周原遺址與西周青銅器, Beijing: Kexue, 2004.

Chang, Kwang-Chih, *Early Chinese Civilization: Anthropological Perspectives*, Cambridge, MA: Harvard University Press, 1976.

Shang Civilization, New Haven: Yale University Press, 1980.

Art, Myth, and Ritual: The Path to Political Authority in Ancient China, Boston: Harvard University Press, 1983.

Charlton, Thomas H., and Deborah L. Nichols, "The City-State Concept: Development and Applications," in *The Archaeology of City-States: Cross-Cultural Approaches*, Washington: Smithsonian Institution Press, 1997, pp. 1–14.

Chen, Changyuan 陳昌遠, "Zhou dai jingtian zhidu jianlun" 周代井田制度簡論, in *Xian Qin shi lunwenji* 先秦史論文集, Xi'an: Renwen zazhi, 1982, pp. 141–53.

Chen, Fudeng 陳复澄, and Wang Hui 王輝, "Jijian tongqi mingwen zhong fanying de Xi Zhou zhongye de tudi jiaoyi" 幾件銅器銘文中反映的西周中葉的土地交易, *Liaohai wenwu xuekan* 遼遼文物學刊 1986.2, 77–85.

Chen, Gongruo 陳公柔, "Ji Jifu hu Zha zhong jiqi tongchu de tongqi" 記幾父壺柞鐘及其同出的銅器, *Kaogu* 1962.2, 88–101. Printed in Chen Gongruo, *Xian Qin liang Han kaoguxue luncong* 先秦兩漢考古學論叢, Beijing: Wenwu, 2005, pp. 71–78.

"Xi Zhou jinwen zhong de Xinyi Chengzhou yu Wangcheng" 西周金文中的新邑成周與王城, in *Qingzhu Su Binqi xiansheng kaogu wushiwu nian lunwenji* 慶祝蘇秉琦先生考古五十五年論文集, Beijing: Wenwu, 1989, pp. 386–97 (reprinted in Chen Gongruo, *Xian Qin liang Han kaoguxue luncong* 先秦兩漢考古學論叢, Beijing: Wenwu, 2005, pp. 33–48).

Chen, Gongruo 陳公柔, and Zhang Changshou 張長壽, "Yin Zhou qingtong rongqi shang niaowen de duandai yanjiu," 殷周青銅容器上鳥紋的斷代研究, *Kaogu xuebao* 1984.3, 268–69.

Chen, Hanping 陳漢平, *Xi Zhou ceming zhidu yanjiu* 西周冊命制度研究, Beijing: Xuelin, 1986.

Jinwen bian dingbu 金文編訂補, Beijing: Zhongguo shehui kexue, 1993.

Chen, Mengjia 陳夢家, *Xi Zhou niandai kao* 西周年代考, Shanghai: Shangwu, 1945.

"Xi Zhou tongqi duandai I–VI" 西周銅器斷代, *Kaogu xuebao* 考古學報 9 (1955), 137–75; 10 (1955), 69–142; (1956.1), 65–114; (1956.2), 85–94; (1956.3), 105–278; (1956.4), 85–122.

Yinxu buci zongshu 殷墟卜辭綜述, Beijing: Kexue Press, 1956.

Chen, Pan 陳槃, *Chunqiu dashi biao lieguo juexing ji cunmie biao zhuanyi* 春秋大事表列國爵姓及存滅表譔異, Taipei: Academia Sinica, 1969.

Chen, Peifen 陳佩芬, *Xia Shang Zhou qingtongqi yanjiu* 夏商周青銅器研究, 6 vols., Shanghai: Shanghai Guji, 2004.

Chen, Zhi 陳直, *Hanshu xinzheng* 漢書新証, Tianjin: Tianjin renmin, 1959.

Chinese Archaeology (Beijing, Institute of Archaeology, CASS), 4 (2004), 29–33, "Inscribed Oracle Bones of the Shang Period Unearthed from the Daxinzhuang Site in Jinan City."

The Chinese Exhibition: A Commemorative Catalogue of the International Exhibition of Chinese Art, Royal Academy of Arts, November 1935–March 1936. London: Faber and Faber, 1936.

Chu, Ren 楚刃, "Xi Zhou meiyou shiqing shilu zhidu ma?" 西周沒有世卿世祿制度嗎? *Jinyang xuekan* 晉陽學刊 1985.5, 30, 86–87.

Conggu tang kuanzhi xue 從古堂款識學 (Xu Tongbai 徐同柏), 16 *juan*, Shanghai: Tongwen shuju, 1886 (preface by Ruan Yan 阮元, 1839).

Creel, Herrlee, "Bronze Inscriptions of the Western Chou Dynasty as Historical Documents," *Journal of the American Oriental Society* (1936), 335–49.

   "The Beginning of Bureaucracy in China: The Origins of the *Hsien*," *Journal of Asian Studies* 22 (1964), 155–83.

   The Origins of Statecraft in China, vol. 1: *The Western Chou Empire*, Chicago: University of Chicago Press, 1970.

Cui, Lequan 崔樂泉, "Shandong diqu Dong Zhou kaoguxue wenhua de xulie" 山東地區東周考古學的序列, *Huaxia Kaogu* 華夏考古 1992.4, 73–97.

Deng, Delong 鄧德龍, *Zhongguo lidai guanzhi* 中國歷代官制, Wuhan: Wuhan daxue, 1990.

Ding, Shan 丁山, "Zha yi kao" 斝夷考, *Zhongyang yanjiuyuan lishi yuyan yanjiusuo jikan* 中央研究院歷史語言研究所集刊 2.4 (1932), 419–22.

Ding, Yi 丁乙 (Zhang Changshou 張長壽), "Zhouyuan de jianzhu yicun he qingtongqi jiaocang" 周原的建築遺存和青銅器窖藏, *Kaogu* 1982.4, 398–401.

Dirlik, Arif, *Revolution and History: The Origins of Marxist Historiography in China, 1919–1937*, Berkeley: University of California Press, 1978.

Du, Jianmin 杜建民, "Xi Zhou tudi zhidu xintan" 西周土地制度新探, *Shixue yuekan* 1992.2, 15–27.

Du, Zhengsheng 杜正勝, *Zhou dai chengbang* 周代城邦, Taipei: Lianjing, 1979.

Duan, Yucai 段玉裁, *Shuowen jiezi zhu* 說文解字注, Shanghai: Shanghai Guji, 1981.

Eberhard, Wolfram, *A History of China*, Berkeley: University of California Press, 1950.

Eisenstadt, S. N., *The Political Systems of Empires*, London: Free Press of Glencoe, 1963.

Emura, Haruki 江村治樹, "Kodai toshi shakai" 古代都市社會, in *In Shū Shin Kan jidaishi no kihon mondai* 殷周秦漢時代史の基本問題, ed. Matsumaru Michio 松丸道雄 *et al.*, Tokyo: Kyūko shoin, 2001, pp. 27–61.

Engels, Frederick, *The Origin of the Family, Private Property and the State*, ed. and intro. Eleanor Burke Leacock, New York: International Publishers, 1972.

Erbai lanting zhai shoucang jinshi ji 二百蘭亭齋收藏金石記 (Wu Yun 吳雲), 4 vols., Wushi, 1856.

Falkenhausen, Lothar von (see also Luo Tai 羅泰), *Suspended Music: Chime-Bells in the Culture of Bronze Age China*, Berkeley: University of California Press, 1993.

   "Issues in Western Zhou Studies: A Review Article," *Early China* 18 (1993), 139–226.

   "Reflections on the Political Roles of Spirit Medium in Early China: The Wu officials in the Zhou Li," *Early China* 20 (1995), 279–300.

   "Late Western Zhou Taste," *Études chinoises* 18 (1999), 143–78.

   "The Waning of the Bronze Age," in *The Cambridge History of Ancient China: From the Origins of Civilization to 221 BC,* ed. Michael Loewe and Edward L. Shaughnessy, pp. 292–351, Cambridge: Cambridge University Press, 1999.

Chinese Society in the Age of Confucius (1000–250 BC): The Archeological Evidence, Los Angeles: Cotsen Institute of Archaeology, UCLA, 2006.

Feinman, Gary M., and Joyce Marcus, eds., *Archaic States*, Santa Fe: School of American Research Press, 1998.

Finer, S. E., *The History of Government from the Earliest Times*, vol. 1: *Ancient Monarchies and Empires*, Oxford: Oxford University Press, 1997.

Finley, M. I., *The Ancient Economy*, updated with foreword by Ian Morris, Berkeley: University of California Press, 1999.

Fitzgerald, C. P., *China: A Short Cultural History*, New York: D. Appleton-Century Company, 1938.

Fox, John W., Garrett W. Cook, Arlen F. Chase, and Diane Z. Chase, "Questions of Political and Economic Integration: Segmentary versus Centralized States among the Ancient Maya," *Current Anthropology* 37.5 (1996), 795–801.

The Freer Chinese Bronzes, 2 vols. (by John Alexander Pope, Rutherford John Gettens, James Cahill, and Noel Barnard), Washington, DC: Smithsonian Institution, 1967.

Fufeng Qijiacun qingtongqi qun 扶風齊家村青銅器群 (Shaanxi sheng bowuguan 陝西省博物館), Beijing: Wenwu, 1963.

Ganshof, F. L., *Feudalism*, trans. Philip Grierson, New York: Harper & Row, 1964.

Gao, Hongjin 高鴻縉, "Mao Gong ding jishi" 毛公鼎集釋, *Shida xuebao* 師大學報 1 (1956), 67–109.

Gaocheng Taixi Shang dai yizhi 藁城台西商代遺址 (Hebei sheng wenwu yanjiusuo 河北省文物研究所), Beijing: Wenwu, 1985.

Garnsey, Peter, and Richard Saller, *The Roman Empire: Economy, Society, and Culture*, Berkeley: University of California Press, 1987.

The George Eumorfopoulos Collection: Catalogue of the Chinese and Corean Bronzes, Sculpture, Jades, Jewellery and Miscellaneous Objects (W. Perceval Yetts), London: E. Benn, 1929.

Granet, Marcel, *Chinese Civilization*, trans. Kathleem E. Inns and Mabel R. Brailsford, London: Kegan Paul, Trench, Trubner, 1930.

La Féodalité chinoise, Paris: H. Aschehoug & Co., 1952.

Gu, Derong 顧德融, and Zhu Shunlong 朱順龍, *Chunqiu shi* 春秋史, Shanghai: Shiji Press, 2001.

Gu, Donggao 顧棟高, "Chunqiu lieguo guanzhi biao" 春秋列國官制表, in *Chunqiu dashi biao* 春秋大事表, pp. 1033–1123, Beijing: Zhonghua Press, 1993.

Gugong qingtongqi 故宮青銅器 (Palace Museum, Beijing), Beijing: Zijincheng, 1999.

Gugong tongqi tulu 故宮銅器圖錄 2 vols. (Guoli gugong zhongyan bowuyuan lianhe guanlichu 國立故宮中央博物院聯合管理處), Taipei: Palace Museum, 1958.

Guo, Moruo 郭沫若, "Zhouguan zhiyi" 周官質疑, in *Jinwen congkao* 金文叢攷, Tokyo: Bunkyūdō, 1932, pp. 80–87.

Nulizhi shidai 奴隸制時代, Beijing: Renmin, 1973 (1st edition, 1954).

Jinwen congkao 金文叢考, 3 vols. Tokyo: Bunkyūdō, 1932 (revised 2nd edition, Beijing: Renmin, 1954).

Liang Zhou jinwen ci daxi tulu kaoshi 兩周金文辭大係圖錄考釋, 8 vols., Beijing: Kexue, 1958 (1st edition, Tokyo: Bunkyūdō, 1935).

"Ze gui ming kaoshi" 夨簋銘考釋, *Kaogu xuebao* 1956.1, 7–10.

"Li qi ming kaoshi" 盠器銘考釋, *Kaogu xuebao* 1957.2, 1–6.

"Fu Shi Li gui kaoshi" 輔師嫠簋考釋, *Kaogu xuebao* 1958.2, 1–3.

"Mishu gui ji Xun gui kaoshi" 弭叔簋及詢簋考釋, *Wenwu* 1960.2, 5–9.

"Shi Ying Jian yan" 釋應監甗, *Kaogu xuebao* 1960.1, 7–8.

"Shiguwen yanjiu" 石鼓文研究, in *Guo Moruo quanji: Kaogu bian 9* 郭沫若全集: 考古編, Beijing: Kexue, 1982, pp. 21–244.

Guodian Chu mu zhujian 郭店楚墓竹簡 (Shanghai Museum), Beijing: Wenwu, 1998.

Haiwai jijin tulu 海外吉金圖錄 (Rong Geng 容庚), 3 vols., Beiping: Yanjing daxue kaoguxue she, 1935.

Haiwai Zhongguo tongqi tulu 海外中國銅器圖錄 (Chen Mengjia 陳夢家), 2 vols., Beiping: Beiping tushuguan, 1946.

Hall, Richard H., "The Concept of Bureaucracy: An Empirical Assessment," *The American Journal of Sociology* 69.1 (1963), 32–40.

Han, Lianqi 韓連琪, "Xi Zhou de tudi suoyouzhi he boxue xingtai" 西周的土地所有制和剝削形態, *Zhonghua wenshi luncong* 1 (1979), 81–102.

Hanshu 漢書 (by Ban Gu 班固), 12 vols., Beijing: Zhonghua, 1962.

Hansen, Mogens Herman, ed., *A Comparative Study of Thirty City-State Cultures: An Investigation Conducted by the Copenhagen Polis Centre*, Copenhagen: The Royal Danish Academy of Sciences and Letters, 2000.

Hayashi, Minao 林巳奈夫, *In Shū jidai seidōki no kenkyū* 殷周時代青銅器の研究, Tokyo: Kōbunkan, 1984.

Hayashi, Taisuke 林泰輔, *Shōkō to sono jidai* 周公とその時代, Tokyo: Ōkura shoten, 1916.

He, Ziquan 何茲全, "Zhou dai tudi zhidu he tade yanbian" 周代土地制度和它的演變, *Lishi yanjiu* 歷史研究 1964.3, 145–62.

Hengxuan suojian suocang jijin lu 恆軒所見所藏吉金錄 (Wu Dacheng 吳大澂), 2 vols., 1885.

Hobbes, Thomas, *Leviathan*, ed. and intro. C. B. Macpherson, New York: Penguin Books, 1968.

Hou, Wailu 侯外盧, *Zhongguo gudai shehui shi lun* 中國古代社會史論, Beijing: Renmin, 1955.

Hsu, Cho-yun, *Ancient China in Transition: An Analysis of Social Mobility, 722–222 BC*, Stanford: Stanford University Press, 1965.

"Some Working Notes on the Western Chou Government," *Zhongyang yanjiuyuan lishi yuyan yanjiusuo jikan* 中央研究院歷史語言研究所集刊 36 (1966), 513–24.

"The Spring and Autumn Period," in *The Cambridge History of Ancient China: From the Origins of Civilization to 221 BC*, ed. Michael Loewe and Edward L. Shaughnessy, Cambridge: Cambridge University Press, 1999, pp. 570–76.

Hsu, Cho-yun, and Katheryn Linduff, *Western Chou Civilization*, New Haven: Yale University Press, 1988.

"Hu gui gai ming zuotan jiyao" 虎簋蓋銘座談紀要, *Kaogu yu wenwu* 1997.3, 81.

Hu, Houxuan 胡厚宣, "Yindai Fengjian zhidu kao" 殷代封建制度考, in *Jiagu xue Shang shi luncong: I* 甲骨學商史論叢: 初集, Chengdu: Qi Lu daxue guoxue yanjiusuo, 1944, pp. 31–111.

Huaimi shanfang jijin tu 懷米山房吉金圖 (Cao Zaikui 曹載奎), 2 *juan*, Wuxian, Caoshi, 1839 (Japanese edition, Kyoto: Bunsekidō, 1882).

Huang, Benji 黃本驥, *Lidai zhiguan biao* 歷代職官表, Shanghai: Zhonghua, 1965.

Huang, Mingchong 黃銘崇, "Yindai yu Dongzhou zhi nongqi jiqi yiyi" 殷代與東周之弄器及其意義, *Gujin lunheng* 古今論衡 6 (2001), 67–88.

Huang, Ranwei 黃然伟, *Yin Zhou qingtongqi shangci mingwen yanjiu* 商周青銅器賞賜銘文研究, Hong Kong: Lungmen Bookstore, 1978.

Huang, Shengzhang 黃盛璋, "Tongqi mingwen Yi Yu Ze de diwang jiqi yu Wuguo de guanxi" 銅器銘文宜虞夨的地望與吳國的關係, *Kaogu xuebao* 1983.3, 295–305.

"Pu yu xinkao" 逋盂新考, *Renwen zazhi* 1982.5, 98–102.

Huang, Zhanyue 黃展岳, "Han Chang'an cheng nanjiao lizhi jianzhu de weizhi jiqi youguan wenti" 漢長安城南郊禮制建築的位置及其有關問題, *Kaogu* 1960.9, 52–58.

Iijima, Taketsugu 飯島武次, *Chūgoku Shū bunka kōkogaku kenkyū* 中国周文化考古学研究, Tokyo: Dōseisha, 1998.

Itō, Michiharu 伊藤道治, *Chūgoku kodai ōchō no keisei* 中国古代王朝の形成, Tokyo: Sōbunsha, 1975.

"Kyūei shoki kō: Sei-Shū ki tochi shoyū keitai ni kansuru shiken" 裘衛諸器考--西周期土地所有形態に関する私見, *Tōyōshi kenkyū* 37.1 (1978), 35–58.

Chūgoku kodai kokka no shihai kōzō 中国古代王朝の支配構造, Tokyo: Chūō kōronsha, 1987.

Jianghan kaogu 江漢考古.

Jigu zhai zhongding yiqi kuanzhi 積古齋鐘鼎彝器欵識 (Ruan Yuan 阮元), 10 *juan*, 1804 (reprint, Wuchang: Chongwen shuju, 1879).

Jijin wenlu 吉金文錄 (Wu Kaisheng 吳闓生), 1932.

Jin, Jingfang 金景芳, *Gushi lunji* 古史論集, Jinan: Qilu, 1982.

Jinchu Yin Zhou jinwen jilu 近出殷周金文集录, 4 vols. (Liu Yu 劉雨 and Lu Yan 盧岩), Beijing: Zhonghua, 2002.

Jones, A. H. M., *The Later Roman Empire 284–602*, 2 vols., Oxford: Basil Blackwell, 1964 (reprint, Baltimore: Johns Hopkins University Press, 1992).

Jungu lu jinwen 攗古錄金文 (Wu Shifen 吳式芬), 9 vols., Haifeng: Wushi, 1895 (completed before 1956).

Junxian yiqi 濬縣彝器 (Sun Haibo 孫海波), Henan: Tongzhiguan, 1937.

Kaizuka, Shigeki 貝塚茂樹, *Chūgoku no kodai kokka* 中国の古代国家, Kōbundō, 1952.

Kamenka, Eugene, *Bureaucracy*, Oxford: Basil Blackwell, 1989.

Kane, Virginia C., "Aspects of Western Chou Appointment Inscriptions: The Charge, the Gifts, and the Response," *Early China* 8 (1982–83), 14–28.

Kankarō kikin zu 冠斝樓吉金圖 (ed. Umehara Sueji 梅原末治), Kyoto: Kobayashi shuppanbu, 1947.

Kaogu 考古 1960.7, 36–39, "Han Chang'an cheng nanjiao lizhi jianzhu jizhi qun fajue jianbao" 漢長安城南郊禮制建築基址群發掘簡報.

1965.9, 447–50, "Shaanxi Chang'an Zhangjiapo Xi Zhou mu qingli jianbao" 陝西長安張家坡西周墓清理簡報.

1986.1, 22–27, "Chang'an Zhangjiapo Xi Zhou Jingshu mu fajue jianbao" 長安張家坡西周井叔墓發掘簡報.

1989.11, 1041–44, "Hubei Yicheng chutu Cai guo qingtongqi" 湖北宜城出土蔡國青銅器.

1990.1, 20–31, "Beijing Liulihe 1193 hao damu fajue jianbao" 北京琉璃河1193號大墓發掘簡報.

1991.10, 910–18, "Shandong Huangxian Guicheng yizhi de diaocha yu fajue" 山東黃縣歸城遺址的調查與發掘.

2002.9, 3–26, "Shaanxi Fufeng xian Yuntang Qizhen Xi Zhou jianzhu jizhi 1999–2000 niandu fajue jianbao" 陝西扶風縣雲塘齊鎮西周建築基址1999–2000年度發掘簡報.

2003.6, 3–6, "Jinan shi Daxinzhuang jizhi chutu Shang dai jiaguwen" 濟南市大辛莊遺址出土商代甲骨文.

2004.1, 3–6, "Shaanxi Zhouyuan yizhi faxian Xi Zhou muzang yu zhutong yizhi" 陝西周原遺址發現西周墓葬與鑄銅遺址.

Kaogu jinghua 考古精華 (Institute of Archeology, CASS), Beijing: Kexue, 1993.

Kaogu nianbao 考古年報 (Shaanxi Provincial Institute of Archeology).

Kaogu tu 考古圖 (Lü Dalin 呂大臨), 10 *juan*, 1092 (Dade edition, 1299; Boruzhai edition, 1368).

Kaogu yu wenwu 考古与文物 1981.4, 27–28, "Mugong gui gai mingwen jianshi" 穆公簋蓋銘文簡釋.

1982.2, 6, "Meixian chutu wang zuo Zhongjiang bao ding" 眉縣出土王作中姜寶鼎.

1986.4, 4–5, "Yaoxian Dingjiagou chutu Xi Zhou jiaocang qingtongqi" 燿縣丁家溝出土西周窖藏青銅器.

1989.3, 7–9. "Shaanxi Ankang shi chutu Xi Zhou Shimi gui" 陝西安康市出土西周史密簋.

1998.3, 69–71, "Shaanxi Chang'an xian chutu Xi Zhou Wu Hu ding" 陝西長安縣出土西周吳虎鼎.

2003.3, 3–12, "Shaanxi Meixian Yangjiacun Xi Zhou qingtongqi jiaocang" 陝西眉縣楊家村西周青銅器窖藏.

Karlgren, Bernhard, "Yin and Chou in Chinese Bronzes," *Bulletin of the Museum of Far Eastern Antiquities* 8 (1936).

Keightley, David, "The Religious Commitment: Shang Theology and the Genesis of Chinese Political Culture," *History of Religions* 17.3–4 (1978), 214–20.

"The Late Shang State: When, Where, and What?" in *The Origins of Chinese Civilization*, Berkeley: University of California Press, 1983, pp. 523–64.

"The Shang: China's First Historical Dynasty," in *The Cambridge History of Ancient China: From the Origins of Civilization to 221 BC*, ed. Michael Loewe and Edward L. Shaughnessy, Cambridge: Cambridge University Press, 1999, pp. 268–88.

The Ancestral Landscape: Time, Space, and Community in Late Shang China (*ca. 1200–1045 BC*), Berkeley: Institute of East Asian Studies, 2000.

Kern, Martin, "Shi Jing Songs as Performance Texts: A Case Study of 'Chu Ci' (Thorny Caltrop)," *Early China* 25 (2000), 49–111.

Kezhai jigu lu 愙齋集古錄 (Wu Dacheng 吳大澂), 26 vols., Shanghai: Hanfenlou, 1918 (preface 1896).

Kimura, Hideumi 木村秀海, "Rokushi no kankōsei ni tsuite: Rei hōson meibun o chūshin ni shite" 六師の官構成について--盠方尊銘文を中心にして, *Tōhōgaku* 東方學 69 (1985), 1–13.

"Sei-Shū kansei no kihon kōzō" 西周官制の基本構造, *Shigaku zasshi* 史学雑誌 94.1 (1985), 38–66.

Kokyū hakubutsuin 故宮博物院, vol. 12: *Seidōki* 青銅器, ed. Higuchi Takayasu 樋口隆康, Tokyo: Nihon hōsō shutsuban kyōkai (NHK), 1998.

Laoniupo 老牛坡 (Xibei daxue lishixi 西北大學歷史系), Xi'an: Shaanxi renmin, 2002.

Legge, James, *The Chinese Classics,* vol. 3: *The Shoo King, or Book of Historical Documents,* Hong Kong: University of Hong Kong Press, 1960 (reprint of London: Henry Frowde, 1865).

Lewis, Mark, "Ritual Origins of the Warring States," *Bulletin de l'École Française d'Extrême-Orient* 84 (1997), 73–98.

"Warring States Political History," in *The Cambridge History of Ancient China: From the Origins of Civilization to 221 BC,* ed. Michael Loewe and Edward Shauhgnessy, Cambridge: Cambridge University Press, 1999, pp. 605–8.

"The City-State in Spring-and-Autumn China," in *A Comparative Study of Thirty City-State Cultures: An Investigation Conducted by the Copenhagen Polis Centre,* ed. Mogens Herman Hansen, Copenhagen: The Royal Danish Academy of Sciences and Letters, 2000, pp. 359–73.

The Construction of Space in Early China, Albany: State University of New York Press, 2006.

Li, Boqian 李伯謙, "Shu Ze fangding mingwen kaoshi" 叔夨方鼎銘文考釋, *Wenwu* 2001.8, 39–41.

"Meixian xinchu Lai pan yu Da Ke ding de shidai" 眉縣新出逨盤與大克鼎的時代, in *Disi jie guoji Zhongguo guwenzi xue yantaohui lunwen ji* 第四屆國際中國古文字學研討會論文集, Hong Kong: Chinese University of Hong Kong, 2003, pp. 89–96.

Li Chaoyuan 李朝遠, *Xi Zhou tudi guanxi lun* 西周土地關係論, Shanghai: Renmin, 1997.

Lidai zhongding yiqi kuanzhi fatie 歷代鐘鼎彝器款識法帖 (Xue Shanggong 薛尚功), 20 *juan,* stone edition, 1144 (Wanyue shanren edition, 1588).

Li, Fang 李昉, *Taiping yulan* 太平御覽, Shanghai: Zhonghua shuju, 1960.

Li, Feng 李峰, "Huanghe liuyu Xi Zhou muzang chutu qingtong liqi de fenqi yu niandai" 黄河流域西周墓葬出土青銅禮器的分期与年代, *Kaogu xuebao* 1988.4, 383–419.

"Ancient Reproductions and Calligraphic Variations: Studies of Western Zhou Bronzes with Identical Inscriptions," *Early China* 22 (1997), 1–41.

"Tayūtei meibun o meguru rekishi chiri teki mondai no kaiketsu: Shū ōchō no seihoku keiryaku o kaimei suru tameni, sono ichi" 多友鼎銘文を巡る歴史地理的問題の解決：周王朝の西北経略を解明するために、その一, in *Chūgoku kodai no moji to bunka* 中国古代の文字と文化, Tokyo: Kyūko shoin, 1999, pp. 179–206.

"The Decline and Fall of the Western Zhou Dynasty: A Historical, Archeological, and Geographical Study of China from the Tenth to the Eighth Centuries BC," unpublished PhD thesis, University of Chicago, 2000.

" 'Offices' in Bronze Inscriptions and Western Zhou Government Administration," *Early China* 26–27 (2001–2002), 1–72.

"Literacy Crossing Cultural Borders: Evidence from the Bronze Inscriptions of the Western Zhou Period (1045–771 BC)," *Bulletin of the Museum of Far Eastern Antiquity* 74 (2002), 210–421.

" 'Feudalism' and Western Zhou China: A Criticism," *Harvard Journal of Asiatic Studies* 63.1 (2003), 115–44.

"Succession and Promotion: Elite Mobility during the Western Zhou," *Monumenta Serica* 52 (2004), 1–35.

"Textual Criticism and Western Zhou Bronze Inscriptions: The Example of the Mu Gui," in *Essays in Honour of An Zhimin,* ed. Teng Chung and Chen Xing-can, Hong Kong: Chinese University of Hong Kong, 2004, pp. 280–97.

"Ouzhou Feudalism de fansi jiqi dui Zhongguo lishi fenqi de yiyi" 歐洲 Feudalism的反思及其對中國歷史分期的意義, *Zhongguo xueshu* 中國學 術 24 (2005), 8–29.

Landscape and Power in Early China: The Crisis and Fall of the Western Zhou, 1045–771 BC, Cambridge: Cambridge University Press, 2006.

"Xi Zhou jinwen zhong de Zheng di he Zheng guo dongqian" 西周金文中的 鄭地和鄭國東遷, *Wenwu* 2006.9, 70–78.

"Transmitting Antiquity: The Origin and Paradigmization of the 'Five Ranks'," in *Perceptions of Antiquity in Chinese Civilization* (Würzburger Sinologische Schriften), ed. Dieter Kohn and Helga Stahl, Heidelberg: Edition Forum, 2008, 103–34.

Li, Jiahao 李家浩, "Xian Qin wenzi zhong de xian" 先秦文字中的縣, *Wenshi* 文 史 28 (1987), 49–58.

Li, Xiaoding 李孝定, *Jiaguwen zi jishi* 甲骨文字集釋, 14 vols., Taipei: Academia Sinica, 1965.

Li, Xueqin 李學勤 (see also Zhou Yuan 周瑗), "Meixian Lijiacun tongqi kao" 郿 縣李家村銅器考, *Wenwu caokao ziliao* 文物參考資料 1957.7, 58–59.

"Xi Zhou jinwen zhong de tudi zhuanrang" 西周金文中的土地轉讓, in *Shix- ue lunwen xuan* 史學論文選, Beijing: Guangming ribao, 1984, pp. 69–74.

"Xi Zhou jinwen de liushi bashi" 西周金文的六師八師, *Huaxia kaogu* 華夏 考古 1987.2, 207–10.

Xinchu qingtongqi yanjiu 新出青銅器研究, Beijing: Wenwu, 1990.

Zhongguo qingtongqi gaishuo 中國青銅器概說, Beijing: Foreign Language Publisher, 1995.

"Shi Guodian jian Zhai Gong zhi guming" 釋郭店簡祭公之顧命, *Wenwu* 1998.7, 44–45.

Li, Xueshan 李雪山, *Shang dai fenfeng zhidu yanjiu* 商代分封制度研究, Beijing: Shehui kexue, 2004.

Liji 禮記, in *Shisanjing zhushu* 十三經註疏, Beijing: Zhonghua, 1979, pp. 1221– 1696.

Liu, Li, and Xingcan Chen, *State Formation in Early China*, London: Duckworth, 2003.

Liu, Xinyuan 劉心源, *Qigu shi jijin wen shu* 奇觚室吉金文述, China: 1902.

Liu, Yu 劉雨, "Duoyou ding de shidai yu diming kaoding" 多友鼎的時代與地 名考訂, *Kaogu* 1983.2, 152–57.

"Xi Zhou jinwen zhong de sheli" 西周金文中的射禮, *Kaogu* 12 (1986), 112–21.

Liu, Zongyuan 柳宗元, "Fengjian lun" 封建論, in *Liu Zongyuan ji* 柳宗元集, Taibei: Huazheng, 1990, pp. 69–76.

Liulihe Xi Zhou Yan guo mudi 琉璃河西周燕國墓地 (Beijing shi wenwu yanji- uso 北京市文物研究所), Beijing: Wenwu Press, 1995.

Loewe, Michael, "The Administrative Documents from Yinwan: A Summary of Certain Issues Raised," posted at the website of the Society for the Study of Early China (www.lib.uchicago.edu/earlychina/res); visited on February 15, 2005.

ed. *Early Chinese Texts: A Bibliographical Guide*, Berkeley: Institute of East Asian Studies, University of California, 1993.

The Government of the Qin and Han Empires, 221 BCE–220 CE, Indianapolis: Hackett Publishing Co., 2006.

Lu, Liancheng 盧連成, "Zhou du Yu Zheng kao" 周都域鄭考, in *Guwenzi lun- ji* 古文字論集(*Kaogu yu wenwu congkan* 考古与文物叢刊 no. 2), Xi'an: 1983, pp. 8–11.

"An di yu Zhao Wang shijiu nian nanzheng" 斥地与昭王十九年南征, *Kaogu yu wenwu* 1984.6, 75–79.

"Xi Zhou Ze guo shiji kaolue jiqi xiangguan wenti" 西周夨國史跡考略及其相關問題, in *Xi Zhou shi yanjiu* 西周史研究 (Monograph of *Renwen zazhi*人文雜誌叢刊 no. 2), Xi' an: 1984, pp. 232–48.

"Xi Zhou Feng Hao liangjing kao" 西周豐鎬兩京考, paper presented in the conference for the 30th anniversary of the establishment of Shaanxi Provincial Institute of Archaeology and the Banpo Museum, Xi'an: 1988, pp. 1–56.

"Chariot and Horse Burials in Ancient China," *Antiquity* 67 (1993), 824–38.

Lü, Wenyu 呂文郁, *Zhou dai caiyi zhidu yanjiu* 周代采邑制度研究, Taipei: Wenjin, 1992.

"Zhou dai wangji kaoshu" 周代王畿考述, *Renwen zazhi* 1992.2, 92–101.

Luo, Tai 羅泰 (Lothar von Falkenhausen), "Xi Zhou tongqi mingwen de xing-zhi"西周銅器銘文的性質, in *Kaogu xue yanjiu* 考古學研究 6 (Festschrift for Professor Gao Ming), Beijing: Kexue, 2006, pp. 343–74.

Luo, Xizhang 羅西章, "Zai Shou gui ming luekao" 宰獸簋銘略考, *Wenwu* 1998.8, 83–87.

"Zhouyuan qingtongqi jiaocang jiqi youguan wenti de tantao" 周原青銅器窖藏及其有關問題的探討, *Kaogu yu wenwu* 1988.2, 40–47.

Ma, Chengyuan 馬承源, *Shang Zhou qingtongqi mingwen xuan* 商周青銅器銘文選, 4 vols., Beijing: Wenwu, 1986–90.

"Jinhou Su bianzhong" 晉侯蘇編鐘, *Shanghai bowuguan jikan* 上海博物館集刊 1996.7, 1–17.

MacIver, R. M., *The Modern State*, London: Oxford University Press, 1955.

Maisels, Charles, "Models of Social Evolution: Trajectories from the Neolithic to the State," *Man* 22.2 (1987), 340–43.

Early Civilizations of the Old World: The Formative Histories of Egypt, The Levant, Mesopotamia, India and China (London: Routledge, 1999).

Maspero, Henri, "Le Régime féodal et la propriété foncière dans la Chine antique," *Mélanges posthumes sur les religions et l'histoire de la Chine, III. Études historiques*, Paris: 1950, pp. 111–46.

Masubuchi, Tatsuo 增淵龍夫, "Sen Shin jidai no hōken to gunken" 先秦時代の封建と郡県, *Hitotsubashi daigaku kenkyū nenpō: Keizaigaku kenkyū* 一橋大学研究年報：経済学研究 12 (1958), 175–298.

Chūgoku kodai no shakai to kokka 中国古代の社会と国家. Tokyo: Kōbundō, 1960.

Matsui, Yoshinori 松井嘉徳, "Shū no kokusei: Hōkensei to kansei o chūshin toshite" 周の国制：封建制と官制を中心にして, in *In Shū Shin Kan jidaishi no kihon mondai* 殷周秦漢時代史の基本問題, ed. Matsumaru Michio 松丸道雄 *et al.*, Tokyo: Kyūko shoin 2001 pp. 89–112.

Shūdai kokusei no kenkyū 周代国制の研究, Tokyo: Kyūko shuin, 2002.

Matsumaru, Michio 松丸道雄, "Inkyo bokuji chū no tenryōchi ni tsuite: Indai kokka kōzo kenkyū no tameni" 殷墟卜辭中の田獵地について--殷代國家構造研究のために, *Tōkyō daigaku tōyō bunka kenkyūjo kiyō* 東京大學東洋文化研究所紀要 31 (1963), 1–163.

"In Shū kokka no kōzō" 殷周国家の構造, in *Iwanami kōza: Sekai rekishi* 岩波講座：世界歴史, Tokyo: Iwanami shoten, 1970, pp. 49–100.

"Sei Shū seidōki seisaku no haikei: Shū kinbun kenkyū, joshō" 西周青銅器製作の背景――周金文研究序章, *Tōyō bunka kenkyūjo kiyō* 東洋文化研

究所紀要 72 (1977), 1–128 (reprint Matsumaru Michio, ed., *Sei Shū seidōki to sono kokka* 西周青銅器とその国家, pp. 11–136, Tokyo: Tōkyōdaigaku, 1980).

"Sei Shū seidōki chū no shokō seisakuki ni tsuite: Shū kinbun kenkyū, jo no 2" 西周青銅器中の諸侯製作器について—周金文研究—序の2, *Tōyō bunka* 東洋文化 59 (1979), 1–48 (reprint Matsumaru Michio, ed., *Sei Shū seidōki to sono kokka* 西周青銅器とその国家, Tokyo: Tōkyōdaigaku, 1980, pp. 137–84).

"Sei Shū kōki shakai ni mieru henkaku no hōga: Ko tei mei kaishaku mondai no shohoteki kaiketsu" 西周後期社會に見える変革の萌芽—曶鼎銘解釈問題の初歩的解決, in *Nishijima Sadao hakase kanreki kinen: Higashi Ajia shi ni okeru kokka to nōmin* 西嶋定生博士還暦記念—東アジア史における国家と農民, Tokyo: Yamakawa, 1984, pp. 29–74.

"In jin no kannen sekai" 殷人の観念世界, in *Chūgoku no In Shū bunka-Symposium* 中国の殷周文化—シンポジウム, Tokyo: Yomiuri shinbun, 1986, pp. 121–46.

"Sei Shū kinbun chū no hōsei shiryō" 西周金文中の法制資料, in *Chūgoku hōsei shi: Kihon shiryō no kenkyū* 中国法制史—基本資料の研究, ed. Shiga Shūzō 滋賀秀三, Tokyo: Tokyo daigaku, 1993, pp. 3–55.

"In Shū Shunjū shi sōsetsu" 殷周春秋史総説, in *In Shū Shin Kan jidaishi no kihon mondai* 殷周秦漢時代史の基本問題, ed. Matsumaru Michio *et al.*, Tokyo: Kyūko shoin, 2001, pp. 3–26.

Matsumaru, Michio 松丸道雄, and Ken-ichi Takashima 高嶋謙一, *Kōkotsu moji jishaku sōran* 甲骨文字字釈総覧, Tokyo: Tokyo daigaku, 1993.

Matsumaru, Michio 松丸道雄, and Nagata Hidemasa 永田英正, *Chūgoku bunmei no seiritsu* 中国文明の成立, Tokyo: Kōdansha, 1985.

Matsumoto, Mitsuo 松本光雄, "Chūgoku kodai no yū to min, jin to no kankei" 中国古代の邑と民、人との関係, *Yamanashi daigaku gakugei gakubu kenkyū hōkoku* 山梨大学学芸学部研究報告 3 (1952), 81–91.

Mencius (trans. David Hinton), Washington DC: Counterpoint, 1998.

Miyazaki, Ichisada 宮崎市定, *Chūgoku kodaishi gairon* 中国古代史概論, Kyoto: Toshisha daigaku, 1954.

"Chūgoku jōdai ha hōkensei ka toshi kokka ka" 中国上代は封建制か都市国家か, *Shirin* 史林 33.2 (1958), 1–20.

Mu tianzi zhuan 穆天子傳, in *Sibu beiyao* 四部備要 vol. 77, Shanghai: Shangwu, 1936.

Musha, Akira 武者章, "Sei Shū satsumei kinbun bunrui no kokoromi" 西周冊命金文分類の試み, in *Sei Shū seidōki to sono kokka* 西周青銅器とその国家, ed. Matsumaru Michio, Tokyo: Tōkyō daigaku, 1980, pp. 241–324.

Neimenggu wenwu kaogu 内蒙古文物考古1982.2, 5–7, "Zaomeng faxian de daxing qingtongqi" 昭盟發現的大型青銅器.

Nickinovich, David, "Bureaucracy," in *Encyclopedia of Sociology*, ed. Edgar F. Borgatta, New York: Macmillan Reference USA, 2000, pp. 233–34.

Nienhauser, William H. (ed.), *The Grand Scribe's Records*, vol. 1: *The Basic Annals of Pre-Han China*, Bloomington: Indiana University Press, 1994.

The Grand Scribe's Record, vol. II: *The Basic Annals of Han China*, Bloomington: Indiana University Press, 2002.

Ningshou jiangu 寧壽鑑古 (Qianlong Emperor), 16 *juan*, Shanghai: Hanfenlou, 1913 (completed before 1779).

Nishijima, Sadao 西嶋定生, *Chūgoku kodai no shakai to keizai* 中国古代の社会 と経済, Tokyo: Tokyo University Press, 1981.

Nivison, David, "The Dates of Western Chou," *Harvard Journal of Asiatic Studies* 43 (1983), 481–580.

Qigu shi jijin wenshu 奇觚室吉金文述 (Liu Xinyuan 劉心源), 20 *juan*, China: 1902.

Pangu lou yiqi kuanzhi 攀古廔彝器款識 (Pan Zuyin 潘祖蔭), 2 vols., Beijing: Pangxi zhai, 1872.

Pankenier, David, "Astronomical Dates in Shang and Western Zhou," *Early China* 7 (1981–82), 1–37.

Prestwich, Michael, *Armies and Warfare in the Middle Ages: The English Experience*, New Haven: Yale University Press, 1996.

Průšek, Jaroslav, *Chinese Statelets and the Northern Barbarians in the Period 1400– 300 BC*, New York: Humanities Press, 1971.

Pugh, D. S. *et al.*, "Dimensions of Organization Structure," *Administrative Science Quarterly* 13.1 (1968), 65–105.

Pulleyblank, Edwin, "Ji and Jiang: the Role of Exogamic Clans in the Organiza- tion of the Zhou Polity," *Early China* 25 (2000), 1–27.

Ogata, Isamu 尾形勇, and Kishimoto Mio 岸本美緒 ed., *Chūgoku shi* 中國史, Tokyo: Yamakawa, 1998.

Qi, Sihe 齊思和, "Zhou dai ximing li kao" 周代錫命禮考, *Yanjing xuebao* 燕京 學報 32 (1947), 197–226.

Qing'ai tang jiacang zhongding yiqi kuanzhi fatie 清愛堂家藏鐘鼎彝器款識法 帖 (Liu Xihai 劉喜海), 1 *juan*, 1838.

Qingtongqi tushi 青銅器圖釋 (Shaanxi sheng bowuguan 陝西省博物館 and Shaanxi sheng wenwu guanli weiyuanhui 陝西省文物管理委員會), Bei- jing: Wenwu, 1960.

Qiu, Xiqui 裘錫圭, "Shi Qiang pan mingwen jieshi" 史墙盤銘文解釋, *Wenwu* 1978.3, 25–32.

   Gu wenzi lunji 古文字論集, Beijing: Zhonghua, 1992.

   "Tan Zenghou Yi mu zhong qing mingwen zhong de jige wenti" 談曾侯乙墓 鐘磬銘文中的幾個問題, in *Gu wenzi lunji*, Beijing: Zhonghua, 1992, pp. 418–28.

Qu, Yingjie 曲英傑, "San pan tushuo" 散盤圖説, in *Xi Zhou shi yanjiu* 西周史 研究 (Monograph of *Renwen zazhi* no. 2), Xi'an: 1984, pp. 325–33.

Qufu Lu guo gucheng 曲阜魯國故城 (Shandong sheng wenwu kaogu yanjiusuo 山東省文物考古研究所 et al.), Jinan: Qilu, 1982.

Rawson, Jessica, "Statesmen or Barbarians? The Western Zhou as Seen through their Bronzes," *Proceedings of the British Academy* 75 (1989), 89–93.

   Western Zhou Ritual Bronzes from the Arthur M. Sackler Collections, Washington, DC: Arthur M. Sackler Foundation, 1990.

   "Western Zhou Archaeology," in *The Cambridge History of Ancient China: From the Origins of Civilization to 221 BC*, ed. Michael Loewe and Edward Shaughnessy, Cambridge: Cambridge University Press, 1999, pp. 420–21.

Reynolds, Susan, *Fiefs and Vassals: The Medieval Evidence Reinterpreted*, Oxford: Clarendon Press, 1994.

Rhee, Song Nai, "Sumerian City-States," *The City-State in Five Cultures*, ed. Rob- ert Griffeth and Carol G. Thomas, Santa Barbara: ABC-Clio, 1981, pp. 1–30.

Rong, Geng 容庚, *Shang Zhou yiqi tongkao* 商周彝器通考, 2 vols., Beiping: Har- vard-Yenching Institute, 1940.

Jinwen bian 金文編 (reedited and enlarged). Beijing: Zhonghua, 1985 (1st edn, 1925).

Sahlins, Marshall, "The Segmentary Lineage: An Organization of Predatory Expansion," *American Anthropologist* 63.2, Part 1 (1961), 322–45.

Sandai jijin wencun 三代吉金文存 (Luo Zhenyu 羅振玉), 20 *juan*, Baijuezhai, 1936.

Schaberg, David, *A Patterned Past: Form and Thought in Early Chinese Historiography*, Cambridge, MA: Harvard University Asia Center, 2001.

Sena, David M.,"Reproducing Society: Lineage and Kinship in Western Zhou China," unpublished PhD thesis, University of Chicago, 2005.

Sen'oku seishō 泉屋清賞 (Hamada Kōsaku 浜田耕作) 6 vols., Japan, 1919.

Service, Elman, *Origins of the State and Civilization: The Process of Cultural Evolution*, New York: W. W. Norton & Company, 1975.

Shaanxi chutu Shang Zhou qingtongqi 陝西出土商周青銅器, 4 vols. (Shaanxi sheng kaogu yanjiusuo 陝西省考古研究所 *et al.*), Beijing: Wenwu, 1979–84.

Shang Zhou jinwen luyi 商周金文錄遺 (Yu Xingwu 于省吾), 1 vol., Beijing: Kexue, 1957.

Shangcunling Guo guo mudi 上村嶺虢國墓地 (Zhongguo kexueyuan kaogu yanjiusuo), Beijing: Kexue Press, 1959.

Shanghai bowuguan cang qingtongqi 上海博物館藏青銅器 (Shanghai bowuguan 上海博物館), Shanghai: Renmin, 1964.

Shanghai bowuguan jikan 上海博物館集刊 1996.7, 1–17, "Jinhou Su bianzhong" 晉侯蘇編鐘.

Shangshu 尚書, in *Shisanjing zhushu* 十三經註疏, Beijing: Zhonghua, 1979, pp. 113–258.

Shanzhai yiqi tulu 善齋彝器圖錄 (Rong Geng 容庚), Beiping: Harvard-Yenching Institute, 1936.

Shang Zhou qingtongqi mingwen xuan 商周青銅器銘文選, see Ma Chengyuan.

Shaughnessy, Edward L. (see also Xia Hanyi 夏含夷), "'New' Evidence on the Zhou Conquest," *Early China* 6 (1981–82), 66–69.

  "The Date of the 'Duo You *Ding*' and Its Significance," *Early China* 9–10 (1983–85), 55–69.

  "On the Authenticity of the *Bamboo Annals*," *Harvard Journal of Asiatic Studies* 46.1 (1986), 149–80.

  "Extra-Lineage Cult in the Shang Dynasty," *Early China* 11–12 (1985–87), 186.

  "Zhouyuan Oracle-Bone Inscriptions: Entering the Research Stage?" *Early China* 11–12 (1985–87), 146–63.

  "Historical Geography and the Extent of the Earliest Chinese Kingdoms," *Asia Major* 2.2 (1989), 13–18.

  "The Role of Grand Protector Shi in the Consolidation of the Zhou Conquest," *Ars Orientalis* 19 (1989), 51–77.

  Sources of Western Zhou History: Inscribed Bronze Vessels, Berkeley: University of California Press, 1991.

  "The Duke of Zhou's Retirement in the East and the Beginnings of the Minister–Monarch Debate in Chinese Political Philosophy," *Early China* 18 (1993), 41–72.

  "Western Zhou History," in *The Cambridge History of Ancient China: From the Origins of Civilization to 221 BC*, ed. Michael Loewe and Edward L. Shaughnessy, Cambridge: Cambridge University Press, 1999, pp. 292–351.

"New Sources of Western Zhou History: Recent Discoveries of Inscribed Bronze Vessels," *Early China*, 26 (2001), 73–98.

Shengshi jijin: Shaanxi Baoji Meixian qingtongqi jiaocang 盛世吉金：陝西寶鷄眉縣青銅器窖藏 (Shaanxi sheng wenwuju 陝西省文物局), Beijing: Beijing chubanshe, 2003.

Shiji 史記 (by Sima Qian 司馬遷), 10 vols., Beijing: Zhonghua, 1959.

Shijing 詩經 (Book of Poetry), in *Shisanjing zhushu* 十三經註疏, Beijing: Zhonghua, 1979, pp. 259–630.

Shiliu changle tang guqi kuanzhi kao 十六長樂堂古器款識考 (Qian Dian 錢坫), 4 *juan*, 2 vols., 1796 (reprint, Shanghai: Kaiming shuju, 1933).

Shim, Jaehoon, "The 'Jinhou Su Bianzhong' Inscription and Its Significance," *Early China* 22 (1997), 43–75.

Shima, Kunio 島邦男, *Inkyo bokuji kenkyū* 殷墟卜辭研究, Hirosaki: Hirosaki daigaku Chūgokugaku kenkyūkai, 1958.

Shirakawa, Shizuka 白川静, "In no ōzoku to seiji no keitai" 殷の王族と政治の形態, *Kodaigaku* 古代学 3.1 (1954), 19–44.

"Kinbun tsūshaku" 金文通釈, *Hakutsuru bijutsukanshi* 白鶴美術館誌, 56 vols., Kobe, 1966–83.

"Shaku shi" 釋史, in *Kōkotsu kinbungaku ronshū* 甲骨金文学論集, Kyoto: Hōyū Shoten, 1974, pp. 1–68.

"Shaku shi" 釋師, in *Kōkotsu kinbungaku ronshū* 甲骨金文学論集, Kyoto: Hōyū Shoten, 1974, pp. 207–305.

Shouxian Caihou mu chutu yiwu 壽縣蔡侯墓出土遺物 (Anhui sheng wenwu guanli weiyuanhui 安徽省文物管理委員會 *et al.*), Beijing: Kexue, 1956.

Shuangjian chi jijin wenxuan 雙劍誃吉金文選 (Yu Xingwu 于省吾), Beijing: 1933.

Shuowen jiezi 說文解字 (by Xu Shen 許慎), Beijing: Zhonghua, 1963.

Si, Weizhi 斯維之, "Xi Zhou jinwen suojian guanming kao" 西周金文所見官名考, *Zhongguo wenhua yanjiu huikan* 中國文化研究彙刊 7 (1947), 1–25.

"Fengjian kaoyuan" 封建考源, in *Xian Qin shi lunwen ji* 先秦史論文集, Xi'an: Renwen zazhi, 1982, pp. 33–42.

Sicker, Martin, *The Genesis of the State*, New York: Praeger, 1991.

Skinner, Quentin, "The State," in *Political Innovation and Conceptual Change*, ed. Terence Ball, James Farr, and Russell L. Hanson, Cambridge: Cambridge University Press, 1989, pp. 90–131.

"How We Acquired the Concept of the State (and What Concept[s] We Acquired)?" paper presented at the Columbia Conference on the "State," February 2006, New York.

Skosey, Laura, "The Legal System and Legal Tradition of the Western Zhou, CA. 1045–771 B.C.E.," unpublished PhD thesis, University of Chicago, 1996.

Southall, Aidan, *Alur Society: A Study in Processes and Types of Domination*, Cambridge: W. Heffer & Sons Limited, 1956.

"The Segmentary State in Africa and Asia," *Comparative Studies in Society and History* 30.1 (1988), 52–82.

"The Segmentary State: From the Imaginary to the Material Means of Production," in *Early State Economy*, ed. Henri Claessen and Pieter Van De Velde, New Brunswick: Transaction Publishers, 1991, pp. 75–96.

"Urban Theory and the Chinese City," in *Urban Anthropology in China*, ed. Greg Guldin and Aidan Southall, Leiden: E. J. Brill, 1993, pp, 19–40.

Strayer, Joseph R., "Feudalism in Western Europe," in *Feudalism in History*, ed. Ruthton Coulbourn, Princeton: Princeton University Press, 1956.

Feudalism, Princeton: D. Van Nostrand Company, 1965.

Sun, Xingyan 孫星衍, *Shangshu jingu wen zhushu* 尚書今古文注疏, Beijing: Zhonghua, 1986.

Sun, Yirang 孫貽讓, *Guzhou shiyi* 古籀拾遺 (Sun Yirang 孫詒讓), 3 *juan*, 1888.

Zhou qing shulin 籀廎述林, 1916.

Taiping yulan 太平禦覽, 4 vols. (by Li Fang 李昉), Beijing: Zhonghua, 1960.

Takashima, Ken-ichi "The Causative Construction with *shi* in Shang Chinese," paper presented at the Sixteenth Annual International Conference on Chinese Paleography, Guangzhou, November 2006, pp. 1–20.

Takeuchi, Yasuhiro 竹內康浩, "Shunjū kara mita godōshakusei: Shūsho ni okeru hōken no mondai" 春秋から見た五等爵制--周初における封建の問題, *Shigaku zasshi* 史學雜誌 100.2 (1991), 40–144.

Tang, Lan 唐蘭, "Zuoce Ling zun ji Zuoce Ling yi ming kaoshi" 作冊令尊及作冊令彝銘考釋, *Guoli Beijing daxue guoxue jikan* 國立北京大學國學集刊 4.1 (1934), 22–25.

"Yihou Ze gui kaoshi" 宜侯夨簋考釋, *Kaogu xuebao* 1956.2, 79–83.

"Xi Zhou jinwen duandai zhong de Kang Gong wenti" 西周金文斷代中的康宮問題, *Kaogu xuebao* 1962.1, 15–48.

"Yong yu mingwen jieshi" 永盂銘文解釋, *Wenwu* 1972.1, 58–62.

Tang Lan xiansheng jinwen lunji 唐蘭先生金文論集, Beijing: Zijingchen, 1995.

Taozhai jijin lu 陶齋吉金錄 (Duan Fang 端方), 8 *juan*, Shanghai: Youzheng shuju, 1908.

Tengzhou Qianzhangda mudi 滕州前掌大墓地 (Zhongguo shehui kexueyuan kaogu yanjusuo 中國社會科學院考古研究所), Beijing: Wenwu, 2005.

Thatcher, Melvin P., "A Structural Comparison of the Central Government of Ch'u, Ch'i, and Chin," *Monumenta Serica* 33 (1977–78), 140–61.

"Central Government of the State of Ch'in in the Spring and Autumn Period," *Journal of Oriental Studies* (Hong Kong) 23.1 (1985), 29–53.

Tongdian 通典, 5 vols. (by Du You 杜佑; punctuated edn), Beijing: Zhonghua, 1988.

Trigger, Bruce, "The Evolution of Pre-Industrial Cities: A Multilinear Perspective," in *Mélanges offerts à Jean Vercoutter*, ed. Francis Geus and Florence Thill, Paris: Éditions Recherche sur les Civilisations, 1985, pp. 343–47.

Early Civilization, Cairo: American University in Cairo Press, 1993.

"Shang Political Organization: A Comparative Approach," *Journal of East Asian Archaeology* 1 (1999), 43–62.

Twitchett, Denis, and Michael Loewe, *The Cambridge History of China*, vol. 1: *The Ch'in and Han Empires*, Cambridge: Cambridge University Press, 1986.

Udy, Stanley H., "'Bureaucracy' and 'Rationality' in Weber's Organization Theory: An Empirical Study," *American Sociological Review* 24.6 (1959), 791–95.

Utsunomiya, Kiyoyoshi 宇都宮清吉, *Kandai shakai keizaishi kankyū* 漢代社会経済史研究, Tokyo: Kōbundō, 1955.

Vandermeersch, Leon, *Wangdao ou la Voie Royale*, vol. 1, Paris: École Française d'Extrême-Orient, 1977.

Waley, Arthur, trans., *The Book of Songs: the Ancient Chinese Classics of Poetry*, ed. Joseph R. Allen, New York: Grove Press, 1996.

Wan, Changhua 萬昌華, "Junxian zhi qiyuan lilun de lishi kaocha" 郡縣制起源理論的歷史考察, *Qi Lu xuekan* 齊魯學刊 2000.5, 77–80.

Wang, Guimin 王貴民, "Shangchao guanzhi jiqi lishi tedian" 商朝官制及其歷史特點, *Lishi yanjiu* 歷史研究 1986.4, 107–19.

   Shang Zhou zhidu kaoxin 商周制度考信, Taipei: Minwen, 1989.

Wang, Guowei 王國維, "Shi shi" 釋史, in *Guantang jilin* 觀堂集林, 2 vols., pp. 159–66, Shijiazhuang: Hebei Jiaoyu, 2001.

Wang, Hanzhang 王翰章, "Hu gui gai ming kaoshi" 虎簋蓋銘考釋, *Kaogu yu wenwu* 1997.3, 78–80.

Wang, Hui 王輝, "Xi Zhou jinei diming xiaoji" 西周畿內地名小記, *Kaogu yu wenwu* 1985.3, 26–31.

Wang, Jian 王健, *Xi Zhou zhengzhi dili jiegou yanjiu* 西周政治地理結構研究, Zhengzhou: Zhongzhou guji, 2004.

Wang, Rencong 王人聰, "Xi Zhou jinwen shen jing yici bushi" 西周金文鬺京一詞補釋, *Kaogu yu wenwu* 1987. 2, 49–50.

Wang, Shiren 王世仁, "Han Chang'an cheng nanjiao lizhi jianzhu (Datumencun yizhi) yuanzhuang de tuice" 漢長安城南郊禮制建築（大土門村遺址）原狀的推測, *Kaogu* 1963.9, 501–15.

Wang, Yiliang 王貽梁, "Yelun Xi Zhou renguan zhidu" 也論西周任官制度, *Huadong shifan daxue xuebao* 華東師範大學學報 1989.1, 90–96.

Wang, Yuzhe 王玉哲, "Xi Zhou jinwen zhong de zhu he tudi guanxi" 西周金文中的 "貯" 和土地關係, *Nankai xuebao* 1983.3, 47–53.

Wang, Zhengzhong 王震中, *Zhongguo wenming qiyuan de bijiao yanjiu* 中國文明起源的比較研究, Xi'an: Shaanxi renmin, 1994.

Wang, Zhongwen 汪中文, *Liang Zhou guanzhi lungao* 兩周官制論稿, Gaoxiong: Fuwen, 1993.

Weber, Max, "Bureaucracy," in *From Max Weber: Essays in Sociology*, trans. and ed. H. H. Gerth and C. Wright Mills, New York: Oxford University Press, 1946, pp. 196–244.

   The Theory of Social and Economic Organizations, trans. and ed. A. M. Henderson and Talcott Parsons, Glencoe: Free Press, 1947.

Weihua ge jigu lu bawei 韡華閣集古錄跋尾 (Ke Changji 柯昌濟), 15 *juan*, 1935 (completed 1916).

Wenbo 文博 1987.2, 17–25, "Meixian chutu yipi Xi Zhou jiaocang qingtong yueqi" 眉縣出土一批西周窖藏青銅樂器.

Wenhua dageming qijian chutu wenwu 文化大革命期間出土文物 (Zhanlan gongzuozu 展覽工作組), vol. 1, Beijing: Wenwu, 1972.

Wenwu 文物 1975.10, 68–69, "Ji Shaanxi Lantian xian xin chutu de Yinghou zhong" 記陝西藍田縣新出土的應侯鐘.

   1977.8, 27–28, "Ji Shaanxi Lantian xian xin chutu de Yinghou zhong yiwen buzheng" 記陝西藍田縣新出土的應侯鐘一文補正.

   1978.3, 1–18, "Shaanxi Fufeng Zhuangbai yihao Xi Zhou qingtongqi jiaocang fajue jianbao" 陝西扶風莊白一號西周青銅器窖藏發掘簡報.

   1979.1, 23–26, "Hebei sheng Yuanshi xian Xizhangcun de Xi Zhou yizhi he muzang" 河北省元氏縣西張村的西周遺址和墓葬.

   1979.10, 27–34, "Shaanxi Qishan Fengchucun Xi Zhou jianzhu jizhi fajue jianbao" 陝西岐山鳳雛村西周建築基址發掘簡報.

   1980.4, 27–38, "Fufeng Yuntang Xi Zhou guqi zhizao zuofang yizhi shijue jianbao" 扶風雲塘西周骨器製造作坊遺址試掘簡報.

1981.3, 10–22, "Fufeng Shaochen Xi Zhou jianzhu qun jizhi fajue jiaobao" 扶風召陳西周建築群基址發掘簡報.

1985.2, 1–8, "Fengxiang Majiazhuang yihao jianzhu qun yizhi fajue jianbao" 鳳翔馬家莊一號建築群遺址發掘簡報.

1991.5, 84–85, "Shandong sheng Longkou shi chutu Xi Zhou tong ding" 山東省龍口市出土西周銅鼎.

1993.3, 11–30, "1992 nian chun Tianma-Qucun yizhi muzang fajue baogao" 1992年春天馬–曲村遺址墓葬發掘報告.

1994.1, 4–28, "Tianma-Qucun yizhi Beizhao Jin hou mudi di erci fajue" 天馬–曲村遺址北趙晉侯墓地第二次發掘.

1994.8, 1–21, "Tianma-Qucun yizhi Beizhao Jin hou mudi di sici fajue"天馬–曲村遺址北趙晉侯墓地第四次發掘.

1994.8, 22–33, 68, "Tianma-Qucun yizhi Beizhao Jin hou mudi di sanci fajue" 天馬–曲村遺址北趙晉侯墓地第三次發掘.

1995.7, 4–39, "Tianma-Qucun yizhi Beizhao Jin hou mudi di wuci fajue" 天馬–曲村遺址北趙晉侯墓地第五次發掘.

2001.8, 4–21, "Tianma-Qucun yizhi Beizhao Jinhou mudi diliuci fajue" 天馬–曲村遺址北趙晉侯墓地第六次發掘.

2003.6, 5–17, "Shaanxi Meixian Yangjiacun Xi Zhou qingtongqi jiaocang fajue jianbao" 陝西眉縣楊家村西周青銅器窖藏發掘简報.

2004.4, 90, "Guo guo bowuguan shoucang de yijian tong xu" 虢國博物館收藏的一件銅盨.

Wenwu cankao ziliao 1955.5, 58–62, "Jiangsu Dantu xian Yandunshan chutu de gudai qingtongqi" 江蘇丹徒縣煙墩山出土的古代青銅器.

1957.4, 5–10, "Zuguo lishi wenwu de you yici zhongyao faxian: Shaanxi Meixian fajue chu sijian Xi Zhou tongqi" 祖國歷史文物的又一次重要發現：陝西眉縣發掘出四件西周銅器.

Wheatley, Paul, *The Pivot of the Four Quarters: A Preliminary Enquiry into the Origins and Characteristics of the Ancient Chinese City*, Chicago: Aldine Publishing Company, 1971.

Wu, Kuang 吳匡, and Cai Zhemao 蔡哲茂, 'Shi X" 釋鼐, *Gugong xueshu jikan* 故宮學術季刊, 11.3 (1993–94), 88–85.

Wu, Qichang 吳其昌, *Jinwen lishuo shuzheng* 金文歷朔疏証, 2 vols., Shanghai: Shangwu, 1936.

Wu, Shifen 吳式棻, *Jungu lu jinwen* 攗古錄金文, China: Wushi, 1895.

Wu, Zhenfeng 吳鎮烽, *Jinwen renming huibian* 金文人名彙編, Beijing: Zhonghua 1987.

Xia, Hanyi 夏含夷 (Edward Shaughnessy), *Wengu zhixin lu: Shang Zhou wenhua shi guanjian* 溫故知新錄：商周文化史管窺, Taibei: Daohuo, 1997.

"Fu bu fu, zi bu zi: Shilun Xi Zhou zhongqi Xun gui he Shi You gui de duandai" 父不父，子不子：試論西周中期詢簋和師酉簋的斷代, *Zhongguo guwenzi yu guwenxian* 中國古文字与古文獻 1 (1999), 62–64.

"Cong Lu gui kan Zhou Muwang zaiwei nianshu ji niandai wenti" 從親簋看周穆王在位年數及年代問題, *Zhongguo lishi wenwu* 2006.3, 9–10.

Xia Shang Zhou duandai gongcheng: 1996–2000 nian jieduan chengguo baogao 夏商周斷代工程1996–2000 年階段成果報告 (Xia Shang Zhou duandai gongcheng zhuanjiazu夏商周斷代工程專家組), Beijing: Shijie tushu, 2000.

Xiao, Yishan 蕭一山, *Qing dai tongshi* 清代通史, 5 vols., Beijing: Zhong hua, 1986.

Xiqing gujian 西清古鑒 (ed. Liang Shizheng 梁詩正 *et al.*), 40 *juan*, Beijing: Qing Court (Wuyingdian), 1755 (reprint, Shanghai: Hongwen shuju, 1888).

Xiqing xujian jia bian 西清續鑑甲編 (ed. Wang Jie 王傑 *et al.*), 20 *juan* (supplement: 1 *juan*), Shanghai: Hanfenlou, 1910 (completed 1793).

Xiqing xujian yi bian 西清續鑑乙編 (ed. Wang Jie 王傑 *et al.*), 20 *juan*, Beiping: Beiping guwu chenliesuo 1931 (completed 1793).

Xu, Lianggao 徐良高, and Wang Wei 王巍, "Shaanxi Fufeng Yuntang Xi Zhou jianzhu jizhi de chubu yanjiu" 陝西扶風雲塘西周建築基址的初步研究, *kaogu* 2002.9, 27–35.

Xu, Shaohua 徐少華, *Zhou dai nantu lishi dili yu wenhua* 周代南土歷史地理与文化, Wuhan: Wuhan daxue, 1994.

Xu, Tianjin 徐天進, "Zhougongmiao yizhi de kaogu suohuo ji suosi" 周公廟遺址的考古所獲及所思, *Wenwu* 2006.8, 55–62.

Xu, Zhongshu 徐仲舒, and Tang Jiahong 唐嘉弘, "Lun Yin Zhou de waifu" 論殷周的外服 in *Xian Qin shi lunji* 先秦史論集, Xian: Renwen zazhi, 1982, pp. 53–57.

Xuanhe bogu tu 宣和博古圖 (or *Bogu tulu* 博古圖錄) (ed. Wang Fu 王黼 *et al.*), 30 *juan*, ca. 1110 (preface after 1123; Jiang Yang edition, 1528).

Xue, Shanggong 薛尚功, *Lidai zhong ding yiqi kuanzhi* 歷代鐘鼎彝器款識, Shenyang: Liaoshen shushe, 1985.

Xunxian xincun 濬縣辛村 (by Guo Baojun 郭寶鈞), Beijing: Kexue, 1964.

Yan, Yiping 嚴一萍, "Mieli guyi" 蔑歷古意, *Zhongguo wenzi* 中國文字 10 (1962), 1–13.

Yan Zhu 閻鑄, "Junxian zhi de youlai" 郡縣制的由來, *Beijing shiyuan xuebao* 北京師院學報 1978.3–4, 53–59.

Yang, Kuan 楊寬, "Lun Xi Zhou jinwen zhong liushi bashi he xiangsui zhidu de guanxi" 論西周金文中六㠯八㠯和鄉遂制度的關係, *Kaogu* 1964.8, 414–19.

    "Zailun Xi Zhou jinwen zhong liushi he bashi de xingzhi" 再論西周金文 "六㠯" 和 "八㠯" 的性質, *Kaogu* 1965.10, 525–28.

    "Xi Zhou wangchao gong qing de guanjue zhidu" 西周王朝公卿的官爵制度, in *Xi Zhou shi yanjiu* 西周史研究 (monograph of *Renwen zazhi* no. 2), Xi'an: 1984, pp. 100–13.

    "Xi Zhou zhongyang zhengquan jigou pouxi" 西周中央政權機構剖析, *Lishi yanjiu* 1984.1, 78–91.

    Xi Zhou shi 西周史, Shanghai: Shanghai renmin, 1999.

Yang, Shuda 楊樹達, *Jiweiju jinwen shuo* 積微居金文說, supplemented, Beijing: Zhonghua, 1997 (1st edn, Beijing: Kexue, 1952).

Yates, Robin D. S., "State Control of Bureaucrats under the Qin: Techniques and Procedures," *Early China* 20 (1995), 351–52, 57.

    "The City-State in Ancient China," in *The Archaeology of City-States: Cross-Cultural Approaches*, Washington, DC: Smithsonian Institution Press, 1997, pp. 71–90.

Yin, Shengping 尹盛平, *Zhouyuan wenhua yu Xi Zhou wenming* 周原文化與西周文明, Nanjing: Jiangsu jiaoyu, 2005.

Yin, Weizhang 殷瑋璋, and Cao Shuqin 曹淑琴, "Zhou chu Taibao qi zonghe yanjiu" 周初太保器綜合研究, *Kaogu xuebao* 1991.1, 1–21.

Yin Zhou jinwen jicheng 殷周金文集成, 18 vols. (Institute of Archeology, CASS). Beijing: Zhonghua, 1984–94.

Yinxu de faxian yu yanjiu 殷墟的發現與研究 (Institute of Archeology, CASS), Beijing: Kexue, 1994.

Yoshimoto, Michimasa 吉本道雅, "Sei Shū satsumei kinbun kō" 西周冊命金文考, *Shirin* 史林 74.5 (1991), 38–66.

"Kokusei shi" 國制史, in *In Shū Shin Kan jidaishi no kihon mondai* 殷周秦漢時代史の基本問題, ed. Matsumaru Michio 松丸道雄 *et al.*, Tokyo: Kyūko shoin 2001, pp. 63–88.

Yu, Xingwu 于省吾, "Luelun Xi Zhou jinwen zhong de liushi he bashi jiqi tuntian zhi" 略論西周金文中的六𠂤和八𠂤及其屯田制, *Kaogu* 考古 1964.3, 152–55.

"Guanyu 'Lun Xi Zhou jinwen zhong liu shi bashi he xiangsui zhidu de guanxi' yiwen de yijian" 關於〈論西周金文中六𠂤八𠂤和鄉遂制度的關係〉一文的意見, *Kaogu* 1965.3, 131–33.

Yunqing guan jinwen 筠清舘金文 (Wu Rongguang 吳榮光), 5 *juan*, Yunqing guan, 1842.

Zhang, Changshou 張長壽, "Lun Jingshu tongqi: 1983-86 nian Fengxi fajue ziliao zhi er" 論井叔銅器: 1983- 86 年灃西發掘資料之二, *Wenwu* 1990.7, 32–35.

Zhang, Changshou 張長壽, Chen Gongruo 陳公柔, and Wang Shimin 王世民, *Xi Zhou qingtongqi fenqi duandai yanjiu* 西周青銅器分期斷代研究, Beijing: Wenwu, 1999.

Zhang, Maorong 張懋鎔, *Guwenzi yu qingtongqi lunji* 古文字與青銅器論集, Beijing: Kexue, 2002.

Zhang, Yachu 張亞初, "Lun Lutaishan Xi Zhou mu de niandai he zushu" 論魯臺山西周墓的年代和族屬, *Jianghan kaogu* 1984.2, 23–28.

"Shangdai zhiguan yanjiu" 商代職官研究, *Guwenzi yanjiu* 古文字研究 13 (1986), 82–114.

Yin Zhou jinwen jicheng yinde 殷周金文集成引得, Beijing: Zhonghua, 2001.

Zhang, Yachu 張亞初, and Liu Yu 劉雨, *Xi Zhou jinwen guanzhi yanjiu* 西周金文官制研究, Beijing: Zhonghua, 1986.

Zhao, Guangxian 趙光賢, "Cong Qiu Wei zhuqi ming kan Xi Zhou de tudi jiaoyi" 從裘衛諸器銘看西周的土地交易, *Beijing shifan daxue xuebao* 北京師範大學學報 1979.6, 16–23.

Zhou dai shehui bianxi 周代社會辨析, Beijing: Renmin, 1982.

Zheng, Jiexiang 鄭傑祥, *Shang dai dili gailun* 商代地理概論, Zhengzhou: Zhongzhou guji, 1994.

Zheng, Tianting 鄭天挺, *Qing shi* 清史, vol. 1, Hong Kong: China Books, 1994.

Zhensong tang jigu yiwen 貞松堂集古遺文 (Luo Zhenyu 羅振玉), 16 *juan*, 1930.

Zhensong tang jigu yiwen buyi 貞松堂集古遺文補遺 (Luo Zhenyu 羅振玉), 3 *juan*, 1931.

Zhongguo lishi wenwu 中國歷史文物 2004.1, 4–10, 35, "Shi You ding yu Shi You gui" 師酉鼎與師酉簋.

2006.3, 4–6, "Lu gui kaoshi" 褱簋考釋.

Zhongyuan wenwu 中原文物, 1984.4, 13–16, "Nanyang shi beijiao chutu yipi Shen guo qingtongqi" 南陽市北郊出土一批申國青銅器.

Zhou, Fagao 周法高, *Jinwen gulin* 金文詁林, 14 vols., Hong Kong: Chinese University of Hong Kong Press, 1975.

Zhou jinwen cun 周金文存 (Zou An 鄒安), 6 *juan*, Shanghai: Cangsheng mingzhi daxue, 1916.

Zhou, Yuan 周瑗 (Li Xueqin 李學勤), "Jubo Qiu Wei liang jiazu de xiaozhang yu Zhouli de benghuai: Shilun Dongjiacun qingtongqi qun" 矩伯裘衛兩家族的消長與周禮的崩坏: 試論董家村青銅器群, *Wenwu* 1976.6, 45–50 (revised and reprinted, Li Xueqin, *Xinchu qingtongqi yanjiu* 新出青銅器研究, Beijing: Wenwu, 1990, pp. 98–109).

Zhou, Ziqiang 周自強, "Chonglun Xi Zhou shiqi de gongtian he sitian," 重論西周時期的公田和私田, *Shilin* 1987.1, 1–10.

Zhouli 周禮, in *Shisanjing zhushu* 十三經註疏, Beijing: Zhonghua, 1979, pp. 631–943.

Zhu, Fenghan 朱鳳翰, *Shang Zhou jiazu xingtai yanjiu* 商周家族形態研究, Tianjin: Tianjin guji, 2004.

   "Zuoce Ban yuan tanxi" 作冊般黿探析, *Zhongguo lishi wenwu* 中國歷史文物 2005.1, 6–10.

   "Zhabo ding yu Zhougong nanzheng" 柞伯鼎與周公南征, *Wenwu* 2006.5, 67–73.

Zhu, Fenghan 朱鳳翰, and Yao Qingfang 姚青芳, "Shi You ding yu Shi You gui," 師酉鼎和師酉簋, *Zhongguo lishi wenwu* 2004.1, 4–10, 35.

Zhu, Youzeng 朱右曾, *Yi Zhou shu jixun jiaoshi* 逸周書集訓校釋, Hubei: Chongwen shuju, 1877.

Zhuiyi zhai yiqi kuanzhi kaoshi 綴遺齋彝器款識考釋 (Fang Junyi 方濬益), 30 *juan*, Shanghai: Hanfenlou, 1935 (completed 1894).

Zhuiyi zhai yiqi kuanzhi kaoshi gaoben 綴遺齋彝器款識考釋稿本 (Rong Geng 容庚), manuscript.

Zhushu jinian 竹書紀年, in *Sibu congkan* 四部叢刊, Shanghai: Shangwu, 1920.

Zong, Desheng 宗德生, "Shilun jinwen zhong de Zhou" 試論金文中的周, *Nankai xuebao* 南開學報 1985.2, 55–58.

Zou, Junmeng 鄒君孟, and Du Shaoshun 杜紹順, "Xi Zhou tudi suoyouzhi wenti qianjian" 西周土地所有制問題淺見, *Huanan shifan daxue xuebao* 1987.3, 53–59.

Zungu zhai suojian jijin tu chuji 尊古齋所見吉金圖初集 (Huang Jun), 4 *juan*, Beijing: Zunguzhai, 1936.

Zuozhuan 左傳, in *Shisanjing zhushu* 十三經註疏, Beijing: Zhonghua shuju, 1979, pp. 1697–2188.

General Index

affiliated settlements (*shuyi* 屬邑), 174, 187, 281, 293
Albrew, Martin,
  summary of Weber, 4
Alur society, 278, 290–92
  compared with Western Zhou, 292–93
  see also segmentary state
ancestral worship, 15, 162, 214
ancient bureaucracies, 1
  examples suggested (Weber), 5
  see also bureaucracy
ancient Chinese state, 271
  problems in applying sociopolitical models, 283–84
Anyang 安陽, 25, 30, 167, 264,
appointment inscriptions, 13, 103, 118, 214, 236
  date of, emergence, 104
  definition of, 13
  general structure, 110
  geographical distribution, 99
  number of, 104, 302
  see also bronze inscriptions
appointment ritual, 103, 214,
  as bureaucratic procedure, 111, 144
  details reconstructed, 105–10
  regularities, 119–22
  see also appointment inscriptions
archery ritual, 262
aristocratic estates,
  ownership of, 155
  fragmentation of, 156–58
  see also landed property, lineage
Asiatic mode of production, 279, 286,
assistantship, 199, 201, 224–25,
  supported by statistics, 224–25,
Attendant Scribe (*Yushi* 禦史), 56, 310
August Father (Huangfu 皇父), 90, 147,

Ba 灞 River, 157
baigong 百工, *see* "Hundred Officials"
Balazs, Etienne, 6, 97
Ban Gong 般宮, 115, 162
bang 邦, 45, 183
  conceptual difference from *guo* 國, 47
  condition of, 183
  administration of, 183–88

bangbo 邦伯, 45
bangjun 邦君, 132, 183
Bangjun Li 邦君屬, 178, 183, 220
Beetham, David, 4
Beizhao 北趙 cemetery, 257
  see also regional state, Jin
Beizhong 備仲, 132
Bi 畢, 152, 166, 180
Bi Pond (Biyong 璧廱 or Bichi 璧池), 152, 261,
Bielenstein, Hans, 6
  on number of Han officials, 1
Bin 敳 Garrison, 82, 133
Binxian 彬縣, 101
Biyong 璧廱, *see* Bi Pond
Blakeley, Barry B.
  on segmentary state, 279–80
bo 伯 (Elder, as seniority order), 44, 241, 243
Bo Maofu 伯懋父, 264
Bo Sufu 伯俗父 (Shi Sufu 師俗父),
  see Shi Su
Bo Wufu 伯吳父, 249
Bo Xifu 伯犀父, 226
Bo Yifu 伯邑夫, 84
Bo Yongfu 伯雍父, 226
Book of Documents (*Shangshu* 尚書), 55, 61, 245, 246, 295
Book of Poetry (*Shijing* 詩經), 14, 63, 180, 246, 295
  poems about domestic banquet, 16
Book Scribe (*Shushi* 書史), 310
Border Protector (*Yufang* 馭方), 38, 140,
Bright Hall (*mingtang* 明堂), 152,
bronze inscriptions, 256
  background of creation, 11–14
  documentary nature of, 17–18
  as evidence for official career, 218
  as historical documents, 13
  numbers of, 2
  publicly displayed, 19–20
  reasons for inscribing, 19
  of regional states, 236, 247
  as "religious document" (Falkenhausen), 14, 19
  social contexts of, 15–20
  see also appointment inscriptions, inscribed bronzes

Brown, Elizabeth
  attack on "feudalism," 288–89
Bureau (*liao* 寮), 58
  meaning for Zhou administration, 53–54
  staff of, 53
  number of, 66
bureaucracy, 3,
  characteristics of, 4
  and democracy, 5
  definition of, 4–5, 141, 190,
  of Han China, 1
  ideal or *pure* type, 4, 6
  operational characteristics, 96–97,
  post-Weberian studies, 6
  pre-modern, 5
  of Roman Empire, 1
  see also ancient bureaucracies, Weber,
    Albrow, Kamenka
bureaucratic official
  characteristics of, 190
  see also Western Zhou officials
bureaucratization
  causes of, 302
  of Western Zhou government, 94–95, 301

cai 采 (estate), 45
Cai 蔡, 130, 199
Caoyanzhuang 曹演莊, 25
Catching Foal (*zhiju* 執駒), 153
ce 冊, 112
ceming 冊命, *see* appointment ritual
Chang 長 group, 242
Chang, Kwang-Chih, 47, 60, 275
  on multiple functions of Shang-Zhou cities,
    164
Chen, Gongrou 陳公柔, 251
Chen Jian 臣諫陳, 98, 265
Chen, Mengjia 陳夢家, 24, 114, 249
  on the meaning of *pi* 㽙, 200
Chengzhou 成周, 33, 35, 52, 99, 140, 162, 257,
    267, 285
  administration of, 52
  as eastern administrative center, 101
  as military base, 267
Chief (*Yinshi* 尹氏; = Chief Interior Scribe),
    90
Chief Document Maker (*Zuoce yin* 作冊尹),
    93, 219, 311
Chief Interior Scribe (*Neishi yin* 內史尹),
    75–77, 84, 93, 219, 309
  high prestige of, 76
  role in appointment ritual, 109
Chief Minister (*xiang* 相), 253
Chinese bureaucracy, 6
  origin of, 1–2, 7
  as patrimonial, 5, 7
  see also ancient bureaucracies
Chu 楚, 130
"Chuci" 楚茨, 14
Ci 此, 131

city-state, 174, 180, 271
  application to China, 273–75
  classical examples of, 272
  criticism of, 284–87
  definition of, 272–73
  Maya city-states, 272
  Sumerian city-states, 272
city-state kingdom (Lewis), 273
cities,
  administration of cities, 168–69
  composition of Western Zhou city, 159–64
  "Consumer City," 164,
  in Greco-Roman civilization, 167
  multiple functions of, 164
"Committee of High Officials," 84–85, 137,
    232–33, 253
Confucian School, 8
Contribution Hall (Xian Gong 獻宮), 117
Creel, Herrlee, 1, 6, 13, 48, 99, 290, 294
  bureaucracy and feudalism, 7
  on feudal state, 277
  rejection of Shang "Fengjian" system, 27
  on selection of officials, 191
  on Western Zhou government, 93
  see also feudalism

Da 大, 181
Danfeng 丹鳳, 194
Danfu 亶父 (Grand King), 30
dasitu 大嗣徒, *see* Grand Minister of Multitudes
Dengbo 鄧伯, 257,
dian 典 (to document), 17
dian 甸, 45,
Dingbo 定伯, 44, 84
Director of the Imperial Clan (*zongzheng*
    宗正), 67
District Administrator (*Lijun* 里君), 45, 51, 52,
    180–81, 313
Document Maker (*Zuoce* 作冊), 57–58,
    61, 310
  decline of the office in mid-Western Zhou,
    76
  Document Maker Ling 令, 51
  in regional states, 250
Document Maker and Interior Scribe (*Zuoce
    neishi* 作冊內史), 310
dongguo 東國 (eastern states), 48
Dongyi 東夷 (Eastern Barbarian), 34, 264
Dou Bi 豆閉, 132, 183
Du, Zhengsheng 杜正盛
  on city-state, 275
Duke (*gong* 公), 122
Duke of Bi (Bigong 畢公), 56, 60
Duke Grand Scribe (*Gong Taishi* 公太史),
    56, 308
Duke of Mao (Maogong 毛公), 40, 85, 139
Duke Ming (Minggong 明公, or Ming Bao
    明保), 50, 51, 60, 260
Duke Mu (Mugong 穆公), 79, 131
Duke Mu 穆 of Qin, 256

Duke of Shao (Shaogong 召公), 31, 60
Duke Wu (Wugong 武公), 131
    authority of Duke Wu, 140–41
Duke Yi (Yigong 益公), 137
Duke of Zhou (Zhougong 周公), 18, 43, 60,
    225, 245–46
    role in consolidation of Zhou power, 31
duoma 多馬, 29
"Duoshi" 多士, 193
duoya 多亞, 29
duoyin 多尹, 29
Duoyou 多友, 140

Eight Armies (*bashi* 八師), 33, 78, 264, 265
    civil offices in, 78–90
    organization during mid-Western Zhou, 78
Emura, Haruki 江村治樹
    on Shang-Zhou cities, 274
Erlitou 二裏頭, 276, 284
European fiefs, 48, 245, 290

Falkenhausen, von Lothar, 13, 18, 19
    on religious meaning of bronze inscriptions,
    13–14
    on date of "ritual reform," 38
family (*jiazu* 家族), 156
    of Han 函, 162
    of Liang Qi 梁其, 162
    of Qiu 裘, 162
    of Rong 榮, 162, 163
    of Wei 微, 162
    of Zhong 中, 162
Fang 方 enemies, 25
Fangbo 方伯 (Elder of the Fang), 26, 30
fanjing 繁荊, 193–94
Fansheng 番生, 64, 65
fayue 伐閱, 227, 229
Feinman, Gary M., and Joyce Marcus,
    rejection of "segmentary state," 291
Fen 汾 River valley, 39
Feng 豐 (or Fengjing 豐京), 79, 159
feng 封, 48, 182
Fengchu 鳳雛, 116, 153,
Fengjian 封建 System of Zhou, 45
    evidence in bronze inscriptions, 43
    practice of, early Western Zhou, 48, 98
    practice in late Western Zhou, 39
Fengxiang 鳳翔, 103, 159
feudal state, 271
    application to China, 277–78
    definition of, 277
feudalism, 7, 245, 277, 288, 289
    contrast to bureaucracy, 7
    Marxist concept of, 278
    of Western Zhou (Creel), 9–10
feudo-vassalic institutions, 289
fields (*tian* 田), 37, 158, 173, 176, 180
    condition of, 176–77
Finer, S. E.,
    on bureaucracy in ancient China, 7
    reviews of, 7
    standing army and bureaucracy, 79

Five Cities (*wuyi* 五邑), 77, 164–65, 174,
    220, 285
    administration of, 166–67
    meaning explained, 78
    identification of, 166
    institution of, 165–67
"Five Ranks", 290
Foal Palace (Ju Gong 駒宮), 115, 162
    see also Catching Foal
fuyong 附庸, 154

Gao 高 family, 251
Gebo 格伯, 17
Geng Ying Gong 庚嬴宮, 115
gong 宮 (building compound), 114
    as administrative "offices", 116–17, 142
    archeological discoveries, 116
    classification of, 115
    number of, mentioned in inscriptions, 114
gong 公, *see* Duke
Gong Taishi 公太史, *see* Duke Grand Scribe
Gong Zhong 公仲, 259
government service, 199
    balance of appointments, 201–15
    career structure in, 200–201
    chances for new appointment, 212–13
    criteria for promotion, 226–29
    patterns of promotion, 224
    patterns of recruitment, 216–17
    promotion of officials, 214, 217–24, 233
    see also Western Zhou government, Western
      Zhou officials
Grand Invocator (*Taizhu* 太祝), 58, 77, 311
    in regional states, 254, 255
Grand Marshal (*Taishi* 太師), 59, 90, 313
Grand Minister of Multitudes (*dasitu* 大嗣徒),
    82
Grand Protector (*Taibao* 太保), 18, 59, 241, 257
Grand Scribe (*Taishi* 太史), 55, 57, 76, 176, 308
    Grand Scribe X 旟, 88
    Grand Scribe You 友, 55
    in regional states, 254, 255
Grand Secretariat (*taishiliao* 太史寮), 53, 66, 76,
    88, 92–93, 117, 254
Grand Superintendent (*Taizai* 太宰), 312,
    250, 252
Grand Supervisor of Construction (*da sigong*
    大司工)
    in regional states, 249
Grand Supervisor of Horses (*Zhong sima* 冢
    嗣馬), 82, 308
Grand Supervisor of Land (*Zhong situ* 冢嗣土),
    81, 223, 307
Grand Temple (*taimiao* 太廟), 119, 140, 143,
    153, 162
Great Left (*dazuo* 大左), 78
great settlement (*dayi* 大邑), 25, 174, 281, 297
Griffeth, Robert, and Carol G. Thomas
    on city-state, 272–73
Gu Donggao 顧棟高, 253
guanzhi 官制 (system of offices), 43
Guicheng 歸城, 172, 265

Guifang 鬼方, 243
guo 國, 47, 286
Guo Cong 爾從, 176, 177, 184
Guo 國family, 251
Guo, Moruo 郭沫若, 8, 63, 85, 114, 193, 223, 264
Guo Wengong 虢文公, 49
Guo Xuangong 虢宣公, 49
Guodian 郭店, 200
guoren 國人 (Townspeople), 172, 173, 180, 286
Guozhong 虢仲, 98, 267, 268

Hai 害, 130
Hancheng 韓城, 101
Hansen, Mogens Herman
  on territorial state, 275
Heaven's Mandate, 31, 33, 60, 292, 295, 301
Han Dynasty (206 BC–9 AD)
  number of officials, 1
hereditary appointment to offices
  traditional view of, 191
  evidence in bronze inscriptions, 192–94, 199
  number of, in Western Zhou inscriptions, 201
  decline over time, 214–15
Heyang 合陽, 101
High God (*shangdi* 上帝), 295
hou 侯, 45
  in Shang contexts, 27
  meaning in Zhou contexts, 44, 48
Hou, Wailou 侯外廬
  on city-state, 274
Hsu, Cho-yun, 2, 54, 220, 256
  on Zhou government, 10
Hsu, Cho-yun, and Katheryn Linduff, 2, 10
  on the important of Interior Scribe, 75
  on Five Cities, 165
  on selection of officials, 191–92
Hu 曶,
  career development, 223
Hu 滹 River, 101
Hu, Houxuan 胡厚宣
  on Shang "Fengjian" system, 27
Hua Gong 華宮, 115
Huaiyi 淮夷, 35, 38, 85, 140, 226, 247, 266
  invasion of Zhou territories, 35–36
huan 還
  meaning of, 170–71
Huang Ranwei 黃然偉, 112
"Hundred Officials" (*baigong* 百工), 45, 51

imperial bureaucratic states, 235
inscribed bronzes
  domestic use of, 15–16
  durability of, 19
  publicity of, 19–20
  see also, bronze inscriptions
Inspecting Scribe (*Shengshi* 省史), 56, 310
Inspector (*jian* 監), 248, 251, 254, 255
Inspector Elder (*Jianbo* 監伯), 252
institution of the Zhou king,
  King's Legion (*wanghang* 王行), 81
  King's officials (*zhen zhishi* 朕執事), 67, 88

King's people (*wangren* 王人), 67, 241
  power to make appointments, 142, 145–47
  regularity of conducts, 144
  role in administration, general, 141–43
  role in appointment ritual, 142–43, 144
  see also, Royal Household Administration
Interior Scribe (*Neishi* 內史), 75, 176, 308–9
  Interior Scribe Nian 年, 75, 119
  Interior Scribe Wu 吳, 76
  Interior Scribe Wuqi 無㛪, 88
  role in appointment ritual, 109
Invocator (*Zhu* 祝), 58, 77, 311
Itō, Michiharu 伊藤道治, 73, 74, 81, 178
  on bronze inscriptions, 12
  establishment of regional states, 243
  on land ownership, 156
  on *li* district, 182
  on "Six Districts," 82, 172
  on the social contexts of bronzes, 16
  on transaction of land, 177–78

ji 季 (as seniority order), 44
Ji Li 季歷, 30
Jiabo 家伯, 90
jian 建, 48
Jian 監, *see* Royal Inspector
Jifu 幾父, 251
Jinhou 晉侯, 44
Jing Li 井利 (or Li 利), 225
Jingbang 井邦, 47
  see also Polity of Jing
Jingbo 井伯, 44, 77, 84, 118, 121, 132
  as Supervisor of Horses, 42
  initial appointment as Grand Supervisor of Horses, 82
Jingshu 井叔, 223, 228
"Jiugao" 酒誥, 45, 246

Kaizuka, Shigaki 貝塚茂樹
  on city-state, 274
Kang Gong 康宮 (Kang Temple), 69, 114, 121, 142, 153
Kang Shao Gong 康邵宮, 105
Kangbo Mao 康伯毛, 264
"Kanggao" 康誥, 45, 245, 246, 249, 295
Kanghou Tu 康侯圖, 249
Kangshu 康叔, 246
Kanmenka, Eugene, 1, 5
  on development of bureaucracy in China, 6
  on Egyptian bureaucracy, 70
Ke 克, 43, 157, 220, 241–42, 263
Keightley, David
  on Shang state, 25, 26, 273, 301
  on Shang government, 28, 60
  acceptance of "segmentary state" model, 280, 292
Kern, Martin,
  analysis of *Shijing* poem, 295
Kimura, Hideumi 木村秀海, 81
King Cheng, 240
King Gong, 72
King Kang, 240

King Li, 38
King Mu, 34, 37
King Wen, 30
    as recipient of Heaven's Mandate, 294
King Wu, 30, 240
    as recipient of Heaven's Mandate, 295
King Xiao
    abnormal succession, 34
King Xuan, 39, 252
Kuang Ji 匡季, 37

Lai 逨, 79, 131, 215
    career development, 221
landed property, 150
    different ownerships, 151
    royal grant of, 36–37, 157–58
Lantian 藍田, 157, 263
Laoniupo 老牛坡, 25
Learning Hall (Xue Gong 學宮), 115, 152, 153
Left and Right Camps (*zuoyouxi* 左右戲),
    78–79, 166, 193
Lewis, Mark, 30, 276, 284, 286
    on city-state, 273, 274
Li 盠 (or Lifu 盠父), 79, 131
li 里, 180
    administration of, 181–182
    area calculation of, 180
    condition of, 180,
    ownership of, 182
Li, Boqian 李伯謙, 259
Li, Chaoyuan 李朝遠, 150, 181
Li, Feng (previous), 2, 33
    rejection of "Western Zhou feudalism," 290
    on social contexts of bronze inscriptions,
      14–15
    translocation of regional states, 252
    on Zhou government, 10–11
Liang 量, 131
Liangtian 量田, 179
liao 寮, *see* Bureau
liaoren 寮人 (Staff of the Bureau), 53
Liji 禮記, 49
lijun 里君, *see* District Administrators
Linduff, Katheryn, 10
lineage (*zongzu* 宗族)
    Lineage of Jing 井, 103, 155, 183
    Lineage of Guo 虢, 155, 162, 227
    Lineage of San 散, 40, 113, 155, 178, 184,
      186
    residences in cities, 154–55
    segmentation of, 158
"Lineage Law" (*zongfa* 宗法), 248, 301,
lineage settlement (*zuyi* 族邑), 174, 187, 293
    as essential unit of Shang and Zhou societies,
      281
Linzi District 林菑里, 181, 182
Liu, Li, and Xingcan Chen, 283
    archeological evidence presented for Shang
      cities, 25
    on territorial states prior to Anyang, 276
    on settlement system, 284

Liulihe 琉璃河, 172, 241, 259, 263
liuxiang 六鄉 (Six Districts), 172, 173
local administration
    of cities, 159–73
    definition of, 149
    of rural areas, 173–89
    officials of San, 186
    officials of Ze, 185
    see also Western Zhou government
Loewe, Michael,
    on number of Han officials, 1
Longkou 龍口, 251, 265
Luhou 魯侯, 44
Luo Tai 羅泰, *see* Falkenhausen
Luoyi 洛邑, 31
Lü Fuyu 呂服余, 132
Lü, Wenyu 呂文郁, 49

Ma, Chengyuan 馬承源, 64, 74, 179, 219, 227
Ma 馬 group, 242
MacIver, R. M.
    definition of the state, 237
Mai Gong 麥宮, 115
Mai 麥-group bronzes, 261
Maisels, Charles, 282, 286
Manchu state, 62
Manager of the Lineage (*zongren* 宗人), 254
Mao 卯, 157, 177
Maobo Qian 毛伯遷, 225
Maogong Ban 毛公班 (or Maofu Ban 毛父班),
    132, 225
    see also Duke of Mao
Marshals (*Shishi* 師氏), 78, 88, 151, 191, 312–13
Master of Horses (*quma* 趣馬/*zouma* 走馬),
    90, 194, 217
Masters of Horses and Charioteers of the
    Five Cities (*wuyi zuoma yuren* 五邑走
    馬馭人), 79, 194
Matsui, Yoshinori 松井嘉德, 282
Matsumaru, Michio 松丸道雄
    on bronze inscriptions, 11–12
    on Shang state, 26
    conceptualization of *yi* settlement, 173
    discussions of settlement state, 281–82
Matsumoto, Mitsuo 松本光雄, 281
Marxist historiography, 9, 150, 275
Meixian 眉縣 bronzes, 79, 221
Mencius (*Mengzi* 孟子), 180
Mesopotamia, 2
Mian 免, 168
    career development, 223–24
miao 廟 (Temple), 114
    see also Grand Temple, Kang Gong, Zhou
    Temple
"Middle Western Zhou Reform," 10, 38
mid-Western Zhou transition, 36–38, 77
mieli 蔑歷, 120,
    meaning of, 226–29
    relation to appointment ritual, 229
    see also, fayue 伐閱, 227, 229

Military Hall (Shi Gong 師宮), 117
Ministry (*qingshiliao* 卿事寮), 16, 51–52, 60, 66, 72, 83, 88, 114, 117
minor lines (*xiaozong* 小宗), 248
Minor Superintendent (*shaozai* 少宰), 254
Mishu 密叔, 133, 194
Miyazaki, Ichisada 宮崎市定, 274
Mu Gong 穆宮, 153
Mugong 穆公, *see* Duke Mu
Musha, Akira 武者章, 99
  on appointment inscriptions, 104
"Mushi" 牧誓, 55
Muye 牧野 (or Mushi 牧白), 31, 265,

nan 男, 44, 45
Nangong Liu 南宮柳, 131
Nanji 南季, 131, 200
Nanzhong 南仲, 90–91
neiguo 內國 (inner states), 48
Neishi 內史, *see* Interior Scribe
Neishi yin 內史尹, *see* Chief Interior Scribe
New People (*xinmin* 新民), 246
Nine Camps (*jiuxi* 九戲), 79
Notitia Dignitatum, 8

official appointment
  to civil administrative offices, 131
  to military duties, 131–32
  to Royal Household administration, 130–31
  see also appointment ritual, government service
official title
  definition of, 43
  criteria of, 42–43
oracle-bone inscriptions, 25
  possible bias on Shang government, 29–30
  of Zhou, 26, 30

Pengsheng 倗生, 17, 113
Pang 莽 (or Pangjing 莽京), 152, 159, 166, 261, 262
pi 疋 (to assist), 194
  meaning of, 199–200
Pingdingshan 平顶山, 251, 263
Polity of Jing (Jingbang 井邦), 183
Pre-dynastic Zhou, 30
primary line (*dazong* 大宗), 248
Prime Minister (*qingshi* 卿士), 90
prime root (*zong* 宗), 264
principal official (*zhengli* 正吏), 250
proto-state, 291
Protector Ming (*mingbao* 明保),
  see Duke Ming
Provisioner (*Shanfu* 膳夫), 40, 90, 312
  political status of, in late Western Zhou, 91–92
  Provisioner Fengsheng 豐生, 112
  Provisioner Geng 駬, 92
  Provisioner Ke 克, 92
  Provisioner Shan 山, 131

Provisioner Shi 豕, 92
  in regional states, 251,
Průšek, Jaroslav, 250,

Qi Army (*Qishi* 齊師), 266
Qiang 羌 group, 242
Qiangjiacun 強家村, 227,
Qianzhangda 前掌大, 250
Qianzhong 遣仲, 137, 139
Qijiacun 齊家村, 163, 251,
qing 卿, 122
qingshiliao 卿事寮, *see* Ministry
Qiongbo 琼伯, 84
Qiu Wei 裘衛, 156–57, 163, 178, 181, 220
Qiu, Xigui 裘錫圭, 48
Qiyi 岐邑, *see* Zhou
Qizhen 齊鎮, 116
Queen Jiang 姜, 69, 257
Qufu 曲阜, 243, 249

rank society, 291
Rawson, Jessica, 24
  on date of "ritual reform," 38
regional government
  general organization, 249–52
  reflected in textual records for Spring and Autumn period, 252–55
  structural and operational characteristics, 255–57
regional rulers (*zhuhou* 諸侯), 45, 49, 51, 151, 251, 260, 288
  military assistance to Zhou king, 247, 257, 264–68
  personal visit to the Zhou capital *Zongzhou*, 260–64
  rights and obligations of, 245–48, 296,
  as royal officials, 259,
regional states
  administrative autonomy, 98–99
  as cluster of *yi* settlements, 243
  definition of, 238
  as elements of the Western Zhou state, 98, 235
  founding of, 33
  land and population of, 238–39
  joint military campaigns with Zhou royal court, 98
  nature of, 290
  relationship with central court, 256–68
regionalism, 247
Renfang 人方, 228
Reynolds, Susan
  criticism of European "feudalism," 289
ritual,
  definition of, 14
  religious-ritual, 14, 16
  see also appointment ritual, archery ritual
Roman Empire, 1, 8, 302
Rong Dui 榮兌, 221
Rong 戎 people, 18, 265

Rongbo 榮伯, 44, 84, 101, 119, 132, 137, 221
  as host in appointment ritual, 142
Rongji 榮季, 225
royal domain (*wangji* 王畿), 49, 190, 236
  administration of, 159–88
  alleged size of, 49
  composition of, 159
  social structure of, 149–59
Royal Household (*wangjia* 王家), 67, 69, 76,
    90, 134, 151, 223
  branch at Bi 畢, 69, 130, 152
  growth during mid-Western Zhou, 67–70
Royal Household Administration, 67, 88, 91
  officials of, 130–31, 136, 151, 158,
  see also institution of the Zhou king
Royal Inspector (*Jian* 監), 99, 314
Royal Kinsmen (*gongzu* 公族), 66, 254
ruler–subject relationship, 290
ryōdo kokka 領土国家 (or *ryōiki kokka*
    領域国家), *see* territorial state

sacrificial vessel (*zunyi* 尊彝), 16, 17
Sahlins, Marshall,
  criticizing "segmentary state," 291
Sanxingdui 三星堆, 25
Sanyousi 三有嗣, *see* Three Supervisors
Scribe (*Shi* 史), 55–57, 75, 230, 309–10
  Scribe Er 兒, 56
  Scribe Guosheng 史虢生, 92, 112
  Scribe Qiang 牆, 198
  Scribe Mi 史密, 265
  Scribe Miao 繆, 92
  Scribe Song 頌, 92
  Scribe Tian 䛘, 17, 55
segmentary lineage system, 278, 292
  principles of, 291
segmentary state, 271, 290, 291
  application to China, 279–80
  definition of, 278–79
Sena, David, 49, 155,
settlement (*yi* 邑), 48, 158, 171–73, 198, 269, 273
  condition of, 175–76
  as basic social unit, 178
  hierarchy of *yi* settlements, 187, 280–81, 297
  see also, great settlement, lineage settlement,
    affiliated settlement
settlement state, 174, 271, 276
  development of the concept, 280–82
  meaning in Western Zhou contexts, 296–97
  value of, as theoretical model, 293
Shan 山, 131,
Shanbo 單伯, 44, 84, 179
Shang government, 27–29, 60
Shang state, 25, 60, 293
  geographical dimensions, 25–26
  hegemonic religion-focused, 26, 60, 292
Shangshu 尚書, *see Book of Documents*
Shamanism, 28
Shanfu 膳夫, *see* Provisioner
Shaochen 召陳, 116

Shaughnessy, Edward, 2, 13, 27, 35, 109
  on Zhou government, 10
  on relation between Xun and Shi You, 198
Shengshi 省史, *see* Inspecting Scribe
Shenji 爾季, 92
  career development, 219–20
Shi 史, *see* Scribe
  differentiated from *shi* 事 and *shi* 使, 55
Shi 師 (marshal), 122
  as "ex-military officer," 232
  as civil administrative officials, 232
  see also Marshals
Shi Chen 師晨 (or Bo Chen 伯晨), 168, 200,
    215
  career development, 219
Shi Dui 師兌, 166
  career development, 220–21
Shi Gong 㵺宮, 115
Shi Hefu 師穌父 (or Bo Hefu 伯穌父;
    Gongbo He 共伯和), 38, 142, 166, 197,
    220, 221
Shi Hu 師虎 (or Hu 虎), 132, 166, 193, 230
  personal network of, 133
  official career, 192–96, 217–18
Shi Huafu 師華父, 92, 220
Shi Ju 師遽, 231
Shi Ke 師克, 230
Shi Kuifu 師奎父, 132, 231
Shi Li 師釐, 130, 197, 214
Shi Liang Gong 師量宮, 115
Shi Lu Gong 師彔宮, 119, 163, 219
Shi Maofu 師毛父, 132
Shi Qin Gong 師秦宮, 115
Shi Shi 師事, 230
Shi sima 師嗣馬, *see* Supervisor of Horses of
    the Army
Shi Sima Gong 師嗣馬宮, 115, 121–22, 163
Shi Su 師俗 (or Shi Sufu 師俗父, or Bo Sufu
    伯俗父), 74, 84, 119, 120, 137, 200, 232, 265
Shi Tian Gong 師田宮, 115
Shi Tong 師同, 231
Shi Wang 師望, 227
Shi Xi 師戲, 195
Shi Xi Taishi 師戲太室, 133
Shi Xun 師詢, 131, 198, 230
Shi Ying 師穎, 131
Shi You 師酉, 198
Shi Yuan 師寰, 266
Shi Yun 師瘨, 132
Shi Zhen 師朕, 231
Shi Zifu Gong 師汿父宮, 115, 163
Shijing 詩經, *see Book of Poetry*
Shirakawa, Shizuka 白川靜, 115, 137
Shishi 師氏, *see* Marshals
"Shiyue zhi jiao" 十月之交 (*Shijing*), 90
si 嗣 (to be in charge), 42
Sigong 嗣工, *see* Supervisor of Construction
Skinner, Quentin, 236, 237
Skosey, Laura, 37, 74
Sima 嗣馬, *see* Supervisor of Horses

Situ 嗣土, *see* Supervisor of Land
Situ 嗣徒, *see* Supervisor of Multitudes
Six Armies (*liushi* 六師), 33
    organization during mid-Western Zhou, 78
    civil offices in, 78–80
Six Districts (*liuxiang* 六鄉), 82
"Songgao" 崧高, 246
shu 叔 (as seniority order), 44
shu 書, 112
Shu Ze 叔夨 (or Shu Yu 叔虞), 257
Shuigou 水溝, 172
Shuowen jiezi 說文解字, 200
Shushi 書史, *see* Book Scribe
Social History Controversy, 150
    see also Marxist historiography
Song 頌, 130
Southall, Aiden, 291
    on segmentary state, 278–79
sovereignty, 238, 294
Spring and Autumn Annals (*Chunqiu* 春秋), 253
Spring and Autumn period, 245, 250
Spring Plowing Ritual, 71
state, 236, 237, 272
    concept of, 236–38
    state of Cai 蔡, 98, 251, 267
    state of Deng 鄧, 99, 257
    state of Guo 虢, 236
    state of Huan 桓, 219
    state of Ji 冀 (=紀), 266
    state of Jin 晉, 243, 247, 253, 257, 267
    state of Lai 萊 (Lai 贊), 265, 266
    state of Lu 魯, 33, 236, 243, 249, 253, 260
    state of Lü 呂, 39, 252
    state of Qi 齊, 33, 35, 251
    state of Qin 秦, 236
    state of Song 宋, 253
    state of Southern Shen 南申, 41, 250, 252
    state of Shen 申, 39, 220, 246
    state of Teng 滕, 33
    state of Wey 衛, 93, 236, 246, 249, 253, 263, 265
    state of Xing 邢, 15, 43, 98, 247, 250, 261, 265
    state of Yan 匽 (燕), 33, 236, 241–42, 259, 263
    state of Yang 楊, 39, 103, 221
    state of Yi 宜, 43, 174, 238–39
    state of Ying 應, 236, 251
    state of Zheng 鄭, 99, 250, 253
    state of Ze 夨, 40, 113, 184
    see also Western Zhou state, regional states
Su 蘇, 99
sui 遂, 172
suitu 遂土, 73, 172
Superintendent (*Zai* 宰), 59, 70, 90, 224, 311, 254
    as head of royal household administration, 69, 83
    Superintendent Cai 蔡, 69, 130, 199
    Superintendent Hu 曶, 70, 130, 219
    Superintendent Hong 弘, 105

Superintendent Li 利, 132
    Superintendent Shou 獸, 136
Supervisor of Cities (*Sicheng* 司城), 254
Supervisor of Construction (*Sigong* 嗣工), 54, 71, 90, 307
    in regional states, 249, 253
    Supervisor of Construction Yangfu 楊父, 123
    Supervisor of Construction Yongyi 雍毅, 112
Supervisor of Horses (*Sima* 嗣馬), 54, 82, 307
    in regional states, 253
    Supervisor of Horses Gong 共, 119, 169
    Supervisor of Horses Jingbo 井伯, 131
    Supervisor of Horses Shou 壽, 132
Supervisor of Horses of the Army (*Shi situ* 師嗣馬), 308
Supervisor of Land (*Situ* 嗣土), 54, 71, 74, 90, 306
    in regional states, 249
    Supervisor of Land Shi Ying 師穎, 71, 131
Supervisor of Lawsuits (*Sikou* 嗣寇)
    in regional states, 253
    uncertainties of the office, 74
Supervisor of Marshes (*Yu* 虞), 187, 313
Supervisor of Multitudes (*Situ* 嗣徒), 90, 306
    in regional states, 249, 253
    relation to Supervisor of Land, 73–74
    Supervisor of Multitudes Nanzhong 南仲, 132
    Superintendent of Multitude Yebo 液伯, 131
Suyi 夙夷, 101, 267,

Taishi 太史, *see* Grand Scribe
Taishi 太師, *see* Grand Marshal
Taishi Gong 太師宮, 115
taishiliao 太史寮, *see* Grand Secretariat
Taixi 薹西, 25
Taizai 太宰, *see* Grand Superintendent
Taizhu 太祝, *see* Grand Invocator
Tang, Lan 唐蘭, 114–15
    on system of Zhou temples, 162
    calculation of the size of *li*, 180
    on *mieli*, 227
Tenghou 滕侯, 44
territorial administration, 288
territorial state, 271
    application to China, 275–77
    contrast to city-state, 275
Thatcher, Melvin P.
    on regional governments, 251, 253, 256
Three Affairs (*sanshi* 三事), 51, 52
Three Supervisors (*Sanyousi* 三有嗣), 54, 60, 70, 83–84, 88, 151, 269, 305–6
    administrative levels, 73
    of the cities, 168–69
    in military organization, 81
    name lists of, in central bureaucracy, 72
    in regional states, 255
    in rural areas, 187
    service by multiple officials, 72–73
tian 田, *see* fields

Tiger Servants (*huchen* 虎臣), 88, 151, 195, 266
Tong 同, 131
toshi kokka 都市国家, *see* city-state
Trigger, Bruce
  on city-state, 272
  on territorial state, 275, 287
tutian 土田 (land and field), 154

unitary state, 292
Upper Palace (Shang Gong 上宮), 152, 153
use of written documents, 109, 111–14

vassalage, 290
village-state, 282

Wang 望, 130
Wang, Guomin 王貴民, 29
Wang, Zhongwen 汪中文, 123
wangji 王畿, *see* royal domain
wangjia 王家, *see* Royal Household
Weber, Max, 3, 4, 96, 103, 117, 141, 190
  bureaucratization, 94, 302
  characterization of bureaucracy, 4
  ideal or *pure* type of bureaucracy, 4
  on career of officials, 217
Western Zhou officials, 190–91, 199, 218, 224
  bureaucratic features of, 233–34
  career track, 217
  social background of, 215–16
  see also government service
Western Zhou government, 2, 8, 42, 52, 230
  causes of bureaucratization, 94
  headquarters in Chengzhou, 52
  condition of sources for, 2
  expansion in mid-Western Zhou, 83
  as first bureaucracy in China, 2
  geographical sphere of operation, 99
  hierarchy of authority, 136–41
  hierarchy of offices, 83–84
  interpersonal relations, 122–33
  organization described in inscriptions, 50–54, 63–66, 85–90
  problems in previous studies, 8–11
  process of bureaucratization, 94–95, 301
  relevance of *Zhouli*, 8
  working patterns, 133–35, 139
Western Zhou state, 2, 26, 33, 34, 38, 49, 224, 235, 271, 293
  bifurcation of, 44–47, 97
  compared with Alur society, 292–93
  compared with Shang state, 300–301
  conceptual difference from Zhou Royal House, 70
  as congregation of *yi* settlements, 299, 303
  decline of political power, 35
  as delegatory kin-ordered settlement state, 271, 294, 299
  outline of political history, 30–41
  qualification as state, 237–38

reorganized under King Xuan, 39
  time-period, 24
  see also state
wei 衛, 45
Wei 渭 River valley, 26, 36, 103
Well-Field (*jingtian* 井田), 150
Wenxian 溫縣, 99
Wet Palace (Shi Gong 濕宮), 152
Wheatley, Paul, 159
Wu 吳, 130
Wu 攴, 131
Wu Dafu 吳 (虞) 大父, 179
Wu Taibo 吳太伯, 131
Wugeng 武庚, 31
Wugong 武公, *see* Duke Wu
Wuhui 無惠, 132
"Wuyi" 無逸, 193

Xi Gong 犀宮, 115
Xia, Hanyi 夏含夷, *see* Shaughnessy
Xia-Shang-Zhou Chronology Project, 195
xian 縣 (county), 170–71, 276
xiang 鄉, 172
xiangsui 鄉遂 (District and Suburb), 172
Xianyun 玁狁, 38, 85, 91, 101, 141, 221
xiaochen 小臣
  in Shang context, 29
Xing 擤, 130
Xing Jiang 邢姜, 250
Xinghou 邢侯 (Ruler of Xing), 44, 261
Xingong 新宮 (New Temple), 231
Xingtai 邢臺, 262
Xinjing 新京 (New Capital), 172
Xinyi 新邑 (New Settlement), 172
Xuan 玄 River, 101
Xue Gong 學宮, *see* Learning Hall
Xunan 許男, 44
Xunyi 旬邑, 101

Yan 顏 family, 181–82
Yan, Yiping 嚴一萍
  on *mieli*, 227
Yanhou 燕侯, 44
Yang 楊 (Supervisor of Construction), 131
Yang 養, 132
Yang, Kuan 楊寬, 122
  on the different roles of Dukes of Zhou and Shao, 59
  on hereditary succession to offices, 191
  on "Six Districts," 172
Yaoxian 耀縣, 178
Yates, Robin
  on city-state, 273
yeren 野人 (country people), 172, 180
yi 邑, *see* settlement
Yi 宜, 174
Yi Gong 夷宮, 153
Yigong 益公, 84
yiren 邑人, 121, 286
Yin 殷, 131

Yinghou 應侯, 44
Yoshimoto, Michimasa 吉本道雅, 104
Yong 永, 157, 168
Young Boys (*xiaozi* 小子), 151
youzhe 右者 (Right-person), 122, 123, 134, 147
   role explained, 67
   role in appointment ritual, 108–9
   relationship with appointees, 123–33
   number of, 123–31
   see also appointment ritual
Yu 虞, *see* Supervisor of Marshes
Yu, Xingwu 于省吾, 173
Yuan 袁, 130
Yuanshi 元氏, 98, 265
yufang 馭方, *see* Border Protector
Yuntang 云塘, 115, 163
yushi 御事, 29
Yushi 禦史, *see* Attendant Scribe

Zai 宰, *see* Superintendent
   as Shang office, 28
Zha 戲 group, 242
Zhabo 柞伯, 267
Zhai Gong 濂宮, 115
Zhang, Changshou 張長壽, 169, 179, 223
Zhang, Yachu 張亞初, and Liu Yu 劉雨, 8
   studies of Western Zhou government, 42
   on the official title *shi*, 230
Zhangjiapo 張家坡, 223
Zhao Gong 昭宮, 142, 153
zhen 毗-fields, 241
Zheng 鄭, 121, 155, 159, 166, 168, 224, 228, 232, 241, 243
Zheng, Jiexiang 鄭傑祥, 25
Zhengbo 鄭伯, 249
Zhengfu 政父, 178
Zhenghuan 鄭還, 170
Zhengzhou 鄭州, 284, 285
zhong 仲 (as seniority order), 44
Zhong Qi 仲齊, 249

Zhong sima 冢嗣馬, *see* Grand Supervisor of Horses
Zhong situ 冢嗣土, *see* Grand Supervisor of Land
Zhong Taishi 仲太師, 147
Zhongyun 仲允, 90
Zhou 周 (or Zhouyuan 周原), 26, 117, 153, 155, 159
   as center of aristocratic lineage residences, 162–63
   status of, 160
Zhou conquest, 31, 300
Zhou *fangbo* 周方伯, 26
Zhou Shi 周師, 223
Zhou Temple (Zhou Miao 周廟), 162
Zhou theory of state, 31, 292, 295
zhoubang 周邦, 47
Zhougongmiao 周公廟, 172
Zhouguan 周官 (Zhou Offices), 8
Zhouli 周禮 (Zhou Rites), 8, 82, 173, 180
Zhu 祝, *see* Invocator
Zhu Fenghan 朱鳳翰, 156,
zhuhou 諸侯, *see* regional ruler
zhujian 諸監 (Many Inspectors), 251
zhuyin 諸尹 (Many Ministers), 45, 51
zi 子 (Prince), 26
   in Shang contexts, 26–27
Zongzhou 宗周 (Hao 鎬), 5, 117, 159, 247, 257, 260, 263
zongzu 宗族, *see* lineages
Zouzi 棸子, 90
zuo 作 (to be), 42
Zuoce 作冊, *see* Document Maker
   as Shang office, 28
Zuoce neishi 作冊内史, *see* Document Maker and Interior Scribe
Zuoce yin 作冊尹, *see* Chief Document Maker
"Zuoluo" 作洛, 152
Zuozhuan 左傳, 99, 243, 268